THE BEGINNER'S GUIDE TO

DAVINCI RESOLVE 16

by Paul Saccone and Dion Scoppettuolo

The Beginner's Guide to DaVinci Resolve 16

Paul Saccone and Dion Scoppettuolo

Blackmagic Design

www.blackmagicdesign.com

To report errors, please send a note to learning@blackmagicdesign.com.

Series Editor: Patricia Montesion

Series Director: Dion Scoppettuolo

Editor: Bob Lindstrom

Contributing Authors: Daria Fissoun, Mary Plummer, Patrick Inhofer, Casey Faris

Cover Design: Blackmagic Design

ISBN 13: 978-0-xxxxxxx-x-x

Contents

Foreword

Welcome to **The Beginner's Guide to DaVinci Resolve 16**

DaVinci Resolve 16 is the only post production solution that brings editing, color correction, audio post and visual effects together in the same software application! The most exciting thing about DaVinci Resolve 16 is the revolutionary new cut page, which is designed specifically for editors that need to work quickly and on tight deadlines. It's an alternate edit page with a streamlined interface and new tools designed to help you work faster than ever before.

DaVinci Resolve 16 also includes even more advanced color correction, powerful new editing options on the traditional edit page, vastly improved Fairlight digital audio tools and even faster 2D and 3D visual effects compositing on the Fusion page. DaVinci Resolve 16 enables you to switch between creative tasks without having to export or translate files between different applications!

Best of all, DaVinci Resolve 16 is absolutely free! Plus, we've made sure that the free version of DaVinci Resolve actually has more features than any paid editing system. That's because at Blackmagic Design we believe everybody should have the tools to create professional, Hollywood caliber content without having to spend thousands of dollars.

I hope you'll enjoy using DaVinci Resolve 16 and we can't wait to see the amazing work you produce!

Grant Petty
Blackmagic Design

Getting Started

Welcome to **The Beginner's Guide to DaVinci Resolve 16**, the official Blackmagic Design Training and Certification book that teaches editors, artists and students how to edit, composite, color correct, and mix audio in DaVinci Resolve. All you need is a Mac or Windows computer, the free download version of DaVinci Resolve 16, and a passion to learn

This official step-by-step training guide covers the basics of editing, visual effects, motion graphics, color correction and audio so you can start creating your own Hollywood caliber film and video today!

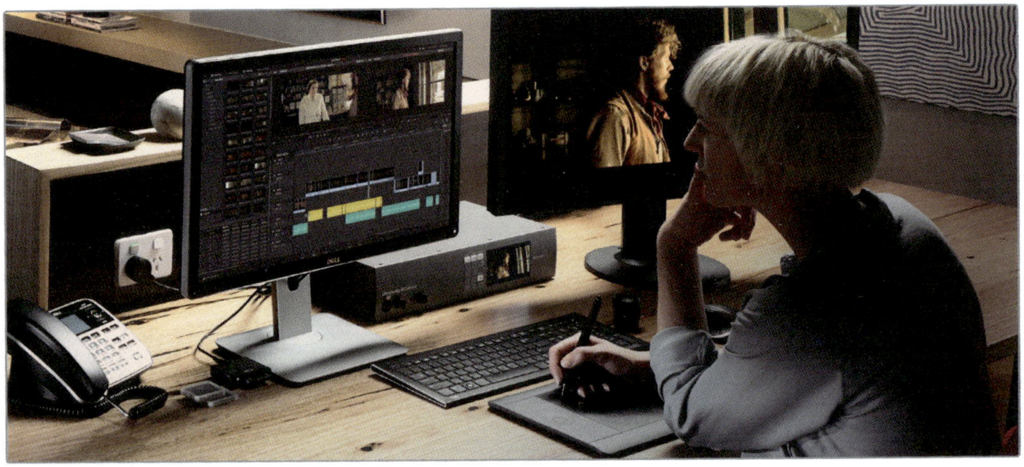

What You'll Learn:

- How to edit, add effects and post to the web, fast using the new cut page.
- How to setup projects, import media and use metadata to speed up your work.
- Marking selections, editing clips in the timeline, and context sensitive trimming.
- How to retime clips, add transitions and pan and scan photos.
- Working with new title templates, creating your own titles and adding animation.
- How to navigate the Fusion page, use a node based interface for visual effects compositing.
- Primary and secondary corrections using DaVinci Resolve's legendary color tools.
- How to match shots, use color management, create looks, grade multiple clips.
- How to use PowerWindows, track objects in a shot, use curves and add ResolveFX.
- Audio sweetening and mixing using the Fairlight audio tools.
- Record voice over directly into the timeline
- Use new FairlightFX to improve audio quality
- How to deliver projects to a variety of formats and share directly to YouTube and Vimeo.
- Dozens of tips and tricks throughout the book that will transform how you work!

The Blackmagic Design Training and Certification Program

Blackmagic Design publishes several training books that take your skills farther in DaVinci Resolve 16. They include:

- The Beginner's Guide to DaVinci Resolve 16
- Advanced Editing with DaVinci Resolve 16
- Color Correction with DaVinci Resolve 16
- Fairlight Audio Post with DaVinci Resolve 16
- Fusion Visual Effects with DaVinci Resolve 16

Whether you want to learn more advanced editing techniques, color grading, or sound mixing, our certified training program has a learning path for you.

After completing this book, you are encouraged to take a one-hour, 50-question online proficiency exam to receive a certificate of completion from Blackmagic Design. The link to the online exam for this beginner's guide can be found on the Blackmagic Design training web page.

For more information on the Training and Certification Program and to find one of our Training Partners in your area please visit www.blackmagicdesign.com/products/davinciresolve/training.

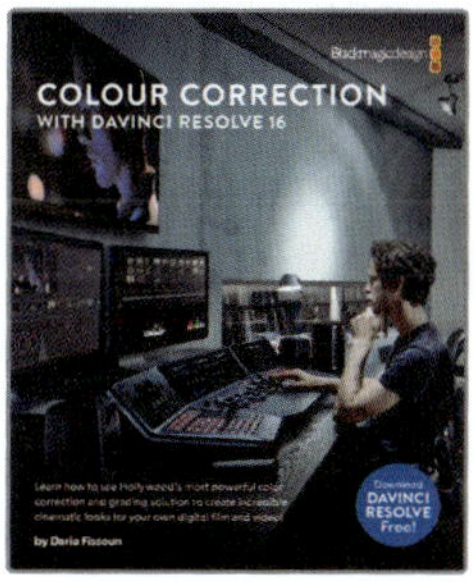

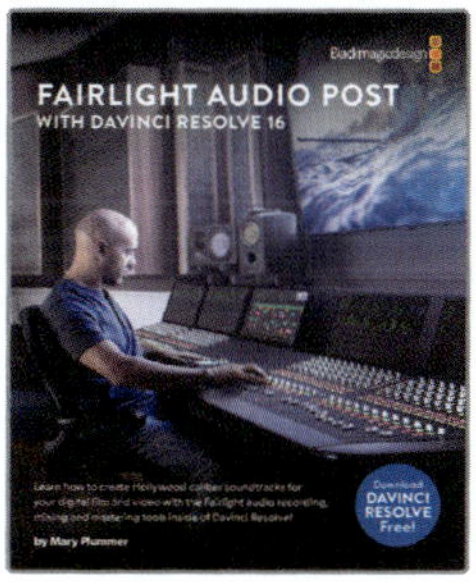

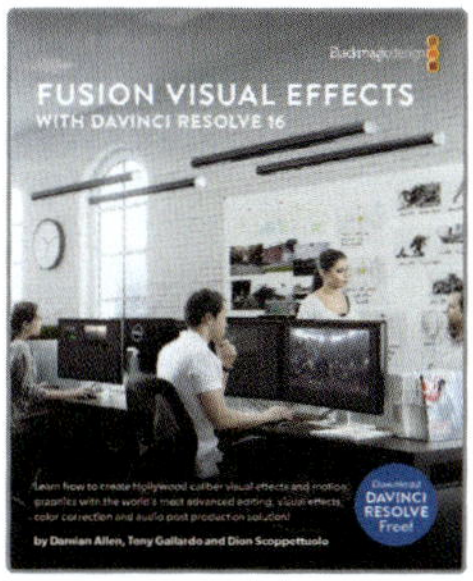

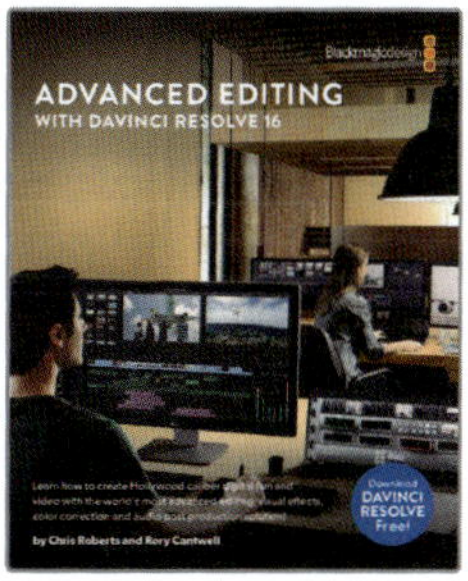

System Requirements

This book supports DaVinci Resolve 16.1 for Mac and Windows. If you have an older version of DaVinci Resolve, you must upgrade to the current version to follow along with the lessons.

NOTE The exercises in this book refer to file and resource locations which will differ if you are using the version of software from the Apple Mac App Store. For the purposes of this training book, if you are using macOS we recommend downloading the DaVinci Resolve software from the Blackmagic Design web site, and not the Mac App store.

Download DaVinci Resolve

To download the free version of DaVinci Resolve 16.1 or later from the Blackmagic Design website:

1. Open a web browser on your Windows or Mac computer.
2. In the address field of your web browser, type: www.blackmagicdesign.com/products/davinciresolve.
3. On the DaVinci Resolve landing page, click the Download button.
4. On the download page, click the Mac or Windows button, depending on your computer's operating system.
5. Follow the installation instructions to complete the installation.

When you have completed the software installation, follow the instructions in the following section, "Copying the Lesson Files," to download the content for this book.

Copying the Lesson Files

The DaVinci Resolve lesson files must be downloaded to your Mac or Windows computer to perform the exercises in this book. After you save the files to your hard disk, extract the file and copy the folder to your Documents folder.

To Download and Install the DaVinci Resolve Lessons Files:

When you are ready to download the lesson files, follow these steps:

1. Connect to the Internet and navigate to: https://www.blackmagicdesign.com/dvres/intro-to-resolve-16

   The download will begin immediately.

   The IntroToResolve16Tutorials.zip file is roughly 7GB in size.

2. After downloading the zip file to your Mac or Windows computer, open your Downloads folder, and double-click IntroToResolve16Tutorials.zip to unzip it if it doesn't unzip automatically. You will end up with a folder named R16 Intro lessons that contains all the content for this book.
3. From your Download folder, drag the "R16 intro lessons" folder to you Documents folder.

You are now ready to begin Lesson 1, Creating a story in the cut page.

Acknowledgments

We would like to thank the following individuals for their contributions of media used throughout the book:

- Brian J Terwilliger, Terwilliger Productions for "Living In the Age of Airplanes"
- Nuyen Anh Nguyen, Second Tomorrow Studios for "Hyperlight"

Lesson 1

Introduction to Editing in the Cut Page

Whether you use DaVinci Resolve on a Mac, Windows, or Linux computer, this training guide will teach you how to take a project from its initial setup to a final output. You'll become familiar with the standard menus and buttons, as well as essential editing, effects, color correction, and audio sweetening workflows.

These first two lessons are used as an introduction to the revolutionary new cut page which is designed for speed so you can edit projects fast. You can import media, edit, trim, add transitions, titles, mix audio and output your programs all from within the cut page itself. You don't even have to use the rest of DaVinci Resolve's features if you don't need too!

Time

This lesson takes approximately 90 minutes to complete.

Goals

The remaining lessons in this book will go into detail on the media, edit, fusion, color, fairlight and deliver pages.

Let's get started!

Starting in the cut page

When it comes to editing, there isn't a one size fits all approach. That's why DaVinci Resolve 16 has two different editing interfaces, the cut page and the edit page. The new cut page is for fast turn around jobs that need to get edited and published quickly. It's perfect for editing news, video blogs, online promos, educational content and more. The traditional edit page features a wider range of features and works in a more traditional way. You can choose either page, depending on what feels the most suited to your needs.

This book will teach you how to use both pages. The exciting part is that you can switch back and forth between the cut and edit pages at any time.

In designing the cut page, Blackmagic Design took a step back and put a lot of thought into how to innovate and make editing faster. The cut page and the edit page provide different interfaces for these two very different cultures of editors. The cut page removes wasteful steps and anything that could slow you down. Every click or action you do on the cut page has a direct result. There are no wasted clicks or optional settings to configure. The page works hard at anticipating what you want to do and helps you get there faster. Let's start exploring the cut page by opening DaVinci Resolve and importing clips.

NOTE At this point you should have downloaded the content for this book, and located that content in your Documents folder as described in Getting Started.

1. First start by launching the DaVinci Resolve application.
2. Double-click the Untitled thumbnail to open a new project.

   DaVinci Resolve will open and display the page last used.

3 At the bottom of the window, click the cut button to switch to the cut page, if necessary.

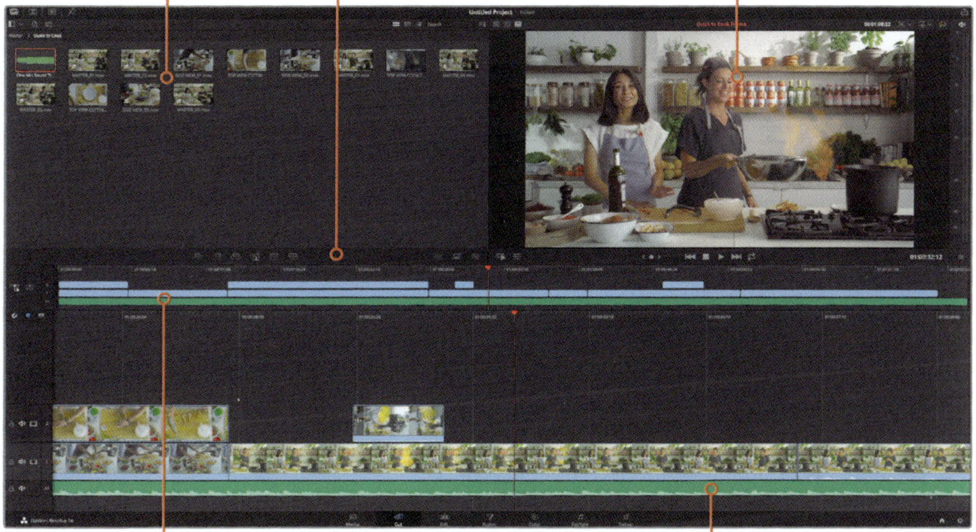

In the upper left area is the media pool. This is where all the clips in your project can be sorted, organized and reviewed. When starting a project, you Import clips into the media pool using the buttons in the upper left corner.

4 In the upper left corner of the media pool, click the import media folder button.

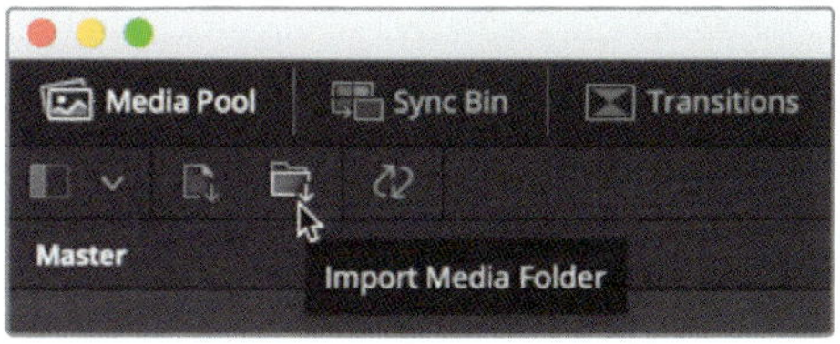

TIP The import file button allows you to import one or more selected audio, video or graphic clips from a folder.

5 In the dialog that appears, navigate to the Documents folder, where you placed the R16 Intro lessons folder.

6 Within that folder, select the Lesson 01 folder, then the Quick to Cook folder and click open.

A useful dialog appears informing you that the clips you are importing are different than the default 1920 x1080 full HD video resolution and frame rate that DaVinci Resolve uses. Using this dialog you can switch Resolve's settings to match the clips' format, without having to open a settings window.

7 Click Change to have the settings in DaVinci Resolve match the size and frame rate of the incoming clips.

All the media imports into of the media pool and the folder is made into a bin. Every project contains one bin to start with, called the master bin. The master bin contains all other bins and your timelines.

8 Double click the Quick to Cook bin.

Bins, like folders, can be used to organize your clips into categories. You can create multiple bins and have them all accessible without any wasted space.

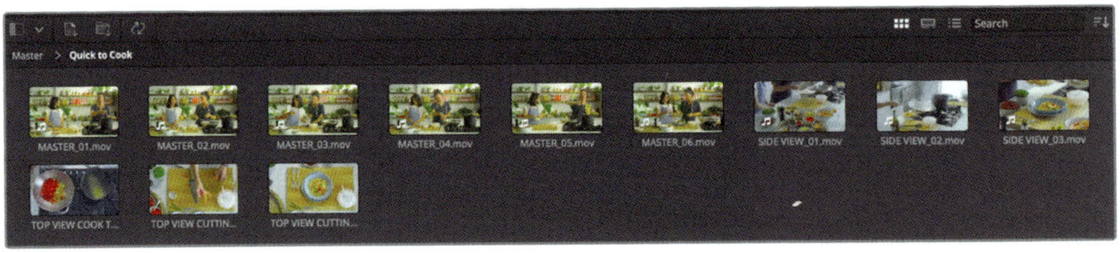

NOTE Depending on your computer's screen resolution, the layout seen in the images in this book may appear differently compared to the layout you see on your display.

Clips in a bin can also be quickly sorted in different ways.

9 Click the sort pop up menu and choose timecode.

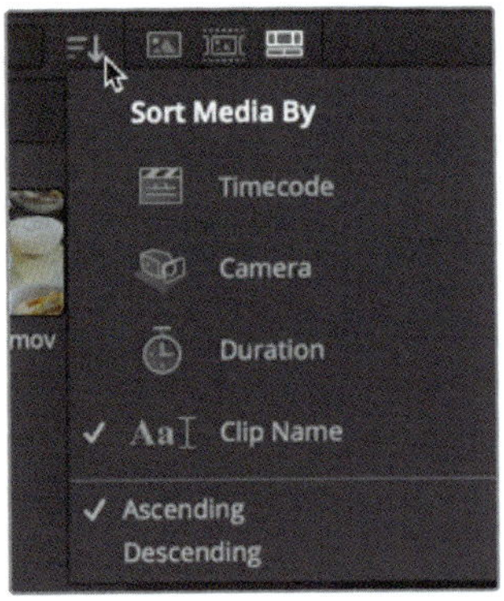

TIP Timecode is a number containing hours, minutes, seconds and frames, which is assigned to each frame of digital video when the clip is recorded. Referencing this eight digit number, it can be easier to locate a given frame of video.

The clips rearrange in the bin based on the time of day they were recorded. Before you move on you'll want to save and name this project because we will continue with it in lesson 2.

10 Choose File > Save project and name the project Cooking Show.

We'll use the clips from this bin to quickly put together a story.

The project you create in the next two lessons is designed to give you a tour of the cut page. You'll learn all the essentials of the cut page and how quickly you can edit, enhance, and share a project.

Adding clips to a timeline

Once you have media in a bin, you can start reviewing the clips to select the ones you want to use in the story you are creating. You can play clips in the larger viewer by double clicking them in the media pool.

1 Double click the first clip titled master 01.

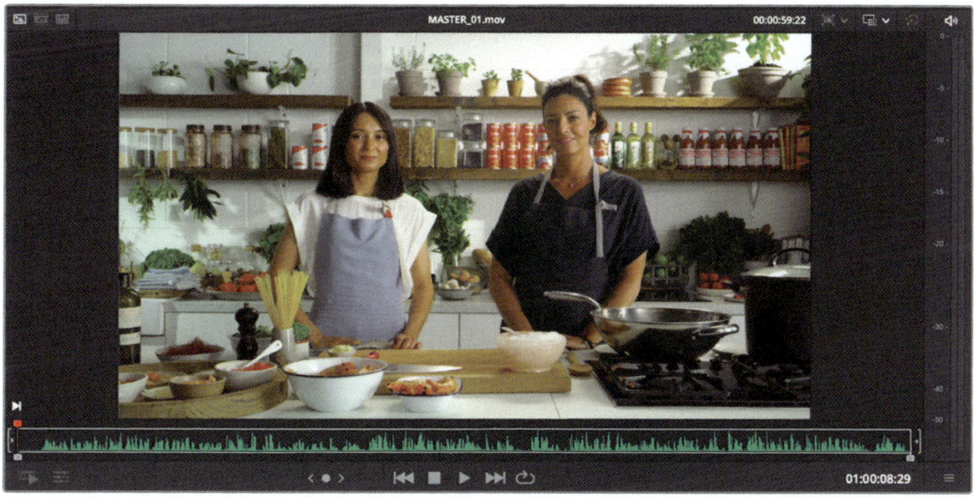

The viewer now shows the clip with the audio waveform under it. You can play a clip by pressing the spacebar.

2 Press the spacebar to play the clip in the viewer.

The is the main take in this cooking show. Since our host doesn't start speaking immediately, we can cut off the beginning of this clip before we add it to the timeline.

3 At the bottom of the viewer, drag the white in point handle so it is just before the host begins to speak.

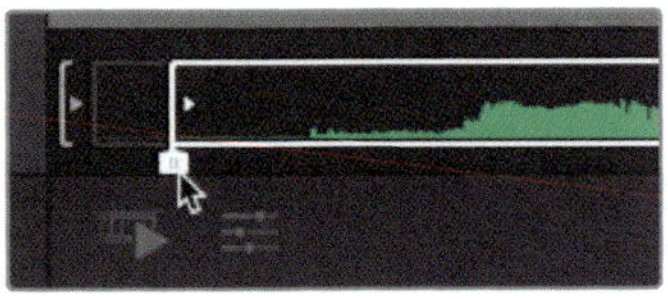

As you drag, the audio waveform zooms in automatically, making it easier to position the in point just before the host speaks.

4 With the in point set, drag the master 01 clip from the media pool down into the lower timeline window.

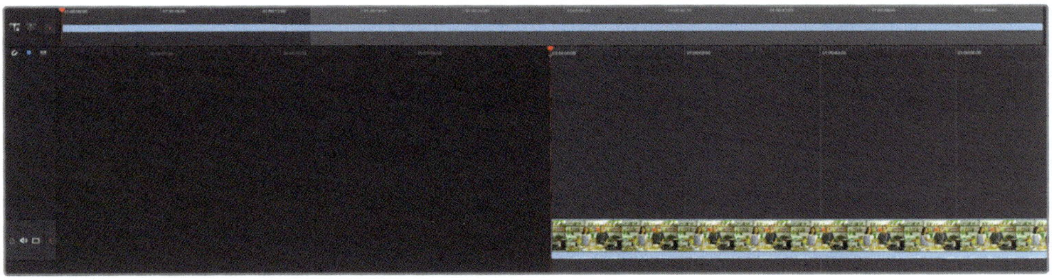

Adding a clip to an empty timeline window creates a new timeline and saves it into the master bin. All timelines created in the cut page are saved into the master bin, making them very easy to locate.

The trimmed clip becomes the first clip of your story. The viewer switches automatically to show you the clip in the timeline.

The timeline is a bit different from what you may be familiar with because there are actually two timelines. The upper timeline shows the entire length of your story. Having the entire timeline always visible makes it incredibly easy to move around, no matter how long the timeline gets.

5 In the upper timeline, click in the right end of the time ruler to move the red play head to the end of the edit.

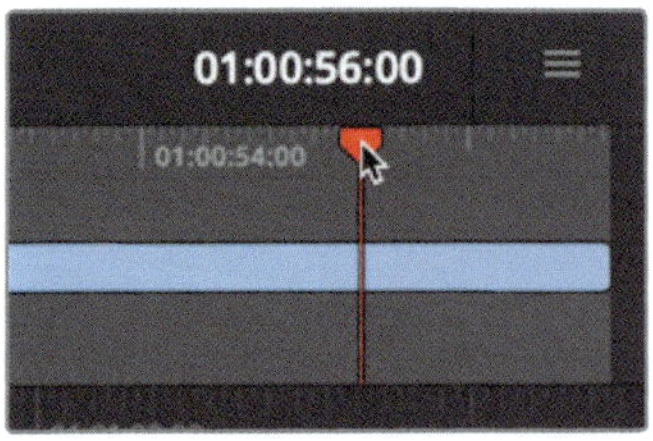

The red play head shows the location in the timeline for the frame displayed in the viewer. Moving the play head updates the frame in the viewer to match.

6 Drag the play head in the upper timeline, back to the left end until you are at the beginning of the edit.

The lower timeline shows a more zoomed in, detailed view of the current position. In the lower timeline, the play head always remains in the center while the timeline scrolls under it.

7 Press the spacebar to play the timeline until you hear the chef on the right say “prawn and basil spaghettini” (about 1/3rd of the way through the clip).

Since this is meant to be a short promotional video that you will share on the web, the part we just played is a good introduction for our story. Now, you can split this clip into two sections by adding a cut just after the chef say’s “spaghettini”. You can refine the play head position by scrubbing the in the lower timeline time ruler.

8 In the lower timeline, drag the time ruler right and left until the play head is just after the chef on the right says “spaghettini”.

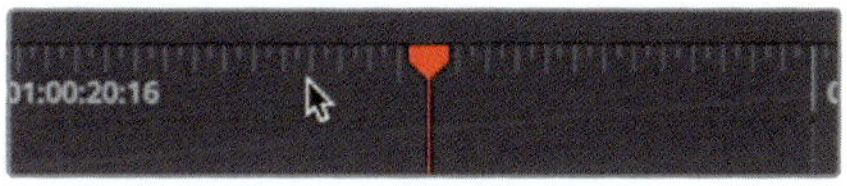

9 On the left side of the toolbar, click the split button to cut the clip at the play head position.

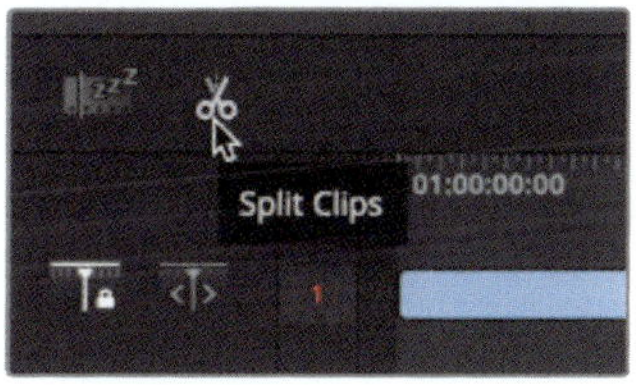

Splitting a clip in two using the split button creates what is called a *through edit*. This added cut or through edit in the timeline allows us to keep the first part of the clip and delete the unwanted part.

10 Select the section of the clip to the right of the play head and press the delete (macOS) or Backspace (Windows) key to remove that part of the clip.

We have a great opening clip to promote this show. The next steps will be to find the parts from other clips that we may be interested in using.

Reviewing clips using source tape

Rather than double clicking each clip and playing them one by one in the viewer, you can find specific clips faster using the source tape feature.

Back when editing was done using videotape, finding and reviewing content was easy because you could just shuttle up and down the tape to find the right area. Shuttling up and down a tape also provided the critical benefit of familiarizing you with the content. The source tape in the cut page brings back that old concept and completely modernizes it to help you find the shots that you need fast.

Let's quickly review some of our cooking shots using the source tape, so we know what we can use in our story.

1 From the upper left corner of the viewer, click the source tape button.

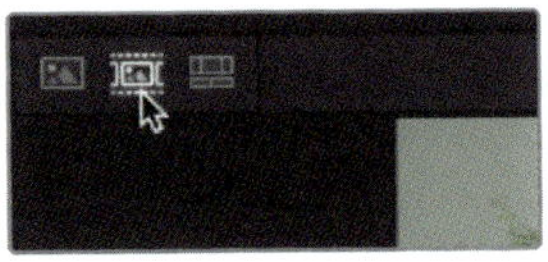

Clicking the source tape button places all the clips from the current bin into the viewer, as a single long clip. Thing white lines visually separate each clip along the audio waveform.

> **TIP** If the current bin contains other bins, the clips from the nested bins will be displayed in source tape mode as well.

2 Using the red play head under the viewer, drag through the entire source tape to view all the clips in the bin.

As you drag through the source tape, the current clip is highlighted in the bin as well.

> **TIP** Changing the sort order in the bin changes the order the clips are displayed in the source tape.

3 Drag back to the beginning of the source tape's string of clips.

To really review all the clips we are working with, you need to play through them and not just skip over them by dragging. The quickest way to review clips is to use the fast review feature.

4 Click the fast review button to play quickly through all the clips in the source tape string of clips.

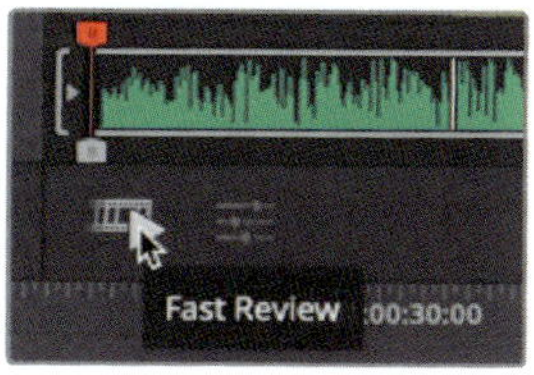

The fast review button plays through the clips at faster speeds for longer clips. When you reach one of the shorter clips, fast review will automatically slow down playback a bit so you don't miss shorter clips. This gives you a quick and easy way to review new material which is important if you're editing unfamiliar clips that someone else has shot. Once you review the content, you should have a good idea of a few shots you might like to use as you start to assemble your edit in the timeline.

Appending clips to the timeline

Once you have reviewed your content, you can start assembling the rest of the clips into your timeline. Instead of dragging, you can easily append clips one after another to the end of your timeline, building your story as you go. Since we have a good opening, let's look for a good ending to our promo.

1 While in the source tape, drag the play head to the last clip where the women pick up the finished plate and prepare to eat from it.

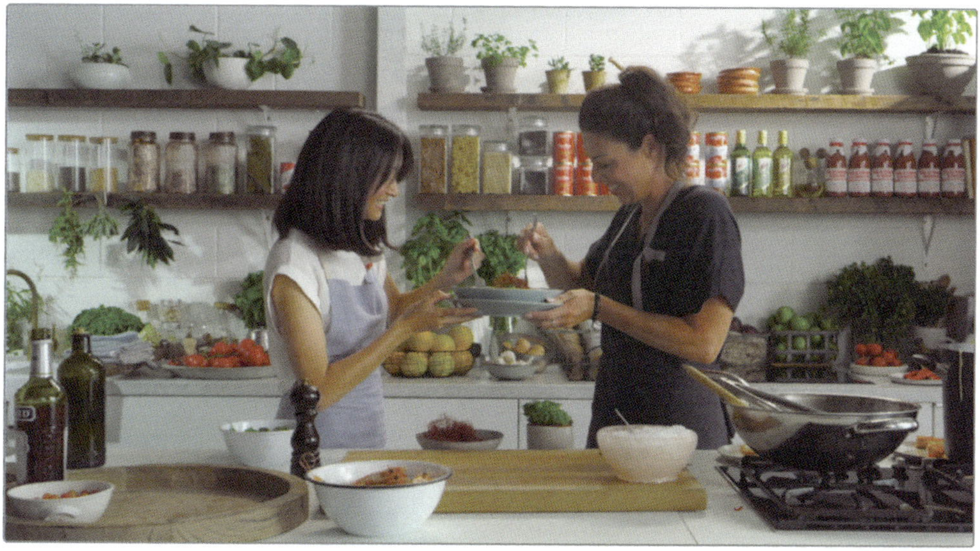

TIP A timecode display for the current play head position is located in the lower right corner of the viewer. You can use that to position the play head around 00:08:20 :00

2 Press I to mark an in point and then press O to set an out point after the host says "Make sure you join us next time".

To add this clip to the end of the timeline, you can use the append button. The append button always adds the marked clip to the very end of your timeline, regardless of where your timeline play head is located.

3 In the toolbar, click the append button to add the selected region to the end of the timeline.

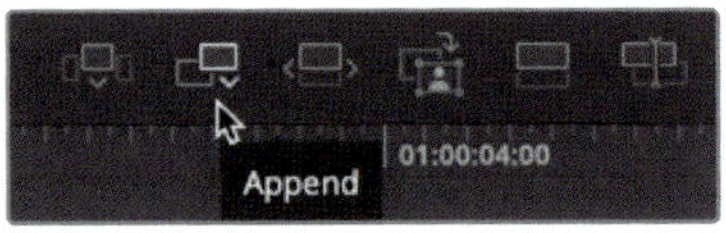

4 Normally, you would keep working down the source tape, adding clips into the timeline as you go. In this case, let's check our edit by dragging the play head before the new clip you added to the end, then press the spacebar to review the edit.

The append edit is one of the easiest editing types since it just adds the current source clip to the end of your timeline. It doesn't matter where your timeline play head is located or if there is an in point. Using the other edit buttons will give you additional options on where edits are placed.

Remember the advantage of the source tape is you can keep throwing clips into the timeline as you go and quickly build complex edits. The viewer will stay on the source tape so you don't waste mouse clicks selecting clips after each edit.

Marking In and Out with precision

Although dragging through clips using the mouse pointer is very straight forward, when trying to set in and out points on longer clips, it is fairly difficult to be precise. That's because moving the mouse pointer even by one or two pixels can jump several frames or even seconds if you have a longer clip. A more precise method of setting an in or out point is to use the scratch trim buttons located under the viewer, on either side of the waveform. Let's see how it works.

1 While still in the source tape viewer, drag the play head near the end of the first clip where the chef picks up the pasta for the first time.

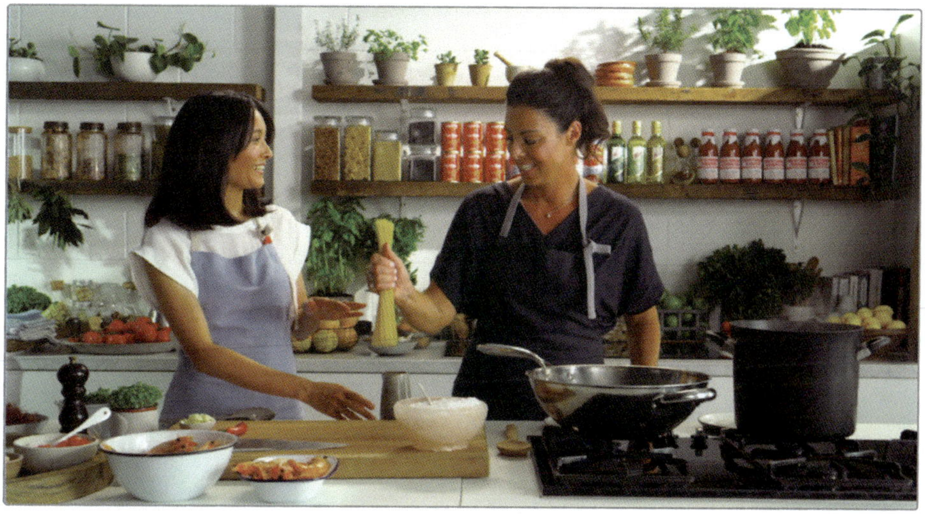

2 Press the I key on your keyboard to mark the start also called an in point.

3 Under the viewer, from the left side of the audio waveform display, drag the scratch trim button to move slowly across the clip and precisely set the in point just before the chef says “so this is spaghettini” .

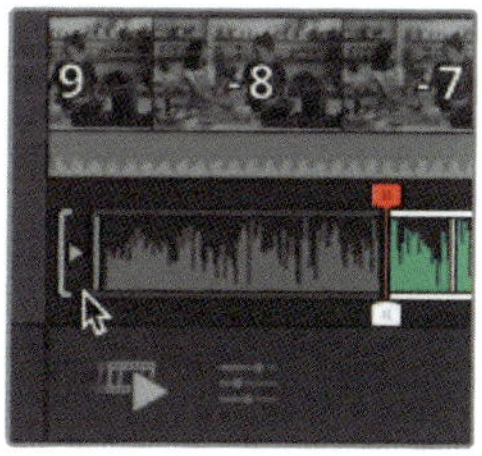

This scratch trim button is used to reposition the in point on the clip with incredible control and precision no matter the length of the clip in the viewer.

Dragging the scratch trim button moves the in point in consistently small increments no matter if the clip is 5 seconds or 5 minutes long. This gives you much better control over selecting the exact range you want to use in your program.

NOTE Scratch trim is very important when using the source tape, as you could have lots of clips in your bin and loaded into the viewer. For even greater precision in trimming in and out points, the DaVinci Resolve Editor Keyboard has a large search dial that makes accurate trimming even faster.

The audio waveform under the viewer is magnified to show a more detailed view of the audio as you move across a clip with the scratch trim button.

4 With the in point set, press shift-I to go to the in point.

5 Press spacebar to play until you hear the host say "So what are we moving on to" then press O to mark the end also called the out point.

By dragging the right side scratch trim button, you can refine the current out point.

6 Drag the right side scratch trim button back and forth to ensure you are positioned just after the chef says "moving on to" but before the clip ends.

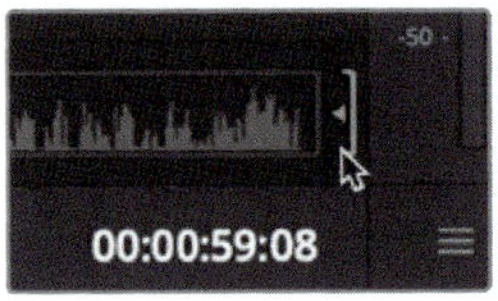

You now have an in and out point and can add this clip into the timeline. Instead of only adding clips to the end of the timeline, you can insert clips between two cuts by dragging directly into the upper timeline.

7 Drag directly from the viewer in between the two clips in the upper timeline.

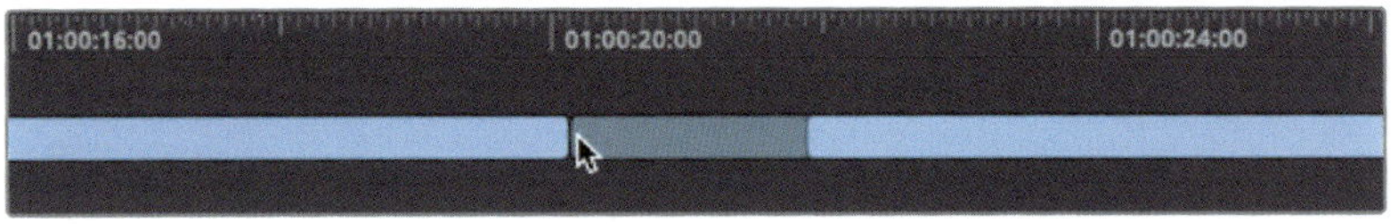

The existing clips separate to make room for the clip you drag between them.

8 Release the mouse to insert the clip into the timeline.

TIP Dragging a clip from the media pool or the viewer, on top of a clip in the timeline and immediately releasing the mouse, will perform a ripple overwrite. Releasing the mouse after 3 seconds will perform a standard overwrite.

9 As before, lets take a moment to view our edit by going to the upper timeline, drag the play head before the new clip, then press the spacebar to review the clip you added to your story.

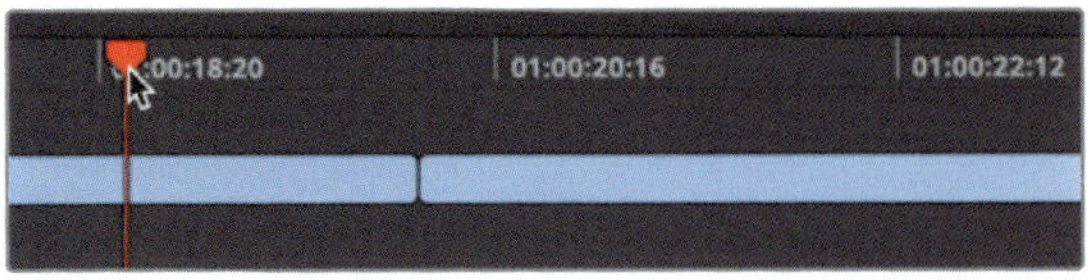

Drag and drop, as well as the append edit button, are just two quick examples of the editing functions in the cut page. There are other, very smart editing tools that we will explore as well.

Using intelligent editing tools

Many of the editing tools in the cut page have extra intelligence built in to help you make better decisions. Even the familiar edit types like insert are given a bit more intelligence than you might normally expect. Let's first locate the timeline play head where we want a new clip inserted.

10 In the upper timeline, move the playhead near the start of the last clip.

11 Click the source tape button above the viewer, then drag through until you see the flames from the flambé.

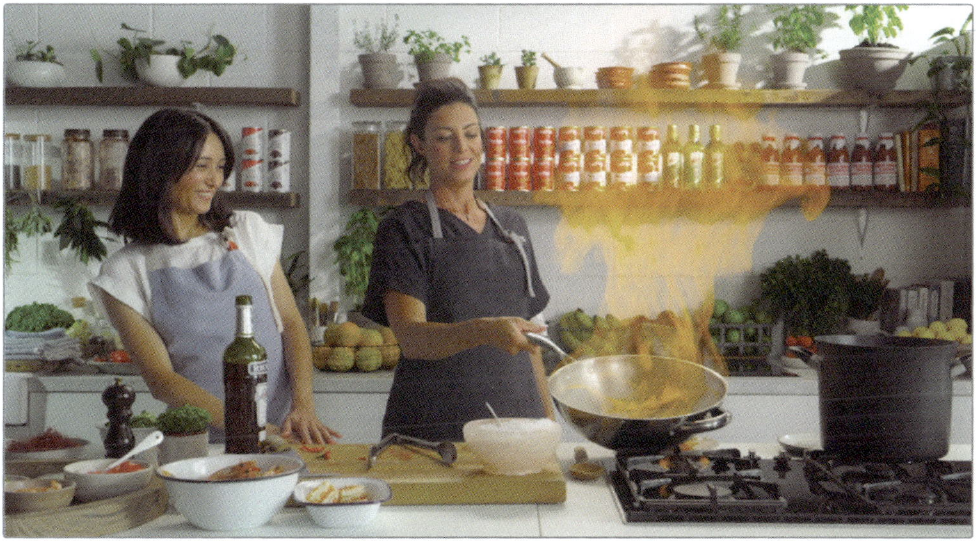

Setting an in point just before the flames appear is a great starting point for the next clip we add to our story. Similar to the scratch trim controls, you can use the jog control to slowly move back and forth to find the perfect starting point. Unlike the scratch trim controls, the jog control does not set in and out points as it only moves the play head. It is up to you to set the in and out points with the keyboard.

12 Drag over the jog control to move the play head backwards just after the chef says "it caramelizes beautifully" and just before she says "so here we go."

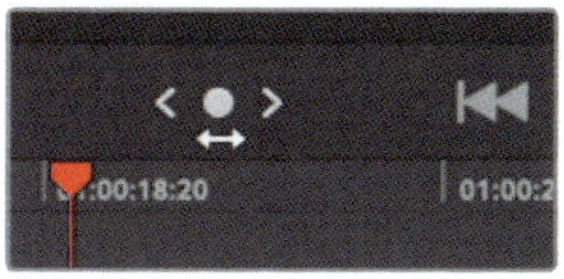

13 Press I to mark an in point.

14 Drag over the jog control again to move the play head forwards until the chef says "eyebrows OK? Intact?" and press O to mark an out point.

With the timeline play head already near the cut where you want this new clip inserted, the smart insert button will handle the rest.

15 Click the smart insert button in the toolbar.

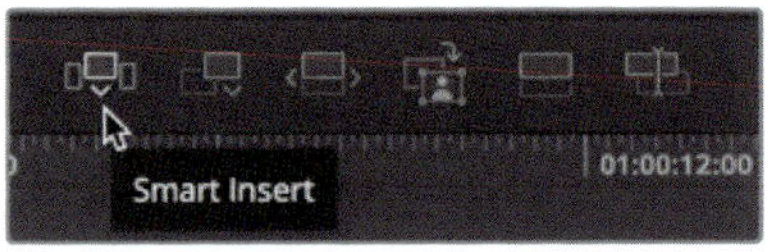

The smart insert finds the nearest edit point and inserts the source clip in between the two existing clips in the timeline.

16 Play your timeline from just before the new clip you inserted to review it.

When performing a smart insert, the play head does not have to be directly over the cut point; it just has to be near enough to the cut where you want the source clip inserted. Let's try another example.

17 Position the play head anywhere near the start of the clip you just inserted.

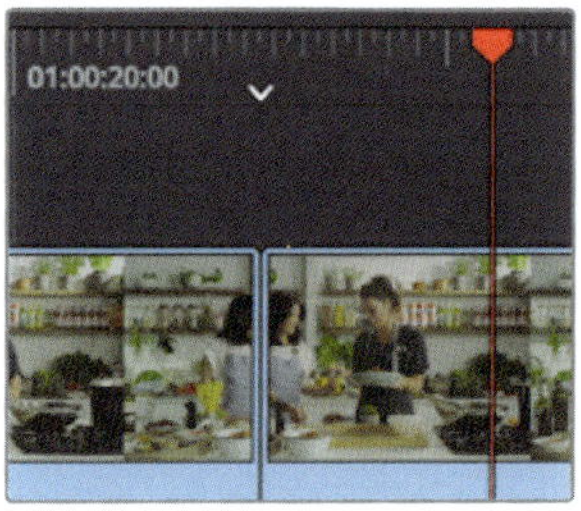

This time, notice the small down arrow icon in the lower timeline time ruler, above the cut. This is called a smart indicator.

The smart indicator shows where the insert will take place. When you position the play head in the timeline, the smart indicator automatically appears, showing you where the nearest cut is located.

18 In the upper left of the viewer, click the source tape button or press Q on your keyboard.

19 In the source tape viewer, drag over the third clip, the side view.

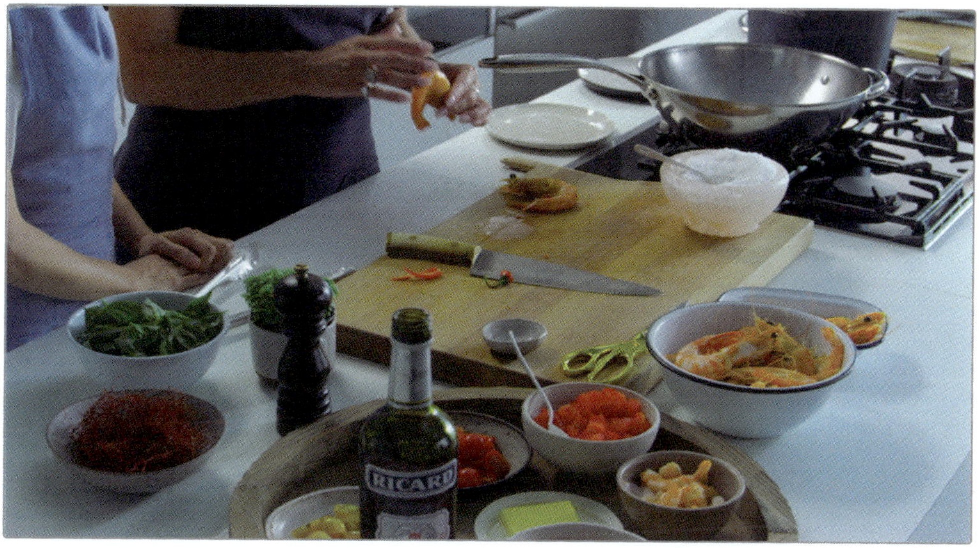

20 Use the jog control to position the play head near the start of the clip, just after the host says "There's a bit of a technique to that isn't there?"

21 Mark an in point and continue jogging through the clip until the chef says "a bit of muscle" and they both laugh. Then mark an out point.

With the play head near the cut where you want this new clip inserted, you can again use smart insert button.

22 Click the smart insert button in the toolbar.

23 Play your timeline from the beginning to review it.

Again, the smart insert finds the nearest cut point and it inserts the source clip in between the two existing clips in the timeline.

Creating a close up angle

Now that we have a timeline roughly created, we'd like to add a few cutaways or even replace clips that might last a bit too long. The cut page can give you a bit more assistance in finding areas that need attention. One easy way to have the cut page help is to use the boring detector.

1 On the far left of the toolbar click the boring detector button.

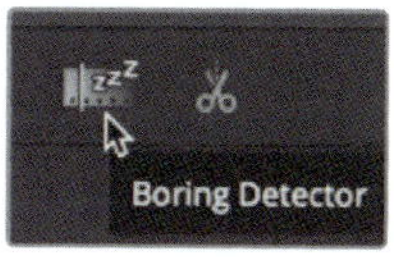

The boring detector window that opens allows you to define clips that may be too long as well as clips that may be too short. You can use this window to highlight areas in the timeline you consider to be too long or too short for this program.

2 Using the top slider in the window, change the value to 15. This sets the analysis to highlight areas of clips that extend longer than 15 seconds.

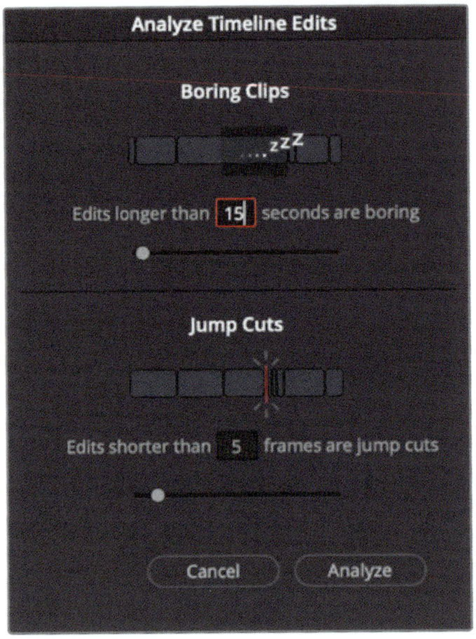

The bottom slider in the window can be used to locate jump cuts or any cut shorter than a specified duration. The default setting of 5 seconds is suitable for our program, so we can leave that alone.

3 Click the Analyze button to turn the analysis on and see the results of the settings.

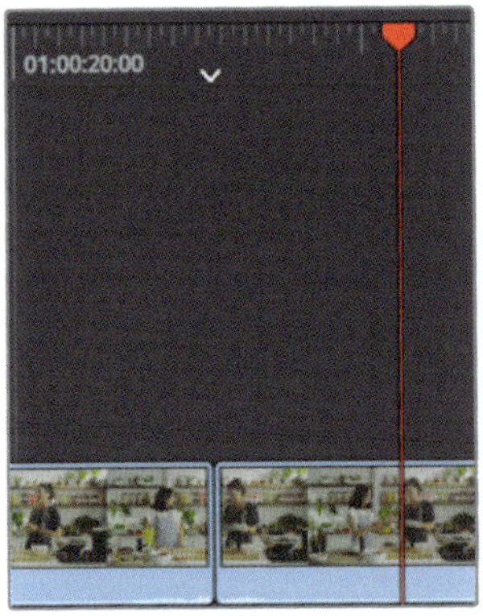

Two areas in the upper timeline are highlighted, showing us where clips extend longer than 10 seconds. As we make changes to these sections, the analysis updates, so we'll have real time feedback as long as the boring detector button is enabled. Let's start at the beginning and fix the first clip indicated by the analysis as too long.

4 Play the timeline from the start and stop when the host says "really quick..".

We can make this opening a bit more interesting by cutting to a close up of the host as she introduces herself and the chef. Unfortunately, we don't have a close up, but we can make one using the close up edit in the cut page.

5 Using the lower timeline time ruler, move the timeline so it is positioned right after the host says "really quick".

6 Click the close up edit button in the toolbar.

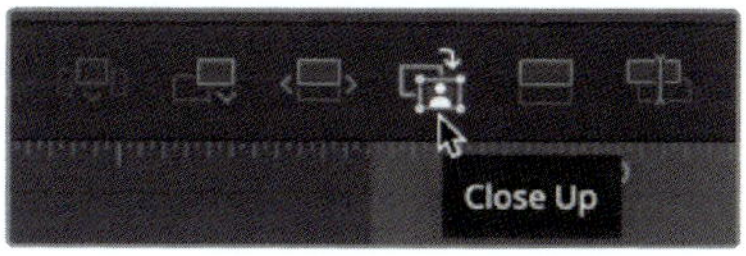

A five second close up is edited into the timeline on a second video track, making this opening a bit more interesting to watch.

Using the close up edit button, there is no need to load a clip into the viewer. It's smart enough to locate the same clip and the exact frame where the playhead is located, then edit it into the timeline on to video track 2, scaling it up to create a close up. It uses the DaVinci Neural Engine to locate the faces in the shot and keep them centered in the frame.

7 Move the playhead back towards the start of the clip and play over your new close up.

TIP You can change the close up edit's default 5 second duration using the Still setting in the User Editing Preferences.

Creating new close up camera angles is one of the many reasons why it helps to capture your clips using a camera like the Blackmagic Pocket Cinema Camera. Even though your timeline may be HD, if the source clips are at a higher resolution, the close up will be sharper.

Adding a simple cut away

To make the opening even more enticing, we'll use a clip of the finished dish at the start of our program while the chef introduces the dish. This is often called a cutaway since we are cutting away from the main action to show a related but different shot.

1 Starting at the first clip in the timeline, use the lower timeline to position the play head at the end of the close up you added to video track 2.

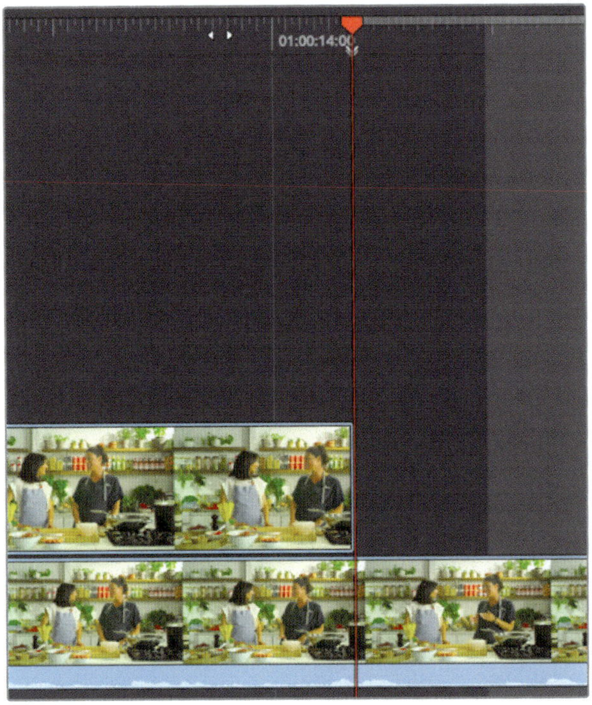

For this cutaway, we would like the new clip to play over the end of the master shot on V1 where the chef describes the dish she will make. To ensure the clip starts and stops precisely over this area, we can mark an in and out point in the timeline.

2 Press I to mark an in point.

3 Drag in the lower timeline's time ruler to the end of the clip and mark an out point.

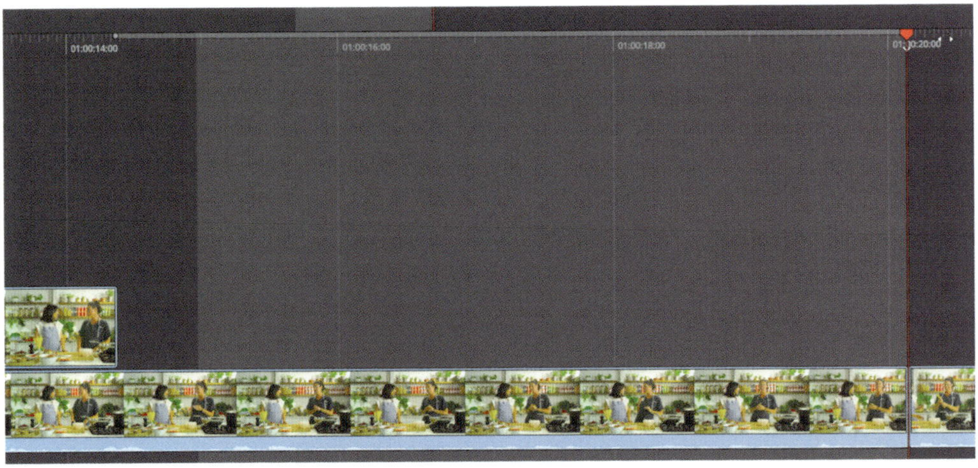

As you move the upper or lower timeline to find a location, you will feel the play head snap to any cut point. This helpful snapping action will make sure you are directly over the cut when you mark the out.

4 Click the source tape button or press Q to return to viewing all the source clips in the viewer.

5 In the source tape, locate the third clip from the end which shows a top view of the cutting board

6 Position the play head just as the chef grabs the pepper mill and brings it into frame.

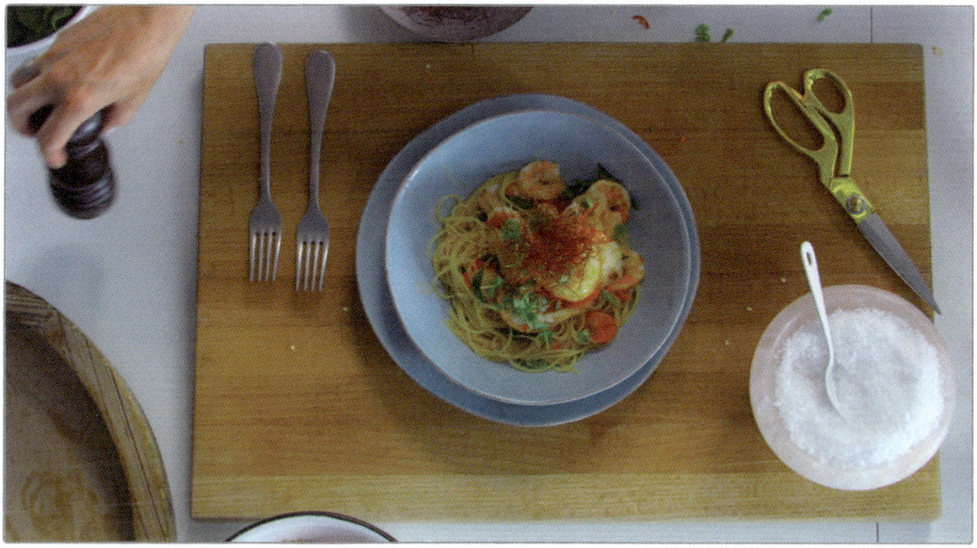

7 Press I to mark an in point.

You will only need an in point since you already have an in and out set in the timeline. This is traditionally called a three-point edit.

8 In the toolbar, click the place on top button to create your cutaway.

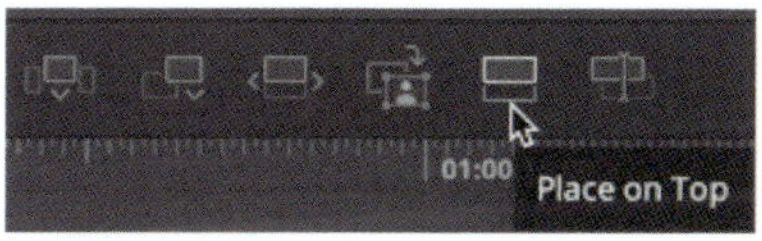

9 Move to the start of the timeline and play over the new addition.

Similar to the close up edit, the place on top edit puts the new cut on top of the one in the timeline but without the zoom in effect. The audio can still be heard from the original clip.

Replacing a clip with ripple overwrite

The last shot is also highlighted as being a little too long. Since the first part of this shot just has them slurping noodles, we'll cut the clip into two sections and then replace the first half with something more interesting.

1 In the upper timeline, move to the last clip in the timeline, where they have mostly eaten the noodle but before the host turns to the camera.

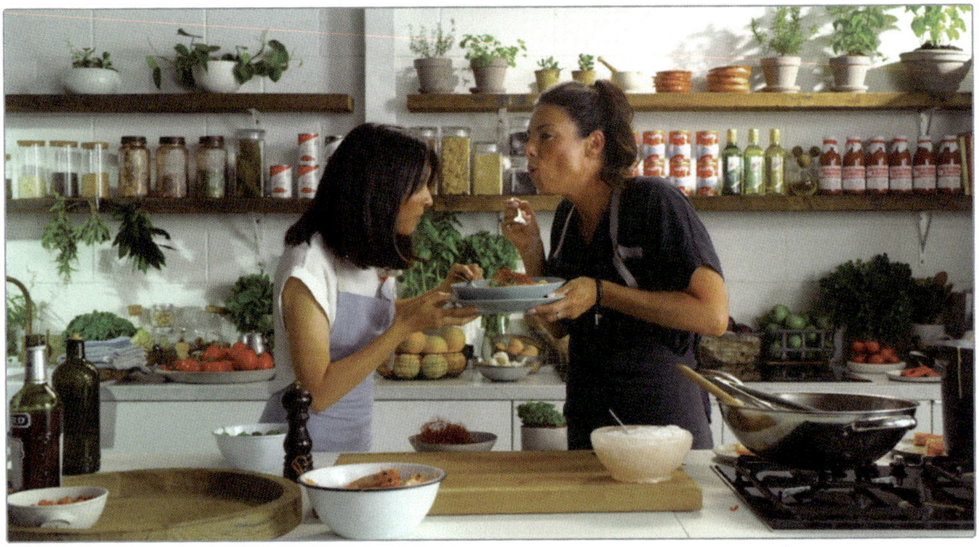

2 To split the clip, click the split button on the left side of the toolbar to create a through edit.

   The last part of this clip is a good way to end our story but we'll replace the first half of them eating with another clip from our source tape.

3 Position the timeline play head anywhere over the first half of the clip you just divided in two.

   When replacing one clip with another, it does not matter where you position the timeline play head as long as it is somewhere over the clip you want to replace.

4 Click the source tape button or press Q to return to viewing all the source clips in the viewer.

   The transport controls under the viewer includes buttons for play and stop. While using source tape, you also have go-to-next and previous clip buttons. This can be a quick and easy way to jump to different clips in the source tape.

5 Under the source tape viewer, click the go-to-next clip button a few times until you are at the next to last clip and you see the side view close up of the empty plate.

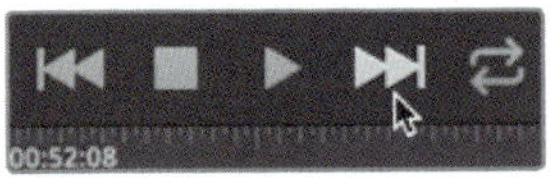

We'll use this shot to replace the one that is currently in the timeline.

6 Press I to mark an in point, and mark an out point after she says "micro basil".

   You could insert this new clip and then delete the old one from the timeline but that seems like a lot of extra work. Instead, you can use the ripple overwrite button.

7 In the toolbar click the ripple overwrite button.

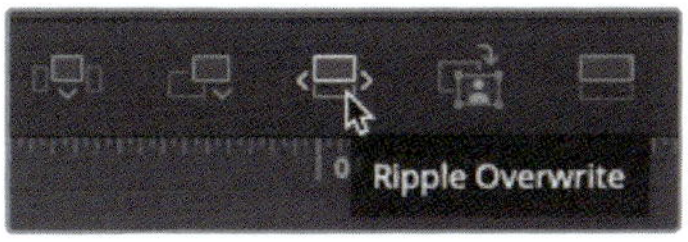

8 In the timeline, back up to the previous clip to review your new edit.

   The ripple overwrite replaces whichever clip your play head is over in the timeline with the clip you are currently viewing and have marked in the source viewer. If the clips are different lengths, the source clip in and out are used for the length of the new clip.

Editing multiple camera angles

The content for this cooking show used multiple cameras and each camera used time of day for its timecode number. The result is that each camera has the same time stamp on every frame. With all the cameras synced to the same timecode, you can save much time in editing in several ways. One significant way the cut page takes advantage of multiple synced cameras is through a new bin type called a sync bin.

1 Move the timeline back a few of clips to where the chef is cutting the prawn on the cutting board.

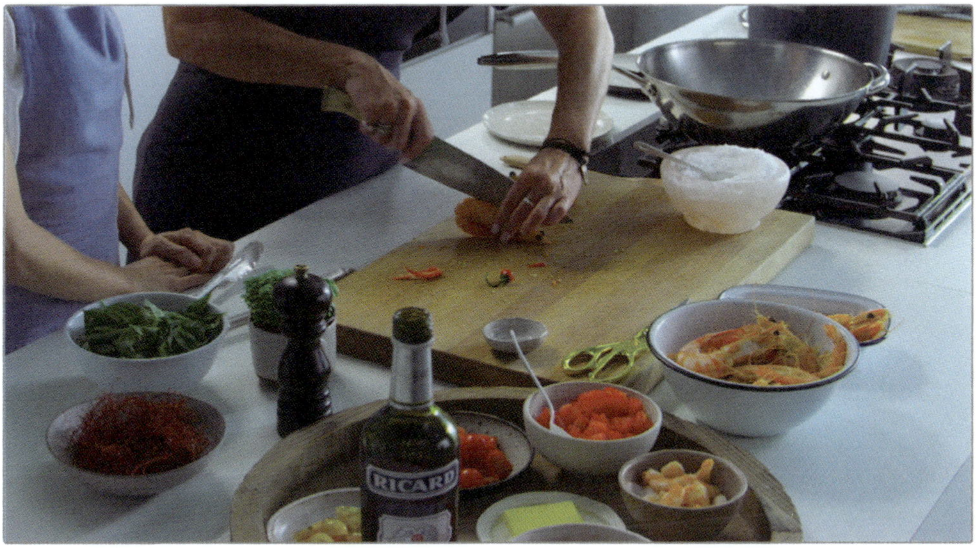

The boring detector highlights the end of this clip as being a bit too long. It might be nicer to break this shot up and switch to a few different angles while cutting the prawns. We can switch to the sync bin to see the other camera angles available at this time.

2 Click the sync bin button above the media pool.

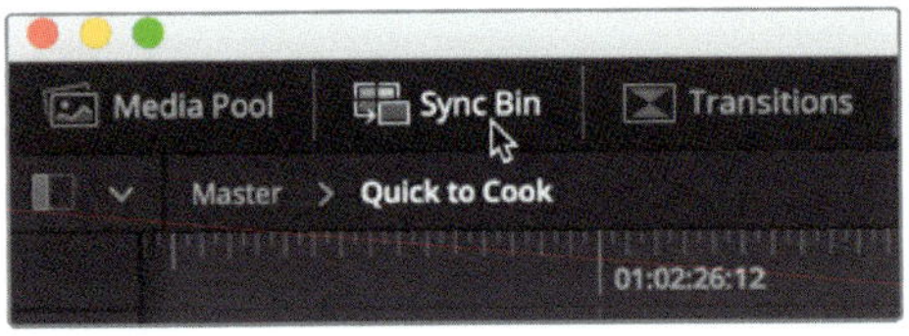

The sync bin arranges clips based on the camera # and their time code. All the camera angles in the bin that match the current timeline location are displayed under the sync bin play head.

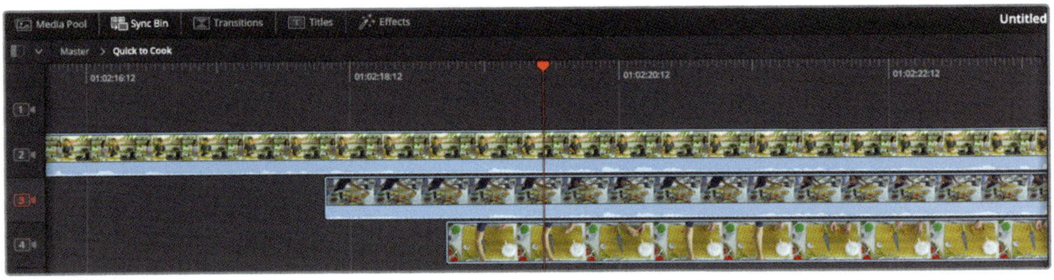

You control the sync bin using the timeline play head.

TIP If your clips do not have camera #s, you can add camera # using the media page metadata inspector.

3 Drag the timeline play head backwards and forwards over your program to see the different synced camera angles display in the sync bin.

As you drag, various clips in the sync bin start and stop based on if they are in sync with the current timeline play head. The viewer displays a multi view of all the synced camera angles, highlighting the one currently used in the timeline.

4 Drag the timeline play back to the side view where the chef start to cut the prawn, just before she says “cutting the prawn in half”.

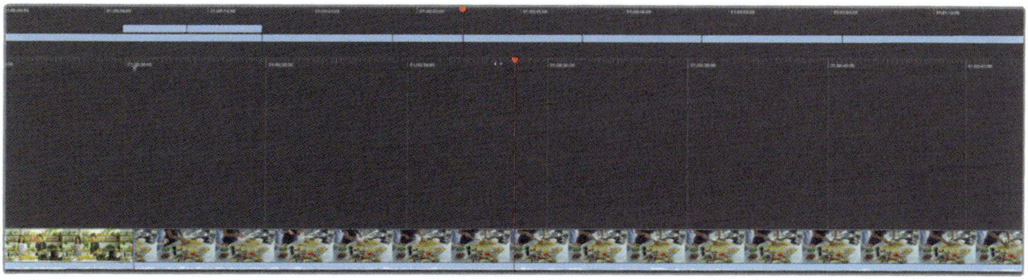

To select a new angle you want to use you just click in the viewer.

5 Click camera 2, the master shot of the two women.

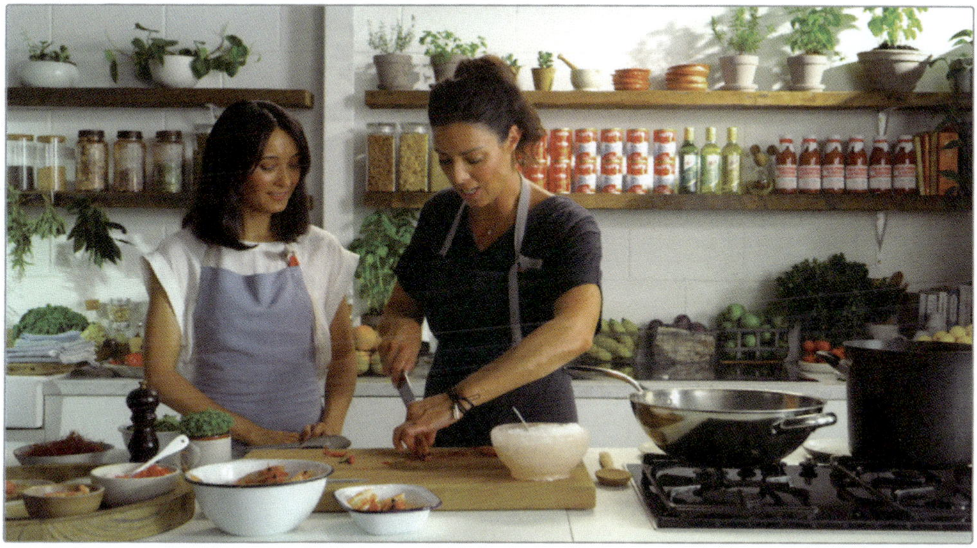

The in point of camera 2 is automatically set to match the current timeline location. The out point is set at a default 5 seconds duration. To make the edit, we’ll use the source overwrite button.

6 In the toolbar, click the source overwrite button.

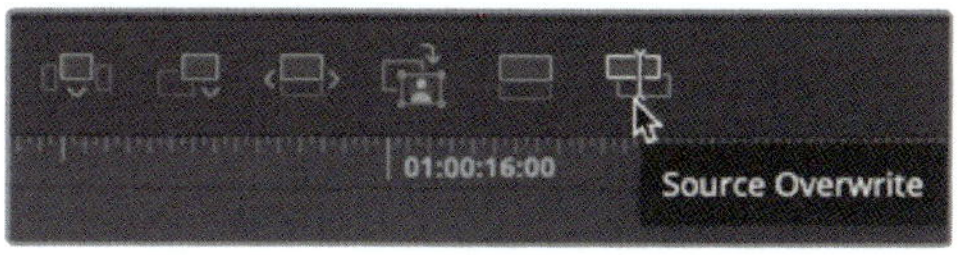

The source overwrite adds the new camera angle on top of the existing video track. Since the source overwrite takes full advantage of the matching timecode, the angles line up perfectly and the action remains in sync. Performing a source overwrite places the timeline playhead at the end of the newly added clip, so you are ready to make another edit.

7 In the viewer, click camera 4 to switch to the top view of the cutting board.

   If you want to change the in or out point you can use the scratch trim controls to refine them before you make the edit.

8 On the far bottom right of the viewer, drag the scratch trim out button to the left, and stop after the chef's lays out the second shrimp on the table.

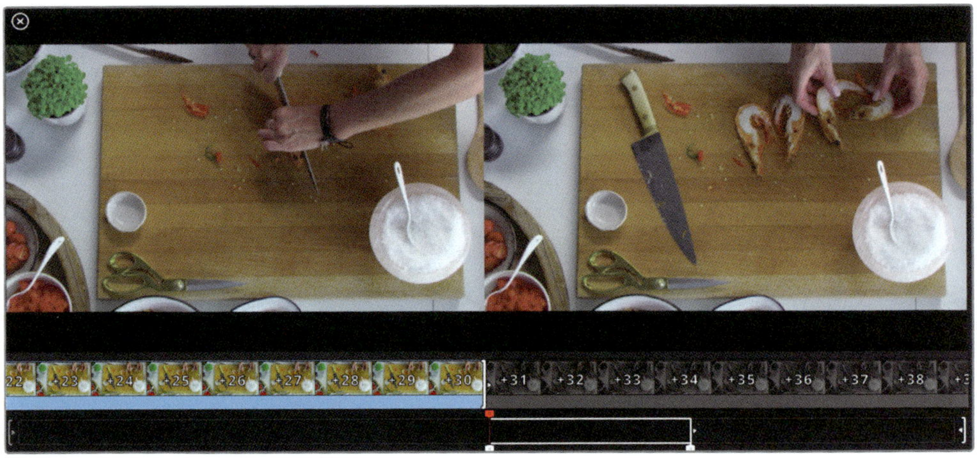

9 Click source overwrite to add another perfectly synced clip to the timeline.

   With two edits made quickly, let's review this new area of our timeline.

10 Above the viewer, click the timeline button to view the timeline.

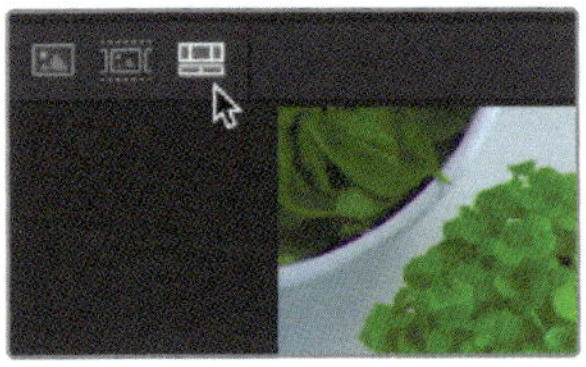

11 In the upper timeline, move the timeline play head back to where you started, seeing the side view of the cutting board.

12 Play the timeline to review the edits.

   The beauty of the sync bin is that you can see all the shots at the same time and pick whichever you like best.

Syncing clips

You are not always going to have clips with matching timecode. So, built into the cut page is a sync window where you can align clips in a variety of ways other than timecode.

1 Click on the media pool button to hide the sync bin.
2 To the right of the import folder button, click the sync window button.

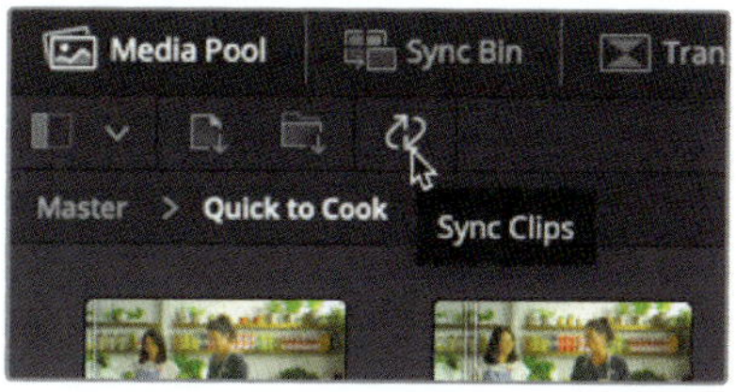

The sync window opens to show all the clips in the current bin and their sync relationships. The sync window defaults to sync by timecode but you can also use it to sync by audio, In point or out point as well.

3 Click the audio button.

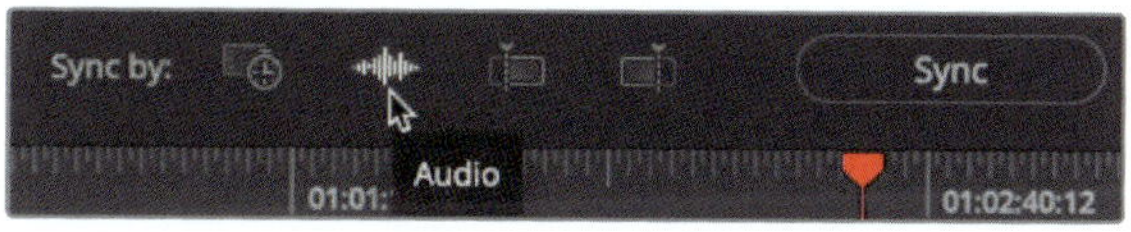

If all the camera angles have audio recorded, you can sync based on the matching audio waveforms.

4 Click the in point button.

When the in or out point button is selected, clips will sync based on the in or out points you have set. However, at anytime you can drag clips in the sync window to align them manually. Since we have timecode, we'll return to the timecode settings.

5 Click the timecode button.

With your choice made for how to sync the clips, clicking the sync button will perform the alignment.

6 Click the sync button, then in the lower right corner of the window, click save sync.

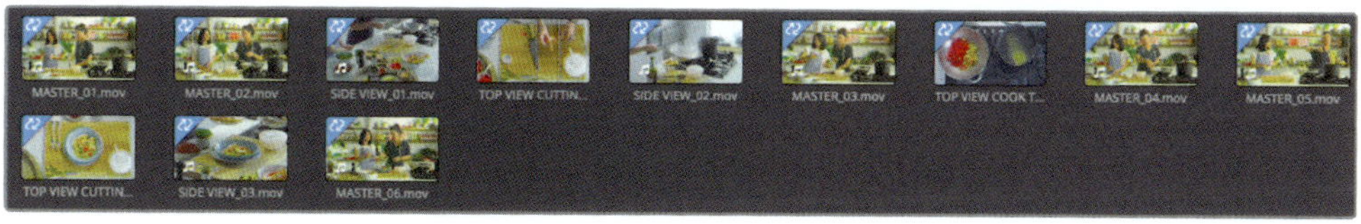

Saving the sync window applies a sync label in the upper left corner of all the clips that you have synced. This helps to identify clips that are not yet aligned with other clips.

The sync window lets you sync non-timecode sources like action cams and mobile phone clips with your professionally recorded content.

Trimming edits

As simple as adding clips to the timeline can seem, you often need to modify the in or out point after the clip gets added to the timeline. Instead of splitting clips and deleting sections, you can fine tune a clip's start point or end point using the cut page's trimming features. In the cut page, there are three areas where you can trim a clip. The upper timeline is for making large scale changes, the lower timeline for smaller changes and directly in the viewer for very precise, frame by frame trimming.

1 Move the timeline play head to the start of the next to last clip, the side view of the finished dish.

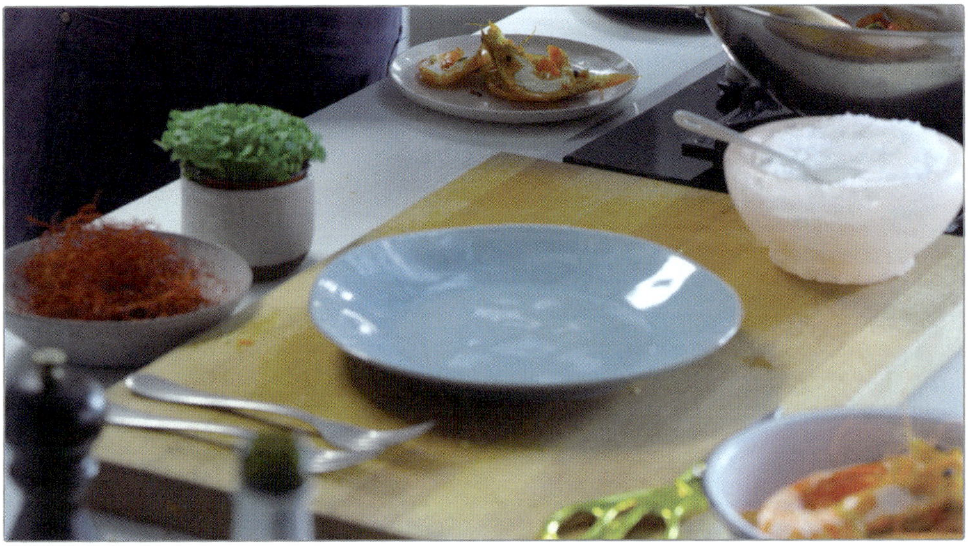

When making small, accurate trims, trimming can be performed using the lower timeline.

2 In the lower timeline, move the mouse pointer over the right side of the cut at the start of the clip.

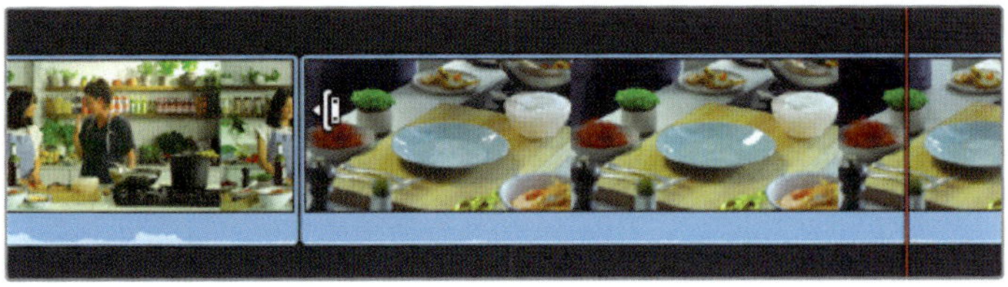

The cursor changes to the ripple trim cursor that can be used to lengthen or shorten a clip's duration. With the cursor to the right side of the cut, you are selecting to trim the in point, or "head" of the cut.

3 Drag the in point until the clip begins just before the plate of the prawns comes into the frame.

TIP The red highlight that appears when you select this in point indicates there are no additional frames available to extend this clip.

As you drag, the viewer goes into trim mode, with a 2 up view to show you the last frame of the clip you are trimming and the first frame of the next clip.

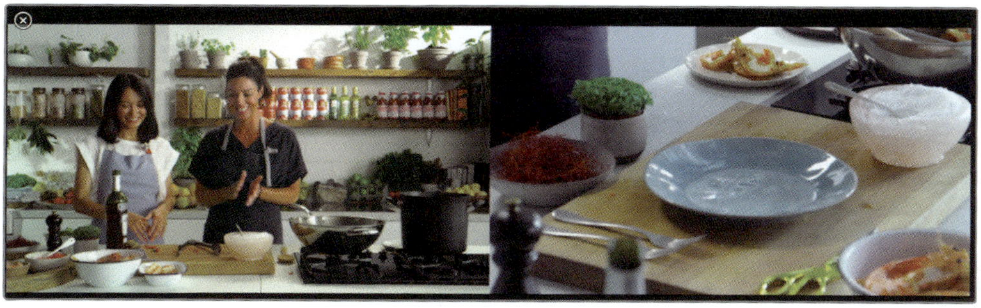

TIP The white outline that is displayed in the lower timeline as you trim shows the remaining frames you have in the source clip.

This 2-up side-by-side display is designed to show how the action and framing from the two sides of a cut will match up (or not). For trimming longer cuts, you can also trim in the upper timeline.

4 Move the play head to the start of the second clip on video track 1 in your timeline.

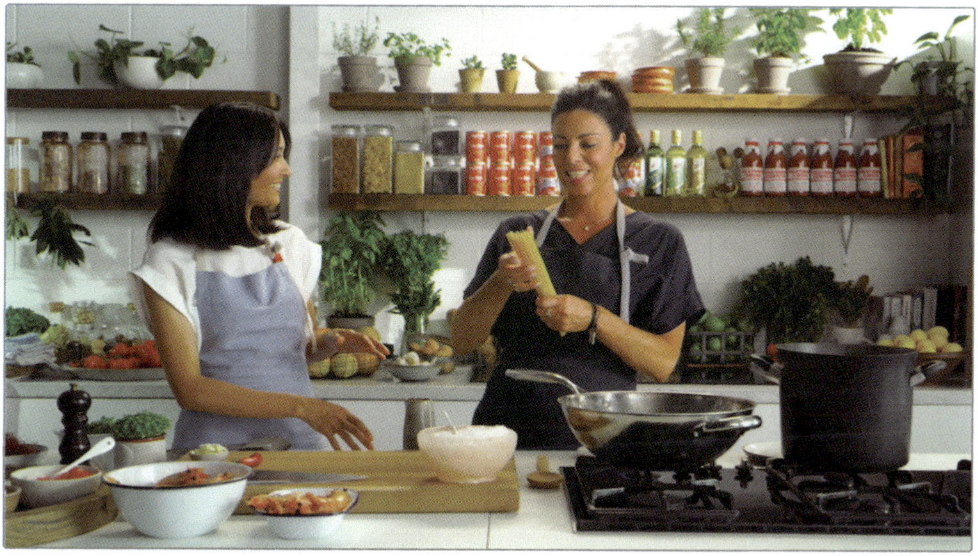

5 Play over the master shot to hear the chef describe spaghettini as angle hair pasta.

This clip can be more concise if we trim the end so the clip stops after the chef says "sometimes it's called angle hair pasta".

Just like the lower timeline, the upper timeline is a fully functional timeline where you can move clips around and trim them. It is especially convenient when dealing with longer clips.

6 In the upper timeline, position the mouse pointer over the end of the clip you want to trim.

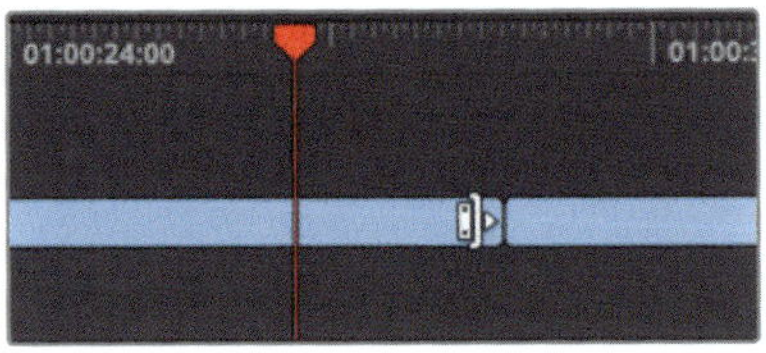

When the cursor is to the left side of the cut, it will trim the out point, or "tail" of the cut.

7 Drag the out point until after the chef says "sometimes it's called angle hair pasta"

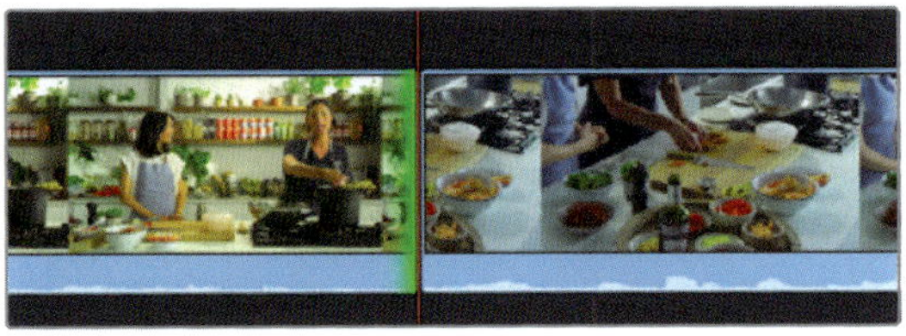

When trimming an in or out point on video track 1 the cut page performs a ripple trim. Ripple trimming pulls in all the clips after the trim point, leaving no empty space when shortening the clip (much like the delete that you performed earlier in this lesson.)

Even the clips on video track 2 move based on the trimming that happens on video track 1. This ensures all the cut aways stay in sync with the master video 1 track even as you trim.

Fine tuning a trim in the viewer

When it comes down to trimming out just a few frames to match action perfectly or remove a single word at the start or end of a clip, the place to do that is within the viewer. The viewer's trim editor has single frame trim buttons and easy visuals for trimming precisely the amount you want.

1 Use the upper timeline to go the start of the 3rd clip on video track 1. This shows the side view of the prawns being cut.

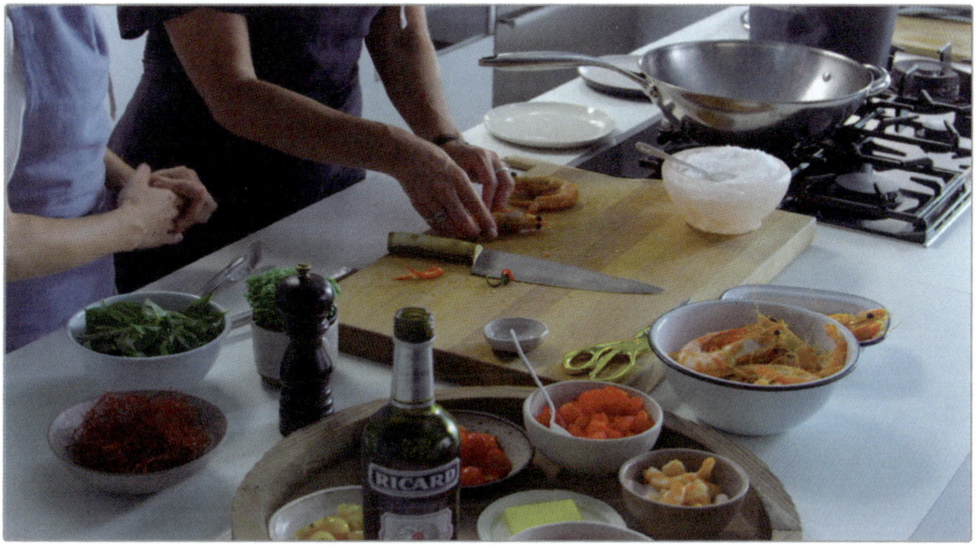

2 Play over the start of the clip and listen to the audio.

As you play over the beginning of the clip you'll hear the chef start out with the word "yeah". You'll want to cut this unnecessary word out from the start of this clip. It's only a few frames so it can be tricky to do by dragging in the timeline.

3 Move the mouse pointer over the start of the cut point and click to select it.

When you select any clip to trim, the viewer shows the trim editor.

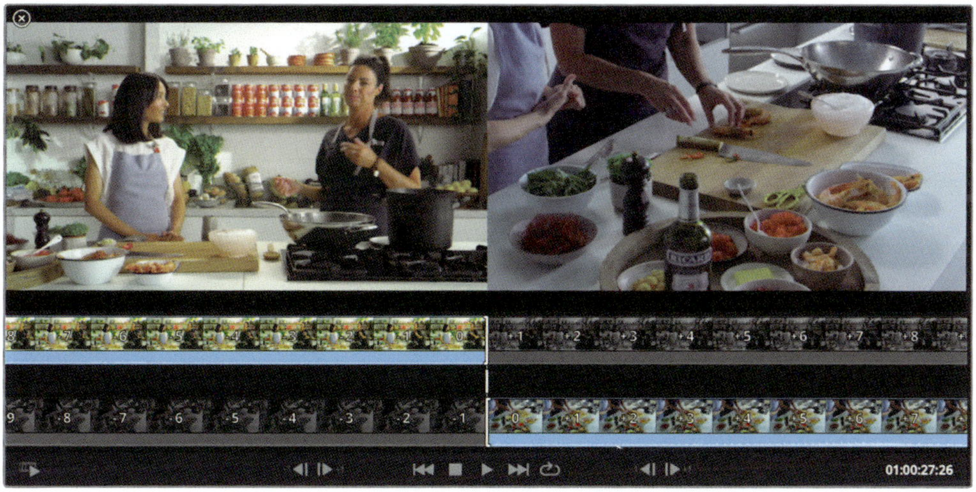

The viewer's trim editor show a close up view of the previous outgoing clip and the next incoming clip. The transition point is identified by a white vertical line in the center of the film strips. This is often called an A/B trimmer since the outgoing clip also called the A side, appears as a filmstrip on the left, and the incoming clip called the B side appears on the right.

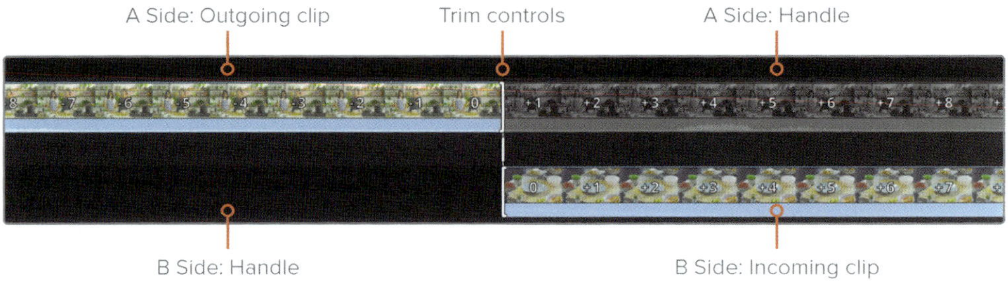

The shaded parts of the filmstrip show the unused sections of the clips that can be used to extend either clip. Since we've already established that the B side incoming clip has no additional handle, there is no shaded part for this clip.

You can ripple trim either of the cuts by dragging the trim control on its filmstrip. You can also trim both sides of the transition simultaneously by dragging the trim control in the gray area between the two clips.

But for very small trims you can use the single frame buttons for the outgoing side or the incoming side.

4 In the viewer, click 5 to 8 times on the +1 frame button under the incoming clip to remove the word yeah.

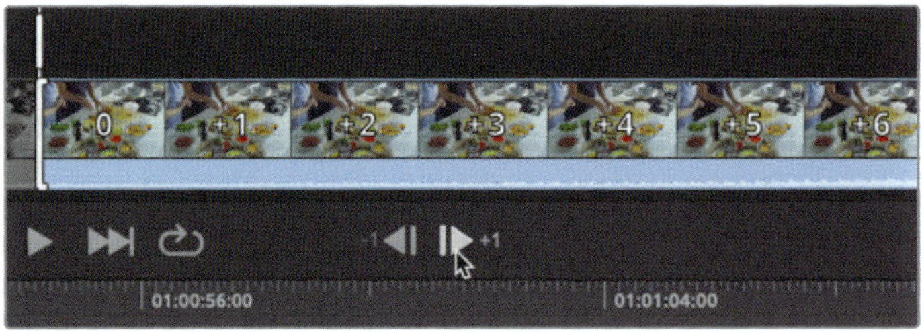

5 Reposition the timeline play head and play over the start of the clip to hear the new in point.

Trimming a few frames removed the word yeah from the start of the clip. You can see how much easier it is to use the viewer buttons when trimming small, precise areas.

Rolling trims

Whereas ripple trimming adds or removes frames from a single side of a cut (In point or out point), rolling trims simultaneously trim both sides of the cut. You can perform rolling trims where ever it is most convenient, the upper timeline, lower timeline or directly in the viewer.

1 Play over the second set of cut away clips on video track 2 of the prawns getting cut.

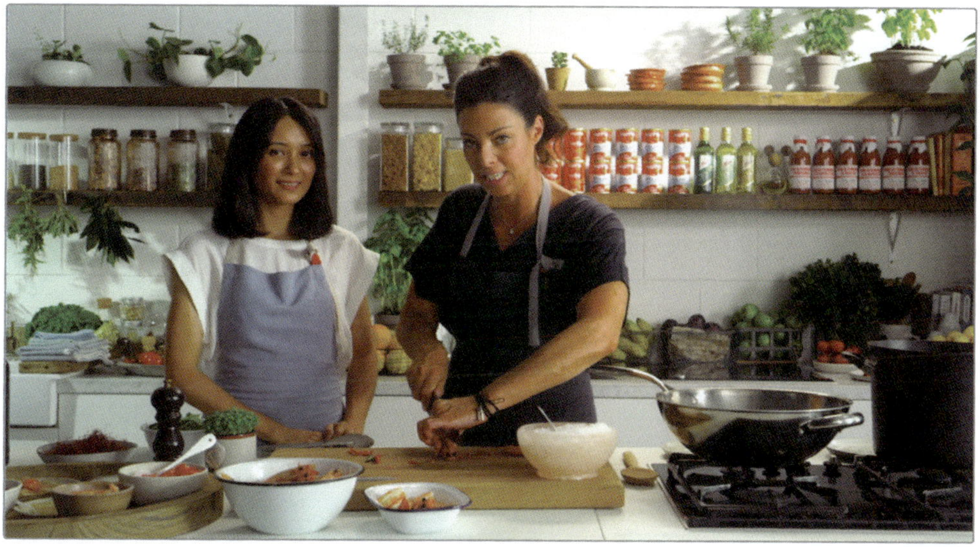

This will make for a better cut if we switch just as the chef's hand pushes palm down on the knife. In this situation, we don't want to extend one shot while leaving the other alone. We want to move the cut just a bit later by extending the master shot a few seconds and cutting away from the top view. This is where a rolling trim will help. Again, since this trim is only a couple of seconds, it will be better to perform this in the lower timeline to see more detail.

2 In the lower timeline, move the mouse pointer directly over the cut point between the side view and the top view on V2.

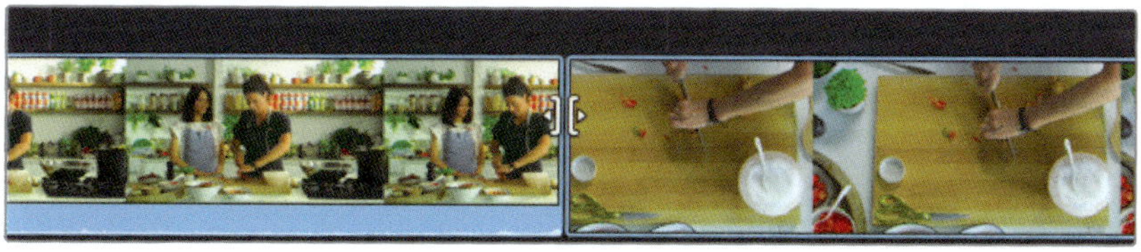

Moving the mouse pointer directly over the center of the cut point displays the rolling trim pointer. As you drag the cut in either direction, both the out point of the side view and in point of the flaming pan clip are trimmed, and the viewer shows both frames updating.

3 Drag the cut to the right until you see the hand palm down on the knife.

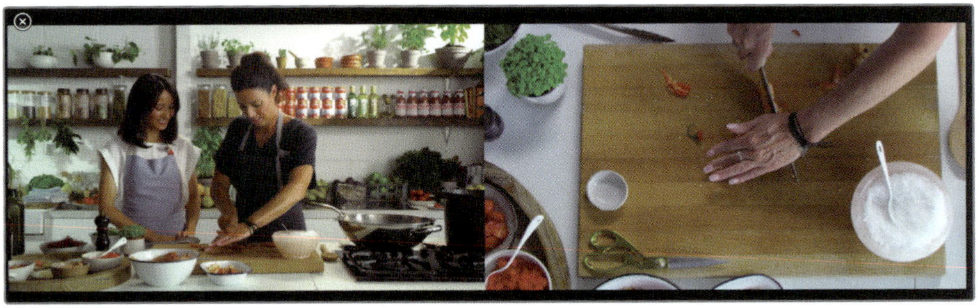

TIP You can perform rolling trims in the upper timeline or in the viewer as well.

4 From the lower timeline time ruler, drag the timeline so the play head is just before the two clips on V2 and play to review the change.

Since rolling trims remove an equal amount from one side of a cut as it takes off from the other side, the overall duration of your timeline remains the same.

Trimming a cut away on V2

Although the steps to make a rolling trim on video track1 or track 2 are identical, only video track 1 clips perform a single sided ripple trim. Instead, single sided trimming on video track 2 opens gaps when a clip is made shorter or overwrites the next clip when a clip is extended.

1 In the upper timeline, move the play head to the first cutaway, the close up clip of the two women.

It will be nicer to cut to this close up a bit earlier just after the host introduces Emma, the chef. Trimming the close up to extend the beginning will not ripple trim the remaining cutaway clips on video track 2 that come after it.

2 In the lower timeline, position the mouse pointer over the start of the close up shot on video track 2.

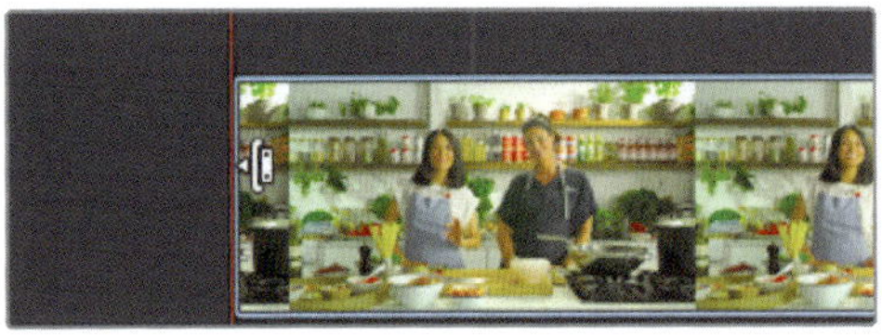

This will trim the in point, or "head" of the cut and although the mouse cursor changes to the same trim cursor you get when ripple trimming a clip on video track 1, this will not be a ripple trim.

3 Drag the in point to the left until you see the host turn her head towards the chef.

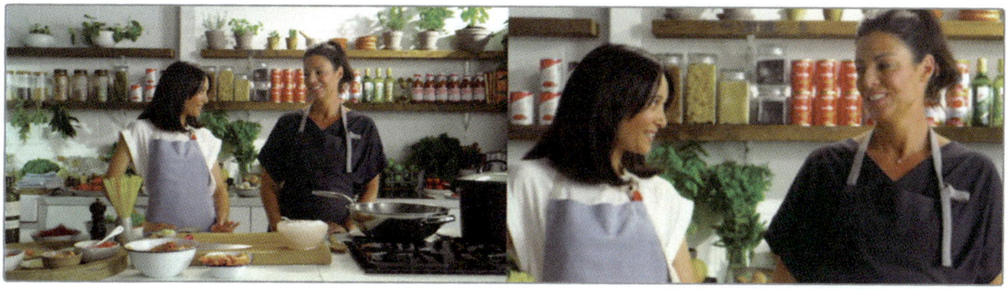

Notice when you trim how all the remaining clip on video track 2 never ripple their position in the timeline. They remain in the same exact location.

4 Play over the beginning of the timeline to see the new starting point for the close up.

When trimming in the cut page – the lower timeline, the upper timeline and the viewer's trim editor perform accurate trimming that can quickly get you the results without a lot of different tools and extra clicking.

Slipping clips

As you refine your timeline, making a clip longer or shorter isn't always going to be the best adjustment. Occasionally, you'll want to use a portion of the source clip that is either earlier or later than what is currently in the timeline. In other words, you want to shift the range without changing the clip's duration or position in the timeline. This trim is called **slipping** a clip.

1 Use the upper timeline to move back over the second cutaway clip in the timeline.

2 Move the mouse pointer over the detailed thumbnails of the clip in the lower timeline.

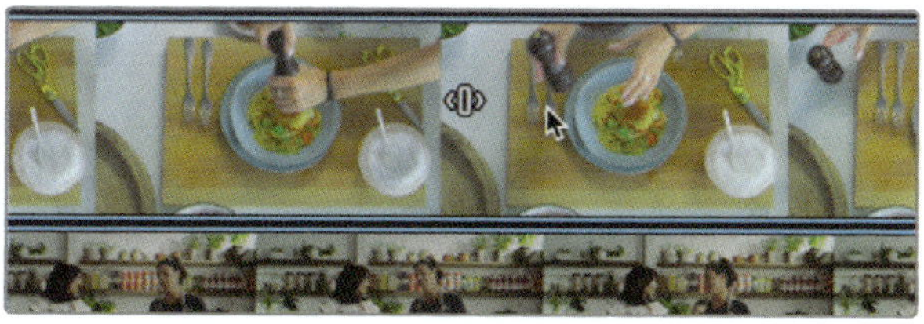

If you look closely at the clips in the lower timeline, you will see a slip edit icon on the clip at about the mid point of the clip. The slip icon allows you to drag the clip left or right to shift the source clip earlier or later while leaving the clip in the same location in the timeline .

3 Drag the slip icon to the left to select a range that is later in the clip.

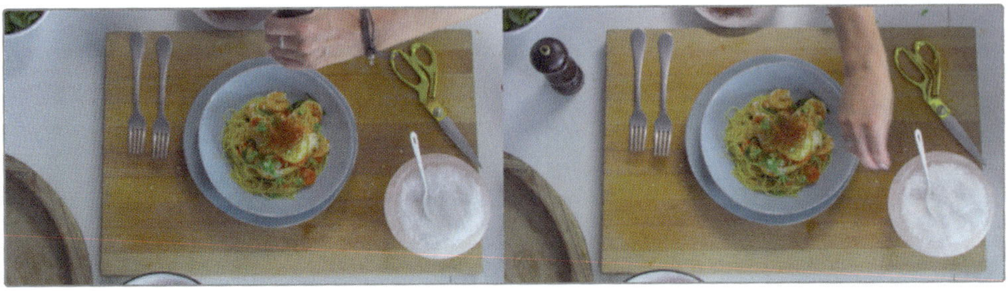

As you drag, the viewer changes to a 4-up display that allows you to compare all relevant outgoing and incoming frames. The most important frames are the upper two frames, which show the starting and ending frames of the clip being slipped. The lower frames show the clips on either side of the one you are slipping. This display enables you ensure you are starting and ending the clip exactly the way you want without guessing.

4 Stop dragging once the dish leaves the right frame but before the hand on the left frame reaches in for the salt.

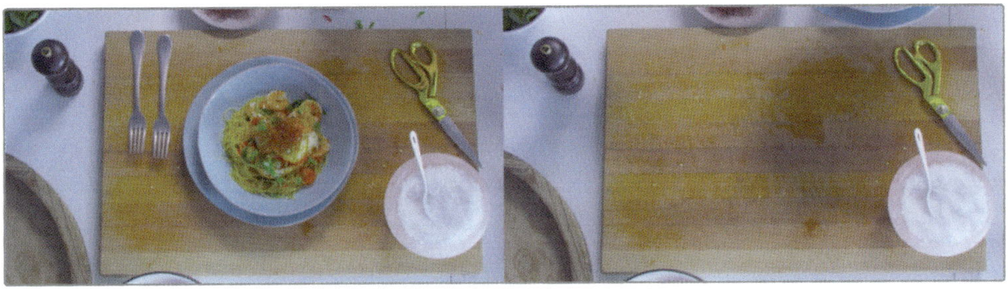

Slipping a clip is most often used subtly as we have done here. You'll find that you will slip clips just a few frames to get the perfect match with clips that surround it. In the next lesson, you'll learn how to enhance this video in the cut page using audio and video effects.

Lesson Review

1 True or False: Importing a folder of media from the operating system automatically makes the folder into a bin.

2 True or False: The only way to view clips is to view them strung out in source tape mode.

3 True False: Source tape mode is based on the bin you are viewing and the sort order of that bin.

4 True or False: Source overwrite requires that two clips be synced.

5 True or False: Trimming can only be performed in the upper timeline or the lower timeline.

Answers

1. True. Importing a folder of media from the operating system automatically makes the folder into a bin.
2. False. You can view clips from a bin in source tape mode or, if you double click a clip in a bin you can view that clip individually.
3. True. Source tape mode is based on the bin you are viewing and the sort order of that bin.
4. True. Source overwrite requires that two clips be synced.
5. False. Trimming can be performed in the upper timeline, the lower timeline or directly in the viewer.

Lesson 2

Adding effects and publishing in the cut page

In this chapter, you'll continue working on the Quick to Cook promo you started in lesson 1. If you haven't completed that lesson, return to it and follow the steps so you can continue with this lesson.

You have completed most of the editing for this promo. We may still add one or two more clips, but the overall focus in this lesson is learning the different ways the cut page can enhance the appearance of our promo. You'll learn how to apply and modify different visual transitions that can help ease the passage from one shot to another. We'll also take a look at titles, filter effects, audio adjustments, and finally output and upload to web streaming services all from within the cut page!

Time

This lesson takes approximately 60 minutes to complete.

Goals

Mixing audio

Most productions will include some music and this short promotion video is no exception. Let's import the audio, listen to the music and then add it to the timeline.

1 Open DaVinci Resolve and open the Cooking Show project you created in the previous lesson.
2 Play over the timeline to review the entire story you have created.

   It's looking very good but we can make it sound better.

3 In the media pool, double click the Quick to Cook bin to open it.
4 In the upper left corner of the media pool, click the Import media button.

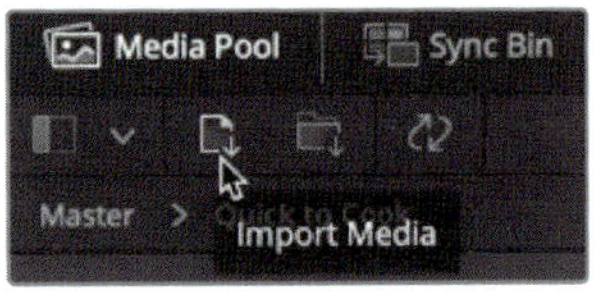

5 In the dialog that appears, navigate to the Documents folder, where you placed the R16 Intro Lessons folder.
6 Within that folder, select the Lesson 02 folder, then select the One Min Sound Track file and click open.
7 In the media pool, double click the One Min Sound Track clip to load it into the source viewer.

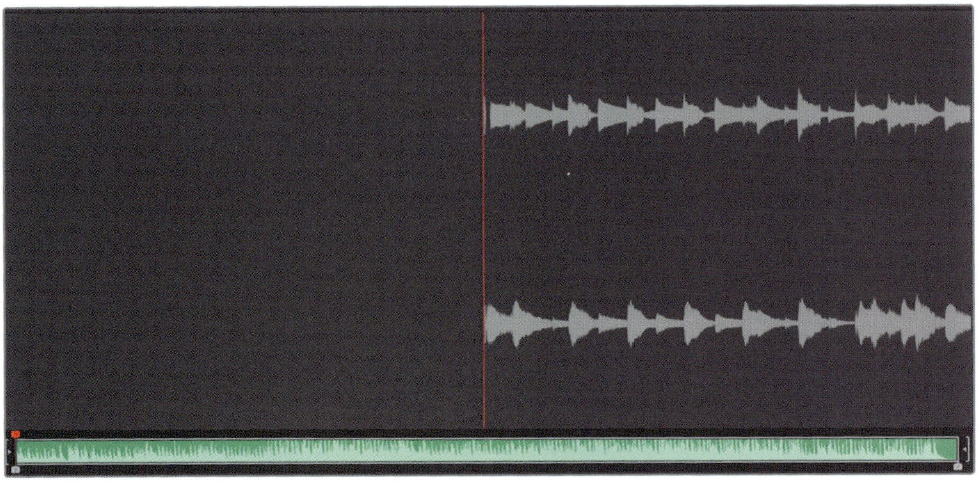

Clips that contain only audio and no video have a unique appearance in the viewer. The entire audio waveform is displayed at the bottom of the viewer and a zoomed-in portion of the waveform is displayed above it.

8 Press the spacebar to play a few seconds of the music clip, and press spacebar again to stop playback.

You will add the entire music track because it is exactly one minute long, which is the target length of your short project. Currently, you have only one audio track that goes along with the video. However, DaVinci Resolve automatically adds an audio track when you drag an audio clip below the main track in the timeline.

9 From the center of the media pool, drag the One Min Sound Track clip below the tracks in the upper timeline. Make sure to position it all the way to the left edge of the upper timeline so that the music begins at the start of the story you have created.

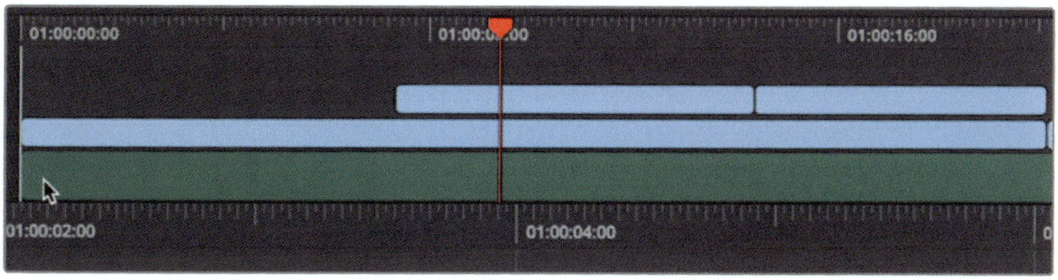

Let's hear how it sounds with the video.

10 Drag the timeline play head to the start of the timeline, and then press spacebar to watch the entire timeline.

Adding the sound track is fine but to get it to sound correct you need to set the level so it the music plays quietly under the women talking.

Adjusting audio levels

When you played the timeline, the women could not clearly be heard over the music. You need to lower the volume of the music so that it enhances the story without overpowering the talking.

1 In the upper timeline, click the One Min Sound Track clip to select it.

With the music track selected, you can use the viewer toolbar to make volume adjustments.

2 In the lower left corner of the viewer, click the tools button to open the viewer toolbar.

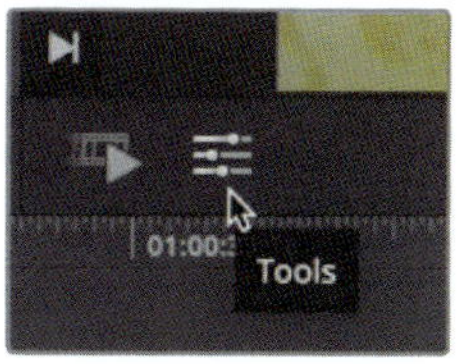

The viewer toolbar contains various audio and video controls depending on what is selected in the timeline. Because you selected an audio clip, a volume slider is displayed so you can play the timeline and adjust the music's volume simultaneously.

3 Drag the play head to the start of the timeline.
4 Press the spacebar to begin playback.
5 Drag the volume slider to the left until it is somewhere just over half way, or wherever it sounds appropriate to you compared to the women speaking.

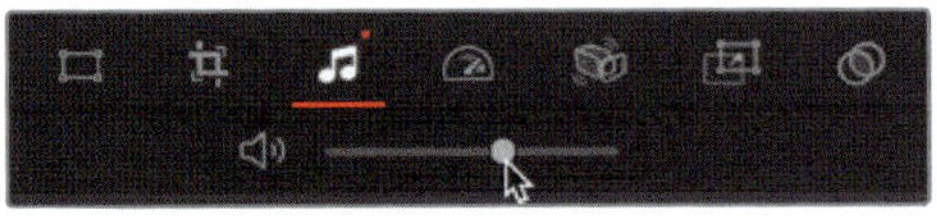

6 When you are done setting the volume level, press the spacebar to stop playing the timeline.
7 In the lower left of the viewer, click the tools button to hide the viewer toolbar.

   The sound level of the music is set more appropriately but other areas of the women speaking are still too loud.

Muting audio clips

The audio from some of our cut away clips is combined with the audio from the master track, making them much louder. Since the audio is identical, we only need to hear audio from the original clip.

1 In the upper timeline, move the timeline play head over the second set of cut away clips on video track 2. (cutting the prawns).

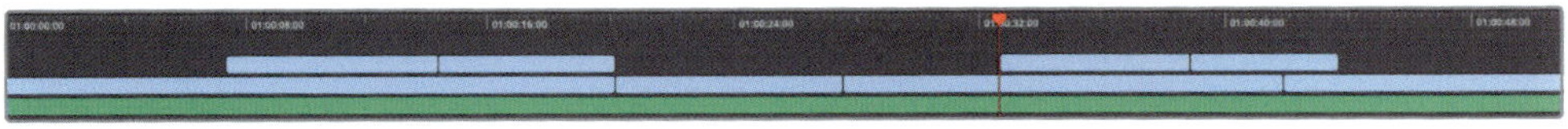

2 Play over the cut away clips and listen to the audio carefully.

   The audio is significantly louder when the cut aways are on screen. The audio is combined from both video tracks. You can mute the entire cut away track or mute just selected clips in the timeline.

3 Drag a selection rectangle around the second set of two cut away clips on video track 2.
4 In either the upper or lower timeline, right click over the selected clips and choose Mute from the menu.

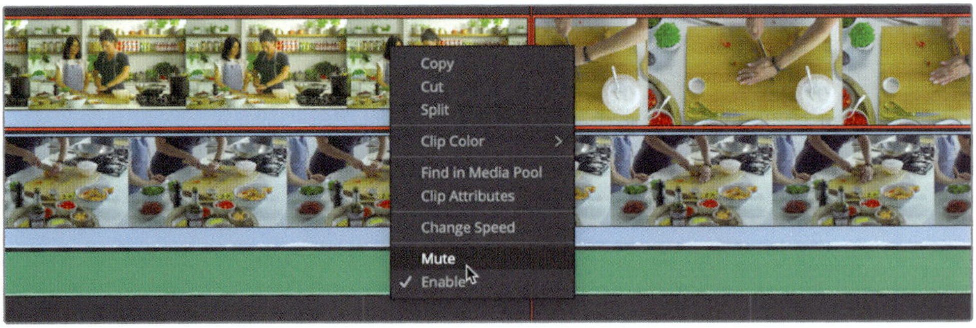

5 Back up in the timeline and press spacebar to hear the improved sounding audio.

You have multiple ways to adjust audio levels in DaVinci Resolve, but using the cut page tools is one of the easiest ways. You'll learn more about setting audio levels and audio post production in Lessons 8 and 9. In this lesson, let's turn towards adding some video effects.

Switching transitions

A transition is the change over from one clip to the next. You've used one type of transition already in the first lesson. The straight cut is the most common transition used but there are others. You may have seen them many times on TV and in films, even if you didn't consciously make note of them. Other than the straight cut, the most common video transition is the cross-dissolve, which is an overlapping fade between the end of one clip and the beginning of the next. It is often used to convey a passage of time. Let's explore creating a cross dissolve in the cut page and a few other transitions as well.

1 Play over the last cut between the side view of the finished dish and the two women eating the noodles.

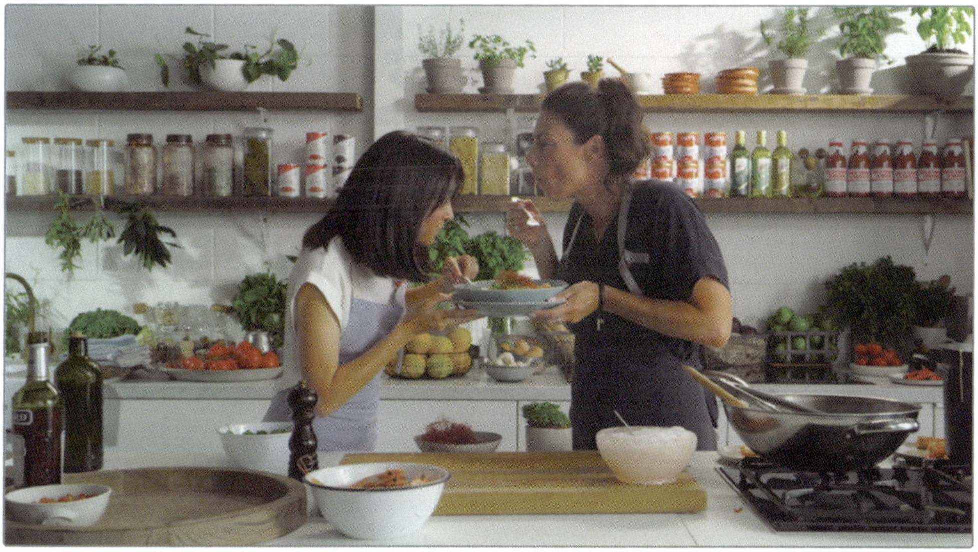

Since there is some passage of time between these two clips, it might be nicer to have a cross dissolve between the two. That is an easy and quick thing to do just by positioning the play head near the cut where you want the transition.

2 Position the play head near the next to last cut in the timeline. Make sure the smart indicator is over the last cut.

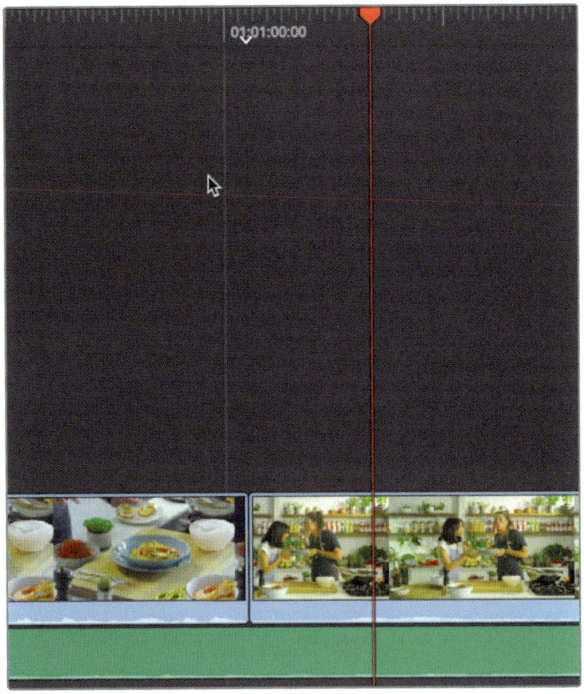

In the toolbar are three transition buttons that can be used to switch between different transition types.

3 In the toolbar, click the cross dissolve button to switch the transition to a half second cross dissolve.

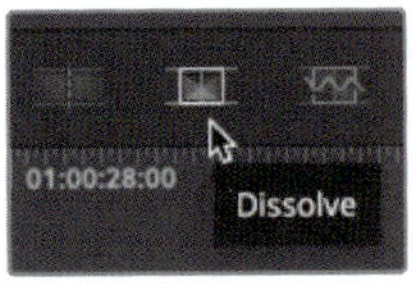

A cross dissolve icon is added on to the timeline at the cut point to show the added transition and give an indication of its duration.

4 Move the play head before the cross dissolve and play the timeline to see the new transition.

It would be great if the default half second dissolve duration fit every scene perfectly, but it won't. It may cut off some of the action or just last too long. Whatever the reason, at some point you will want to change the dissolve duration. The easiest and most straightforward way to do so is by dragging in the timeline.

5 Move the mouse pointer over the right edge of the transition icon in the lower timeline.

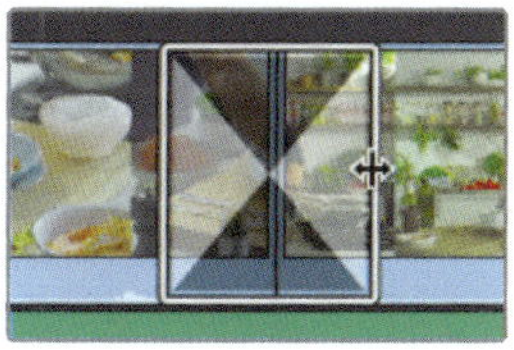

The mouse pointer changes to a resize cursor.

6 Drag the right edge of the transition out to extend the duration of the cross dissolve to 1:00.

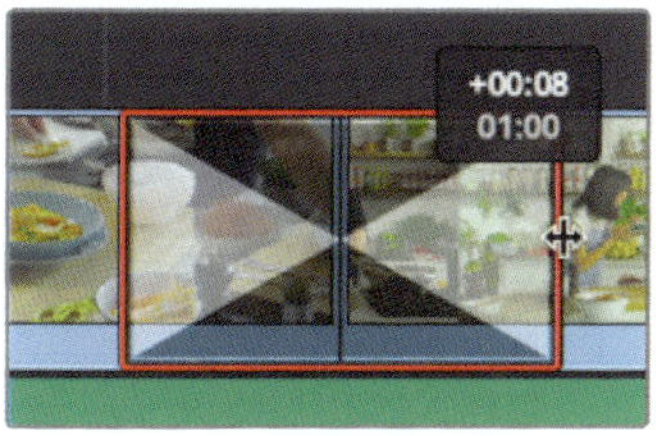

The tool tip that appears as you drag shows the current duration as well as the amount you have added to each side of the transition.

7 Move the play head before the cross dissolve and play to review your change.

You can switch transitions for clips on video track 2 as well.

8 Move the play head back near the end last cut away on video track 2.

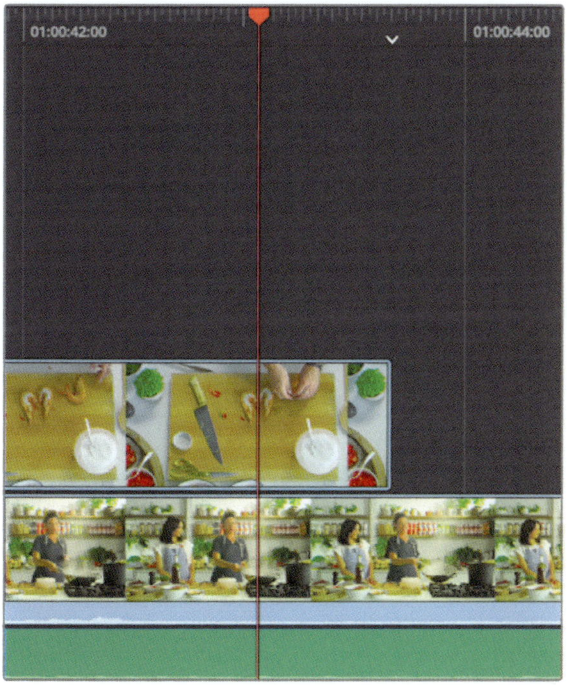

9 In the toolbar, click the cross dissolve button to switch the transition to a half second cross dissolve.

10 Move the play head before the cross dissolve and play to review the addition.

This transition doesn't seem to work as nicely as the first one, but it is easy to switch back from the cross dissolve to a cut using the toolbar buttons.

11 Again move the play head near the transition at the start of the top view clip on video track 2.

12 In the toolbar, click the cut button to switch the transition back to a cut.

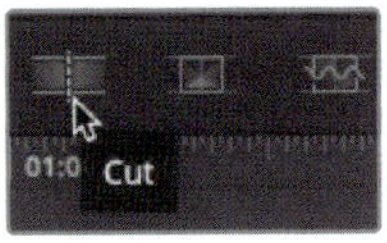

You can also work in the upper timeline since it is a fully functional timeline. The upper timeline can be used to drag the transition icon and change its duration.

Fixing small jump cuts

The third of the three transition buttons located in the timeline is smooth cut. Smooth cut is a sophisticated transition that can be used to fix small jump cuts that may be created when editing.

1 In the upper timeline, move to the second clip on video track 1.

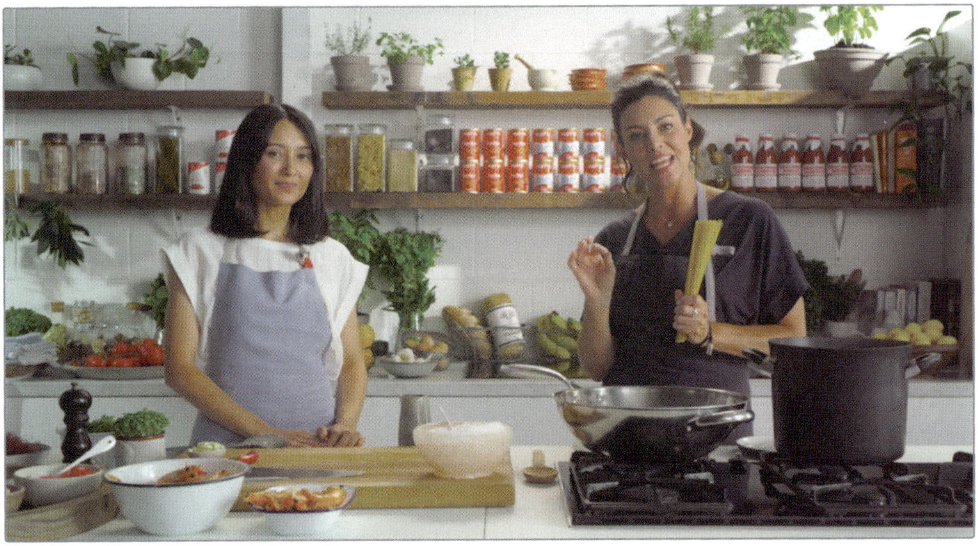

2 Play from the start of the clip until it ends.

Sometimes the on camera talent may not be at ease with being on camera. They can stumble over words or repeat themselves. Removing these slight speaking errors can make the talent seem more professional. Our chef say "umm" in the middle of her explanation of what spaghettini is and this would sound better without it. So, let's cut that out.

3 First, in the lower timeline header, click the lock icon next to the A1 track so we do not accidently cut or delete the music sound track.

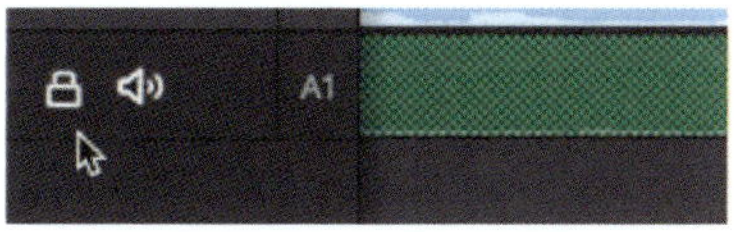

4 Now, in the lower timeline's time ruler, drag to position the play head right before the chef says "umm".

5 On the far left of the toolbar, click the split button to add an edit at the current location in the timeline.

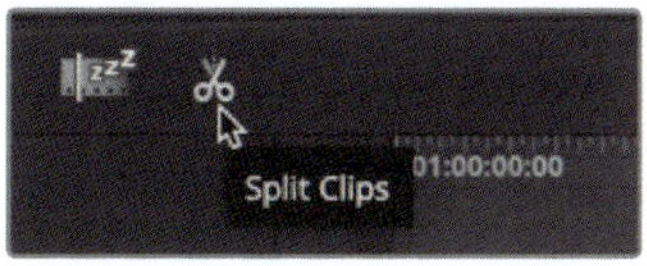

6 Drag the time ruler to position the play head after the chef says "umm" and make another through edit.

7 Select the small segment you have created in the lower timeline and press the delete (macOS) or backspace (windows) key to remove the segment.

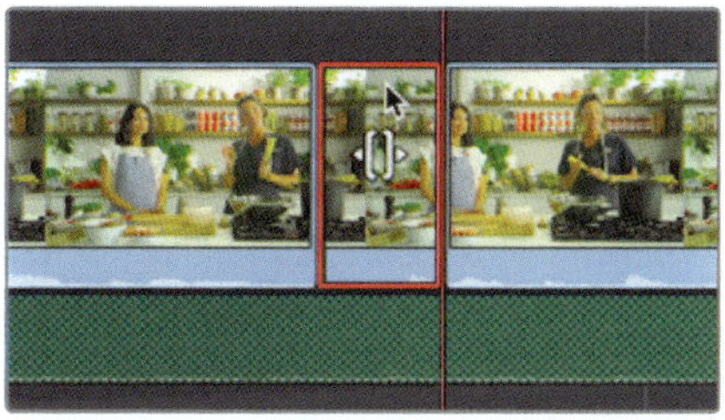

Deleting clips on video track 1 is just like trimming, in that it always ripple deletes and closes up the gap created by the removed segment.

8 Play from the start of the clip until it ends to see and hear what we have done.

Although this sounds great, the missing frames we deleted have created a jump cut.

TIP A jump cut is an abrupt switch between two clips that appear very similar in content and framing. Jump cuts are usually avoided because they are jarring to the audience although at times they can be used as a creative choice.

9 Move the play head near the cut we just created.

10 In the toolbar click the smooth cut button to add the transition.

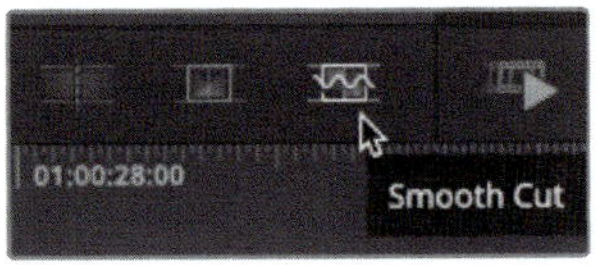

Smooth cut smooths out the transition so it looks like one continuous clip by generating new frames in between the two clips. But before you play it, It works best when it is used for a very short duration of around three or four frames so let's change the duration. When making such a small, precise change, just like trimming, it is easier to use the viewer.

11 In the upper or lower timeline, click on the smooth cut transition to select it.

The viewer now shows the trim edit controls and the smooth cut transition between the two film strips. You can drag the transition using the viewer's controls and frame numbers to guide you.

12 In the viewer, drag the smooth cut transition in towards the center until it reaches the 4 frame mark on the film strip.

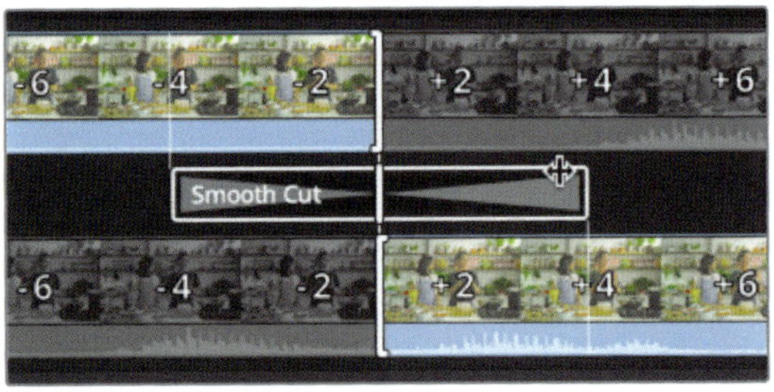

13 Move the play head before the transition and play to see the seamless transition created by the smooth cut.

The jump cut is invisible because it is a perfect situation for a smooth cut transition. For the best results use smooth cut on subtle but jarring cuts between two similar clips. If the clips are significantly different the smooth cut transition won't be able to find similarities in their content and framing to make it seamless.

Adding transitions from the effects library

The three transition buttons are not all the transitions in DaVinci Resolve. Other transitions can be added from the transitions browser.

1 Position the play head near the next to last cut in the timeline where you added the cross dissolve earlier.

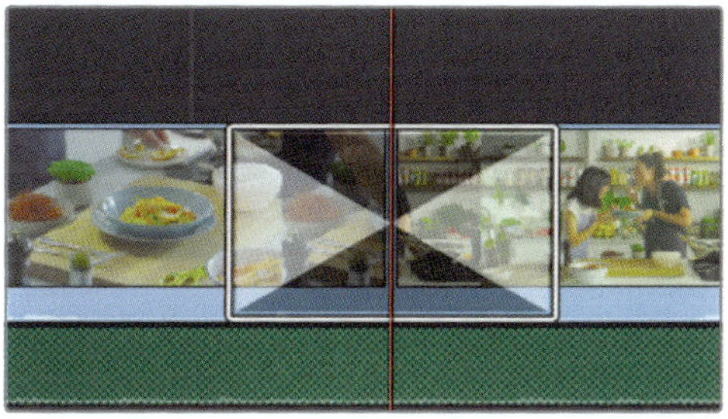

You can add transitions from the transitions browser on to straight cuts or other transition types just by drag and drop.

2 In the upper left corner of the DaVinci Resolve window, click the transitions button.

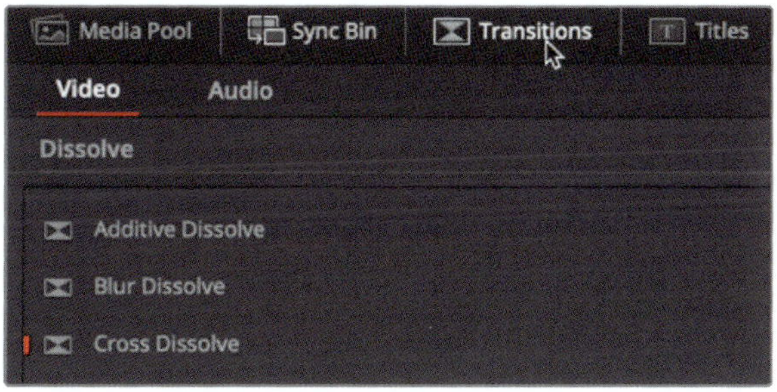

The transitions browser is a list of different transitions categorized by style.

3 In the top dissolve category, drag the Dip to Color Dissolve transition on top of the existing cross dissolve in the lower timeline.

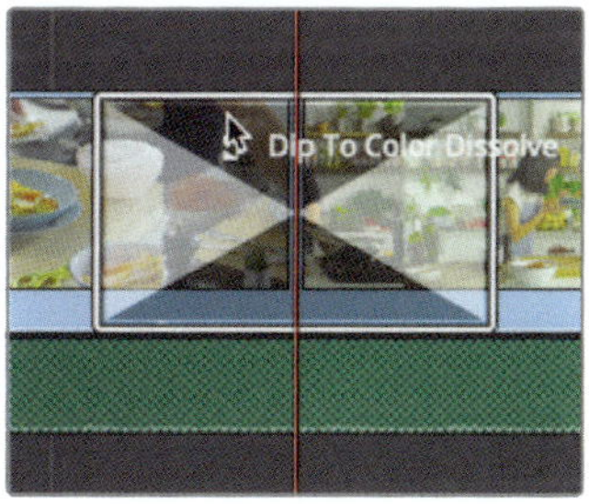

4 Play over the new transition to see the change.

The Dip to Color Dissolve transition is a cross dissolve that transitions to a pure white color in the middle of the transition.

TIP You can add a transition from the transition browser to multiple cuts at once by selecting all the clips in the timeline, then right clicking over the transition in the browser and choosing "add to selected edit points and clips".

It is more than likely you will end up using the cut, dissolve and smooth cut buttons most often because they are the most common types of transitions. However, it is always nice to have creative choices since every project requires a different style. The transition browser gives you more than two dozen different options which you can try out and have fun with!

Resizing and stabilizing clips

OK, let's fix a few things that have stood out since the earlier lesson. One of the cut away clips we added used the master shot of the two women as the chef cut the prawns. Let's take a look in case you don't remember it.

1 Position the play head over the second set of cutaways, where you muted the audio and play over the first cut away clip.

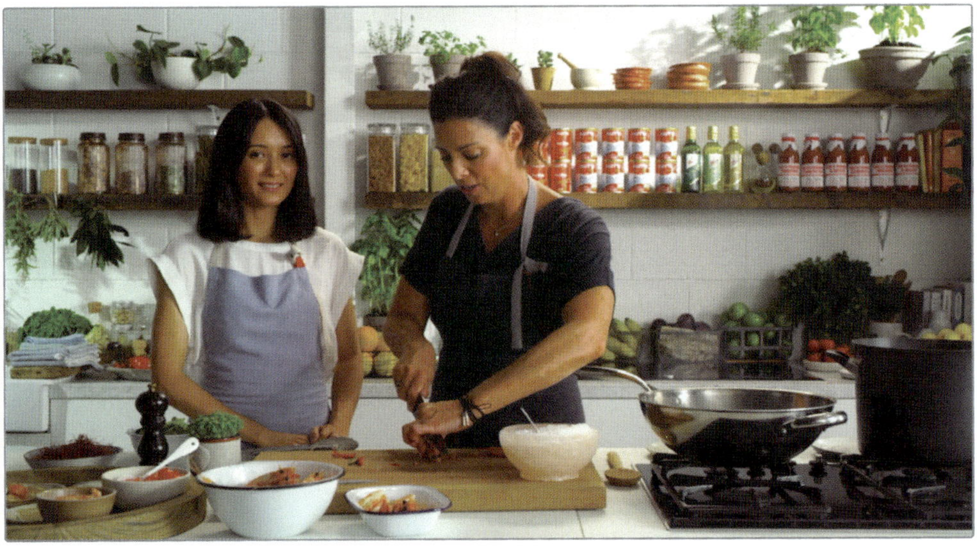

Maybe you noticed when we added this clip, the host is looking directly into the camera for most of the shot. We can fixing this by reframing the shot using the same viewer toolbar we opened when fixing the audio volume.

2 Select the clip in the timeline and position the play head over the center of the clip so you can see the host looking into the camera.

3 In the lower left corner of the viewer, click the tools button.

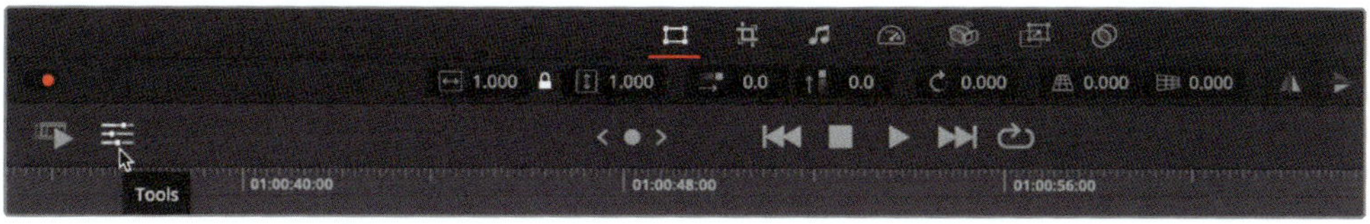

The viewer toolbar defaults to show the transform controls which are used to scale, reposition, rotate and flip the clip. You can use the number field in the toolbar or, the on screen controls in the viewer. Although the number field appears as a field you type in, fields like this in DaVinci Resolve can also be used like sliders.

4 On the left side of the viewer toolbar, drag the mouse pointer over the resize number field until it is around 1.7.

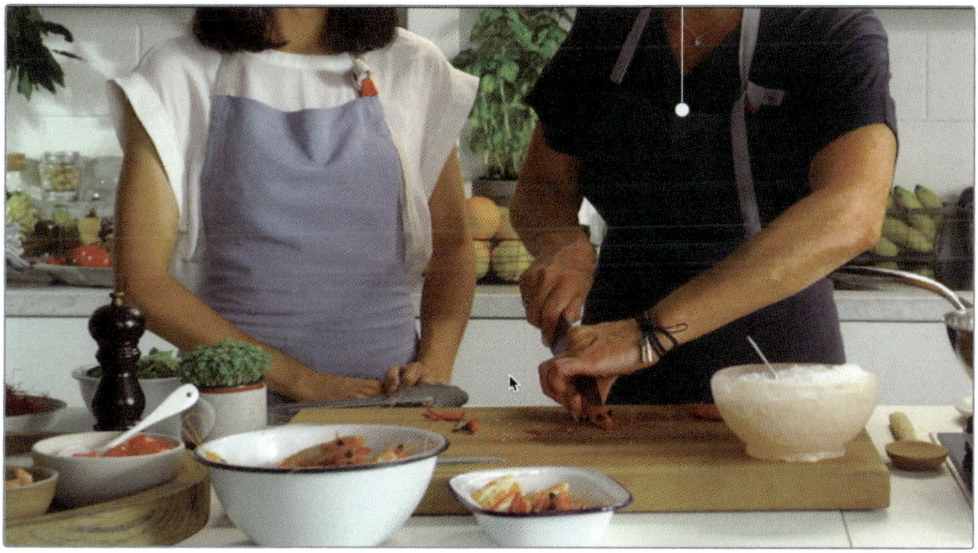

With the frame scaled up, you can use the on screen controls in the viewer to reposition it so the host's face is out of the frame.

5 Drag up in the viewer to cut off the faces of the two women and center them in the frame.

6 Back up the play head and watch the reframed clip.

Let's move on to the next cut away clip in the timeline.

7 Play over the next cut away clip.

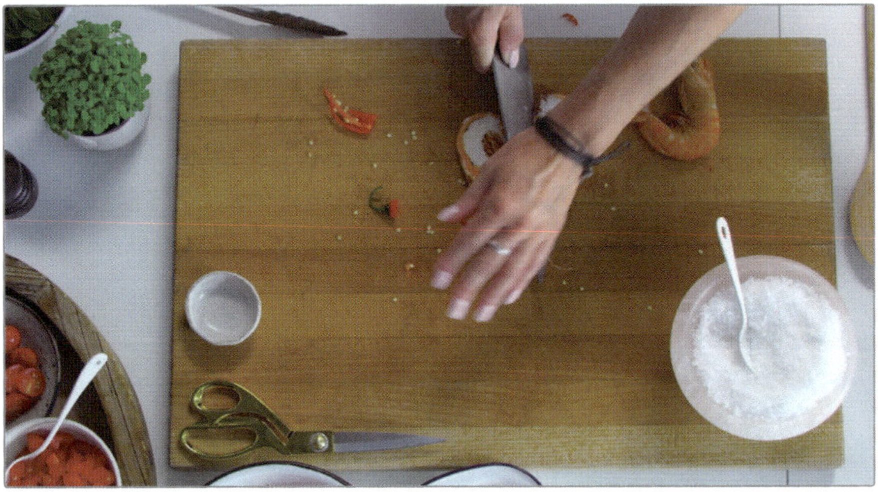

Something that maybe was not as noticeable when the clip was added, is the slight shaking of the camera when the knife pushes down hard to cut the prawn. Fixing that using another of the tools in the viewer toolbar is incredibly simple.

TIP You can click the circular reset button on the far right side of the viewer toolbar to reset the parameters for the currently displayed tool.

8 Select the top view cutting board clip in the timeline.

9 In the viewer toolbar, click the camera button.

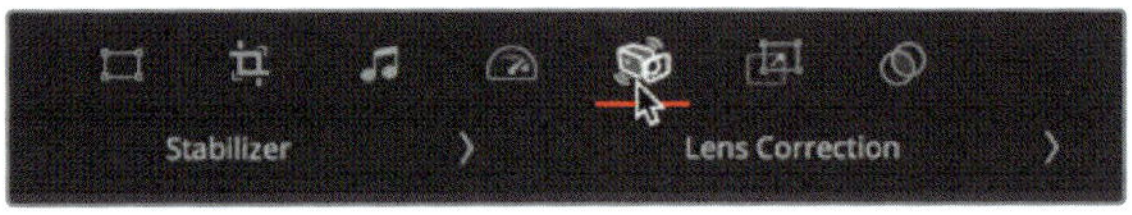

The camera button includes two tools for fixing common camera problems. Lens correction is for fixing wide angle lens distortion and image stabilization is for smoothing out shaky camera work.

10 Click stabilization to open the stabilization controls.

Using the default settings, the stabilizer with smooth out wobbly camera work but leave the primary motion. This can be useful is you have a handheld shot the follows someone around. You want to keep the general motion of the camera but want to smooth out the bumps. In our case, we want to lock off the camera and remove all motion as if it were on a tripod.

11 Click the camera lock icon to switch from smoothing the camera motion to removing all camera motion from the clip.

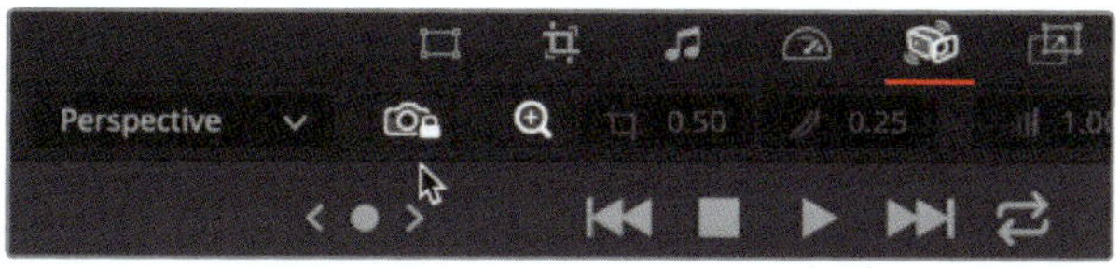

12 Click the stabilize button to begin the process.

Stabilization quickly analyzes the motion and then removes it.

13 One the analysis is complete, play over the clip to see the results.

You can compare any adjustment you make in the tools panel to the original clip by disabling the adjustment.

14 On the left side of the viewer toolbar, click the stabilizer switch to disable the stabilization and view the original clip.

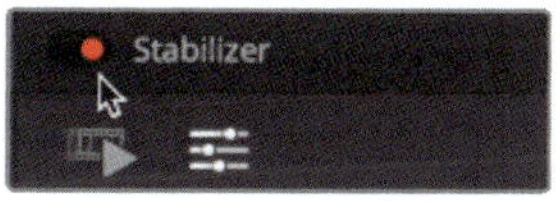

15 Play over the clip to see the original clip, then click the switch again to enable stabilization.

That's a really easy fix for any camera motion problems you may have.

Changing a clip's speed

Another tool in the viewer toolbar is the speed control. You can use the speed control to make a clip play back faster or slower and even change speeds over time. Let's take the flambé clip and slow it down a bit to make it even more dramatic.

1 Position the play head over the flambé clip in the timeline.

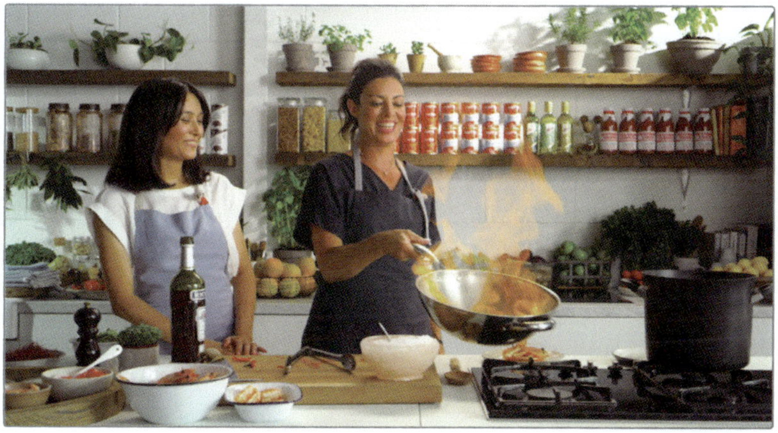

2 Select the clip and in the viewer toolbar click the speed button.

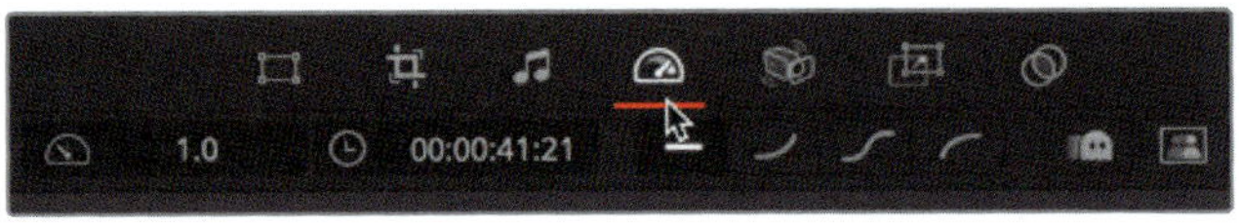

The first number field on the left is the percentage of speed for the currently selected clip. When set to 1.0 the clips plays back at 100% speed. Setting the value to 0.5 will cause the clip to play back at 50% speed.

3 Hover the mouse pointer over the speed percentage field.

Using this virtual slider you can drag in the value field to change the number.

4 Drag the mouse to the left over the number until you have decreased the speedo to around 0.7 (70%).

As you make the speed slower, the clip is extended pushing the rest of the timeline down.

> **TIP** Clips on video track 2 never ripple the timeline, so slowing the speed of a clip on video track 2 will not extend a clip's duration.

5 Back up the play head to the start of the clip and then play the timeline to view the speed change.

The speed change is good but it doesn't have to last the entire length of the clip.

6 Move the play head just before the host says "wow"

7 Click the split button in the toolbar to add an edit.

The first half is perfect for the slow motion but when they start to speak and laugh, it would be better if we return to the actual speed.

8 Select the right side of the split clip you just created.

9 In the viewer toolbar, click the reset button to the left of the speed number field.

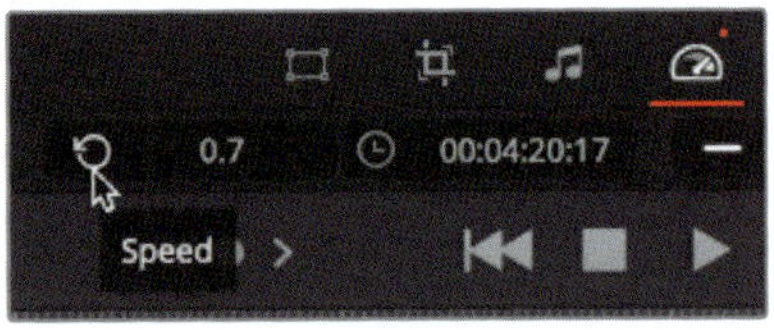

10 Back up the play head to the start of the clip and then play the timeline to view the speed change.

That makes for a much more exciting clip for our promo.

Adding a title

Your promotional video needs a title. Producing a good title whether as the opening or as a simple lower third is an art form that uses typography, color, and animation in creative ways, drawing from graphic design principles that date back centuries. Maybe expectations for this one minute promo are not so lofty, but we can still create some great looking titles, really quickly using the title browser in the cut page.

1 In the upper-left area of the screen, click the title browser button.

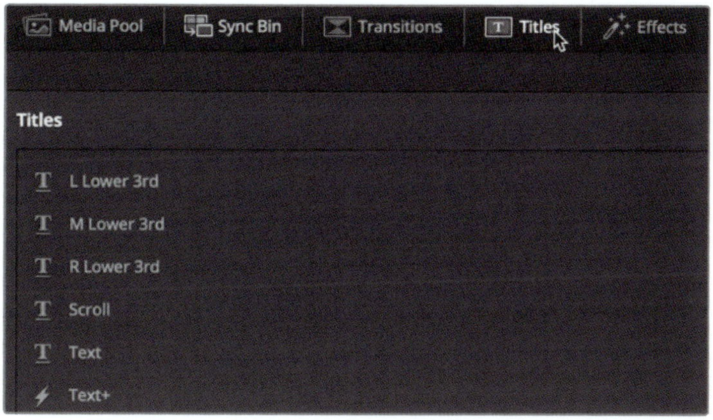

The title browser consists of basic titles at the top where you can create a title from a blank page and over two dozen Fusion animated title templates in the lower half of the browser. Let's use one of the lower third title templates to introduce the prawn and basil spaghettini dish the chef is making.

2 Scroll down the list of title templates until you locate the Lower 3rd Simple Vertical 1 Line template.

3 Drag the Lower 3rd template to the upper timeline, directly above the second cut away clip.

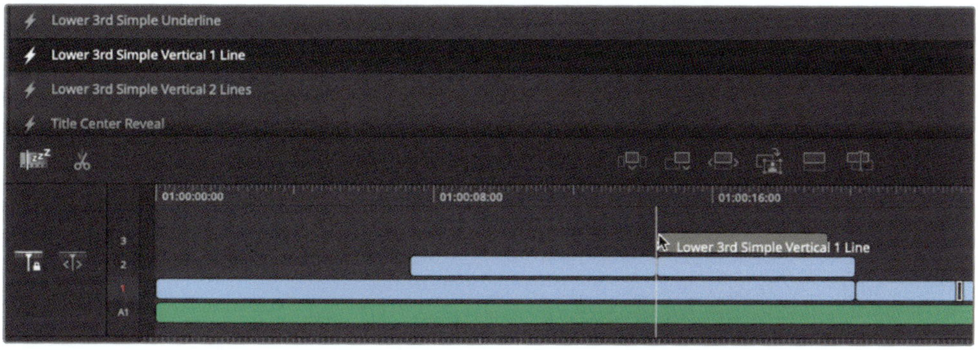

Some templates like this one, when placed over a video clip have a transparent background so the video clip is visible behind the text in the viewer.

4 In the upper timeline, move the play head over middle of the newly added title to see the title and the video under it.

The default title is displayed in the viewer but you can change the text and modify other title parameters using a floating inspector.

5 Select the title clip in the upper timeline and open the viewer toolbar.

6 In the viewer toolbar, click the title button and then click Open Inspector to open a floating Inspector window.

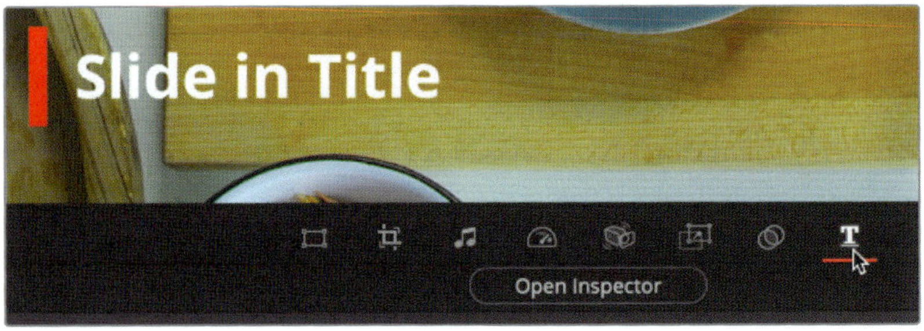

7 In the floating inspector window that opens, type Prawn and basil spaghettini.

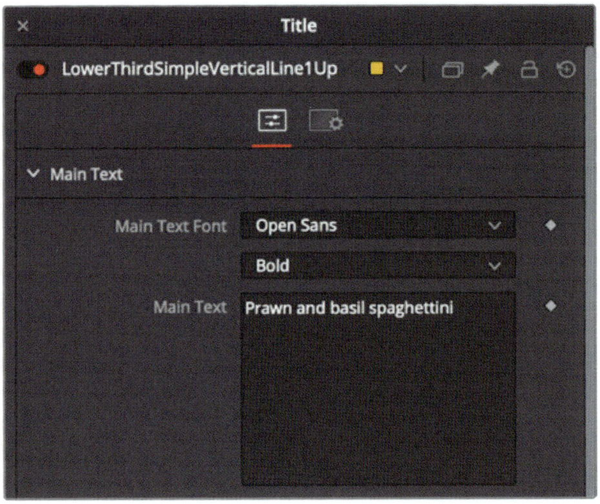

The floating inspector has all the standard controls for formatting this template. You can change the font, typeface, size, and even change the color of the red line. The animation remains intact, making it easy to customize the look without having to deal with keyframes.

8 Click the close button in the upper left corner of the floating inspector window.

9 Move the timeline play head just before the title clip and play to see the animated lower third.

That's how easy it is to add, type and format titles in the cut page!

Using the effects library

Now let's say we want the text to pop out a bit more from the background. This can be super easy to do using the filter effects that come with DaVinci Resolve.

1 In the upper-left area of the screen, click the effects library button.

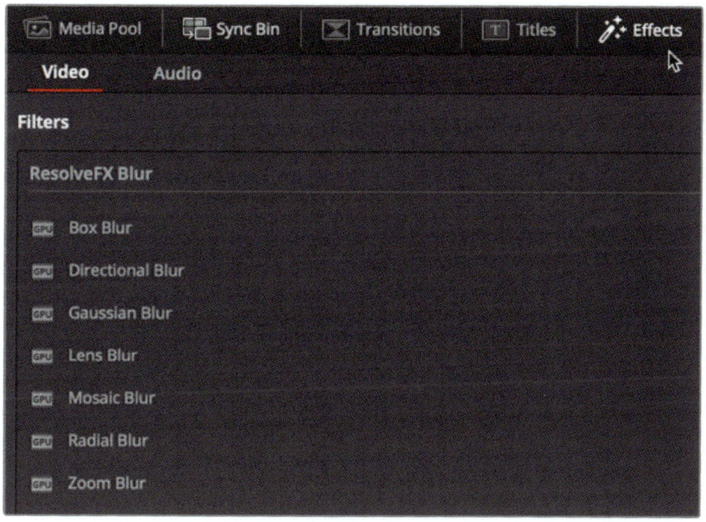

DaVinci Resolve includes high quality and very unique filter effects called Resolve FX, that are easily accessible in the effects library. Some Resolve FX are only available in the DaVinci Resolve Studio version of the software, but they will show up with a watermark so you can try them out if you are using the free version. For the price of an inexpensive suite of plug-ins you can have access to all of them, as well as other features in the editing, color, Fairlight and Fusion pages. However, there are plenty to play around with even if you are using the free version of DaVinci Resolve.

2 Scroll down the list of effects to find the vignette effect.

3 Drag the vignette effect on the top view cutting board clip, which is under the title in the upper timeline.

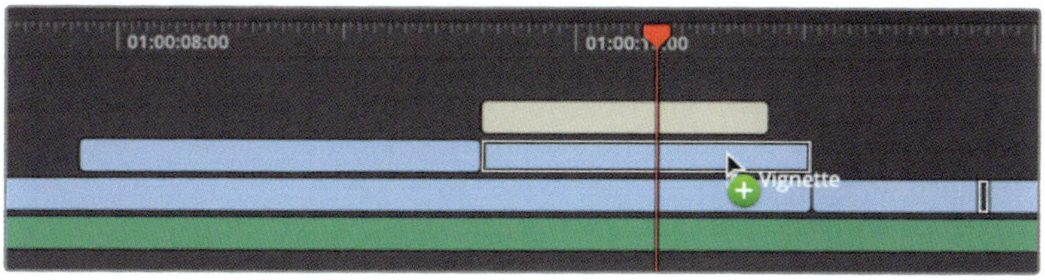

The background video clip behind our title is now darker from the vignette. However, you can edit the effect similarly to the title.

4 In the upper timeline, select the cutting board clip where you applied the vignette effect.

5 In the viewer toolbar, select the effects button then click the open inspector button.

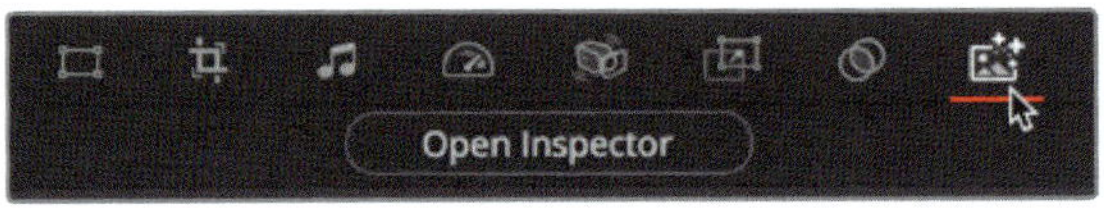

The floating inspector window opens, this time showing controls for the vignette.

6 Increase the size to around 0.7 so you can see more of the image.

7 Click the Color swatch to open the OS color picker and select a white color.

The color changes the vignette from a darker moody appearance to a lighter one that better fits the mood of our cooking show.

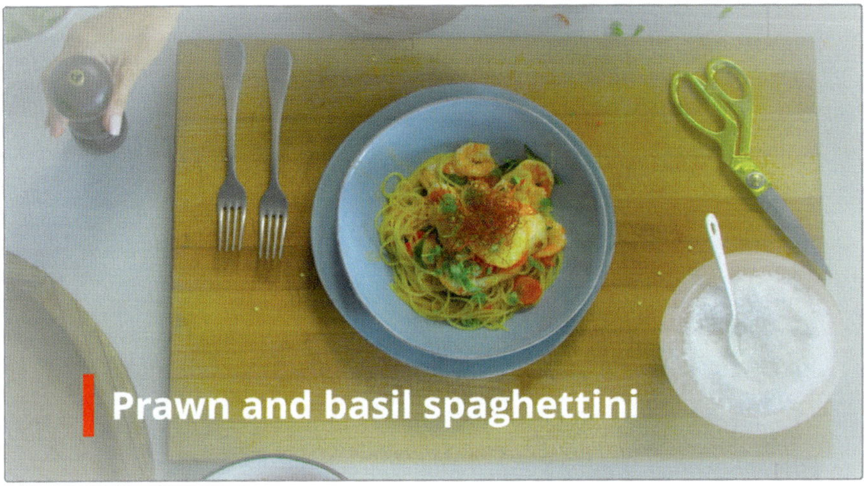

8 When you are done adjusting the color, click the close button on the color picker and click the close button in the upper left corner of the inspector window.

TIP You can click the trash can icon in the upper right of the inspector to remove the effect.

Next, we can even add a little movement to this background clip to make the opening really dynamic.

Panning and zooming clips

The background clip under the title uses just a static camera, but we can add more visual interest by introducing a slight camera move. DaVinci Resolve has a unique auto-animated effect that pans and zooms videos and photos to add a classic smooth camera move to otherwise static shots.

1 In the upper timeline, select the cutting board clip where you applied the vignette effect.

2 In the viewer toolbar, click the dynamic zoom button.

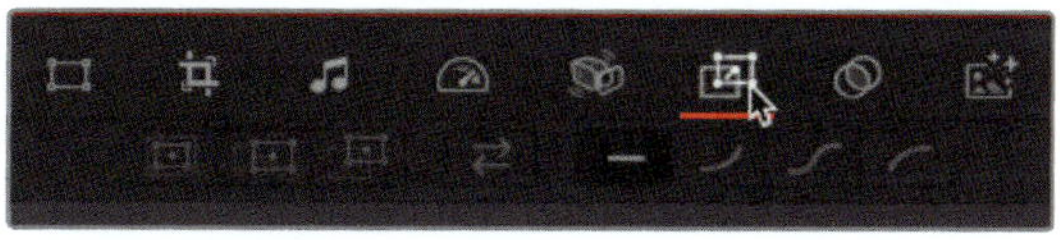

Unlike other tools in the viewer toolbar, the dynamic zoom controls are disabled by default, so you first need to enable them.

3 Click the switch to enable dynamic zoom.

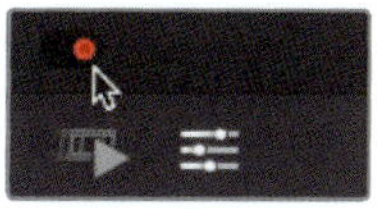

The dynamic zoom button turns red and the effect is applied, so you can now play the clip to see the results.

4 Position the play head at the start of the title.

5 Press the spacebar to play the clip and see the results.

Dynamic zoom adds a nice, smooth zoom-out to this clip.

But instead of pulling out of the clip, let's draw the audience in by reversing the direction and zooming into the clip.

6 In the viewer toolbar click the swap button.

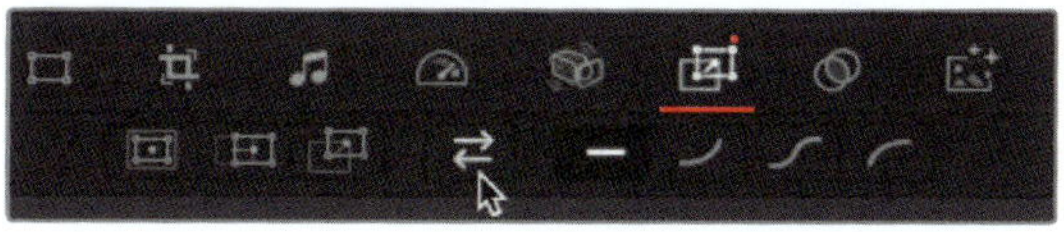

Clicking the swap button changes the direction of the animation. Instead of animating out to show more of the clip, the selected clip now animates in, zooming into an area of the cutting board.

7 Press the spacebar to review your animation change.

You've added some movement to hold attention without detracting from the title. The subtle animation that you added to this clips draws you into the whole movie more than a static shot.

Applying audio effects

Audio is often a forgotten aspect when making a video. But the audio in your edit can have a more powerful impact on an audience than any single filter effect or animation. Although we were able to change the volume, there still remains a problem in our audio track that is a bit more challenging to repair.

1 Position the play head at the start of the timeline and play the entire story you have created. As you play, pay particular attention to the audio.

You may have noticed (especially if you were wearing headphones) that audio from the side view camera only plays out of the left channel. The rest of the audio is stereo, playing out of both the left and right channels. Luckily, DaVinci Resolve has an incredibly powerful page called Fairlight, for professional digital audio mixing and sound design. However, some of that power can be used right from within the cut page, similarly to how we use the ResolveFX to add a vignette.

2 At the top of the effects library click the audio tab.

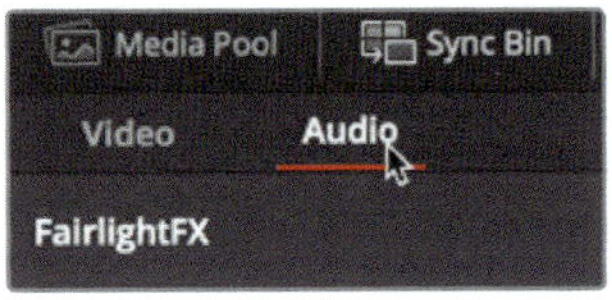

The Fairlight FX in the audio tab are high quality audio processing effects that can be used to improve soundtracks in your production. We'll use one here than can reformat a stereo clip where only one channel has actually been recorded.

3 In the upper timeline move the play head over the third edit in the timeline where the side view of the cutting board is shown.

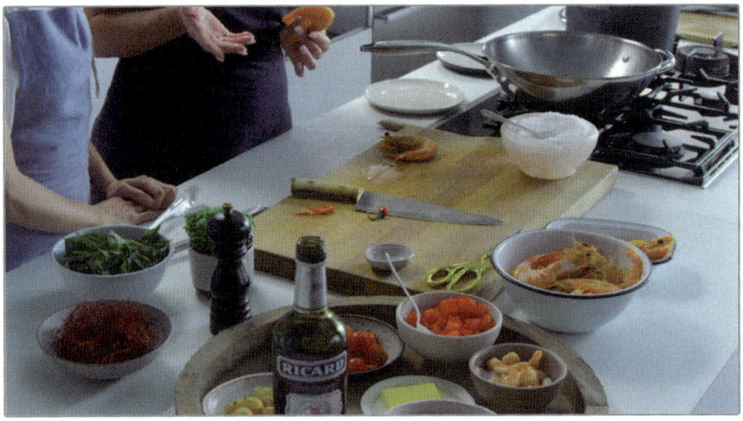

This clip is a stereo audio clip but only the left channel was recorded.

4 In the effects library scroll down the list of FairlightFX . When you locate the stereo fixer effects, drag it on the side view video clip on video track 1 .

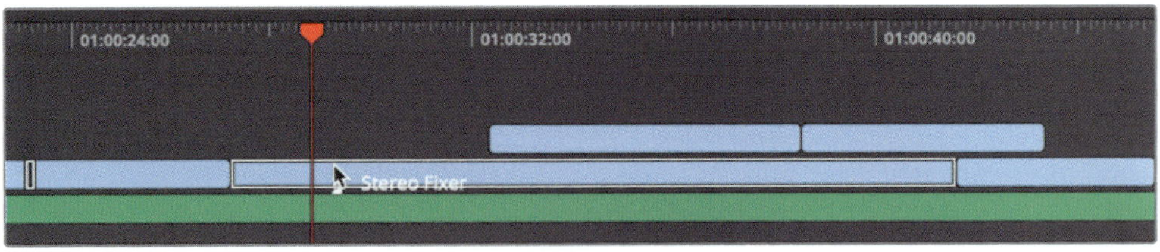

TIP You can drag effects onto the upper or lower timeline depending on which you find easier to target.

The stereo fixer custom controls are displayed once you apply it to a clip.

The controls consist of a series of buttons that you can use to redistribute the single channel sound into stereo.

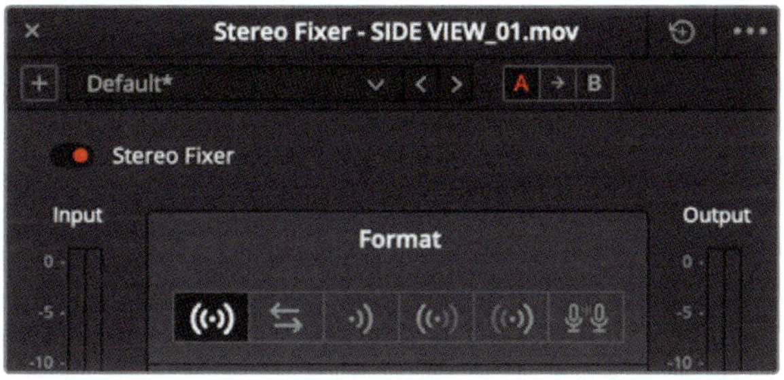

The first button is the default setting and it does not change the audio of the clip. The second button swaps the channels and the third button takes the mix of the two channels to create a single mono channel.

The next button is the choice for us. This option takes the left channel, which contains our good audio and send it to both the left and right output. So we only hear the good audio in both the left and right channel without any additional noise.

5 Click the left only button to create a left channel stereo output.

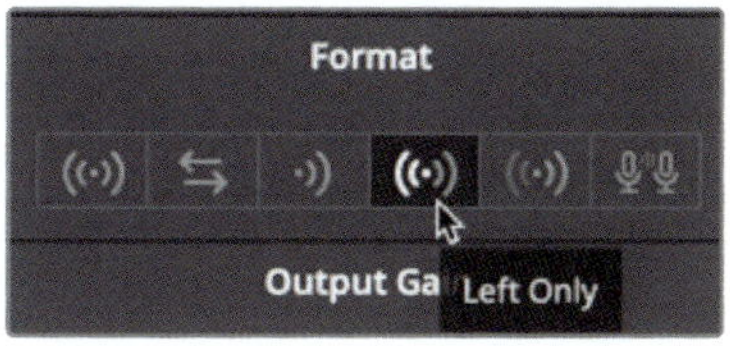

6 Click the close button in the upper left of the custom controls window.
7 Move the play head back to the start of the timeline and play through the audio fix you just created.

Using the viewer toolbar, all the basic things you need are located in one consolidated strip of tools and in inspector panels that appear when needed. From simple resizing, stabilization and speed changes to even more extensive controls for audio and video filter effects accessible all in one place. Everything you need for fast turn around, quick projects is right at your fingertips without ever having to leave the cut page!

Sharing to YouTube and Vimeo

OK, you've created a story and now you need to get it posted to popular streaming web sites as quickly as possible. In the cut page you can upload directly to YouTube or Vimeo as well as create higher resolution master files.

1 In the upper right corner of the cut page, click the quick export button.

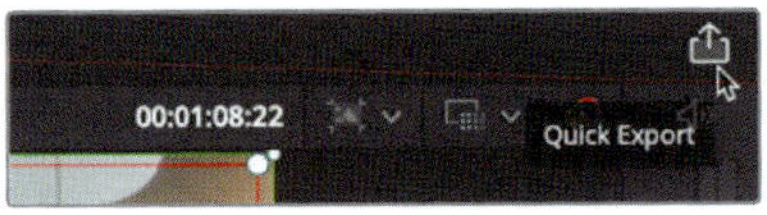

The quick export window includes commonly used presets for creating a movie file of your timeline.

2 Click the Vimeo button.

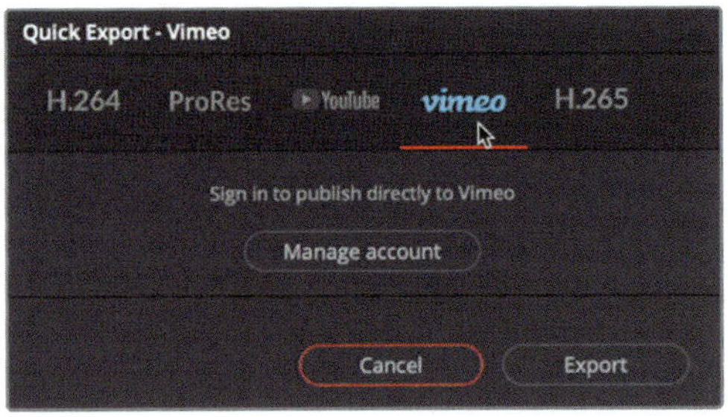

The Vimeo panel shows the input fields for uploading to Vimeo. However, if you haven't already input your account information, all you'll get is a mange account button.

3 Click the manage account button if you haven't input your account information for web streaming sites where you plan to upload your content.

Clicking the manage account button opens the DaVinci Resolve system preferences with the internet accounts panel selected.

Here, you can enter in account information so DaVinci Resolve can upload directly to a web streaming service.

4 Click the sign in button for Vimeo and enter your account information.

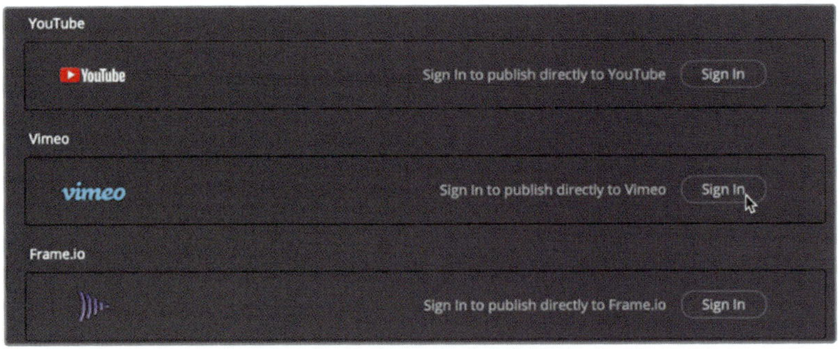

NOTE If you do not have a Vimeo account enter your YouTube account information and follow along by uploading to YouTube in place of Vimeo. If you have neither account, read through the remaining steps to learn how the process can help in the future.

5 When you have completed the sign in process, click save on the preferences window.

The quick export window will now show the preset format for Vimeo based on your timeline.

TIP You'll learn how to create custom settings for rendering movie files in lesson 15: Delivering a final program.

6 Click the directly upload to Vimeo check box.

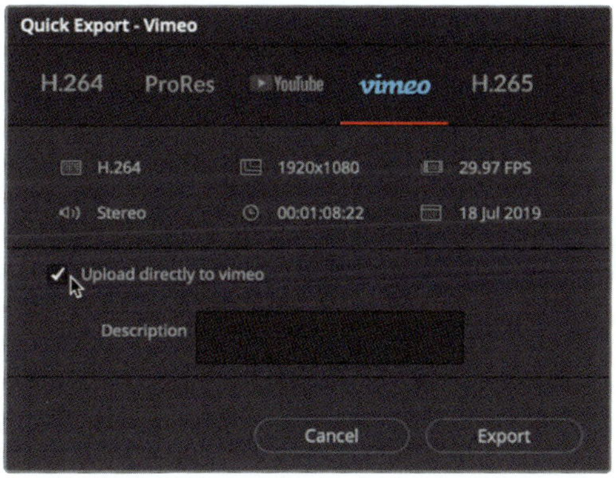

Here, you can enter in a description for this movie. The description you enter here shows up under the movie on the Vimeo page.

7 After you enter in your description, click the export button.

A save dialog opens to choose where the movie file will be saved.

8 Select a hard drive and folder where you want the movie to be saved then click save.

A render process window show the time to completion and upload progress for the movie.

9 Once the upload is complete the render progress window says "Uploading to Vimeo completed" and you can click close on the window.

The name of the movie on Vimeo is the name you gave the timeline. The description you entered shows under the movie in the description area on Vimeo. It is important to know that videos posted are public and viewable by anyone who visits your page on Vimeo.

Editing faster with the DaVinci Resolve Editor Keyboard

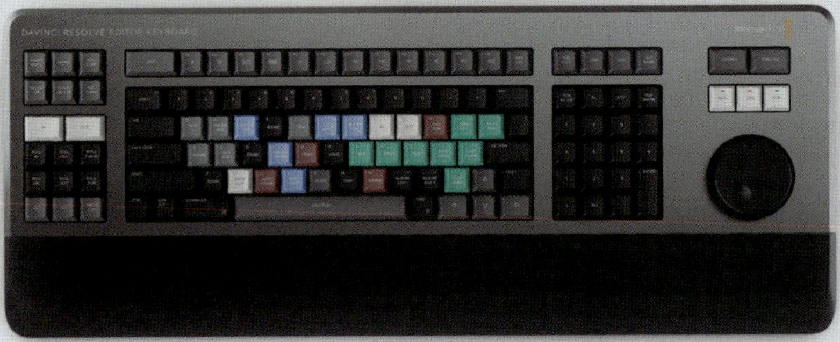

The DaVinci Resolve Editor Keyboard is designed for professional editors who need to work faster and turn around work quickly. More than just a simple keyboard, the DaVinci Resolve Editor Keyboard has been designed as an alternative way to edit that's much faster than a mouse because you can simultaneously use both hands at the same time! It also has dedicated keys for the edit modes and other functions on the cut page.

You also get an integrated search dial built right into the keyboard, which is an accurate way of jogging or scrolling up and down clips or the timeline. There are also buttons above the search dial to switch between source tape and the timeline.

That means you can use 2 hands to edit, so you can work faster because you're able to change position and push buttons at the same time. Your right hand controls the position in a clip or timeline, while your left hand is setting in and out points as well as applying edits.

The keyboard lets you move, mark in and out points, apply an edit, then move again, repeatedly, one after the other, again and again. It's an extremely fast way to work, using both hands at once. You can see why the cut page has been designed to allow multiple edits to happen while staying in the source tape. It does not change to the timeline after each edit, because thats much slower.

To make editing even faster, you can also use the keyboard for trimming. There are trim buttons on the left side below the in and out keys that you can press and hold while using the search dial to accurately adjust edit points. The search dial is big, so trimming is very accurate and very fast! As you saw in the tutorial, the transition selection buttons have dedicated keys that let you change between a cut, dissolve and smooth cut, instantly. That lets you scroll down the timeline while adding and removing dissolves extremely fast.

Everything about the cut page and the DaVinci Resolve Editor Keyboard have been designed for speed. It's an incredibly fast way to get an edit completed and posted in just a few minutes!

Well done! These first two lessons were designed to give you a solid working knowledge of the new cut page and many of its incredibly fast and intelligent tools. But the cut page is just the newest part added to DaVinci Resolve 16. The remainder of this training guide will take you through the other pages for longer format editing, visual effects and motion graphics, audio mixing and color grading.

Lesson Review

1. True or False: All transitions are dragged from the transition browser and applied to the timeline.
2. True or False: To modify the speed, resizing or a filter effect on a clip you only need to move the play head over the clip in the timeline.
3. True False: To disable the dynamic zoom you must rest the parameters back to their default setting.
4. True or False: You can only use the top five title templates while in the cut page. All other title templates are only editable in the edit page.
5. True or False: Quick Export saves a movie to a hard drive and optionally uploads it to a streaming service.

Answers

1. False. You can apply a cross dissolve and smooth cut or switch back to a straight cut using the buttons in the toolbar.
2. False. You must select the clip in the timeline to use the viewer toolbar to modify the effect.
3. False. The switch on the far left side of the viewer toolbar will enable and disable any of the tools.
4. False. You can use all title templates while in the cut page.
5. True. Quick export saves a file and can also upload the file to a streaming service.

Lesson 3

Organizing a New Project

Producing film and video content is a very creative and exciting process. Lessons 1 and 2 gave you a look at that process in the cut page. Now, you're going to start back at the beginning and get a more detailed look at how the media and edit pages handle similar tasks for longer format, more involved projects.

You'll begin by configuring project settings, importing media, grouping clips into folders, and using metadata and smart bins to make it easier to search and sort through large amounts of content.

Time

This lesson takes approximately 45 minutes to complete.

Goals

Configuring essential settings

When you started the project in the lesson 1, you didn't configure any settings at all. In fact, you even didn't give your project a name until the end of the lesson. That project was designed to skip the sometimes dry project setup tasks and jump right into the fun stuff. Now you'll take a step back and correctly set up a new project. To do so, let's return to the project manager.

1 If DaVinci Resolve is closed, open the application to get to the Project manager. If DaVinci Resolve is already open, choose File > Project manager, or press Shift-1.

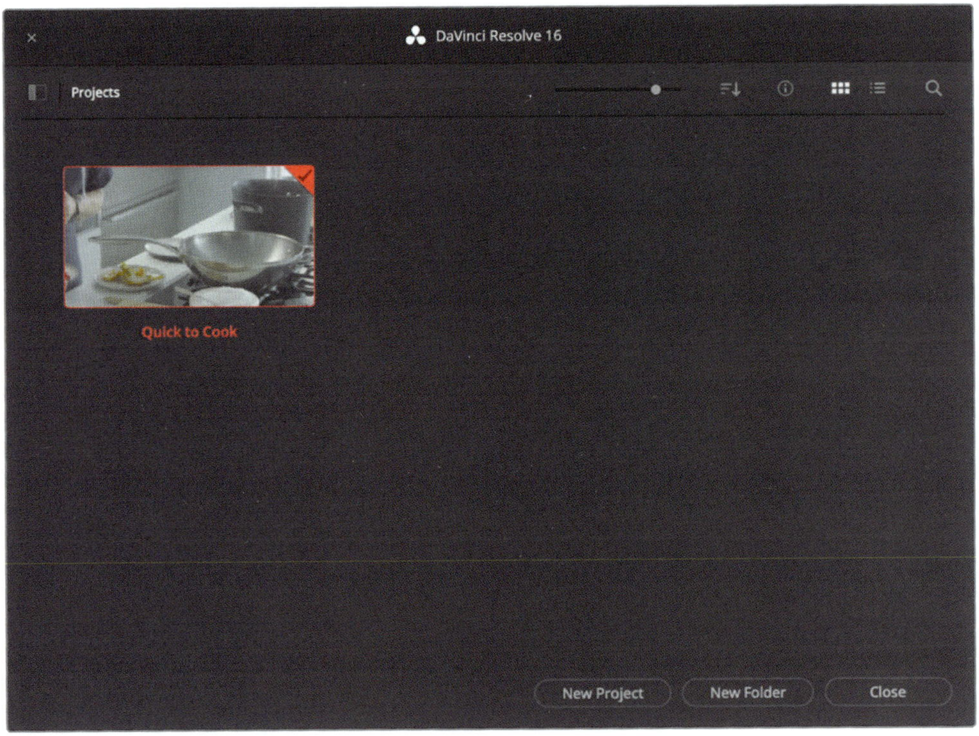

The project manager opens with a thumbnail that represents the project you created in the previous lesson. You'll create a new project in this exercise.

2 At the bottom of the project manager, click the New Project button.

3 In the Create New Project dialog that appears, enter the project name **My New Project**, and click Create.

The new project opens in the edit page.

TIP If the Quick to Cook project is open when you create the new project, the cut page will be displayed. Switch to the edit page to begin this project.

4 To close all the extra panels that you may have opened in previous projects, choose Workspace > Reset UI Layout.

DaVinci Resolve uses default values for project settings such as frame rate for playback, and output resolution. You can customize these values in the project settings window.

5 Choose File > Project settings to open the project settings window.

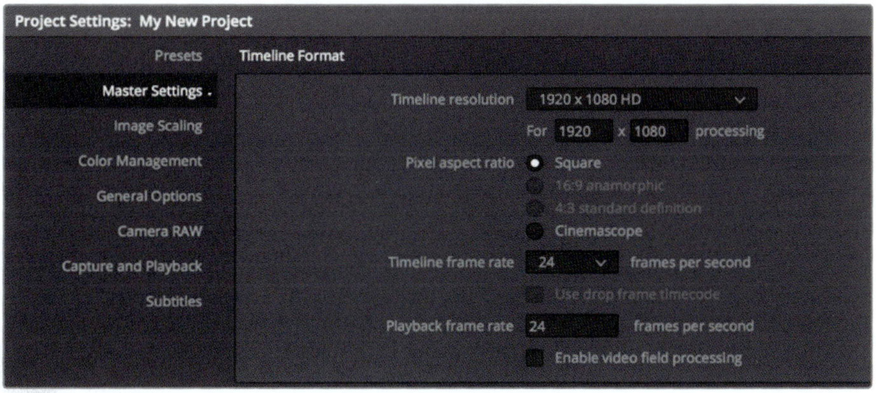

In this lesson, you'll use clips with a frame size of 1280 x 720 pixels running at 23.976 frames-per-second (fps). Let's adjust your project settings accordingly.

6 In the "timeline resolution" pop-up menu, choose "1280 x 720 HD 720P".

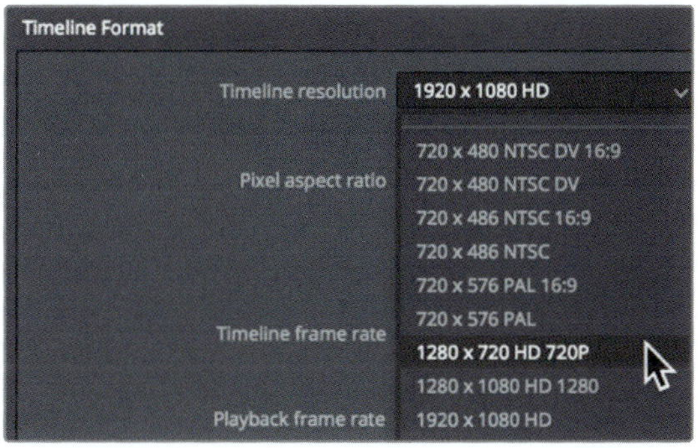

Below the timeline resolution, you can see the timeline frame rate.

7 In the "timeline frame rate" menu, choose 23.976.

8 In the project settings window, click Save to save your changes and return to the edit page.

Although the timeline resolution and frame rate can be customized for each timeline in a project, it is more efficient to set up the default project resolution and frame rate ahead of time. It also leaves less room for operator error. You should set up two other areas before you begin importing clips. Let's start in the preferences window, which is used for configuring DaVinci Resolve settings that do not typically change from project to project.

9 Choose DaVinci Resolve > Preferences, or press Cmd-, (comma) in macOS, or Ctrl-, (comma) in Windows to open the preferences window.

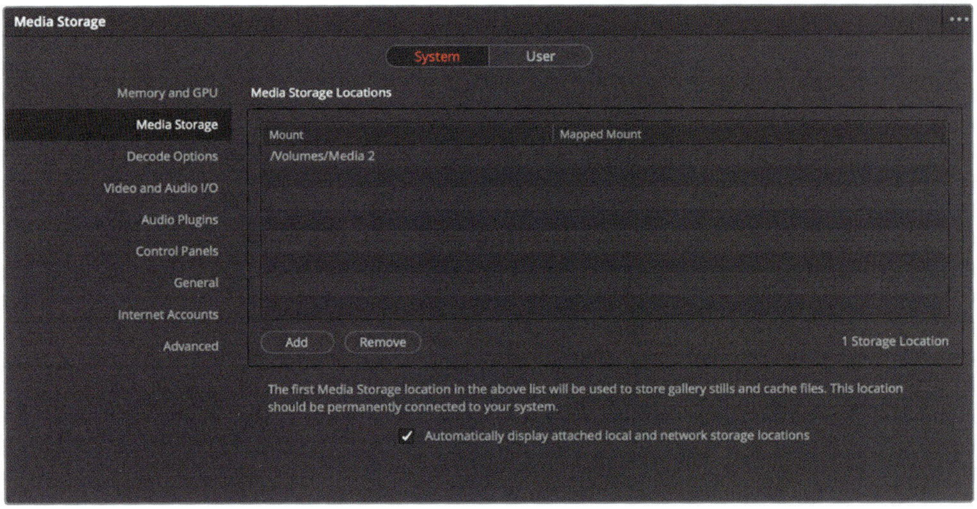

Similar to the project settings window, the preferences window has categories along the left side. The preferences window opens to the media storage category which is the one you'll typically want to set up.

The media storage category allows you to add drives, often called "scratch disks," to your system when using DaVinci Resolve. Throughout the duration of a project, DaVinci Resolve will occasionally create media that must be saved to a hard drive. This may include cached or rendered files, still frames, and various media that is optimized to improve playback performance. Such files are saved to the first hard drive listed in the media storage preferences.

10 If you wish to change the drive used for cached content, click the add button and select your fastest and largest hard drive.

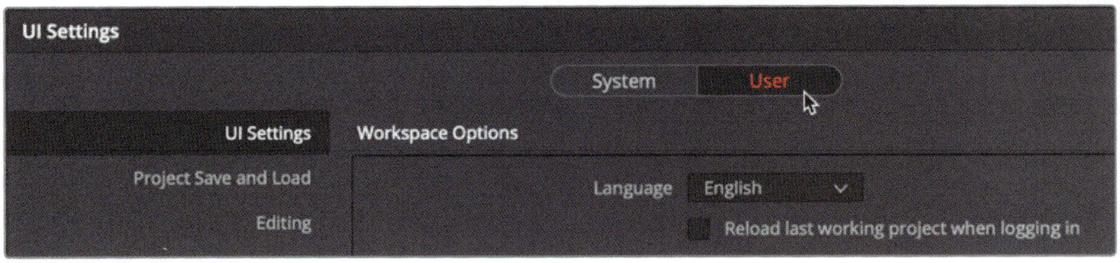

It's almost always advisable to set your scratch disk to the largest, fastest hard drive available to your computer. If you don't specify a scratch disk, your system disk will be used by default.

TIP If you purchased DaVinci Resolve from the macOS App Store, add the fastest largest drive first, then enable "Automatically display attached local and network storage locations". Enabling this check box before adding your scratch disk will cause macOS to add the Mactinosh HD drive as the first drive.

The preference window has two tabs at the top. The default selected tab is the system tab. Its settings, like the media storage settings, are specific to your computer hardware for all projects. The user tab displays preferences that are not saved with a project but saved for use with this workstation.

11 At the top of the preferences window, click the user tab.

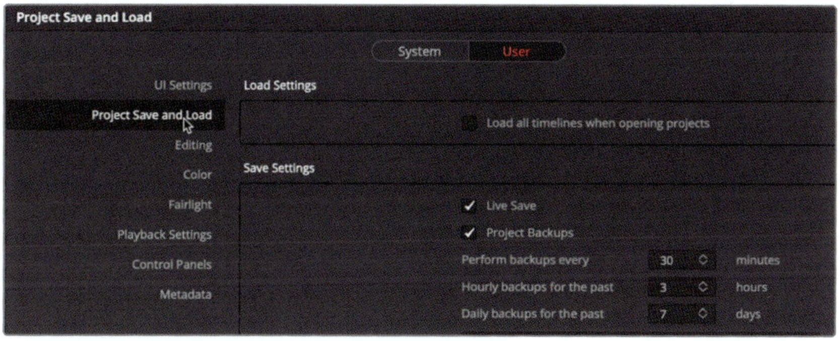

12 Along the left side of the preferences window, click the Project Save and Load category.

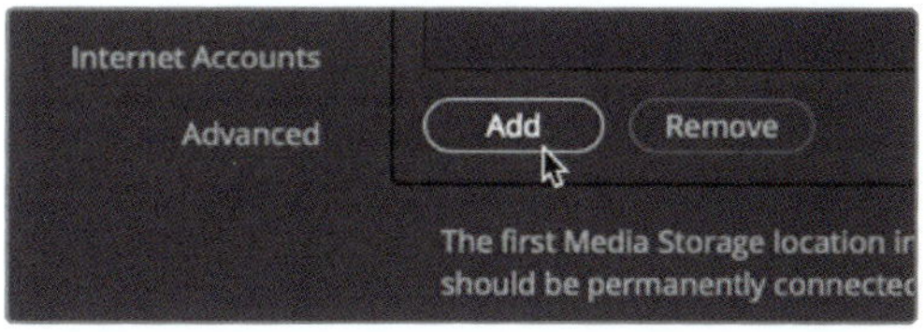

The project save and load settings can configure regularly timed project backups as well as implement a continuously live save mode that always saves your work. Live save is enabled by default on new projects, but you'll need to enable the project backups setting.

13 Click the project backups button to enable the feature.

TIP Keyboard mapping setting is located under the DaVinci Resolve menu and allows you to customize the keyboard shortcuts so that they match other popular editing systems or your own unique layout.

14 Click save to close the preferences window.

TIP Changing some options in preferences will require you to restart DaVinci Resolve.

Now your set up is complete; but before you learn how to import clips, let's get clear about some of the unique aspects of the DaVinci Resolve interface.

Exploring the DaVinci Resolve interface

DaVinci Resolve is organized as a series of interface pages—media, cut, edit, Fusion, color, Fairlight, and deliver—that correspond to the order of most traditional film and video post-production workflows. Each page is accessed by clicking one of six buttons at the bottom of the screen.

1. Click the media page button to switch to the media page.

   The media page is the most efficient page for importing and organizing media, syncing clips, adding metadata, and cloning camera original media. We've already covered the cut page so we'll skip that and go directly to the edit page.

2. Click the edit page button to switch to the edit page.

   The edit page contains all of the professional editing tools you'll need to assemble your program and add titles, transitions, and effects.

3. Click the Fusion page button to switch to the Fusion page.

   The Fusion page is a complete 2D and 3D compositing application for visual effects and motion graphics.

4. Click the color page button to switch to the color page.

   The color page contains DaVinci Resolve's world-class color correction and creative color grading tools as well as keying, stabilization, and filter effects.

5. Click the Fairlight page button to switch to the Fairlight page.

   The Fairlight page is a complete digital audio workstation that has everything you'll need to deliver incredible cinematic soundtracks .

6. Click the deliver page button to switch to the deliver page.

   On the deliver page, you can master to tape, create files for the web, and even output high-resolution files for theatrical distribution.

7. Click the media page to return to the media page.

   You can freely move between these pages to import and manage media, edit in the timeline, create visual effects, color correct, mix audio, and output your program. You'll begin working in the media page.

The media page is divided into five areas:

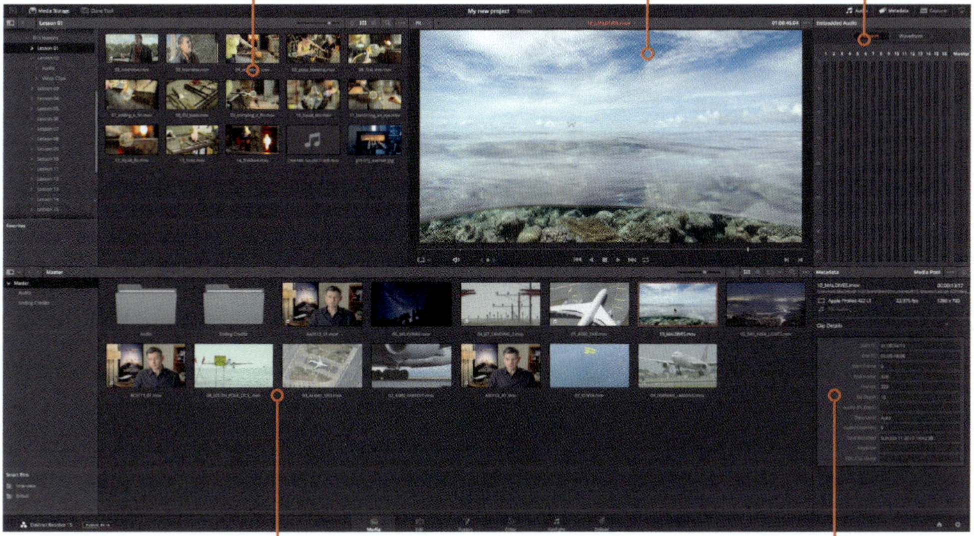

The library browser shows all of the connected drives and the files stored on those drives.

Viewer for previewing video

Audio meters for checking audio levels

The media pool contains all of the media for your current project, organized in bins. You can import files from the drives in the library browser into the media pool for each project.

Metadata editor for viewing, adding, or editing clip metadata

The media page gives you the most flexibility and functionality when it comes to importing media from your hard drives. You'll also perform other tasks here such as media management and clip organization, syncing audio and video clips, and troubleshooting clips that unexpectedly appear offline.

Importing clips

When you are ready to import clips into a project, the most efficient way is through the library browser in the media page. In this browser, you can navigate to any folder or hard drive in which you store your media. When you import clips into your project, they are stored in bins in the media pool.

> **NOTE** The following steps assume that you have copied the R16 Intro lessons folder to your Documents folder. If you copied the files to a different location, use the library browser to navigate to that location.

1 In the library browser sidebar to the left, click the icon of your computer's internal hard drive.

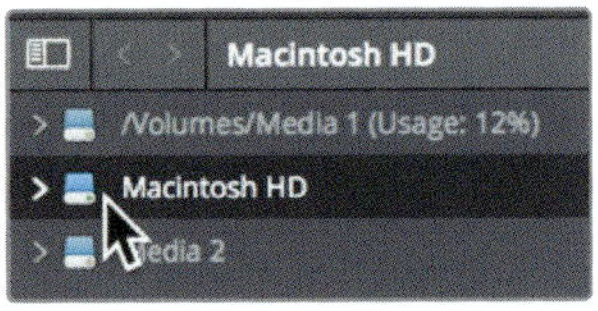

2 In the right panel, navigate to your Documents folder.

3 In the Documents folder, double-click the R16 Intro lessons folder.

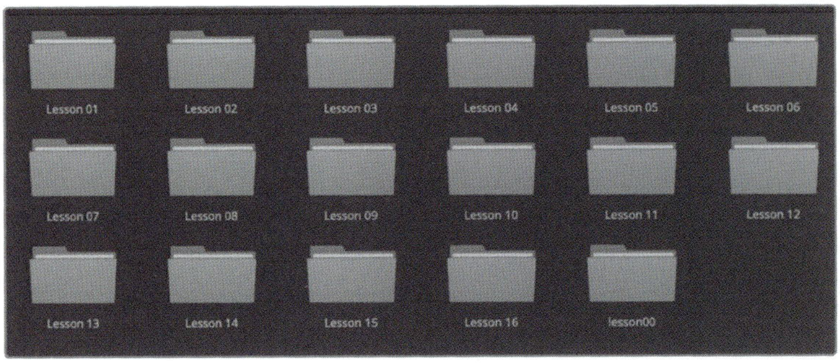

The library displays several subfolders in the R16 intro lessons folder. You'll import clips for this project from the video clips folder located in the Lesson 03 folder.

4 Double-click the Lesson 03 folder, and then double-click the video clips folder to open it.

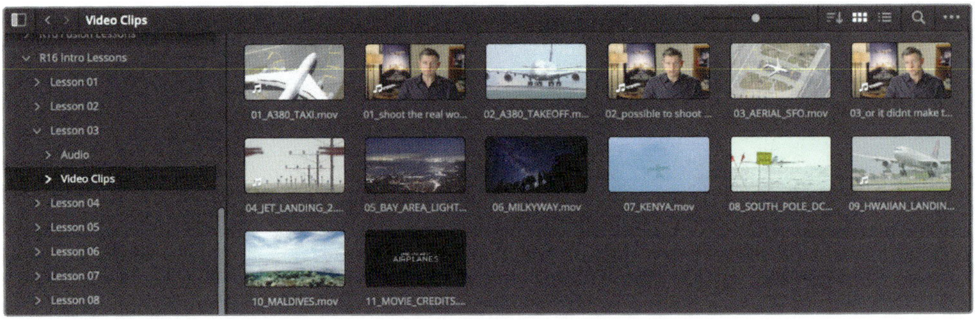

The right panel of the library displays a thumbnail-sized image icon for each of the clips you want to import. You can preview each clip in the viewer.

5 Click any thumbnail to see the clip in the viewer.

6 Press the spacebar to begin playing the clip, and then press spacebar again to stop playback.

After you're finished previewing clips, you can choose to import one or more of them into your project.

7 Choose Edit > Select All to select all the clips displayed in the library, or press Cmd-A (macOS) or Ctrl-A (Windows).

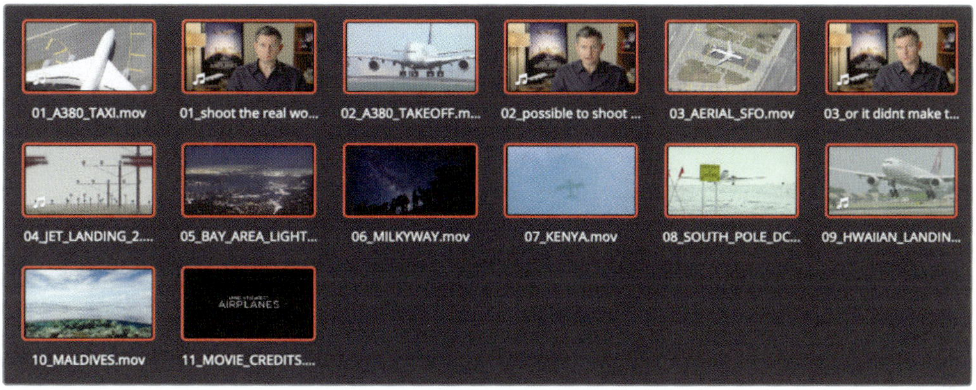

8 Drag any selected clip from the library into the media pool where it is labeled "No clips in media pool".

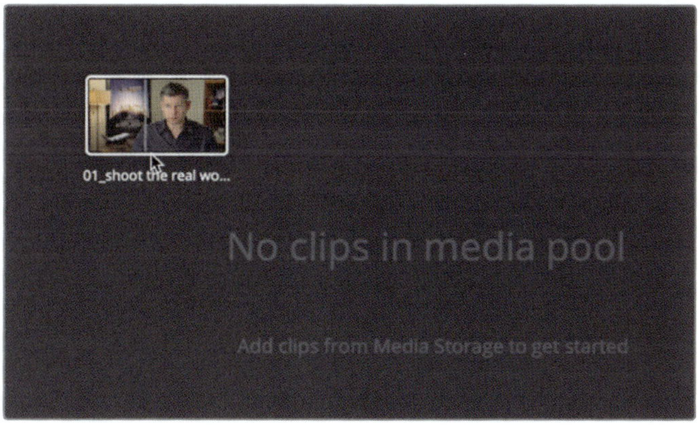

TIP You can also drag clips directly into the media pool from the macOS finder or Windows Explorer.

All the selected clips are added to the master bin in the media pool. Every project always includes a master bin. This master bin contains every clip you add and every new bin you create. It is also important to understand that the clips are not copied, moved, or transcoded when you import them. DaVinci Resolve is completely non-destructive; it simply links to the unaltered files in their current locations on your hard drive.

Importing Folders

Instead of selecting each of the clips you want to import and adding them all to the master bin, you can import an entire folder and automatically create a custom bin.

1 In the upper area of the library, click the back arrow to view the contents of the Lesson 03 folder.

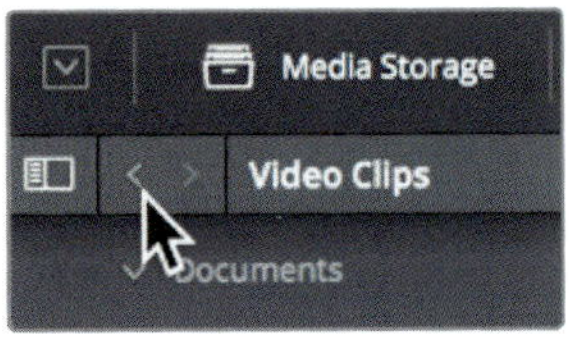

2 Right-click the audio folder, and choose "Add folders and subfolders to media pool (create bins)".

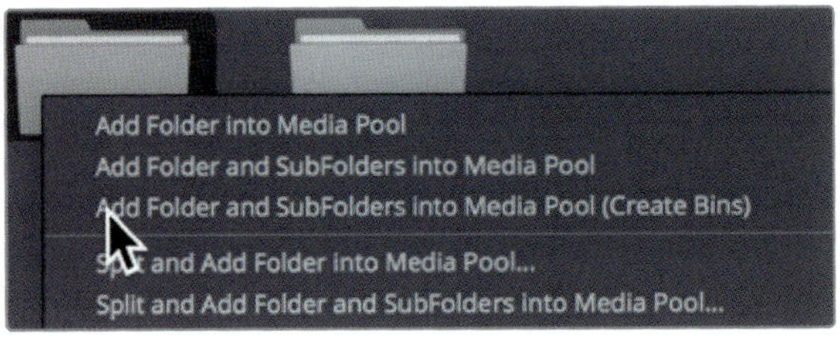

Choosing this menu item creates a bin with the folder's name and adds it to the master bin. All of the clips contained in the folder are imported as part of the new bin.

Reviewing and scrubbing clips

You might want to review and check your clips after you've imported them, especially if you're editing a project that was shot by someone else and you're as-yet unfamiliar with the footage.

1 In the media pool sidebar, select the master bin.

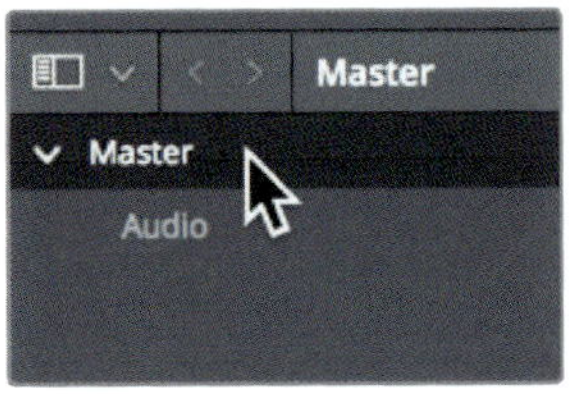

2 In the bin, hover the mouse pointer over any video clip.

When your mouse pointer is located over any clip in a bin, a live preview of the clip is displayed in the viewer. You can move your mouse back and forth over the thumbnail to quickly scrub through it.

NOTE Due to screen and window size differences, the order of clips in your bin may appear slightly different from the figures shown in this lesson.

3 Move the mouse pointer back and forth over the thumbnail to scrub quickly through the clip and see it in the viewer.

TIP Live preview can be disabled in the options menu located in the upper-right corner of the viewer.

The live media preview feature allows you to quickly skim over a clip without having to play it. Still, to edit clips most efficiently, you will need to know their contents intimately. For that purpose, nothing can replace just sitting down and watching a clip play from start to end.

4 While your mouse hovers over the thumbnail, press the spacebar to play the clip.

The clip plays at its native frame rate.

5 Press the spacebar again to stop playback.

The viewer transport buttons include playback as well as other buttons to play a clip in reverse, and move the playhead to the beginning or the end of a clip.

Choosing representative thumbnails

The thumbnail used to represent each clip in the bin is the first frame of that clip. At times, that first frame might not be the best representation of the clip, so it is useful to be able to change it.

1 In the upper-right corner of the media pool, drag the scale slider to increase the size of the thumbnails.

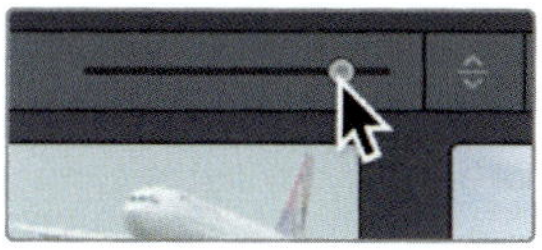

2 Position your pointer over the thumbnail labeled 07_ KENYA.

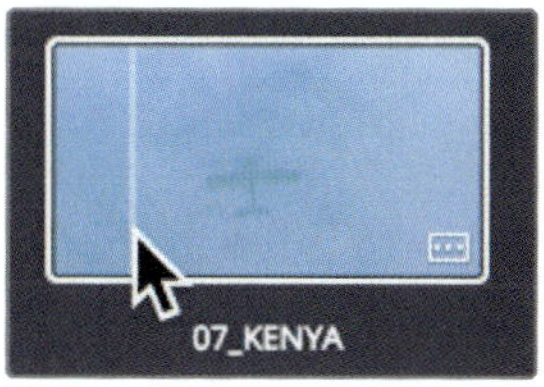

3 Move the mouse pointer left and right over the thumbnail.

As you move the pointer left and right, DaVinci Resolve displays various frames from the clip as if you were fast forwarding and rewinding through it.

4 Move the pointer over the thumbnail until you see the yellow airplane.

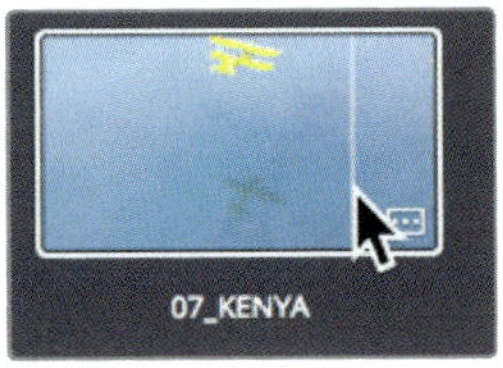

This image will make a better representative frame than the blue water.

5 Right-click the thumbnail, and in the menu, choose set poster frame or press Command-P (macOS) or Ctrl-P (WIndows).

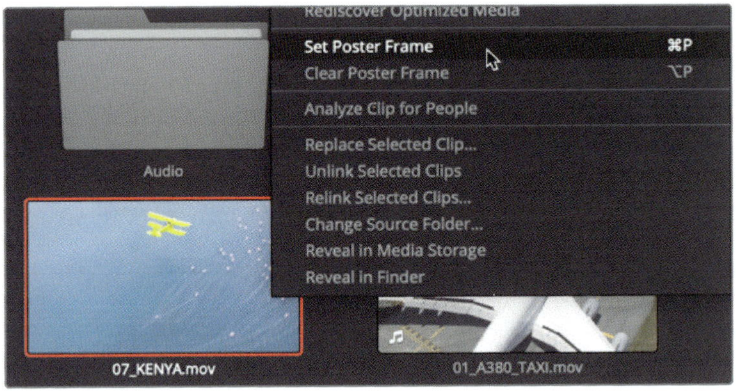

Although setting appropriate poster frames can help a lot when you are searching clips, to truly become familiar with the content you are using, you should always watch each source clip. Once you complete this lesson, take time to review the clips and set poster frames for any other clips that may not currently display the best representative frame.

Viewing clip metadata

In addition to audio and video content, clips can also include information called metadata that describes the content of your clips. Metadata can identify the format, framerate, and resolution, among other data. Some metadata is added automatically to a clip by the camera and audio recorders. You can also add custom metadata, such as keywords, that you can use to help organize your projects more efficiently.

You can view the metadata for a clip and add additional information using the metadata editor.

1 In the master bin, click a clip to load it into the viewer.

Detailed information about the selected clip appears in the metadata editor in the lower-right corner of the media page.

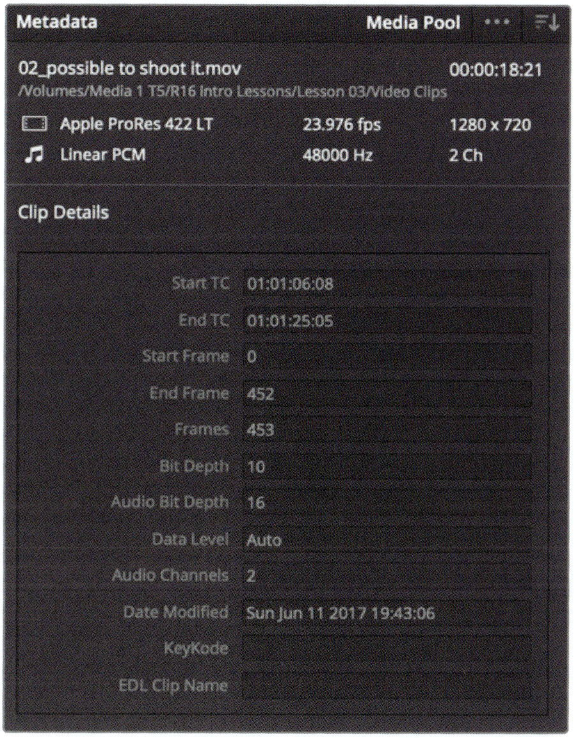

The upper section of the metadata editor displays some essential clip information such as name, duration, and frame size. However, because a production can include an enormous amount of metadata for every clip, a pop-up menu in the upper-right corner of the metadata editor lets you choose other categories of metadata.

2 In the upper-right corner of the metadata editor, in the pop-up menu, choose shot & scene.

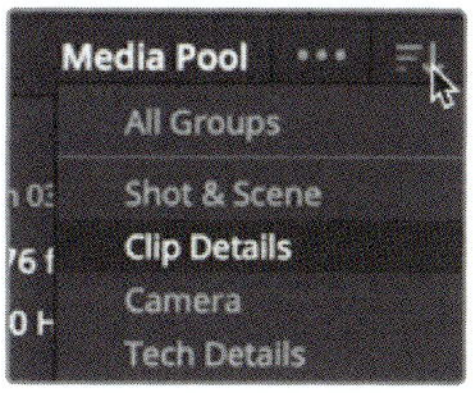

Each category in the pop-up menu contains additional fields and checkboxes. Some may display metadata entered automatically by the camera or other devices, whereas other fields allow you to add custom information that may be helpful in organizing your clips. In the next exercise, you'll add some metadata to clips that will make it easier to locate them.

Adding custom metadata

Standard metadata that is captured or created automatically on set during production is certainly helpful when organizing clips, but adding your own metadata is also important. In almost every project, you'll organize content using some form of metadata. Some of that metadata must be added manually in DaVinci Resolve.

The current lesson has only a few shots from one small scene, so it's not very difficult to stay organized. However, when you're working on larger projects with hundreds, or even thousands, of clips, adding and using metadata can help you save countless hours searching and sorting through clips as you build your edit.

1 In the master bin, select the 01_shoot the real world clip.

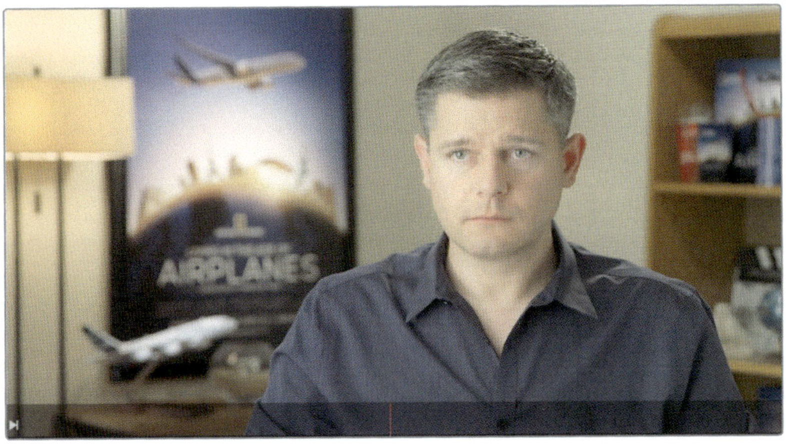

This clip is one of three interview clips that you'll be using. It's a good idea to identify it as an interview clip, so let's add that information as a keyword.

2 In the keywords field of the metadata editor, enter **Interview**.

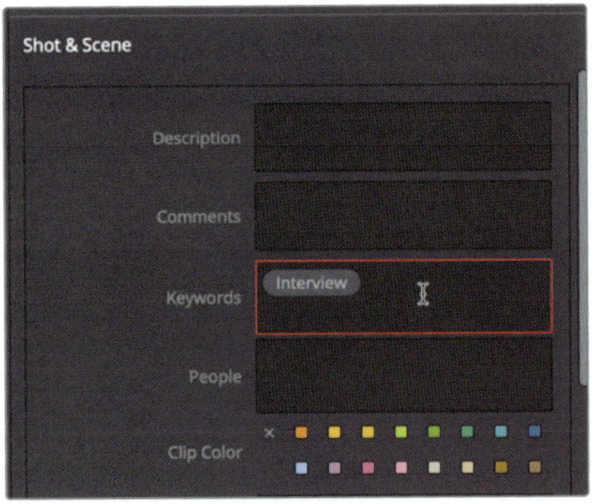

Two other interview clips could also use that "interview" keyword. You can be more efficient by entering the keyword for both clips at the same time.

3 In the master bin, select **02_possible to shoot it** then Cmd-click (macOS) or Ctrl-click (Windows) **03_or it didnt make the movie** to select it, too.

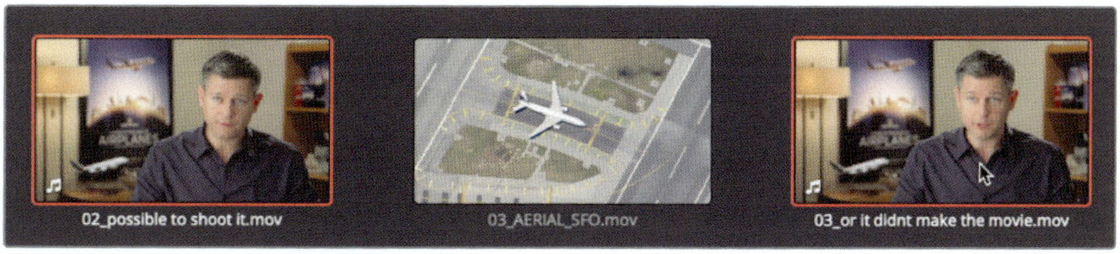

4 With both clips selected, in the keyword field of the metadata editor, enter the letters **INT**.

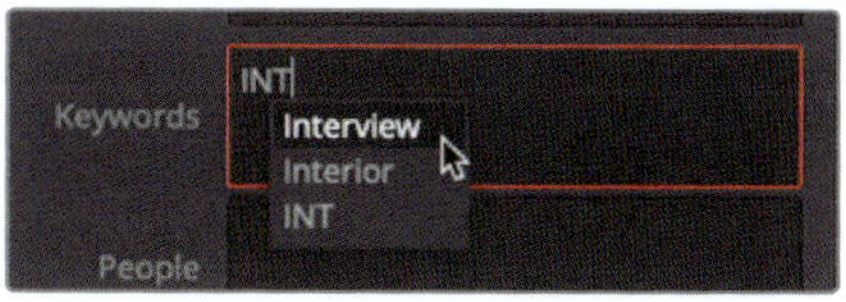

A list of standard keywords and previously entered keywords that start with I-N-T are displayed. It's helpful to select keywords from the list if they are available, rather than running the risk of misspelling.

5 In the pop-up menu, choose "interview" to add that keyword.

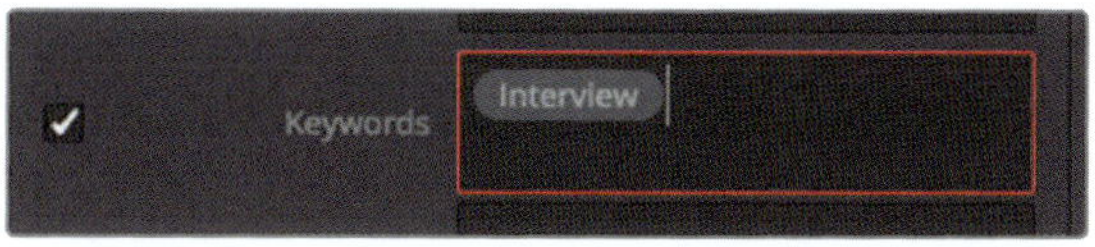

6 At the bottom of the metadata panel, click save to apply the keyword to both clips.

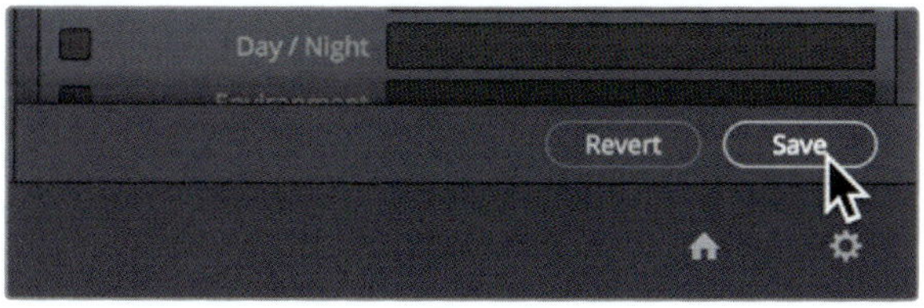

You have tagged interview clips with some important information about their contents. metadata added this way can be used throughout DaVinci Resolve to improve clip organization. Next, you'll learn ways to put that metadata to use as you begin organizing your clips.

Making new bins

Bins are like folders, or containers, for all your clips. Although all the video clips that you import go into the default master bin, it is not very efficient to rely entirely on a single bin to hold all of them. It's like having a filing cabinet and stuffing everything in one folder. A better strategy is to create custom folders or bins and organize your clips in a way that makes it easier for you to find them later.

1 In the media pool, select the master bin.

All the video clips currently in the master bin would be easier to work with (and faster to locate) if they were organized by content. For instance, you could place all of the scenic plane shots in a b-roll bin to distinguish them from the interview clips that you could place in an Interview bin.

2 To create a new bin, choose File > New Bin, or press Cmd-Shift-N (macOS) or Ctrl-Shift-N (Windows).

A new bin with the default name bin 1 is created and added to the media pool. Let's change the name so it fits your project. The names of new bins are immediately available for editing.

3 Type **Ending Credits** as the name of the bin.

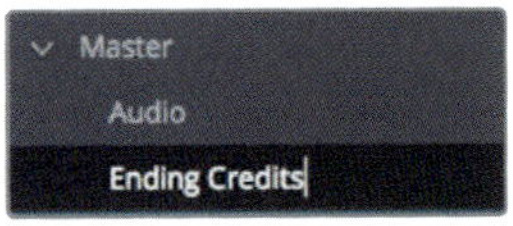

All new bins that you create appear inside the master bin. With a new bin created and named to suit your project, you're ready to start organizing your clips into bins.

4 Select the master bin, and then drag the 11_MOVIE_CREDITS thumbnail onto the Ending Credits bin name in the bin list sidebar. When the Ending Credits bin name highlights, release the mouse button.

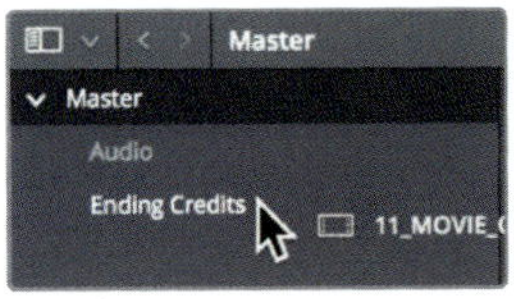

TIP You can open multiple bins at the same time by right-clicking a bin name in the bin list sidebar, and choosing Open As a New Window.

5 In the media pool sidebar, click the Ending Credits bin to view its contents.

You've now successfully moved clips from one bin to another. Although the process of organizing clips is straightforward, it can also be very labor intensive. Let's look at a more efficient way to organize clips.

Displaying keyword smart bins

Smart bins search your entire project to group clips based on metadata that you define. For example, you can create a smart bin that automatically finds all of the audio clips in your project or all of the clips captured using a specific camera. Best of all, a smart bin's contents will continually update as new footage is added to your project. That means you don't have to manually organize footage when using metadata and smart bins. Smart bins are automatically created for any keyword you tag to a clip. They are displayed at the bottom of the bin list.

1 At the bottom of the bin list in the media pool, click the disclosure arrow to reveal the Interview smart bin.

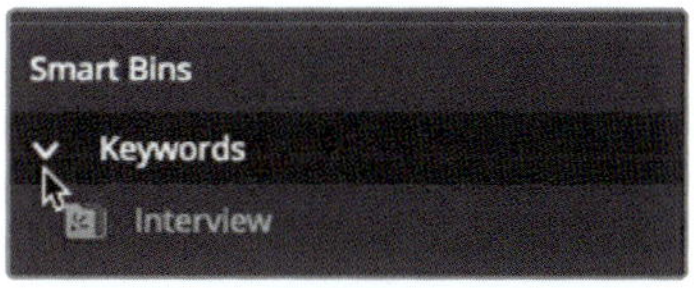

2 Select the interview smart bin to display the clips

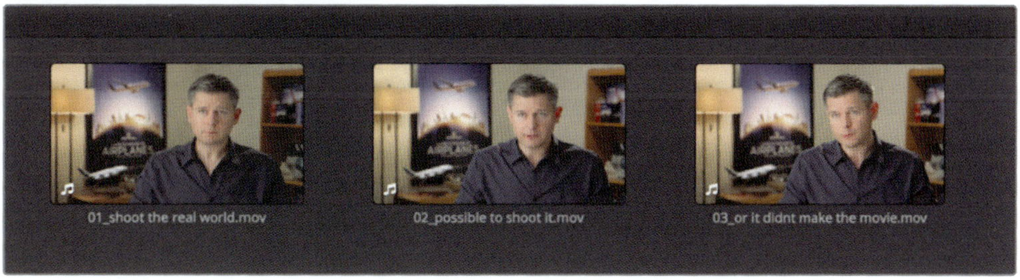

The smart bin appears at the bottom of the media pool and displays all of the clips that contain the keyword. Any new keywords applied to clips will automatically create a smart bin and display in the smart bin section of the bin list.

Creating custom smart bins

You just displayed a simple keyword smart bin. But smart bins can be much smarter! You can create custom smart bins that use multiple layers of criteria for more advanced clip selection.

1 Right-click under the Interview smart bin, and in the menu, choose add smart bin.

The create smart bin dialog appears. In this dialog, you set up the rules that determine which clips are automatically added to this custom smart bin. The criteria options are many, enabling you to create smart bins that group clips based on a wide range of auto-generated and manually entered metadata. For this smart bin, you'll look for all of the clips that are **not** interview clips.

2 In the create smart bin dialog, in the name field, enter **B-Roll**.

3 Click media pool properties, and in the menu, choose metadata - shot & scene because this was the metadata category chosen when you entered the interview keyword.

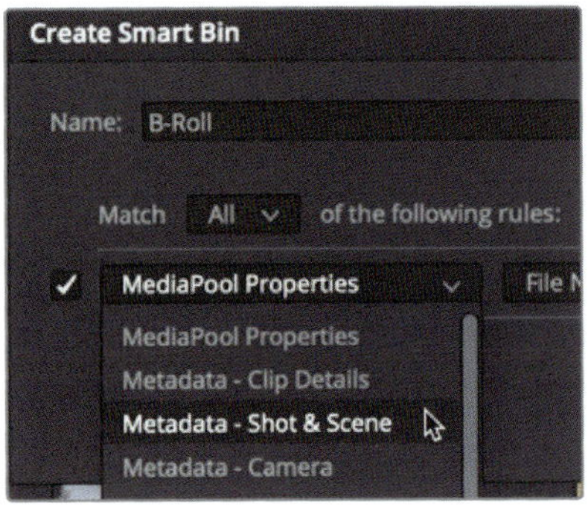

4 Set the metadata type pop-up menu to Keywords,

5 Set the third metadata criteria pop-up menu to "does not contain".

6 In the text entry field, type interview, and click create smart bin.

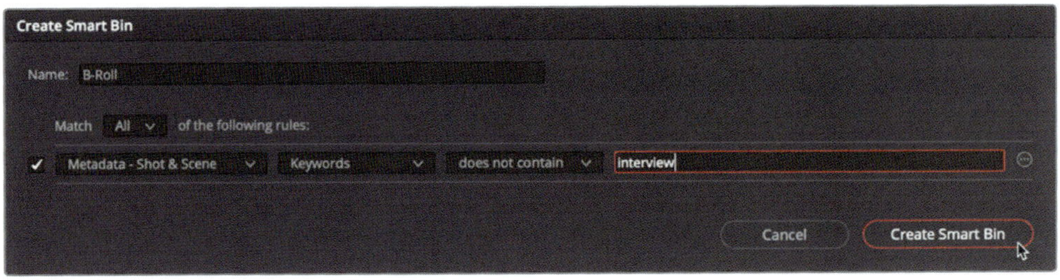

You now have a smart bin that includes all the clips that do not have the keyword Interview applied to them. That identifies most of the clips that you want, but the bin also contains the audio clips in your project. You'd actually like to narrow down this smart bin even further to exclude those audio clips.

7 To edit the smart bin criteria, double-click the B-Roll smart bin.

You can add additional layers of criteria for a Smart Bin which will result in a more selective choice of clips.

8 To the far right of the dialog, click the add filter criteria button to add an additional field for criteria.

9 Change “metadata - shot & scene” to “media pool properties”.

10 Change “file name” to “clip type”.

11 Set the last two menus to “is not” and “audio”.

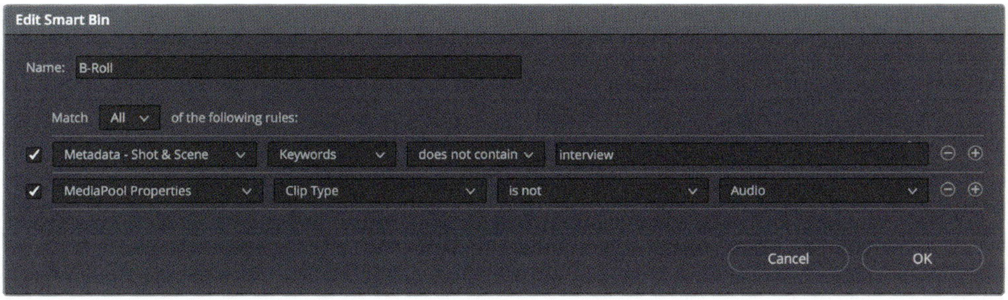

You‘ve now removed all of the audio clips from this smart bin, but you also need to eliminate any timelines.

12 Click the add filter criteria button to add another criteria field.

The new fields use similar criteria as the previous one so you need to change only the last two items.

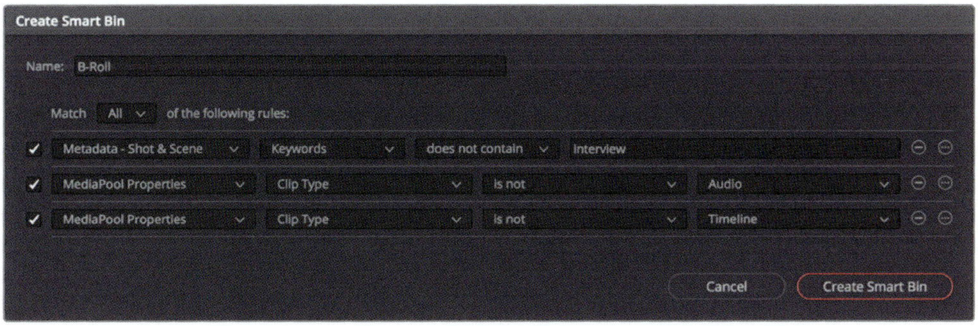

13 Change “is” to “is not” and change the last item from video to timeline.

14 Click OK to close the dialog and update the smart bin.

In the future, when you add the “interview” keyword to new clips in this project, those clips automatically will be added to the Interview smart bin and excluded from the B-Roll smart bin. That’s the beauty of the smart bin. It collects clips based on whatever criteria you identify and continually updates your clip organization.

Saving custom bin views

Beyond organizing clips into bins, you can organize how content appears in those bins. Clips in bins can be shown in list view as well as thumbnail view and can display as much or as little metadata as you'd like.

1 Select the B-Roll bin.

2 At the upper-right of the media pool, click the list view button.

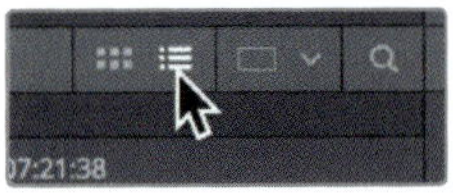

The media pool switches from showing the clips as thumbnails to showing clips in a text list.

In every project, some of the columns in list view will be more important than others. To ensure that you can see the information you'll need most, you can hide and show columns in a bin and then save that customized view as a layout.

3 Ctrl-click (macOS) or right-click (Windows) any column heading to display the bin headings contextual menu.

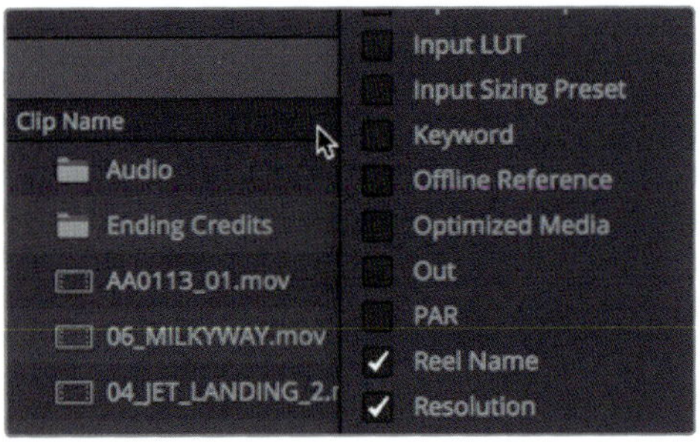

The contextual menu lists all of the columns that you can display in a bin. The headings with a check mark are the currently displayed columns.

4 In the contextual menu, deselect all the check boxes except for Audio CH, Duration, End TC, Resolution, and Start TC.

The columns you deselected are removed from the bin's List view.

You can also sort columns, and therefore the clips, based on the information found in a column.

5 Click the heading for Start TC so that the small arrow next to the name points up.

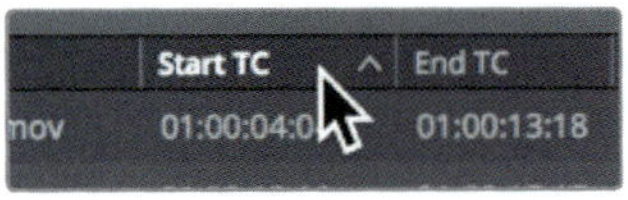

Clicking the heading for any column sorts that column based on its criterion. Clicking the Start TC heading sorts the bin contents in ascending order based on the starting timecode number for each clip. A small arrow pointing up is shown next to the column heading name to indicate that this column is used for sorting as well as indicating the order of the sort.

After making these changes, you have a nice, slimmed-down number of columns that display only the essential information that you might want to see. You can save as many different bin views as necessary and recall them from the menu later. To save a bin view, you can use the same contextual menu.

6 Ctrl-click (macOS) or right-click (Windows) one of the bin column headings, and in the contextual menu, choose create column layout.

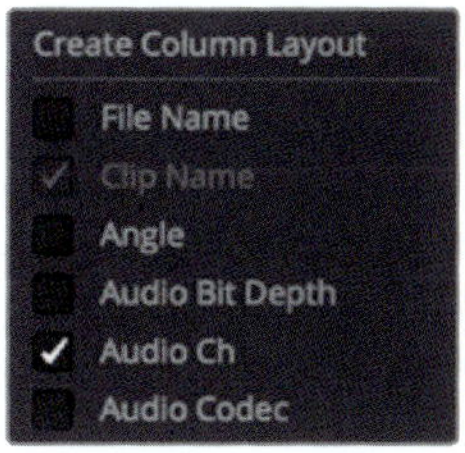

7 Type **Basic View** as the column layout name, and click OK.

You have now set up all the bins, sorted the clips and created a few smart bins based on metadata. You are ready to begin editing your movie trailer. In the next lesson, you'll move to the edit page where you begin assembling clips into a timeline.

Lesson Review

1 True or false? You can can set the timeline resolution and frame rate in the project settings.

2 True or false? Smart bins are created automatically for any keyword you apply.

3 Where are the settings to create auto saves or project backups?

4 Where are the original media files located after you add them into the media pool?

5 True or false? You must first create a bin before you can add clips to the media pool.

Answers

1 True. You can set the timeline resolution and frame rate in the project settings.

2 True. Smart bins are automatically created for keywords.

3 Live save and project backups are located in the User Preferences > Project Save and Load panel.

4 The media files do not change their locations after you add them to the media pool. They remain in their original locations in their original formats and resolutions.

5 False. If no other bin is created in the Media pool, clips are added to the master bin.

Lesson 4

Assembling a Rough Cut

With your content imported and organized, you are ready to start editing in the Edit page. The first pass at developing a timeline is called the **rough cut**. The goal is to place clips in the rough order you'll want them in your final program. It is the equivalent of sketching a picture rather than precisely drawing one. In this lesson, you'll use the edit page and look at the various ways to begin a rough cut. Unlike the cut page, where a fast turn around is the single most important requirement, the edit page is designed for more craft style editing. It is designed for longer form projects and to that end it provides more options in the number of ways you can set up and edit a project.

Time

This lesson takes approximately 50 minutes to complete.

Goals

Creating a timeline

Before you can start editing, you must create a timeline into which you place clips in the order you'll want to use them. DaVinci Resolve 16 projects can contain one or more edited timelines. As you experiment with multiple versions of a timeline, it can be helpful to duplicate your timeline by selecting Edit > Duplicate Timeline. Unlike the cut page, you can place timelines in any bin, not just the master bin. On larger projects with dozens of timeline versions, having a dedicated timelines bin can make it easier to go back and compare versions or locate the exact version you want.

1 If DaVinci Resolve is closed, launch the application to get to the project manager.

2 Double-click the My New Project thumbnail that you created in Lesson 3.

   When you left this project, you were on the media page, but to begin assembling your rough cut, you'll now move to the edit page.

3 At the bottom of the screen, click the edit page button.

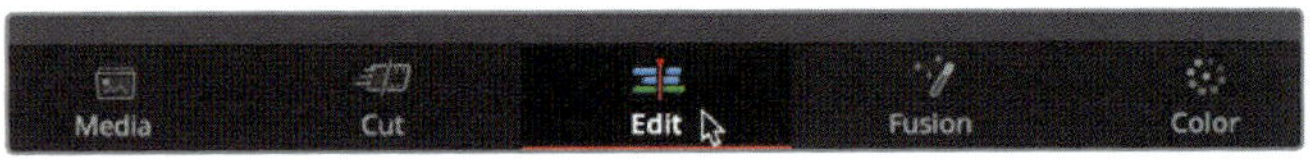

   You'll begin by creating a timeline and a bin that will hold your timeline.

4 In the media pool sidebar, select the master bin, and choose File > New Bin to create a new bin within the master bin.

5 Name the new bin **Rough Cuts**, and press Return or Enter.

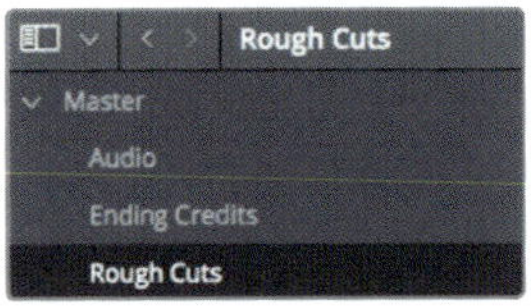

6 With the Rough Cuts bin selected, choose File > New Timeline, or press Cmd-N (macOS) or Ctrl-N (Windows).

   When the new timeline dialog appears, you can give the timeline a new name.

7 Name the timeline **First Rough Cut**, and click create.

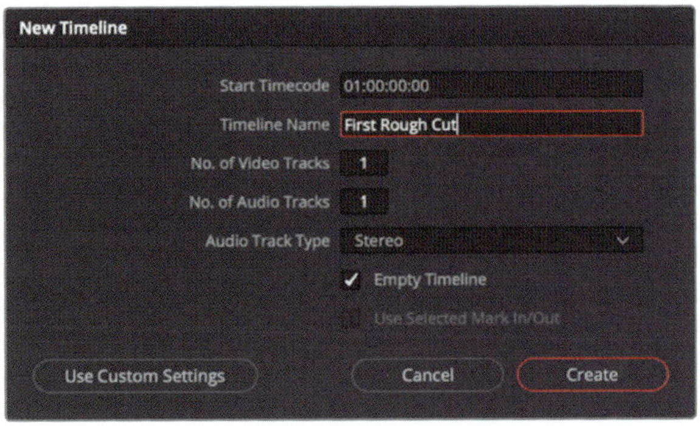

> **TIP** You can click the use custom settings button to override the project settings for the timeline format, frame rate, monitoring and output configuration.

An empty timeline is added to the timeline editor and the name of the timeline is displayed above the timeline viewer, just as the name of the viewed clip is displayed above the source viewer. An icon for that timeline is added to the Rough Cuts bin.

You can make timelines even easier to locate by assigning a color to the Rough Cuts bin so it stands out from the other bins in your list.

8 In the bin list, right-click the Rough Cuts bin.

9 In the contextual menu, choose Color Tag > Cyan to assign a cyan color to the Rough Cuts bin.

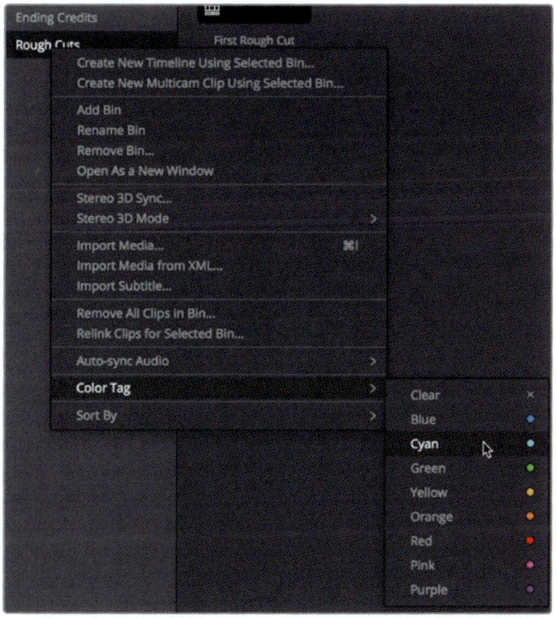

Yes, the bin does appear black, but that is only because it is still selected. When you switch to a different bin in the next exercise, you'll see the correct cyan color. So, let's move on and add clips to your timeline.

Making the first edit

A large part of the editing process is selecting your shots. You are not only selecting which clips to include in the project; you are also selecting the portion of the clip you wish to use. In Lesson 1 you learned how to identify a range using the in and out points in the cut page, now you'll learn a similar process for the edit page.

1 Select the Interview smart bin, and click the thumbnail view button to display the clips as thumbnails.

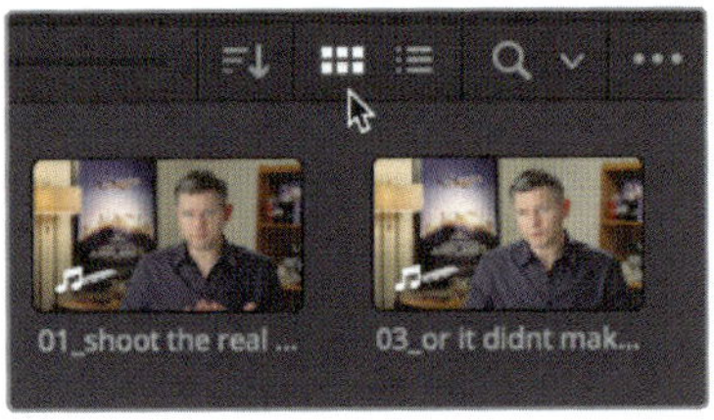

2 In the smart bin, double-click the 01_shoot the real world clip to load it into the source viewer.

Because this clip has dialog, you can use an audio waveform overlay to quickly locate the portion of the clip you want to include in your timeline.

3 In the options menu above the source viewer, choose show zoomed audio waveform.

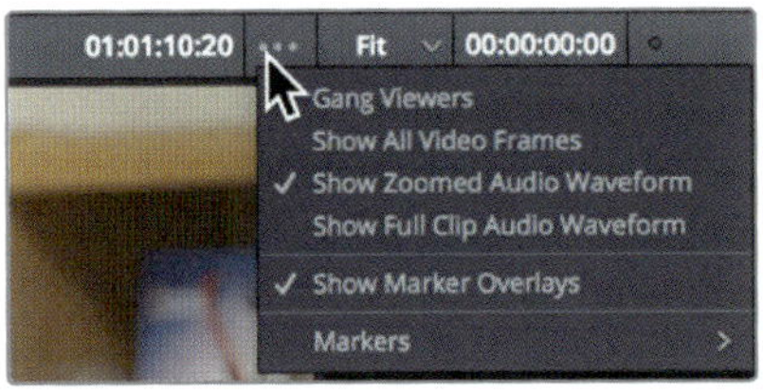

An audio waveform for the video clip is displayed under the viewer. The waveform shows where audio begins and ends, as well as quiet or loud sections.

4 Move to the start of the clip and press the spacebar again to play the clip, then press the spacebar to stop playback when the interviewee says, "In this film." (Notice that the audio waveform begins at this point.)

5 Press the left arrow key to nudge the position of the playhead 10 frames before the word, "In." You can use the audio waveform to guide you.

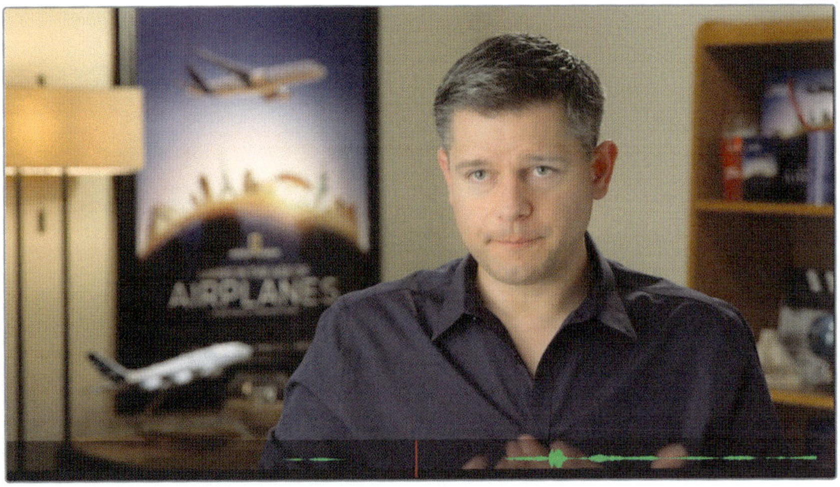

6 Press the I key to mark an in point.

7 After marking an in point, play the clip for roughly 10 more seconds until the man says, "making all the things possible." Then press the spacebar to stop playback.

8 Again, use the arrow keys to nudge the playhead right after the word "possible", and press the O key to mark an out point.

> **TIP** You can press Option-I (macOS) or Alt-I (Windows) to clear an in point; press Option-O (macOS) or Alt-O (Windows) to clear an out point; and press Option-X (macOS) or Alt-X (Windows) to clear both the in and out points.

It always a good idea to verify your selected range by playing from the In point to the out point.

9 Choose Playback > Play Around/To > Play In to Out, or press Option-/ (slash) in macOS, or Alt-/ (slash) in Windows.

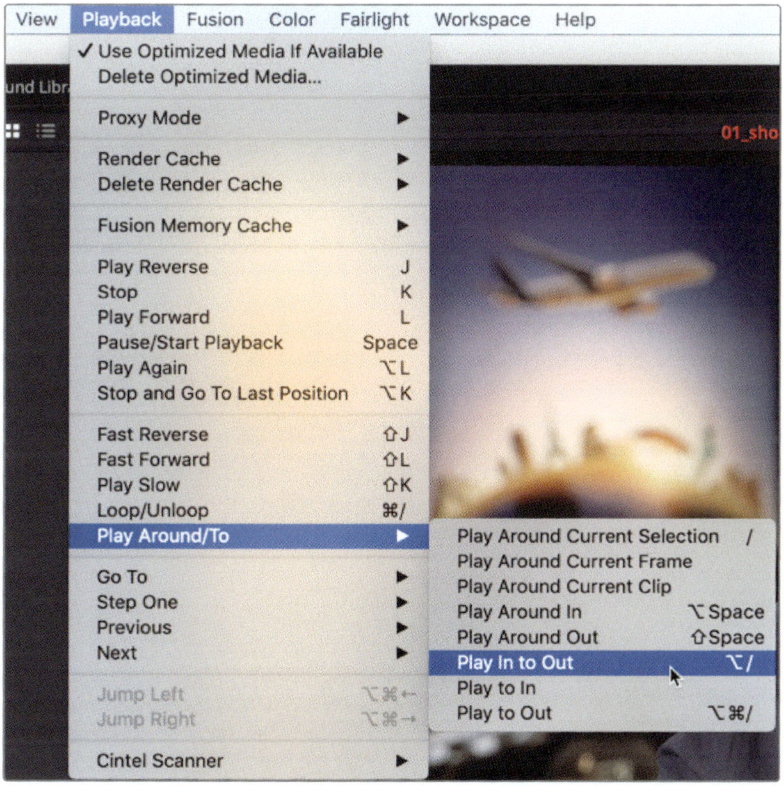

Playing the clip from the In point to the out point is a good way to see if your selected range is correct. If it isn't, feel free to go back and set the marks again.

When you are ready to add your first clip to the timeline, the easiest way to see all of the available editing functions is to use the edit overlay.

10 Drag from the center of the source viewer into the timeline viewer but do not yet release the mouse button.

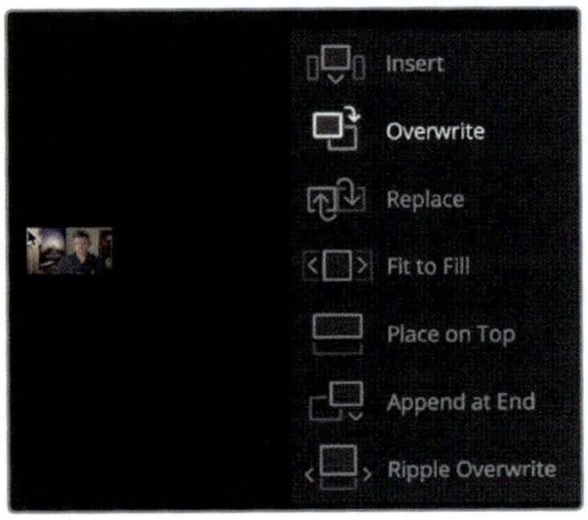

The edit overlay appears in the timeline viewer displaying seven edit functions which differ slightly from the cut page:

- **Overwrite** covers up a clip (or part of a clip) in your timeline using the new clip.
- **Insert** adds the clip to the timeline at the location of the playhead. Everything is split and moved down to make room for the new clip.
- **Replace** substitutes a clip in the timeline with a new clip without using any In or Out points.
- **Fit to Fill** changes the speed of a clip to fit a specified length.
- **Place on Top** positions one clip on top of another for blending or compositing. (Same as cut page)
- **Ripple Overwrite** replaces a clip of one length with a clip of another and ripples the timeline based on the difference in duration. (Same as cut page)
- **Append at End** adds new clips after the last clip in the timeline, regardless of where the playhead is located. (Same as cut page)

The overwrite edit is the default highlighted function which means that you can release the mouse button anywhere in the timeline viewer to perform that edit. Because you have nothing else in the timeline, overwrite is a fine choice for this edit.

11 Release the mouse button to perform an overwrite edit.

12 Drag the timeline playhead back to the start of the timeline, and press spacebar to play a little bit of the first edit.

> **TIP** If at any time you make a mistake, DaVinci Resolve allows you to undo your most recent steps. You can choose Edit >Undo several times to undo multiple steps, or choose Edit > Undo List and select the last step you want performed from the list of previous steps.

Although you've only edited one clip into your timeline, this process of marking in and out points and choosing an editing function from the edit overlay is a process that you will perform over and over when creating a rough cut. So, in the next exercise you'll repeat the process but learn to do it a bit more quickly, especially when adding longer clips.

Scrubbing with JKL keys

Using the JKL keys can help you quickly scan through clips. It's like using the fast forward and rewind buttons on your DVR so you can find exactly the right frame. The L key plays forward, the J key plays backward, and the K key stops playback. Tapping the L or J keys multiple times will speed up playback. Holding down K while tapping L or J will playback in slow motion. Let's give it a try.

1 In the Interview smart bin, double-click the 02_if it was possible clip to load the clip into the source viewer.

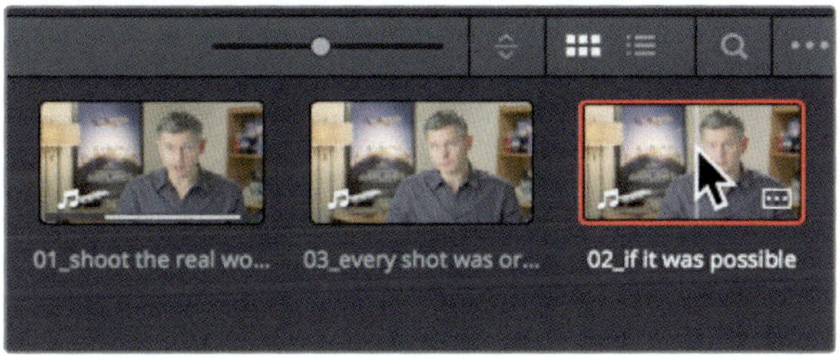

You are going to look for a point near the start of this clip where the man says, "If it was possible to shoot it, we wanted to go shoot it." The J and L keys can scrub over a clip at twice the speed or half the speed which makes it much faster to locate an exact spot rather than playing through the clip at normal speed. Let's start by placing your fingers correctly on the keyboard

2 If you are right handed, leave your right hand on the mouse and place your left ring finger on the J key, middle finger on K, and right index finger on L. If you are left handed place your index finger on J, middle finger on K, and ring finger on L.

> **TIP** Using the keyboard customization from the DaVinci Resolve menu, you can remap the keyboard to better configure the J-K-L key functionality for your comfort.

It can take bit of getting used to these hand positions, but let's start by just playing forward.

3 Tap the L key to play the clip at normal speed, and then press K to pause it when you hear the line you are looking for: "Ah, if it was possible to shoot it."

More than likely, you overran the beginning of the line. That isn't a problem because you can play backward using the J key.

4 Press the J key to go back near the start of the sentence, and press K to pause playback when you arrive there. Don't forget to use the audio waveform as a guide to locate where the sentence starts.

When you are near the start of the sentence, you can be more precise by playing at half speed using key combinations. The combination of the J and K keys for playing backward at half speed and the K and L keys to play forward at half speed can make it easier to pinpoint timeline locations.

5 Press J and K together to play backward at half speed, and then press K and L together to play forward at half speed until you are closer to the start of the sentence.

You can even use these keyboard shortcuts to nudge one frame forward and one frame back rather than moving your hand down to press the arrow keys.

6 Hold down the K key and tap the J key to nudge one frame back, and then hold down the K key and tap the L key to move one frame forward. Keep repeating those keyboard shortcuts until you are exactly at the start of the sentence, being careful not to include the "ah" at the start of the sentence.

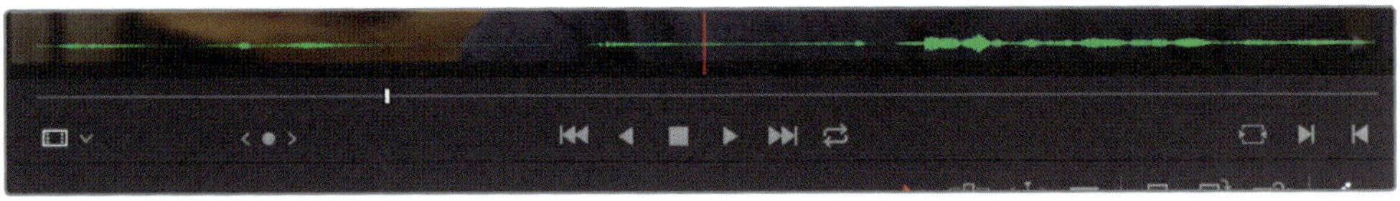

7 Press the I key to mark an In point.

Now let's use the same J-K-L scrubbing technique to locate an Out point. You'll look for the sentence about 10 seconds farther in, where he says, "Every shot was original and every shot was real."

8 Tap the L key twice to play the clip at double speed, then press K to pause when you hear the line you are looking for: "Every shot was original and every shot was real."

When you get close to the correct location, you'll want to switch to half speed playback and one-frame nudging.

9 Press J and K together and K and L together until you are closer to the end of the sentence.

10 Hold down the K key and tap the J or L key to move one frame at a time until you locate the exact end of the sentence, "Every shot was original and every shot was real."

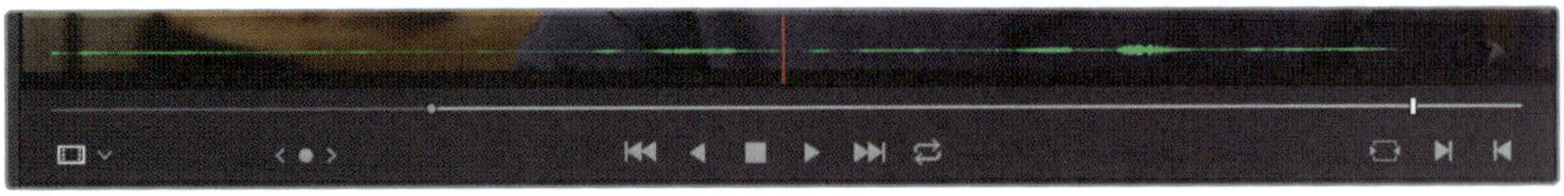

11 Press the O key to mark an out point.

12 Choose Playback > Play Around/To > Play In to Out, or press Option-/ (slash) in macOS, or Alt-/ (slash) in Windows, to review your range.

You can now edit this range into your timeline. Just as you more efficiently placed the in and out point using the JKL keys, you'll now speed up the actual edit using the toolbar.

13 Position the playhead at the end of the last clip in the timeline.

Although you can mark in and out points in the timeline, the timeline playhead will act as an implicit In point if neither mark exists.

The toolbar below the source and timeline viewers contains many of the most common functions that you'll use during editing. It even includes the three most commonly used editing functions: insert, overwrite, and replace.

14 In the toolbar, under the source and timeline viewers, click the overwrite button, or press F10 on the keyboard.

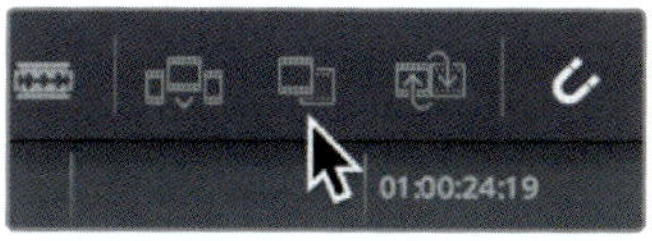

The second clip is added directly after the first clip in the timeline. Using the edit overlay or clicking one of the three edit buttons in the toolbar are both acceptable methods of making edits into your timeline. The method you choose is up to you and your style of editing. This lesson will continue to use these two methods, as well as introducing you to others to help you decide which is right for you.

Inserting clips into a timeline

Editing clips sequentially into the timeline can only take you so far. You'll eventually need to place new clips between two existing timeline clips. If you don't have an In point marked in the timeline, the playhead will be used instead. Unlike the cut page where the smart insert goes to the nearest cut, the insert edit on the edit page requires you to be more precise with the playhead poisiton.

1 Position the playhead at the start of the timeline and play the two clips you have added so far.

The two interview clips create a jarring cut because they are very similar looking. This jarring cut is called a **jump cut** because it appears as if the person abruptly jumped from one position to another. You can eliminate an unwanted jump cut by inserting a different clip between the two interview clips.

2 Position the playhead between the two interview clips in the timeline. As you drag, the playhead should snap to the cut point, ensuring that you are in the right spot.

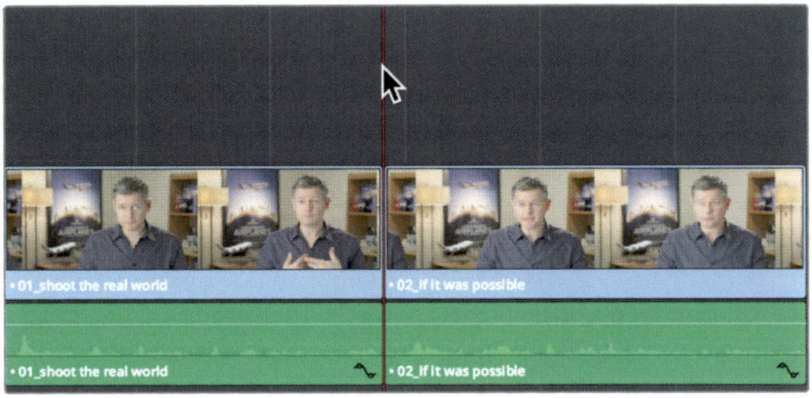

TIP The snapping behavior can be disabled by clicking the snapping button in the toolbar, or pressing N.

3 In the bin list, click the B-Roll smart bin, and double-click the 08_SOUTH_POLE_DC3 clip to load it into the source viewer.

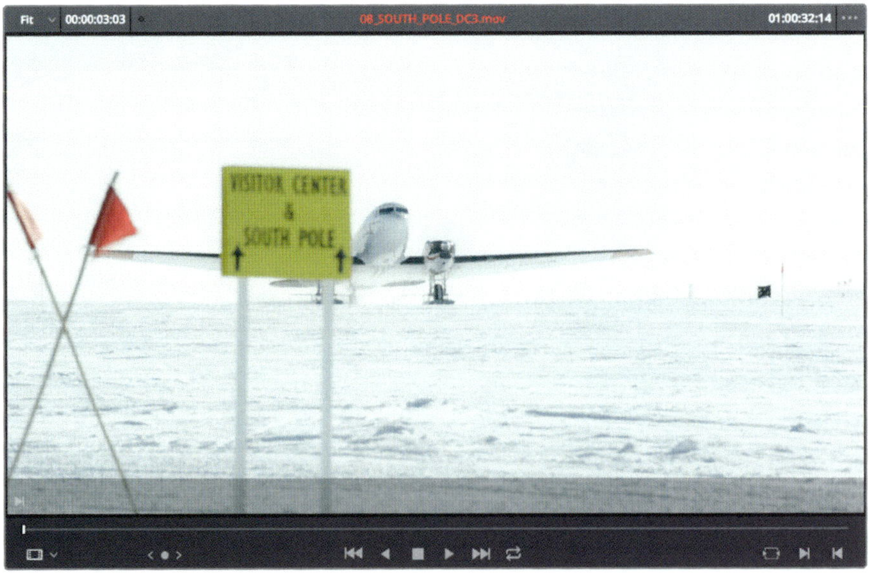

4 Move to the start of the clip and press spacebar to play this clip.

The clip of a plane taking off from the South Pole is a good one to add between these two interview clips because it goes with his comments about getting impossible shots.

5 From the beginning of the clip, drag the source viewer's jog bar until you see the tail of the plane emerge from behind the sign.

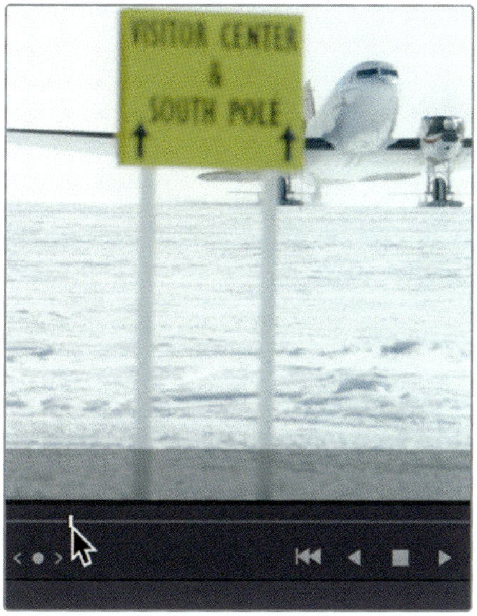

This spot in the clip gives you a little buffer room from the very first frame so it will work as your in point.

6 Press the I key to mark an in point in the source viewer.

This shot doesn't have a lot of action and it isn't very long, so you will use all of it.

As noted by the highlighted section of the jog bar, if no out point is set, DaVinci Resolve will use the remaining part of the clip to the end.

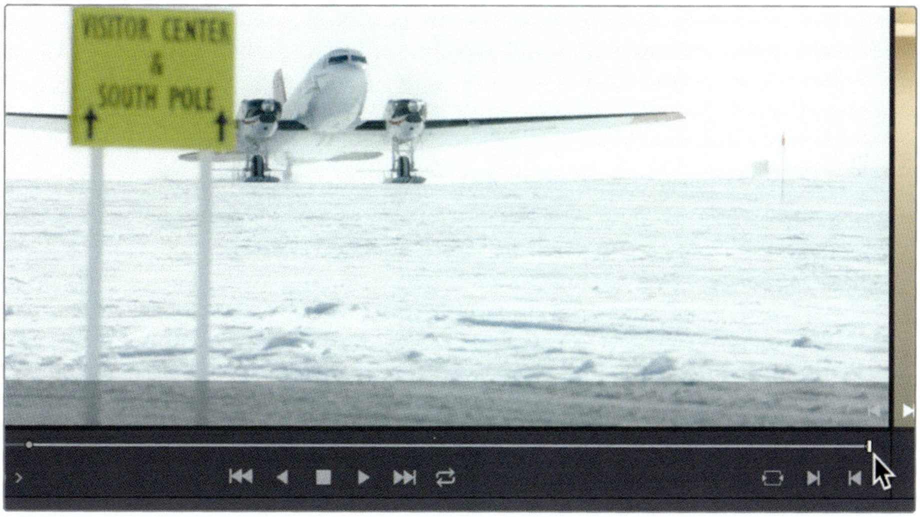

7 To make the edit, drag from the center of the source viewer into the timeline viewer. When the edit overlay appears, drag over the word "Insert" and release the mouse button.

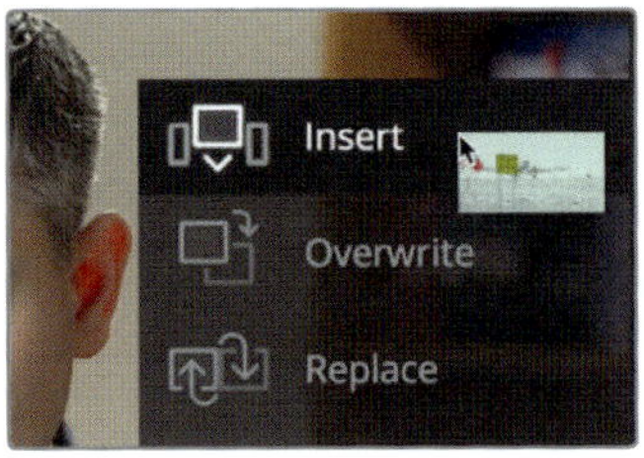

When you choose Insert in the edit overlay, the source clip is added to the timeline by pushing the second clip in the timeline to the right to make room. The overall duration of the timeline is extended by the duration of the added clip.

8 Drag the timeline playhead to the start of the timeline, and press spacebar to view the new edit.

> **TIP** Pressing the Home and End keys will move you to the start or end of the timeline, respectively. Some Mac keyboards do not have Home and End keys. When using one of those keyboards, press Fn-left arrow to move to the start of the timeline and Fn-right arrow to move to the end.

Splitting a clip with an insert

Not every insert you perform must be placed between two existing clips in the timeline. In some instances, you may want a new clip to split an existing clip in two. Let's learn how to deal with that situation.

1 Position the timeline playhead at the start of the second interview, if necessary.

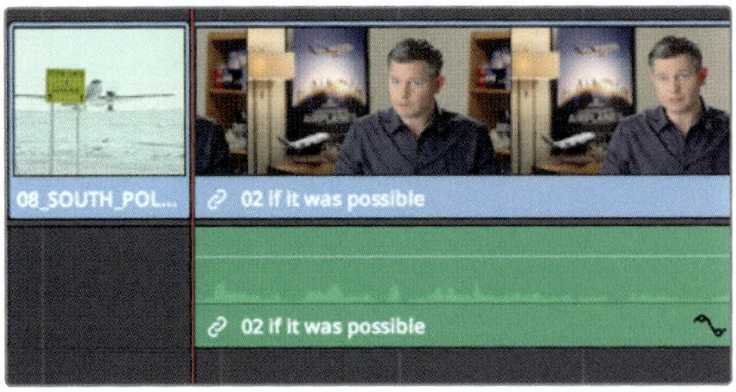

2 Press spacebar to watch and listen to this clip.

This long interview clip would be better if you split it up into two smaller clips. Also, that last line, "It was really important, every shot was original and that everything was real," would be a lot more impactful if it stood alone at the end of this trailer.

3 Press the J+K and K+L keys to play slowly over the last two sentences and locate the space between the sentences "It didn't make the movie" and "It was really important."

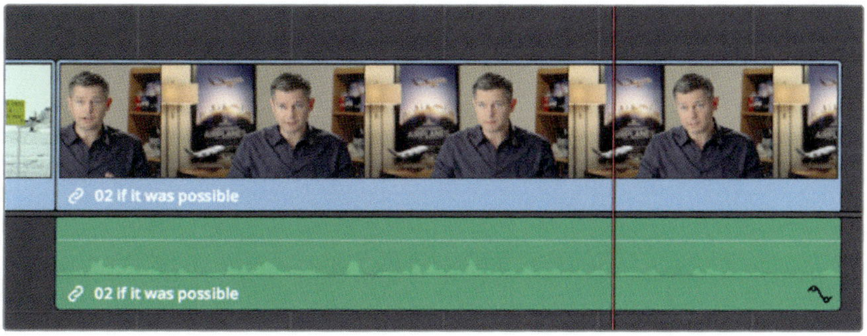

This brief gap between the two sentences is where you will insert a new clip. It can be easier to locate that small gap when you zoom into the timeline waveform.

4 In the toolbar, drag the zoom slider to the right to zoom in to the interview clip and see more detail in the audio waveform.

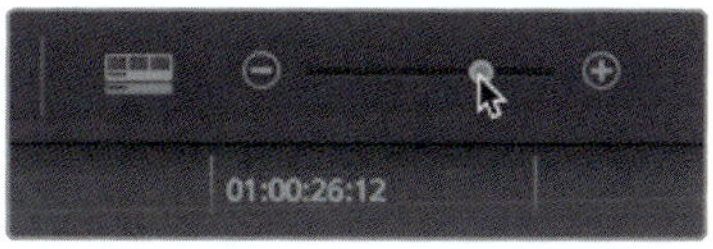

5 Press the J+K and K+L keys to refine your location between the sentences "It didn't make the movie" and "It was really important."

You can leave your playhead in this location and set in and out points on the source clip.

6 In the B-Roll smart bin double-click the **06_MILKYWAY** clip to load it into the source viewer.

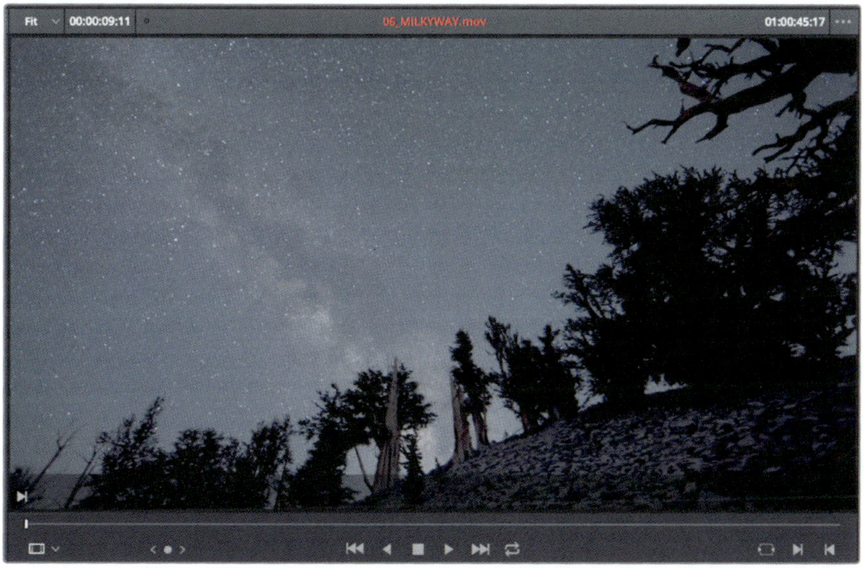

7 Move to the start of the clip and press spacebar to watch this clip and stop playback somewhere in its middle.

For this edit, you will use the entire clip. If you do not enter any marks on a source clip, DaVinci Resolve uses the entire clip.

Instead of using the edit overlay to choose an edit, this time you'll perform the Insert edit using the toolbar edit button. The insert edit button provides the same editing function as choosing "Insert" in the overlay. The method you choose depends only on your preferred style of editing.

8 In the toolbar, click the insert button, or press the F9 key.

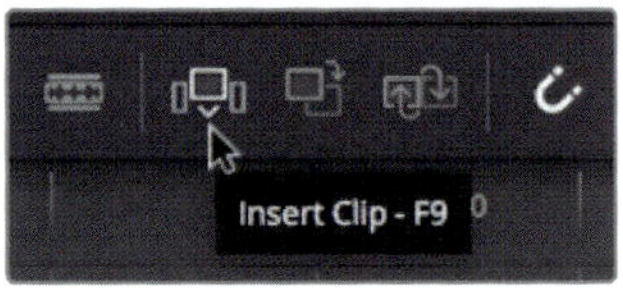

TIP To use the function keyboard shortcuts in macOS, go to System Preferences > Keyboard and enable "Use F1, F2 etc. keys as standard functions keys".

The insert edit splits the timeline clip at the playhead position and places the new clip at that point in the timeline. It will be easier to see if you zoom out the timeline.

9 Choose View > Zoom > Zoom to Fit, or press Shift-Z, to see the entire timeline.

10 Position the timeline playhead at the start of the second interview clip, and press spacebar to review the last half of the timeline.

An insert edit is one of the most basic edits you will perform. However, it is important to understand that once you insert a new clip, all of the other clips in the timeline are pushed farther down the timeline to make room for the new clip. Your overall timeline duration is therefore increased.

Using timecode

Up until now, you've placed clips in your timeline using sound and picture as a rough guides. An alternative guide is to use timecode numbers. Using timecode lets you specify the exact duration of a clip before you edit it into the timeline.

1 In the B-Roll bin, double-click the 05_BAY_AREA_LIGHTS clip to load it into the source viewer.

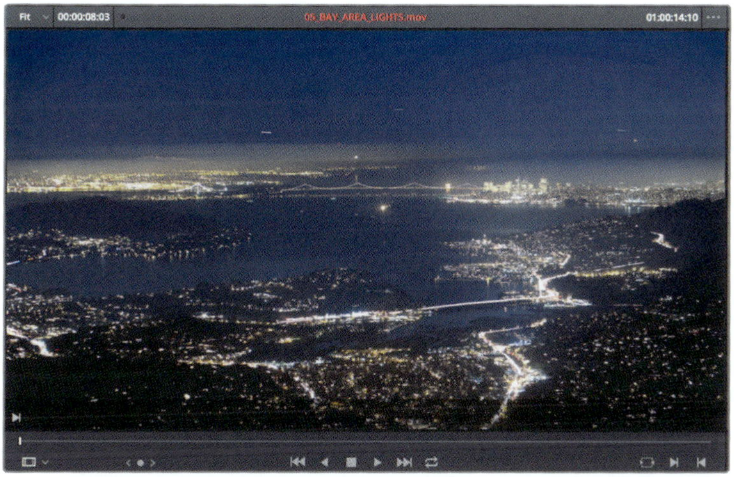

You can type an offset number to move the source viewer's jog bar or the timeline playhead forward or backward by a specific number of seconds and frames. You first identify the direction in which you want to move the playhead. To move forward, you press the + (plus) key on the keypad.

2 Move to the start of the clip, and type **+100**. Press Return or Enter to move the playhead forward one second.

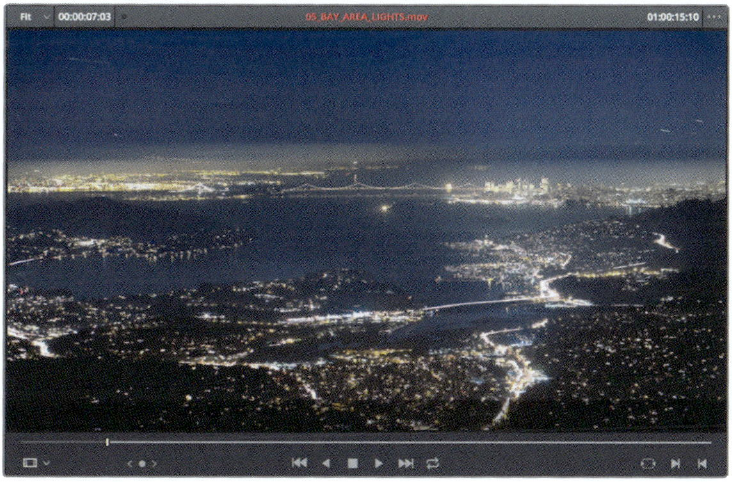

TIP When using a keyboard without a number pad, press Shift-= (equals sign) to enter a + (plus sign).

You'll use this frame for your in point.

3 Press I to mark an in point.

You can also identify a playhead location by exact seconds and frames if you have precise values you want to use. Let's move ahead four seconds and 10 frames in this clip.

4 Type **+410**, and then press Return or Enter.

The playhead jumps forward four seconds and 10 frames. You'll use this frame for your out point.

5 Press O to mark an out point

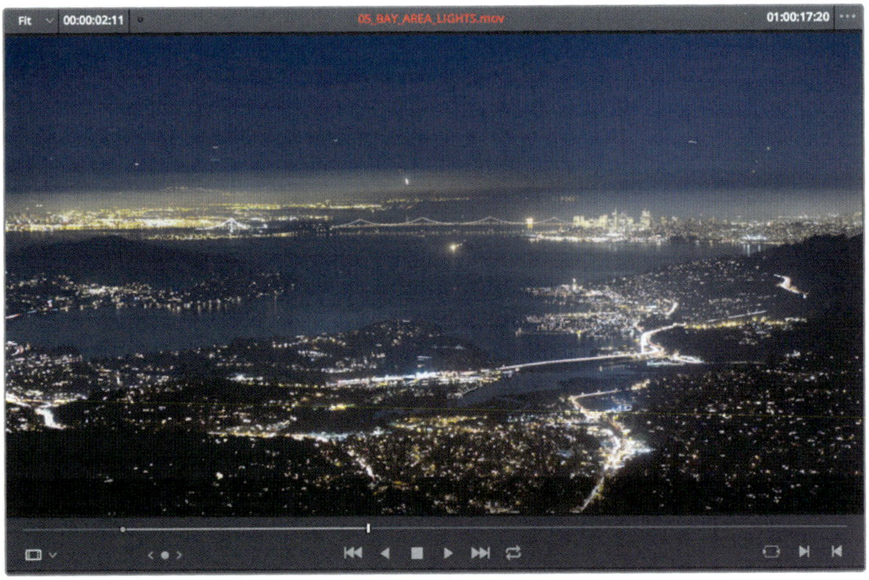

Let's position the timeline playhead where you want to insert the clip.

6 In the timeline, position the playhead at end of the 06_MILKYWAY clip.

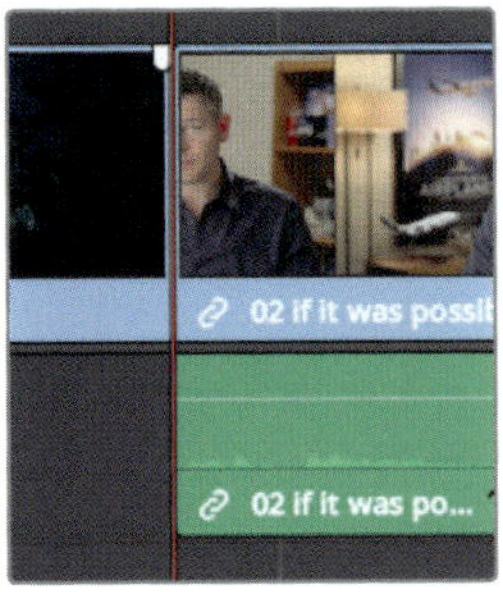

7 In the toolbar, click the insert button, or press the F9 key to Insert edit the clip.

8 Press Shift-Z to see the entire timeline. Then position the timeline playhead at the start of the second interview clip, and press spacebar to review the last half of the timeline.

When you start to rely on keyboard shortcuts for a lot of your editing, it is important to be aware of which viewer is active. You want to make sure you are moving the playhead and marking in and out points in the correct viewer before you tap a keyboard key or you will be setting those points in the wrong places. The best way to know which viewer is active is by looking at the clip or timeline name above the viewer. The active viewer appears in red.

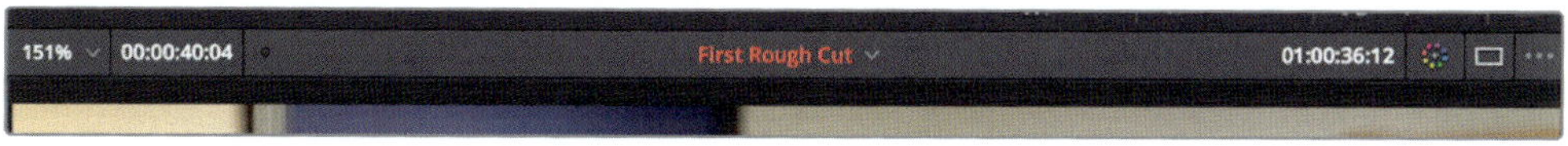

9 Press the Q key to activate the source viewer.

The Q key is a toggle, so it will switch between activating the timeline or the source viewer.

The insert and overwrite edit functions you have used so far are the two most commonly used edits throughout a program. After performing the edit a few times, you should more fully understand the usefulness of an insert edit. Let's make the case for the overwrite edit.

Overwriting video only

When creating a rough cut, you may want to replace the footage of your interview subject with B-roll, which is secondary footage that illustrates what he or she is discussing. You may choose to do this to refocus the audience's attention, hide problems with the existing video, or enhance the subject's commentary. This is called a cut-away because the visual temporarily cuts away from the main action. Although you can perform a cut away, using the place on top function as you did in the cut page, on the edit page you also can perform a cut-away using an overwrite edit.

1 In the timeline, position the playhead between the **08_SOUTH_POLE_DC3** clip and the second Interview clip, **02_if it was possible**.

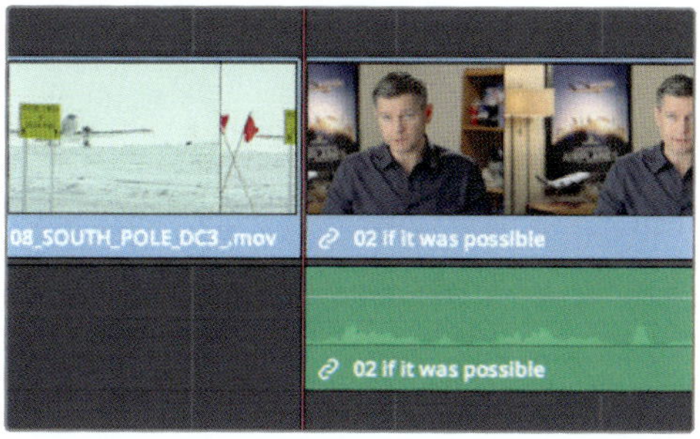

2 Press spacebar to play the interview.

The first line is, "If it was possible to shoot it you wanted to go shoot it." Instead of having him onscreen during that time, it would look nicer to have one of those impressive, almost impossible shots. This time, you'll make an in and out point in the timeline because you know you would like the duration of the new shot to be the length of that first sentence.

3 In the timeline, position the playhead between the 08_SOUTH_POLE_DC3 clip and the second Interview clip, 02_if it was possible.

4 Press I to mark an in point.

5 Press spacebar to play the interview and stop playback when the interviewee finishes the line, "If it was possible to shoot it, you wanted to go shoot it."

6 Press O to mark an out point.

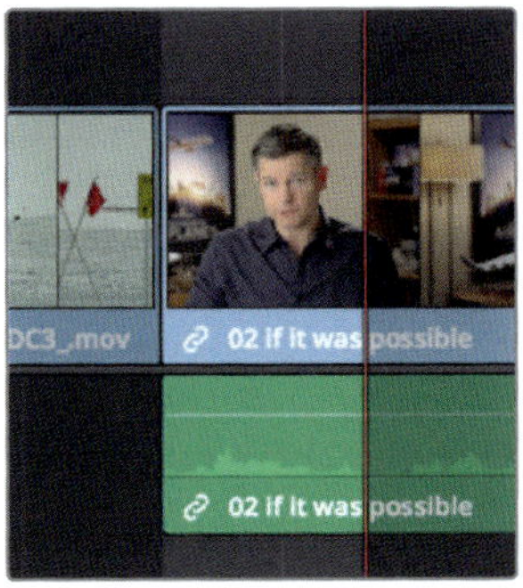

Now you'll look for a clip to edit into that location.

7 In the B-Roll bin, double-click 04_JET_LANDING_2 to load it into the source viewer.

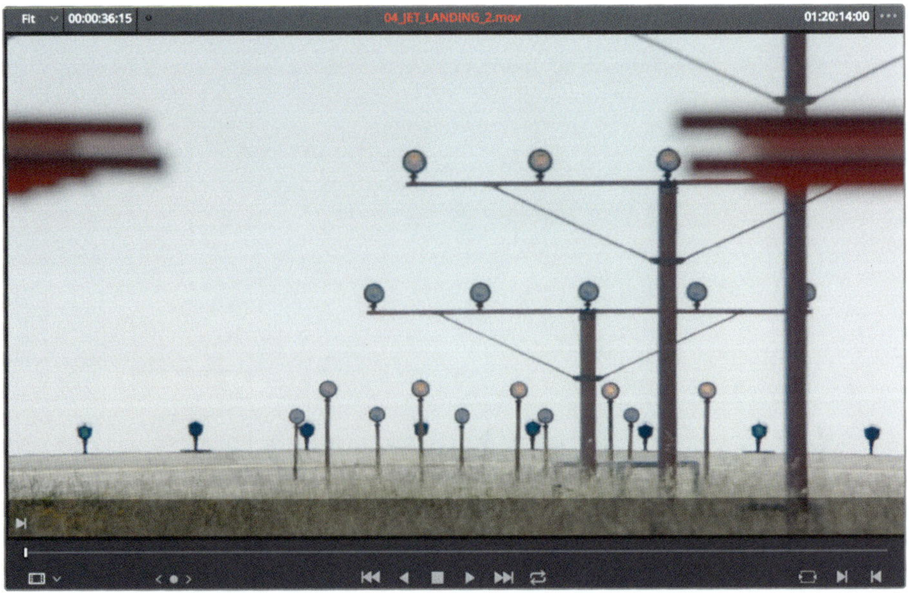

8 Move to the start of the clip and press spacebar to play the clip.

This is a well-framed shot of a large jet landing. Let's mark an in point just as you see the landing wheels at the top of the screen.

9 Drag the source viewer jog bar from the beginning of the clip until the wheels of the plane are visible in the frame.

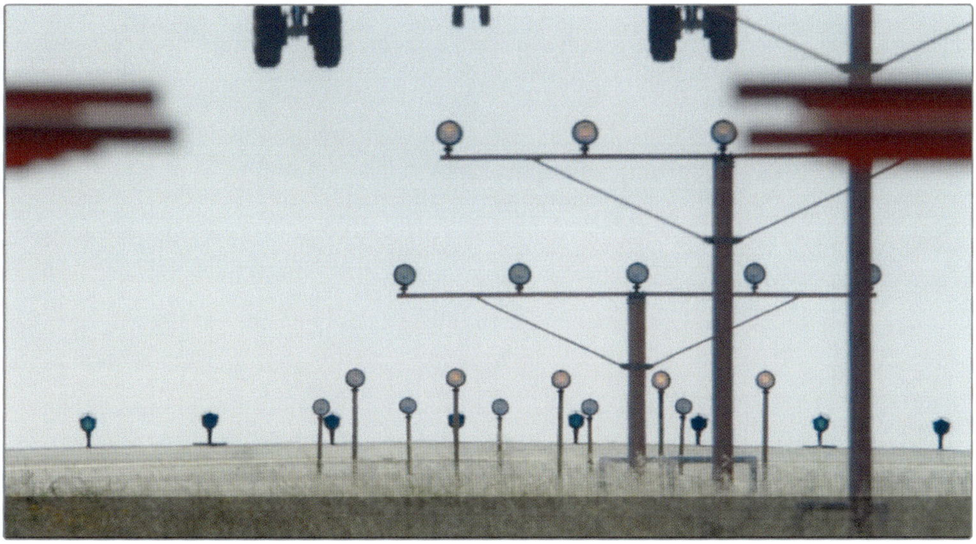

You need to mark only an in point on this source clip because you already have the duration set in the timeline.

10 Press I to mark an in point.

You'll use an overwrite edit to replace the area marked in the timeline. But you don't want to overwrite the audio track of this clip. You want to continue to hear the voice of the interview subject while viewing the new 04_JET_LANDING_2 shot. So, you need a way to replace only the video content of the timeline while retaining the audio of the original clip.

The timeline has destination controls that display which video and audio tracks from the source clip are edited into the timeline. By default, the destination controls are enabled in both the V1 (Video 1) and A1 (Audio 1) source tracks, as indicated by the orange outline around the track number.

11 In the timeline track header, click the A1 destination control to disable it.

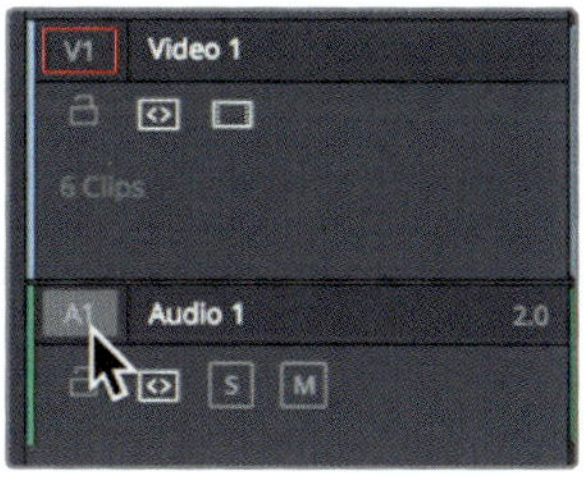

The destination control displays no outline when it is disabled. As a result, audio source material on A1 will not be edited into the timeline.

12 In the toolbar, click the overwrite button, or press F10.

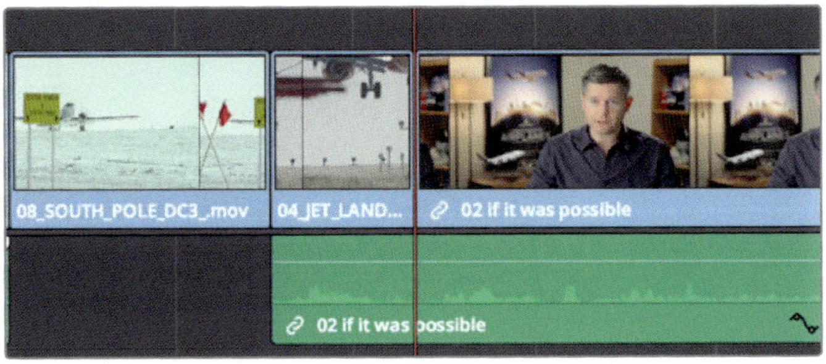

The overwrite edit caused a few seconds of the second interview clip to be covered by the new 04_JET_LANDING_2 clip. The audio from the interview, however, remained, and can be heard even when the cut-away is visible.

13 In the timeline, position the playhead between the 08_SOUTH_POLE_DC3 clip and the 04_JET_LANDING video clip.

14 Press spacebar to play over the interview.

This is a short sample of some common editing functions. Other functions on the edit page like append at end and place on top are identical to the cut page's append and place on top functions. However, the two pages do have differences even in editing techniques. let's take a look at a few of those next.

Editing from a bin

If the clips you are working with do not contain audio of any importance and you just want to add a few clips to the timeline as a montage, you can set marks using the thumbnails in the media pool instead of loading each clip into the source viewer. You'll do this for the final three clips you will add to your program.

1 At the top of the media pool, drag the scale slider to the right to increase the size of the thumbnails.

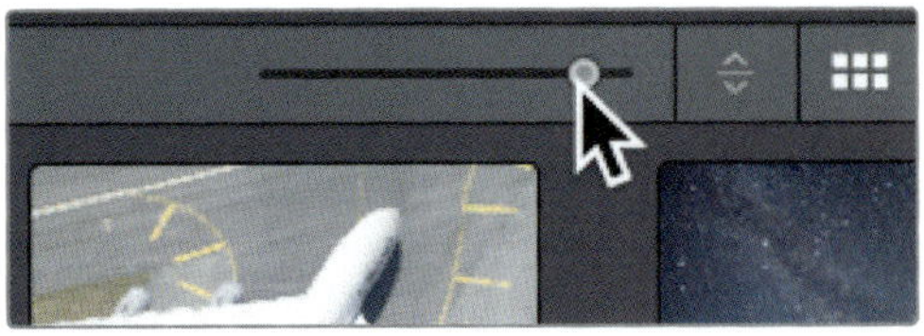

When working with thumbnails in the bin, it can be helpful to give you a larger target.

2 Select the B-Roll smart bin, and hover your mouse pointer over **01 A380 TAXI**.

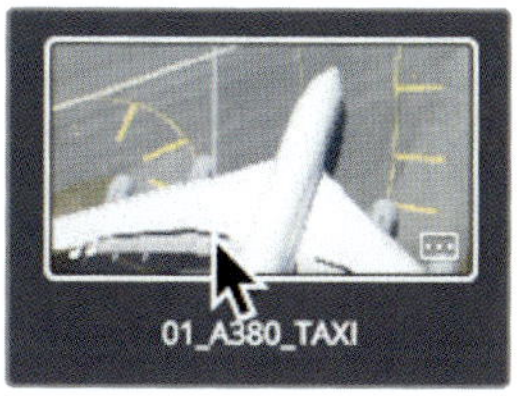

3 Move your mouse back and forth over the thumbnail to preview the frames in the viewer.

This is a quick way to preview clips and set in and out points without explicitly loading the clip in the viewer.

4 Skim the mouse pointer all the way to the left of the thumbnail to the start of the clip, and press I to set an in point

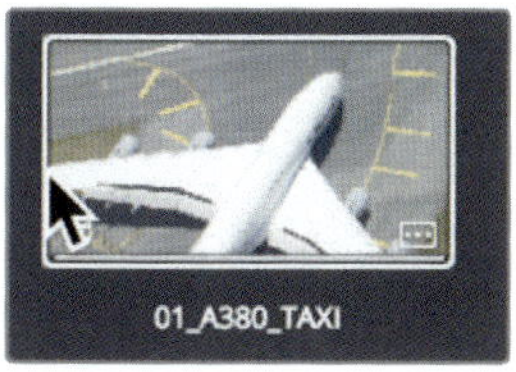

A thin white line appears at the bottom of the thumbnail to indicate the presence of an in point.

5 Skim to the right on the thumbnail until the plane is pointing straight up to the top of the frame, and press O to set an out point.

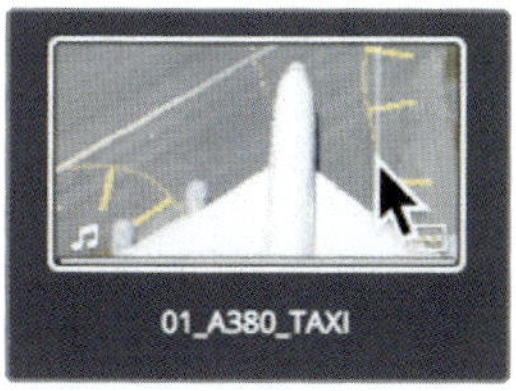

The white line at the bottom of the thumbnail stops three-quarters of the way across the thumbnail to display a relative duration compared to the entire length of the clip. Let's set in and out points on two more clips using the same technique.

6 Hover your mouse pointer over **02_A380_TAKE OFF**.

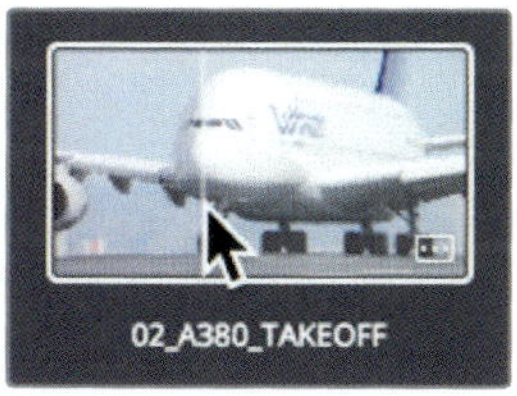

7 Skim the mouse pointer all the way to the left of the thumbnail to the start of the clip, and press I to set the in point

8 Skim to the right on the thumbnail until the you can no longer see the Lufthansa name on the plane, and press O to mark an out point.

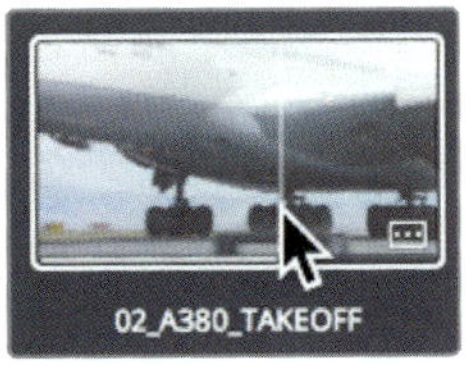

9 Hover your mouse pointer over 09_HAWAIIAN_LANDING.

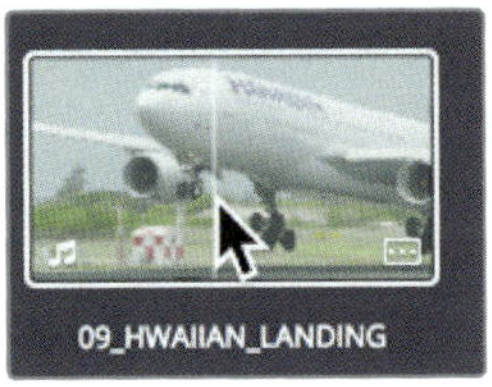

10 Mark an in point at the start of the clip, and an out point in the middle of the clip.

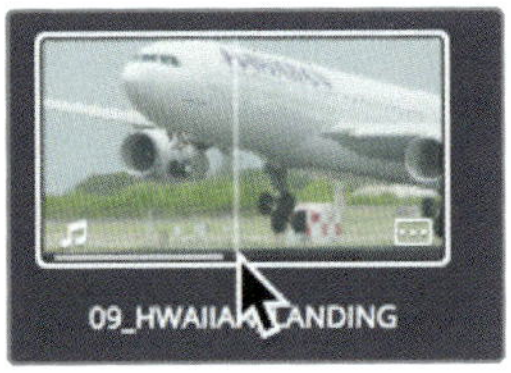

To place these clips into the timeline, you learned in Lesson 1 that you can drag from a bin directly to the timeline, but this method limits you to an overwrite edit. A more flexible method is to drag clips from the bin to the edit overlay in the timeline viewer.

11 Position the timeline playhead at the start of the 11_MOVIE_ CREDITS clip.

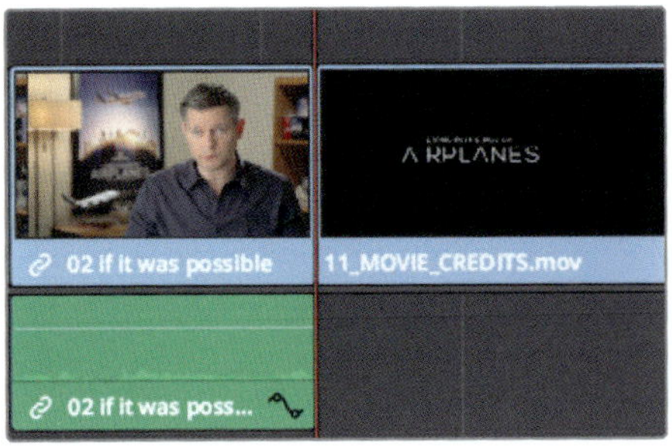

12 In the media pool, click the 01_A380_TAXI clip, and then Cmd-click (macOS) or Ctrl-click (Windows) the 02_A380_TAKE OFF and the 09_HAWAIIAN_LANDING clips.

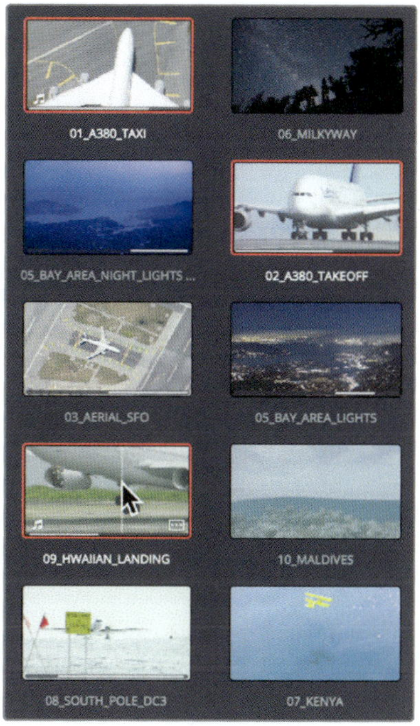

The three clips are outlined in red to indicate that they are selected.

13 Drag the clips directly into the timeline viewer, and when the edit overlay appears, move the pointer over Insert and release the mouse button.

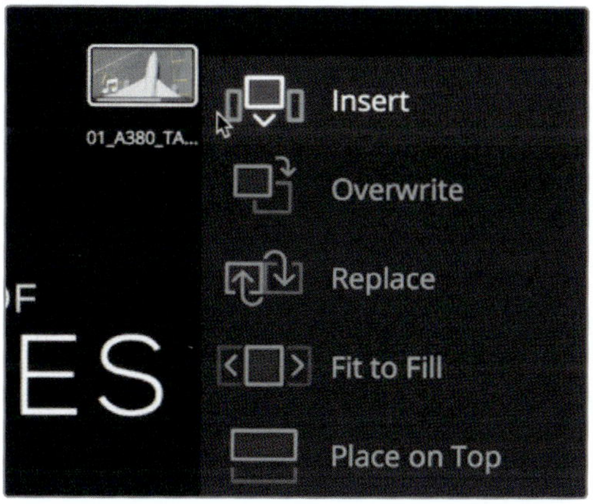

All three clips are inserted into the timeline based on the order they are displayed in the bin. Let's zoom the timeline to fit the window and play this program from the beginning.

14 Choose View > Zoom > Zoom to Fit, or press Shift-Z, to see the entire timeline in the window.

15 Go to the start of the timeline, and choose Workspace > Viewer Mode > Cinema Viewer, or press Cmd-F (macOS) or Ctrl-F (Windows), to play the entire program in full screen view.

Combining the technique of marking points in the bin with the edit overlay options makes drag-and-drop style editing much more flexible and viable as an advanced editing technique.

Replacing a shot

When reviewing your rough cut, you'll often realize that your first choice of shots is not always the best. Editing comes down to a lot of trial and error. You'll try out an arrangement, pacing, and juxtaposition of clips, and then think of a better way. Doing so leads to replacing shots in your timeline with those that you think will work better. The replace edit function which is unique to the edit page, is designed to make that process easy.

1 In the timeline, drag the playhead over the **04_JET_LANDING_2** clip.

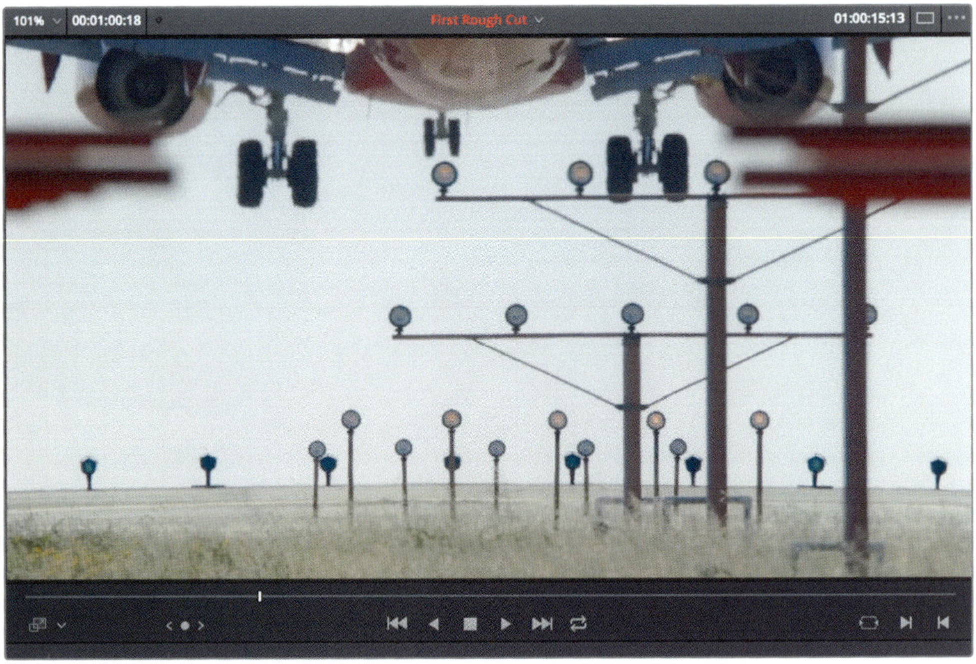

Although this is a nicely framed shot, you need a more spectacular shot at this point in the trailer. Luckily, you have a shot that like that in your B-Roll Smart Bin.

2 In the B-Roll smart bin, double-click the **10_MALDIVES** clip, and press spacebar to view it in the source viewer.

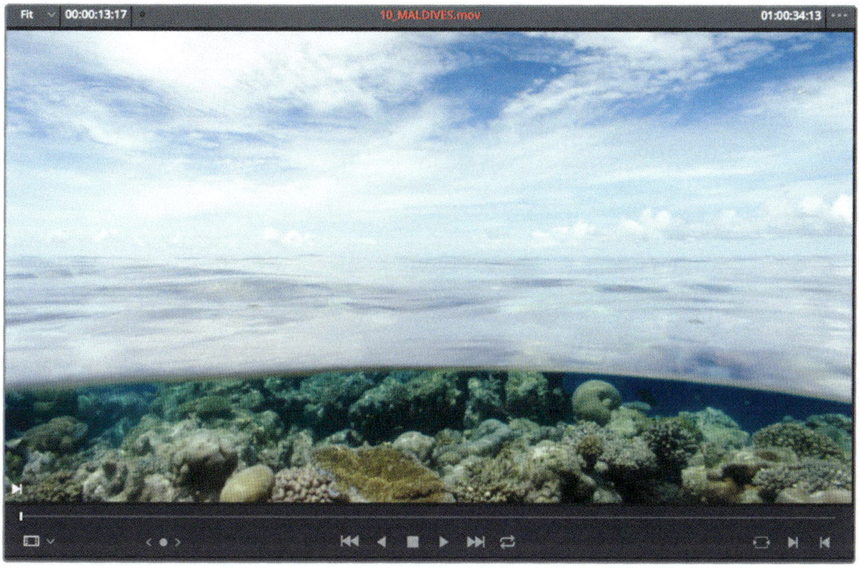

You would like to have the plane fly in from overhead about a third of the way into the clip. Without setting any marks, the replace edit will swap one shot for another by aligning the current frame in the source viewer with the current frame in the timeline.

3 In the timeline, position the playhead over the center of **04_JET_LANDING_2** clip.

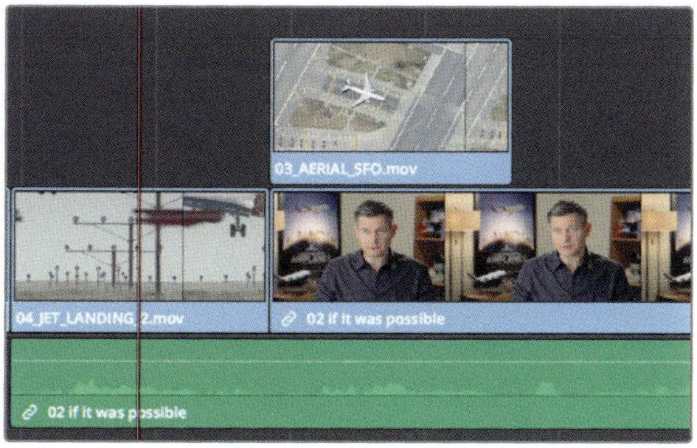

Zooming into the clip in the timeline will make it easier to position the playhead more precisely.

4 In the toolbar, drag the zoom slider to the right to zoom in on the clip, or press Cmd-= (equals sign) in macOS, or Ctrl-= (equals sign) in Windows.

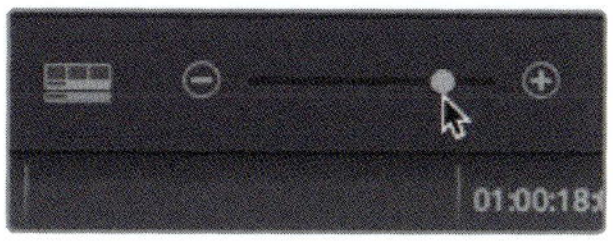

> **TIP** Zooming is always centered on the current position of the playhead, even if the playhead is offscreen.

5 Move the playhead roughly one-third of the way into the 04_JET_LANDING_2 clip. Around the time when you first see the jet engines enter the frame.

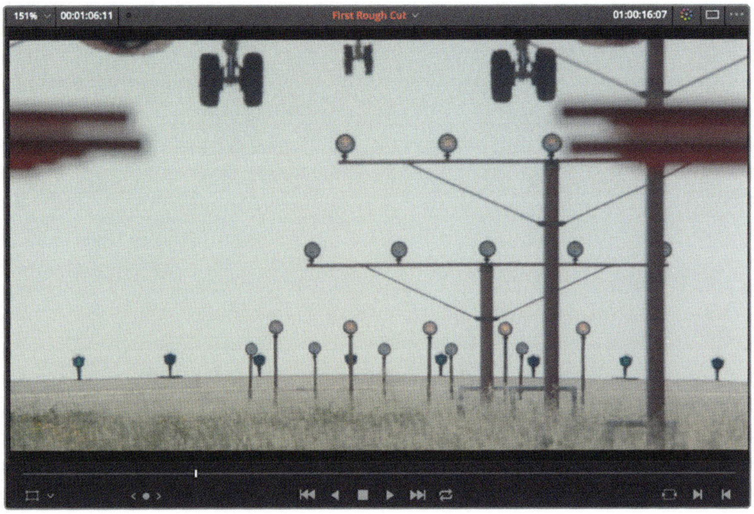

This is the time location when you want the plane to come into the frame on the 10_MALDIVES shot.

6 In the source viewer, drag the jog bar until you first see the plane coming into frame.

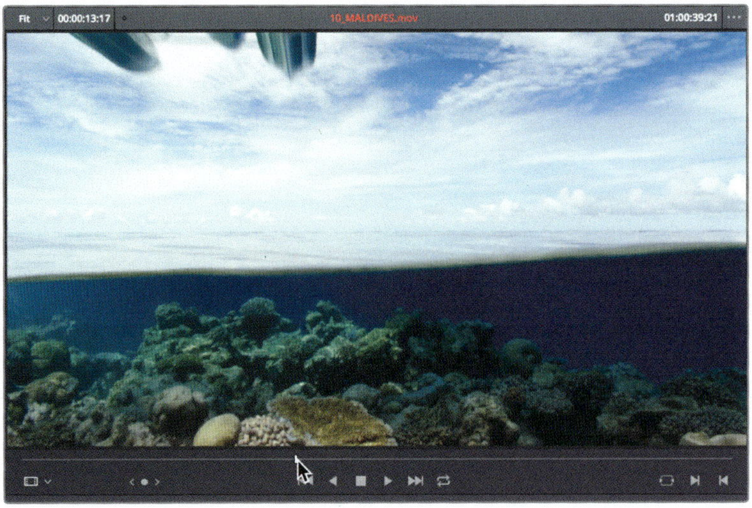

With the playheads aligned, you can use the replace edit button in the toolbar.

7 In the toolbar, click the replace edit button, or press F11.

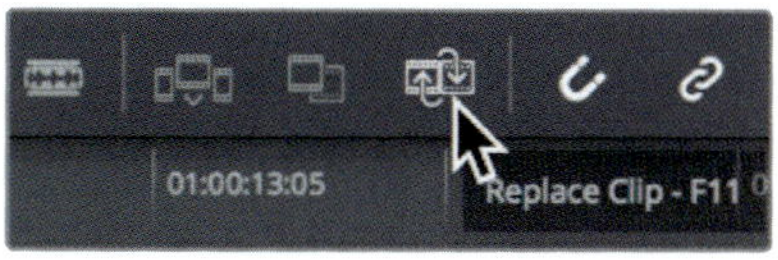

The replace edit figures out the in and out points you need based on the timeline clip you are replacing.

8 Choose View > Zoom > Zoom to Fit, or press Shift-Z, to see the entire timeline.

9 Drag the playhead to the start of the timeline and play the program you have created so far.

Whenever you have a spare moment while you are editing, it is always a smart idea to take a step back and watch the entire program. Sometimes you forget what the big picture is like because you spend so much time fiddling with specific clips.

Lesson Review

1 To edit a clip between two existing clips, which edit function would you use?

2 How can you tell which viewer is the active viewer?

3 True or false? Pressing the K and J keys together will play the project in reverse at half speed.

4 How can you simultaneously move multiple clips from the bin and insert them into the timeline?

5 True or false? Typing a positive number (+) will move the playhead to the left, towards the start of the timeline.

Answers

1 The Insert editing function will add a new clip into the timeline by splitting two existing clips to make room for the new clip.

2 The active viewer displays the clip or timeline name above the viewer, highlighted in red.

3 True. Pressing J will play in reverse. Pressing K+J will play in reverse at half speed.

4 Drag multiple clips from a bin into the timeline viewer, and use the edit overlay to select any editing function, including Insert.

5 False. Positive values move the playhead to the right, toward the end of the timeline.

Lesson 5

Moving Clips in the Timeline

Like the cut page, the timeline is much more than just a view of the edits you make. Once you start putting a project together, the timeline quickly becomes the hub of all activity. It is the place where you will move segments around, split clips in half, and delete segments altogether. Knowing how to operate in the timeline will improve your editing skills.

Time

This lesson takes approximately 30 minutes to complete.

Goals

Importing projects and relinking media

When someone sends you a DaVinci Resolve 16 project from another computer or you want to move a project from one computer to another, you need to import the project file and relink the media.

For instance, if you were moving from a desktop computer to a portable laptop to edit on-the-go, you would export the project from the desktop computer and import it on the laptop.

In this lesson, you'll import a project that contains several pre-made timelines that are slight variations on the timeline you created in the previous lesson. The timeline for this lesson is set up so you can learn how to move, delete, and split clips.

1 Open DaVinci Resolve 16, if necessary; or if DaVinci Resolve is already open, choose File > Project manager.

2 In the project manager, right-click in an empty area, and in the contextual menu, choose Import Project.

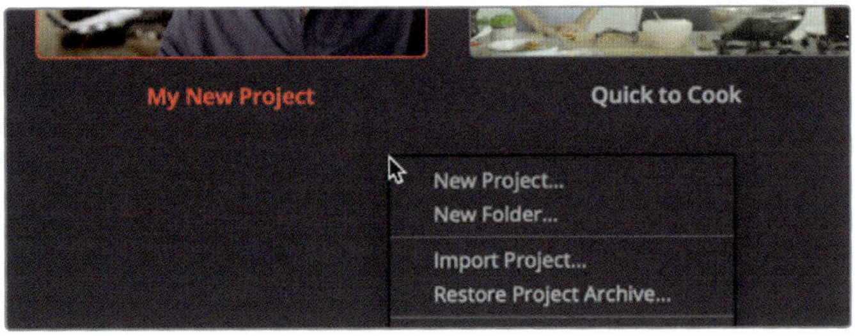

NOTE To export a project, you can right-click the project in the project manager, and choose Export, or choose File > Export Project while a project is open.

3 In the open dialog, select R16 Intro lessons folder > Lesson 05 > Age of Airplanes.drp then click open. The project is imported but the media may not yet be linked to the clips. The project contains only the metadata for clips and timelines. It has no media associated with it. Links between the clip and timeline metadata and the media can break when media is copied or moved from one computer to another, or when folder names are changed. When necessary, you can easily relink the media to all of the clips and timelines in a project.

4 Double-click the Age of Airplanes project to open it.

5 In the media pool sidebar, select the master bin, and double-click any clip to open it in the source viewer.

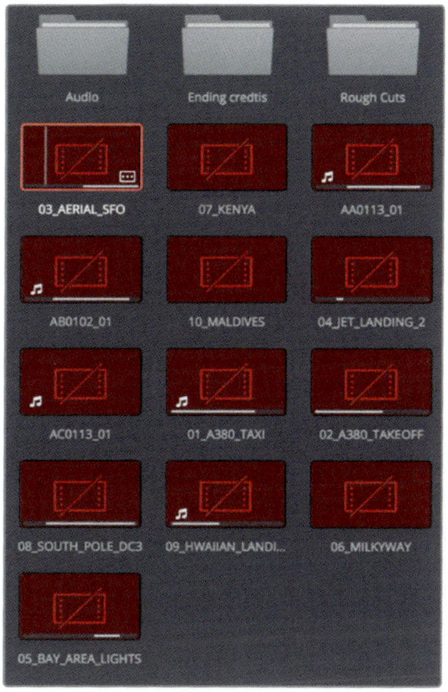

These clips are offline. You need to guide DaVinci Resolve to the locations of the media so it can relink the media and clips to the project. You can do so just by selecting the bins that contain the offline clips, which in this case, is every bin in the project.

Because the master bin contains every bin and all the clips in the project, you can just relink from the master bin.

6 Ctrl-click (macOS) or right-click (Windows) the Master bin, and in the contextual menu, choose “Relink Clips for Selected Bins”.

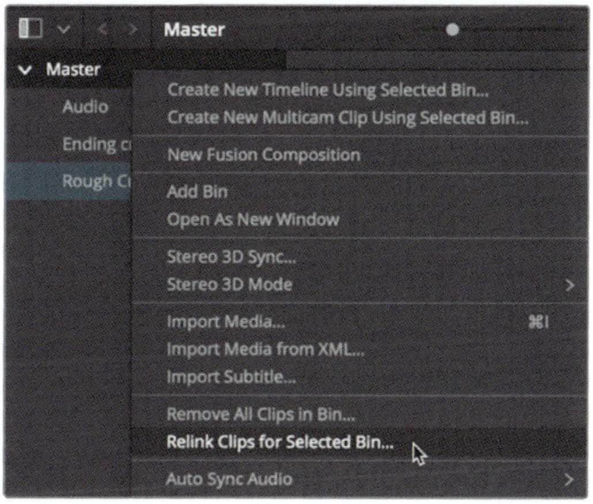

7 In the select source folder dialog, select the Documents > R16 Intro lessons folder. Click OK.

   Relinking the master bin automatically relinks all of the clips in all of the bins, as well as the timelines in those bins.

8 In the Rough Cuts bin, double-click the **01 Cut Copy paste** timeline to load it into the timeline viewer.

9 Play the timeline to review the cuts that you will work with in this lesson.

This timeline is a slimmed-down version of the one you created in Lesson 4. It does, however, include a new music track that, as you will see, can cause some hurdles when you start cut, copy, and pasting clips in the timeline.

Color coding clips

Additional clips within a timeline can slow you down when trying to locate a single shot. You can make it easier to find that shot by assigning a color to different clip groups. The assigned color will appear in the timeline whenever a clip from that group is used.

1 In the Bin list, select the Interview smart bin.

2 Click any clip in the media pool, and choose Edit > Select All, or press Cmd-A (macOS) or Ctrl-A (Windows), to select all of the clips in the bin.

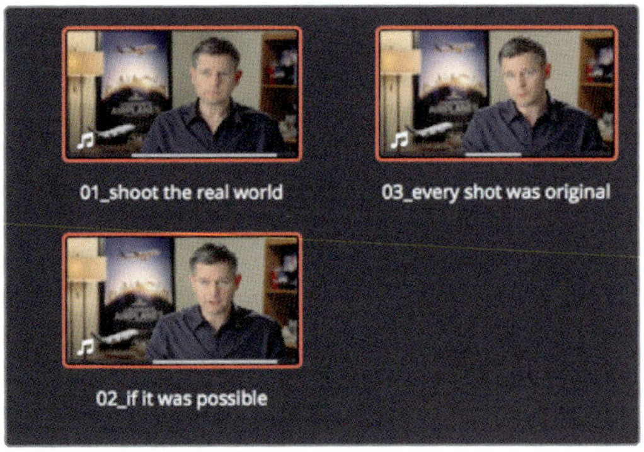

3 Right-click any one of the selected clips, and in the menu, choose Clip Color > Navy.

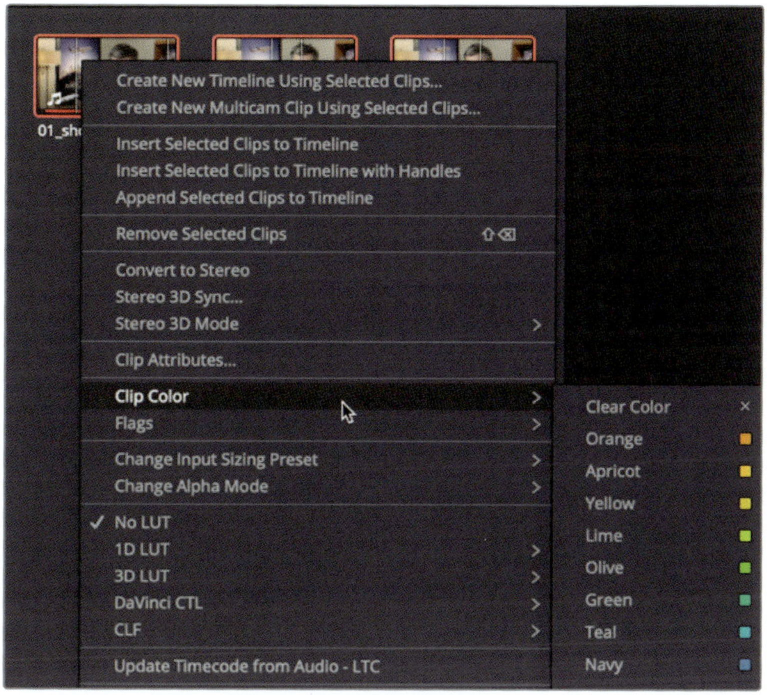

Now let's color code all the B-Roll clips.

4 In the bin list, select the B-Roll Smart Bin.

5 Click any clip in the media pool, and choose Edit > Select All, or press Cmd-A (macOS) or Ctrl-A (Windows), to select all the clips in that bin.

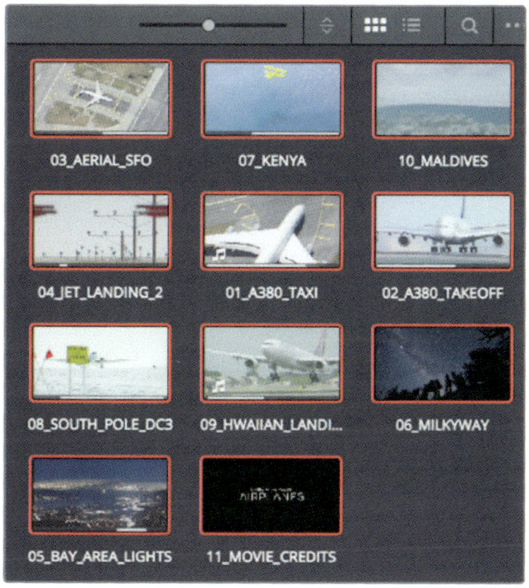

6 Right-click any one of the selected clips, and in the contextual menu, choose Clip Color > Brown.

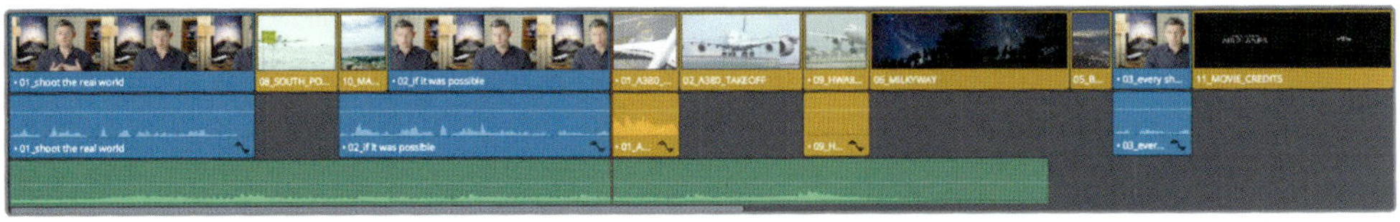

All the timeline clips from the Interview and the B-Roll bins are now color coded to navy blue or brown. As you make changes in the timeline, the differentiation in color will make it easier for you to locate these categories of clips.

Deleting clips without leaving a gap

Knowing when and how clips should be deleted is almost as important as knowing where to place clips in the timeline. You can delete clips and leave a gap, or you can delete clips and automatically close the gap. In your timeline, if you were trying to line up your picture to music, you might seem to have too many clips. You'll need to delete at least one and possibly more.

1 In the timeline, position the playhead at the end of the middle interview clip.

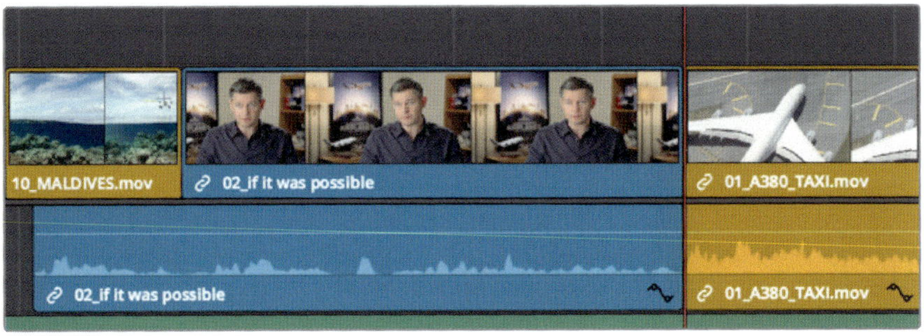

2 Press spacebar to play until the end of the movie.

Because we have three similar plane clips in a row, one of the three can be deleted. The most likely culprit is the slow-moving Hawaiian Landing clip. To remove a selected clip from the timeline in the edit page: simply press the delete key and it will leave a gap in the timeline. But what if you wanted it to act more like the cut page, and not leave a gap? In this situation, you want to remove the clip but have all the clips to the right move left to close up the gap. This type of deletion is often called a **ripple delete** because the change ripples through the rest of the timeline.

3 In the timeline, select the 09_HAWAIIAN_LANDING clip.

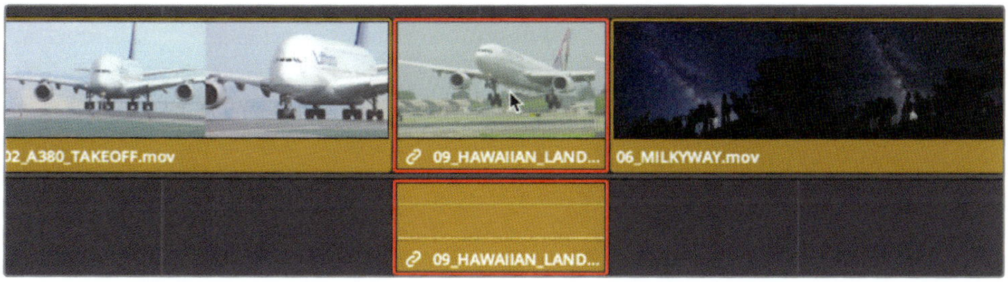

Because the audio and video tracks are part of the same clip, they are both selected in the timeline.

4 Choose Edit > Ripple Delete, or press Shift-Delete or Shift-Backspace.

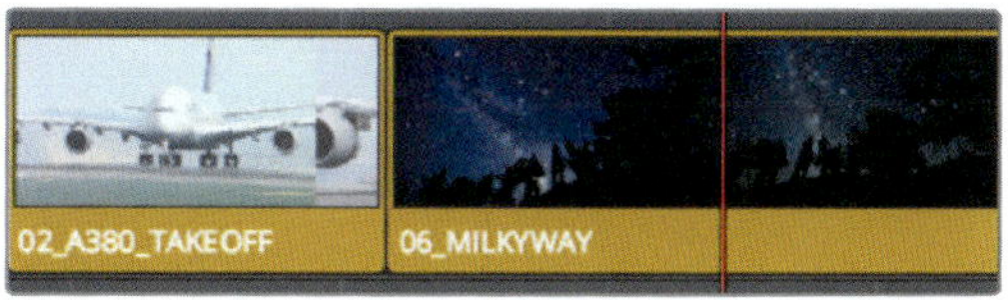

Both the audio and video tracks of the clip are removed, or extracted, from the timeline, but not deleted from the bin or your hard drive. In addition, the gap is closed up because all of the clips positioned after the 09_HAWAIIAN_LANDING clip shift to the left.

Deleting video or audio content separately

As you played over those three jetliner clips, you heard some ambient sound of the crew talking. What if you wanted to delete only the audio contents from clips in the timeline and leave their video contents in place?

1 In the timeline, position the playhead over the middle interview shot.

2 Play the timeline and listen carefully to the audio during the 01_A380_TAXI shot.

You can hear directions being called out, along with some undesirable helicopter noise. You'll want to retain the video of this clip in the timeline, but remove its audio. In the previous exercise, you found that when you select a clip, DaVinci Resolve automatically selects both its video and audio tracks. To remove the crew noise but leave the clip's video track in the timeline, you'll need to unlink the two tracks so you can select them separately.

3 In the toolbar, click the linked selection button, or press Cmd-Shift-L (macOS) or Ctrl-Shift-L (Windows).

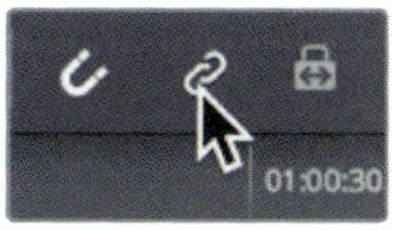

The linked selection is no longer highlighted, indicating that the function is disabled. With the association between video and sync audio track temporarily disabled, you can move and delete them independently.

TIP You can temporarily disable the linked selection button without going to the toolbar by Option-clicking (macOS) or Alt-clicking (Windows) a clip.

4 In the timeline, select the audio track of the 01_A380_TAXI clip.

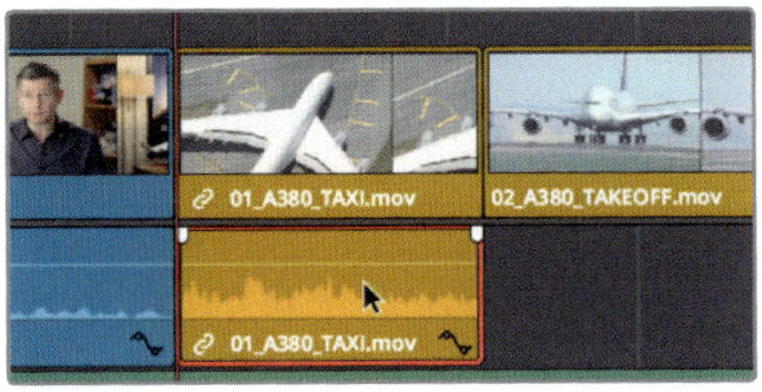

Only the audio track is outlined in red.

5 Press delete or backspace to remove the audio track.

The audio is now removed from the timeline, but the video track remains.

6 In the toolbar, click the linked selection button, or press Cmd-Shift-L (macOS) or Ctrl-Shift-L (Windows), to re-enable the link behavior.

It is usually a good idea to keep the linked selection button enabled so that clips that have audio and video in sync are not accidentally separated.

Deleting a range within a clip

Often with interview clips, or "talking heads," you won't want to delete an entire clip as often as you'll want to remove repetitive sentences or fumbled words. For this, you need to delete just a portion of audio somewhere within the clip.

1 In the timeline, position the playhead at the start of the 10_MALDIVES clip.

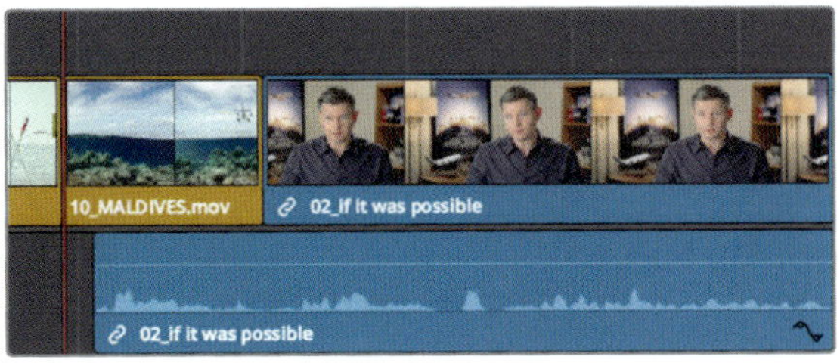

2 Play the timeline and listen carefully to the audio during the interview shot.

You can tighten up this interview by removing the redundant statement, "Stay at that location longer." When deleting small ranges within a clip, it is best to zoom into the timeline area you will be working on.

3 In the toolbar, drag the zoom slider to the right until the **02_if it was possible** interview clip almost fills the entire timeline window.

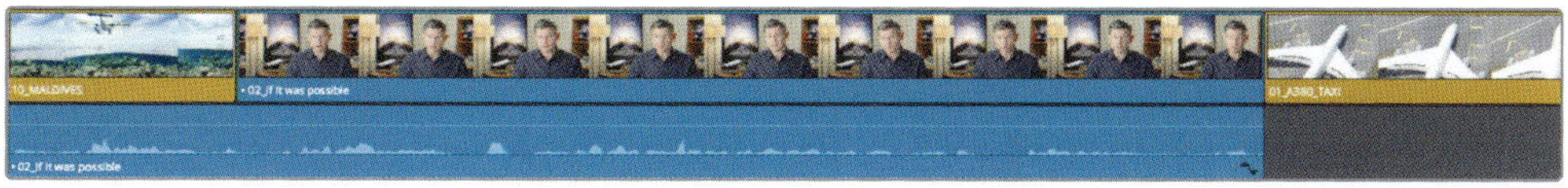

Zooming in will help you identify the sentence by giving you a more detailed view of the audio waveform. Using the waveform as a guide, you'll mark the range you want to delete using in and out points.

4 Use your J-K-L keys to slowly play back and forth over the interview clip until you locate the start of the line, "stay at that location longer."

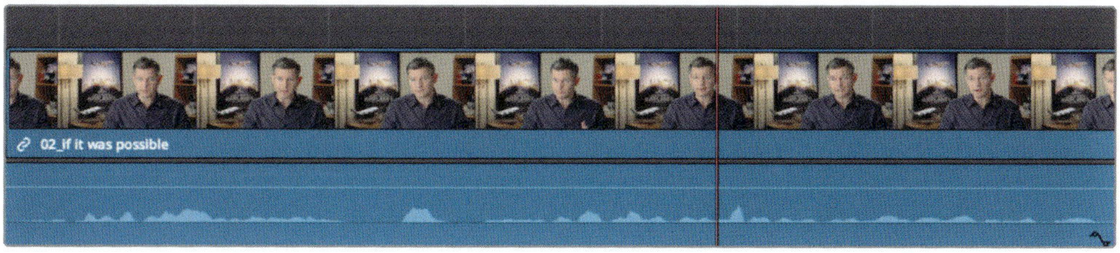

5 When the playhead is located before the word "stay," press I to mark an in point. This is the start of the range you will delete. Now let's look for the out point.

6 Press your J-K-L keys to slowly play back and forth over the interview clip until you locate the end of the line, "stay at that location longer."

7 When the playhead is located after the word "longer," press O to mark an out point.

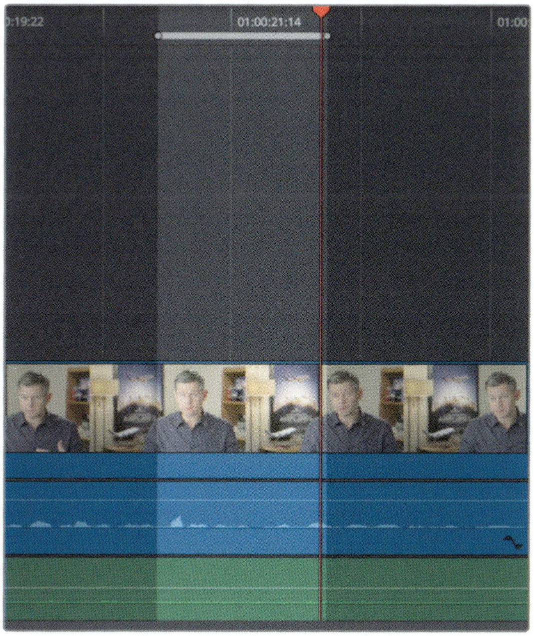

With the range identified, you can delete it, or more precisely, ripple delete it so you don't leave a gap in the timeline. However, if you deleted the range right now, you'd run into a problem. To see the problem, let's delete the range, observe the problem, and then figure out how to solve it.

8 Press Shift-Delete/Backspace to remove the range.

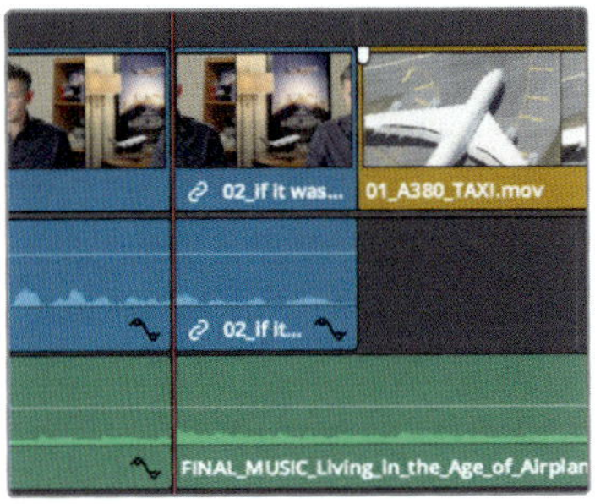

The range between the in and out points is deleted on the interview, but is also deleted on the music track. You need to not only identify the range, but also identify the individual tracks in which you want the deletion to occur. DaVinci Resolve includes auto select buttons on each track to help with this situation.

9 Choose Edit > Undo, or press Cmd-Z (macOS) or Ctrl-Z (Windows), to undo the previous operation.

10 In the timeline track header, on the Audio 2 track, click the auto select button to disable that track.

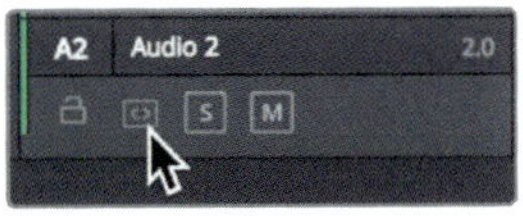

The auto select buttons are incredibly important buttons to be aware of because they perform so many different functions when editing in the timeline. For your current purposes, you only need to be aware that these buttons will identify the tracks to operate on when they are enabled and will exclude the tracks on which they're disabled.

11 Press Shift-Delete/Backspace to remove the range on tracks V1 and A1.

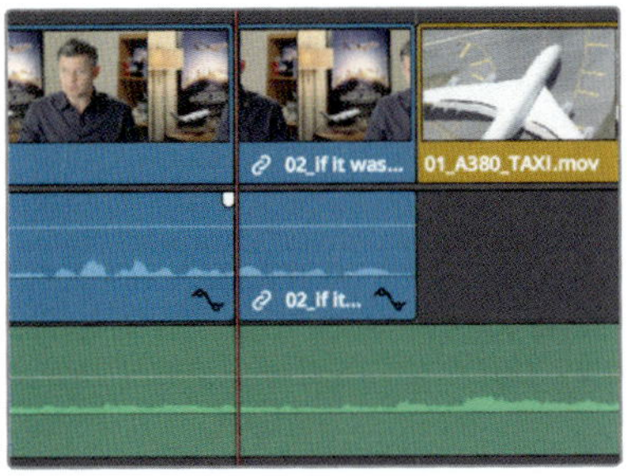

Let's review the deletion.

12 Move the playhead to the start of the 10_MALDIVES shot, and press the spacebar to play over the deleted region.

Don't be too concerned with the jump cut you just created, you can easily fix that using a place on top edit or the smooth cut transition you learned in the cut page. Often when editing, you'll create audio that sounds exactly as you want it to sound, and then later fix jump cuts when all of the audio is in place.

13 In the timeline track header, on the A2 track, click the auto select button to enable it so you don't forget to do so later.

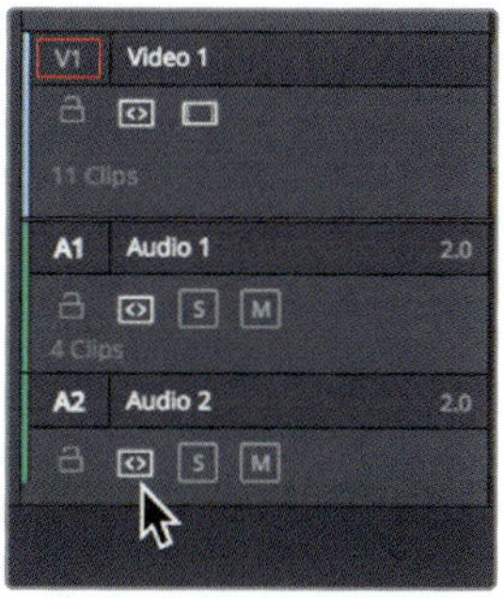

Although creating a backup isn't all that critical in this training project, when you start making dramatic changes to any rough cut, such as deleting lots of clips, it's a good idea to duplicate your timeline so you can return to a previous version.

Splitting clips

In some cases, you might want to create space between sentences to improve pacing. In this example, instead of identifying the range you want to delete, you'll identify a frame where you want to split a sentence. The easiest way to do so is using the razor edit mode.

1 At the bottom of the timeline, drag the scroll bar to center the cut between the 10_MALDIVES and the 02_if it was possible interview clips in the window.

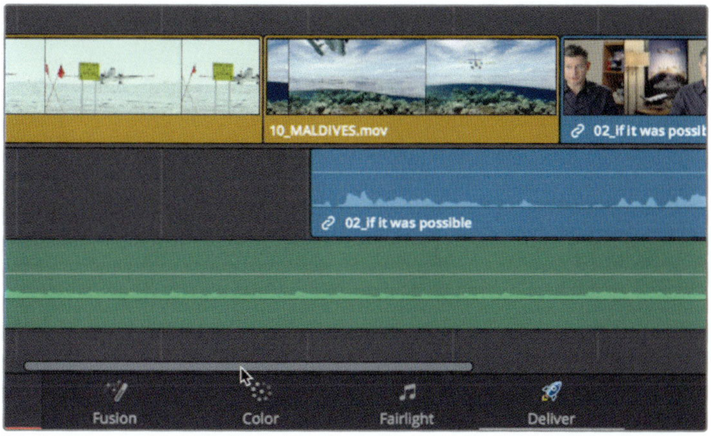

2 Drag the timeline playhead to the start of the 10_Maldives clip.

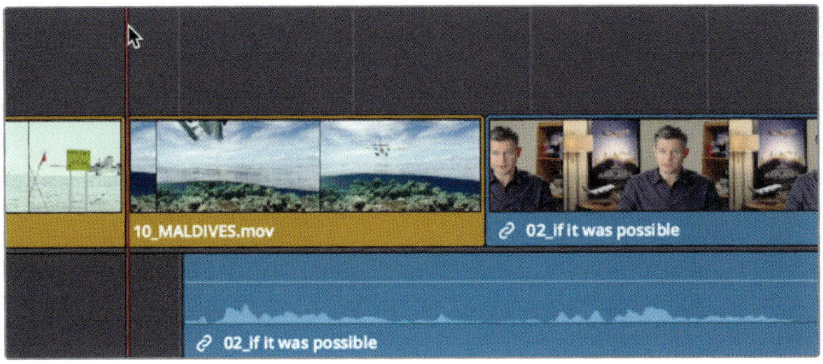

3 Press the spacebar to play the timeline, and stop playback when the audio from the interview says, "If the weather wasn't right."

Creating some separation from the first sentence—"If it was possible to shoot it, you wanted to go shoot it"—seems like the right thing to do because that is a complete thought that you want the audience to soak in. You'll need to split that sentence from the rest of the clip.

4 Position the playhead on the cut between the 10_MALDIVES and the 02_if it was possible interview clips because that is where the sentence ends.

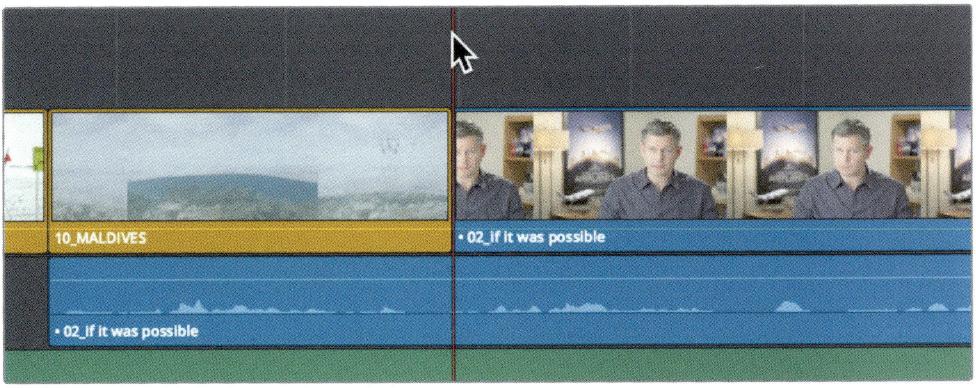

In the razor edit mode, you can split clips into sections just like the split (scissors) function in the cut page. Unlike the cut page the razor edit mode works by clicking on the clip you want to split. Here, you can use it here to split just the audio track.

5 In the toolbar, click the razor edit mode tool, or press B.

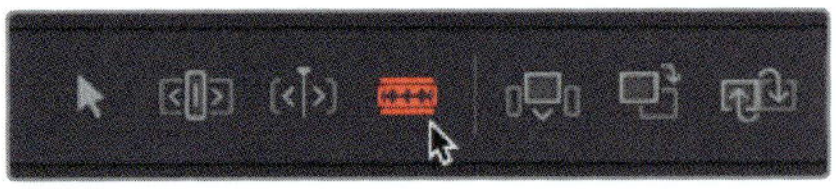

With the razor edit mode tool selected, anywhere you click in the timeline will divide that clip.

6 Position the left edge of the razor blade pointer directly over the playhead on the audio track, and click to split the clip.

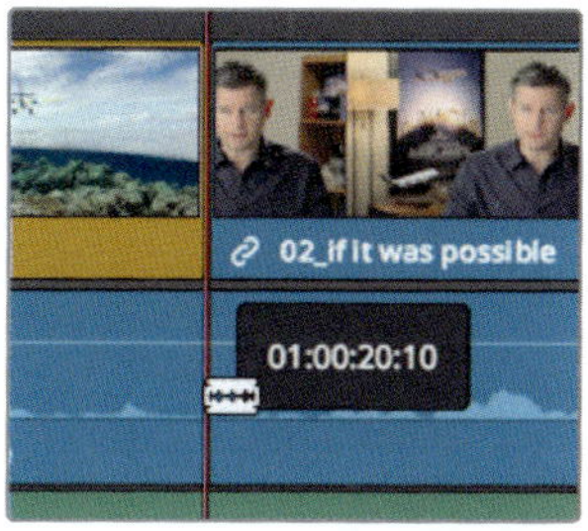

The clip is divided based on where the left edge of the razor blade pointer was located when you clicked. You now have a separated clip that you can reposition.

TIP To split every clip under the playhead that has a track with auto select enabled, choose Timeline > Split Clip, or press Cmd-\ (backslash) in macOS, or Ctrl-\ (backslash) in Windows.

7 Click the selection mode button, or press the A key.

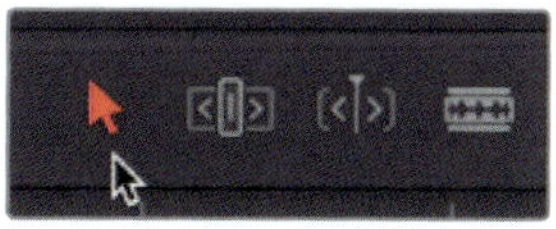

With the clip successfully split, you can now separate it from the interview that comes directly after it.

8 In the timeline, select the split audio track.

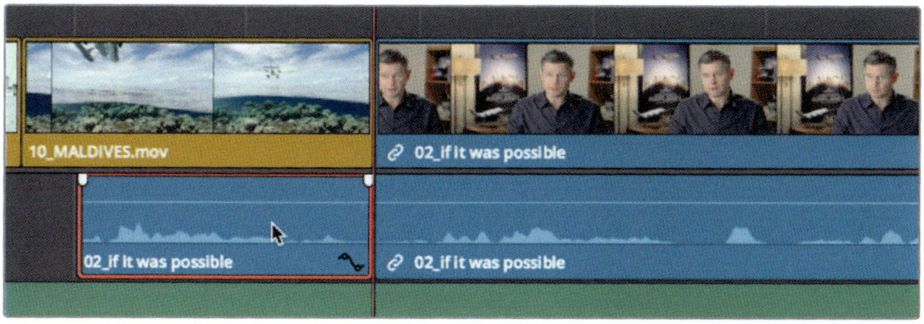

To create one second of silence, you can use the same technique that you used when you entered timecode values to move the source viewer's playhead.

9 To move the clip one second earlier in the timeline, type **-1.** (minus, 1, period), and press Enter or Return.

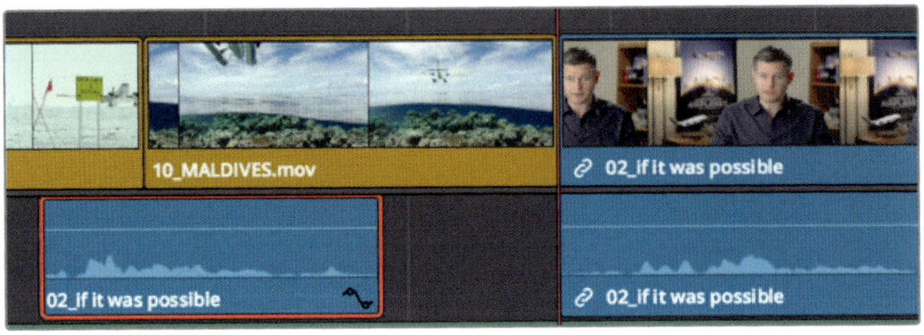

TIP You can nudge the selected clip one frame at a time by pressing, (comma) to move one frame left or . (period) to move one frame right. Pressing Shift-, (comma) or Shift-. (period) nudges the playhead five frames to the left or right, respectively.

The audio moves one second toward the beginning of the timeline.

10 In the toolbar, click the linked selection button, or press Cmd-Shift-L (Mac) or Ctrl-Shift-L (Windows), to enable it again.

11 Choose View > Zoom > Zoom to Fit, or press Shift-Z, to see the entire timeline.

TIP Shift-Z acts as a zoom toggle. Press the key combination once to zoom all the way out to see the entire timeline. Press it again to return to the previous zoom level.

12 Position the playhead at the end of the first interview clip and press the spacebar to play the timeline until you see the 01_A380_TAXI clip in the viewer.

The result of splitting the clip may or may not be perfect. It all depends on how precisely you selected the cut points. It will become easier to make precise adjustments when you learn more trimming options in Lesson 6.

Cutting and pasting clips

Dragging or entering time values are fine ways to move clips when no other clips are in the way. However, when other clips are in the timeline, you'll not only need to decide what the clip you're moving will do, but also what the other clips in the timeline will do because of the move. Unless you want to overwrite the other clips as you drag or move a clip, you'll need to ripple the timeline.

1 Position the playhead at the start of the 01_A380_TAXI clip in the timeline.

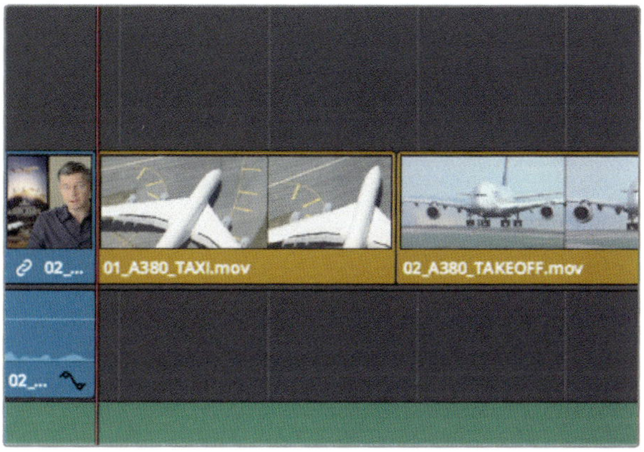

2 Press the spacebar to play to the end of the timeline

DaVinci Resolve has some useful cut/copy/paste operations that work on clips you've selected in the timeline. They can be very helpful when moving clips from one end of the timeline to the other, such as the two A380 jets clips you have at the end of this timeline.

3 In the timeline, click the 01_A380_TAXi clip to select it, and then Cmd-click (macOS) or Ctrl-click (Windows) the 02_A380_TAKE_OFF clip to select both clips.

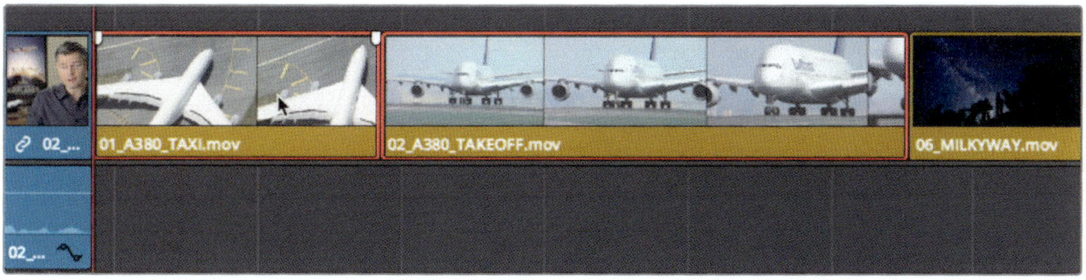

To remove the clips from their current locations with the intent to relocate them, you can cut them from the timeline.

4 Choose Edit > Ripple Cut, or press Cmd-Shift-X (macOS) or Ctrl-Shift-X (Windows).

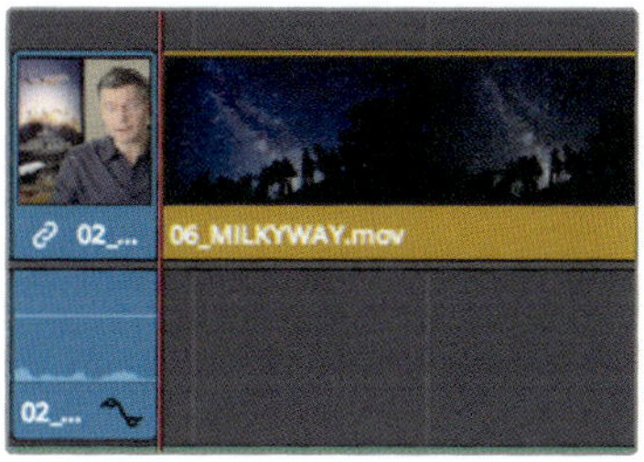

The ripple cut extracts the clips from the timeline, and closes up the gap. Unlike a ripple delete, the clips are kept in memory ready to be pasted into another location.

5 In the timeline, position the playhead at the end of the first interview clip.

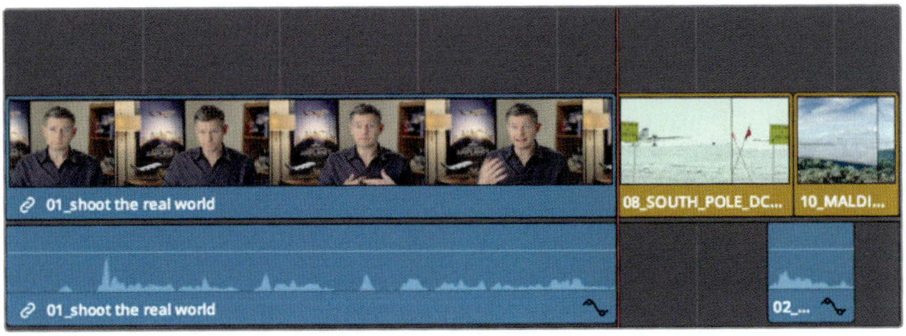

6 In the timeline header, click the Audio 2 auto select button because you want to paste onto only the Video and Audio 1 tracks.

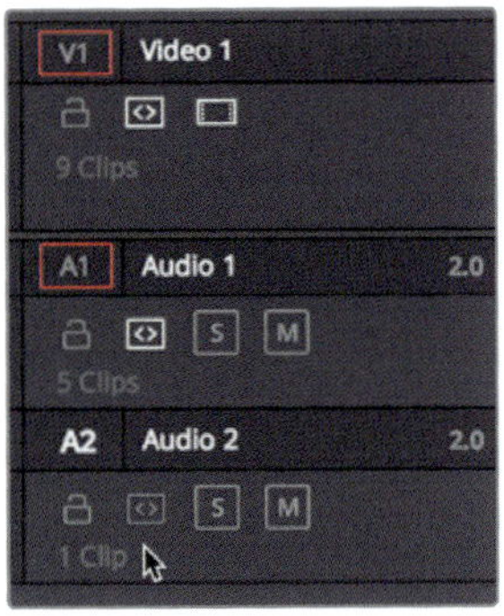

7 Choose Edit > Paste Insert, or press Cmd-Shift-V (macOS) or Ctrl-Shift-V (Windows).

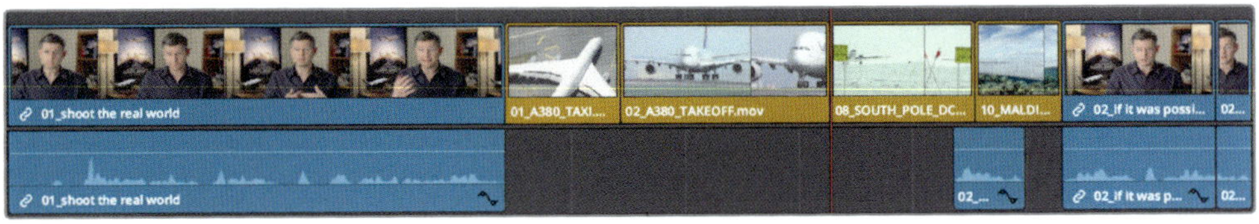

The clips are inserted at the position of the playhead. The paste insert function is identical to inserting clips using the Insert button in the toolbar or the edit overlays.

Swapping clip positions

If you don't have to move a clip over more than two or three clips, you can just swap its position.

1 In the timeline, click the 05_BAY_AREA_LIGHTS clip to select it.

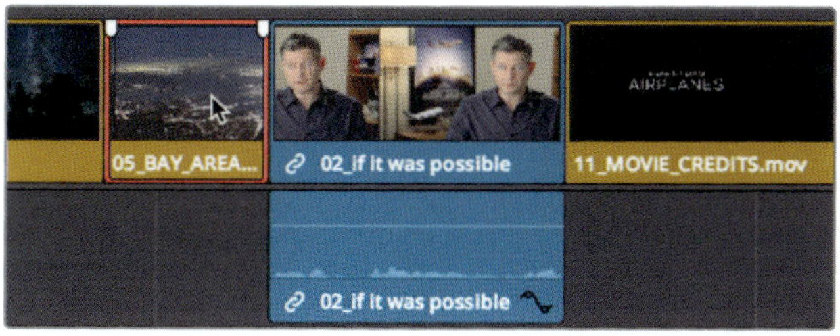

2 Drag the clip to the right. Once you begin dragging, hold down Cmd-Shift (macOS) or Ctrl-Shift (Windows) until you are at the start of the 11_MOVIE_CREDITS clip.

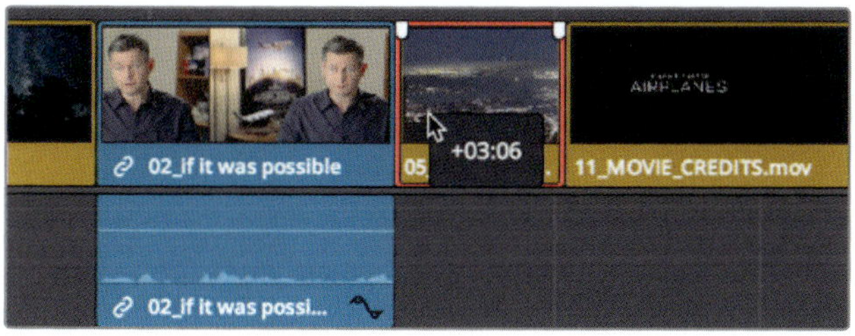

The 05_BAY_AREA_LIGHTS clip and the last interview clip swap positions.

Because you've made a lot of large changes, this seems like a good time to sit back and watch your entire movie.

3 Drag the playhead to the start of the timeline, and press Cmd-F (macOS) or Ctrl-F (Windows) to play the timeline and review your changes.

This cut looks very nice, but it still is not fully aligned to the music and some of the shots are too long. These timing problems cannot be addressed by merely moving clips around. You need to extend and shorten clips using trim techniques you will learn in the next lesson.

Lesson Review

1 What's the advantage of using relink from the master bin?

2 Where do you find the link selection button which allows you to select either the video or the audio on the timeline?

3 In the toolbar, what does clicking the razor blade icon allow you to do in the timeline?

4 What does pressing Shift-Z do?

5 True or false? To move a clip in the edit page timeline, you must hold down the Shift key.

Answers

1. Relinking from the master bin relinks all of the clips in every bin.
2. The link selection button is located in the edit page toolbar.
3. It allows you to split a clip into sections in the timeline.
4. It toggles between showing the entire timeline in the window and returning to the previous magnification level.
5. False. As long as the selection mode tool is the active tool in the toolbar, you can move a clip without using any keyboard modifiers.

Lesson 6

Refining a Timeline

The real artistry of editing is achieved in the pacing of the clips you assembled in the timeline. Pacing is refined by shortening or extending clips by a few seconds or even just a few frames to get the perfect timing between the two.

The edit page in DaVinci Resolve includes many of the same precision trimming tools that you learned in the Cut page plus a number of unique techniques you can use to address your creative needs. In this lesson, you'll learn how multiple trimming methods can help you pace your program perfectly.

Time

This lesson takes approximately 50 minutes to complete.

Goals

Customizing the Layout for Trimming

DaVinci Resolve lets you customize and save your user interface layouts to make various workflows easier. For example, the current interface layout has somewhat small dual viewers that are unsuitable for trimming. Before you dive into trimming, let's optimize your layout for that process.

1 Open DaVinci Resolve if necessary, and then open the Age of Airplanes project.

2 In the Rough Cuts bin, double-click the 02 Trim Rough Cut timeline to load it into the timeline viewer.

   This timeline is similar to the one you worked on in the previous lesson with slight adjustments made for the following exercises.

   While trimming, you will work with only your timeline clips, so you can optimize your workspace by hiding the Media pool and the source viewer. This will give you a larger area for the timeline and the timeline viewer.

3 In the upper-left user interface toolbar, click the Media pool button to hide the Media pool.

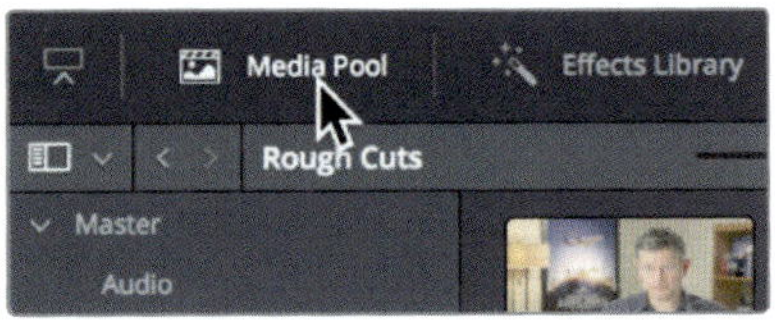

   Hiding the Media pool already gives you a lot more room for the viewers and timeline.

4 In the upper-right corner of the interface, click the single viewer mode button to hide the source viewer.

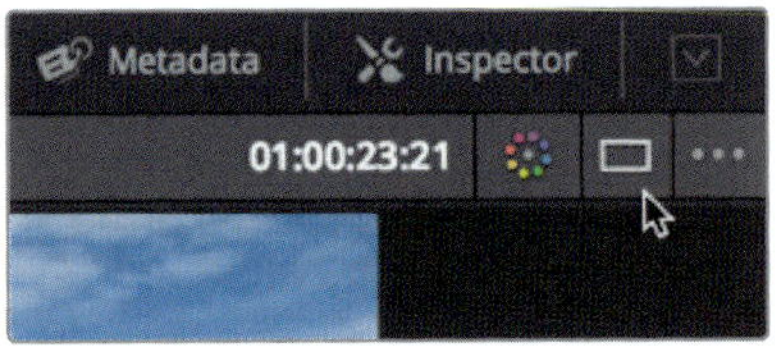

   The timeline viewer now moves to the center of the screen. With the extra horizontal space, you can increase the size of the viewer by taking away some space from the timeline.

   The timeline has a horizontal divider that separates the toolbar from the viewers. You can drag down that divider to allow more room for the viewers and less to the timeline tracks. Because you don't need too much vertical space for your timeline, this will work out well while trimming.

5 Position the mouse pointer between the toolbar and the transport controls.

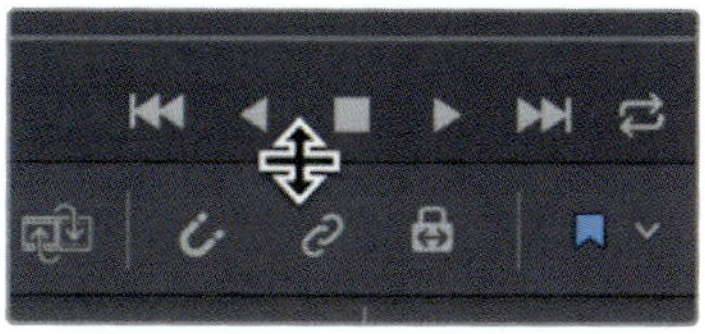

6 When the pointer changes to a resize cursor, drag down the horizontal divider while leaving a little bit of room above the video track in the timeline.

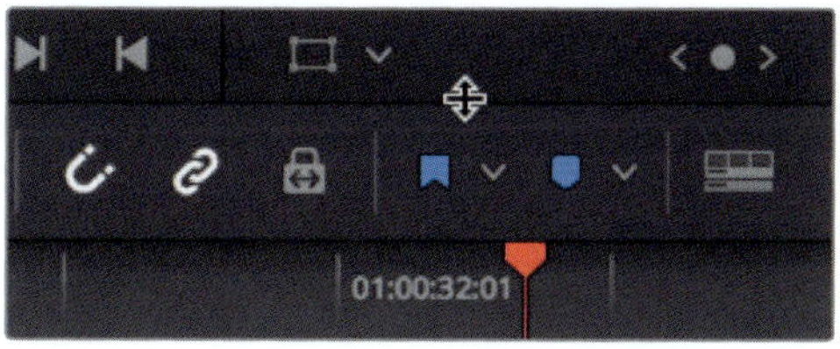

You can save this layout as your Big Trim layout and use it in all of your projects.

7 Choose Workspace > Layout Presets > Save Layout as Preset.

8 In the dialog, enter **Big Trim** as the layout name, and click OK.

Now that you have an optimized big trim layout, you can get to work trimming and refining your program.

Trimming to the Playhead

One of the fastest ways to remove frames from the start or end of a clip is sometimes called tops and tails trimming. This trimming style is used heavily in broadcast news-type programs, but it is useful for all types of programs. The concept is to loosely edit-in clips by adding more of the clip than you really want. Then, you'll remove frames from the start (top) of the clip or the end (tail) of the clip by positioning the playhead where you would like to locate the new start or end. Let's begin this trimming lesson at the start of the timeline. You don't have to play the entire timeline, but it is worth looking at the first clip to see how it can be improved.

1 Choose View > Zoom > Zoom to Fit, or press Shift-Z, to see the entire timeline in the window.

2 Position the playhead at the start of the timeline, and play it to review the first two clips.

The first clip isn't wrong, but it could be improved by shortening both its start and end. Let's start by trimming some of the silence from the start of the clip.

3 Position the playhead at the start of the timeline.

4 In the toolbar, drag the zoom slider to the right until the first clip fills half of the timeline window.

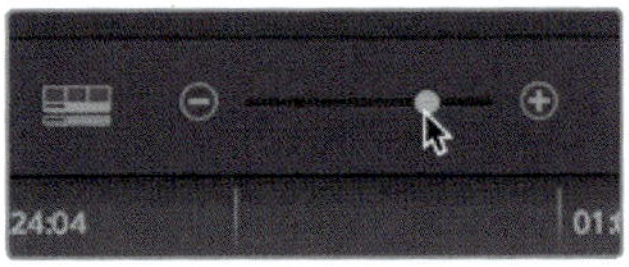

5 Position the playhead between the words "so" and "in this film." Use the audio waveform as a guide to position the playhead between the words.

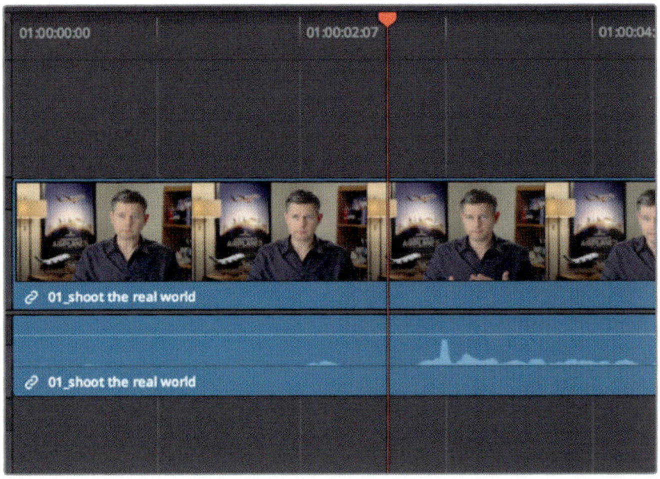

This playhead position is where you want the clip to start. You can perform the trim-to-playhead function using two different tools. Let's first apply the selection mode tool that you are already using.

6 Choose Trim > Trim Start, or press Shift-[(left bracket).

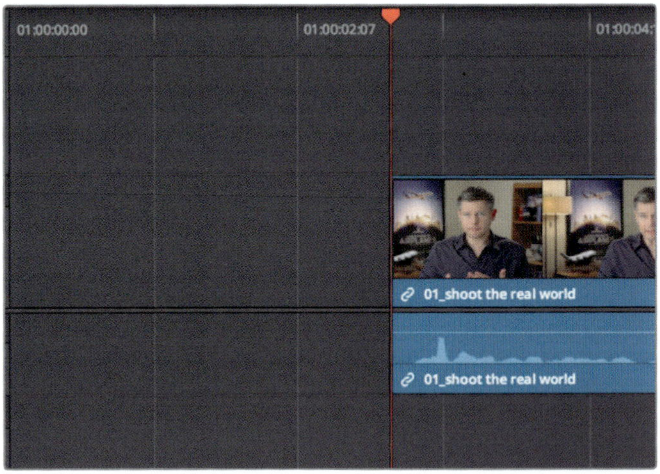

The start of the clip is trimmed to the playhead position. Let's review the change.

7 Position the playhead at the start of timeline, and press the spacebar to listen to the first clip.

8 Although the clip starts on the correct word, it no longer starts at the beginning of the timeline. A gap now exists between the start of the timeline and the first clip. You'll have to undo that trim, and try another tool.

9 Choose Edit > Undo, or press Cmd-Z (macOS) or Ctrl-Z (Windows), to undo the previous trim.

10 In the toolbar, select the trim edit mode tool, or press T.

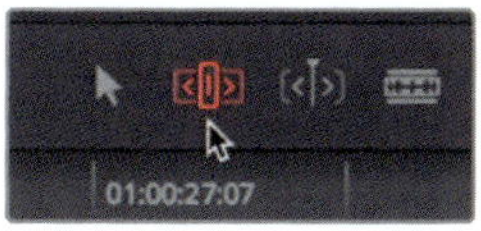

The trim edit mode tool is the most flexible tool to use when you want to shorten and lengthen clips in the timeline. The primary difference between the trim edit mode tool and the selection mode tool, is that trim edit mode ripples the timeline instead of leaving gaps. Let's see it in practice.

11 Again, position the playhead between the words "so" and "in this film."

12 Choose Trim > Trim Start, or press Shift-[(left bracket).

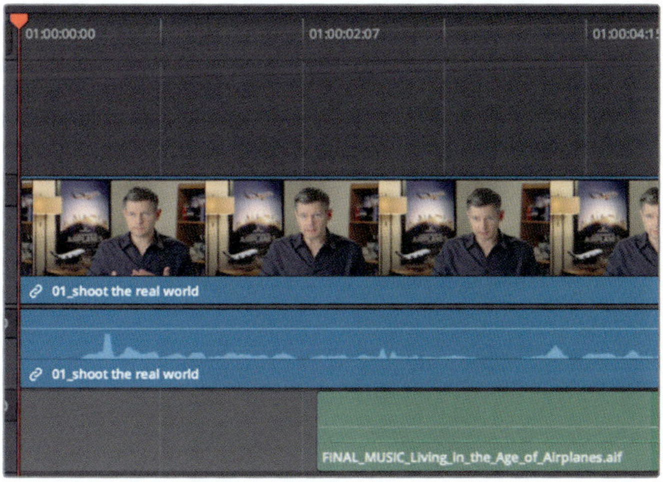

The same beginning frames are trimmed from the clip, but now the clip starts at the beginning of the timeline and the change ripples through the rest of the timeline, thereby shortening the overall duration. Let's look at the end of this clip.

13 Position the playhead at the start of the timeline, and play over the first clip.

A more powerful ending to this clip would be after the statement, "Shoot the real world."

14 Position the playhead at the end of the statement, "Shoot the real world," while ensuring that you do not include any of the following sentence.

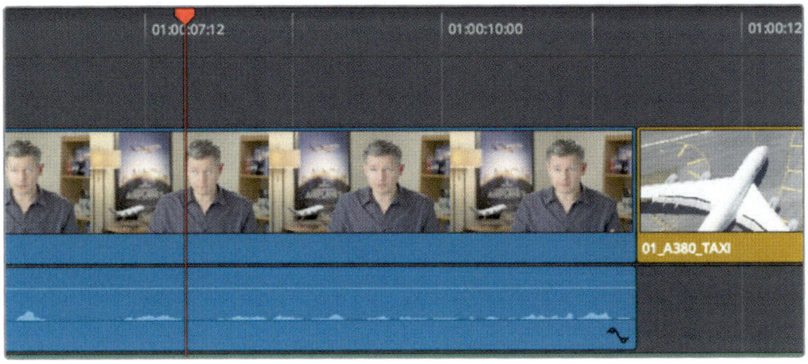

TIP You can press the Left and right arrow keys to nudge the playhead one frame forward or backward to position it more precisely.

Instead of using the trim start function, you can use the trim end function to remove frames from the end of the clip.

Because you have the trim edit mode selected, removing all the frames from the playhead to the end of the clip will ripple the timeline, as did the ripple delete function you used in the previous lesson. But just as you disabled auto select in the previous lesson for the music track so you didn't delete a portion of the music, you also need to disable auto select here so you don't trim the end of the music.

15 Click the auto select button to disable it on Audio 2.

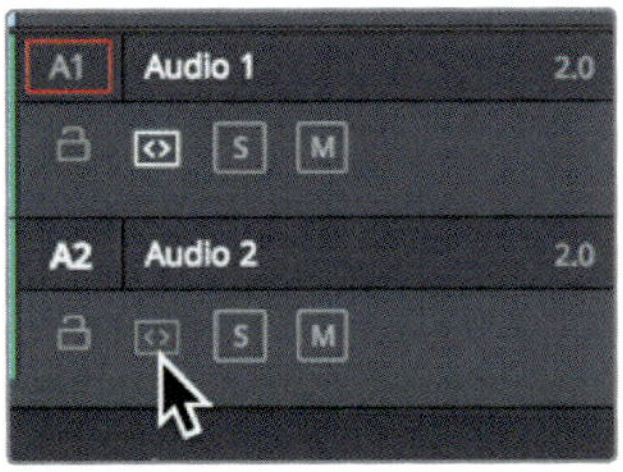

16 Choose Trim > Trim End, or press Shift-] (right bracket).

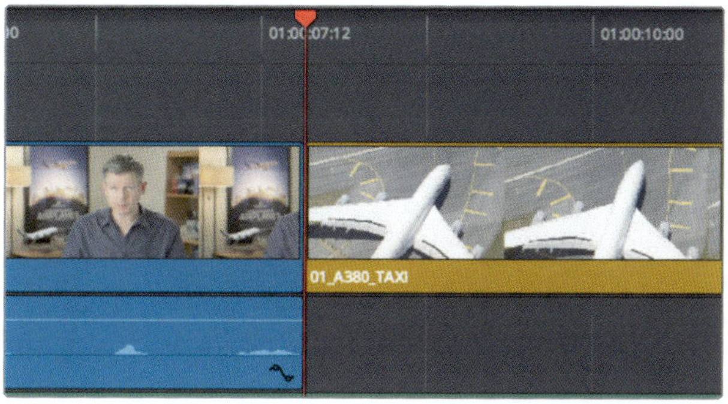

The end of the clips on Video 1 and Audio 1 are trimmed to the playhead but the music track remains unchanged. The remaining clips in the timeline are shifted to the left by the same number of frames that you just removed.

17 In the toolbar, select the Selection mode tool, or press A.

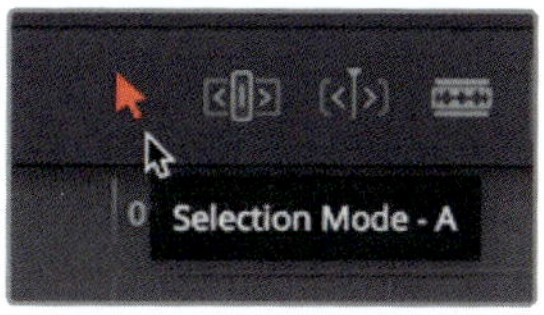

18 Position the playhead at the start of timeline, and start playback to review your top and tail trims.

You should have two take-aways from this exercise. The first (and obvious) one is that trim start and trim end are two very quick ways to tighten your edits through an entire timeline. The second and more fundamental take-away is that the Selection mode tool opens gaps while the trim edit mode tool ripples the timeline.

Ripple Trimming

The multiple ways you can use the trim edit mode makes it fast, precise, and flexible. Let's look at another clip to decide how trimming might improve it.

1 Position the playhead at the end of the interview clip you just trimmed.

2 Play the timeline to view the next three clips, until the interview subject returns to the screen.

The shot of the Maldives starts too late. The water plane is already overhead when the clip begins. You need to add more frames to the beginning of the Maldives shot so it starts with the plane out of the frame. Let's zoom in and center that clip in the timeline window.

3 Position the playhead at the start of the 10_MALDIVES clip.

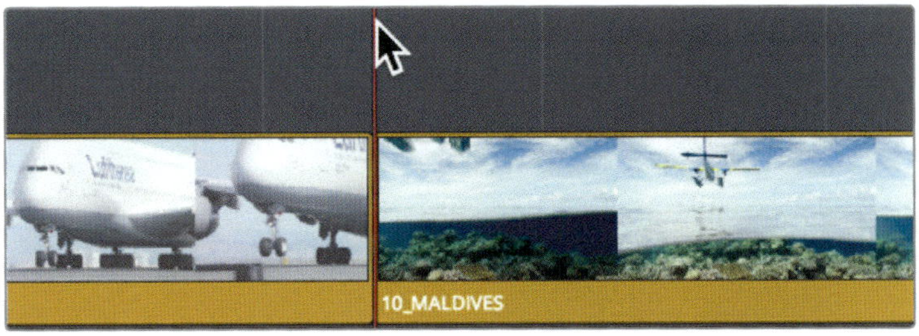

4 Below the timeline, drag the scroll bar to the right to center the playhead.

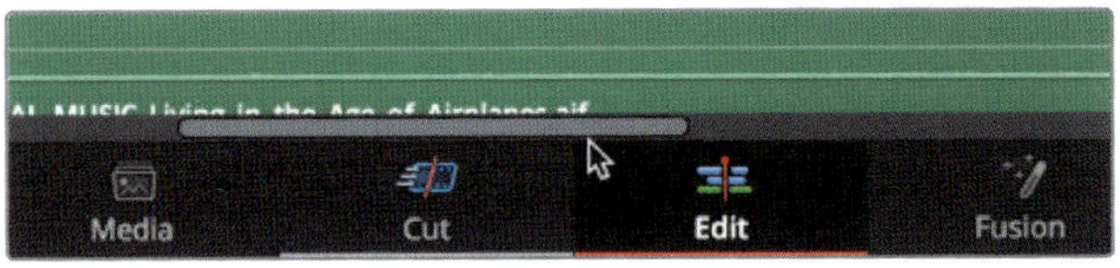

5 In the toolbar, drag the zoom slider to the right to increase the size of the 10 MALDIVES clip in the timeline.

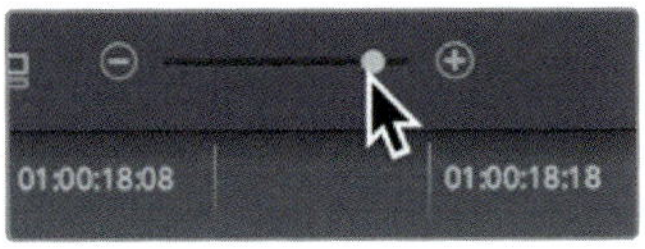

You now have two choices. You can use the Selection mode tool to add frames to the beginning of the Maldives, and thereby overwrite some of the end frames on the A380 clips that comes before it. Or, you can use the trim edit mode tool and ripple the timeline, thereby leaving the A380 clip unchanged.

Because the A380 clip is fine as it is, let's choose to ripple trim.

6 In the toolbar, click the trim edit mode button, or press T.

With the trim edit mode selected, you can no longer use the cursor to select clips and move them in the timeline. Now, the primary purpose of the cursor is to select a cut point and the side of that cut point you want to trim.

7 Position the trim edit mode cursor at the end of the 02_A380_TAKEOFF clip.

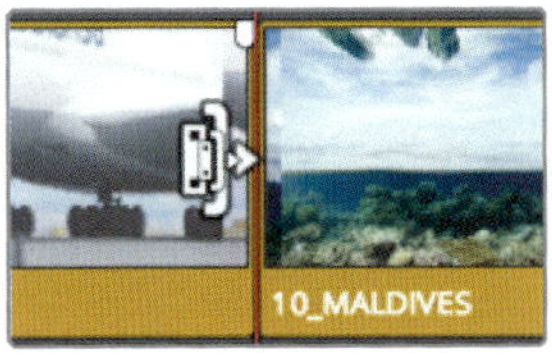

The cursor changes to the ripple trim cursor that you use to lengthen or shorten a clip's duration. When the cursor is to the left of the cut, it will trim the end, or tail, of the cut.

8 Position the trim edit mode cursor over the beginning, or head, of the **10_MALDIVES** clip.

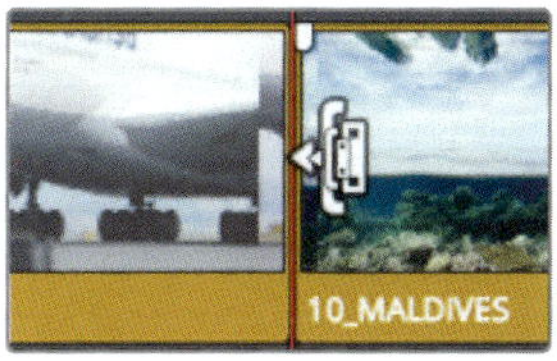

When the cursor is on the right side of the cut, you can trim the head of the clip. This is where you want to trim.

9 Drag the head of the cut slightly to the left and hold the cursor there for a moment.

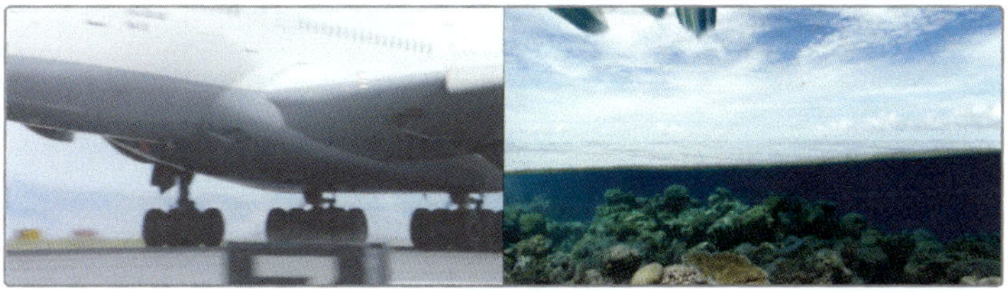

As you drag, the timeline viewer splits to show you the last frame of the outgoing clip on the left and the first frame of the incoming clip on the right. This two-frame side-by-side display is designed to show how the action and framing from the two sides of a cut will match up (or not).

10 Continue dragging left until the **10 MALDIVES** plane is off the screen.

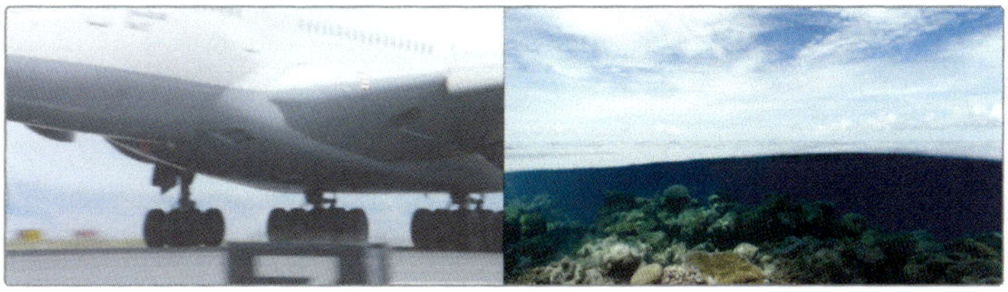

> **TIP** When dragging to trim, the cut point may snap to the playhead and make it difficult to precisely position the trim. When this happens, tap the N key to disable snapping as you trim.

When removing frames, a ripple trim pulls in all the clips after the trim point to close the gap and also changes the overall duration of the timeline.

11 To review the trim point, choose Playback > Play Around/To > Play Around Current Frame, or press / (slash).

TIP The number of seconds played before and after any play around command is determined by the pre-roll and post-roll settings in the editing user preferences.

Although trimming in the edit page timeline is similar to the cut page, there is one major difference. Only V1 ripple trims in the cut page. However, in the edit page, if the trim edit mode tool is selected, all trimming will ripple the timeline no matter which track you are trimming.

Trimming using Numbers

When you are a trimming specific number of frames, instead of dragging the cut point using a visual guide, it is easier to use the keyboard to enter the exact number of frames you want to move, or to nudge the trim one frame forward or backward.

1 Make sure the start of the 10_MALDIVES clip is still selected with the trim edit mode tool.

From the previous review of this trim, you can see that the plane still comes in too abruptly. Let's add one second more to the start of this clip. Instead of trying to drag one second precisely, you can enter the number using the keypad.

2 Type **-1.** (minus, one, period), and press Return (macOS) or Enter (Windows).

One second is added to the start of the 10_MALDIVES clip. Using a negative number to add frames may seem a bit counterintuitive, but the positive and negative values are based on the timeline direction. Moving a clip or cut point to the left is a negative move, whereas moving to the right is a positive move.

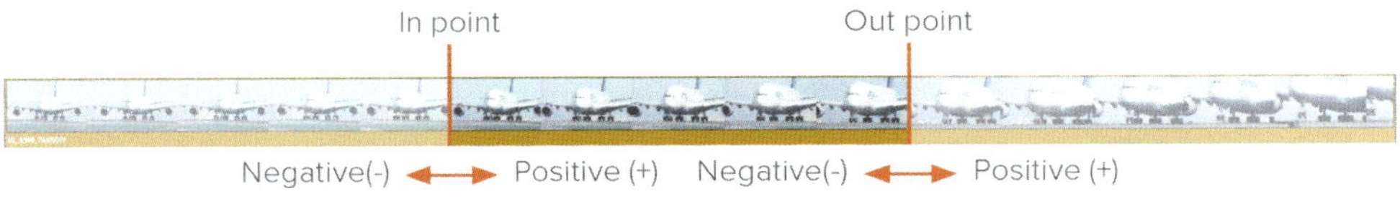

3 To review the cut, choose Playback > Play Around/To > Play Around Current Frame, or press / (slash).

You can continue to enter seconds and frames to refine the precise starting point for the Maldives clip. But you can also quickly nudge the cut one frame at a time by pressing the, (comma) and . (period) keys.

4 To remove three frames from the start of the Maldives clip, press the . (period) key three times.

TIP Pressing Shift-, (comma) or Shift-. (period) trims in five-frame increments.

5 To review the trim point, choose Playback > Play Around/To > Play Around Current Frame, or press / (slash).

6 To return one frame to the start of the Maldives clip, press the, (comma) key once.

> **TIP** Choosing Playback > Loop and then playing around the current frame allows you to use the . (period) and, (comma) keys on-the-fly as you loop over the transition.

Whether you use the number pad or drag to trim is really your choice. Although using the number pad may be faster, it is also less visual. When trimming by dragging you are better able to see the frames, but you sacrifice work speed. The right choice for you is whichever method you feel most comfortable with in any given situation.

Selecting Tracks to Trim

So far in this lesson you've trimmed only video clips. What happens when you select a clip that includes an audio track? This is where trimming in the edit page gives you a bit more flexibility than the cut page.

1 Press Shift-Z to view the entire timeline, and then position the playhead between the 06_MILKYWAY and 02_If it was possible clips.

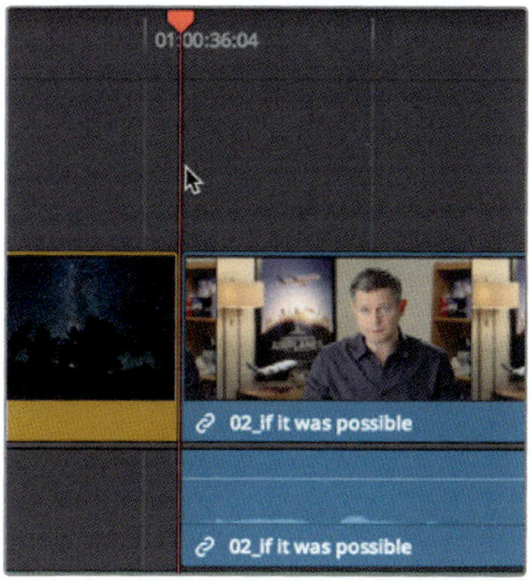

2 In the toolbar, drag the zoom slider to zoom in on these two clips.

> **TIP** In macOS, press Cmd-+ (plus sign) or Cmd- - (minus sign) to incrementally zoom in and out of the timeline. In Windows, press Ctrl-+ (plus sign) or Ctrl- - (minus sign) to incrementally zoom in and out of the timeline.

3 Click the trim edit mode button, or press T, to enter trim edit mode, if necessary.

4 Place the pointer over the right side of the cut point, over the start of the **02_If it was possible** clip.

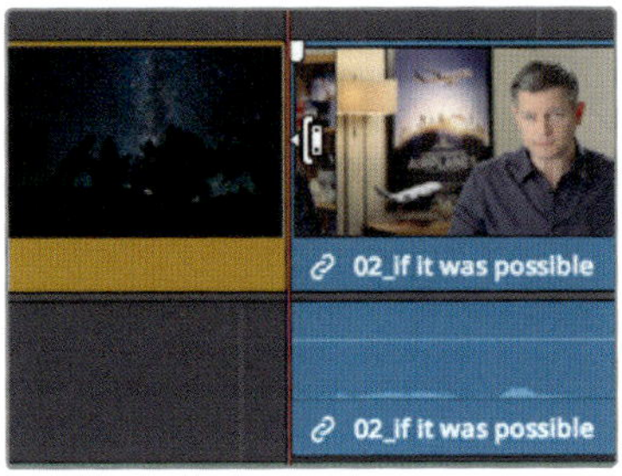

5 Click to select the start of the **02_If it was possible** clip for ripple trimming.

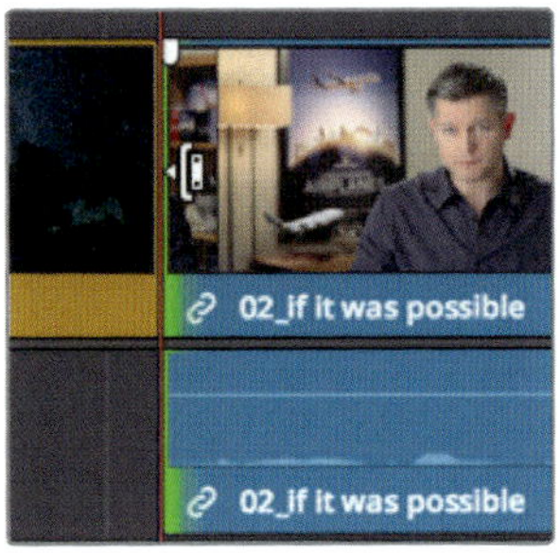

Even though you selected only the video track, both the video and audio tracks are selected. The audio and video are from the same interview clip, so they are linked. This behavior is similar to moving clips in the timeline with the linked selection button enabled.

6 In the empty timeline area above the video track, click to deselect the edit point.

7 Click the linked selection button to disable it.

TIP You can also hold down the Option key (macOS) or the Alt key (Windows) to temporarily select the video edit point without disabling the linked selection button.

8 Once again, select the start of the 02_If it was possible clip for ripple trimming.

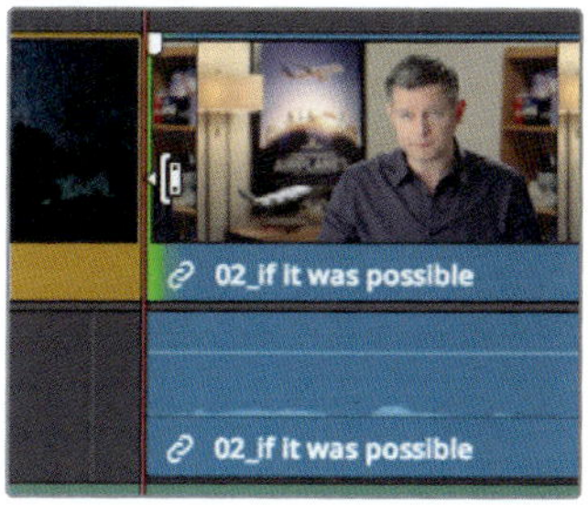

With the linked selection function disabled, only the video edit point is selected.

9 To review the selected cut, choose Playback > Play Around/To > Play Around Current Frame, or press / (slash).

Offsetting the video from the audio so that one is seen or heard sooner than the other is a technique used in editing to improve program flow. Often called **J-cuts** and **L-cuts**, these edits are most commonly used in dialog scenes, but they can be used here to lead you into the next shot with more continuity. To further increase continuity, let's start his voice a few seconds before the picture.

10 Drag the cut to the right about one second until you are between the statements "It was really important" and "Every shot was original." Use the audio waveform in the audio track as a guide to position the video cut in the gap between the sentences.

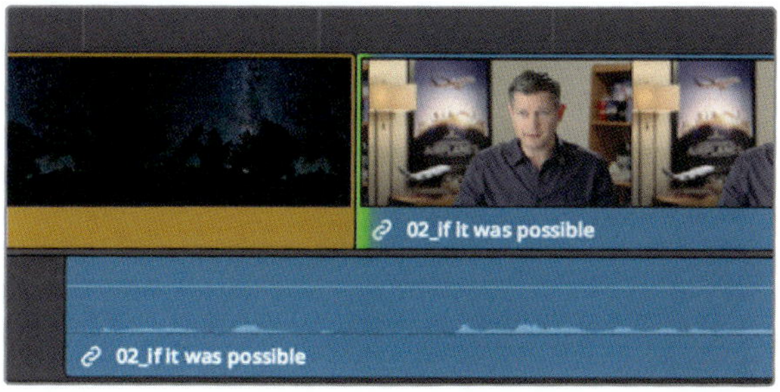

TIP Enabling Trim > Dynamic Trim allows you to use the J-K-L keys for trimming.

Before you review that cut, it is worth taking a short detour and asking why the audio track moved under the 06_MILKYWAY clip when you trimmed the video track? That has a lot to do with the state of the auto select button that you used earlier in this lesson.

Here, the auto select function was trying to keep your timeline in sync while you were trimming. To more fully understand how this works, let's trim a bit more, this time with auto select disabled for the audio track.

11 On Audio 1, click the auto select button to disable it.

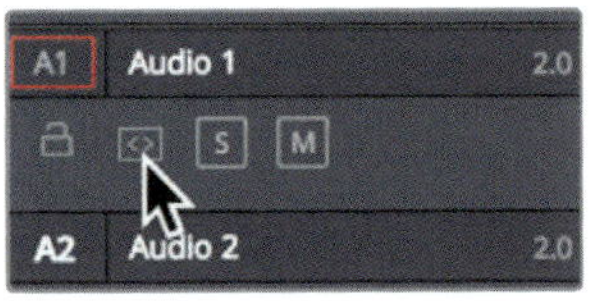

12 Again, select the start of the 02_If it was possible clip and drag it to the right for a few frames.

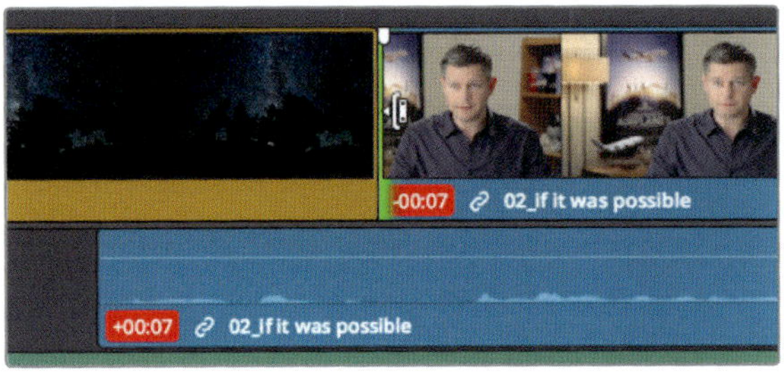

Because you disabled the auto select button for the Audio 1 track, it didn't adjust when you trimmed frames from the video track. Consequently, the audio went out of sync with the now-short video track. The red badges indicate that the number of frames in the audio and video tracks are out of sync. With more understanding of auto select, let's undo that action and finish up the lesson.

13 Choose Edit > Undo, or press Cmd-Z (macOS) or Ctrl-Z (Windows), to undo the previous trim.

14 On Audio 1, enable the auto select button.

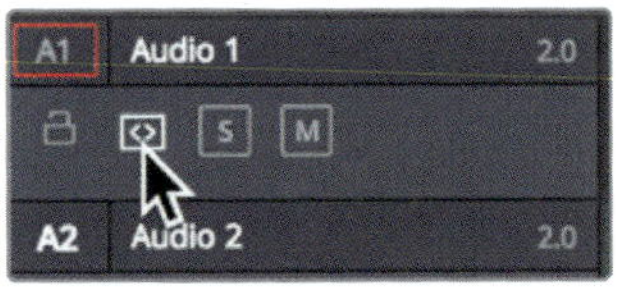

15 Click the linked selection button to enable linked clips.

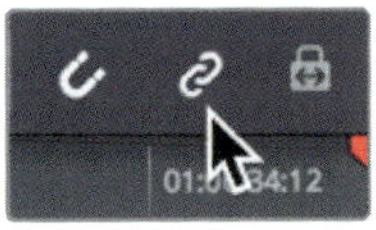

16 In the toolbar, select the Selection mode tool, or press A.

Finally, let's review the trim you made.

17 Position the playhead at the start of 06_MILKYWAY clip, and review your J-cut.

Keeping audio and video in sync is always a concern (and a chore) for editors. The linked selection function is invaluable in assisting you with that effort on a clip-by-clip basis and the auto select buttons are invaluable on a timeline basis. Although it's necessary to disable both in some situations, it's good practice to enable them most of the time.

Using Roll Trimming

While a ripple trim alters a single side of a cut point, Roll trims simultaneously trim both the end of the outgoing clip and the start of the incoming clip. These types of trims are useful when you want to retain the overall timeline duration or want to ensure your timeline stays in sync.

1 In the timeline, position the playhead at the end of the 06_MILKYWAY clip.

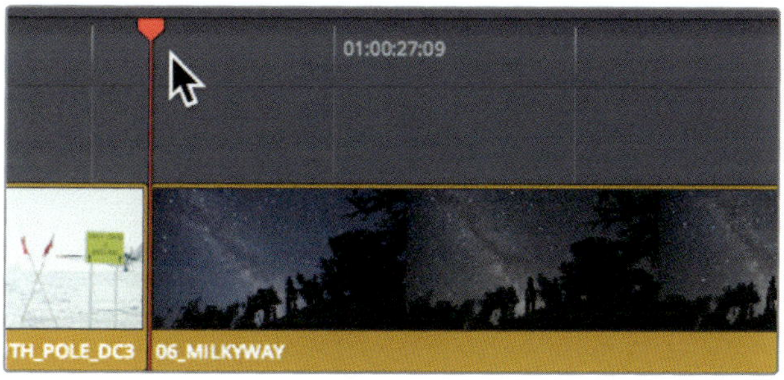

2 Press the spacebar to play through the end of the 05_BAY AREA_LIGHTS clip.

For this trim, you will need to trim only the video track because the audio in this interview ends where you want it, when he says, "Everything was real." However, the two shots would flow better if you heard the word "real" while the Bay Area shot was onscreen. Just a small overlap is all you need.

3 In the toolbar, click the linked selection button to disable it.

A rolling trim can be performed using either the Selection mode tool or the trim edit mode tool. The behavior for a roll trim is exactly the same no matter which tool you use. So, you can leave your Selection mode tool selected.

4 Center the mouse pointer over the video cut point.

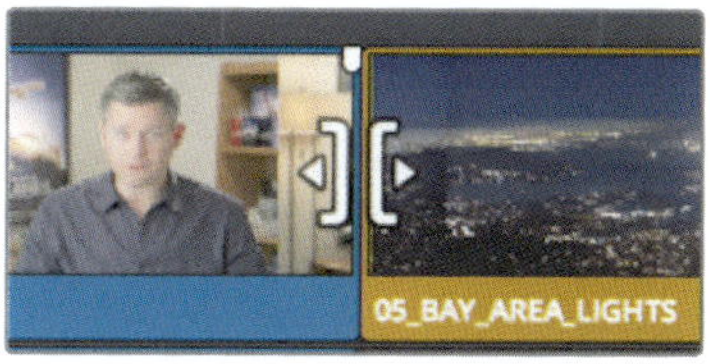

When the mouse pointer is centered over the cut, the cursor changes to a roll trim cursor.

5 On the video track, click the cut point to select both the end of the 02_if_it_was_possible interview clip and the start of the 05_BAY AREA_LIGHTS clip.

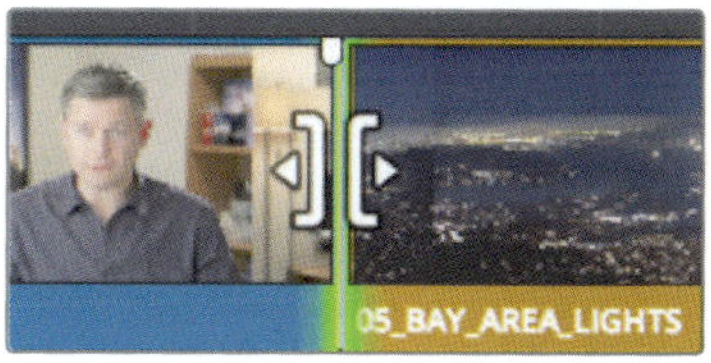

TIP When a cut point is selected with the ripple or roll cursor, pressing the U key toggles between each side of the edit to select that side for trimming.

With both sides of the cut selected, any adjustments will be made equally to both sides of the cut. Removing frames from the end of the interview clip will add frames to the start of the Bay Area clip and vice versa.

6 Drag the cut to the left until the playhead is just before the words "was real." In the audio track, use the audio waveform as a guide to position the video cut just before those words.

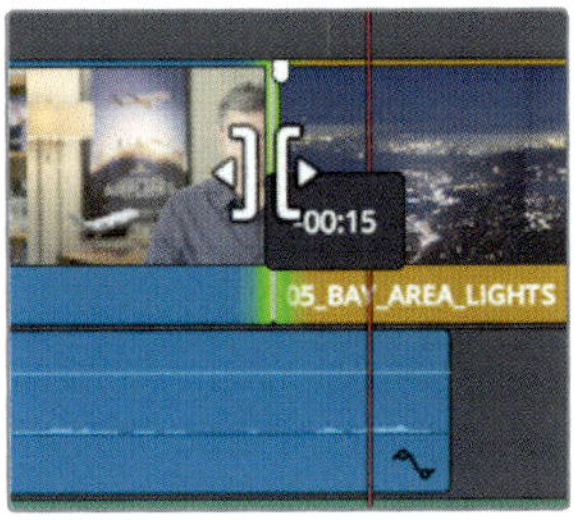

Let's play the transition to see your results.

7 To review the cut, choose Playback > Play Around/To > Play Around Current Frame, or press / (slash).

You can continue to refine the cut by pressing the, (comma) and . (period) keys to nudge it into the exact spot you want.

Slipping a Clip

Slipping a clip so that you shift the range without changing the clip's duration or position in the timeline is done slightly differently than in the Cut page. Slipping in the edit page can only be performed when you are in trim edit mode.

1 Choose View > Zoom > Zoom to Fit, or press Shift-Z, to see the entire timeline.

2 Position the playhead at the start of the 01_A380_TAXI clip.

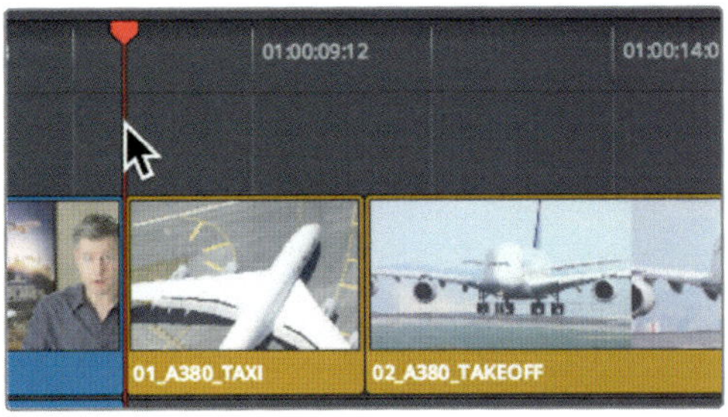

3 Press the spacebar to play the timeline until you see the 10_MALDIVES clip.

The 02_A380_TAKEOFF clip starts a bit slow and ends before the plane is out of the frame. Could you trim both ends of the cut to fix this? Sure, but you could perform the same correction more quickly using the slip tool.

4 Position the playhead over the 02_A380_TAKEOFF clip, and in the toolbar, drag the zoom slider until you fill the timeline window with the A380 clip and the clips on either side of it.

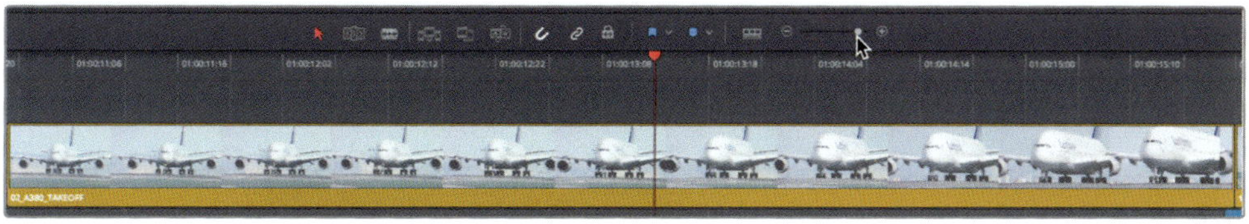

5 Click the trim edit mode button, or press T.

Just as when you chose between ripple or roll trims, the placement of the mouse pointer is important when choosing the slip cursor.

6 Place the mouse pointer over the upper-middle region of the 02_A320_TAKEOFF clip.

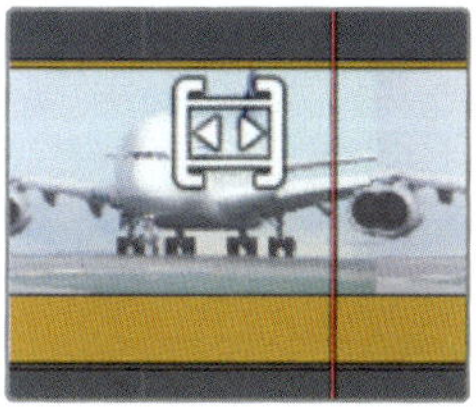

The cursor changes to a slip cursor. With the slip cursor in place, you're ready to slip the clip.

7 Drag to the left to slip the clip until you see the plane leave the frame in the upper right of the viewer.

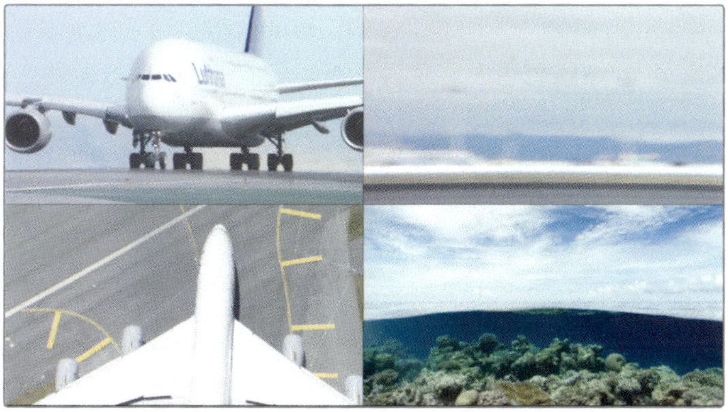

As you drag, the same 4-up display you viewed in the Cut page is shown in the edit page. This allows you to compare all relevant outgoing and incoming frames. The upper two frames show the starting and ending frames of the clip being slipped. The lower-left frame shows the previous clip's unchanging last frame, and the lower-right frame shows the next clip's unchanging first frame.

NOTE Depending upon the window configuration and the size of your display, you may need to stop dragging a clip, reposition the mouse, and then resume dragging.

Having the plane leave the frame completes the action of the take-off and makes for a more pleasing clip.

8. Position the playhead before the slipped clip, and then play the timeline to review your edit.

   This looks good but it could be improved if you didn't cut to the Maldives shot exactly as the plane leaves the frame. You need to add five frames of the plane out of frame before you cut.

   Once you click a clip with the slip tool, you can use keyboard shortcuts to slip left or right in one- or five-frame increments.

9. Press Shift-, (comma) to slip the clip five more frames.

10. Position the playhead before the slipped clip, and play the timeline to review your edit.

    If that looks good to you, then leave it as it is. If you feel the clip needs more or less "breathing room" before you cut to the next clip, use the keyboard shortcuts to refine it.

11. When you are done, in the toolbar, select the selection mode tool, or press A.

Slipping a clip is most often used more subtly than you have done here. You'll find that you frequently will slip clips just a few frames to get a perfect match with the surrounding clips.

Trimming with the Selection Tool

When you trimmed in the Cut page on video track 2 in Lesson 1, it opened up a gap or over wrote the incoming clip. To get that same behavior in the edit page, you use the standard selection tool instead of the trim edit mode. The difference being that trimming with the selection tool in the edit page will perform the same way no matter which track you trim on. It does not ripple trim; instead, it opens gaps when a clip is made shorter or overwrites the next clip when a clip is extended.

1 Choose View > Zoom > Zoom to Fit, or press Shift-Z, to see the entire timeline.

2 Position the playhead at the start of the 08_SOUTH_POLE clip.

To fix the jump cut you created earlier, you can add frames to the start of the south pole clip. Doing this with the selection tool will over write the clip prior and not ripple the timeline.

3 Position the mouse pointer over the head of the south pole clip.

A Resize Trim cursor appears that is similar to the ripple trim cursor. However, the results are different when compared to using the Trim tool.

4 Drag to the left until the short interview segment is overwritten.

Now, let's see what happens when you shorten a clip with the selection tool.

5 Press the spacebar to play the timeline until you see the 05_BAY_AREA_LIGHTS clip.

06_MILKYWAY is a long clip. It would be better to shorten it. You could just overwrite a new clip to cover up part of the 06_MILKYWAY clip, but in many cases you can't do that. For instance, maybe you haven't yet imported the clip or you haven't decided which clip you want to use. Still, you may want to shorten the clip and leave the gap as a placeholding reminder. For whatever reason, opening gaps is a valuable trimming function that you can apply with the selection mode tool.

6 Position the playhead over the center of the 06_MILKYWAY clip.

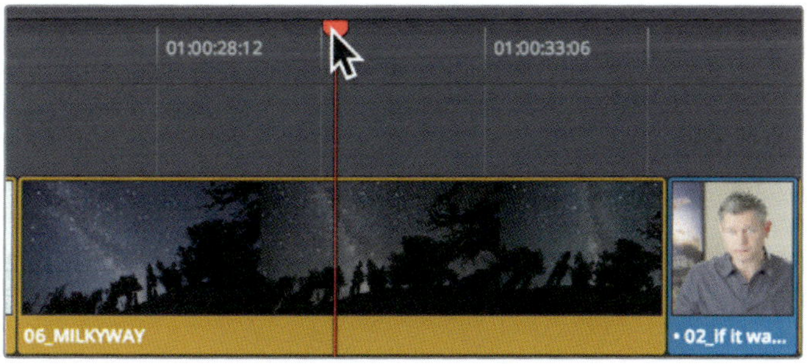

7 In the toolbar, drag the zoom slider to increase the size of the clip in the window.

8 Hover the mouse pointer over the start of the 06_MILKYWAY clip.

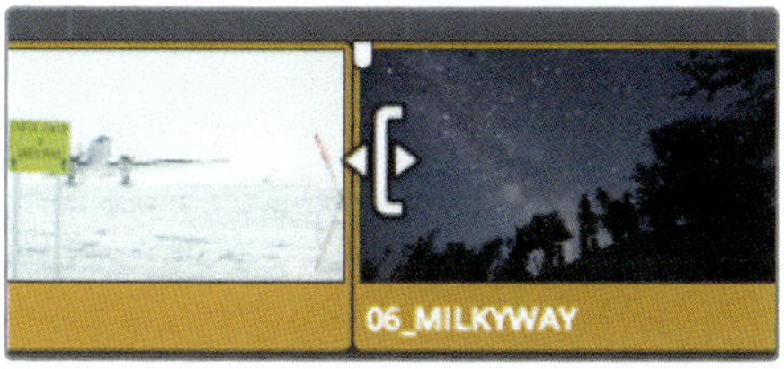

9 Drag the start of the 06_MILKYWAY clip to the right until the tool tip displays +4:00.

Unlike using the ripple trim tool, when using the trim edit tool, trimming one side of an edit using the selection mode tool leaves a gap.

Marking a Gap

You can't leave the gap in your program so you will have to fill it with a clip. Let's look in the B-Roll bin for a clip to fill this gap.

1 Choose Workspace > Reset UI Layout to unhide the Media pool, and display the source viewer.

2 In the B-Roll bin, double-click the 07_Kenya clip to load it into the viewer, and press the spacebar to play it.

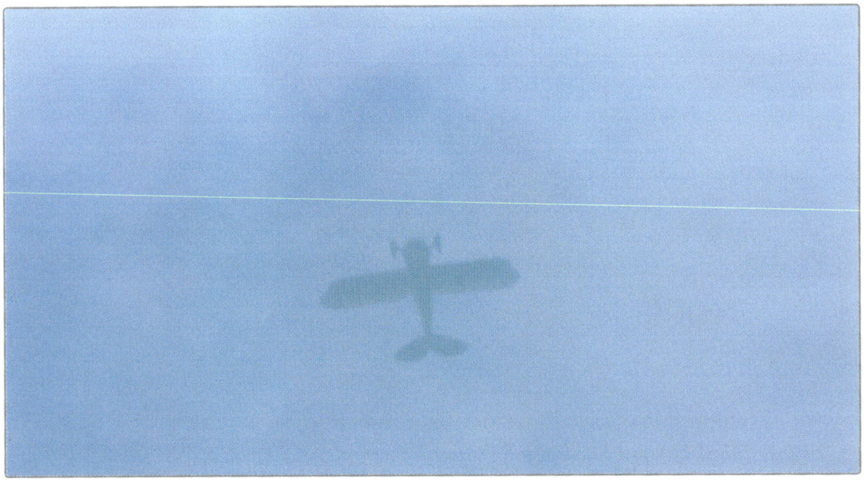

The 07_KENYA clip is the only clip in the bin that you haven't used, so it is a good candidate for filling the gap.

3 In the viewer, drag the jog bar back until the plane's reflection in the water points straight up.

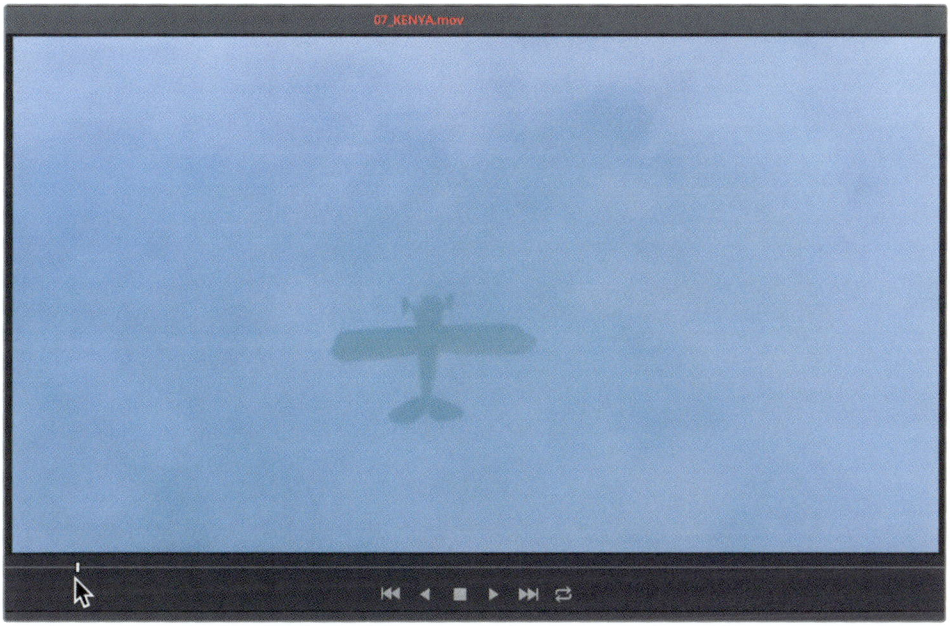

You'll mark your In point here.

4 Press I to mark an in point on the source clip.

The gap is the range in the timeline you are trying to fill, so you needn't add an out point on the source clip; but you will need to mark in and out points in the timeline based on the duration of the gap.

5 Drag the timeline playhead into the center of the gap.

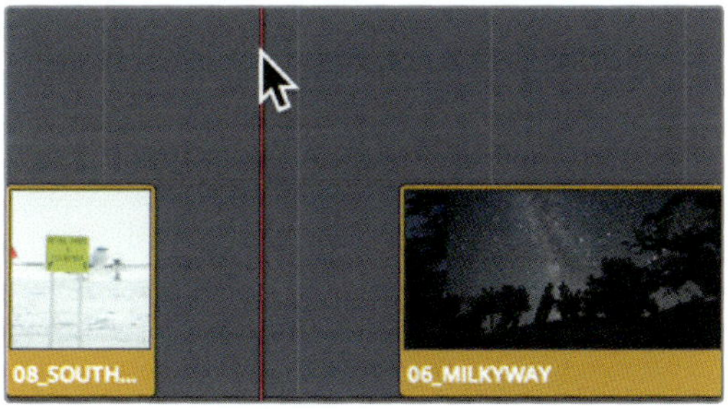

Instead of moving the playhead, marking an In point, moving the playhead again, and marking an out point, you can use the Mark Clip command to mark the clip under the playhead.

6 Choose Mark > Mark Clip, or press X.

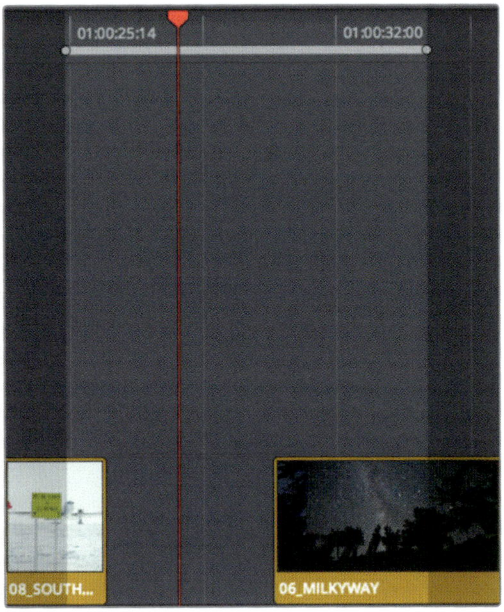

The Mark Clip command added in and out points in the timeline, but it used the audio track on A2 as the duration to mark. You really want to ignore the audio track and use the gap. This is another use case for auto select. It helps keep tracks in sync when trimming and identifies the tracks when deleting a range (as you did in Lesson 4). Here, auto select will allow you to target the track you want the Mark Clip command to use when setting in and out points.

7 In the timeline header, disable the auto select buttons for Audio 2 leaving Video 1 Audio 1 with auto select buttons enabled.

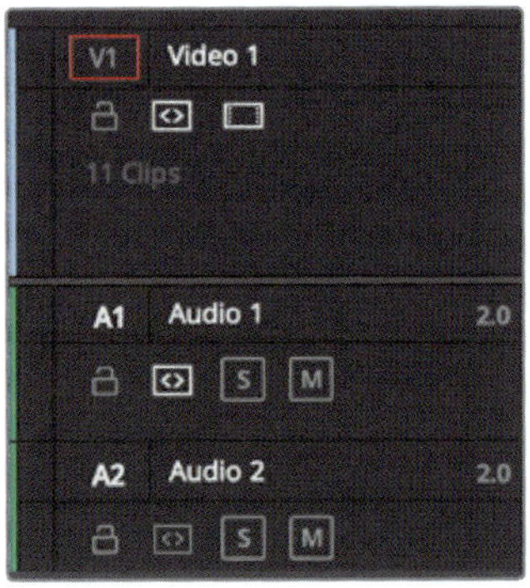

8 Choose Mark > Mark Clip, or press X.

> **TIP** When multiple video tracks have Auto Select enabled, the lowest numbered video track is the target track.

With auto select enabled on Video 1, the Mark Clip command correctly used the gap duration to set the in and out points. All that is left to do is make the edit.

9 In the toolbar, click the overwrite button to edit-in the **07_KENYA** clip.

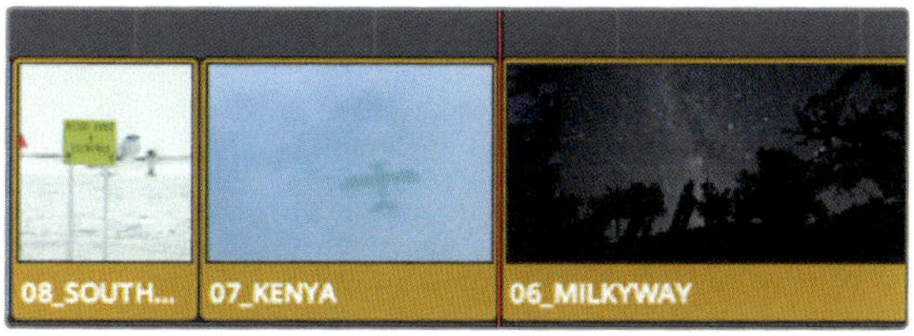

This is the same behavior you saw on the very first exercise in this lesson when using the trim start function opened a gap between the start of the timeline and the first clip. It is a fundamental behavior to keep in mind.

Lesson Review

1 When using Trim Start or Trim End, how do you ignore a track?

2 Where do you find the command to save a customized layout preset?

3 When trimming a transition, what is the significance of the two-up display in the timeline viewer?

4 What's the difference between a roll trim and a ripple trim?

5 When double-clicking a clip in the timeline, will adjusting the in and out points change the timeline?

Answers

1 In the timeline header, disable the track's auto select button.

2 You can save a layout preset in the Workspace menu.

3 The left side of the two-up display shows the last frame of the outgoing clip, whereas the right side shows the first frame of the incoming clip.

4 A roll trim will adjust the durations of both of the clips that share the trim point. A ripple trim will shorten or lengthen the selected side of the trim.

5 Yes. This is called trimming in the source.

Lesson 7

Applying Transitions and Effects

Once you have the basic structure of a scene, you can begin to open up a whole new avenue of creativity by adding graphics and effects. It doesn't matter what type of program you are creating; these additions can be as simple as a cross-fade or as fantastic as a morphing transition. Many effects are subtle, even hidden, while others are meant to be attention grabbers. In this lesson, you'll work with a sampling of DaVinci Resolve 16's tools for creating visual interest in the Edit page; but more importantly, you'll learn the concepts of adding transitions and effects so you can confidently continue to explore on your own.

Time

This lesson takes approximately 50 minutes to complete.

Goals

Fading Clips In and Out

Many programs start with a fade transition (fade-in) and end with one (fade-out). When you fade, you are mixing two elements. One element is a video clip and the other is a completely black frame, or in DaVinci Resolve, an empty part of the timeline.

1 Open the Age of Airplanes project, if necessary.

2 In the Rough Cuts bin, double-click the 03 Transitions and FX rough cut.

Because you will be altering the video track in this lesson, you can modify the layout again to suit your needs.

3 Choose Workspace > Layout Presets > Big Trim > Load Preset to use your previously created layout.

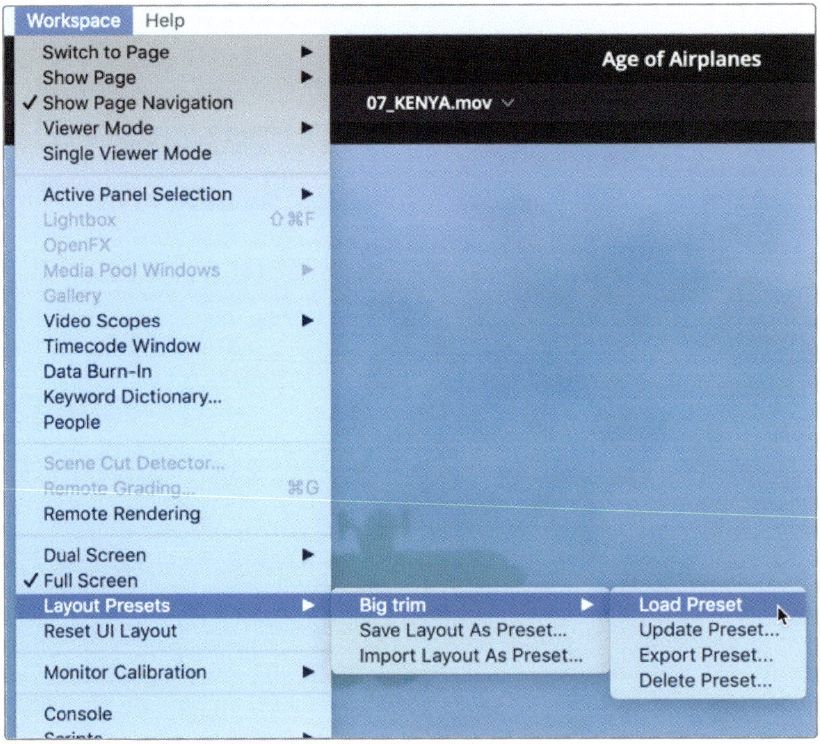

You'll also customize the timeline view to make the audio tracks smaller and the video track larger.

4 Click the Timeline View Options menu.

5 Drag the Audio Track Height slider all the way to the left.

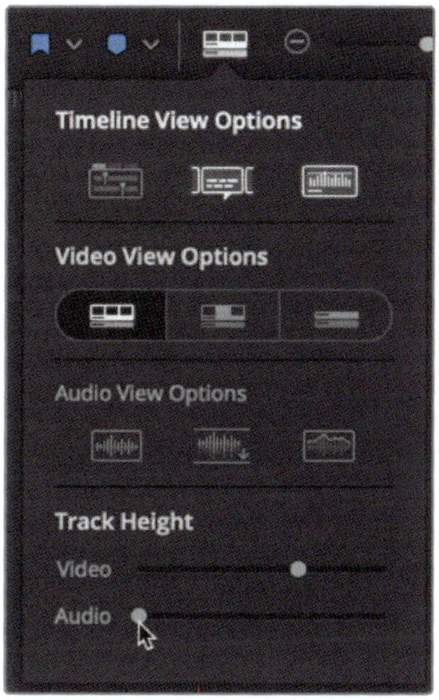

6 Drag the Video Track Height slider about mid-way, and click the Timeline View Options button again to hide the options.

7 Position the playhead at the start of the timeline.

8 To begin this trailer, you'll add a very quick fade-in.

9 In the timeline, place the pointer over the 01_shoot the real world clip.

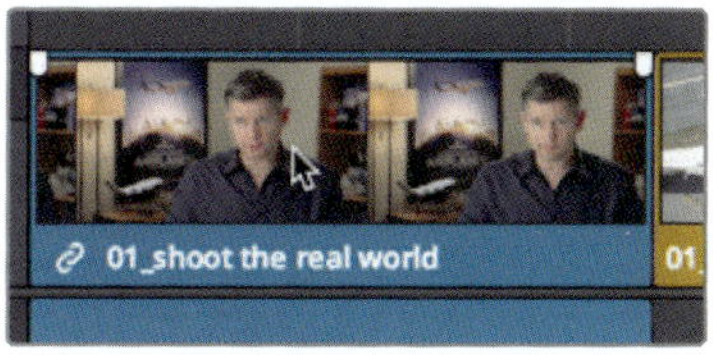

As with audio clips, two fade handles—video fade handles, in this case—appear in the upper-left and upper-right corners of the clip.

10 At the start of the clip, drag the handle toward the center of the clip until the tool tip reads +00:10.

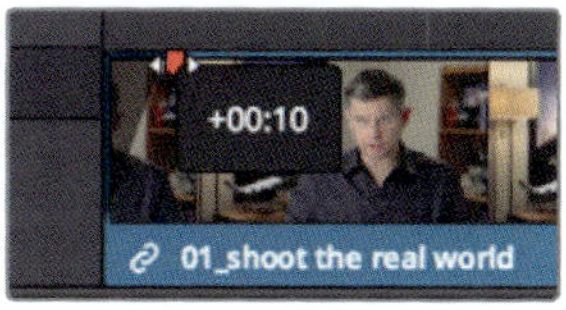

You've added a 10-frame fade-in to the start of the scene.

11 Play the start of the timeline to watch the fade.

> **TIP** You can drag the playhead from the start of a clip to where you want the fade-in to end, and then in the Trim menu, choose Fade In to playhead.

Adjusting fade handles is a fast and easily accessed method for placing and refining fades-in and -out.

Adding Cross Dissolves

You can add the same transitions you applied in the Cut page. The Effects library includes all the same options. However, the method of applying the standard cross dissolve is different. The quickest way to add a cross-dissolve is through the menu option or keyboard short cut.

1 In the timeline, go to the third red marker.

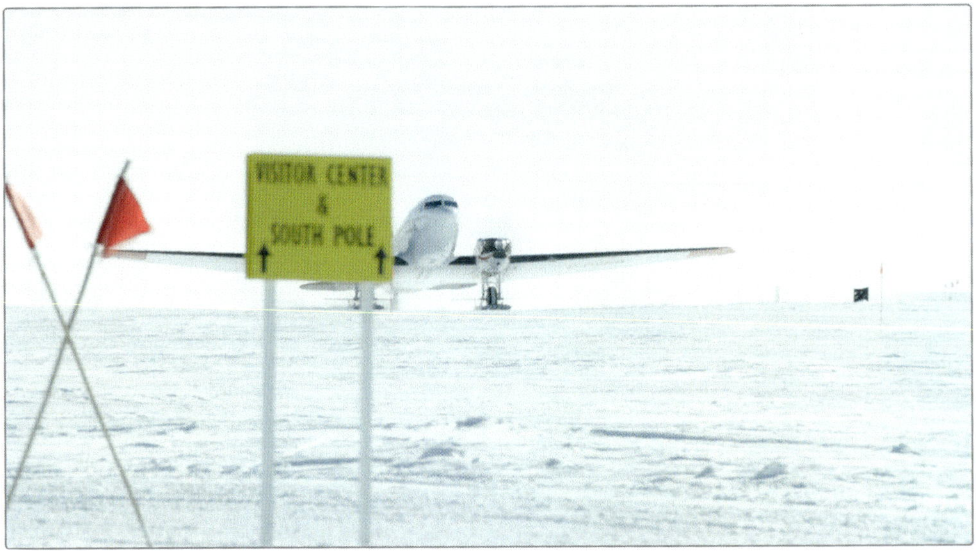

2 Play over 08_SOUTH_POLE_DC3 and the next clip, 07_KENYA.

You would like to blend these two clips softly into each other. To achieve this, you'll add the default cross dissolve transition.

3 Drag the zoom slider to zoom in to the clips you'll be working on.

> **TIP** You can hold down the middle mouse button to pan in the timeline.

4 As if you were going to perform a rolling trim, locate the mouse pointer directly over the edit between 08_SOUTH_POLE_DC3 and 07_KENYA.

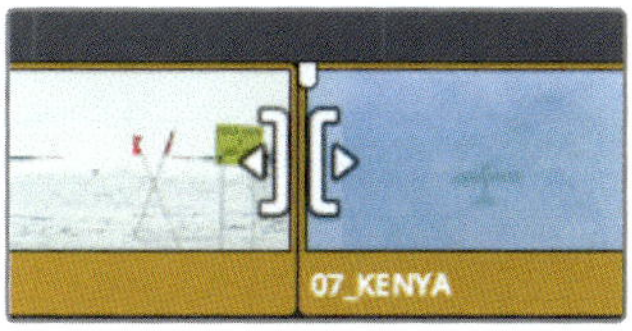

5 When the pointer changes to a rolling trim cursor, click the cut to select it.

The green rolling trim handles appear on both sides of the edit point.

6 Choose Timeline > Add Transition, or press Cmd-T (macOS) or Ctrl-T (Windows).

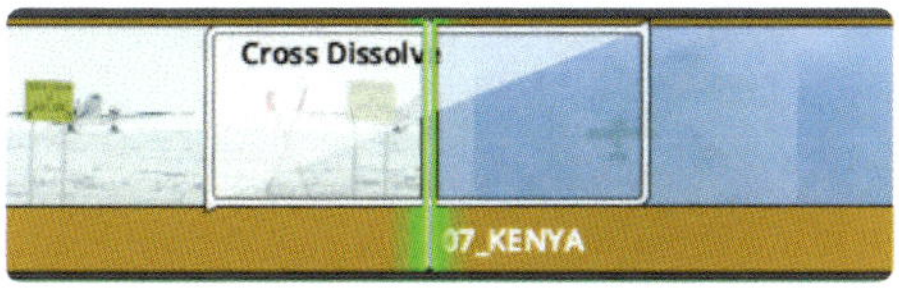

A dissolve with a one-second duration is added to the edit point.

TIP You can change the default transition duration in the editing category of the user preferences window.

When creating a transition, frames from the two clips will overlap. That is, half of the transition frames are taken from the unused portions of the outgoing clip and half from the incoming clip. These video handles, which you used for trimming in Lesson 6, are now used to extend clips to support the transition.

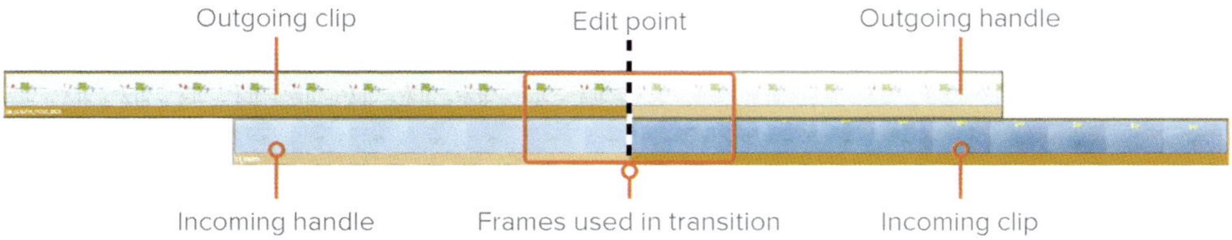

7 Play the two clips to view the dissolve.

TIP To remove a transition, zoom in and select it using the selection tool, and press Delete.

Shortening and Lengthening Transitions

Changing the duration of a transition can be done just like the Cut page, by dragging the transition directly in the timeline.

1 Place the mouse pointer over the right edge of the dissolve between 08_SOUTH_POLE_DC3 and 07_KENYA.

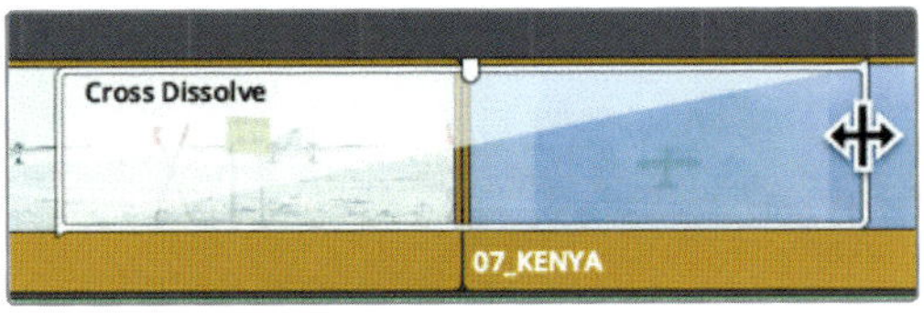

2 Drag the right edge in toward the edit until the tool tip reads -00:06.

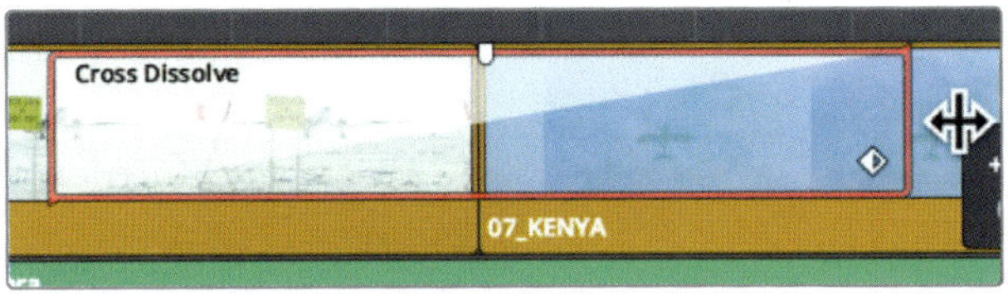

As you drag, the transition is shortened by six frames on both sides of the edit for a total decrease of 12 frames. This dissolve transition is aligned to the center of the cut, so the transition will remove the same number of frames on each side of the cut regardless of how short you make it. How long can you make a transition? That depends upon the length of the two source clips in the bin.

3 Drag the right edge away from the edit until the selected edit will not extend any further.

The transition can extend only so far because you will eventually run out of handles on one of the clips, which means that no more media is available to create a longer transition.

Customizing Transitions

Each transition has several adjustments that you can use to customize its appearance. Some of the simpler transitions, such as the cross dissolve, have fewer parameters than specialty transitions such as wipes. In every case, customization controls appear in the Inspector.

1 Double-click the Cross Dissolve transition in the timeline to open it in the Inspector.

> **TIP** If you are finding it difficult to select a transition, drag the zoom slider to zoom in on the timeline until you can select the transition icon without accidentally selecting the cut point.

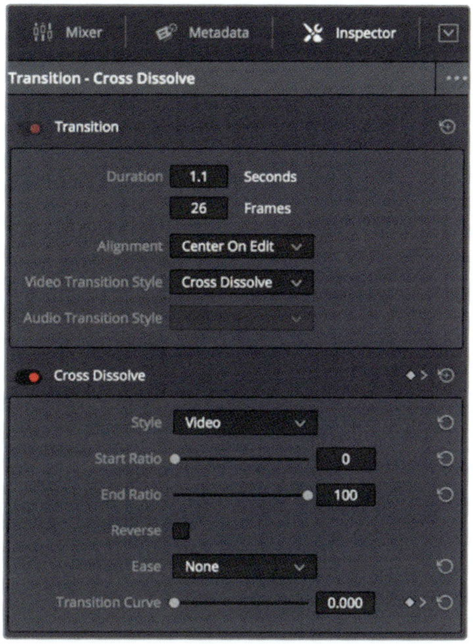

The Inspector displays the transition parameters. The upper half of the Inspector has parameters that are common to all transitions. These include Duration, Alignment, and Transition Style. The lower half has parameters specific to the current transition.

2 In the Alignment pop-up menu, choose Start On Edit.

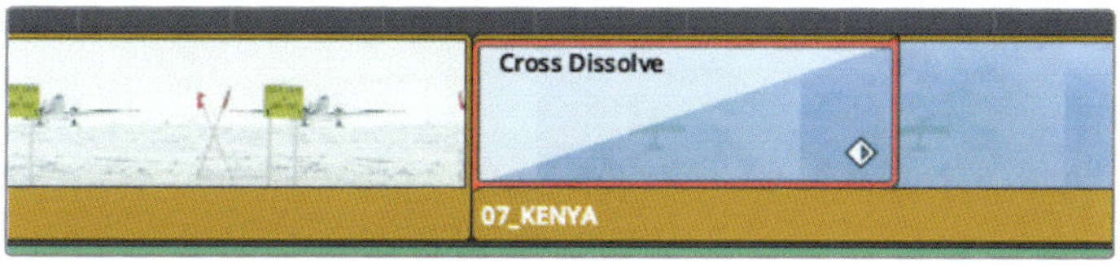

Previously, half of the dissolve's duration started before the edit point; now it begins at the edit point.

3 In the Cross Dissolve Style menu, choose Film.

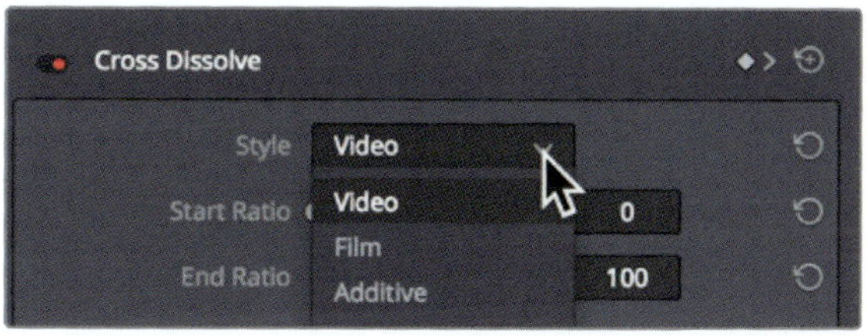

The Style menu allows you to choose from a variety of Cross Dissolve styles. The Film dissolve mimics the subtle luminance and acceleration response of a dissolve optically generated for film. You can further increase the acceleration curve by choosing an Ease In & Ease Out acceleration.

4 In the Ease menu, choose In & Out to create a smoother transition.

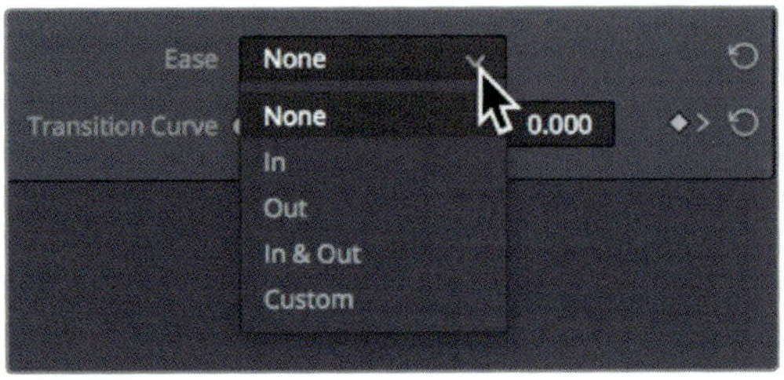

5 Play the modified Film Dissolve to view your changes.

Now that you have customized a transition, you'll learn how to save it for repeated use.

Saving Custom Presets

After customizing a transition, you can save that transition and its customizations into the Effects Library for use in future projects.

1 In the timeline, right-click the customized Cross Dissolve transition.

2 In the pop-up menu, choose Create Transition Preset.

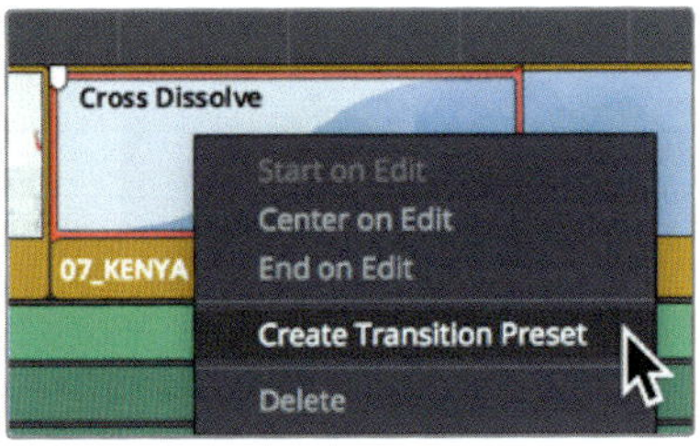

3 In the Transition Preset dialog, enter the name **Cinema Dissolve**, and click OK.

Saved presets are saved into the Effects Library.

4 In the upper-left area of the Interface toolbar, click the Effects Library button.

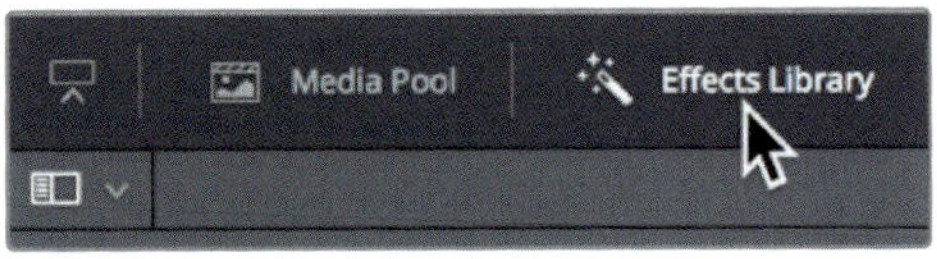

The Effects Library contains all transitions, titles, and filter effects. The categories along the left side make it easy to find the effect type you are looking for.

5 In the sidebar, select the Video Transitions category.

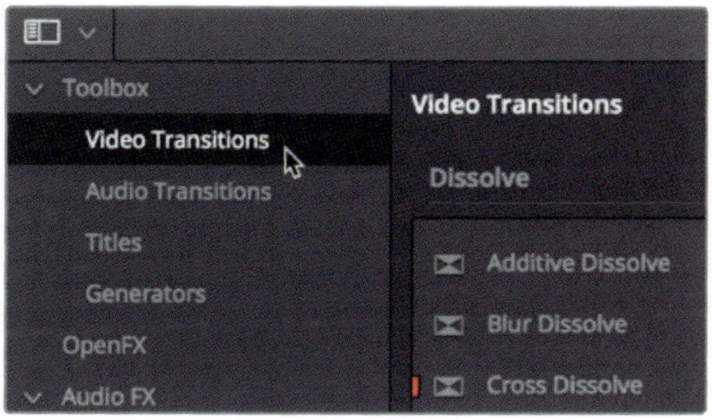

All custom presets are located at the bottom of the effects library in the User section. The icons are highlighted in yellow to make them easier to identify.

6 Scroll to the bottom of the Effects Library to locate your saved preset.

If your saved preset is something you plan on using as a signature transition throughout a program, you may want to save it as the standard transition. The standard transition has the benefit of being the transition that can be added from the Timeline > Add Transition menu or a keyboard shortcut.

7 In the Effects Library, right-click your saved preset, and choose Set As Standard Transition.

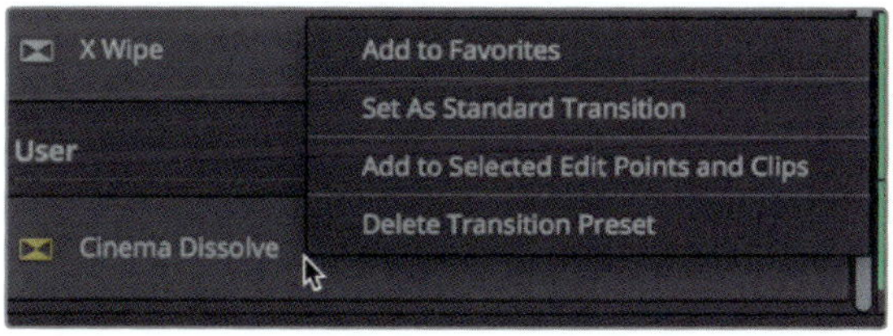

The new standard transition has a red tag to the left of its name to identify it as the standard transition. It is now the standard transition for all projects you create on this system.

Applying Transitions and Filters from the Effects Library

Like the Cut page, the edit page includes many types of transitions, each with a unique visual style. Other transitions may not be as useful storytelling tools as the dissolve, but they can be handy in specific situations. Because other transitions are not as commonly used, you add them directly from the Effects Library and not by using a keyboard shortcut.

1 Scroll to the top of the Effects Library.

2 From the Effects Library, drag the Blur Dissolve transition over the existing cross dissolve in the timeline.

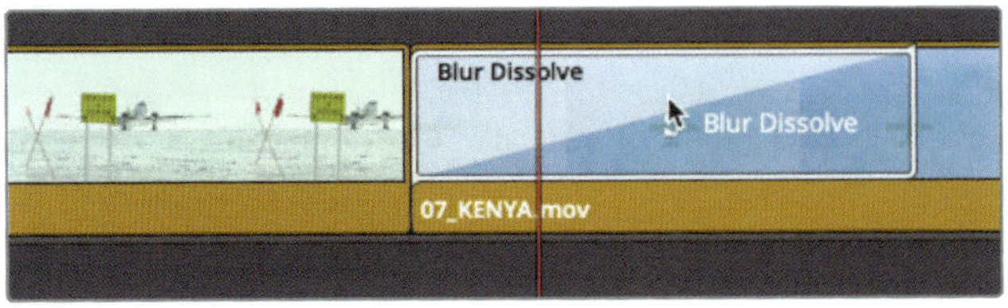

3 Release the mouse button to replace the cross dissolve with the blur dissolve.

The blur dissolve combines a cross dissolve with a horizontal or vertical blur.

4 Play the timeline to view the blur dissolve.

The Inspector has specific controls for each wipe or transition effect you apply.

Applying Filter Effects

The Effects Library also holds filter effects that you can use to create unique visual effects or to solve common visual problems.

1 Press Shift-Z to see the entire timeline.

2 Press Shift-down arrow until you are on the last red marker on the **05_BAY_AREA_LIGHTS** clip.

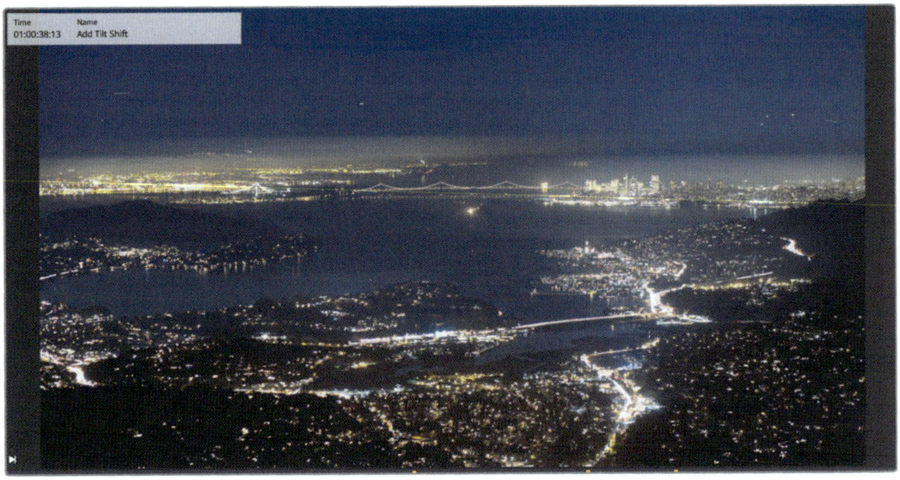

This clip appears a little flat and would look nicer if it were shot with a tilt-shift lens. Luckily, DaVinci Resolve has a built-in Tilt-Shift Blur filter to simulate just such a lens.

3 At the top of the Effects Library click the search button.

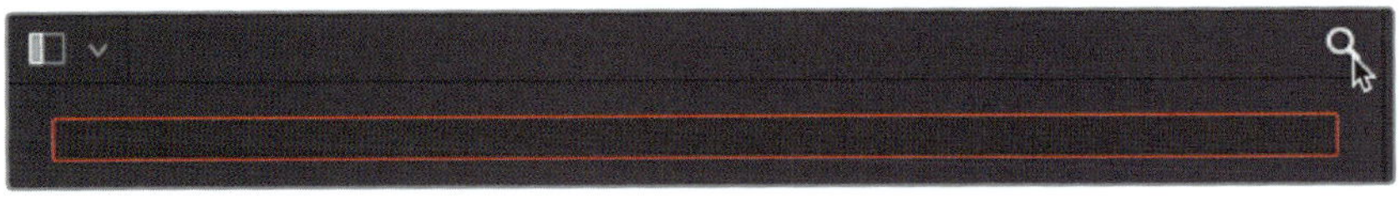

4 In the sidebar category list, select OpenFX, and in the search field, type **Tilt**.

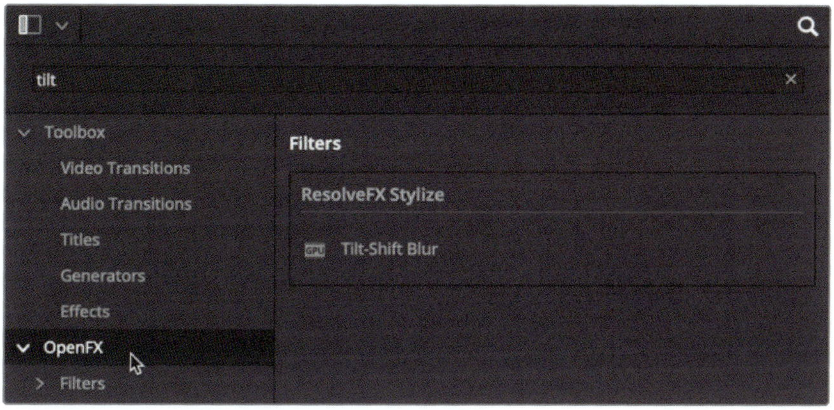

5 Drag the Tilt-Shift Blur filter onto the 05_BAY AREA LIGHTS clip in the timeline.

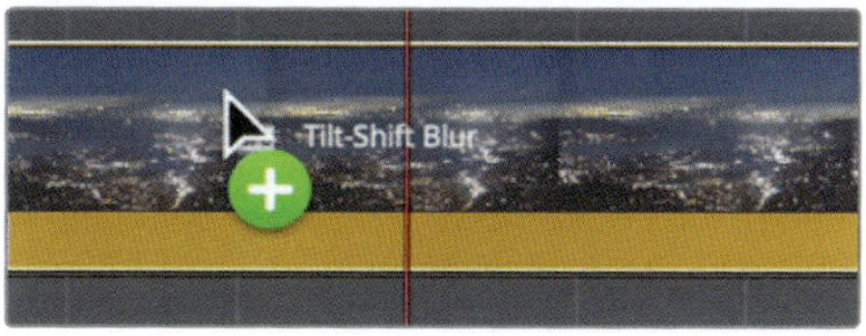

The Tilt-Shift Blur filter is added; but if you are using the free version of DaVinci Resolve, a dialog box indicates that this effect is available only in the Studio version.

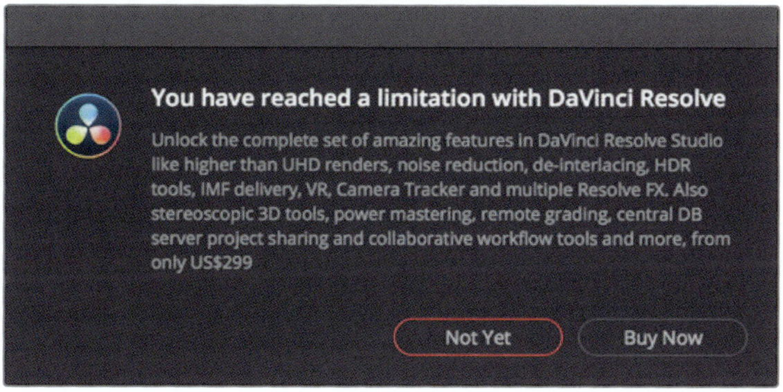

However, you can still try it out without upgrading, although the results will include a watermark.

6 Click Not Yet to continue. You have many parameters available in the Inspector to customize its look.

7 In the timeline, select the 05 BAY AREA LIGHTS clip, and then click the Inspector button in the upper-right corner of the interface.

When a filter effect is applied to a clip, the Inspector will display an OpenFX tab next to the standard Video tab.

8 At the top of the Inspector, click the OpenFX tab.

TIP To reset a single parameter or the entire effect, click the circular Reset button to the right of the Inspector.

You can quickly compare the filtered shot to the original by disabling the effect in the Inspector.

9 At the top of the Inspector, click the Disable button to the left of the filter effect's name. Click it again to enable the effect.

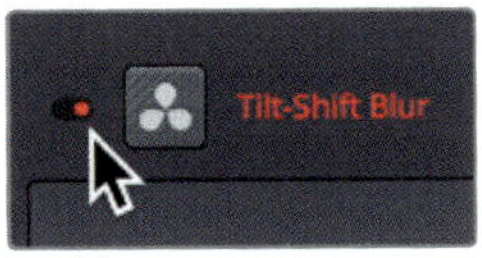

If you are using the free version of DaVinci Resolve, you can remove this effect from the timeline.

10 Click the trash can icon at the top of the Inspector.

Effect choices are neither right or wrong. You can use as many or as few as you think you need to tell your story. The only potential wrong is the end result. You must always ask yourself if an effect helps set the right mood or atmosphere for the story. Does it help to steer audience attention in the right direction? If the answer is yes, then try it. Ultimately, it is your own aesthetic that will help you decide.

Using third-party effect plug-ins

OpenFX is a cross-platform visual effects plug-in standard used byDaVinci Resolve and Fusion software as well as other applications. Popular plug-in packages—such as Boris FX Continuum, Red Giant Universe, and Re:vision Effects' ReelSmart Motion blur can be added to DaVinci Resolve to perform many stylized operations that would be otherwise difficult or impossible to perform using only DaVinci Resolve's standard tools. These plug-ins can be applied in exactly the same ways you would apply other items from the Effects Library.

The installation and licensing of plug-ins is managed by each vendor's installer. Once installed, OpenFX plug-ins appear in the Effects Library and in the OpenFX category.

Reframing Shots

Most of the time, you're going to be editing high-definition (HD) or maybe ultra high-definition (UHD) projects that use a 16×9 aspect ratio. But sometimes you'll need (or want) to edit and view your program using a different aspect ratio. You can do so using the output blanking menu.

1 Choose Timeline > Output Blanking > 2.39.

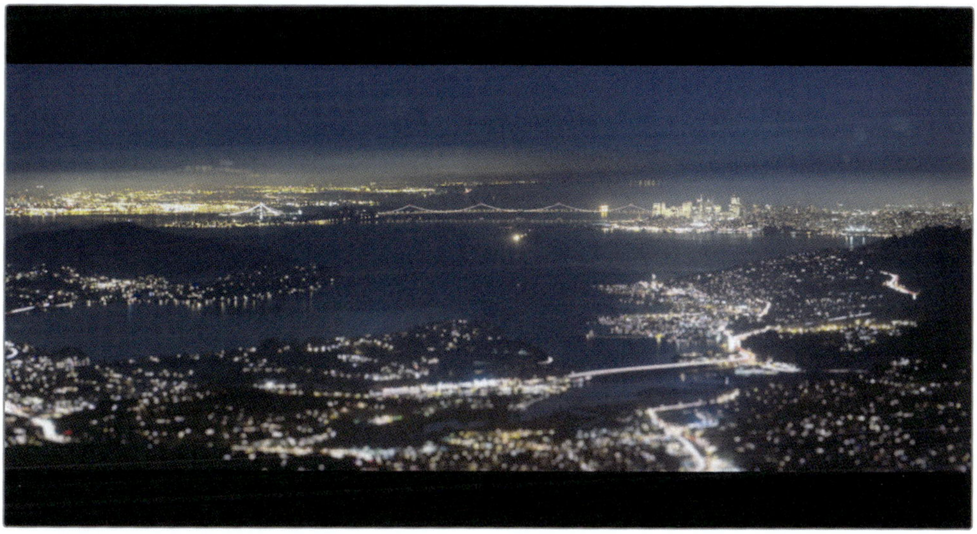

The aspect ratio of 2.39:1, which is used for 35mm theatrical widescreen, is applied in the viewer.

> **TIP** The controls used by the output blanking menu to create masks are located on the Color page in the sizing palette's output sizing mode.

When you apply output blanking, it does not remove the hidden part of the clip, it just covers it up which allows you to reframe clips to better fit the new aspect ratio.

2 Move the playhead over the first interview shot, and in the timeline, select the clip.

The Inspector now shows the video tab controls for the selected clip. These controls include typical parameters for Zoom, Position, Rotation Angle, and Crop.

You can move your subject down in the viewer to give him more head room and make a more pleasing composition.

3 Hover the mouse pointer over the Position Y numeric field.

Any numeric field can be used as a virtual slider just by dragging within the field.

4 In the Y Position numeric field, drag to the left until the value shows -50.00.

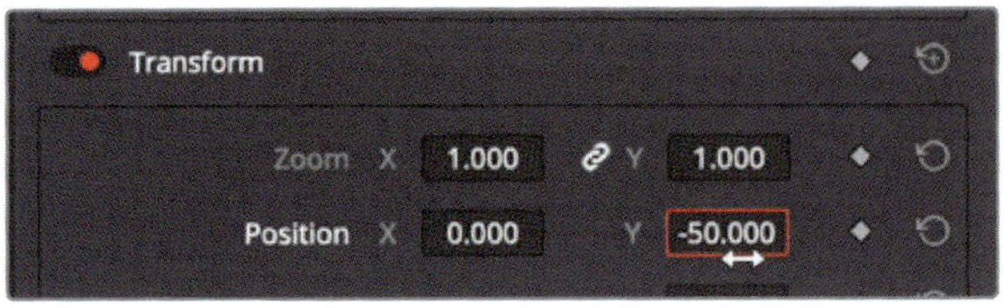

This is better positioning for the subject. You'll have to copy this to the remaining interview shots.

5 Choose Edit > Copy, or press Cmd-C (macOS) or Ctrl-C (Windows).

6 From the timeline menu choose Select clips with Clip Color > Navy. This will select all the interview clips in the timeline since previously in lesson 4, we color coded those clips navy.

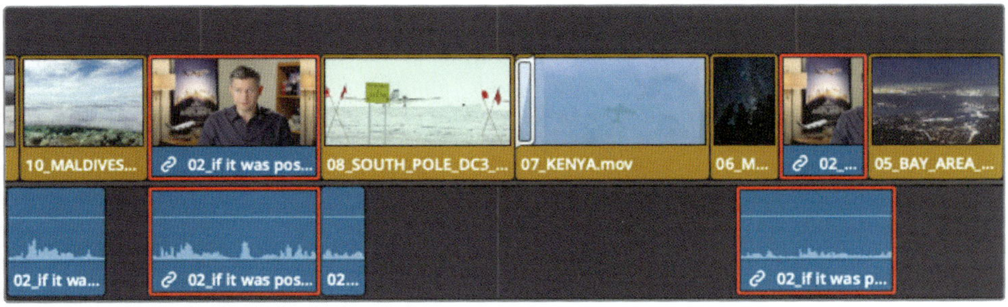

7 Choose Edit > Paste Attributes, or press Option-V (macOS) or Alt-V (Windows), to open the Paste Attributes window.

8 In the Video Attributes category, select the Position checkbox, and click Apply.

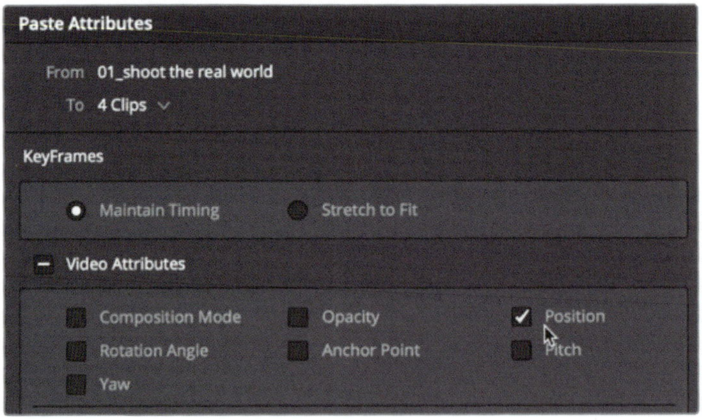

This reposition value applied to the first interview clip is pasted onto the selected interview clips.

TIP Another way to copy and paste effects is to use adjustment clips from the Effects Library. Place an adjustment clip above clips on a new track on the timeline, add an effect to the adjustment clip, and then re-use it over any other clips you want. Any effect on the Adjustment clip is applied to all clips below it in the timeline

Using Onscreen Controls

You can apply common transform operations such as position, scale, and rotation using onscreen controls in the viewer, rather than dragging virtual sliders in the Inspector. Let's reframe a shot by resizing it in the viewer.

1 Press Shift-down arrow to go to the last red marker on the **05_BAY_AREA LIGHTS** clip.

  This is the last clip before your credits, so to indicate that you are bringing this trailer to a close, let's simulate the camera pulling back and away from the scene. First, you'll use the onscreen control to resize the clip a bit larger.

2 In the timeline, select the first half of the **05 BAY AREA LIGHTS** clip, and move the playhead over it to see the clip in the viewer.

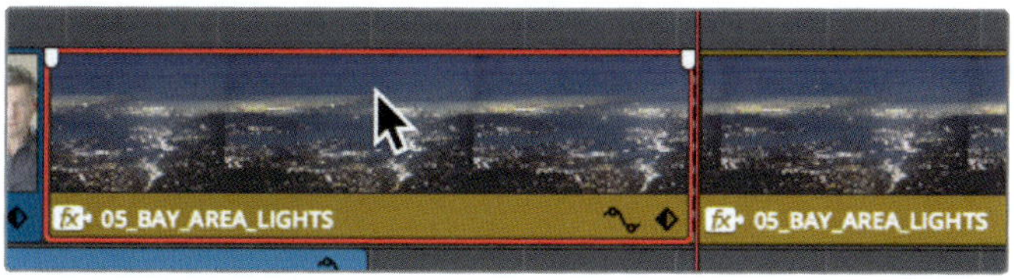

3 In the lower-left corner of the viewer, click the timeline viewer pop-up menu, and choose Transform.

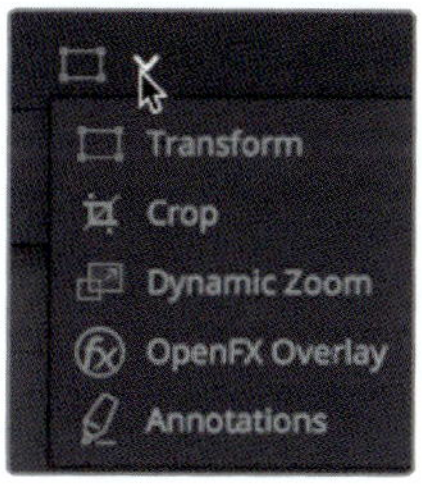

  A bounding rectangle appears in the viewer to show the size and position of the frame.

4 To scale the clip, drag a handle in any corner of the bounding box away from the center until the zoom value shows 1.200.

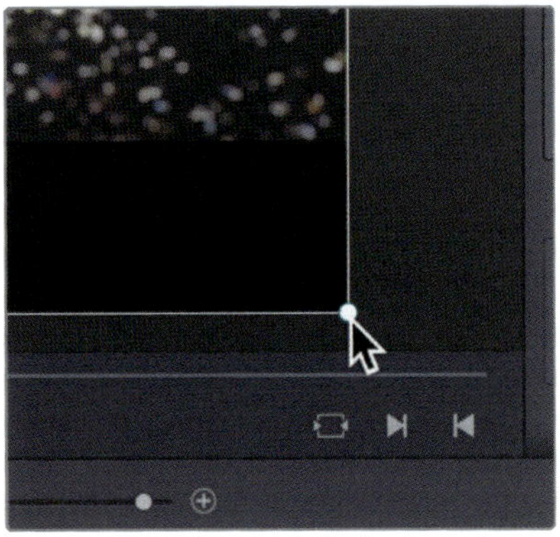

By default, the zoom X and Y values are linked together so the clip is resized equally in X and Y, thereby keeping its normal aspect ratio.

> **TIP** In the magnification menu (in the upper-left of the viewer) you can change how the frame is sized in the viewer.

5 In the lower-left corner of the viewer, click the transform rectangle to hide the onscreen controls.

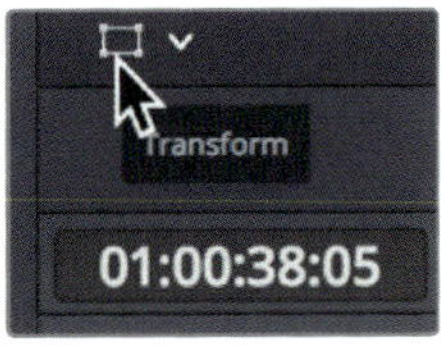

Animating a Resize

Almost every parameter displayed in the Inspector can be animated over time by setting two keyframes. You'll use the current resized frame as the starting keyframe, and then set a new keyframe at the end of the clip.

1 Move the playhead to the start of the **05 BAY AREA LIGHTS** clip.

2 Select the clip to display the controls in the Inspector.

Animating the parameters of an image over time requires that you set keyframes. Keyframes allow you to assign different parameter values to specific frames. DaVinci Resolve then interpolates between the two values to create a smooth animation.

You have already scaled the clip up so now you must position the playhead where you want to scale down the clip.

3 Position the playhead about one-third of the way into the **05 BAY AREA LIGHTS** clip.

Here is where you'll start to scale down the frame, so you'll need to add a keyframe.

4 In the Inspector, click the zoom keyframe button to the right of the Zoom X and Y numeric fields.

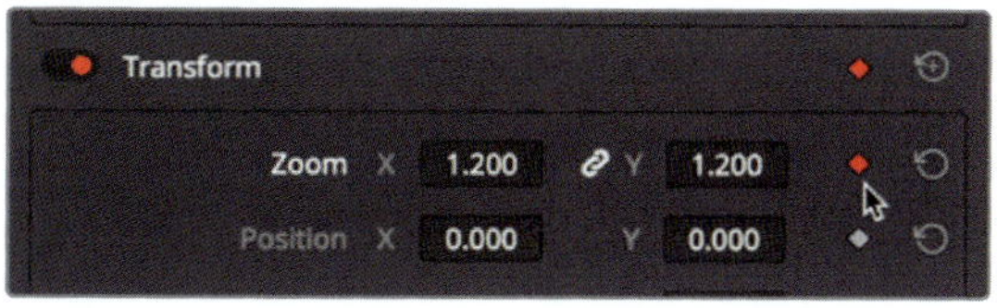

Animating a parameter requires that you set at least two values for it on separate frames. The first keyframe that signifies the start of the animation is now set. You'll set the second value where you want the image to stop scaling.

5 In the timeline, position the playhead about one-third of the way from the end of the **05 BAY AREA LIGHTS** clip.

DaVinci Resolve uses an auto-keyframe model. When a parameter already has one keyframe set, changing the position of the playhead, and then modifying the parameter, automatically adds a second keyframe.

6 Place the cursor over the Zoom X numeric field, and drag to the right until the value is reset to 1.0.

TIP You can double click the parameter name to reset the value to its default.

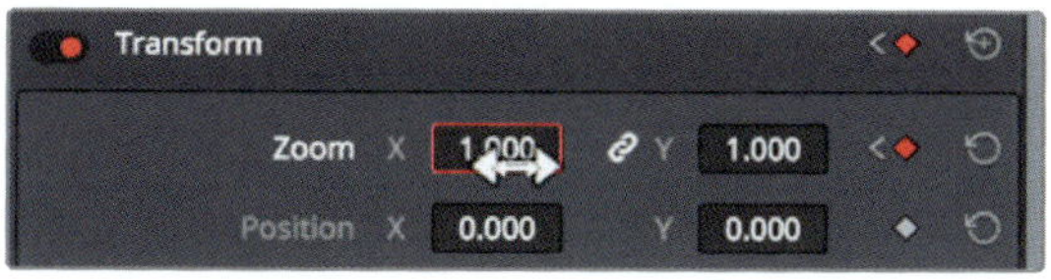

7 Press the / (slash) key to play around the currently selected clip.

You can further control the keyframe position and smoothness of the motion using the ease-in/ease-out commands and the keyframe editor.

8 In the inspector click the go to next keyframe button.

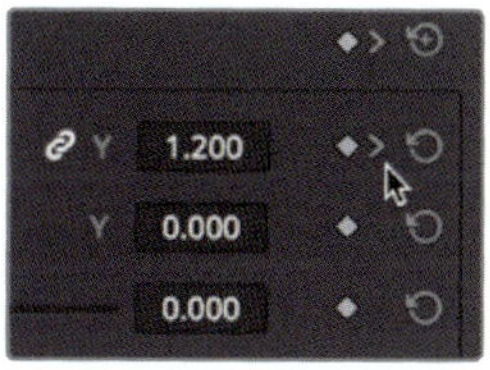

The go to next or previous keyframe icons appear when keyframes have been added to a control. Clicking the button moves the playhead to the keyframe position.

9 Right click over the red diamond keyframe icon and choose ease out.

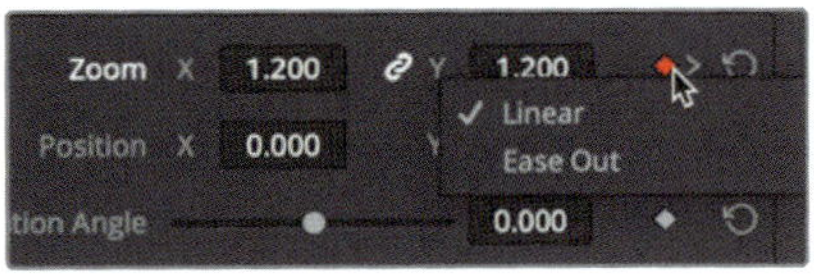

This will smooth the motion as the animation starts.

10 Click the go to next keyframe button to jump to the last keyframe.

11 Right click over the red diamond keyframe icon and choose ease in.

This will smooth the motion as the animation ends. Now, we can adjust timing of the animation as well.

12 Zoom into the timeline to see the **05 BAY AREA LIGHTS** clip clearly.

13 With the clip still selected, in the lower-right corner of the timeline segment, click the diamond-shaped keyframe button.

The keyframe tracks include small white dots that represent each keyframe. Dragging these white dots will change the position of those keyframes.

14 Select the last white keyframe in the keyframe editor and drag it slightly to the right to extend the animation.

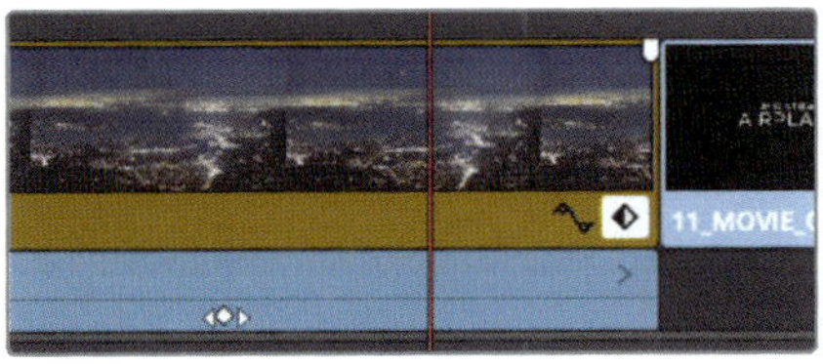

15 Click the keyframe button to close both keyframe displays.

16 Press the / (slash) key to play around the currently selected clip.

Rendering and Background Caching

Depending on the speed of your computer and disk drives, as well as the media file types you are using, all effects may not play back smoothly on your computer. The fps (frames per second) indicator above the timeline viewer shows the actual playback framerate that your computer is achieving. If the number has a red dot next to it, your system is playing your project slower than the actual project frame rate.

To optimize playback performance for complex effects, DaVinci Resolve can automatically render and cache such effects to your disk drive. Although DaVinci Resolve can use three distinct caching systems to render files, this exercise will focus on smart caching for the Edit page.

The first task is to make sure caching is turned on.

1. Choose Playback > Render Cache> Smart.

   The smart cache operates on timeline-specific effects such as transitions, opacity adjustments, and composite mode superimpositions. Regions of the timeline that require caching have a red bar over them, whereas regions that are already cached have a blue bar over them.

   All of this is easy enough, but you have additional settings to customize the caching operation.

2. Choose File > Project settings > Master settings.

   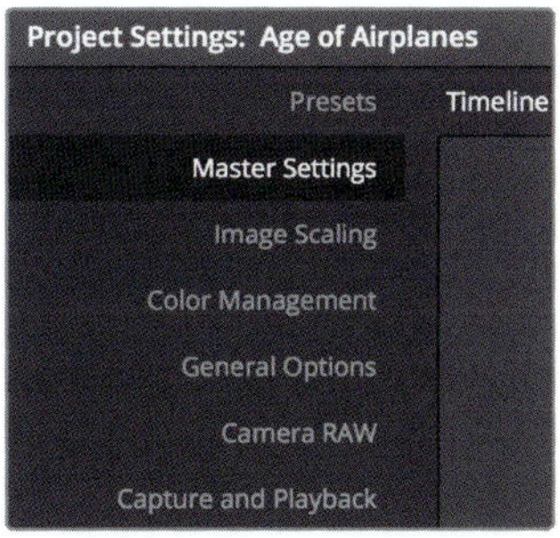

   Master settings include a few Optimized Media settings related to caching. The "Cache frames in" menu sets the compression format that DaVinci Resolve uses to save the rendered files. The choices common to macOS and Windows include uncompressed 10-bit and 8-bit formats, and Avid's DNxHR formats. In macOS, DaVinci Resolve also includes Apple's ProRes compression format.

   The default setting creates a high-quality 10-bit file that will look good in your final output. If you are temporarily working on a portable or a laptop with a slow disk drive, you may want to opt for a marginally lower-quality 8-bit format such as Avid DNxHR HQ or ProRes 422 to enable faster processing. For now, you'll leave this setting at the default value and move on to background processing.

3. Make sure "Enable background caching" is selected.

   When background caching is enabled, effects rendering begins based on the length of time your computer sits idle.

4. In the "Enable background caching" numeric box, enter **3**.

   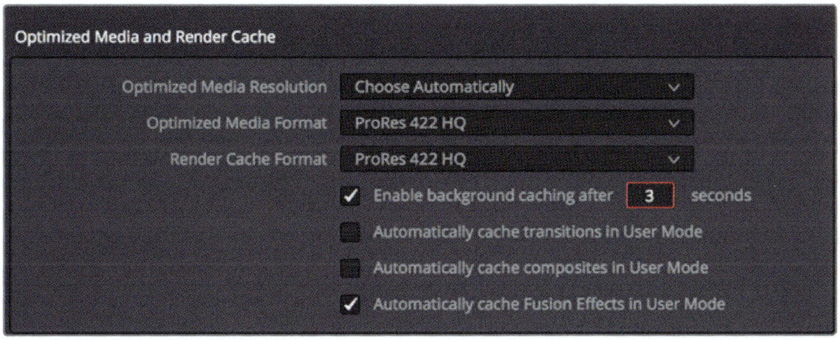

Background caching will now begin to render effects after your computer sits idle for three seconds.

TIP To delete all of the rendered cache files for the current project, choose Playback > Delete Render Cache > All.

Now that your smart caching is set, DaVinci Resolve will automatically render everything necessary to optimize playback for your effects. When you reopen a project, cached clips are still cached; but when you change any cached effect, it will need to be re-cached.

Creating a Constant Speed Change

Changing the playback speed of a clip is done for a variety of reasons. Sometimes it's used to accentuate dramatic action, and sometimes it's used so the timing of a clip fits into a scene. In almost every production genre, you'll have a need to speed up clips, slow them down, and even stop and hold on a frame for a few seconds.

The most common type of speed change is a constant speed change. It uniformly alters the playback of a clip in the timeline to turn it into a slow-motion clip or a fast-motion clip of a single framerate.

1 In the timeline, position the playhead at the start of the 06_MILKYWAY clip.

2 Play over the clip (always a good idea before you change its speed.)

   This clip goes on a bit too fast for a shot of the nighttime sky. You want to slow the speed but not change its duration in the timeline.

3 Select 06_MILKYWAY. Right-click the clip, and in the pop-up menu, choose Change Clip Speed.

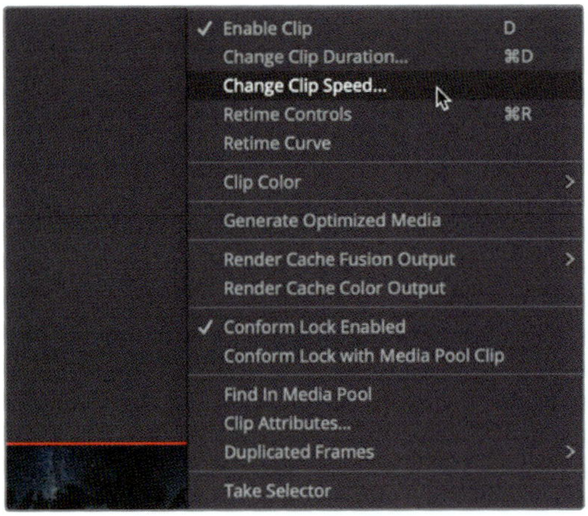

The Change Clip Speed dialog appears with a number of controls for clip playback.

4 In the Speed numeric field, enter **50**, and click Change to close the dialog.

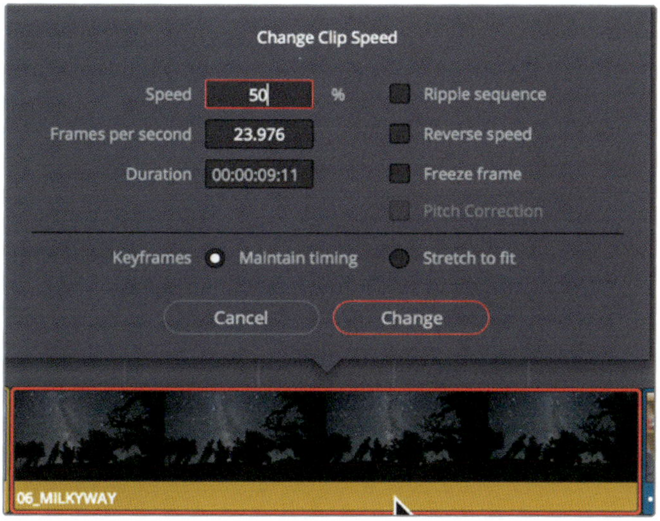

Setting this value to 50% means that the clip will play at half the timeline frame rate — in this case, 12 frames per second. To indicate that the clip's playback speed has been changed, a small speed change icon is displayed next to the clip's name in the timeline.

5 Play the clip to see the speed change results.

When creating a slow-motion clip, the default settings in the Change Clip Speed dialog do not change the overall duration of the clip or the timeline. However, DaVinci Resolve does have tools that allow you to modify the speed of a clip by changing its duration.

Retiming using the Selection and Trim Tools

While the Change Clip Speed dialog creates constant speed changes and retains the clip duration, the retime controls stretch and shrink a clip's duration by slowing it down and speeding it up.

1 Right-click the **06_MILKYWAY** clip, and in the pop-up menu, choose Retime Controls, or press Cmd-R (macOS) or Ctrl-R (Windows).

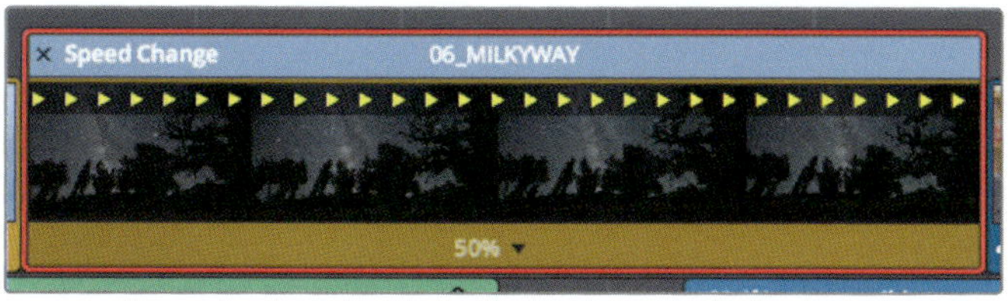

The Speed Change bar appears at the top of the clip in the timeline. The current speed of the clip is listed along the bottom. The speed of a clip is altered by trimming the Speed Change bar in the timeline.

2 In the toolbar, select the trim tool, or press T.

3 Move the pointer to the right edge of the Speed Change bar.

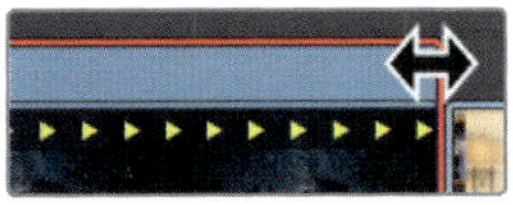

The pointer turns into a double-arrow cursor.

4 Drag the edge of the Speed Change bar to the right to lengthen the clip until the speed display at the bottom of the clip reads 40%.

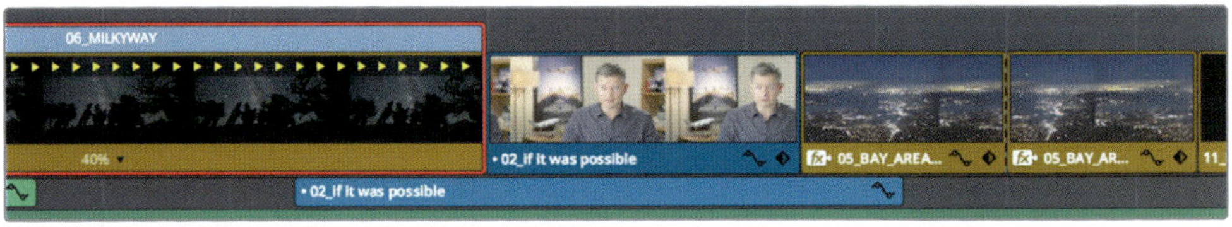

Dragging the Speed Change bar to the left extends the duration of the clip by slowing down its playback speed. When the trim tool is selected, the Speed Change bar ripples the remaining clips in the timeline. However, if you undo that last step, you can see how the same trimming feature can change depending upon which tool is selected in the toolbar.

5 Press Cmd-Z (macOS) or Ctrl-Z (Windows) to undo the previous speed change.

6 In the toolbar, click the Selection mode tool, or press A.

7 Move the pointer to the right edge of the Speed Change bar, and drag to the right until the clip completely overwrites the incoming interview clip.

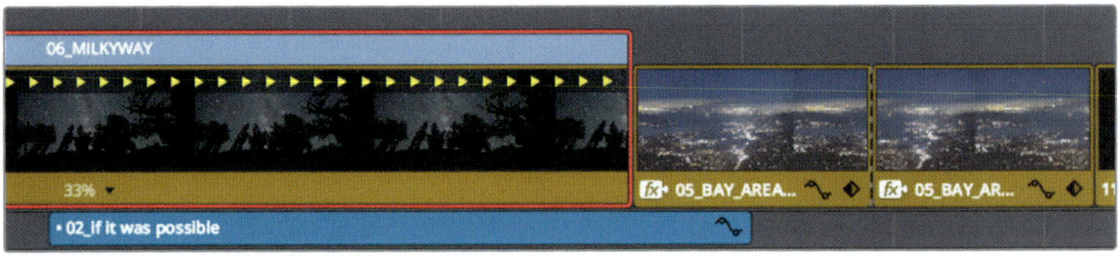

8 Play the retimed clip to see the results.

> **TIP** To return a clip to its original speed, click the clip speed pop-up menu at the bottom of the clip, and choose "Reset to 100%".

With the trim tool selected, the timeline is rippled, thereby pushing the rest of the clips to the right. The clip's duration and the overall timeline duration are extended.

Reversing a Clip

When the retime controls are displayed, you have the option of using a pop-up menu at the bottom of the clip to change the speed instead of trimming it using the Speed Change bar.

1 At the bottom of the 06_MILKYWAY clip, click the retime pop-up menu.

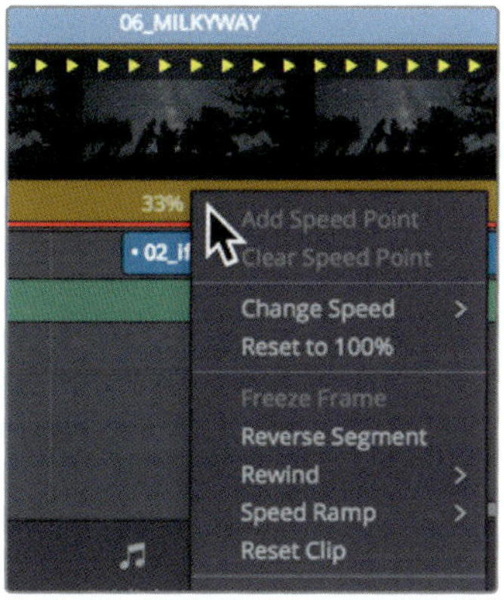

This menu includes options for common slow and fast speeds, as well as the ability to set speed points for variable retiming. Still other options allow you to reset or reverse the playback.

2 In the menu, choose Reverse Segment.

3 Play the retimed clip to see the results.

The clip now plays in the reverse direction at the same speed.

Changing Retime Processing

You can change the way a retimed clip is processed, and thereby change the way it looks. The various retime processing settings located in the Inspector trade speed for quality. Which you choose will depend on the type of movement in your shot and how much processing time you are willing to allow.

1 Select the retimed 06_MILKYWAY clip.

2 Open the Inspector.

3 Scroll to the bottom of the Inspector.

4 Click the Retime Process menu to open it.

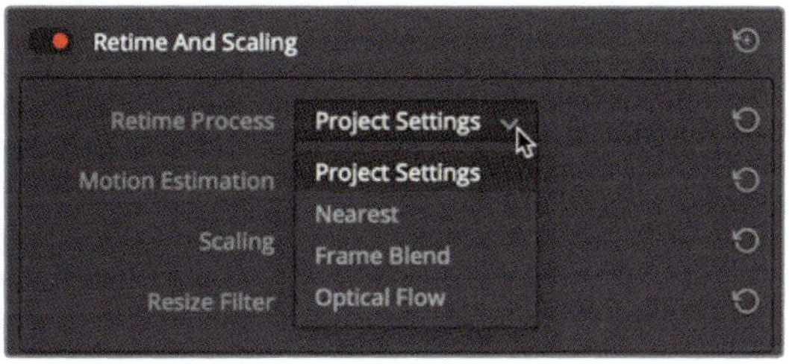

You have three options for processing clip retiming: Nearest, Frame Blend, and Optical Flow.

- Nearest is the fastest processing option but delivers the lowest-quality results. This simple operation duplicates frames to create slow motion which often causes stepping artifacts even in clips that have just a moderate amount of movement. Nearest is the default option set on the Master settings of the project settings.
- Frame Blend is a slightly more processor-intensive option that delivers better-looking results. It also duplicates frames to create slow motion, but then blends them to produce smoother motion. This is the most reliable option and generally delivers acceptable results.
- Optical Flow is the most processor-intensive and highest-quality process. It uses motion estimation and warping techniques to generate new frames from the original source frames. The results can be exceptionally smooth when the motion in a clip is unobstructed. However, if two moving elements cross while moving in different directions (such as legs crossing when walking) or the camera movement is erratic, optical flow processing can cause stretching and tearing artifacts.

> **TIP** The motion estimation pop up menu in includes options that can sometimes improve small tears or stretching artifacts caused by Optical flow.

5. In the menu, choose Optical Flow.

   When Optical Flow is selected, a red bar appears above the clip to indicate that the process needs to cache. If smart caching is enabled, the rendering will be performed in the background and you'll be able to see the results in a few seconds.

6. When the clip is cached, play over the optical flow results to see the smoother motion.

It's a good idea to first try Optical Flow processing to see if it produces acceptable results, and then revert to Frame Blend, as necessary. Optical Flow, unlike the other retime processing types, *requires* that you cache the result.

Lesson Review

1 Why would you be unable to drag a transition to extend its duration in the Edit page timeline?

2 How do you save a custom transition preset?

3 True or false? You set up and enable background caching in the Inspector.

4 What is the minimum number of keyframes required for an animation of the position parameter?

5 If you wanted to change the speed of a clip, what's the difference between using "Change Clip Speed" or "Retime Controls?"

Answers

1. If no media handles are available on either side of the transition, you will not be able to drag the transition to extend its duration.
2. To save a custom transition preset, right-click the tratnsition on the timeline, and choose Create Transition Preset.
3. False. Background caching is set up and enabled in the Project settings.
4. Two keyframes are needed at two different clip locations and of two different values to create an animation.
5. Choosing Change Clip Speed opens a dialog in which you can type specific speed values. Once set, the clip duration remains the same in the timeline while playing back at a different speed. The Retime Controls provide a speed bar above the clip in the timeline, and dragging the speed bar speeds up or slows down the clip by changing its duration.

An Introduction to Audio Post and Sound Design

Chances are you've heard the adages "Seeing is believing" and "A picture is worth a thousand words." However, when it comes to motion pictures, both the visuals and soundtrack are equally important. In fact, a great soundtrack sells the onscreen illusion, manipulates emotions, transports the audience into the scene and captivates their imagination. A lousy soundtrack, on the other hand, keeps the audience at a distance, distracts from the story, and draws attention to production flaws, performance issues, and plot holes.

Audio post production is much more than simply adjusting volume levels and mixing tracks. Transforming production sound into a powerful soundtrack requires time, technical skill, creative vision and execution, as well as a full set of professional audio tools. The good news is that DaVinci Resolve 16 includes the tools to create a professional soundtrack from start to finish. Before you dive into the following audio chapters, it's a good idea to understand the audio post production process and workflow.

Keep in mind that many elements affect the workflow you'll use: the type of project, budget, format, length, deliverables and distribution methods often dictate the size of the post audio team, amount of time, and tools available to get the job done. For this introduction, let's focus on the fundamental post production audio processes necessary for both narrative and documentary style projects. Although the following pages explain the different jobs and stages in audio post production, having the Fairlight page built into DaVinci Resolve means you can perform the same steps on your projects with no additional crew or budget.

What is Audio Post Production?

Let's start with a few basic terms. **Audio post production** refers to the process of making a soundtrack for moving images. Notice the use of "moving images," which encompasses all projects great and small from movie theaters to streaming videos and everything in-between. A **soundtrack** is simply the audio that accompanies a finished project.

How your audience experiences the finished project is greatly influenced by the soundtrack. In fact, a well executed soundtrack may go unnoticed for hours by the audience while it is immersed in show. On the other hand, it takes only a few seconds of an amateurish or sloppy soundtrack to lose the audience not only from the story, but possibly from the theater or to a different channel.

If you've ever recorded or watched a home movie, especially one shot at an exciting public place such as the beach or an amusement park, then you've got first hand experience with some of the inherent challenges in both recording and listening to natural production sound. All those excess environmental sounds and distractions create a need for audio post production to transform raw sound into successful soundtracks with clear dialogue, realistic effects, and lush acoustic soundscapes wrapped in an emotionally powerful score.

What is the Audio Post Production Workflow?

Since the advent of synced sound in motion pictures, the first rule of audio post has been, "Never start working on audio until the picture is locked." Locked suggests that there will be no more changes to the picture edit from this point forward.

In reality, changes always happen. Why does this matter? Because, soundtracks need to maintain a frame accurate relationship with the picture to stay in sync. If they are off by as little as one or two frames, the sight and sound will be noticeably out of sync, a situation that is distracting, unprofessional and likely to lose your audience.

In a traditional post production workflow, changes to locked picture have a cascading snowball effect on audio post. But when you're working with DaVinci Resolve, which is the only professional editing software that includes a full digital audio workstation (DAW), no matter what editing changes are made, you can update your project immediately and efficiently. This gives you tremendous creative flexibility if you are working on your own, because you can go back and forth between editing picture, audio work and color correction as often as needed.

For larger productions, DaVinci Resolve solves the issue of updating, transferring files to other systems, and conforming projects between editorial and audio post because editing and audio post production are done in the same project without ever leaving the application. Best of all, audio post production can start on the exact same timeline that the editor used so you have zero chance of losing frames or going out of sync. Once audio post begins, the editor can use a duplicate timeline to make any new changes. Then the audio editor can easily merge the changes between timelines with DaVinci Resolve's powerful timeline comparison tool.

DaVinci Resolve has the audio tools needed for the highest quality audio post production, and is ideal for small projects yet powerful enough for big Hollywood studios and broadcast productions to use as well. Whether you are working on your own or with a large post production team, you can easily migrate projects to a large facility for experienced audio sound designers and engineers to mix and master the soundtrack.

Now let's break down the different phases and jobs in a traditional audio post production workflow. With DaVinci Resolve you can perform all of these steps as needed by yourself or with a team of audio professionals on your own projects.

Spotting the Soundtrack

A **spotting session** is when the supervising sound editor and the sound designer (often the same person) sit down with the director, editor and composer to look for soundtrack elements that need to be added, fixed or re-recorded. Notes from a spotting session are combined into a spotting list that details music cues, important sound effects, dialogue fixes, and additional audio notes.

DaVinci Resolve has simplified these spotting sessions with the timeline markers that you can use in either the Edit page or Fairlight page. The marker index in the Fairlight page serves as an interactive spotting list, that not only includes information and a thumbnail for each marker, but also moves the playhead to the selected markers position in the timeline.

Production Dialogue Editing

Dialogue editing is the tedious behind the scenes task of splitting dialogue into separate tracks, removing unwanted sounds, replacing individual words or phrases for clarity and balancing separate clip audio levels for consistency. Why go to all that trouble? Because spoken words are as important to a soundtrack as the lead vocals in a hit song. Keep in mind that dialogue editors are responsible for all spoken words including dialogue, narration, and voice over.

Production dialogue editing starts with creating separate tracks for each character, then moving all of those dialogue clips into a specific track. This crucial step is necessary because each voice in a production is different and, therefore, needs to be processed individually with volume normalization, equalization, and effects specific to that voice.

Next, the dialogue editor cleans up the tracks and removes any unwanted human sounds (like tongue clicks and lip smacks). If a distracting sound can be physically cut out, this is the time to do it. Plug-ins and effects can help eliminate unwanted clicks, pops, and noise automatically; but be aware that any processing you add to a clip, can affect a voice, as well.

After the dialogue is cleaned up, the volume levels are balanced to be consistent on each dialogue track. If dialogue can't be used because it is damaged, noisy, or unclear, it must be replaced with audio from other takes or re-recorded. The process of re-recording production dialogue is called **automatic dialogue replacemen**t (ADR) or **looping**.

Dialogue editing can be time consuming and laborious. Once again, DaVinci Resolve includes easy navigation, precision editing tools and shortcuts that can simplify and speed up the process.

Sound Design and Sound Effects Editing

Once the dialogue editing is finished, the creative process begins! The sound designer's creative input to the soundtrack is similar to that of the director of photography for the picture. Sound designers are responsible for the overall acoustic experience for the audience. They also oversee the many individual tracks of sound and music that comprise the soundtrack. These audio tracks include dialogue, ambience, hard sound effects, and foley sounds.

Not only do sound designers determine the aural illusion and mood of the soundtrack, they also create, record, and enhance sound elements that only exist in their imaginations. After all, many projects need sound effects that don't exist in the real world. Where do you go to record dragons, aliens, or zombies? Those sounds must be created or designed from scratch using a combination of real sounds, simulated sounds, and a lot of processing and effects.

While the sound designer determines the depth and detail of the sound effects tracks, the sound effects editor places each sound effect in corresponding tracks. Sound effects fall into four main categories:

Natural sound, also known as **Nat sound** or **production sound**, is anything other than dialogue recorded by a microphone on location during the shoot.

Ambience, or ambient sound, is the realistic conglomerate of sounds that establish a location, such as waves rhythmically crashing and sea birds chattering for remote seaside ambience.

Hard sound effects are so named because they need to be physically synced to picture and are necessary for the story or scene.

Foley sound consists of any character-driven sound effects caused by characters interacting with their onscreen environments. Foley sounds are named after Jack Foley, a legendary sound editor at Universal Studios, who originally developed the technique of recording reenactments on a stage. Foley sound replaces the original production audio for everything from fist fights to footsteps and clothing movement.

Audio editing tools in DaVinci Resolve's Fairlight page are designed specifically for the precision editing and placement required when editing sound effects. And DaVinci Resolve's clip speed changes are perfect for advanced sound design and pitch effects.

Music Editing

Music editing involves placing different music elements into the soundtrack to enhance the mood or story. All soundtrack music falls into one of two categories: music occurring within the scene that the characters can hear, so-called source or **diegetic music**; and **non-diegetic music** that is added in post for the benefit of the audience, the **background score**.

Diegetic music needs special attention to make sure that the volume levels, placement, effects and presence fit the context of the scene.

Non-diegetic music added in post production for emotional effect or impact includes the score, stingers, and stabs. Stingers are singular notes or chords that build tension and suspense. Stabs are quick bursts of music that work like an exclamation point to draw attention to something or someone in the story or narration.

Enhancing and Sweetening Tracks

Once the dialogue tracks are edited and the sound effects and music added, it's time make subtle improvements to the sound of each track so that they work in context with the other tracks in the mix. The tools used to improve the sound in a track are similar in many ways to the tools colorists use to improve individual shots within a scene. Because you are learning to use DaVinci Resolve, and color correction is an integral part of the post production process, it seems fitting to show the similarities between adjusting audio and color.

For all intents and purposes this process could be called audio correction. You manipulate four fundamental elements to enhance or "sweeten" audio tracks so they work together as intended in the final mix: volume level, dynamics, equalization and pan. DaVinci Resolve controls all four of these elements on every track without the need for additional plug-ins or patching.

Volume controls are used to adjust the loudness of a track on a decibel scale, and are similar to luminance (brightness) because both volume and luminance have strict broadcast standards, and are usually the first thing the audience notices in each scene. Volume levels can be adjusted on each clip, track, and the main output, just as luminance (black and white levels) can be adjusted on individual clips, scenes, and output. In DaVinci Resolve, you can change the volume level of a clip in the timeline or Inspector. Track volume is controlled by faders in the mixer. You can also change the volume levels over time using automation.

Dynamics controls adjust the **dynamic range**, which is difference between the loudest and quietest peaks in a track. A track's dynamic range is very similar to contrast within a shot. A track with a high dynamic range has very loud and quiet elements within the track, such as a character whispering and then screaming in the same scene. A low dynamic range would be fairly flat, such as a commercial voiceover in which the volume level of the talent is very even from start to finish. If you have ever worked with a Waveform or Parade scope in the Color page, controlling a track's dynamics is very similar to adjusting the white and black levels of a clip. Just think of white as the loudest you can get (-3db) and black as the quietest.

The Fairlight page mixer includes the four most common dynamics controls in one easy-to-use panel. The compressor is used to narrow the dynamic range by lowering the loudest peaks and bringing them closer to the lowest peaks. The expander, in contrast, expands the dynamic range to increase the difference between the loudest and quietest peaks. The limiter and gate both work as acoustic "brick walls" to limit sound from exceeding a target level (limiter), and to prevent sounds lower than a set threshold from being heard (gate).

Pan controls place the sound of a track within a panoramic stereo field. These controls are used to compose the acoustic experience just as a cinematographer composes the visuals of a shot. Tracks can be precisely located anywhere from left to right to sound as if they come from an offscreen source, or somewhere within the frame. DaVinci Resolve includes advanced pan controls in both the Edit page and Fairlight page with both 2D (stereo) and 3D sound placement for surround sound systems.

Equalization (EQ) controls manipulate specific frequencies to enhance the overall sound, and are just like working with color, saturation, and hue in color correction. For example: the human voice is based on a fundamental frequency shared by millions, the additional frequencies add tonal qualities to "color" the voice and make it unique and recognizable. The primary function of equalization is to lower frequencies that detract from the voice and boost the positive frequencies to improve the overall sound. The Fairlight page mixer includes a six-band **parametric equalizer** on each track which is the perfect tool for enhancing and "sweetening" audio tracks.

Mixing and Mastering

The last step of audio post is mixing the tracks and mastering the output. Assuming that all of the other steps were completed prior to the mix, the process is fairly straightforward. The goal of mixing and mastering is to balance the levels coming from each track so they sound good as a whole. This is accomplished by making subtle changes to the track levels, or combining similar tracks into submixes to make them easier to control with one fader. The final master needs to sound great and meet delivery standards for loudness. Fortunately, the Fairlight page includes everything you need to mix tracks and loudness meters to make sure the levels are right on target.

Now that you understand some of the technical steps and creative tools that are essential in an audio post production workflow, you can dive in to the upcoming lessons and start putting them to use on your own projects!

Lesson 8

Working with Audio on the Edit Page

Depending on the size of your project, you may be responsible for the basic audio tracks or for the entire sound design. Even if you plan to hand off your final mix to an audio editor, you still need to give your client a sense of what that final audio mix may sound like.

On the Edit page, DaVinci Resolve 16 includes audio editing and mixing tools to help you mix your soundtrack. DaVinci Resolve also includes all of the capabilities of a full-blown digital audio workstation (DAW) on its Fairlight page. In this lesson, you will work on the Edit page to create additional audio tracks for sound effects, and then set the audio levels to create a balanced mix.

Time

This lesson takes approximately 45 minutes to complete.

Goals

Working with Markers

You will create your mix using a similar version of the current timeline. Because that timeline already has narration and music in place, you'll begin by identifying areas that could benefit from sound effects. You can use markers to annotate clips in the source, identify a specific time in the timeline, or label a range of time. Such markers are often used as reminders for a task that you want to do later. In this timeline, you'll add markers in the timeline to identify the four areas that need additional sound effects.

1 Open the Age of Airplanes project, if necessary, and choose Workspace > Reset UI Layout.

2 Select the Rough Cuts bin, and double-click the **04 Audio Rough Cut** timeline to open it into the timeline viewer.

3 In the timeline, position the playhead in the middle of the **02_A380_TAKEOFF** clip.

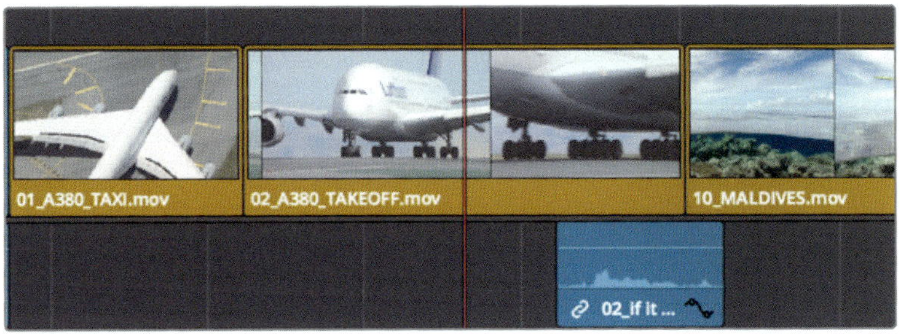

This clip could use a nice big roaring take-off sound. To place a marker here, you must first select the clip.

4 Using the Selection mode tool, click the clip in the timeline.

You can add markers using the marker button in the toolbar.

5 Click the marker button.

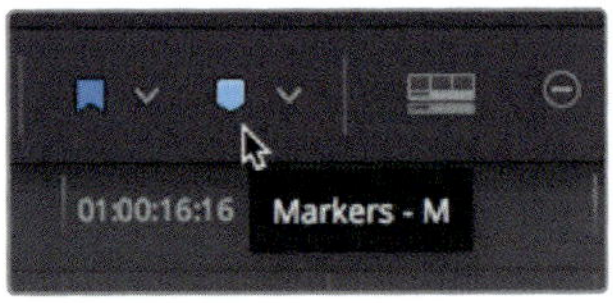

> **TIP** You can turn the marker visibility on and off in the Viewers using the Options menu.

A blue marker is added to the selected clip in the timeline at the current playhead position.

6 On the clip, double-click the blue marker; or select the marker, and press Shift-M to open the marker dialog.

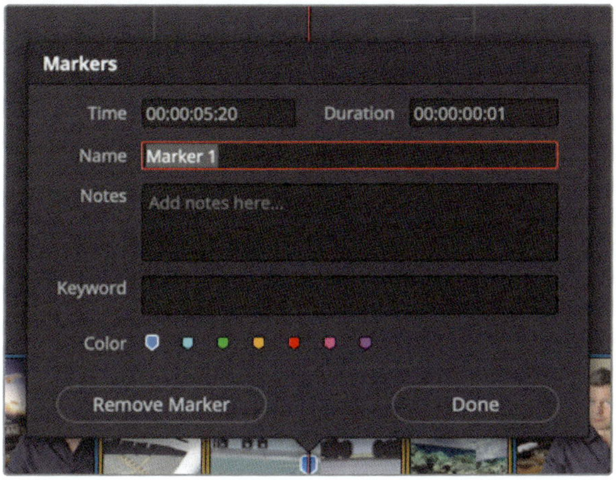

You can change the color of markers to further organize your work. For instance, you could add green markers where graphics were needed and purple markers where effects were needed. You could also add notes to markers that are more descriptive of your changes.

7 Click the red color swatch, and in the Name field, type **SFX**. In the Notes field, type **Add Roaring Take Off**. Click Done.

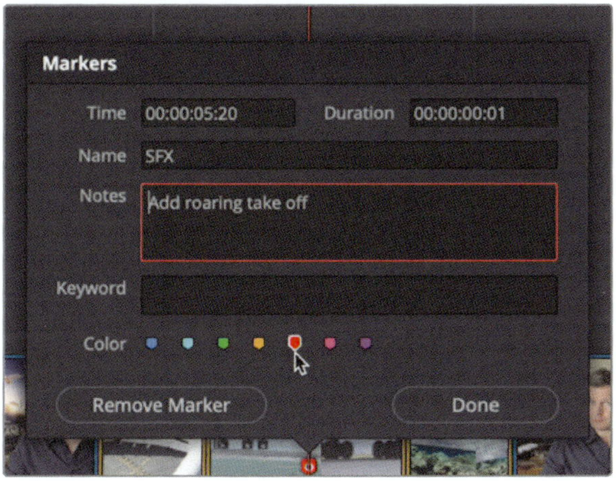

With one clip completed, you have two remaining timeline locations that need markers and notes.

8 In the timeline, position the playhead in the middle of the **10_MALDIVES** clip and select it.

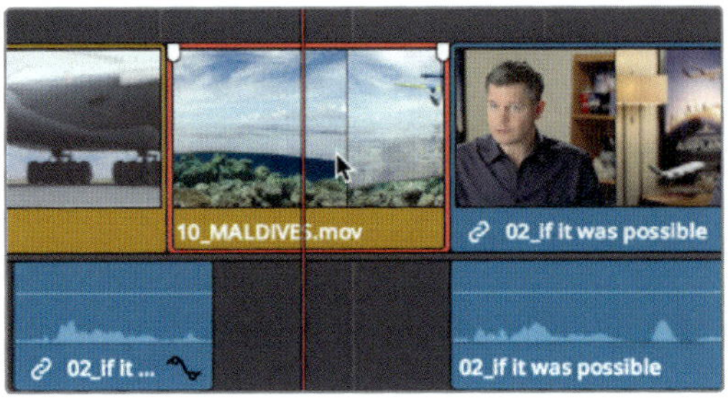

For this clip, you'll use the fastest method, a keyboard shortcut.

9 Press the M key twice.

The first M key press adds the marker; the second press opens the dialog.

10 In the dialog Name field, type **SFX**; in the Notes field, type **Add Overhead Sea Plane**, and make the marker red. Click Done.

> **TIP** To delete a marker, open the Marker dialog, and click the Remove Marker; or select the marker, and press the Delete or Backspace key.

11 Next, position the timeline playhead in the middle of the **08 South_Pole_DC3** clip, and click in the gray area above the clip so nothing is selected in the timeline.

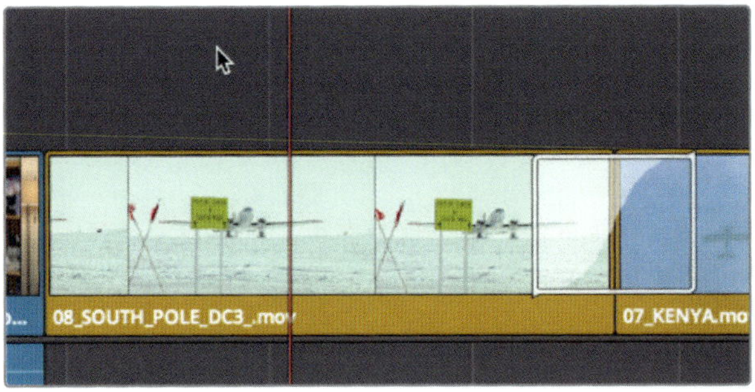

For this clip, you'll use the fastest method of all, a keyboard shortcut.

12 Press the M key.

The marker is added to the timeline ruler under the playhead location. Unlike the other markers applied to the clip, if you were to drag or cut and paste the South Pole clip to a new location in the timeline, the marker would not move with it. With that exception, the marker works exactly the same as the clip markers.

13 Press M again to open the dialog, and in the Name field, type **SFX**. In the Notes field, type **Add Loud Prop Plane**, and make the marker red. Click Done.

> **TIP** Ripple trimming a clip in the timeline will move a marker in the Timeline Ruler to the same duration as the trim.

All your red color markers are added into the program.

Marking a Range of Frames

Markers are not limited to identifying a single frame on a clip or in the time ruler. You can also use them to mark a range of frames. Let's mark a clip range where you want to add a comment about a visual correction you want made to a clip. Because you are no longer marking audio changes, you'll use a new color marker.

1 In the toolbar, drag the zoom slider to zoom in to the 08_SOUTH_POLE_DC3_ where you just added a red marker.

Make sure no clips are selected in the timeline.

2 Position the playhead near the start of the south pole clip.

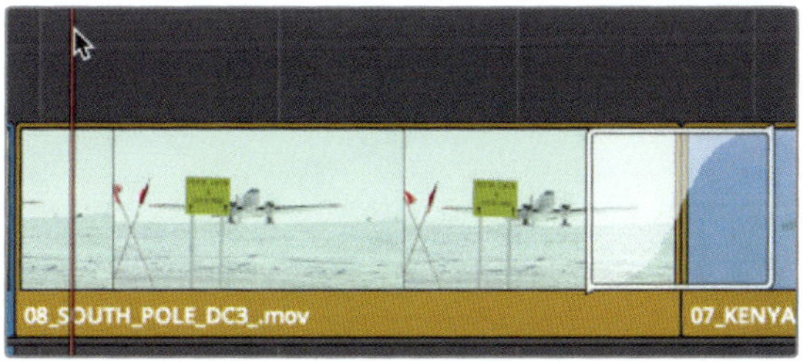

Let's assign yellow as the color for visual effects notes.

3 In the marker menu in the toolbar, choose yellow.

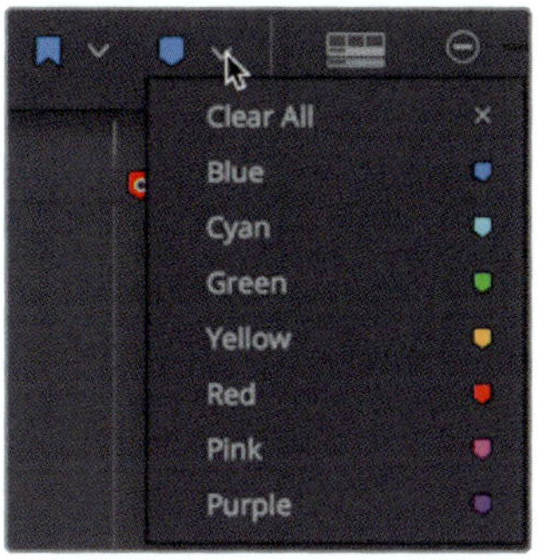

A yellow marker is added to the time ruler.

4 Hold the Option-drag (macOS) or Alt-drag (Windows) the marker to the other end of the clip.

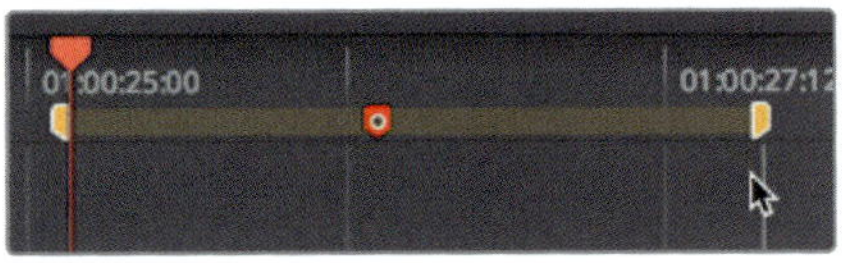

The marker expands to cover the length of the clip. Now you can add a note and even draw on the frames.

5 Press Shift-M to open the Markers dialog.

6 In the name field, enter VFX; and in the notes field, type Move the plane down in the frame. Click Done to close the dialog.

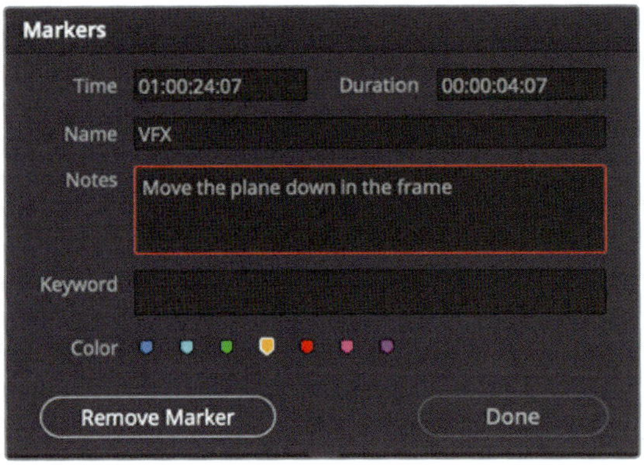

Although in most cases a simple note will provide enough context for any change you may want to make, sometimes a picture is worth more than five or six words.

Annotating on Clips

You can add more details to notes using drawing tools built into each marker. Instead of just typing to move the plane down, you can draw on the frame to show roughly where you want the plane to be placed.

1 In the lower-left corner of the timeline viewer, in the timeline pop-up menu, choose Annotations.

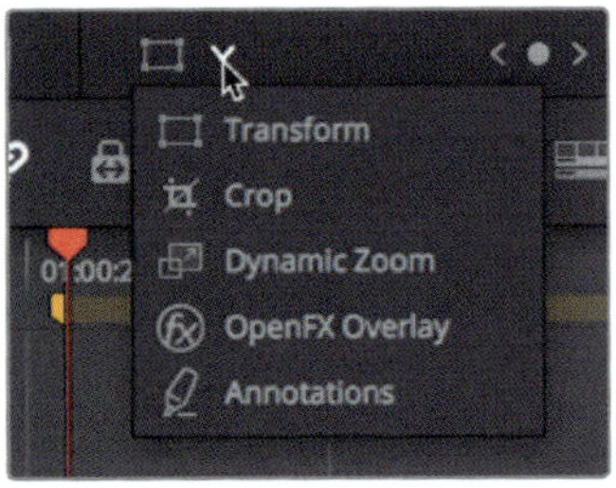

TIP In the timeline viewer pop-up menu, choosing Annotations will automatically add a marker when one doesn't exist at the current position.

Enabling the on-screen controls for annotations adds an annotation toolbar in the upper left corner of the viewer with three options: The draw tool, arrow tool and color pop up.

2 Click the arrow icon; then, starting at the plane's cockpit, drag down to the wheels of the plane.

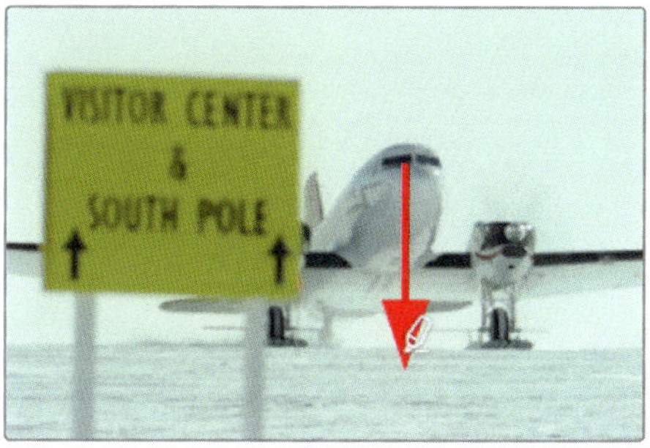

3 In the color pop-up menu, choose yellow.

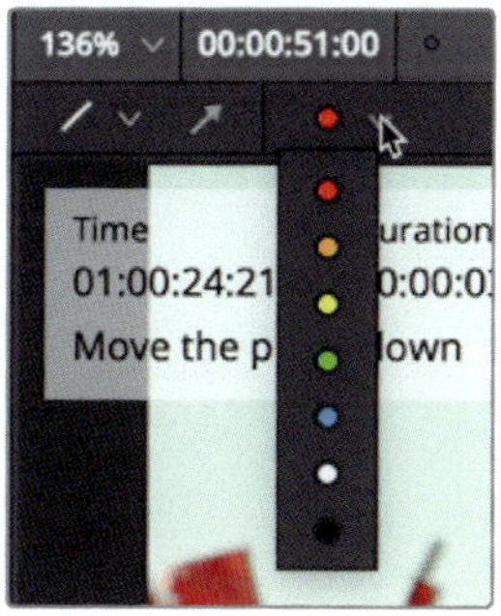

TIP Selecting a line or arrow and pressing the Delete or Backspace key will remove an annotation.

4 In the timeline viewer pop-up menu, click the annotation tool to hide the annotation toolbar.

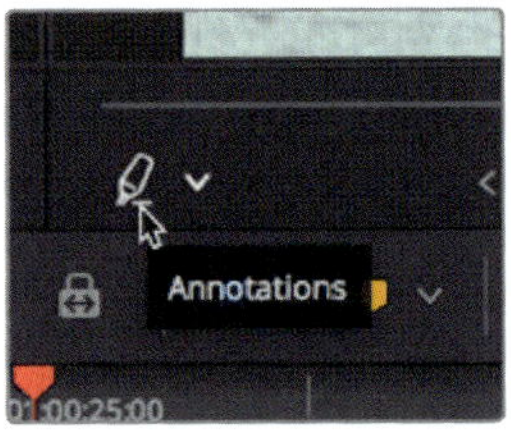

You'll return your attention to the red markers as you continue to work on audio. You'll need to locate sound effects that match your marker notes.

Adding markers in the Source Viewer

You'll also find markers invaluable when applied to source clips. Markers on a source clip can add notes as in the timeline. You also can use markers to identify multiple areas of a clip that you may want to use in your timeline. In this way, markers can be used as placeholders for multiple in and out points.

1 In the Audio bin, double-click the Sound FX clip to open it in the source viewer.

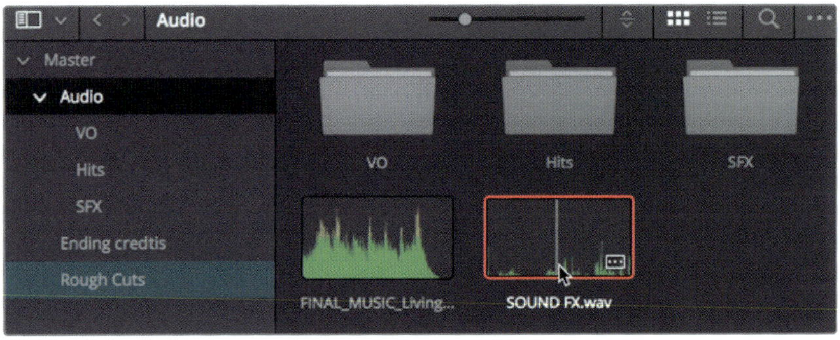

This is a typical sound effects clip that contains many sounds. Let's play it and listen for a sound effect that you might want to use somewhere in your timeline.

NOTE Although the images in this book show bins in specific configurations, it is not critical that your setup match them exactly. Your bins may be in icon view or list view depending on your preference.

2 Play the first five seconds of the **Sound FX** clip.

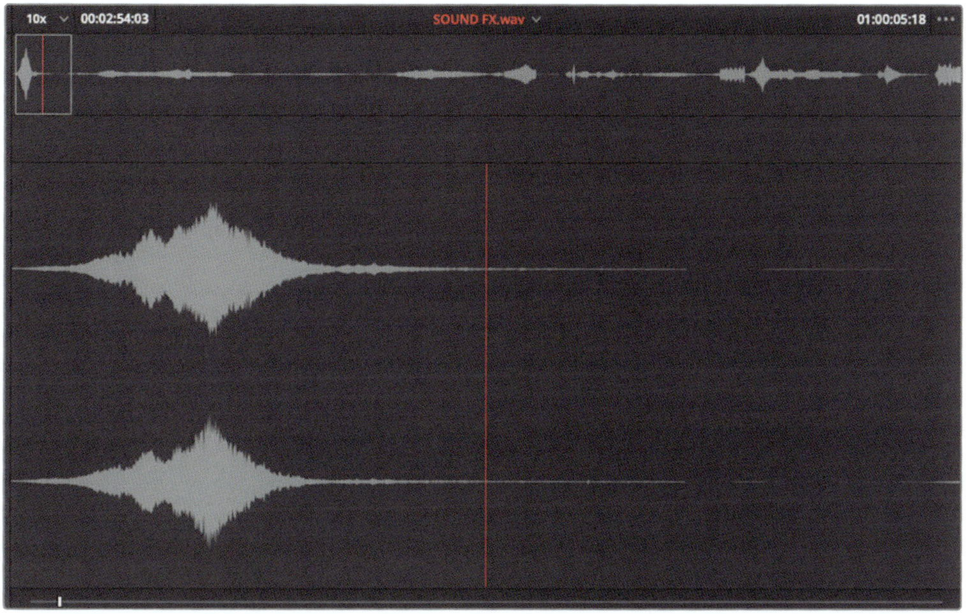

Fortunately, the first sound effect in this clip is a prop plane buzzing. To add a marker to the source clip in the viewer, you can use the same keyboard shortcut.

3 Position the source viewer's jog bar over the peak of the sound effect (the highest part of the waveform).

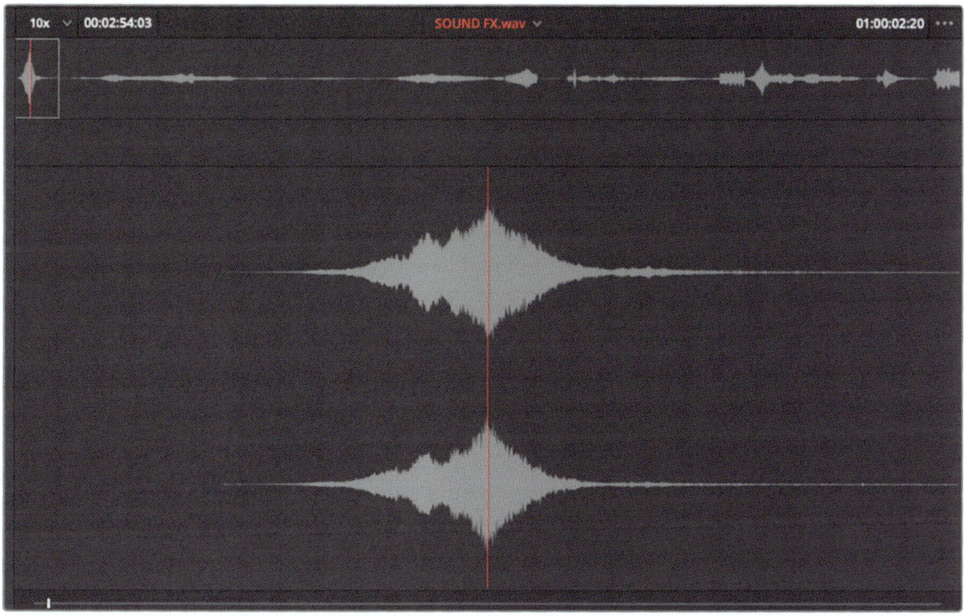

4 Press the M key.

A marker is added to the source clip under the source viewer's jog bar. You also can add notes to source clip markers.

5 Press M again to open the dialog, and in the Name field, type **Plane Overhead**. Click Done.

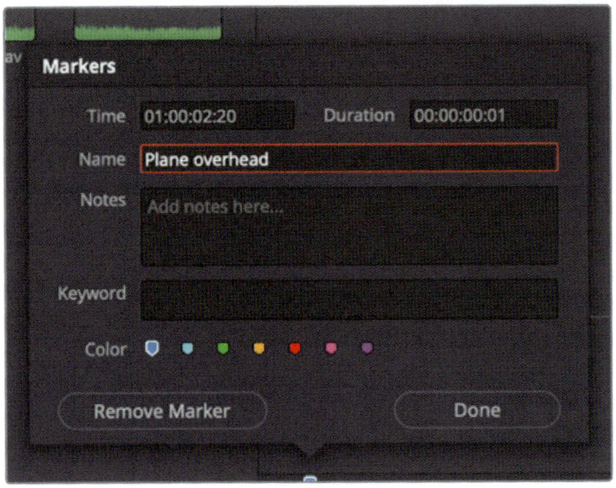

Your first sound effect is marked and identified. The marker will help you locate this effect later when you want to begin editing.

Marking a Range in the Source Viewer

In the source viewer marking a range is a bit different than doing so in the timeline. Dragging out the duration of the marker can be trickier because you can't zoom into the source viewer jog bar. But using marker durations in the source viewer can be very helpful to simulate multiple in and out points on a clip. You can use this function in a long sound effects clip that may contain multiple effects you want to use. Considering the previous marker that you added in the source viewer, you need to locate two more sounds for your program. First, you'll look for a loud prop plane sound for the South Pole shot.

1 In the source viewer, continue playing the Sound FX clip for about 30 seconds.

Somewhere in that 30 seconds is a loud, good-sounding prop plane take-off. Before you decide to use this sound effect, you can use markers to identity a potential range for the South Pole clip. Then, you can continue to search the source clip for possible alternatives.

In the source viewer, position the jog bar where the prop plane sound effect begins.

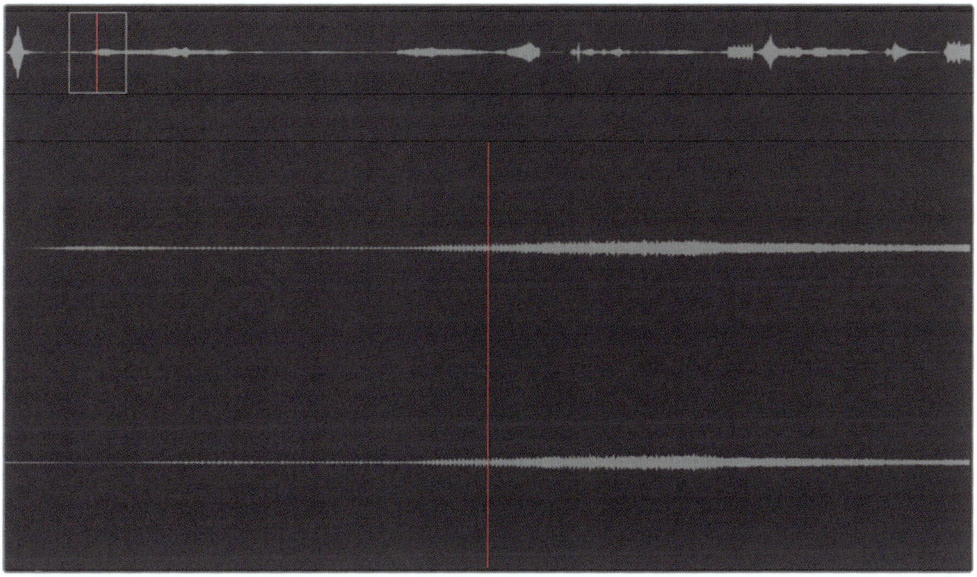

The initial sound of the prop plane engine would not fit the visual of the South Pole plane. You'll need to play a little farther into the sound effect and place a marker when the engine really gets going.

2 Play the clip to find a location where the engine sound is revving loudly.

3 Press M to add a marker in the source viewer.

4 Press M a second time to open the dialog. In the Name field, type **Loud Prop Plane**.

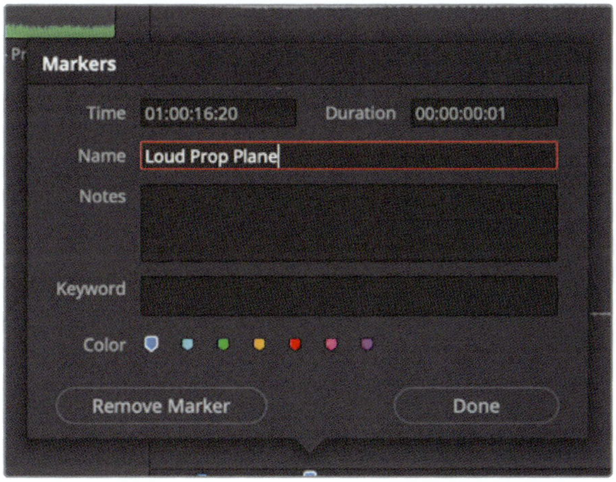

5 To extend the range of the marker, click at the end of the Duration field, and delete the last three digits.

6 Type **300** to create a duration of three seconds, press Enter on the keyboard and click Done.

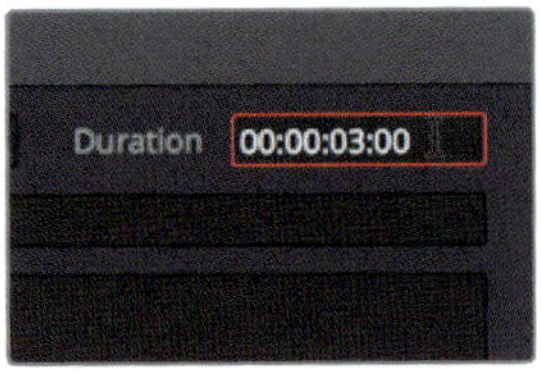

TIP Instead of entering a duration for the marker range, you could Option-drag (macOS) or Alt-drag (Windows) the marker to extend the range.

This time you'll add in and out points around the area you are interested in and then convert them to markers.

This will be a roaring jet taking off for the A380 Takeoff clip.

7 Drag the jog bar slowly across the clip until you hear the loud jet take-off, somewhere near the middle of the clip. (Hint: A medium-sized peak can be found in the audio waveform where the jet sound is located.)

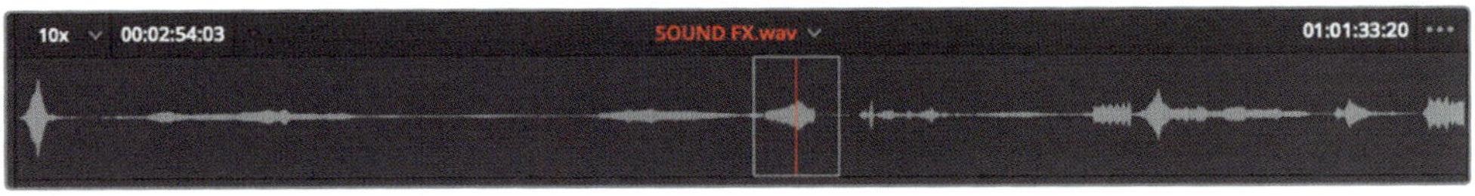

Once you locate the start of the jet sound, you'll use an in and out point to mark the range.

8 In the source viewer, position the jog bar where you hear the jet take-off start.

9 Mark an in point, and then locate the end of the sound and mark an out point.

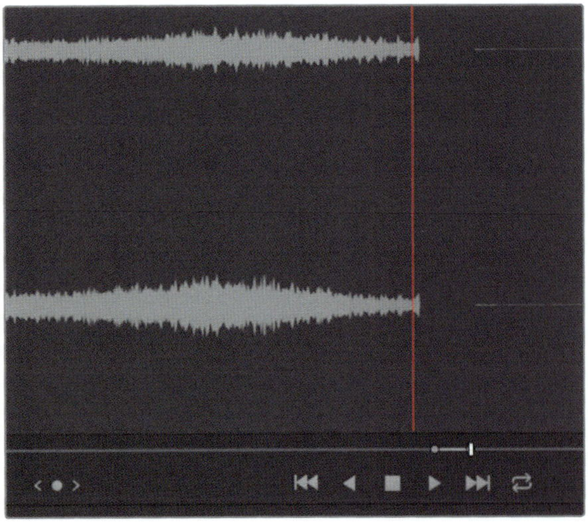

10 Right-click between the marked in and out points, and in the pop-up menu, choose "Convert In and Out to Duration Marker".

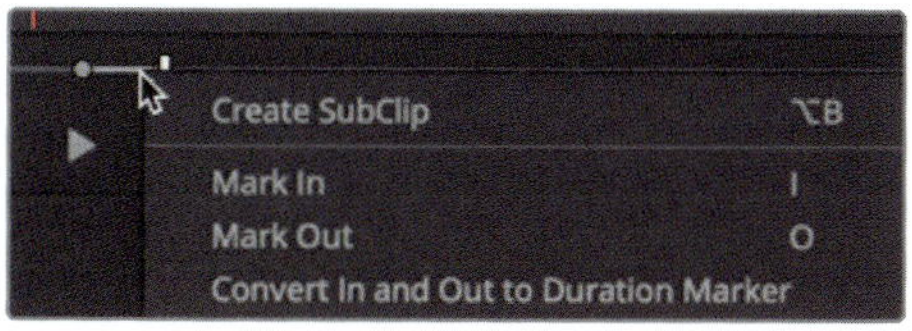

> **TIP** You can also convert duration markers to in and out points in the same contextual menu.

The Duration marker is added to identify the same frames as the in and out points. You can use the same pop-up menu to open the dialog.

11 Right-click in the marker range, and in the pop-up menu, choose Modify Marker.

The dialog opens.

12 In the Name field, type **Roaring Jet Take Off** and click Done.

You've identified sound effects that fill the requirements of the markers in the timeline. Now, you'll edit them into your trailer to enhance the cinematic experience.

Customizing the Interface for Audio

Throughout this lesson you'll work on the audio tracks, so it makes sense to customize the timeline view by increasing the audio track heights so you can more clearly see the audio waveform displays. Doing so will help you locate specific sounds and evaluate the audio more effectively. Furthermore, those waveforms are a handy visual reference to determine the volume of the audio.

To open up more room in the timeline for audio tracks, you can push the tracks up, thereby removing some of the headroom that exists above the video track.

1 Locate the mouse pointer between the video track and the audio tracks in the timeline.

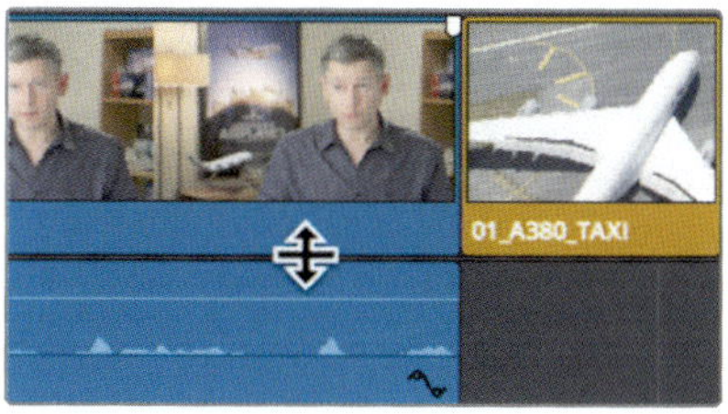

The pointer changes to a resize cursor, indicating that you can drag up or down to assign more or less room to audio or video tracks.

2 Drag up on the horizontal divider that separates the audio and video tracks until the video track is at the top of the timeline.

As you did in the previous lesson, you can change the appearance of the tracks in the Timeline View Options menu.

3 In the toolbar, click the Timeline View Options button to open the pop-up menu.

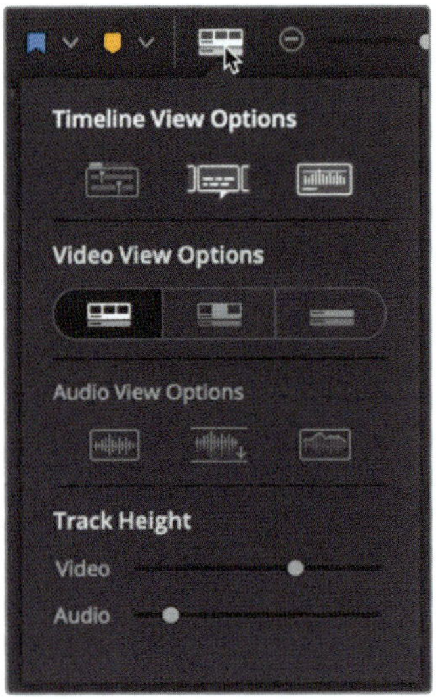

Here you will change the height of the video and audio tracks to suit your upcoming tasks.

4 In the Clip View Options section, click the third track appearance button to the right to collapse the audio and video tracks.

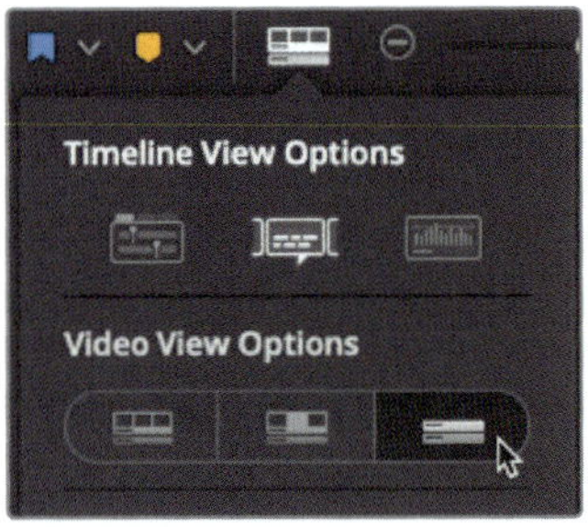

5 At the top of the Timeline View Options, click the third button to enable audio waveforms.

6 Drag the video track height slider all the way to the right to increase the track size.

7 Drag the audio track height slider halfway to the right to increase the track size.

8 In the Timeline View Options, click the audio waveform button to display audio waveforms in the timeline tracks.

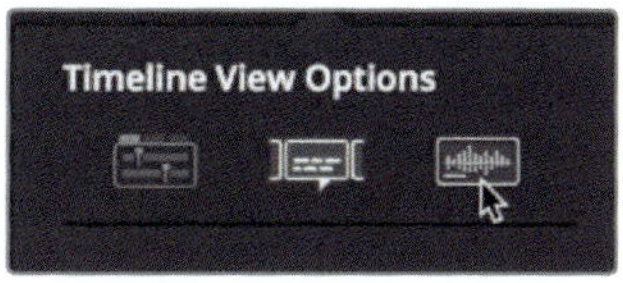

9 Click the Timeline View Options button to hide the pop-up menu.

Now your timeline is better configured for audio editing and mixing. You'll later add other interface elements to help control and monitor the audio; but for now, displaying larger waveforms in the timeline will help you edit in the sound effects.

Adding and Patching Tracks

Your timeline is fairly well organized considering the small amount of audio that it contains. Audio 1 is devoted to the interview and Audio 2 is devoted to music. To keep those tracks organized, you'll insert an empty audio track to accommodate the new sound effects.

1 In the timeline header, right-click the Audio 2 label to open the pop-up menu.

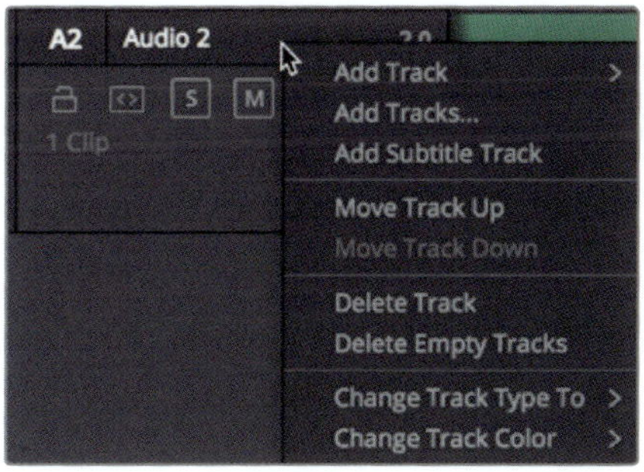

This menu has options to add, move, and delete tracks. Your stereo sound effects need to be edited into a new stereo audio track.

2 In the pop-up menu, choose Add Track > Stereo.

> **TIP** In the timeline, audio clips with multiple channels are displayed as a single audio clip on a single track. When you first create a new audio track, you choose its audio format (mono, stereo, 5.1 surround, or multi-channel). You can, however, change it later.

An Audio 3 track is added to the timeline. Now you need to patch the track so that the audio content in the source clip is edited onto this new Audio 3 track.

3 Drag down the A1 destination control to Audio 3 to align the A1 track in the source viewer with the Audio 3 track in the timeline.

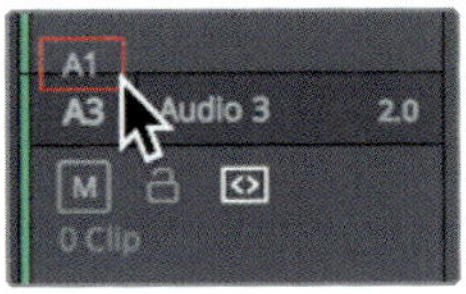

Now that the tracks are patched, you can edit your first sound effect into the timeline. Let's locate that first sound effect.

4 In the source viewer, navigate to the first marker in the clip by choosing playback > Previous Marker three times, or pressing Shift-up arrow three times.

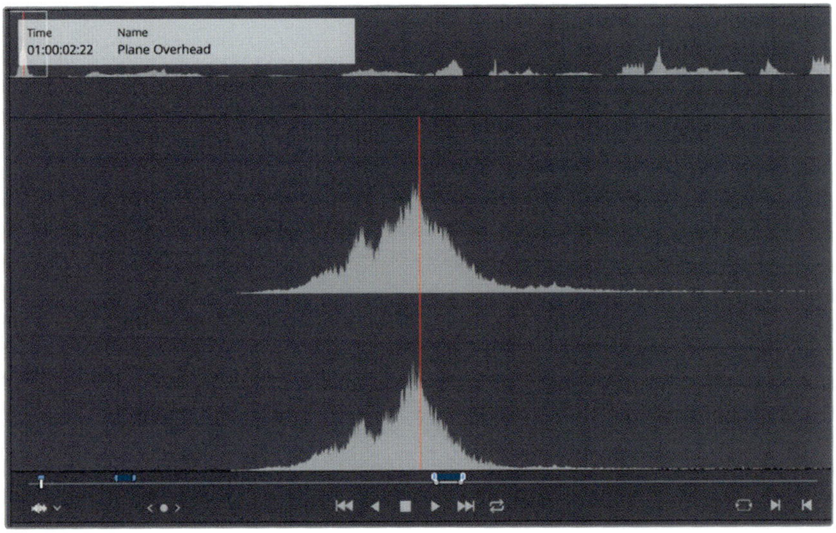

The source viewer should be located at the first marker. The marker overlay in the viewer shows that this is an overhead prop plane. This may work perfectly for the Maldives shot where the plane flies in at the top of the frame.

5 Click in the timeline viewer, or press the Q key, to activate the timeline viewer.

6 Navigate to the marker over the Maldives clip by choosing Playback > Previous Marker, or pressing Shift-up arrow.

One of the best ways to edit sound effects is to use the replace edit that you used previously. When adding sound effects, you typically are trying to match the action in a frame with a precise sync point in the sound effect. Most often these sync points are not at the start or end of a clip, so you need to use another method for aligning the clips. With a replace edit, you can position the jog bar over the sync point of the sound effect, and then position the timeline playhead on the video frame where you want the sound effect sync point to be heard. The source clip is already located on the loudest part of the buzzing overhead plane. That point should line up with the sea plane just entering the top of the frame.

7 Position the playhead on the frame where the nose of the plane and the floats have just entered the frame.

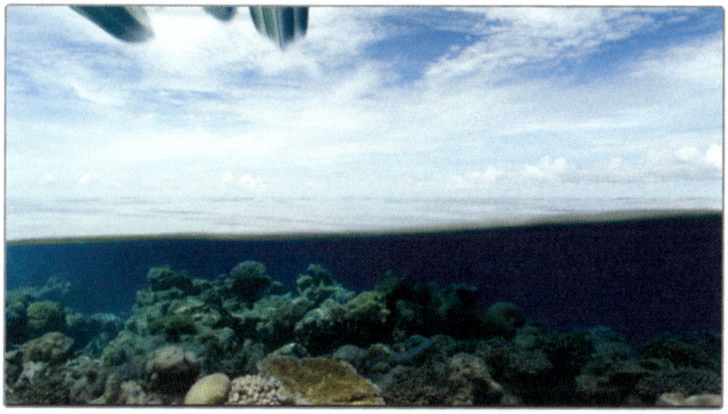

> **TIP** If the playhead is difficult to move precisely, press the N key, or click the snapping button in the toolbar, to disable snapping. The playhead will no longer snap to the marker.

Unlike using a replace edit to replace a clip on the same track, you must set in and out points when replacing a clip into an empty track as you are doing here in Audio 3.

8 Choose Mark > Mark Clip, or press X, to mark in and out points for the duration of the Maldives clip.

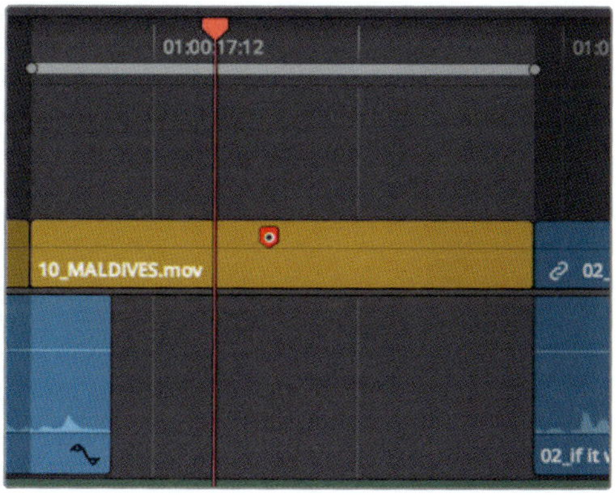

9 In the toolbar, click the replace button, or press F11.

10 Play over the sound effect to hear it synchronized with the picture.

Now you have an organized track layout that places the subject's voice on Audio 1, music on Audio 2, and sound effects on Audio 3. Maintaining media organization throughout your editing stage is always important, but may be even more important when editing audio because you'll often find yourself managing a dozen tracks or more.

Color Coding Tracks

You can organize your tracks even further by adding another layer of color organization. You already color coded the video clips, but you can also color code tracks in the timeline. To make it easier to parse your timeline, let's color code the music track with orange and the sound effects track with green.

1 Right-click the Audio 2 timeline header.
2 In the pop-up menu, choose Change Track Color > Orange.

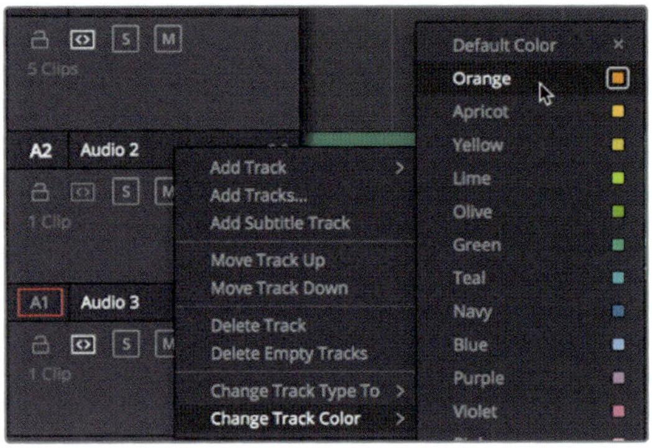

The music clip on Audio 2 changes to the orange color.

3 Right-click the Audio 3 timeline header.
4 In the pop-up menu, choose Change Track Color > Olive.

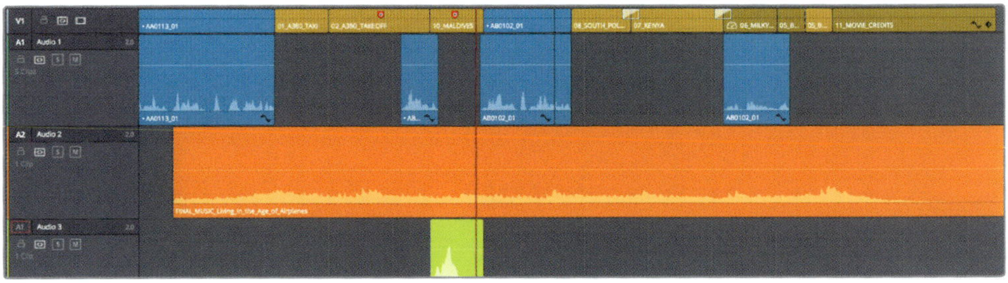

The sound effect clip changes to an olive color. Any new sound effect that you edit onto that track will also assume the olive color. However, when you have assigned a color to a clip in the bin, that color will override the timeline track color.

Finding Markers using the Edit Index

In a short timeline such as the one you have here, navigating to each marker isn't much of a challenge. On more involved projects, however, you'll need a quick way to locate one specific marker among dozens of other markers. The Edit Index is a list view of all the editing events (clips and markers) in the current timeline.

1 At the top of the DaVinci Resolve window, click the Edit Index button.

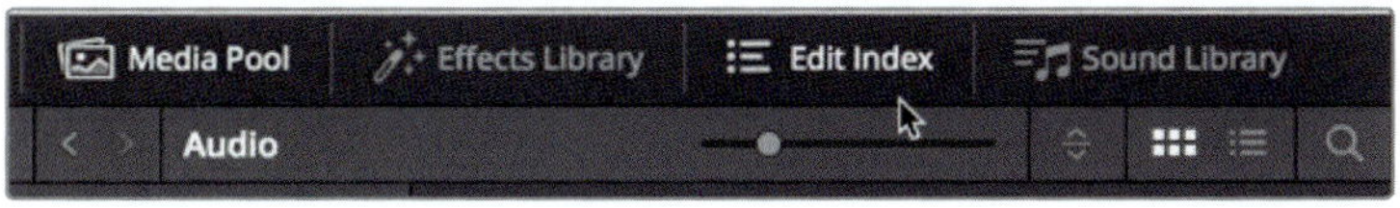

The Edit Index opens below the Media pool, showing all of the editing events and columns of metadata. This is too much information to digest even in a short timeline.

2 In the upper-right corner of the Edit Index, click the options menu.

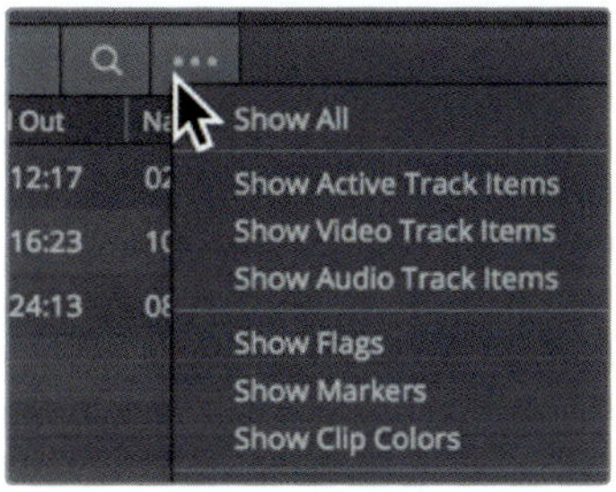

3 Choose Show Markers > Red.

The Edit Index changes to show only the red markers in the timeline, making it much easier to review the list. But you can make it even easier. As with the bin's list view, you can choose to show or hide columns of information.

4 Right-click a column header to open the menu of columns.

5 In this menu, deselect each column except for Number, Color, and Notes.

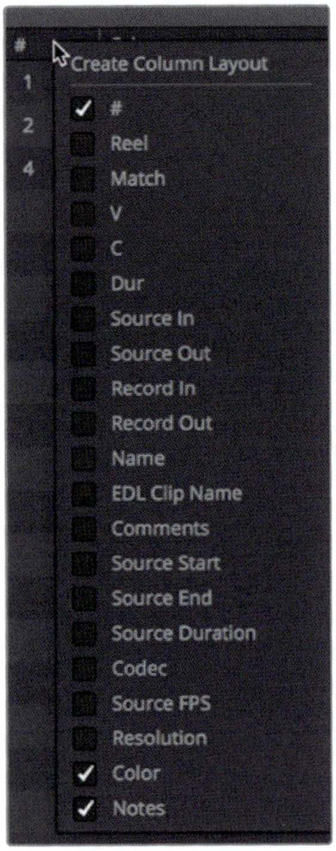

Now you can identify each marker by its color, and the note you entered.

6 Click the red marker that contains the note, "Add Roaring Take Off."

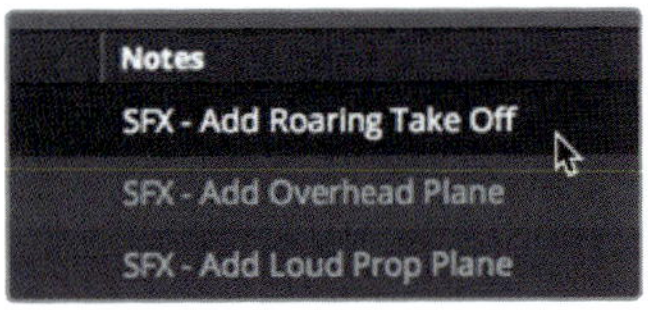

The timeline jumps to the marker on the **02_A380_Takeoff** clip. This is the next clip to which you'll add sound effects. Instead of trying to find the marker in the Source viewer, DaVinci Resolve has an easier way that you'll use next.

Viewing Markers in a Bin

Markers added to source clips can be viewed in the list view of a bin. If the markers have a duration, you can use them like multiple in and out points and edit them directly into the timeline.

1 Above the Media pool, click the list view button.

   The sound effects clip has a disclosure arrow to the left of its name. Clicking this disclosure arrow will display the markers you added to the clip.

2 Click the disclosure arrow next to the Sound FX clip.

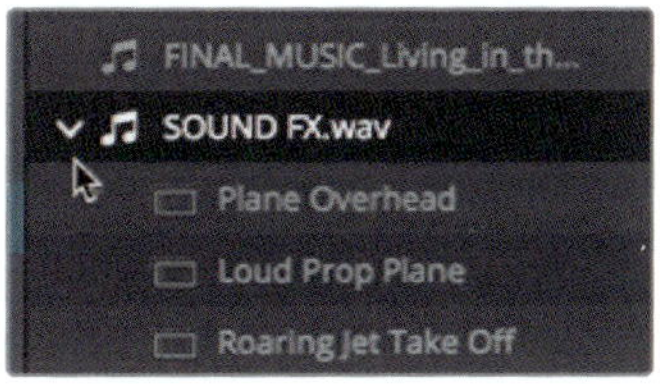

   Each marker on the source clip is displayed under the clip's file name. If these markers have duration, you can just drag them into the timeline, and the duration markers will be used as in and out points for the clip.

3 From the Audio bin, drag the Roaring Jet Take off marker to the Audio 3 track so it aligns with the start of the 02_A380_TAKEOFF clip.

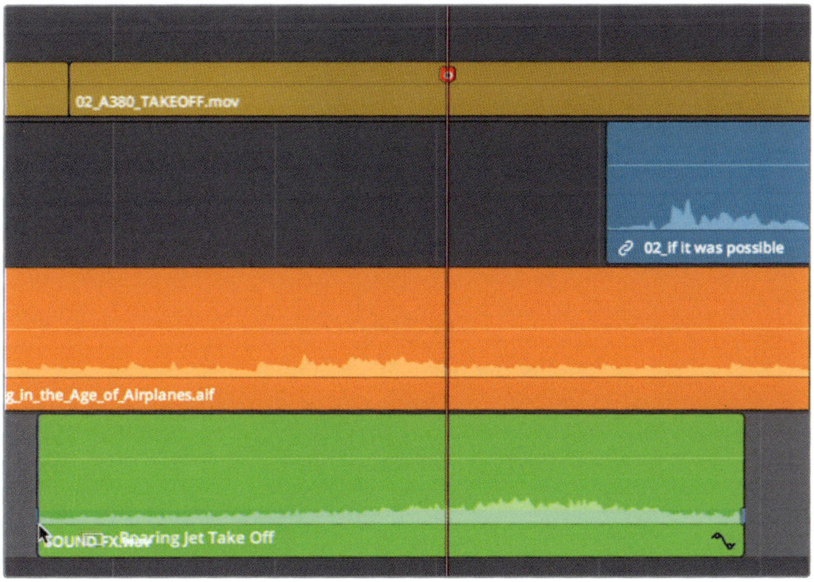

   One more sound effect to add.

TIP Double-clicking the marker in the bin's list view will open the clip into the source viewer with the jog bar placed at the marker.

4 In the Edit Index, click the SFX - Add Loud Prop Plane entry to relocate the timeline playhead to that marker position.

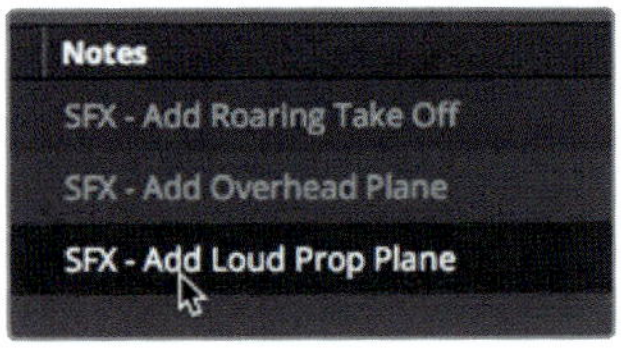

5 From the Audio bin, drag the Loud Prop Plane marker to the Audio 3 track so it aligns with the start of the 08_SOUTH_POLE_DC3 clip.

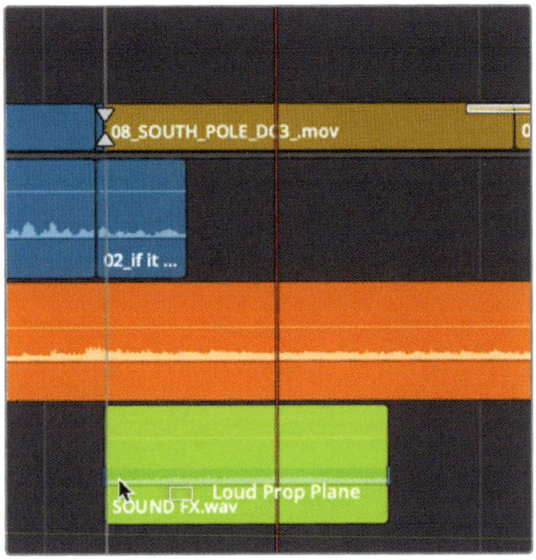

6 Move the playhead to the start of the timeline, and play over your newly added sound effects.

All of your audio tracks, music, narration, and sound effects are now in place.

Linking Clips

Clips that contain audio and video captured together are linked automatically in DaVinci Resolve. That behavior makes it easy to move and trim them together so they stay in sync. However, that is not the case with your newly added sound effects. They have no link to the video they were placed with. However, you can create a sync relationship between them so that when you move one of the video clips that has a sound effect under it, they are attached and move together.

1 In the timeline, select the **02_A380_TAKEOFF** clip.

2 In Audio 3, Cmd-click (macOS) or Ctrl-click (Windows) the sound effect clip directly under **02_A380_TAKEOFF**.

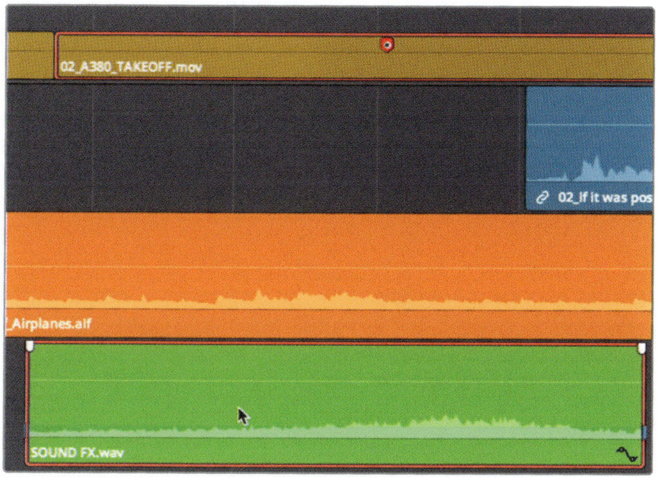

These two clips should stay together if you later want to move the A380 clip or even delete it. To do so, you need to link them together.

3 Right-click the selected **SOUND FX** clip, and in the pop-up menu, choose Link Clips.

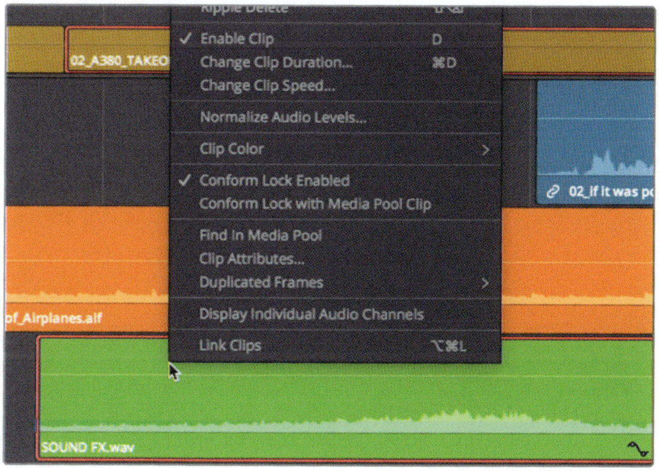

A small link icon appears in the timeline before the clip name. The icon signifies that this audio clip is linked to another clip. If you selected one in the timeline, the other would also be selected just as if they were recorded together.

4 Go through the timeline and link the remaining three sound effects with their respective video clips.

The linked selection button in the timeline toolbar works for these linked clips just as it does for linked clips that were recorded together.

Monitoring, Soloing, and Muting Audio

When you start to edit your audio, the first thing you need to do is sit back and listen. Just play the tracks to hear them in the context of the picture.

1 Press the Home key, and then press the spacebar to play the timeline to its end.

> **TIP** Some Mac keyboards do not have Home and End keys. In their place, press Fn-left arrow to move the playhead to the start of the timeline and Fn-right arrow to move to the end.

To get a sense of the contents of each audio track, you can listen to each track independently by soloing it.

2 Press the Home key to move the playhead back to the start of the timeline.

3 On Audio 1, click the solo button to temporarily silence the other audio tracks.

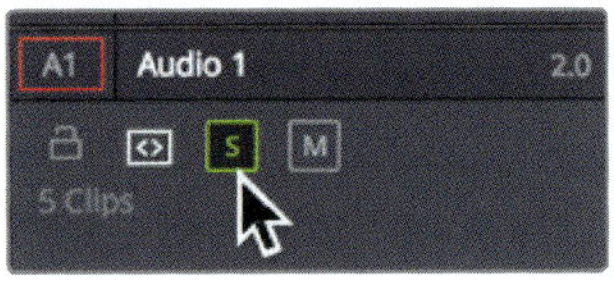

4 Press the spacebar to play the timeline.

Only the interview is heard because the other two tracks are not soloed.

5 While the timeline plays, click the solo button on Audio 3 to hear the sound effects.

You can solo multiple tracks to hear only the track you select.

To accurately monitor the levels of your audio, you can use the audio meters.

6 In the upper-right corner of the DaVinci Resolve interface, click the Mixer button to open the audio mixer.

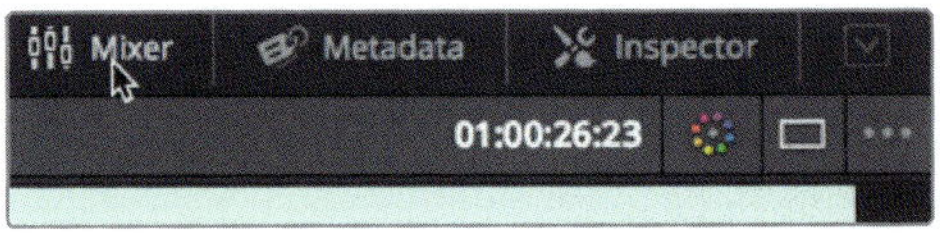

You will use the Mixer panel to monitor each track's audio level while watching the audio meters. Meters are a visual guide for making audio volume and processing adjustments. In DaVinci Resolve, the meters repeatedly generate an average (mean) level with a thin one-pixel line showing you the peak. But here in the Edit page, the goal is really just to create consistency amongst the clips on the same track, so all your narration is at the same level and all your similar sound effects are at a consistent level.

7 Play the timeline to hear the soloed tracks as you watch the meters.

You can see each track's audio displayed in the meters and set the appropriate level for each track.

Reading Meters and Setting Targets

Before you make any clip volume adjustments, it is a good idea to know how to read an **RMS** (root mean square) peak meter such as the one used in the mixer. The meters in the mixer use a *decibel* (dB) *scale* to measure the volume of your audio clips. These meters range from a maximum of 0 dB down to -50 dB. Any audio levels above 0 dB are distorted, so you must always keep audio levels below 0 dB. Although not a hard and fast rule, tracks such as dialog, sound effects, and music generally have target dB levels as good starting points.

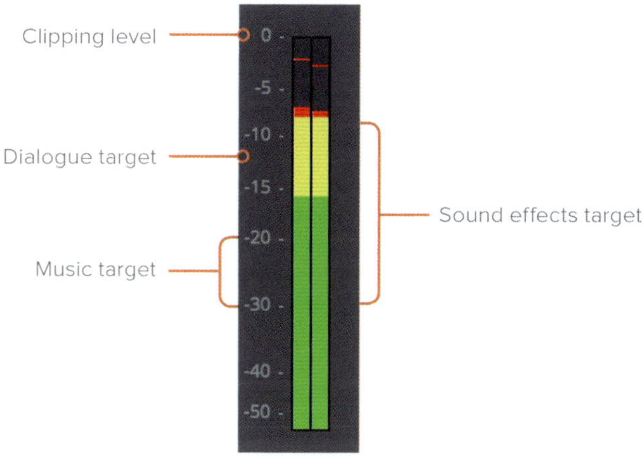

Normal spoken dialogue should average around -12 dB on the meter.

Sound effects have a wider target range because they have such a wide variety; but in general, try to target sound effects to fall between -10 and -30 dB.

Music tracks require a wide dynamic range but should fall between -20 and -30 dB.

These level guidelines are good starting points; but in the end, your ears must be the final judges of what sounds right.

For this first stage of audio mixing, you will target each clip and set its level appropriately for the type of sound it contains. Eventually, all the clips of dialogue should be placed on a single dialogue track and play at roughly the same level. The single-track and common dB-level strategy applies to all the sound effects and all the music. At this stage, however, you needn't be concerned with comparing the dialogue levels to the music or sound effect levels because you are mixing on a clip level. Later, in the Fairlight page, you'll tackle track-level mixing.

Let's start by working with your dialog on audio track 1.

Normalizing Audio

With all video and audio edited into your timeline, you're ready to set the relative audio levels for your project. You'll start by examining the tracks that contain the primary audio – in this case, the interview clips on Audio 1 – and setting those clips to their maximum volume levels.

1 Position the playhead at the start of the timeline.

2 Ensure that only the audio 1 track is solo enabled.

3 Press Shift-Z to see all of the clips on audio 1.

4 Drag a selection around the audio clips on audio 1, or Cmd-click (macOS) or Ctrl-click, (Windows) to select them.

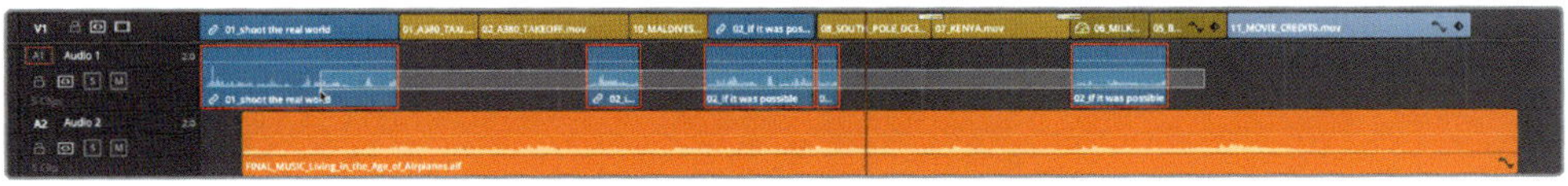

You can quickly maximize the volume for the selected clip using the normalize function.

5 Right-click any of the selected audio clips, and choose Normalize Audio Levels.

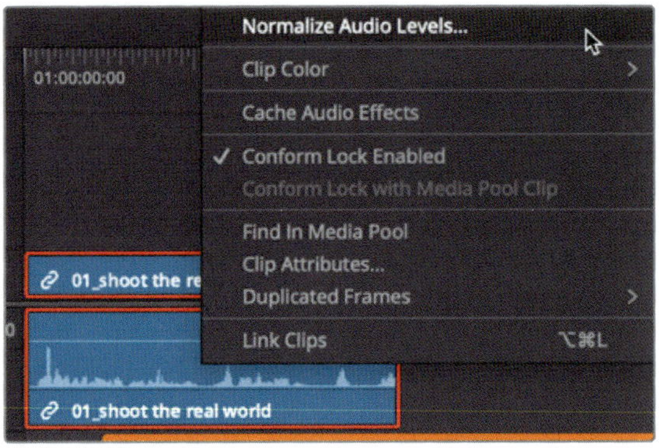

The dialog that appears allows you to amplify the audio by targeting the peaks to reach a specific the dBFS level. For most dialogue and voiceovers, you want the average to land around -12dBFs on the meter, so setting the Normalize peak target can be a bit higher.

6 In the Reference Level field, type -10.

The lower two options in the dialog determine if the highest peak of all the clips is used to set the target reference level, or if the peaks of each selected clip are amplified to reach the target reference level. Because you have a lot of variety in the levels on audio 1, let's individual maximize each clip's peak.

7 Choose Independent.

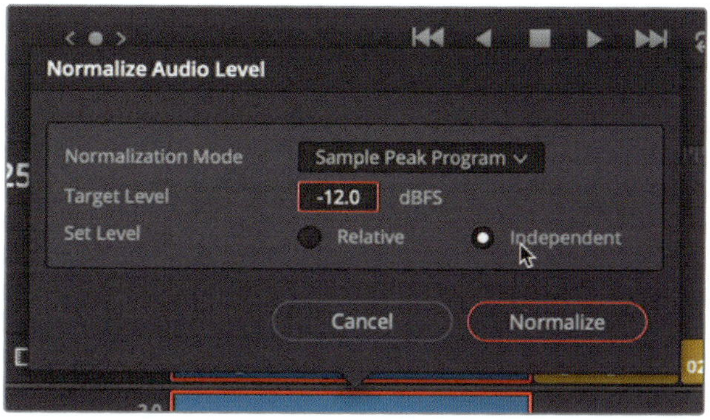

8 Click Normalize, and play over the audio on track 1 to hear what should now be a consistent audio level.

As the audio plays, watch the meters in the mixer. The average levels should be bouncing around 012 dBFS. The loudest peak on the track should never go above the target -10 dBFS.

Setting Levels in the Inspector

As you played over the track, you may have noticed that the next to last clip sounded considerably lower than the others. Because all clips are not identical, some need adjustments in addition to an automatic normalization.

1 Position the playhead over the 4th audio interview clip in the middle of the timeline.

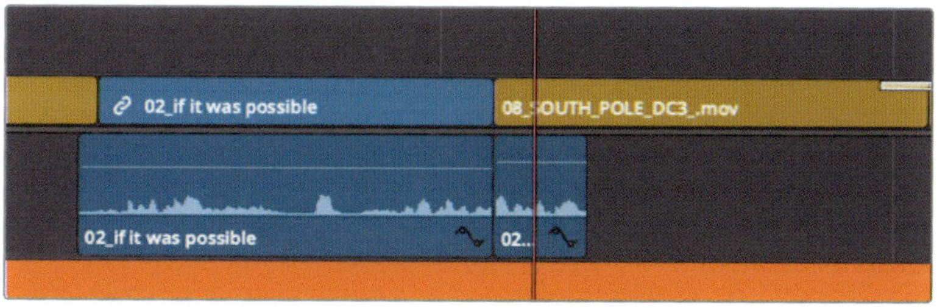

2 Select the audio clip, and click the Inspector button to open the Inspector

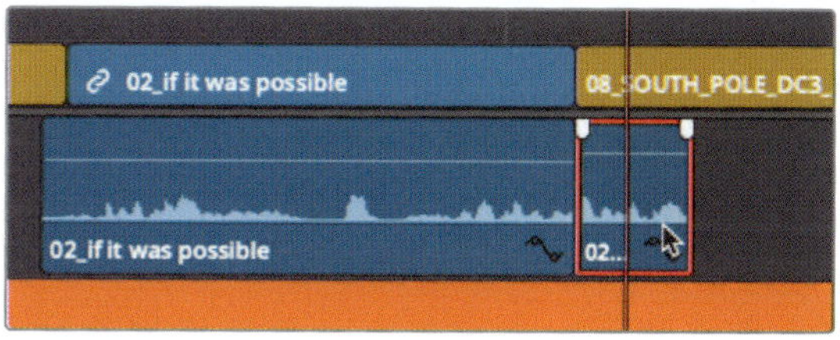

When an audio clip is selected in the timeline, Level, Pitch, and EQ parameters are displayed in the Inspector.

3 Drag the Volume slider to the right until it reaches about 10.

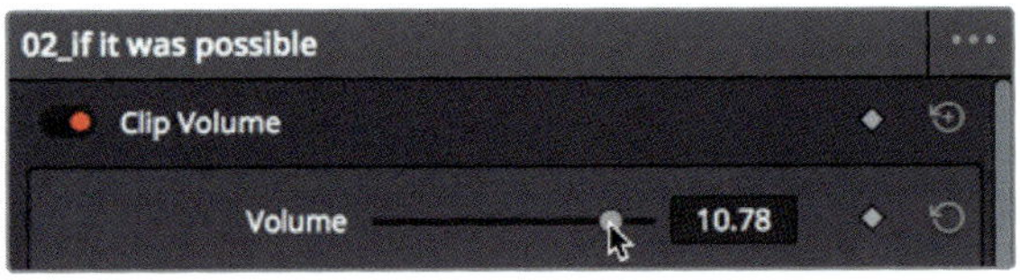

TIP To increase or decrease the volume of a selected clip, press Cmd-Option-+ (plus sign) and Cmd-Option- - (minus sign) in macOS, or Ctrl-Alt-+ (plus sign) and Ctrl-Alt- - (minus sign) in Windows.

4 Play through the clip and watch the meters to ensure that they fall somewhere between -10 and -15 dB. If the meters show levels going consistently above -10 dB, drag the volume slider to the left to lower the clip level.

It is important to optimize levels around -12 dB, otherwise you might be setting your primary clips too low and not taking advantage of the full dynamic range of digital audio recording.

Setting Levels in the Timeline

To perform quick audio level adjustments, you can graphically change a clip's audio level in the timeline using volume curves.

1 In the track header for audio 3, click the solo button to play only the sound effects.

2 Position the timeline playhead at the start of the first sound effect on audio 3.

3 If necessary, drag the scroll bar at the bottom of the timeline so you can see all three sound effects in the timeline window.

4 Play these three sound effects, and on the meters, watch A3 to monitor their levels.

All three sound effects are too loud. They are not meant to be at the same level as a direct hit from a photon torpedo!

You can use the -10 to -30 dB range as a rule-of-thumb target as you set sound effect levels.

5 Place your mouse pointer over the thin white line that runs through the first sound effect audio clip on audio 3.

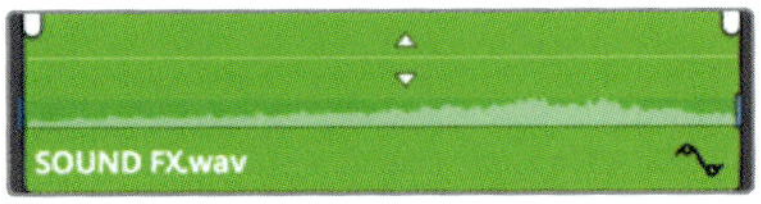

This line in the audio clip is the volume curve and represents the volume level of the clip. Dragging the volume curve (line) down will lower the level just as it would if you dragged the Volume slider to the left in the Inspector.

6 When your mouse pointer changes to an up and down arrow pointer, drag the volume curve down until the tool tip reads roughly -10 dB.

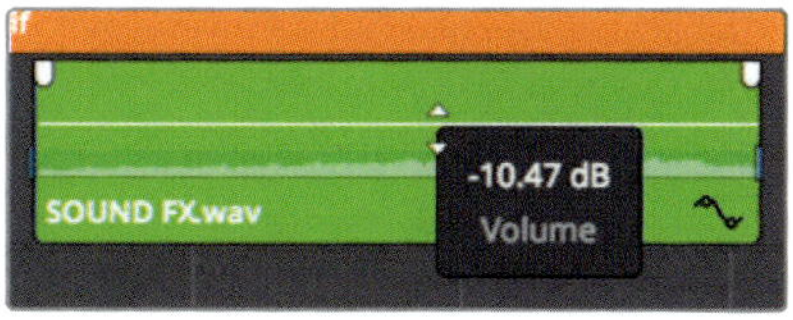

You have now lowered the volume by 10 dB.

> **TIP** The tool tip displays the offset relative to the current level. It is not showing the exact dB level that the audio will reach on the meters. The term dB Full Scale or dBFS expresses exact meter readings, but a simple dB value expresses an offset level.

All the sound effects probably sounded a bit loud on first playthrough. You can easily copy the lowered level of one audio clip to another using the Paste Attributes command you applied in the previous lesson.

7 Select the first sound effect clip on A3.

8 Choose Edit > Copy, or press Cmd-C (macOS) or Ctrl-C (Windows).

9 Select the second sound effect clip on A3, and Cmd-click (macOS) or Ctrl-click (Windows) the third and final sound effect clip on the track to select both clips.

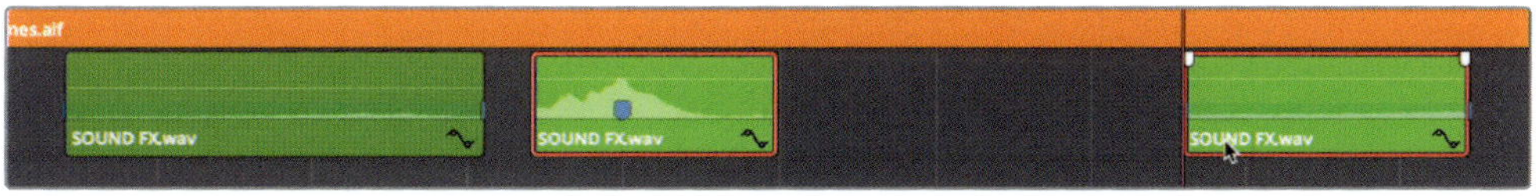

10 Choose Edit > Paste Attributes, or press Option-V (macOS) or Alt-V (Windows).

The Audio Attributes window includes clip attributes that you can copy and paste from one clip to another.

11 Select the Audio Attributes Volume checkbox, and click Apply.

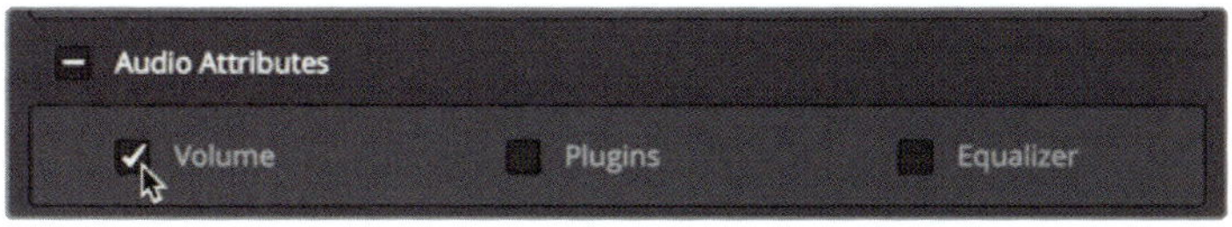

The volume attributes from the first interview clip are pasted onto the selected clips.

12 Play over the timeline. Drag the Volume slider to fine-tune the volume adjustments.

Copying and pasting attributes to set clips at similar levels can save you a lot of time when working with a complex timeline, but you will still need to play through the clips to ensure appropriate levels.

Changing a Level within a Clip

The music track is the final track that you'll integrate into your mix. Level setting here is slightly more involved than with the other tracks because you really want to set two different levels within this one music clip. The music should be at a quiet level as it plays under the interview portion of the timeline, and then gradually increase in volume when the interview stops. You can set multiple levels within a clip in different ways but on the Edit page you'll use keyframes.

1 In the track header, disable the solo buttons for A1 and A2.

   All three audio tracks should now be audible.

   Initially, you'll set a low volume level for the music as the interview begins. You'll want it low enough so that it doesn't interfere with the spoken words but loud enough to add atmosphere to the scene. You can set the level by dragging the volume line directly in the timeline. Again, you will use a general rule of thumb that music should fall somewhere between -20 and -30 dBFS.

2 For the music clip, drag the volume line down until the tool tip reads roughly -20 dB.

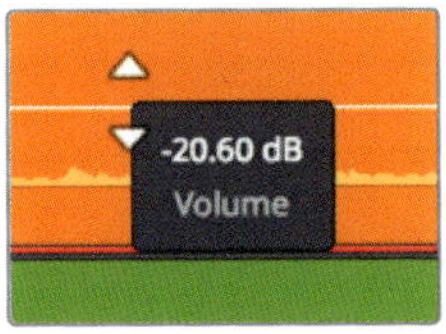

3 Play the timeline with the audio mixed in.

   Dragging the entire level curve has set the clip's overall level. This level should suit the interview portion of the timeline, but it's much too low to underscore the plane shots. By adding keyframes to manipulate the volume line, you can change a clip's volume over time.

4 Position the playhead at the end of the first interview clip.

   Here is where you want the audio to be loud so you will add a keyframe to the music clip.

5 On the music clip, Option-click (macOS) or Alt-click (Windows) the volume line under the playhead position to add a keyframe.

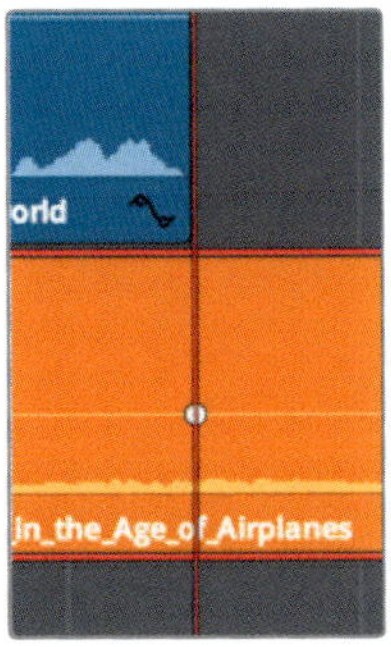

A white dot, the keyframe, is added to the curve. (You may have to move the playhead slightly to see it.) This keyframe marks the point where the music volume should be loud. You now need to set a keyframe before this point to identify where the music should start to crescendo, or ramp up.

6 Click in an empty gray area of the timeline to ensure that no clips are selected.

7 Type **-12**, and press Enter/Return to move the playhead back half a second.

8 Option-click (macOS) or Alt-click (Windows) the level curve under the playhead position to add a keyframe.

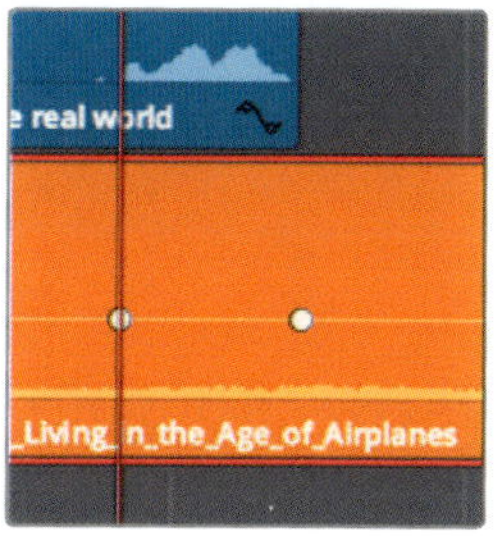

You've now set the duration that the gradual volume change, or ramp, will occur. Changing the vertical position of the second keyframe will cause a ramp up in volume.

9 Position the pointer over the second keyframe on the music clip.

The pointer changes to a move pointer to indicate that it is over a keyframe.

10 Drag the keyframe up until the tool tip reads roughly -10.00 db.

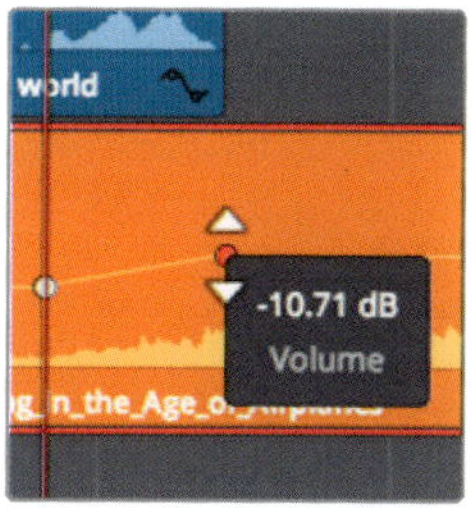

11 Play the first part of the timeline until you hear the mix with the new music ramp.

You've only set the music volume levels under the first interview section. It is now too loud for the rest of the timeline. You could continue to add keyframes and adjust levels for the entire timeline, but let's hold off and complete the adjustments in the Fairlight page in the next lesson.

Adding Audio Fades

Most audio fades are added as a corrective process to soften the incoming or outgoing audio clip. Subtle fades are often applied to narration and dialogue when plosives, particularly those that start with P and B, are too harsh to leave unchanged. You'll also find that you'll use the obvious fade-in and fade-out on music.

1 Play over the start of the timeline until the music begins.

  No matter how low you set this music, it always comes in abruptly. It is meant to build during the interview and hit a crescendo when the first image of the plane appears. You can achieve this slow build up with a reasonably long fade-in.

2 Press Shift-Z to see the entire timeline.

3 In the timeline, place the pointer over the music clip.

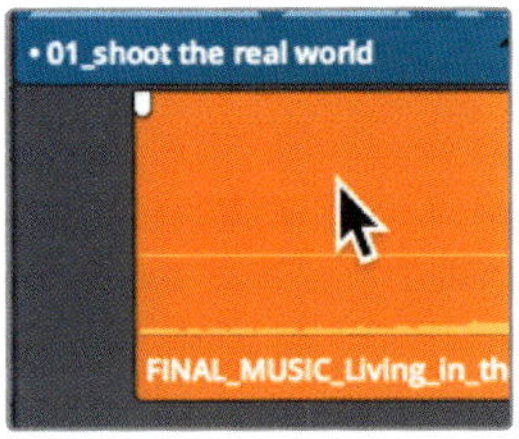

  Audio fade handles appear in the upper-left and upper-right corners of the clip.

4 Drag the left handle in toward the center of the clip until the tool tip reads +2:00

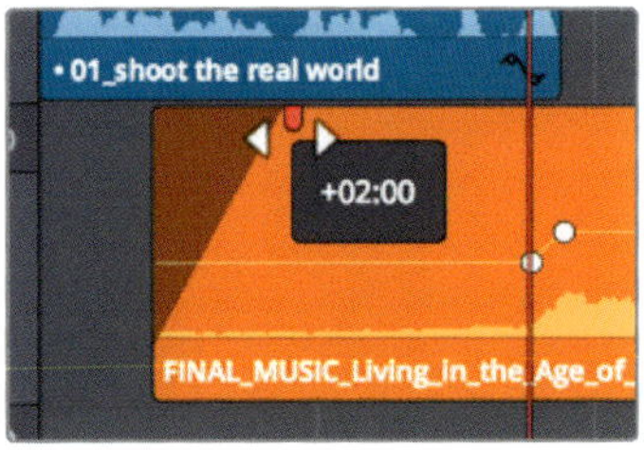

> **TIP** Instead of dragging the fade handle, you could position the playhead where you want the fade-in to stop, and choose Trim > Fade In to playhead.

  You added a two-second fade-in to the start of the clip.

5 Play over the start of the timeline to hear your new fade in.

You can use any combination of fade handles, level curves, and Inspector tweaks that you feel most comfortable with to refine your audio tracks; but these tools and techniques are ultimately just a starting point. To build a true multitrack, cinematic soundtrack, in the next lesson, you'll use DaVinci Resolve's Fairlight page.

Lesson Review

1 What must you select to add a marker to the timeline ruler?

2 Where do you find a list of all the markers on the timeline?

3 How do you add a keyframe to an audio clip's volume line in the timeline?

4 What can you do in the Normalize Audio dialog?

5 True or false? When reading an RMS/Peak meter in the Edit page, audio that is around -5 dbFS is very quiet.

Answers

1 Nothing can be selected in the timeline when you want to add a marker to the timeline ruler.

2 The Edit index can display a list of some or all of the timeline markers.

3 Option-click (macOS) or Alt-click (Windows) the volume line.

4 In the Normalize Audio dialog, you can enter a dbFS value, and thereby set the loudest peak of a selected clip or group of clips to that value.

5 False. When reading an RMS/Peak meter in the Edit page, zero is the maximum level of the system, so -5 dbFS is very loud.

Lesson 9

Mixing Sound in Fairlight: Exploring the Interface

Why do professional productions spend so much time, talent, and (yes) money to create perfect soundtracks? The answer is that high-quality sound is essential to visual storytelling. It is often the difference between an amateur and a professional production.

The Fairlight page in DaVinci Resolve 16 is designed specifically for realizing cinematic-quality sound in your productions. Most importantly, since it is built into your editing application, you can refine the edit, visual effects, color, and sound mix, right up until the time of your final delivery. That integration is what makes DaVinci Resolve a game changer for filmmakers.

In this lesson, you'll navigate the Fairlight page, edit sound effects and narration, record a voiceover, and clean up some background hum using FairlightFX.

Time

This lesson takes approximately 45 minutes to complete.

Goals

Exploring the Interface

Let's talk about workflow. You are almost finished with your edit, and your project is now more or less complete. At some point, you have to move on to audio finishing. Traditionally, all audio post-production was completed separately from editing using standalone audio software. As a result, media conversions and duplication of work were necessary just to share the edited timeline with an audio-post application. You are about to experience how that workflow is accelerated by DaVinci Resolve 16.

1 Open DaVinci Resolve, if necessary; and in the Project manager, open the Age of Airplanes project.

2 In the Rough Cuts bin, double-click the **05 Fairlight Rough Cut** to open it in the timeline.

   This timeline is slightly different from the one you used in the previous lesson. It has all the volume changes you made, along with the keyframing and fade-up on the music track, but it also has more sound effects.

3 At the bottom of the DaVinci Resolve interface, click the Fairlight button.

   That is the one-and-only workflow step required to move from editing to audio post!

   While the interface may appear to be a single large timeline, the Fairlight page is actually divided into four sections.

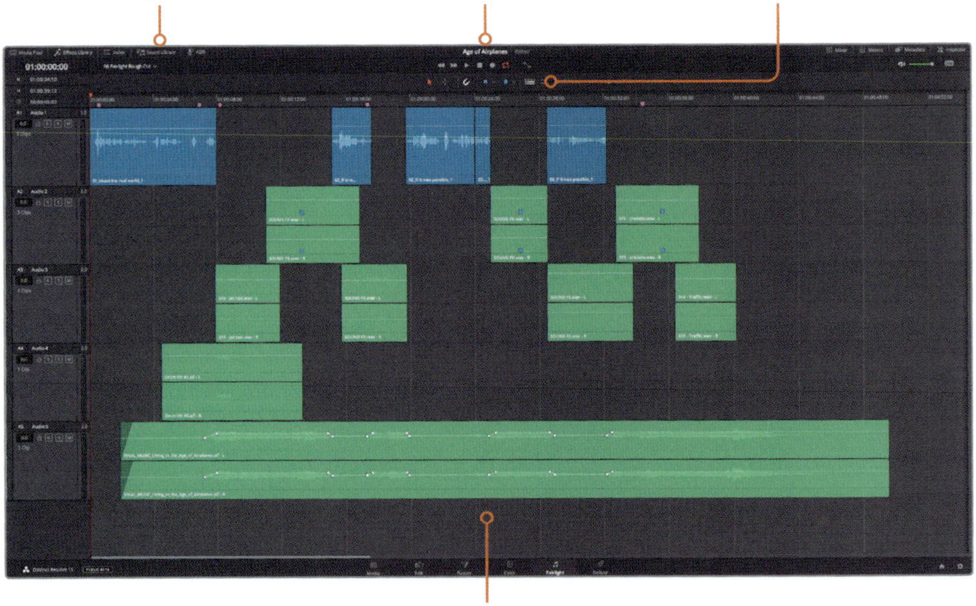

Your current timeline—with the same color-coded tracks, markers, and audio levels that you were viewing in the Edit page—is now available in the Fairlight page. It looks different because the Fairlight page is optimized for multichannel audio recording, editing, mixing, and sweetening. As you can see, the default layout is streamlined to only show the audio timeline. However, in the Interface toolbar, you can open panels as you need them. By default, the media pool, viewer, meters and mixer are hidden.

4 In the upper-right corner of the interface toolbar, click the Meters button to open the Monitoring panel.

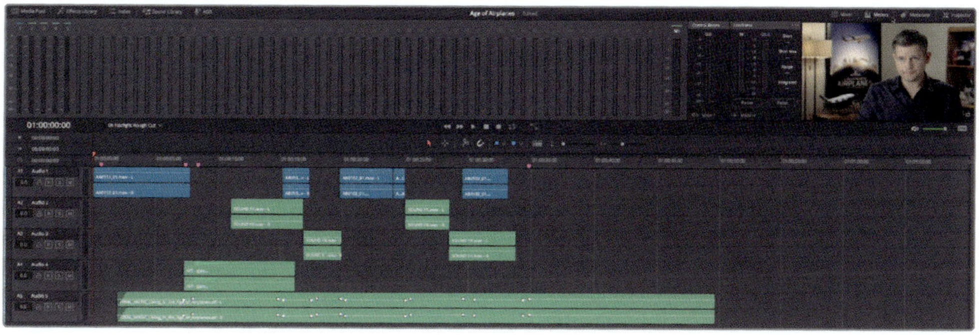

As the name suggests, the monitoring panel displays all of the audio and video contents of the current timeline. There is also an expandable mixer that you can use for balancing track levels.

5 In the interface toolbar, click the Mixer button to show the mixer.

6 Drag the left edge of the Mixer toward the left to expand the mixer until it shows the channel strips for all five tracks.

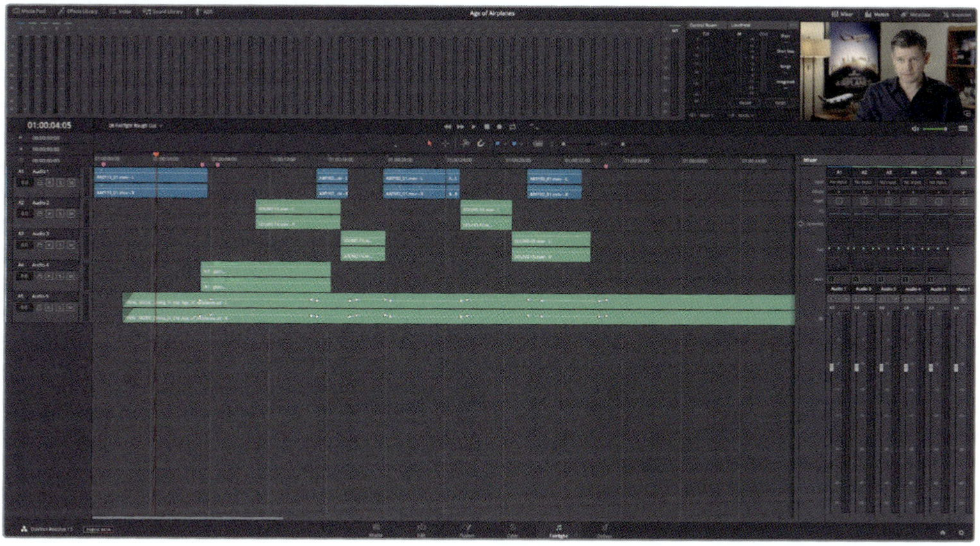

At a glance, you can see that the Fairlight Mixer is loaded with controls, especially at the top where you'll find an Effects slot, EQ, Dynamics, and Pan controls. You'll work more with the mixer later in the lesson. For now, let's play the project. Luckily, many of the playback techniques you learned when using the Edit page will also apply here.

7 Drag the playhead to the start of the timeline, or press the Home key.

8 Press the spacebar to play your project.

9 Press the K key to pause, and then press L twice to fast forward.

10 Press J to play backward.

11 In the transport controls above the timeline, click the Stop button, or press the spacebar again, to stop playback.

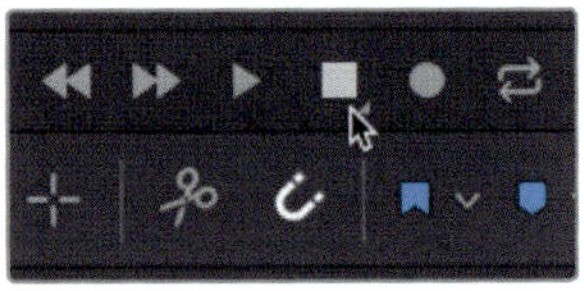

12 Press Shift-Z to fit all the timeline clips horizontally in the page, if necessary.

You'll notice that, unlike the Edit page, each track shows the number of channels it contains. Let's expand the tracks vertically so you can more clearly see the two channels on Audio 1 track.

13 Fit the audio tracks vertically in the timeline window by holding down Shift and scrolling your middle mouse wheel.

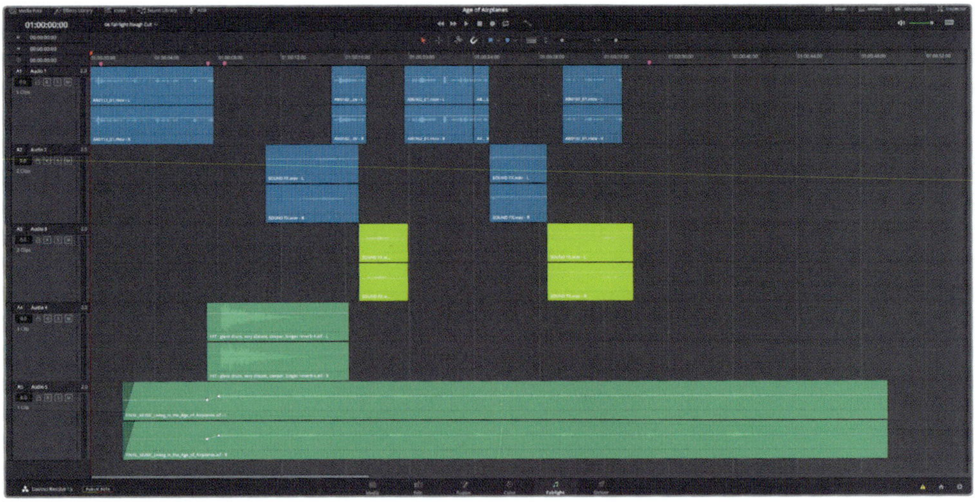

TIP When zooming a Fairlight timeline, the focus remains on the playhead for horizontal zooming and the selected track for vertical zooming.

Other standard transport controls such as play, rewind, and fast forward are also included in the strip of transport controls, along with audio-specific transport controls such as loop and record.

Previewing Video

In a traditional audio-post workflow, an audio editor will need a separate reference video to use as a guide when building the soundtrack. In Resolve, you do not need a reference video because the Fairlight page includes a handy viewer that shows the timeline's video. You can also see the edited clip segments on a video track in the timeline.

1 Press the spacebar, and watch the meters and viewer during playback.

  The meters display all your track and output levels.

2 In the toolbar, click the timeline view options button.

3 At the top of the Timeline View Options pop-up menu, click the video tracks button.

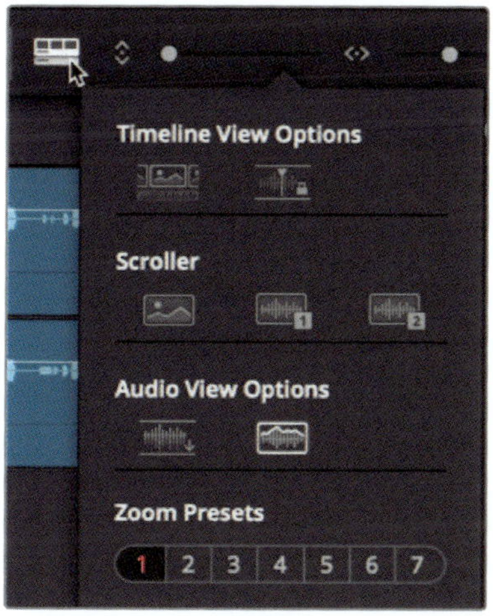

The video track and all the edits appear above the audio tracks in the Fairlight timeline. If you have a Blackmagic DeckLink card or UltraStudio, you also can view the video on a second video display.

Renaming and Color Coding Tracks

Track organization becomes extremely important as you expand the number of audio tracks and need to navigate through them quickly. Instead of trying to remember the track number that you used for different types of tracks, you can rename tracks to describe their contents. For this project, you'll use capital letters to name individual tracks. Using capital letters in track names is common practice in audio post-production because they are easier to read in both the track headers and the audio mixer.

1 Click the Audio 1 track header to select the track.

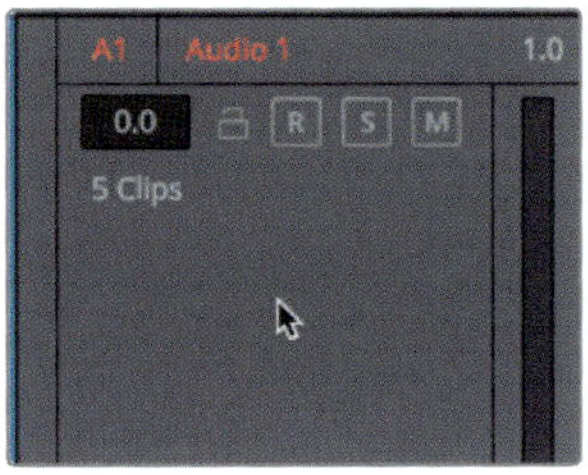

Dealing with a handful of tracks is easy, but imagine that you have fifty tracks or more in your project. Suddenly, you're going to want more than a vague track number to identify each track. Fortunately, DaVinci Resolve allows you to name the audio tracks in the header.

2 On the A1 Track header, double-click the name Audio 1. Type **SYNC**, and press Return.

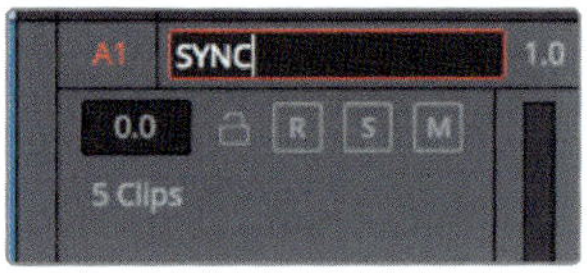

This is the track that contains your sync sound interview. The next two tracks contain sound effects and the last two are for music.

3 Change the names of Audio 2 and Audio 3 to **SFX 01** and **SFX 02**, respectively.

4 Click the Audio 4 track, and rename the track to **DRUM HITS**.

5 Click the Audio 5 track, and rename the track to **MUSIC**.

As you did in the Edit page, you can also better organize tracks by color coding the new tracks in the Fairlight page.

6 Right-click the SFX 01 track header, and choose Change Track Color > Lime.

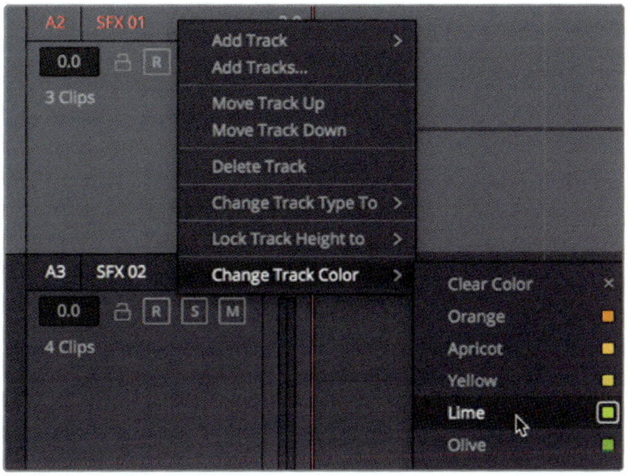

7 Do the same for SFX 02.

8 On the DRUM HITS track, right-click the header, and choose Change Track Color > Yellow.

9 Do the same for MUSIC.

Now, the similar sound-element tracks are color coded to match, thereby making it easier to parse a large timeline. Again, when you're working with only a few tracks, naming and color coding them may seem like overkill; but when your track list starts to grow, you will be glad you started the process in an organized fashion.

Viewing a Spotting List

Communication is essential in post-production because one person seldom does all the work. As a result, it is important to keep a list of the audio tasks you have to do for your project. Even when you plan to do all the editing and audio mixing yourself, most projects develop too many details to keep in your head, so making a list is critical.

Among the items in the list, you should include the basic decisions about where music, sound effects, and additional voice over (VO) should be placed. Those choices are documented in a **spotting list** that is typically created when the director, the sound editor, and the composer watch the program together and identify, or **spot**, where sound effects and music are needed.

Even when you are one person doing everything, you will still need that spotting list of all the audio elements you'll want to add. The Index panel takes much of the work out of creating a **spotting list** by leveraging those markers you added on the Edit page along with any new markers you add in the Fairlight page.

1 In the upper-left of the Interface toolbar, click the Index button.

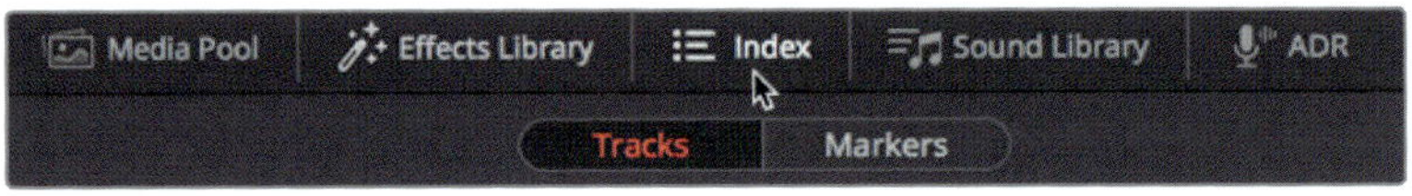

The Index is divided into two tabs. The first tab lists all the tracks in the current timeline. The second tab shows the markers added to the timeline.

2 In the Index, click the Markers tab.

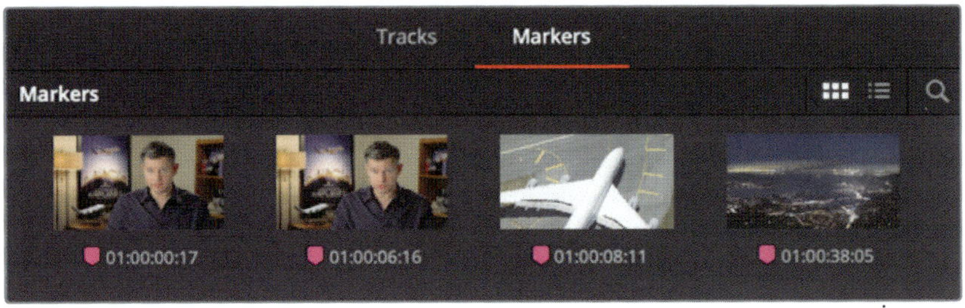

The Markers index shows a thumbnail and timecode location for each timeline marker. It also displays any text typed into the name and notes fields in a list view.

3 At the top of the Index window, click the list view button to view the Index as a list.

In list view, you can use marker information in the columns to help create your spotting list by customizing the columns to show only the information you need.

4 Right-click any one of the column headings, and deselect Start TC, End TC, and Duration to hide those columns in the Index.

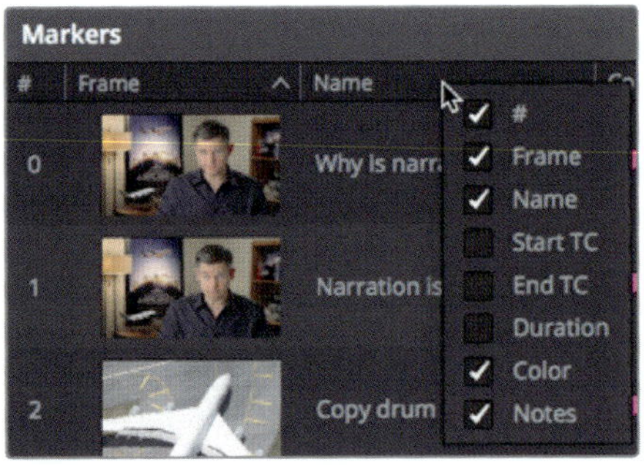

5 Click the Frame column header to sort the markers in the order they appear in the timeline.

Now that the marker spotting list is set up, you can use it as a guide for your upcoming work on the soundtrack.

TIP You can sort markers in ascending or descending order based on any selected column header. For these exercises, you'll sort by the Frames column to keep the markers in the order they appear in the timeline.

6 Double-click the first marker in the list.

TIP In the Fairlight page, press Shift-up and down arrow keys to move the playhead from marker to marker just as you would in the Edit page.

The playhead jumps to the marker position in the timeline. The note attached to this marker asks why the Sync narration is stereo. Although it isn't unusual to find editors cutting dialogue in stereo, spoken word tracks are often recorded and edited in mono.

Changing Track Formats

Whatever spoken words you have in your project, whether they be dialogue, interview, or voiceover, they are probably the primary audio in your timeline. So, it is essential to spend extra time finessing those clips to create a polished soundtrack.

The first step in editing spoken words is to evaluate those recordings. You can learn a lot about a track's recording methods just by looking at the audio clips in the Fairlight timeline.

1 Look at the A1 SYNC track. These clips have two waveforms because they are in a two-channel stereo track.

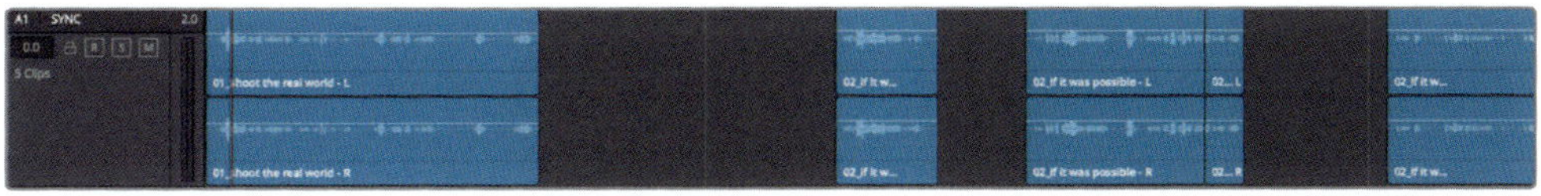

2 On the A1 SYNC track, click the solo button, and play the two channels. The left and right channels sound identical.

It is typical for narration or dialogue to be recorded as mono clips. Because the current waveforms appear identical, and you cannot hear any discernable difference in the left and right channels, you can assume that the channels are identical and that these clips are actually mono recordings. The quickest way to turn these into mono clips to convert the entire track to mono.

3 Right-click the A1 SYNC track header, and choose Change Track Type To > Mono.

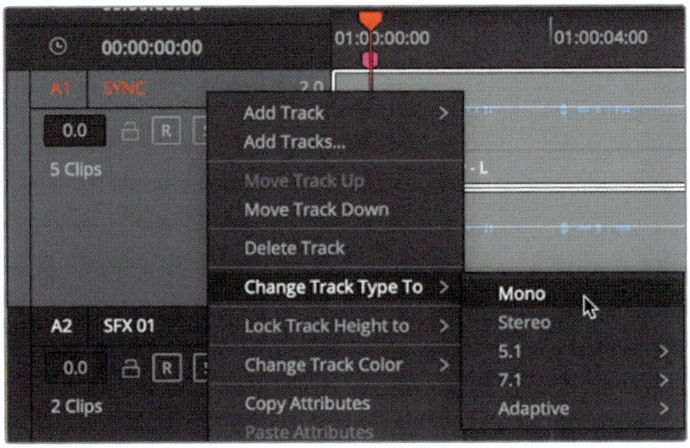

After you convert the track type, three key indicators let you know the track was changed. The label to the right of the track name now reads 1.0 to indicate a mono track. The meter to the right of the track header shows a single volume meter instead of two meters. Lastly, the clips on the track show only one channel.

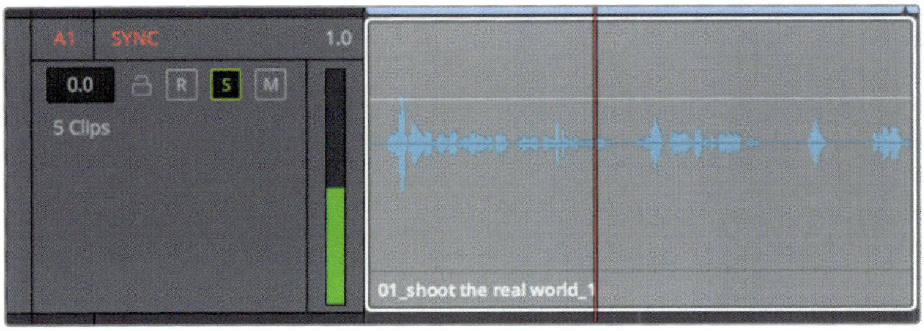

The clips themselves are not modified, however. If you edit or copy one of these clips onto a stereo track, both channels will reappear. Because a mono track can contain only one channel of audio, the left channel (the upper channel as seen in the timeline) is used by default when stereo clips are edited onto mono tracks. Since both channels on these clips were identical, converting the track was the quickest way to make all the clips mono.

Trimming Clips in Fairlight

The next step when cleaning up a spoken word track usually is to refine them using a trimming method similar to one you used in the Edit page. However, the trimming behavior in the Fairlight page is more akin to trimming with the selection tool on the Edit page, and not the trim tool. You can extend or shorten clips without worrying about pushing tracks out of sync because Fairlight never ripple trims clips.

1 In the Index, double-click the second marker.

The playhead jumps to the end of the first timeline clip on the SYNC track. The marker note in the Index claims the narration cuts off too early.

2 In the toolbar, drag the horizontal slider to zoom in to the narration clip until it nearly fills the timeline window.

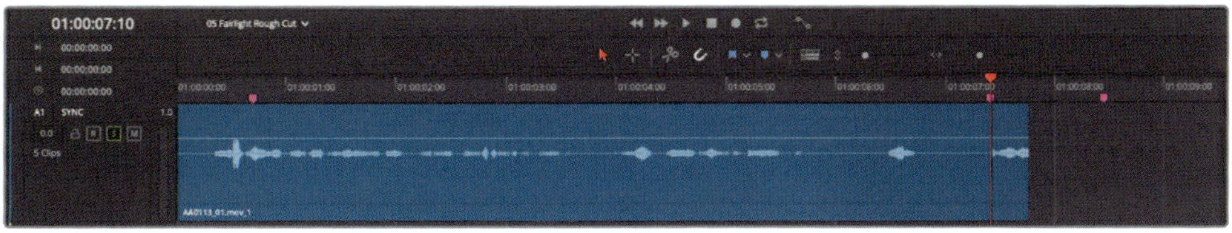

Let's first play over the clip to hear the narration.

3 In the toolbar, click the range selection tool, or press R, and click the clip on the A1, SYNC track.

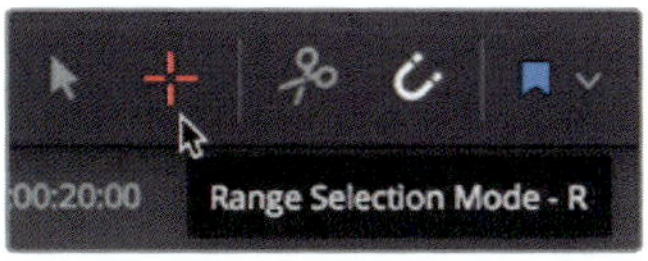

Selecting a clip with the range selection tool marks in and out points around that clip, which makes it easier to play the clip and review the difference between channels.

4 Press Option-/ (slash) in macOS or Alt-/ (slash) in Windows to play the clip from its in to out points.

The last word at the end of this clip ends a bit too soon. You can trim it out to extend the clip and more clearly hear the last word.

5 Press Option-X (macOS) Or Alt-X (Windows) to clear the in and out marks.

6 Place the mouse pointer over the end of the sync narration clip until the mouse pointer changes to a trim cursor.

7 Drag the end of the clip to the right until the last word is fully included in the clip. Use the waveform on the track as a guide to ending the trim.

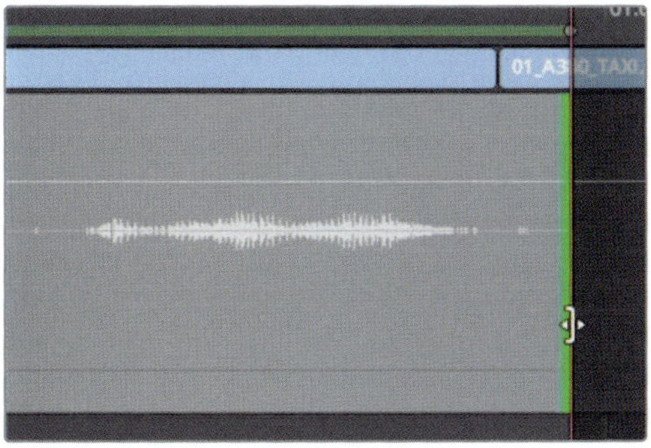

Because you modified only the ending, let's not listen to the entire clip. Just audition the range near the end.

> **TIP** You can split a clip by choosing Timeline > Razor, using the scissors icon in the toolbar, or pressing Cmd-B (macOS) or Ctrl-B (Windows).

8 Position the range selection cursor just below the clip and to the right.

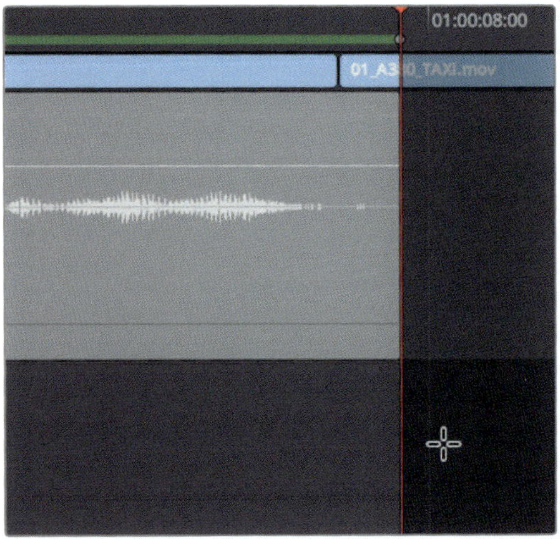

9 Drag a selection rectangle around the end of the clip until you run out of room near the timeline header.

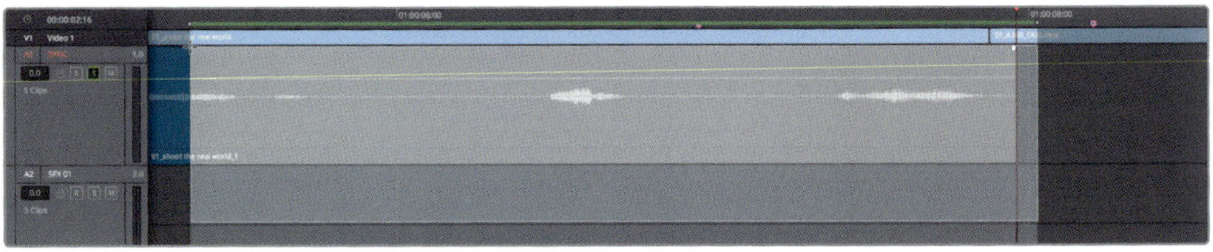

Dragging out the selection range marks in and out points to encompass the selection.

10 Press Option-/ (slash) in macOS or Alt-/ (slash) in Windows to play from the in to out points and hear the new trimmed ending.

11 Press the A key to return to the selection tool, and press Option-X (macOS) or Alt-X (Windows) to clear the in and out marks.

12 Unsolo A1 SYNC.

Trimming in the Fairlight page is not bound by video frames, so you can be very precise with subframe audio trimming.

Aligning Sound Effects

Once your narration or spoken word tracks are edited, you can turn your attention to editing sound effects and music. Sometimes you'll use music which is completely mixed for the entire project, and at other times you'll receive music split into individual music cues. Still other times you'll have mixed music on which you want to add transients or short sound hits that adds an audible exclamation point.

1 Double-click the third marker in the index, "Copy drum hit".

 The playhead jumps to the center of the clip on the drum hit track.

2 Press Shift-Z to see the entire timeline.

3 Solo track A4, DRUM HITS.

4 In the toolbar, click the range selection tool, or press R, and click the clip on the A4, DRUM HITS.

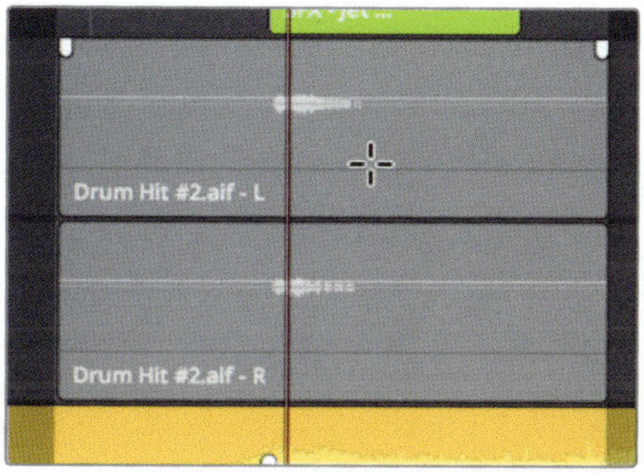

 Let's review the sound on this track to understand what you are about to do.

5 Press Option-/ (slash) in macOS or Alt-/ (slash) in Window) to play from the in to out points.

 This sound is just a single, loud, reverberating drum hit, but it makes a good exclamation point in the sound track. Based on the note in the marker, you'll copy the clip from the start of this track and paste it on the end where the music comes to its conclusion. Keep in mind that copy/paste functions in the Fairlight page are designed to enable precise placement of clips based on the position of the playhead. So, pay close attention to your selections and to your playhead when moving the sound effect.

6 Press the A key to return to the selection tool, and press Option-X (macOS) or Alt-X (Windows) to clear the in and out points.

7 In the timeline, click any empty space to deselect all selected tracks.

8 As you did in Lesson 3, use the J, K, and L keys to position the playhead directly over the start of the drum sound waveform.

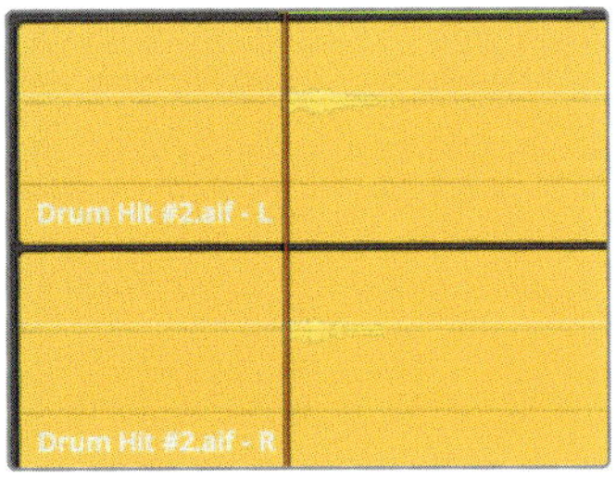

9 Un-solo A4 DRUM HITS.

10 Select the clip in the A4, DRUM HITS tracks, and press Cmd-C (macOS) or Ctrl-C (Windows).

11 Drag the playhead down toward the end of the timeline.

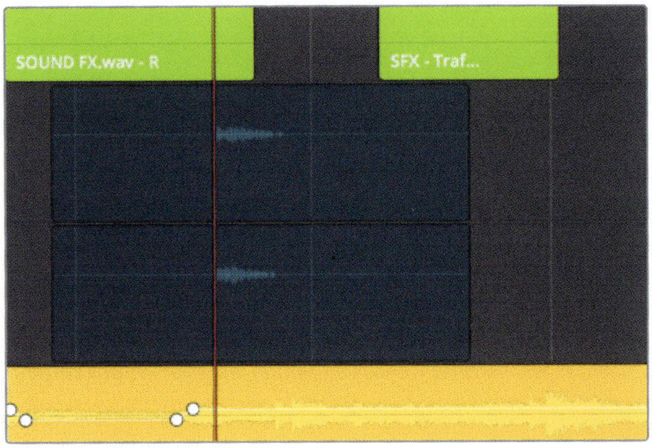

As you move the playhead, the copy of the clip is seen as a translucent clip that follows the playhead. Throughout the move, the playhead maintains its position at the start of the drum hit waveform. This behavior makes it easy to position the drum hit sound exactly where you need it.

12 When the playhead is located at the start of the last video clip in the timeline, as you see the first frame of the ending credit in the viewer, press Cmd-V (macOS) or Ctrl-V (Windows) to paste the clip at that location.

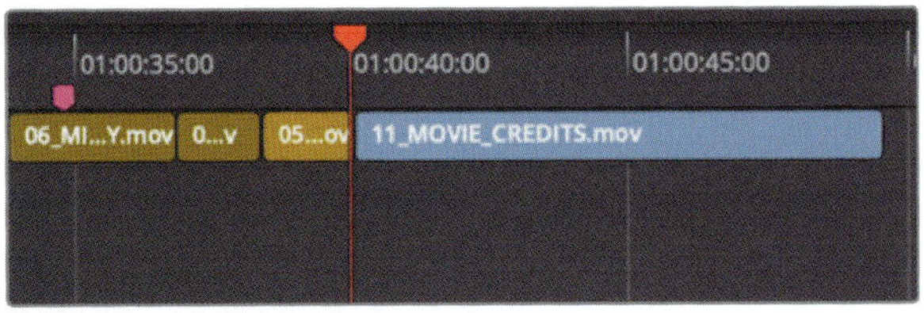

Let's review the new drum hit placement.

13 In the toolbar, click the range selection tool, or press R, and click the last clip on the A4 DRUM HIT track.

14 Press Option-/ (slash) in macOS or Alt-/ (slash) in Windows to play from the in to out points.

15 Press the A key to return to the selection tool, and press Option-X (macOS) or Alt-X (Windows) to clear the in and out points.

If you find that the alignment is not perfect, just as in the Edit page, you can press the, (comma) and . (period) keys to nudge the clip a few frames forward or backward.

Recording Audio in a Timeline

You can record your own voiceover in DaVinci Resolve right in the Fairlight page timeline. All you need to do is set up a microphone, patch the microphone input to a track, arm the track, and start recording.

In this exercise, you'll record a temporary ending voiceover tag for this trailer. Frequently, the voiceover talent can't record his or her lines until after you have started editing the sound. So, you can easily record a temporary VO clip to use as you edit. When the real VO talent arrives, you can use this same recording method to record the final VO directly into the timeline.

NOTE If you don't have a separate microphone, you can use the built-in microphone in your computer for the following exercises. If you lack a microphone entirely, read through the set-up and recording sections and follow along when the recording is finished.

1 If you have a standalone USB microphone, close DaVinci Resolve, and attach the microphone to your computer.

2 In your computer's Sound preferences or settings, set your microphone (or the built-in mic) as the audio input device.

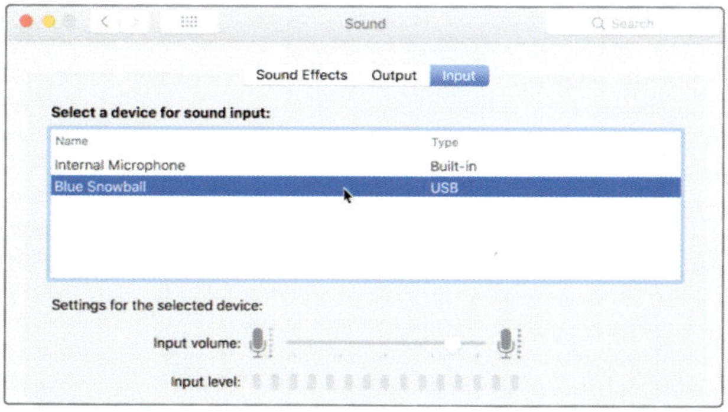

3 In DaVinci Resolve, open the Age of Airplanes project.

4 Choose File > Project settings.

5 Click the Capture and Playback settings.

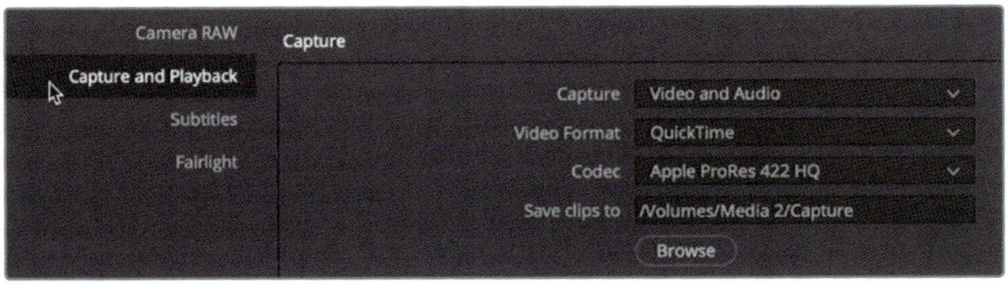

6 In the "Save clips to" field, click the browser button, and choose a location to store your newly recorded audio files.

7 Click Save to close the Project settings window.

8 Hide the Monitoring panel (Meters), and show the Mixer.

Now that your mic is attached and the capture path is set, all you need to do is create a track for your recording and set up the timeline.

Creating and Patching Tracks for Recording

When recording audio onto a track, the important thing to consider is whether you want to record in stereo or mono. By now, you've probably figured out that mono is the preferred format for dialogue and VO.

For this recording, you'll create a new mono track, and use the input settings in the Mixer to patch the microphone to that new track.

1 Right-click any track header, and choose Add Tracks.

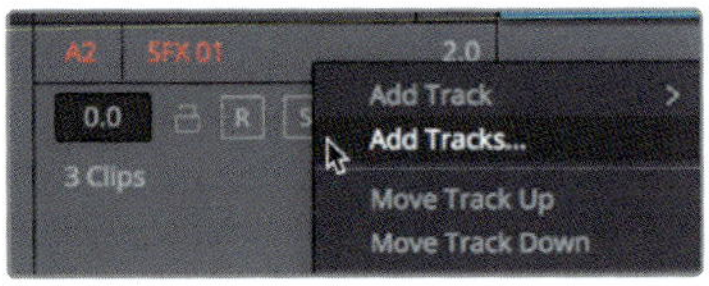

2 In the Add Tracks dialog that appears, set "Number of tracks" to 1, and set Insert Position to Below SYNC. Change the Audio Track Type to Mono. Click Add Tracks.

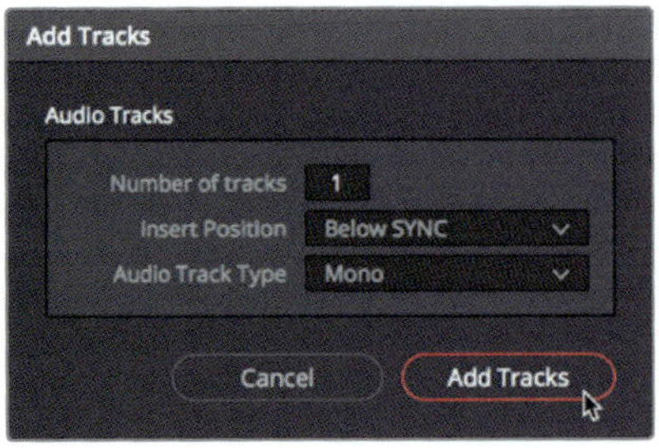

A new mono track appears below A1. Now, you must set the input for this track. To patch a track's input, you can use the input settings in the Mixer.

3 In the track header, double-click the Audio 2 name, and type **VO** because this will be your voiceover track.

4 In the upper-right corner of the window, click the Mixer button to open the mixer.

Input settings appear at the top of each channel strip just below the track number assignment. Tracks without an assigned input display No Input.

5 At the top of the A2 channel strip, in the Input pop-up menu, choose Input.

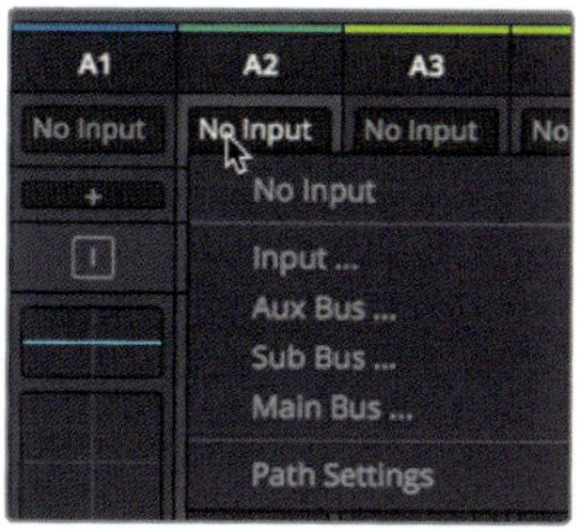

The Patch Input/Output window opens displaying the Source inputs to the left and the Destination tracks to the right.

6 Select the first channel for your microphone as the source, and select the VO track as the destination.

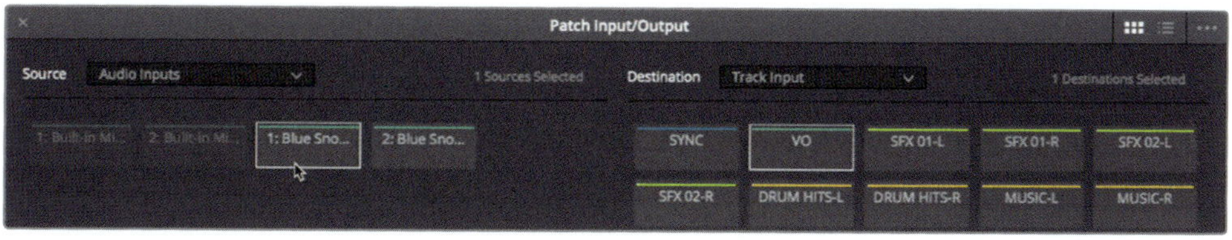

7 At the bottom of the window, click Patch to set your input patch, and then close the window.

Your track is created and patched. Now, you must arm it for recording.

Arming a Track for Recording

Each track header includes an arm button to enable the track for recording. To do so, you must first patch the track with an input, as you've done for the Audio 2 track. The arm button (R button) is available in both the track header and the track's channel strip in the Mixer.

1 In the A2 track header, click the arm button.

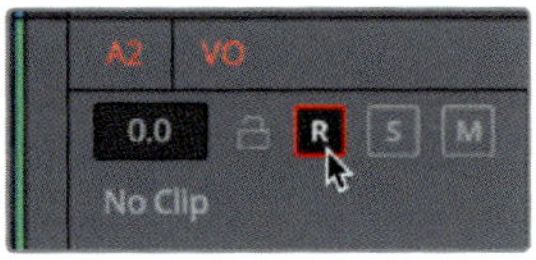

The track name and arm button turn red to indicate that the track is armed for recording.

> **NOTE** Before recording, it's a good idea to know your lines. Here is the ending tag line for the trailer: "In the age of airplanes, we've become explorers once again."

2 Practice your line once or twice prior to recording.

When recording, you do not want any of the other tracks to be audible, or they also will be recorded.

3 Solo track A2 VO.

4 In the transport controls. click the record button. When the playhead starts moving and drawing a red region within the timeline, you are recording. Read the line with your best movie trailer voice. When you are finished, press the spacebar to stop recording.

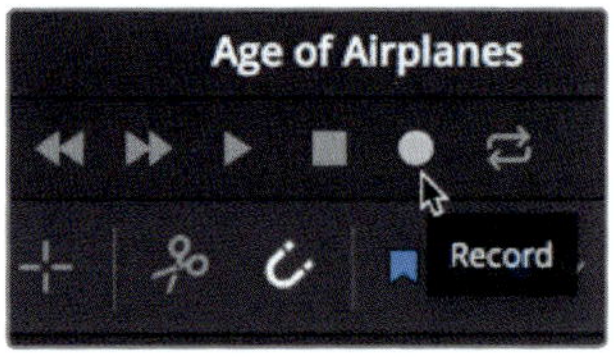

5 Un-solo track A2 VO so you can review the voiceover with the music and sound effects.

6 Play your recording.

7 When you are finished, in the track header, click the arm button to disarm the track.

Even though this temp VO is all you need for this project, DaVinci Resolve's Fairlight audio includes more advanced recording tools for automatic dialogue replacement (ADR), multitrack music recording, and foley sound effects. If you weren't able to record the voiceover, the next exercise will bring you up to date as you work with a professionally pre-recorded voiceover clip.

Modifying Clip Attributes

Although you recorded a fine temporary VO, when the real VO is recorded with professional talent, you'll need to preview it and add it to the timeline. You can access and preview any audio clip in your Media pool within the Fairlight page.

1 In the upper-left corner of the DaVinci Resolve window, click the Index button to close the Index, and click the Media pool to show the bins and clips in this project.

2 In the bin list, select the Audio bin.

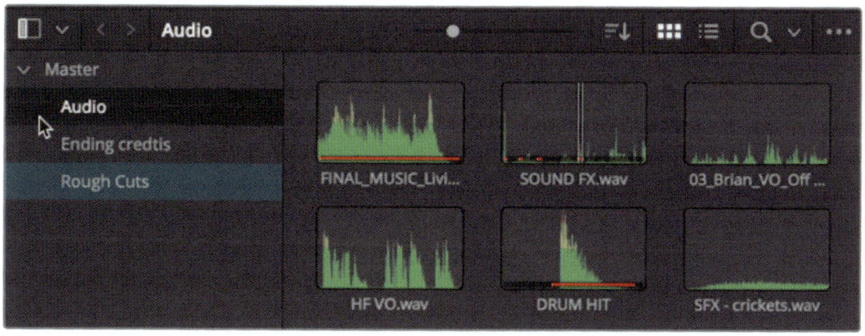

All your audio clips are visible in the bin. You can preview them to find the right clip and edit it into the project.

3 Click the **HF VO** clip to load it in the Media pool preview player at the top of the panel.

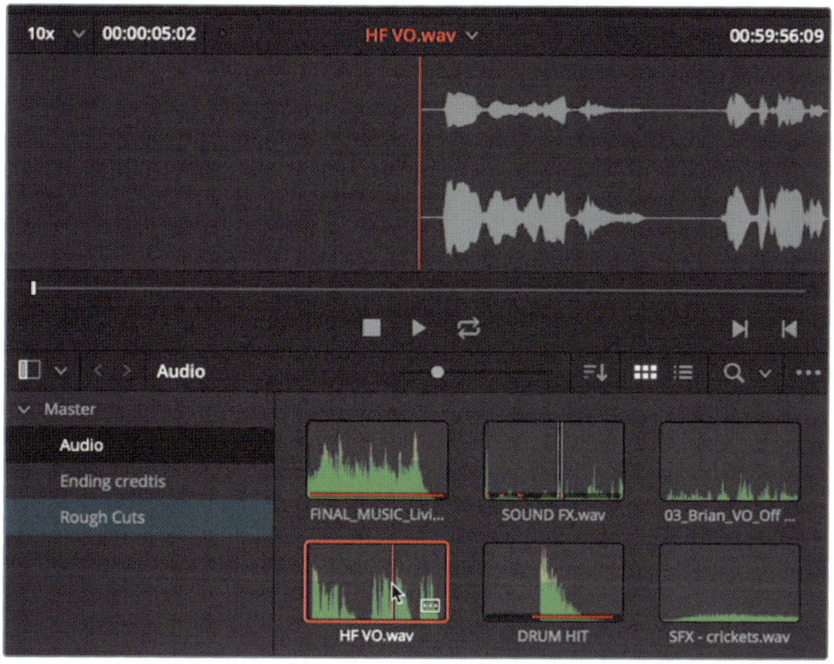

Without playing the clip, the appearance of the two waveforms should tell you that this is a stereo clip. You should also see that the upper channel (channel 1) waveforms peak is lower which indicates it is a quieter channel. Let's give it a listen to hear the difference.

> **TIP** Listening to the differences in channels is easier when using headphones because each ear hears a separate channel of the stereo clip.

The left channel, channel 1, does not sound as clear as the right channel, channel 2. It is often the case that dialogue or interviews are recorded with two microphones. A boom mic is typically the primary and clearest mic while a lavalier or lapel mic is useful primarily as a backup. You now need to ensure that channel 2 is used when you edit your professional VO clip onto your mono track.

4 In the bin, right-click the **HF VO** clip, and choose Clip attributes.

The clip attributes show the format of the audio, as well as all the channel mapping. By default, the left channel is always channel 1 and is the channel used when converting a stereo clip into a mono track. You can change that default behavior in the clip attributes window.

5 In the clip attributes Format pop-up menu, choose Mono.

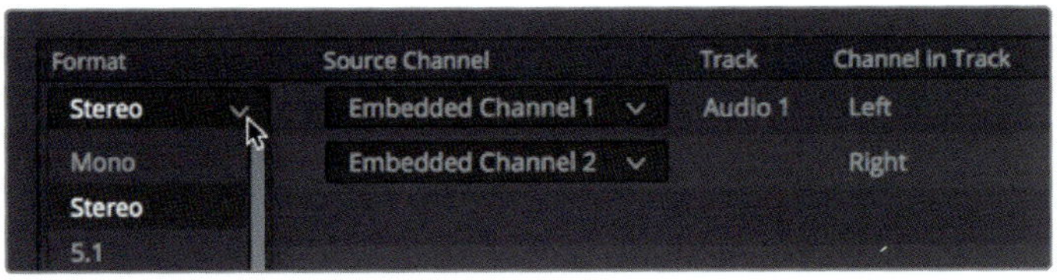

6 Change the Source channel to Embedded Channel 2.

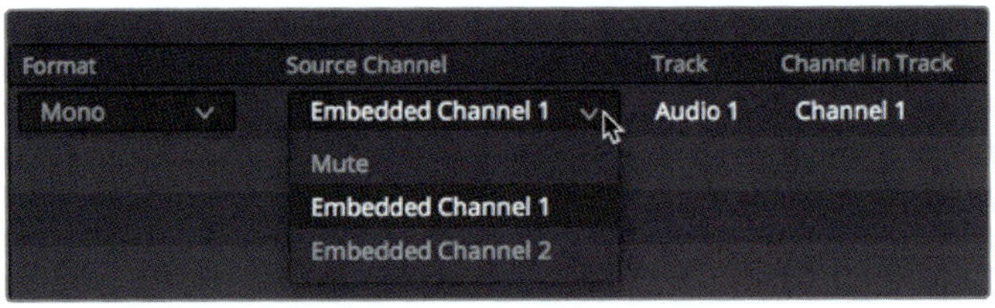

7 Click OK to close the clip attributes window.

You now have a mono clip for your VO that uses channel 2 as its audio source. When you edit this clip into the mono track, you'll be using the good-sounding boom mic recording.

8 In the timeline, select the temporary VO clip you recorded, and press Delete or Backspace to remove it.

9 Position the playhead at the last pink marker, which indicates where the VO should start.

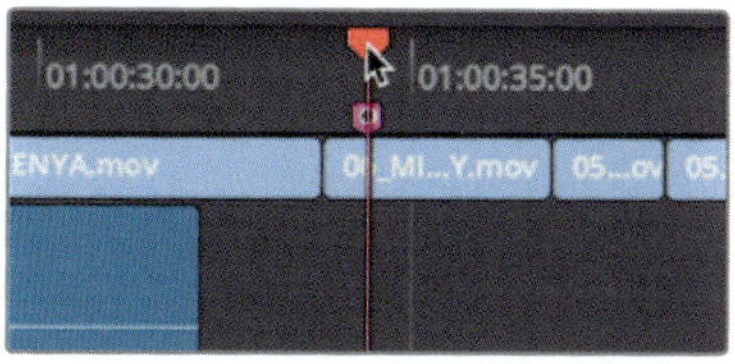

10 Drag the HF VO clip from the Media pool, and place it so the start of the clip lines up with the playhead position in the timeline.

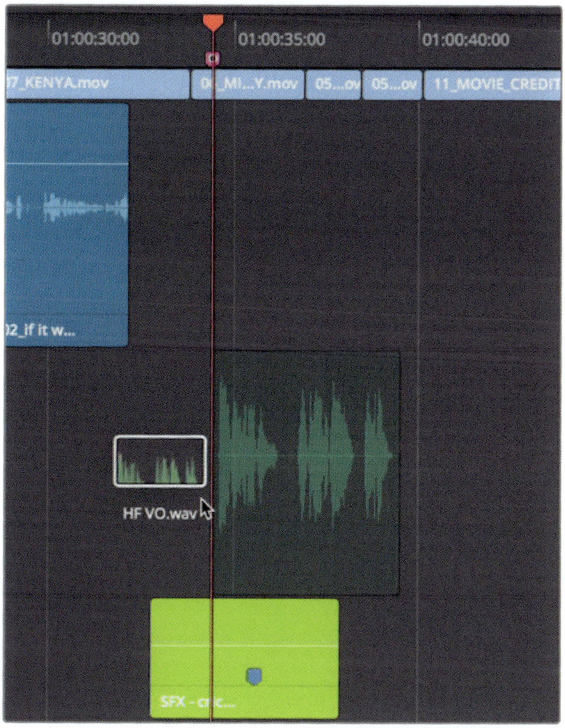

11 Position the playhead just before the new VO clip, and play the timeline to hear the mix of all the tracks.

Now that you know how to set up, remap, and edit your dialogue tracks, you're ready to address the sound quality of your project.

Using Fairlight FX

Fairlight includes a wide range of native audio processing plug-ins that work across all three OS's. When you are using a macOS you also have support for third-party VST and Audio Unit plug-ins. Windows users also have VST plug-in support. You can apply these plug-ins to a single clip or an entire track to fix common problems or to design sounds so they perfectly match the mood of your project.

1 Solo the VO track so you can listen to it independent of the other soundtrack elements.

2 In the toolbar, click the Range selection tool, or press R, and in the timeline, click the VO clip.

3 Press Option-/ (slash) in macOS or Alt-/ (slash) in Windows to play from the in to out points.

   In the VO, you can hear a low-pitched background buzz. This is not an uncommon problem and can happen when an electrical signal seeps into your audio cables. Typically, it is due to poor electrical grounding or poor audio cable shielding.

   You have a convenient tool to minimize this common problem: a notch filter that can block a very narrow band of audio frequencies in your recording. The buzzing hum in this audio clip, as is often the case, is at a frequency of 60 Hz or 50 Hz depending on whether you recorded in North America, Asia, or Europe (due to the AC delivery standards in those continents.) Since this type of buzz is so common and so specific, Fairlight includes a special De-Hummer Fairlight FX plug-in to address the problem.

4 In the upper-left of the Resolve window, close the Media pool, and click the Effects library button to display the Audio FX plug-ins.

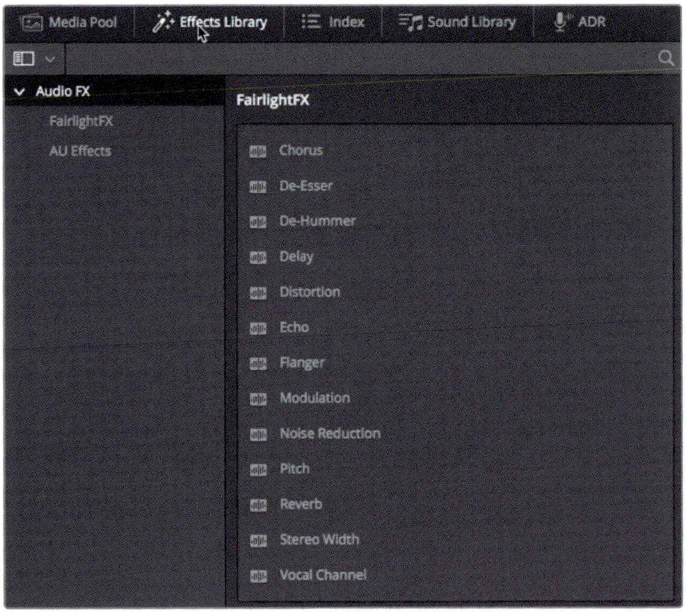

5 In the FairlightFX category, drag the De-Hummer plug-in onto the VO clip in the timeline.

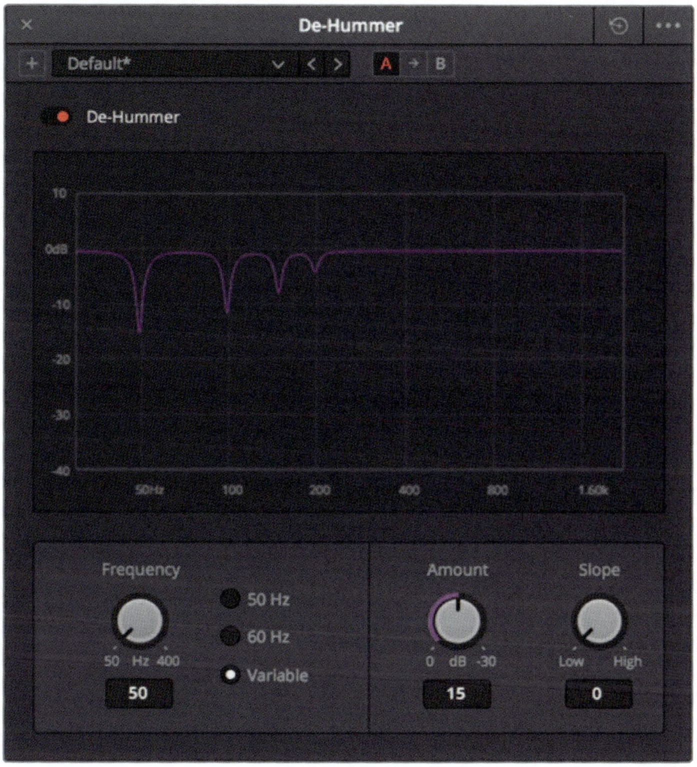

When you apply the plug-in, the De-Hummer dialog opens with controls to specify the type of hum you have.

TIP If the Inspector is open, it will also show controls for the De-Hummer. There you can click the Trash can icon to remove the effect.

6 In the Frequency section, click the 60 Hz button to set the De-Hummer to notch out the 60 Hz frequency.

The graph in the De-Hummer displays frequencies along the bottom. Low frequencies are to the left and higher frequencies are to the right. The dips in the graph indicate the narrow bands of frequencies that are being cut out or diminished in the clip.

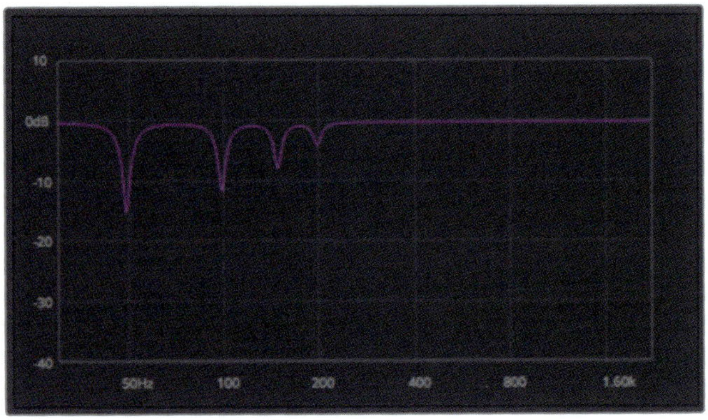

7 In the transport controls above the timeline, click the loop button, and press Option-/ (slash) in macOS or Alt-/ (slash) in Windows to loop the playback from the in to out points.

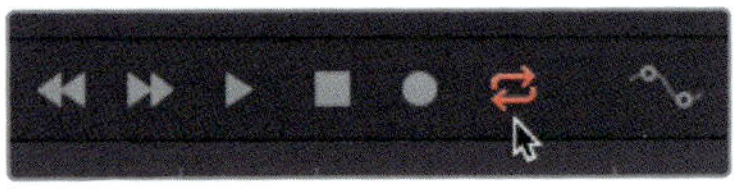

8 As the clip plays, drag the Amount dial to adjust the amount of hum that is removed.

As you drag the Amount dial clockwise, you are lowering the volume of the selected frequencies (60 Hz, in this case) in the voiceover clip. So, you are also altering the sound quality of the voice recording. It's a delicate balance to decide how much hum to remove before you lose too much vocal quality.

Looking at the graph, you might think that by selecting 60 Hz that the filter will notch out only that frequency; but simply removing one frequency may not fix the problem. You can adjust the Slope control to filter out additional frequencies that may be contributing to the unwanted hum.

9 Drag the Slope control until you hear the least hum in the voiceover.

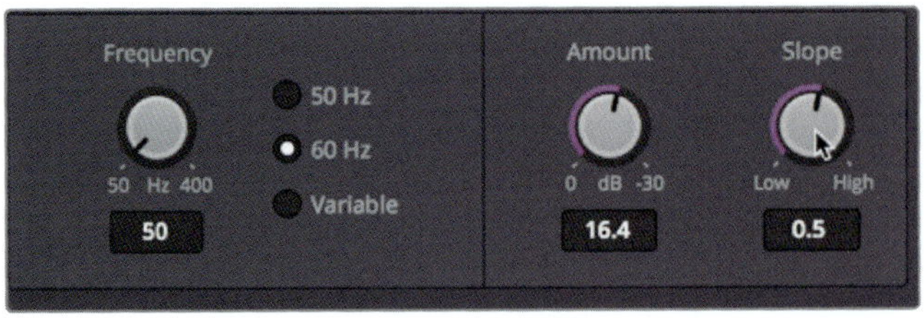

10 When you are done making adjustments, press the spacebar to stop playback; close the De-Hummer window; and in the toolbar, click the selection tool, or press A. Finally, unsolo A2 VO.

The De-Hummer is one of the most frequently used plug-ins, even for picture editors because it addresses a very common problem with very little effort.

Applying Noise Reduction to an Entire Track

In the previous exercise you applied a repair plug-in to an individual clip. You can also apply plug-ins to an entire track, either from the effects inserts at the top of the mixer or by dragging the effect from the Effects Library to the track header in the timeline. In this exercise, you'll apply Resolve's powerful Noise Reduction plug-in to the entire A1 SYNC track and have it sample to noise to automatically remove it.

Since the noise reduction effect requires to have an area on the track where you only hear the noise, you'll have to edit in a short clip of room tone.

1 Return to the edit page, and from the Audio bin load the Room Tone.aiff clip into the source viewer.

2 Mark an In and Out point around any 10 second area of room tone and append it to the end of the timeline on the SYNC track.

3 Return to the Fairlight page.

4 In the Effects Library, drag the Noise Reduction plug-in onto the A1 SYNC track header.

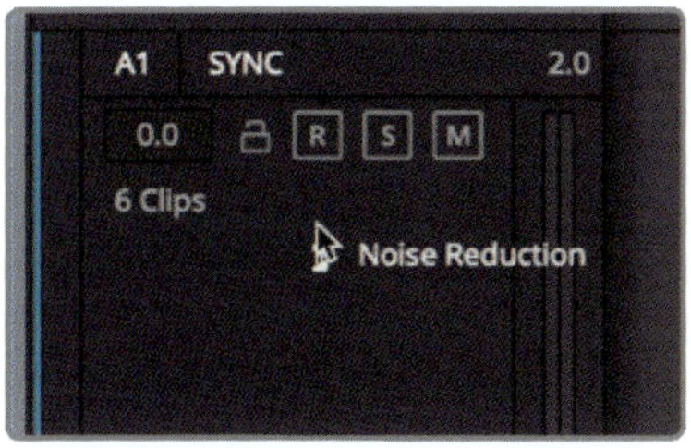

Although the noise reduction has many controls, if you have a few seconds of clean room tone, you can have the noise reduction plugin sample what that sounds like and remove it from the remaining clip on the SYNC track.

5 Solo the Sync track.

6 Click the learn button and play over the 10 seconds of room tone. then stop playback.

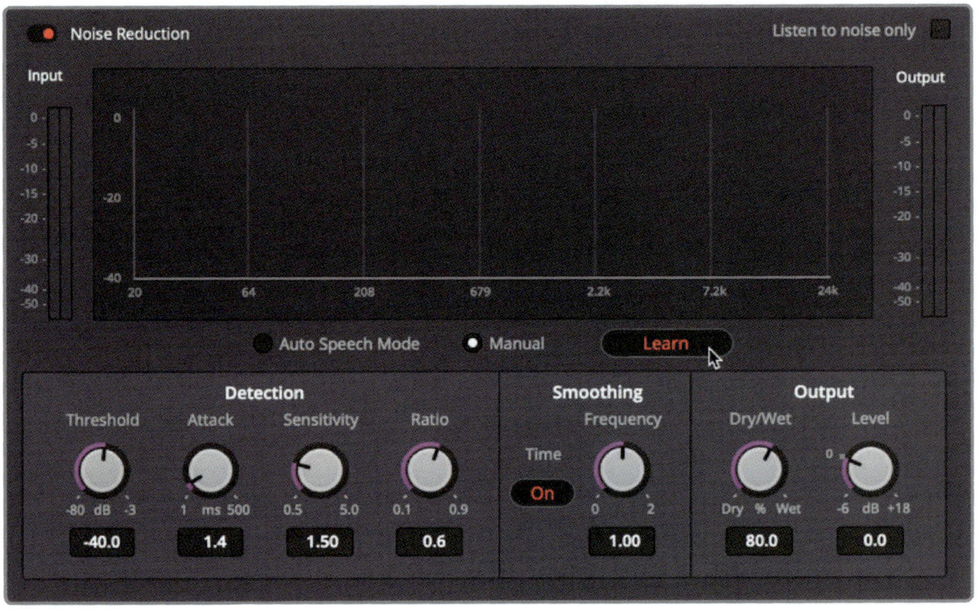

Clicking the learn button and playing over the noise you wish to remove, subtracts that same noise from the other clips on the track. That's the benefit of applying the plugins to a track and editing all clips from one source onto its own track.

7 Move the playhead to the start of the timeline and play to hear the corrected interview clips.

Wow! What a difference noise reduction can make.

8 Click the red bypass switch in the upper-left corner of the dialog to turn the plug-in off. Click the bypass switch again to hear the plug-in.

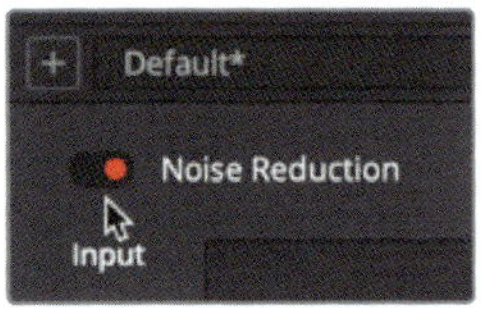

9 When you are finished, stop playback. Close the Noise Reduction dialog.

Noise Reduction is just one of the exciting Fairlight FX plug-ins that come with DaVinci Resolve 16. Now that you have seen how easy it is to apply plug-ins and presets, you can start experimenting with them on your own projects.

Setting Track Levels

Audio balance is the key to the entire sound-mixing process. When you achieve balance in your mix, you have successfully done your job. In the previous lesson you performed volume adjustments at the clip level; but to achieve overall balance, you must now adjust entire tracks relative to one another.

1 In the upper-left corner of the Interface toolbar, click the Effects Library button to close the Effects Library and open more room for the timeline.

2 Make sure the Mixer is still open, and drag its left edge to view the channel strips.

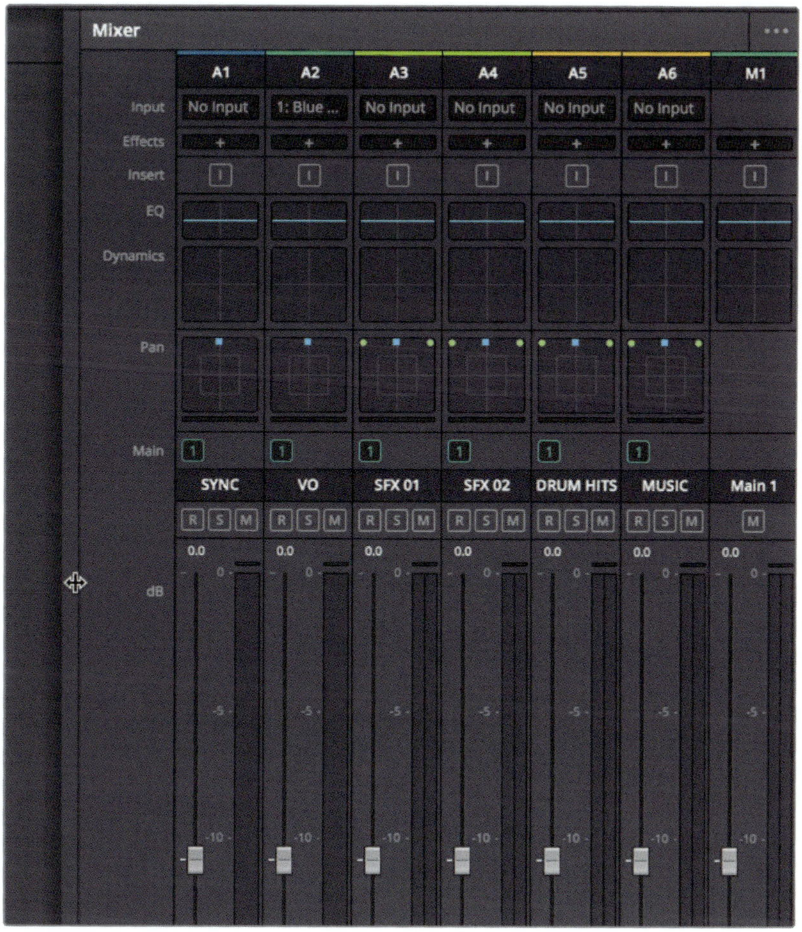

The Mixer panel includes a channel strip for each timeline track and a master audio strip. Each channel strip is color coded based on the track color that you assigned. Unlike the Inspector in which you can adjust the volume of a single clip, mixer fader changes are applied to entire tracks.

3 Press Shift-Z to see the entire timeline. Position the playhead at the start of the timeline, and press the spacebar to play the entire program.

Overall, the sync sound interview clips seem too low. No problem. You can the adjust the volume level for the entire track using the corresponding SYNC fader in the Mixer.

4 Play the timeline again, and drag up the SYNC fader until the interview voice plays a more clearly audible level.

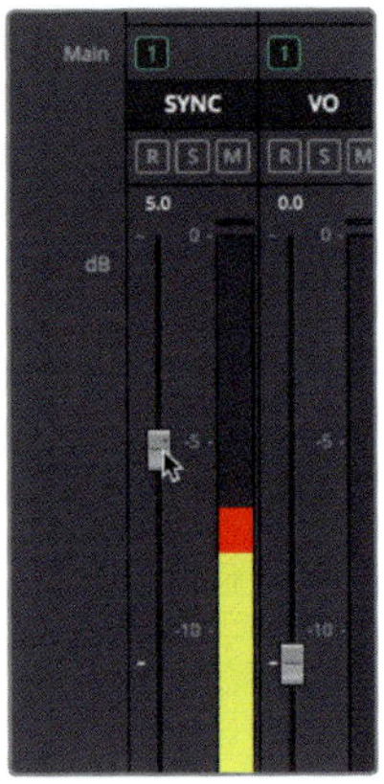

5 Play the timeline again, and adjust the tracks, as needed to achieve a proper balance between all the sound elements.

> **TIP** Using automation control, you can record track level adjustments as you play the timeline. You can learn more about the Fairlight page in the DaVinci Resolve User Manual, as well as the Introduction to Fairlight Audio Post with DaVinci Resolve 16 training manual.

As you adjust overall track levels, it is important to keep an eye on your meters levels, and to monitor the audio results using quality speakers in a calibrated system. Just as you want to view your video content on a calibrated display, you must hear your soundtrack content in an audio-calibrated environment. So, before you complete audio post-production, take off those headphones and prepare your final mix using professionally calibrated speakers.

By now, you've probably heard that sound is half of the video experience. Yet, somehow, sound often gets the least amount of attention when it comes to independent filmmakers. In the words of George Lucas, "Filmmakers should focus on making the sure the soundtracks are really the best they can possibly be. Because in terms of an investment, sound is where you get the most bang for your buck."

Lesson Review

1 On the Fairlight page, which panel shows a viewer for the video?

2 How do you identify the track you want to record on in the Fairlight page timeline?

3 Within a bin, how do you change a stereo clip to mono?

4 True or false? A De-Hummer can remove only 50 and 60 Hz noises from stereo clips.

5 True or false? You can apply Fairlight FX to a clip or an entire track.

Answers

1. On the Fairlight page, the Meters panel (located in the user interface toolbar) shows a viewer for the timeline's video.
2. In the Fairlight page timeline, you select the track you want to record on by clicking the Arm Recording button (R) in the timeline track header.
3. You can change a stereo clip to mono from a bin by right-clicking the clip and choosing Clip attributes.
4. False. The De-Hummer can remove a wide range of frequencies.
5. True. You can apply Fairlight FX to a single clip or to an entire track.

An Introduction to Visual Effects Compositing

When mutants attack or aliens land spaceships on Earth, filmmakers turn to visual effects artists to make those shots reality. You can use visual effects to create images that cannot be realized with live action production. Anything that's too difficult, too dangerous, or even too expensive to capture with a camera, you can create with visual effects compositing.

DaVinci Resolve 16 has the full Fusion visual effects and motion graphics toolset built in, which makes it possible for you to create feature film-quality effects without switching between software applications!

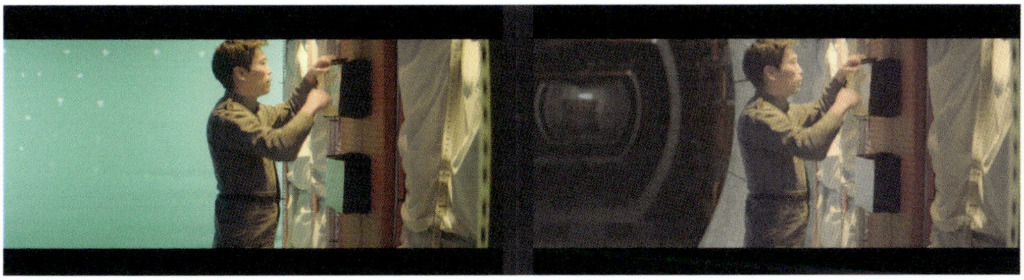

While you can create simple visual effects in the Edit page, you'll find more advanced tools for building sophisticated, photorealistic effects in the Fusion page. It features a flow graph-style interface, known as a node tree, that is designed specifically for visual effects and motion graphics work.

As you read through the following lesson, you'll begin to understand the many tasks you might choose to perform using Fusion's complete 3D workspace and over 250 compositing and visual effects tools. Best of all, it's now part of DaVinci Resolve so you can switch from editing, color grading, and audio post-production to visual effects and motion graphics with a single click!

What is Visual Effects Compositing?

Compositing is the process of combining two or more images to make a unique, new image. But it's not just about combining images. You can composite many different elements such as video clips, animations, text, mattes, particles, and graphics. Sometimes these elements are called layers because they are layered on top of each other to produce the new image.

Many tasks fall under the umbrella of visual effects. Just as with color and audio post-production, visual effects are a huge and exciting part of the creative film-making process. Depending on the type of work you do, you may need to learn some or all of the skills needed to create a finished visual effects shot. Smaller productions often require you to build shots from start to finish; whereas larger studios may have specialized artists dedicated to tasks such as rotoscoping, 3D, particles, lighting, and so on.

Even when you are hired as an editor or a colorist, you will often be asked to produce smaller effects. Like all aspects of post-production, learning the tools and techniques requires practice. Understanding the technology behind the tools will improve your problem-solving skills and efficiency.

As industry deadlines tend to grow shorter, editors and colorists that know how to finish shots quickly and efficiently are in the highest demand. Learning the basics of Fusion visual effects in DaVinci Resolve—along with color correction and audio post-production will make you a more valuable artist and open you up to more jobs.

Getting Started with Visual Effects

Visual effects were once a luxury reserved only for big budget feature films. With the power of Fusion built into DaVinci Resolve, you can add feature film-quality visual effects to any program without a massive budget.

If you think visual effects are only about creating aliens, spaceships, and explosions, you are missing out on the many smaller effects that can improve any project. In fact, the majority of visual effects consist of corrective effects, clean-up work, or inserting subtle hidden effects such as sky and window replacements. These effects don't take long to do and can improve everything from poorly framed b-roll to dull gray skies.

Adding Elements

Weather is unpredictable and when the story calls for snow, you need snow! This is why creating elements such as snow, rain, fog, and even lightning are essential skills of the visual effects artist. You can use the particle system in Fusion to create realistic weather elements that move, fall, and drift naturally.

Sometimes it's just too dangerous to do things on a real set. For example, smoke, flying debris, and fire are always dangerous when actors and an entire crew are involved. In many cases, these elements can be shot separately and you can composite them in later as a safer yet realistic-looking alternative.

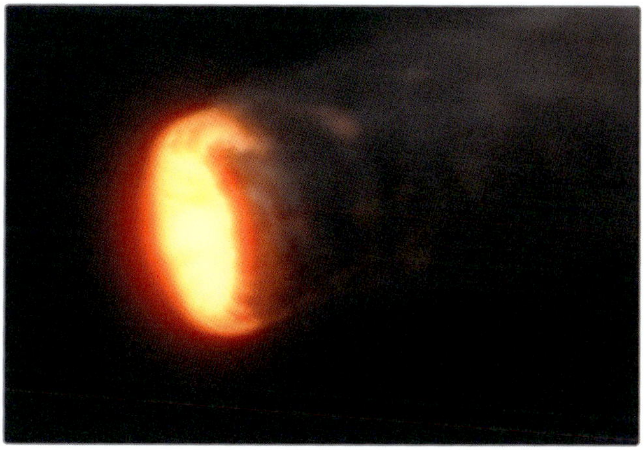

Animals and Kids

The unpredictable nature of working with animals and children can slow each shooting day to a crawl. Being able to divide and conquer a shot by splitting it up and shooting animals separately from main action can ensure that you get the shot completed without schedule overruns. Through seamless compositing, you can combine each section of a frame to create a realistic split-screen composite that looks like one take.

Sky Replacement

A perfect sunset or a bright blue sky with puffy clouds are great backdrops for any scene, but weather is out of your control. When everyone is on-set, the equipment is rented, and the clock is ticking, you've got to get the shot even when the weather isn't cooperating. That's where the (extremely common) art of sky replacement comes in. Fusion's keyers, rotoscoping tools, tracking, and 3D compositing can remove ugly gray skies or salvage overexposed skies. Add in some Fast Noise or volumetric effects and that clear blue sky can include beautiful dramatic clouds that weren't there during the shoot.

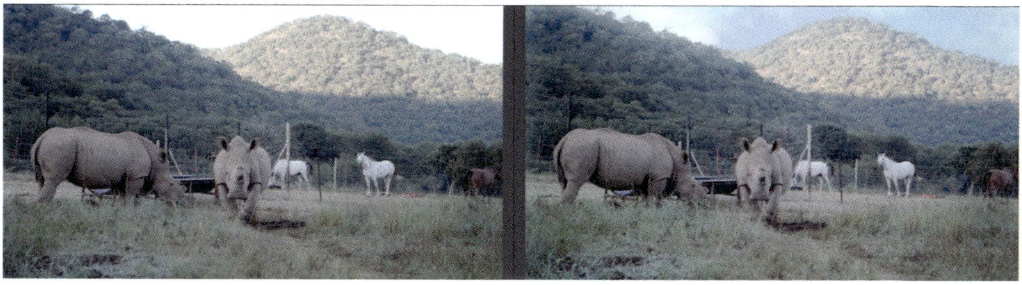

With the 3D controls in Fusion, you also can simulate the light direction, atmospheric haze, and realistic parallax camera movement, all elements that can make the difference between a believable, sky replacement and a cheap, artificial fake.

Performance/Cosmetic Fixes

Correcting or improving an actor's not-quite-perfect performance can avoid the need for expensive reshoots. This common compositing task is rarely noticed by an audience and can be simple to do, depending on the required fix. For instance, a detail often missed during shooting (but painfully obvious in the screening room) is when an actor portraying a dead body involuntarily moves his eyes. Compositing closed eyes from one frame over an entire shot is a skill that can save the shot and be repurposed for many similar fixes. Removing scars, tattoos, or uneven tan lines all use similar techniques and can be performed using Fusion's planar tracker, paint tools, and rotoscoping.

Changing Locations

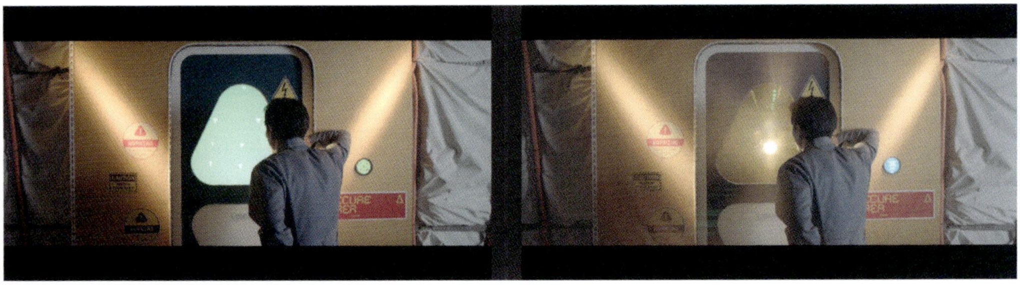

Production budgets always limit where and when you can shoot a scene, but simple environmental enhancements can disguise those limits and change the feel of an entire scene. Such effects can consist of replacing windows in a moving car because you couldn't close down Times Square to shoot your scene, or "moving" the ground-floor apartment location you could afford to a penthouse view. These are not uncommon tasks for the visual effects artist and can be very quick fixes for editors and colorists to perform.

Wire Removal

Visual effects are also used to add realism to already dangerous stunts. Getting performers to fly across the screen either from explosive force or supernatural powers often requires safety harnesses and wire rigs. You can hide those rigs and wires using Fusion's simple clone tools and tracking, a task that editors and colorists can take on in a pinch when the visual effects artists are busy with larger composites. Plus, the wire removal skills you use in Fusion techniques can also apply to removing lighting stands, telephone wires, and unsightly antennas.

Set Extensions

You can take environment enhancements to the next level to create entire set extensions that visually transport your audience to a specific location (while keeping your production safe at home on a sound stage.) Instead of shipping the whole cast and crew to the Himalayan foothills, you can replace the background of your shots with temples and mountains and snow. For period pieces or science fiction, such effects can save enormous amounts of time and money because you don't have to build massive sets. You just construct set fragments around your actors and place green screens in the surroundings. Using the Fusion page during post-production, you can track the camera movement, and replace the green-screen with 3D extensions to your set.

Motion Graphics

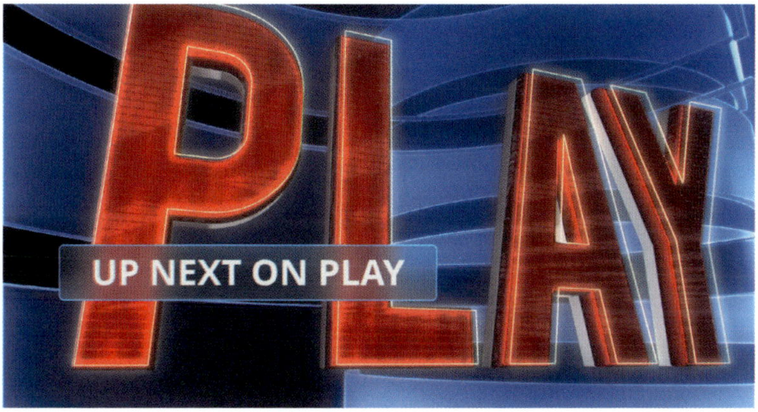

Motion graphics, or motion design, is all about animating graphic elements. It's the marriage of visual effects, animation, and graphic design with the goal of presenting on-screen information. Because information in some form is the objective, text often plays a primary role in almost every motion design project. The Fusion page includes both 2D and 3D typography tools along with creative paint, Bézier shape drawing tools, and incredibly deep spline animation controls. They enable you to create engaging animated designs that communicate, educate, and entertain.

Learning to see

If you want to create high-quality visual effects, you need to be very conscious of how the world appears around you. Visual Effects need to look and feel real or your audience will stop believing. The skill to observe the world around in painstaking detail is just as important as mastering the technical and artistic side of visual effects.

To become a skillful visual effects artist, you must start noticing how light, perspective, and depth appear in the real world, and then bring those observations into your composites.

If all the elements that make up a composite are meant to be in the same location, then you must make sure that light hits them all from the same direction. Simulating relative sizes, parallax motion, and depth to a real-world level of detail is essential to the realism of an effects shot.

As you begin creating visual effects, start small. The Fusion page is very deep and incredibly powerful. The beauty of having Fusion built into DaVinci Resolve is that you can jump into creating visual effects with one click; try something out to see if it will work; and then, depending on your skill and the time available, either pass it off to your visual effects artists or finish it yourself.

Visual effects compositing is about a combination of tools rather than any single filter effect. It takes time, patience, and experience to do well, but it's an incredibly exciting activity that you can learn through experimentation and practice. Eventually, you'll create the most thrilling cinematic moments imaginable.

As Walt Disney said, "It's kind of fun to do the impossible."

Lesson 10

Creating Graphics and Effects in Fusion

Visual effects make the fantastic and impossible look completely realistic. Whether you're in a theater watching the latest studio blockbuster, viewing a show on your iPhone, or at home on a big screen television, visual effects are everywhere. With DaVinci Resolve 16, you have the power to create your own visual effects, so you can transport an audience into completely believable immersive worlds!

Producing visual effects is an exciting craft that takes time and practice to master. But once you do, you'll be able to bring virtually any story to life, no matter how imaginative!

The Fusion page in DaVinci Resolve features all of the tools you need to create visual effects and animated motion graphics using nodes instead of layers. You do so by linking tools together as you would combine building blocks, and then connecting them into an image-processing flowchart.

Time

This lesson takes approximately 90 minutes to complete.

Goals

In this lesson, you'll build some common effects. You'll explore both visual effects and motion graphics in exercises that will teach you how to composite shots, create a green screen key, and design animated titles using Fusion 's powerful text layout and keyframe animation tools. You'll acquire basic skills needed so you can continue to explore the Fusion page on your own, try out additional tools, and customize your own effects.

Exploring the interface

In most editing systems you put together your rough cut and then refine your edited versions in the edit page timeline. If you need compositing or motion graphics work you export frames, open up different software, import the frames and then render out the results for importing back into the edit timeline. In this first exercise we'll open a project that will allow us to take a quick tour of how DaVinci Resolve and the Fusion page simplify that entire process. Let's start by restoring a project and quickly get into the Fusion page.

1 Open DaVinci Resolve, right-click in the Project manager, and choose Import.

2 Navigate to the R16 lessons folder, and in the Lesson 10 folder, open the Hyperlight.drp file and relink the media.

This project has a single timeline that includes three shots requiring some motion graphics and visual effects.

3 In the timeline, move the playhead to the first red marker over the close-up of an actress.

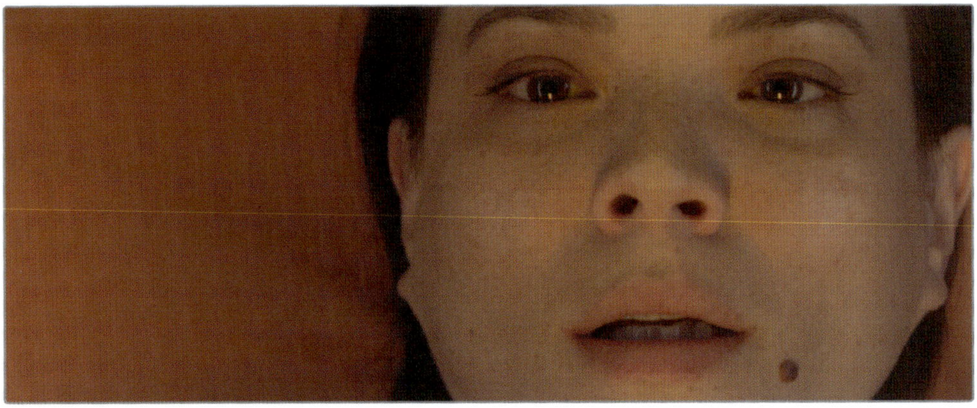

4 Click the Fusion page button, or press Shift-5.

That's all It takes to bring a single shot into the Fusion page where you can apply effects.

But before you start creating those visual effects, let's get familiar with the Fusion page.

The page is organized into four main sections. The two viewers across the top display the images you are working on. Below the viewers, a toolbar includes the most commonly used effects or *tools*. The lower work area, called the node editor, is the heart of the Fusion page where you construct your effects. Finally, the Inspector is to the right.

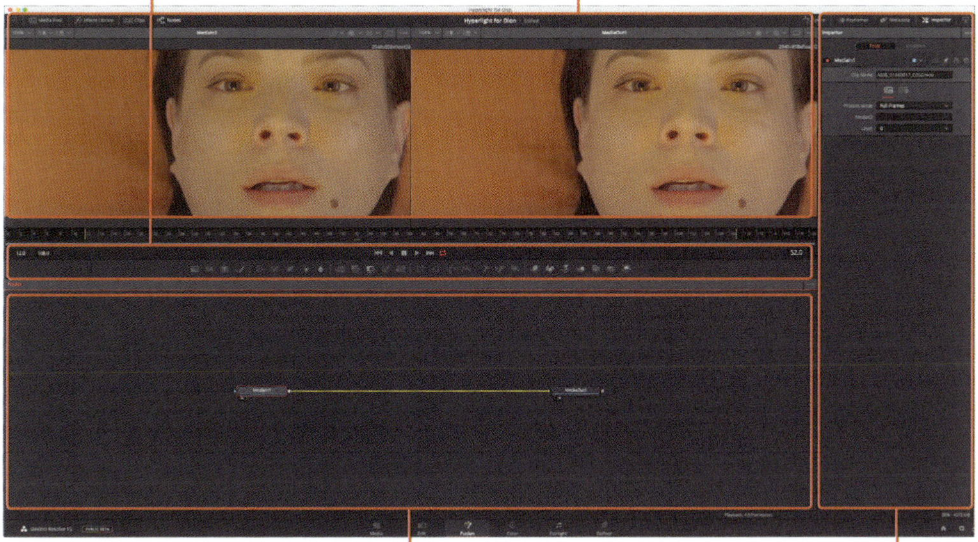

By default, the work area displays the node editor. Fusion does not use a timeline for compositing or applying effects, as does the edit page. Instead, it uses a node tree in which each image or effect is a *node*, as represented by a rectangular icon in the node editor.

Nodes are connected in a flowchart-like style, which makes it easy for you to see the entire structure of a composite and quickly make changes. Working with nodes in Fusion is much faster than hunting through nested stacks of precomposed layers and filters, as you might have to do with a layer-based interface. The node tree flows from one node to the next: one node applies an effect to an image and then passes it to another node for additional processing or output.

5 With the mouse pointer located over an empty gray space in the node editor, hold down the middle mouse button, and drag to pan the node tree into the center of the panel.

Every clip or image file that you bring into the Fusion page is represented by a *media in* node in the node editor. The current media in node represents the clip from the edit page. The *media out* node represents the image that is sent back to the timeline on the edit page.

6 In the node editor, select the media in 1 node, and press the 1 key to display the image in viewer 1 to the left.

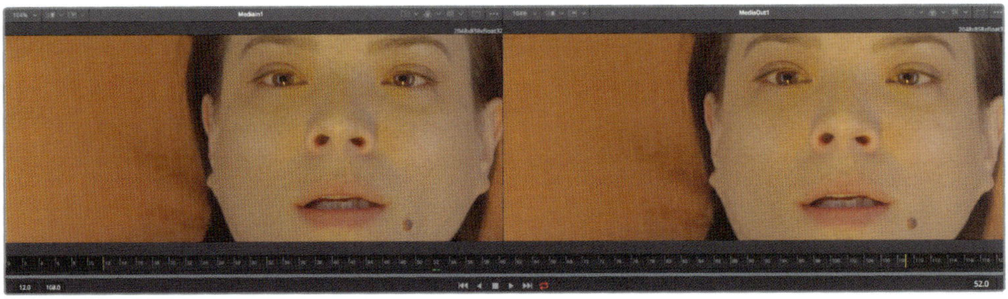

Viewer 1 Viewer 2

TIP The terms *node* and *tool* are used interchangeably to refer to an image-processing operation.

You can rename nodes to describe their function or image.

7 Select the media in1 node. Press the F2 key, and rename the media in 1 node **ACTRESS**.

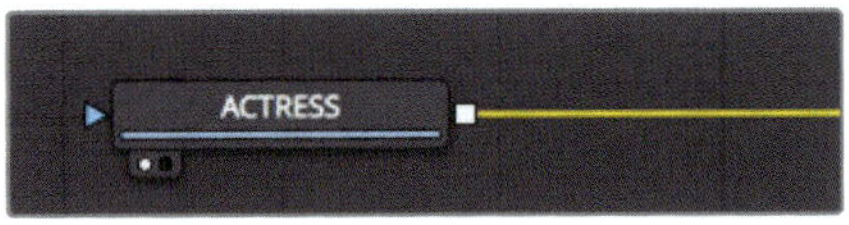

8 Select the media out node. Press the F2 key, and rename the media out node **OUTPUT**.

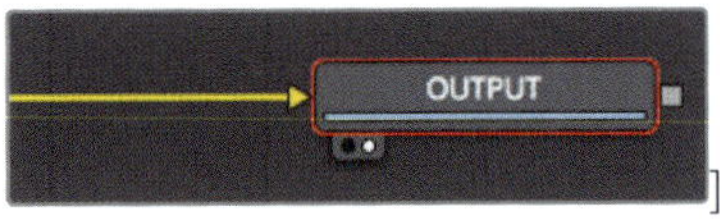

Under the viewers, a time ruler shows the duration of the current effect. Dragging the red playhead in the time ruler moves to different frames just as when dragging the jog bar under the source or timeline viewer in the edit page.

TIP By default, the time ruler and all time fields on the Fusion page display frame numbers. To display timecode, choose Fusion > Fusion settings, and in the defaults panel, configure the Fusion page to do so.

The time ruler shows the entire source clip length, and the yellow lines indicate the *render range*, which is that portion of that clip actually used in the timeline for final rendering.

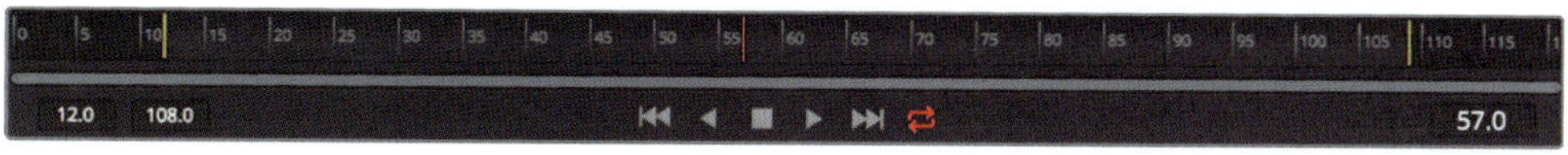

9 Drag the playhead slowly through the render range from the first yellow line on the left to the second yellow line on the right.

As you drag the playhead through the render range, the current time display (to the right of the time ruler) displays the current frame number. To the left of the time ruler, you can see the render range start and end frame.

Under the time ruler, you can drag a two-handled scroll bar to zoom into the render range. This capability can be helpful when a source clip is very long and you are using only a small portion of it in your timeline.

10 At the far left edge of the two-handled scroll bar, drag in toward the center of the time ruler until the yellow line is near the beginning.

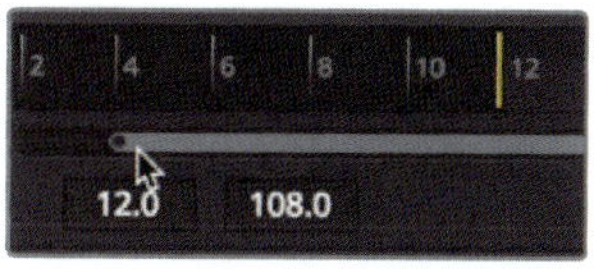

11 At the far-right edge of the two-handled scroll bar, drag in toward the center of the time ruler until the yellow line is near the end.

TIP To reset the render range, right-click in the time ruler, and choose Auto Range Render.

As the playhead moves, a green line appears along the time ruler to indicate frames that are cached into RAM for smoother playback. The more RAM you have in your system, the longer the cached region for RAM playback can be.

TIP You can assign more or less RAM for Fusion RAM playback in the Preferences panel. The amount of RAM assigned to Fusion RAM playback is taken from the total amount assigned to the DaVinci Resolve application.

Adding the first effect

To understand the basic principles of working with nodes instead of layers, let's add a simple effect to this clip. The most common tools or effects that you will want to use are located in the toolbar.

1 Hover your mouse pointer over the first tool in the toolbar to display a tooltip with the name of the tool.

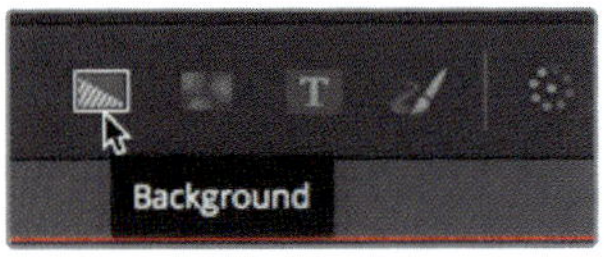

A thin divider separates each of the six toolbar categories. From left-to-right the categories are: generators, color, compositing/transforms, masks, particles, and 3D.

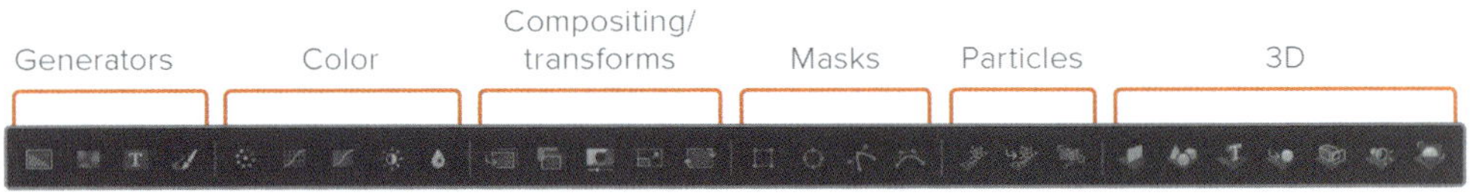

You build effects by connecting tools between the media in and media out nodes. In this example, you'll add a color corrector tool from the color category.

2 Move your mouse over the first tool after the first divider in the toolbar.

3 Drag the color corrector tool over the connection line between the ACTRESS node and the OUTPUT node.

4 When half of the line turns blue, release the mouse button to insert the color corrector tool as a new node.

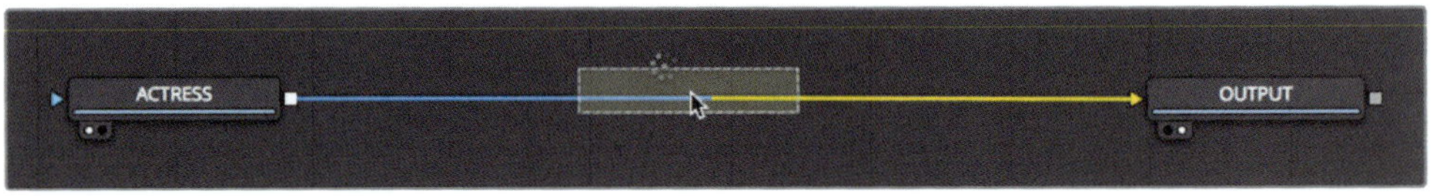

5 In the node editor, select the color corrector, and press the 2 key.

The color corrector results appear in viewer 2, while the original clip remains visible in viewer 1.

When a node is selected in the node editor, the parameters for adjusting that node appear in the Inspector.

6 To give this shot a colder, outer space feel, in the Inspector drag the color indicator towards blue until the ACTRESS has a light blue tint in viewer 2 .

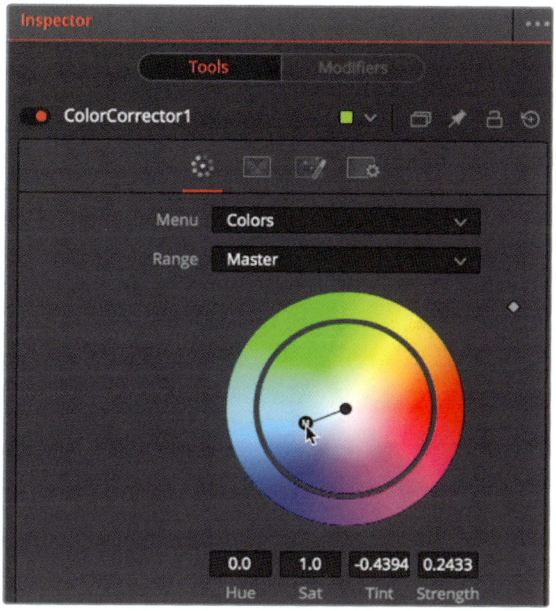

While the results are shown in viewer 2, viewer 1 still displays the original, unaltered ACTRESS image. By using the two viewers to see different aspects of your effect, you can more precisely compare and modify your adjustments.

Any effect you create in the Fusion page is also instantly visible in the timeline in the edit page.

7 At the bottom of the window, click the edit page button, or press Shift-4.

The edit page smart cache renders any Fusion effect in the background as you continue to edit.

TIP If you use DaVinci Resolve's user cache instead of smart cache, you can right click over any Fusion clip in the edit page or color page timeline and choose cache Fusion output > On to manually cache the Fusion effect.

That's just the start of creating this effect, let's return to the Fusion page.

8 At the bottom of the window, click the Fusion page button, or press Shift-5.

It's easy to see how the node tree functions like a flowchart with just a single image. The image comes in at the left, the effect is applied; and at the right, the modified image is sent back to the edit page. However, most visual effects use more than a single image, so next we'll learn how to bring in additional images that don't exist in the edit page timeline.

Adding clips from the media pool

On the most basic level, visual effects are about combining two or more images to make a new image. Although you currently have only a single clip from the edit page timeline in your composite, you can access any clip from your project in the media pool. For the creation of this sci-fi shot, you will add a computer-generated heads-up display (HUD) to make it appear that the actress looking at a computer display.

1 In the upper-left corner of the interface, click the media pool button.

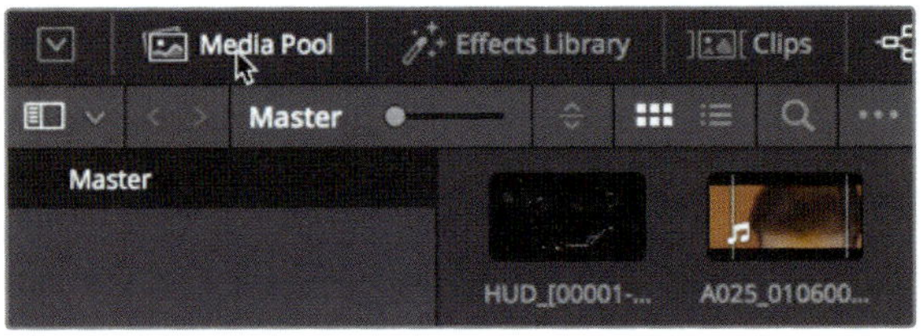

This Fusion page media pool is the same media pool you would find on the edit page and includes the same bins and clips.

> **NOTE** Your bins and node editor may appear different than the pictures displayed in this book due to screen resolution and layout.

2 From the master bin, drag the HUD clip to an empty area of the node editor.

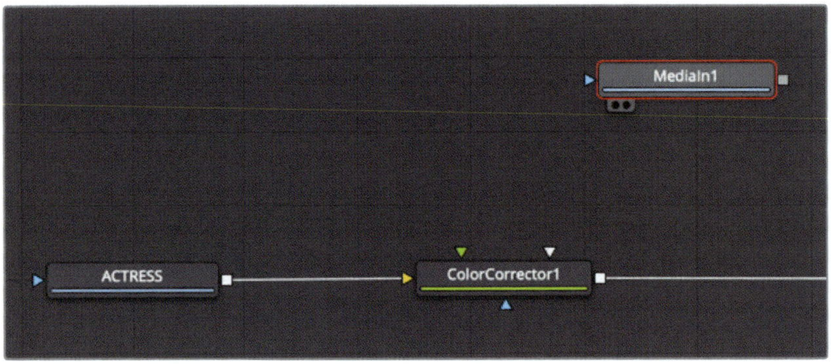

A new media in 1 node is created to represent the clip. The clip is not yet connected to your composite; it is just added to the node editor. Before connecting a clip to your composite, you can learn a lot about it by displaying it in the viewer.

3 Select the media in 1 node, and press F2 to rename the node to **HUD**; then, press 1 to display it in viewer 1.

In the lower-left of the HUD node, a small white dot, called the *view indicator button*, is highlighted to indicate that the node is displayed on viewer 1.

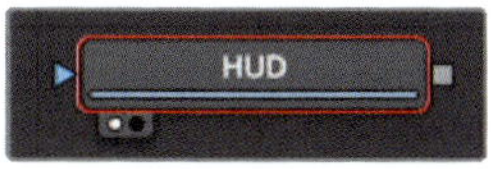

On the OUTPUT node, a second view indicator button is highlighted to the right of the first to indicate that this node is displayed on viewer 2. By displaying the OUTPUT node, viewer 2 will show you the final composite output destined for the edit page timeline.

TIP Switching from the Fusion page to the edit page and back to the Fusion page will switch viewer 2 to display the media out node, regardless of what is selected before you leave the Fusion page.

Viewer 1 displays the HUD graphic with a checkerboard background to indicate that this computer-generated graphic has a transparent area created by the inclusion of an alpha channel.

TIP An alpha channel is a fourth channel that accompanies the red, green, and blue channels of an image. Alpha channels determine which parts of an image are opaque and which parts are transparent.

4 Above viewer 1, click the color controls button; or click in the viewer and press the A key to view the alpha channel in the viewer.

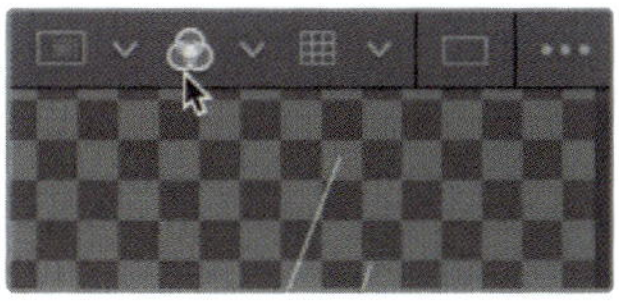

The color controls button now shows the alpha channel of the currently viewed clip.

5 Click the color controls button, or press the A key again, to once again display the full color image.

6 Click the media pool button to close the media pool and provide more room for the node editor and viewers.

With an additional image element added to the node editor, you are ready to begin blending two images together.

Understanding the merge node

The merge node is one of the most important and commonly used tools on the Fusion page. It composites, or blends, two images. You can add the merge node—as you would add other effects—by dragging it from the toolbar and inserting it in the node editor between the color corrector and OUTPUT nodes.

1 Directly after the second divider in the toolbar, drag the merge node into the node editor, and hover it over the connection line between the color corrector and OUTPUT nodes.

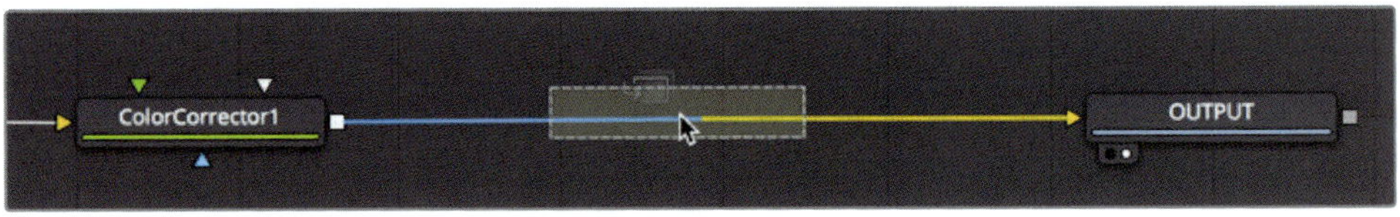

2 When half of the line turns blue, release the mouse button to insert a merge node between the color corrector and OUTPUT nodes.

> **TIP** Shift-dragging a node extracts it from the node tree and enables you to reconnect it at a new location. Alternatively, selecting a node and pressing Delete or Backspace entirely removes that node from the node editor.

The merge node is now connected into the node tree and you can use it to composite the HUD graphic over the shot of the actress. Before you combine the two images, let's explore the merge node in more depth.

A merge node has three inputs: one for a background image (yellow triangle). You can think of this as a clip on V1 in the edit page timeline. The green triangle represents a foreground image, similar to a clip on V2 in the edit page timeline. A third input (blue triangle) is used exclusively for masking. Like all nodes, the merge node also includes an output (white square).

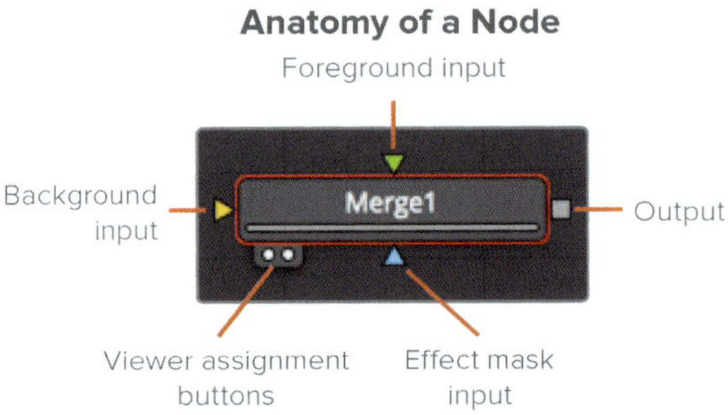

When you insert a merge node, it automatically connects the incoming connection line to the background input. It is up to you to manually connect the foreground image. In this node tree, the shot of the actress via the color corrector is connected to the yellow background input of the merge node.

3 To connect the HUD graphic into the foreground input of the merge node, drag the square output from the HUD node into the green foreground input of the merge node.

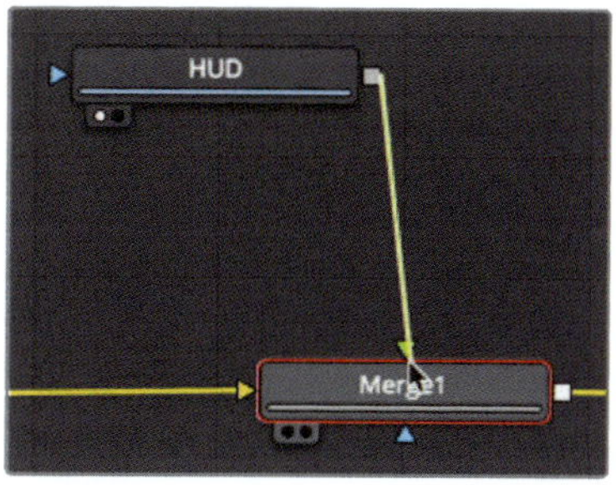

By adding the HUD graphic into the foreground input, you composite that graphic on top of the actress using the graphic's built-in alpha channel transparency.

TIP When using a third display, such as a full-screen broadcast monitor connected via a Blackmagic Design UltraStudio or DeckLink card, you can press 3 on your keyboard to display the node on the third monitor.

4 In the node editor, drag the HUD node below the merge node.

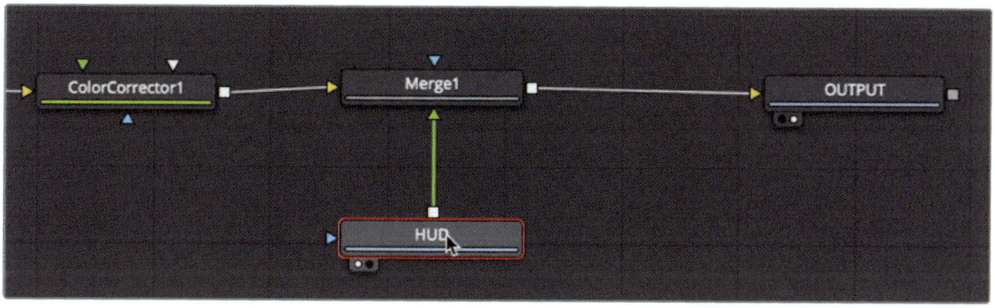

It is important to know that repositioning a node within the node editor in this way only visually organizes your node tree and has no impact on the compositing results. Only the connections made from node to node determine the processing order of images.

5 Return the placement of the HUD node above the merge node.

The merge node is the fundamental building block of almost every composite you will make in Fusion . Although it allows you to connect only two images, understanding how those two inputs interact is crucial because they enable you to link multiple merges and create much more advanced visual effects.

Inserting and adjusting effects

Node order is the single most important concept to understand in any node-based compositing system. Where you insert a node in the tree and the order in which you connect nodes determines the results of your composite.

The frame size of the HUD graphic is slightly larger than the background, so some of it is cut off. You'll need to add a transform node—but in precisely the correct location—to resize the graphic without resizing the background.

1 Just before the third divider in the toolbar, drag the transform tool to an empty place in the node editor.

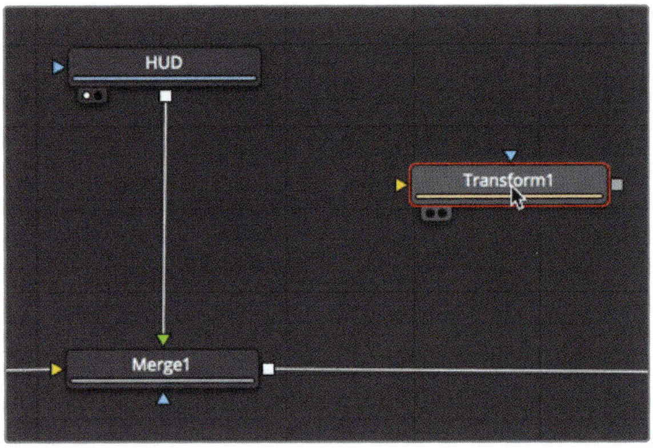

This transform tool must be placed into the node tree so it applies only to the HUD graphic. If you place it after the merge tool, this node will resize the entire shot.

2 Shift-drag the transform node between the HUD and the merge nodes. When the mouse pointer is over the connection line and the line turns blue, release the mouse button to insert the transform node.

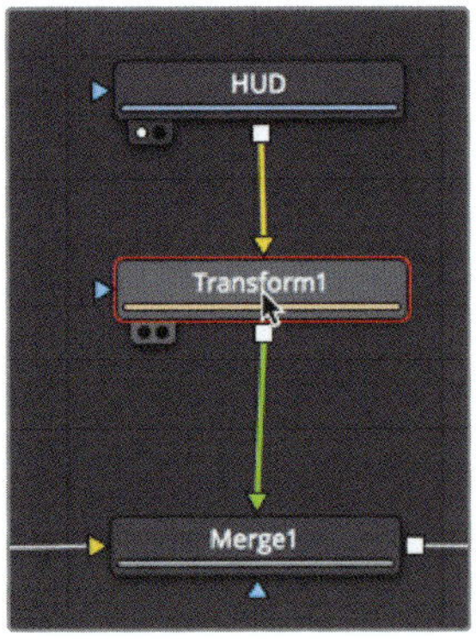

Although you have not made any changes, you can see the original graphic in viewer 1 and the transform adjustments in viewer 2 because it displays the OUTPUT node's results.

TIP In the lower-left corner of the interface, the status bar displays basic metadata about any selected node.

When a node is selected in the node editor, the parameters for adjusting that node appear in the Inspector with on-screen controls displayed in the viewer.

3 In the Inspector, drag the transform size slider to the left to scale down the graphic until the logo on the left is no longer cut off.

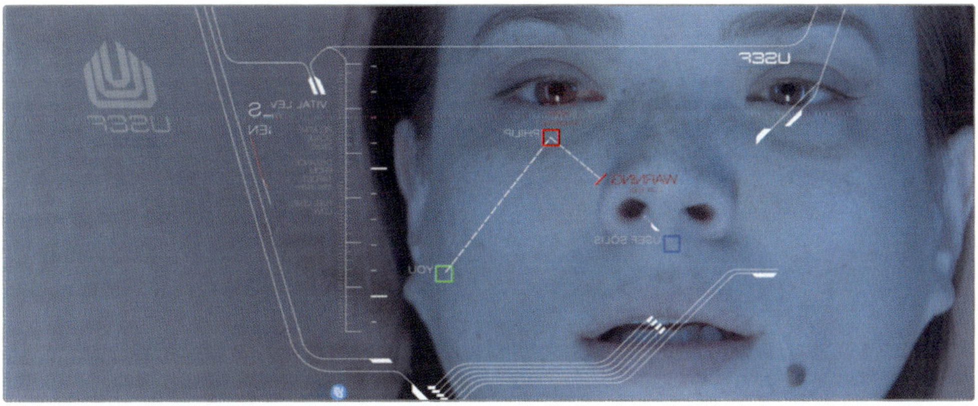

Adding additional effects to the same shot is as easy as clicking the tool in the toolbar.

4 Click the blur tool—located in the toolbar just before the second divider—to insert it directly after the transform node.

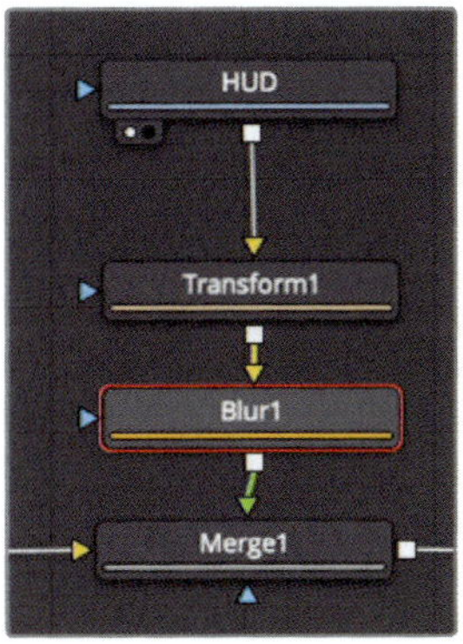

TIP When a node is selected in the node editor, clicking a button in the toolbar will insert the new tool directly after the selected node.

Often, computer graphics must be softened so they appear more natural when composited over live action. Next, you'll add a very small amount of blur to better blend the graphic with the live action background.

5 In the Inspector, drag the blur size slider to around 1.5 to slightly soften the graphics.

> **TIP** If can be easier to enter values rather than dragging sliders when changing controls.

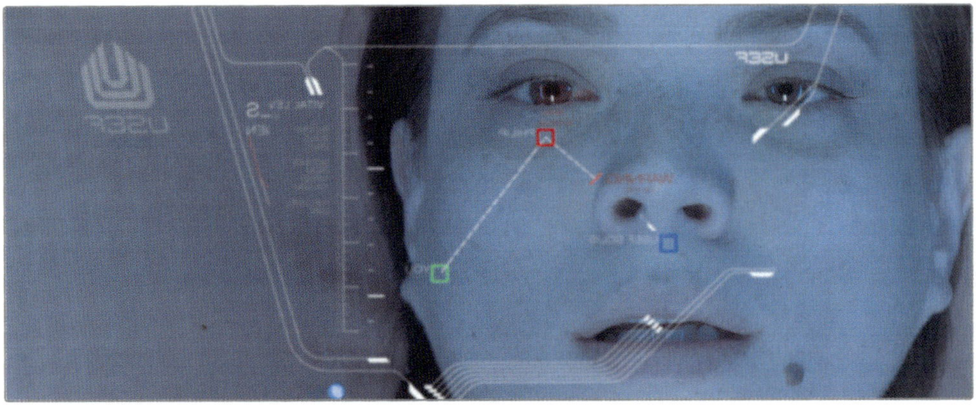

> **TIP** You can temporarily disable a node by selecting it in the node tree, and pressing Cmd-P (macOS) or Ctrl-P (Windows).

Now, let's preview your composite.

6 In the transport controls, above the toolbar, press the first frame button to move the playhead to the start of the render range.

7 Press the Spacebar to play the composite.

The results from the OUTPUT node are visible in viewer 2.

Chaining merge nodes together

Merge nodes only process two images at a time, foreground and background. To add additional images, often called elements or plates, to a composite, you must chain merge nodes together using the output of one merge as the foreground or background of another merge. That's how you'll add a scratched glass element that we'll again get from the media pool.

1. In the upper-left corner of the interface, click the media pool button.
2. From the master bin, drag the glass clip to an empty area of the node editor.
3. Press 1 to see the image in viewer 1, then press F2 to rename this node, GLASS.

   This is the image we will composite over the top of the ACTRESS and the HUD.
4. In the node editor, select the merge 1 node.

   Instead of dragging from the toolbar, selecting a node allows you to click a tool in the toolbar and connect it into the selected node.
5. In the toolbar, click the merge tool.

   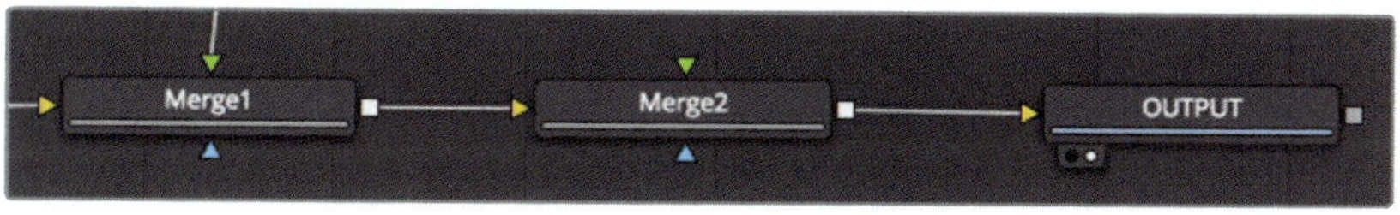

   The output of merge 1 is now connected to the yellow background input of merge 2. You can use the unconnected green foreground input on the merge 2 node to connect the scratched glass image.
6. Drag the output of the GLASS node to the green foreground input of the merge 2 node.

   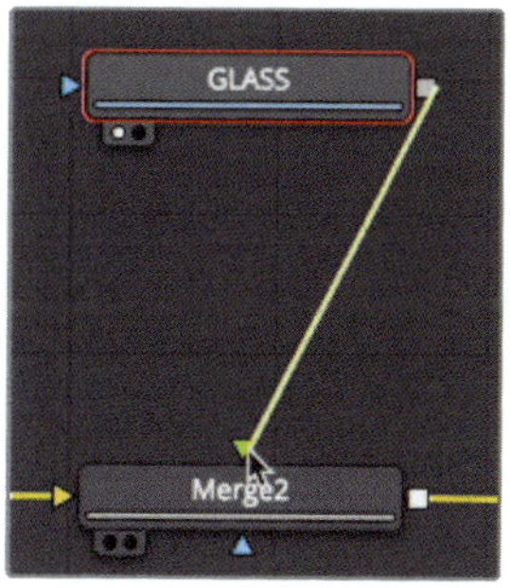

   With the glass node connected, you can use the merge node to blend the images to create more realism.

7 In the node editor, select the merge 2 node; and in the Inspector, drag the blend slider to 0.3 to lower the opacity of glass element.

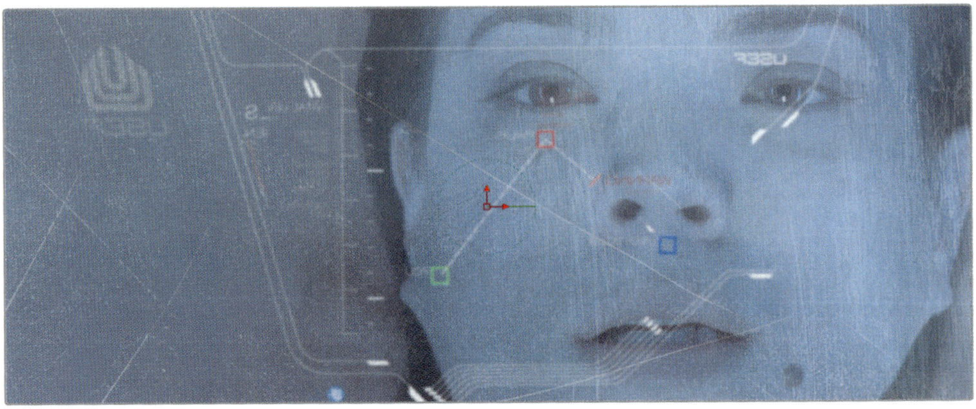

You can find more sophisticated blending operations in the apply mode pop up menu. These settings use simple mathematical operations to blend images based on the color and luminance of the foreground and background.

Although you have a number of choices, the most common apply modes can be defined based on their overall effects on the composite:

- Darken colors: darken and multiply
- Lighten colors: lighten, and screen
- Increase color contrast: hardlight, overlay, and softlight

Because you want the scratches in the glass to be seen clearly, let's use an overlay mode which will composite the scratched glass with more contrast over the top of the actress.

8 In the apply mode menu, choose overlay.

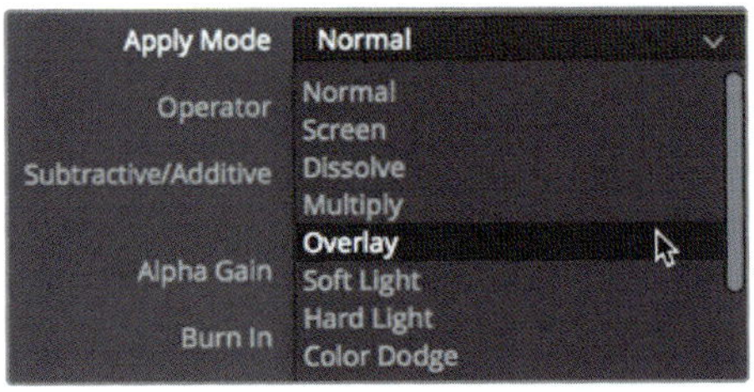

If you wanted to add even more image elements beyond the glass and HUD elements, you could continue chaining merges together. Adding new merge nodes before the existing ones would place new elements behind the current composite.

Masking effects

Effects have an input and an output for connecting other nodes. These connections are color coded with a yellow triangle to represent the primary input and a white square to represent an output. Nodes also have an effect mask input for masking use, as represented by a blue triangle. You can use the mask input to limit the area of the image that is affected by an effect. Let's create a subtle vignette that will darken the area around the actress' face.

1 In the node editor, select the Color corrector node.

   With the selected node being the one directly before the first merge node, any effect we add will only affect the actress.

2 In the toolbar before the second divider, click the brightness contrast tool to insert it into the node tree directly after the actress node.

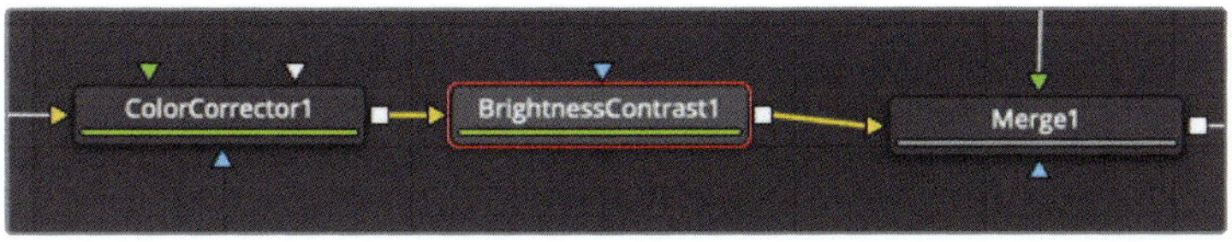

   Let's change the gamma in this node to darken the actress.

3 With the brightness contrast node selected, drag the gamma down to around 0.75.

   You've darkened the entire image considerably. By adding a matte tool, you can limit where that darkness is applied.

4 With the brightness contrast node selected, in the mask category of the toolbar (located after the third divider), click the ellipse mask tool.

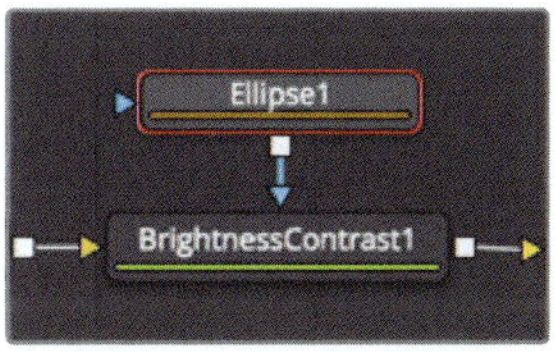

   Because the brightness contrast node was selected, the ellipse tool automatically connects to it. The ellipse is a mask tool, so it automatically connects to the blue effect mask input.

   In viewer 2, the gamma adjustment is now masked inside the ellipse shape. You'll have to invert the ellipse matte so the darkness falls outside the shape.

5 In the Inspector, select the Invert checkbox to reverse the ellipse matte.

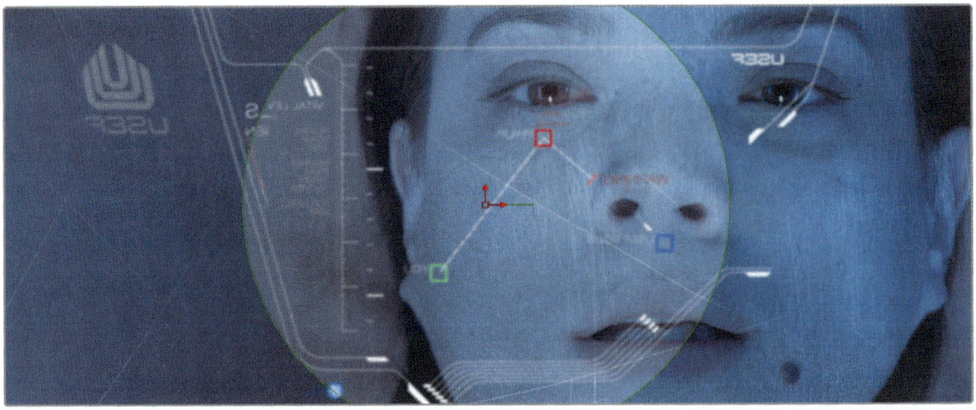

A few more adjustments will make the darkened vignette look even nicer.

6 In the Inspector, refine the ellipse matte by increasing the soft edge slider to create a more gradual transition from the center to the darkened edges.

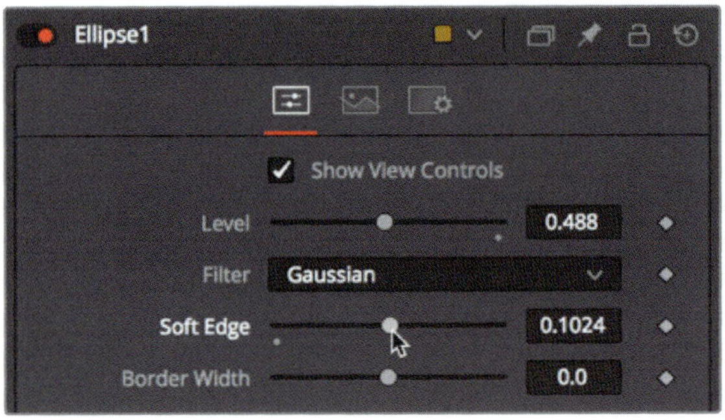

TIP A small gray dot appearing under any parameter slider indicates the default position of that parameter. Clicking the gray dot resets the slider to its default position.

You can use the on-screen controls to change the ellipse shape so it covers more of the wide aspect of the frame.

7 In viewer 2, drag the right edge of the ellipse to expand its width and cover more of the frame.

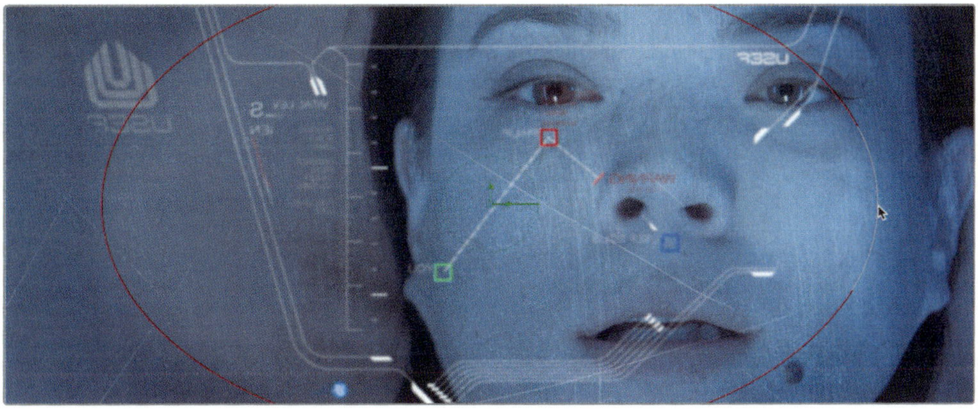

8 In the transport controls, above the toolbar, press the first frame button to move the playhead to the start of the render range, and press the Spacebar to play through the composite.

The first time the composite is played, DaVinci Resolve loads the effect into RAM. A green line under the time ruler indicates the cached regions of the composite. When the entire composite, from the start of the render range to the end, is cached into RAM, the composite plays back in real time.

Adding effects from the effects library

The Fusion page includes more effects than just those in the toolbar. It also includes over 250 tools that you can access in the effects library.

To add more realism to this shot, we should make the HUD appear more realistic and include some lens flares to simulate the effects of light from stars or suns in the area hitting the HUD glass.

Let's start with making the computer screen HUD glow.

1 In the node editor, select the blur1 that is connected to the merge 1 node.

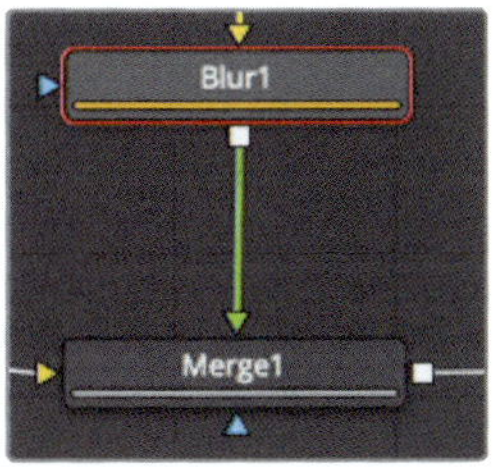

2 In the upper-left of the Fusion page, click the effects library button.

The library is organized by category. There are categories for everything from paint and particles to masking, image filters, tracking, and more.

3 In the Effects library, select the blur category and click the Soft Glow tool to add it to the node editor.

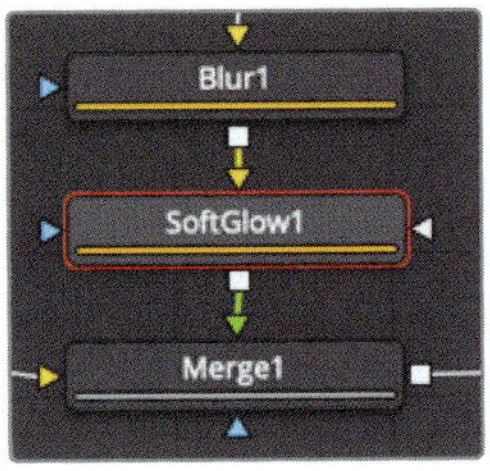

The soft glow gives the HUD a more realistic and dramatic appearance.

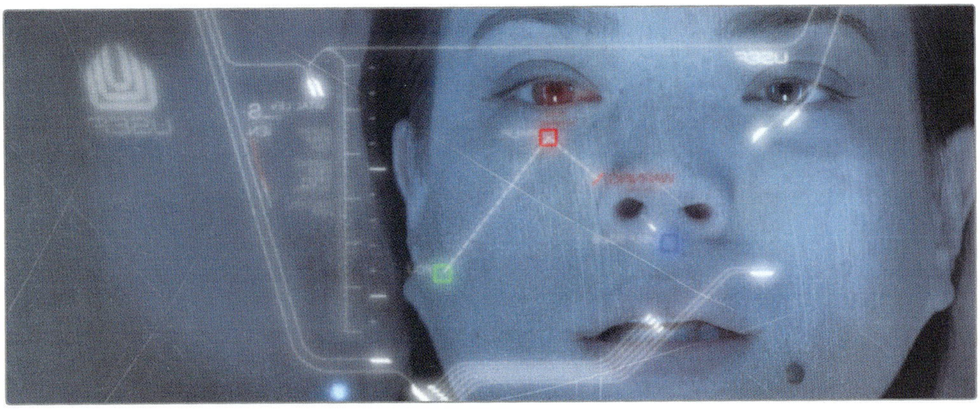

Now we'll add some light reflections.

4 In the effects library, click tools to close the category, then click OpenFX > resolveFX Light.

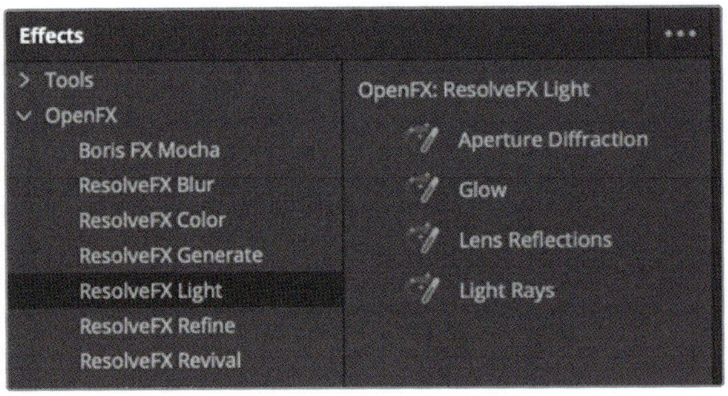

The OpenFX category contains the same filter effects you have in the Effects libraries in the Cut and Edit pages.

5 From the ResolveFX Light category, drag the Lens Reflections tool over the connection line between the Merge 2 node and the OUTPUT nodes. When half of the line turns blue, release the mouse button to insert the Lens Reflections tool as a new node.

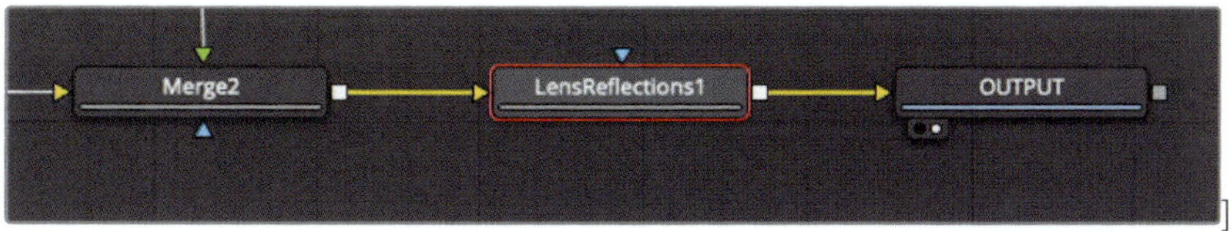

6 In the inspector, increase the Global brightness and Global blur values to suit your taste.

The Lens Reflections effect is used to simulate highlights reflecting off various optical elements within a lens to create flaring and scattering effects based on the motion of highlights in the shot.

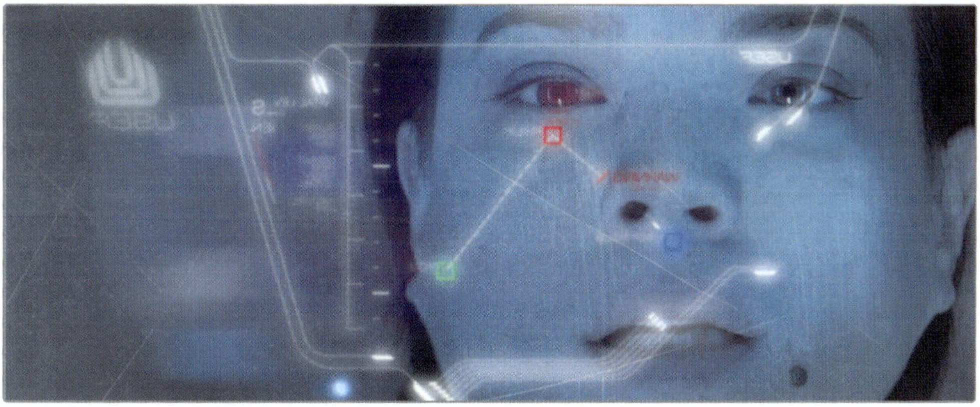

This first exercise was designed to introduce you to the general concepts and workflow for working in Fusion page. Now let's dive a bit deeper into green screen compositing.

Using Layers from the Edit Page

Because Fusion is fully built into DaVinci Resolve, the layering and transforms you perform on the Edit page timeline also carry over into the Fusion page. Let's look at a two-layer section of your Edit page timeline, and see how you can bring those elements into the Fusion page.

1 Click the edit button to switch to the Edit page or press Shift-4.

2 Move the playhead over the second red marker in the timeline

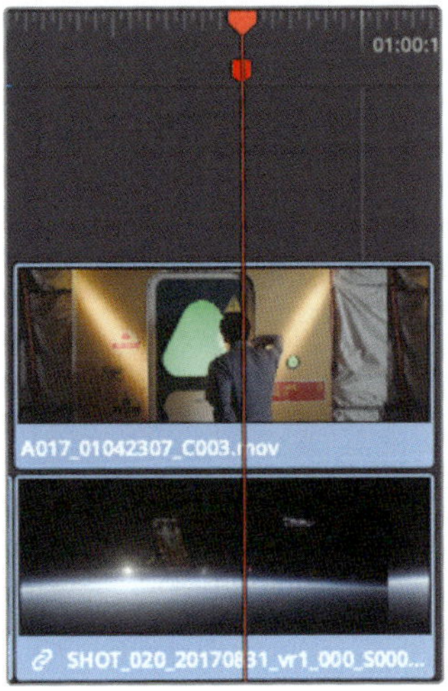

3 In the timeline, select the clip on Video 2. Press D to disable it, and view the Video 1 track.

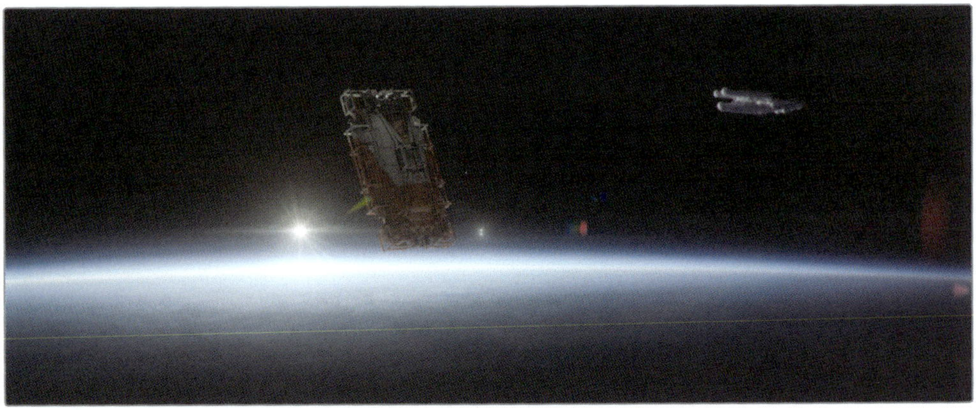

The Video track is a computer-generated spaceship clip. Video 2 has a green screen clip.

4 Press D again to reenable the green screen clip on Video 2.

You can use the Edit page timeline to layer, trim, and align the elements, and then bring multiple clips into the Fusion page. To move multiple clips from the Edit page into the Fusion page, you must create a Fusion clip.

5 In the timeline, select both clips, then right—click, and choose new Fusion clip.

The new Fusion clip is created in the timeline and added to the selected bin. The two layers are collapsed into a container of sorts, yet both layers are still accessible in the Fusion page.

TIP You can display all the layers of a Fusion clip in the edit page timeline by right-clicking the Fusion clip, and choosing open in timeline.

6 With the playhead still positioned over the clip, click the Fusion page button, or press Shift-5.

In the Fusion page, the Node editor shows the clip from Video 1 as a media in 1 node, and the clip from Video 2 as a media in 2 node. Both of these clips are combined in the merge node using the media in 1 output as the background and the media in 2 output as the foreground. To make it easier to keep track of which node is which clip, let's rename them.

7 In the Fusion page, select the media in 1 node, and press the 1 key.

8 Right-click the media in 1 node, and choose Rename, or press F2. Rename the node as PLANET_BKGD.

9 Select the media in 2 node, and press the 1 key.

10 Right-click, the media in 2 node, choose Rename (or press F2), and rename the node as GREENSCREEN_FRGD.

The merge node matches the way the two clips are layered in the timeline, but it does not have keying capabilities. To key the greenscreen shot, you need to add a keyer tool.

Pulling a Green Screen Key

Combining different shots requires a matte, which is a grayscale image that identifies parts of the foreground as transparent and parts as opaque. Unlike the computer-generated alpha channel you used earlier, the live-action shot in your foreground does not include a matte. So, it is up to you to create the matte through the process of keying.

NOTE This exercise uses a green screen, but the process is the same when you are removing blue screen from a shot.

1 In the Node editor, select the GREENSCREEN_FRGD node, and in the upper-left corner of the interface, click the effects library button.

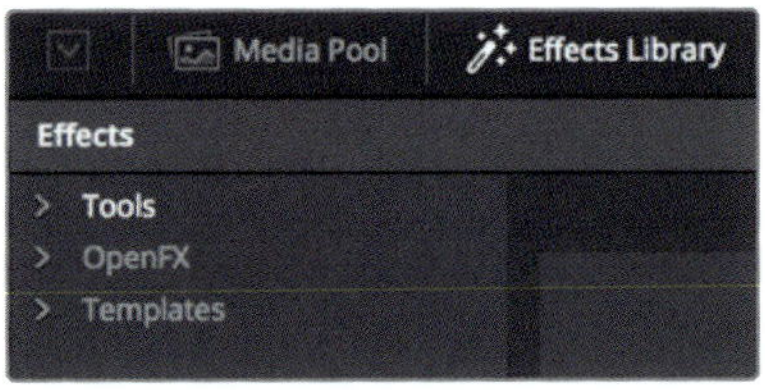

Just as in the Edit page, you have access to all the same ResolveFX in the OpenFX category. But all of Fusion 's compositing tools are found in the Tools categories. Keyers are located in the Tools > Matte category.

NOTE The terms matte and mask are often used interchangeably. In this book, matte refers to a grayscale image that identifies transparent and opaque pixels. A mask is the application of a matte. You use a matte to mask off part of an image.

2 Click the Tools disclosure arrow, and select the Matte category. Click the Delta Keyer once.

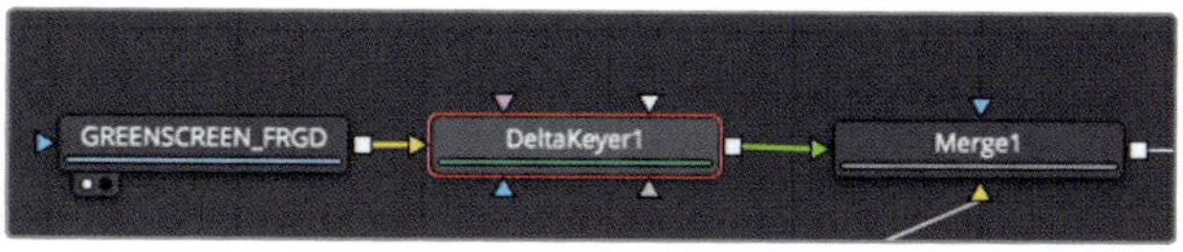

Because the GREENSCREEN_FRGD node was selected in the Node editor, the Delta keyer is connected to the GREENSCREEN_FRGD output.

The Delta Keyer is the most advanced color difference keyer in the Fusion page, and it is very simple to use.

3 Select the Delta keyer node, and press 1 to display its output in viewer 1.

Your first step will be to select the green color in the foreground image that you want to make transparent.

4 In the Inspector, drag the background color eyedropper and move the mouse pointer over the green screen in viewer 1.

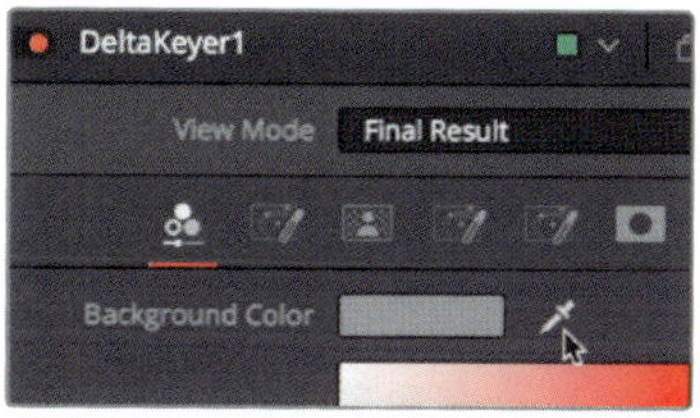

5 Release the mouse button when the green screen is removed and you can clearly see the planet in viewer 2.

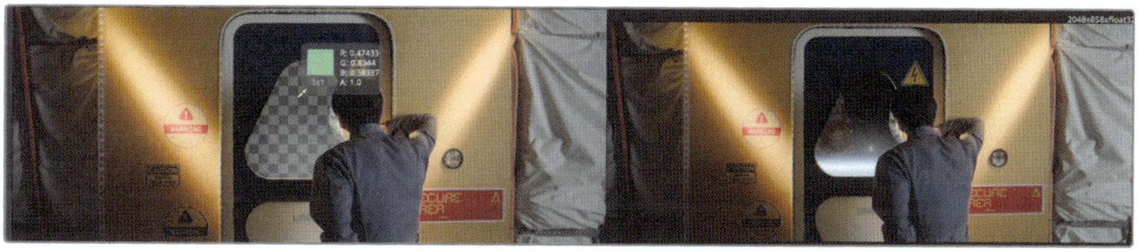

You've now created a matte for the foreground shot by selecting a green color. Even if this looks satisfactory in the viewers, you always need to check the matte to verify that its quality is good.

6 Above viewer 1, click the color controls button.

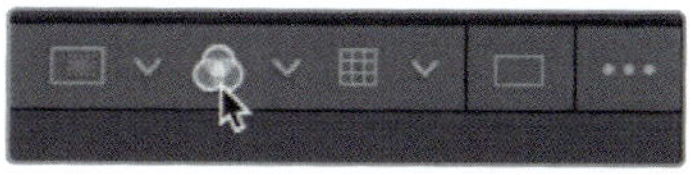

The matte or alpha channel for our live action shot is displayed. Even on the cleanest of green screen keys, such as you have here, you must refine the matte a bit to ensure that areas intended to be opaque appear solidly white and transparent areas appear solidly black.

7 Drag the playhead through the shot and look for areas in the white opaque regions that appear gray. At the same time, look for areas in the black transparent regions that also appear gray.

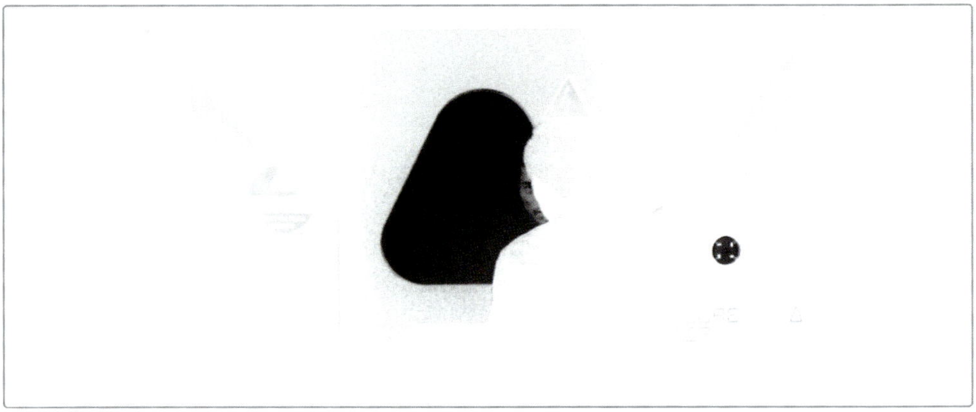

A good quality matte will be solidly black and white where you want full transparency and opaqueness. Gray areas signify semi-transparency which is perfectly acceptable when the shot contains hair, glass, or other translucent materials. This foreground has none of those so it should be solidly black and white. However, as you skim through the clip, you'll see that some areas are gray in the matte. You can increase the density of the matte using the Delta keyers matte tab to fix this.

8 In the Inspector, click the matte tab.

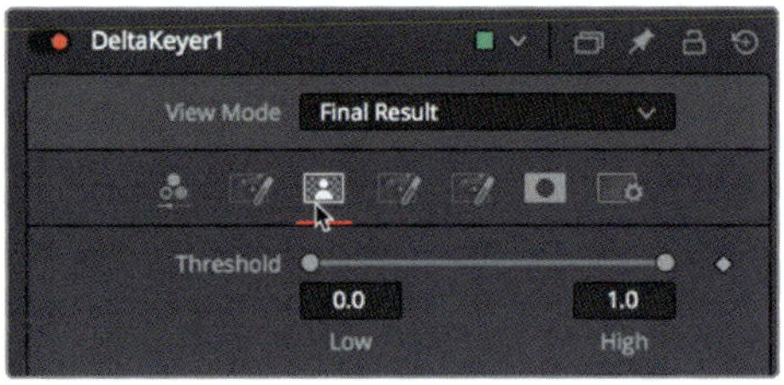

The matte tab contains parameters for modifying the density and edges of the matte. It is the most important tab in the Delta keyer because the quality of your matte determines the quality of the key. At the top of the matte tab are threshold sliders. Adjusting these will set the black-and-white cut-off points. Values that fall below the low threshold setting will be considered pure black and values that fall above the high threshold setting will be considered pure white.

9 Drag the low threshold slider to the right until the black is clear of all gray areas except the reflection of his face and the green button on the right side of the wall.

10 Drag the high threshold slider to the left until the white is clear of all gray areas

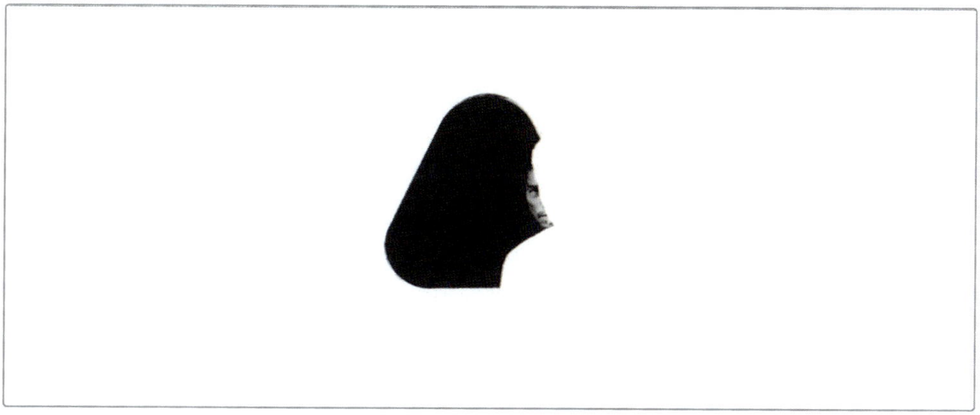

11 Click the color controls button above viewer 1 to return to the color output of the Delta keyer.

12 Press Cmd-left arrow (macOS) or Ctrl-left arrow (Windows) to move the playhead to the start of the render range, and press the spacebar to play through the composite

Depending on the shot's lighting and the foreground objects you are trying to composite, keying can often require many more adjustments, rotoscoping, and even multiple Delta keyers to fix different areas of the shot. However, the basic setup you have done here is the same starting point for every key you will create in Fusion .

Adding a Solid Mask

The remaining task we need to take care of is the small button on the right side of the frame. This was made with the same color green, I assume so we can fill it with some graphic. Right now, it is keying through to show part of the planet in the background. We can prevent this key by adding a small mask around the area to hold out the key. This is referred to as a solid mask.

1 After the third divider line in the toolbar, drag the ellipse mask into an empty area of the node editor, next to the delta keyer.

You can connect multiple masks directly into the Delta keyer to eliminate areas the keyer cannot or should not make transparent.

2 In the viewer, resize and reposition the ellipse over the circular object on the right side of the frame.

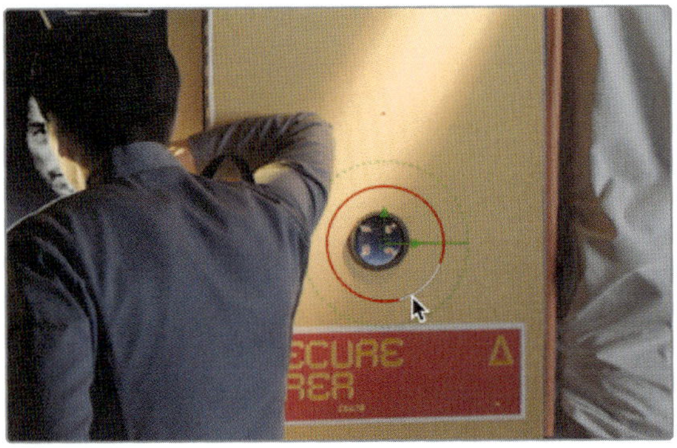

Now you will have to connect it into the Solid mask input on the delta keyer. You can hover the mouse point over any input on a node to reveal the input's name.

3 Hover the mouse pointer over the bright white input on the deltakeyer to reveal the tooltip.

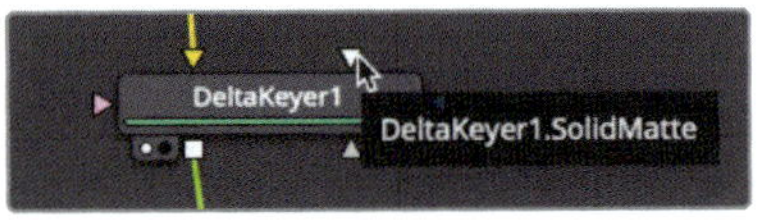

4 With the Solid mask input identified, drag the output of the ellipse mask into the solid mask input on the delta keyer.

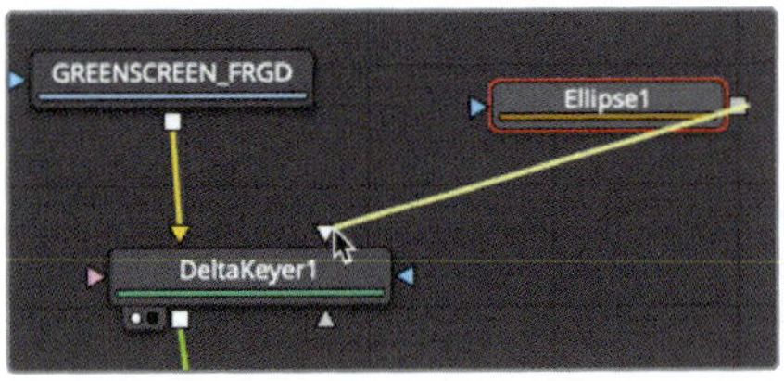

Once the mask is connected, the circular object turns gray instead of transparent. The Delta keyer has controls for how areas covered by a solid matte should react. You can change this behavior in the Solid mask tab in the inspector.

5 Select the delta keyer node, then in the Inspector, click the Mask tab.

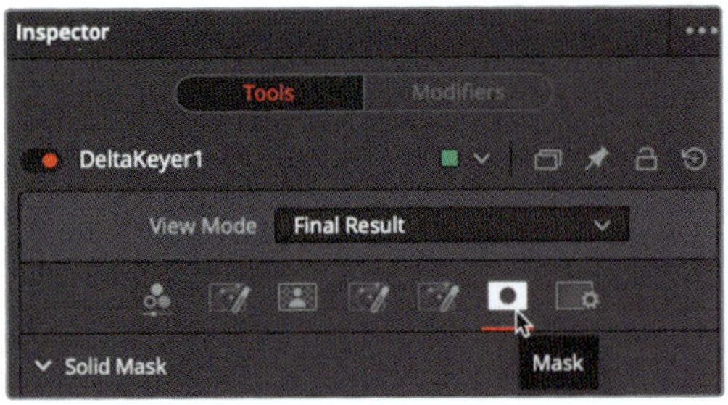

6 Set the Solid Replace Mode menu to hard color, then drag the eye dropper into the viewer to select the red color of the sign.

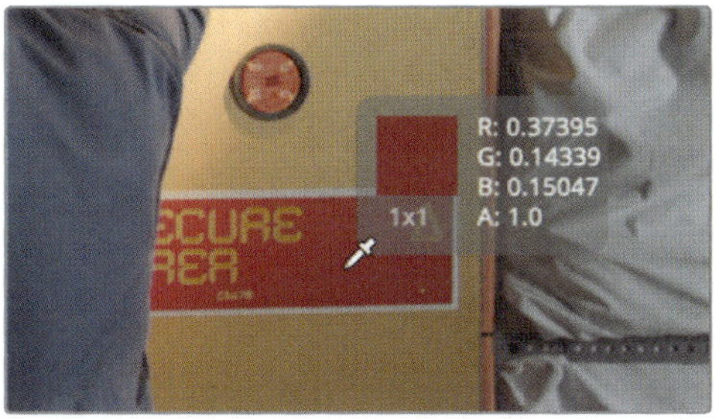

The hard color replaces the green screen color with whatever you select using the eye dropped. Choosing the red color from the sign, blends the object nicely into the set.

Adding text+ in the Edit page

Good graphics—whether they are main titles, still images, or even captions within a program—should convey important information while remaining true to the look of the program. They also must hold the audience's attention. In this exercise, you'll add text in the edit page and then bring it into the Fusion page to create an animated opening title for your sci-fi film.

1 Return to the Edit page and position the playhead over the first clip in the timeline.

2 Open the Effects library and drag the Text+ title above the first clip in the timeline. Then trim it to match the duration of the first clip on V1.

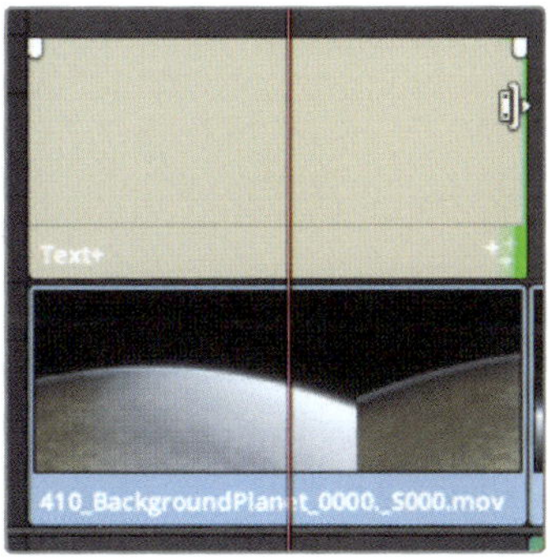

The Text+ title is a title that can be used in both the Edit and Fusion pages. It has all the same controls in both pages so you can start creating a title in the edit page and then move to Fusion without having to redo any work.

3 Select the title in the timeline and open the inspector.

4 In the Inspector's styled text field, type **HYPERLIGHT**.

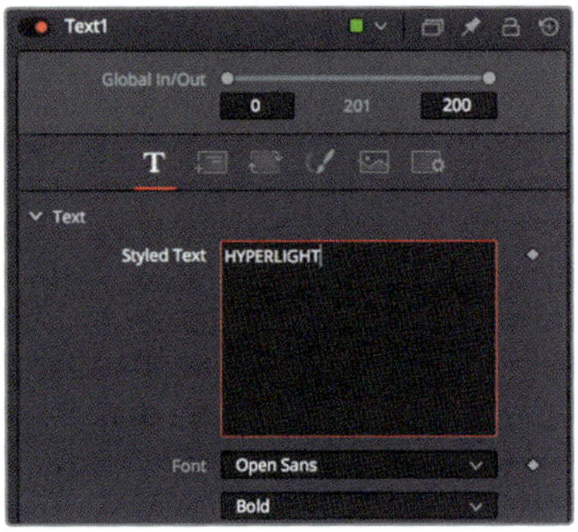

5 Below the Styled Text field, choose the Open Sans font for macOS or SegoeUI for Windows.

6 Below the font selection, set the type face to Light.

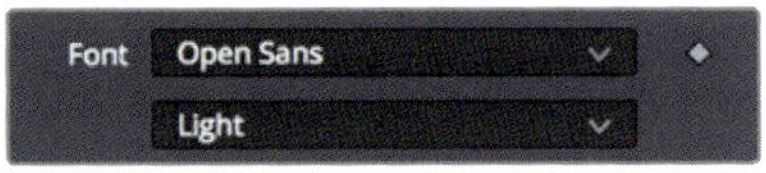

Next, you'll slightly increase the text size.

7 In the Inspector, drag the size slider to increase the text size to around 0.1

The Text+ tool has incredibly flexible styling options called shading elements. They control the style of the fill, outline, border, and shadow of the text.

8 Click the shading tab.

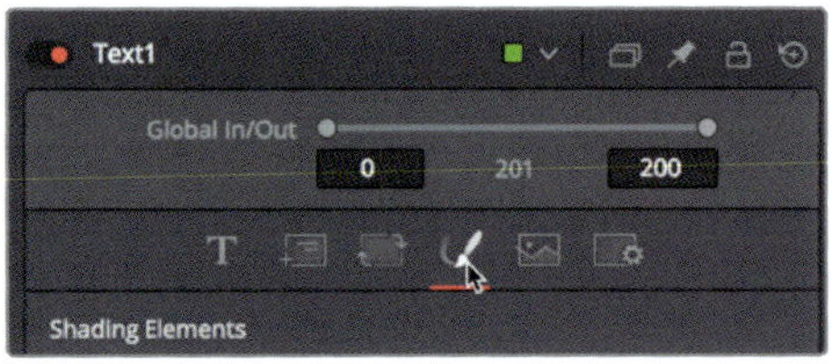

In the shading tab, you can apply text color, outline, shadows, and glows. Instead of using plain white text, let's use a gradient to fill the text.

9 In the properties section of the Inspector, set the type pop-up menu to gradient.

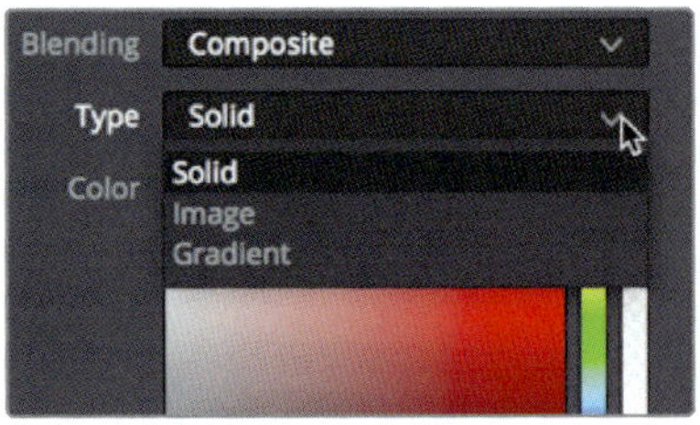

A gradient bar appears with two color stops. The color stop on the left sets the color of the bottom of the gradient and the color stop on the right sets the upper color.

10 Select the color stop on the left, and change the color to light yellow. Select the color stop on the right, and change it to a darker golden yellow.

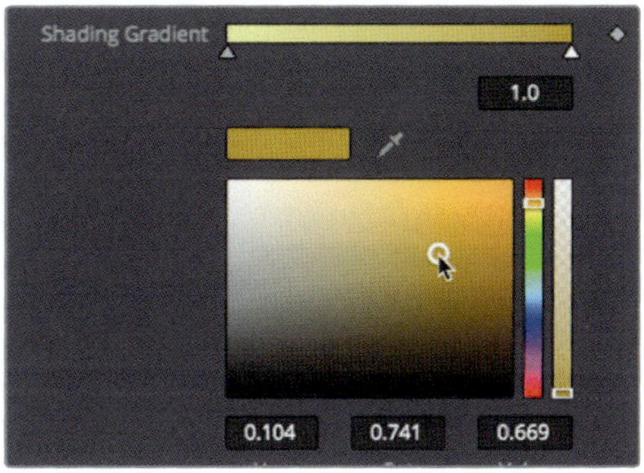

The fill color of text is one of eight shading elements. The remaining shading elements are located in the Inspector in the shading elements pop-up menu. Although you could change all of these elements, the first white fill shading element is the only one enabled by default. Other elements must be enabled individually.

11 In the select element pop-up menu, choose number 3, and select the enabled button to its right.

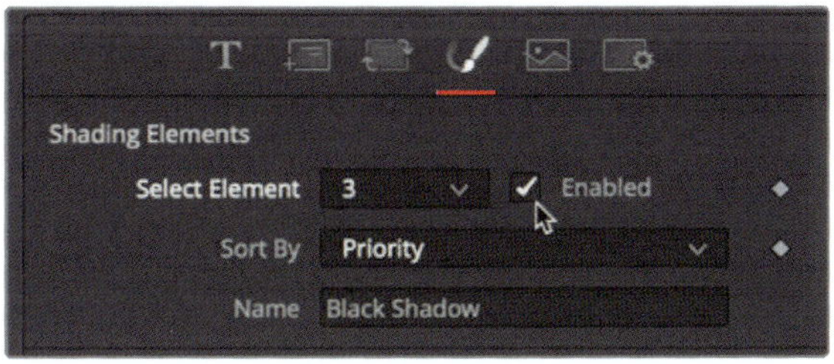

This shading element defaults to a soft drop shadow. Let's reposition the offset of the drop shadow.

12 Scroll down the Inspector, open the position section.

13 Adjust the offset X and Y parameters to position the soft drop shadow below and slightly to the left of the text.

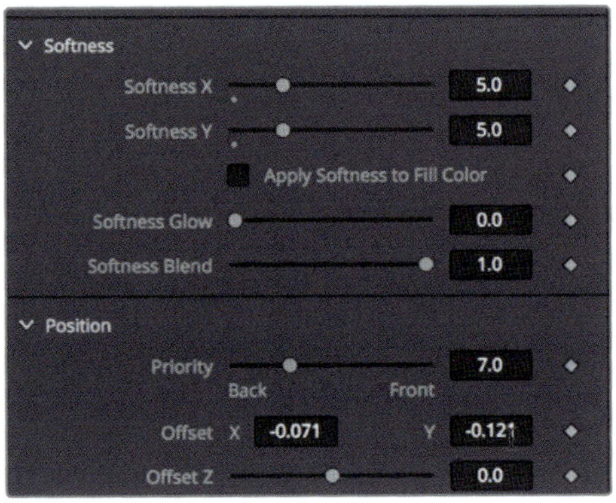

As mentioned, you can add up to eight shading elements to create fills, shadows, outlines, borders, and glows. In addition, you have control over the position, shearing, and rotation of each shading element, so your title design options are nearly limitless.

With the film's title created, you can now bring it into Fusion to add more effects and animate it.

Adding effects to text in Fusion

Since the text+ tool is available in both the Edit page and Fusion, anything you create in the edit page can be enhanced using the Fusion tools, once you transition to the Fusion page.

1 With the playhead over the text+ clip, click the Fusion page button.

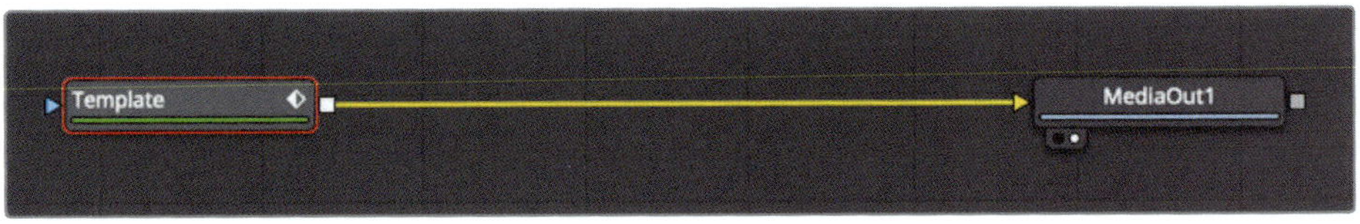

2 From the Fusion Effects Library, select Tools > Effect > and click Rays to add the Rays effect directly after the Template node.

The template node includes all the same controls that the Text+ node did in the Edit page. However, in Fusion you now have access to all the effects included in the Fusion page.

Animating with Keyframes

The ability to change elements over time is a crucial feature of any visual effects and motion graphics application. The Fusion page handles basic keyframe animation in the same manner that you already know from the Edit page, but goes much deeper with full keyframes and spline editors. Let's start by animating the Rays node.

1 Press Cmd-left arrow (macOS) or Ctrl-left arrow (Windows) to move the playhead to the start of the render range.

   As you did on the Edit page in Lesson 7, you'll add a keyframe using the Inspector. In this case, you'll use the Rays Y parameter to have the lights rays pan up over the text.

2 With the Rays tool selected, click the keyframe icon to the right of the Center Y control to add a keyframe, and drag the Y parameter to about 0.9.

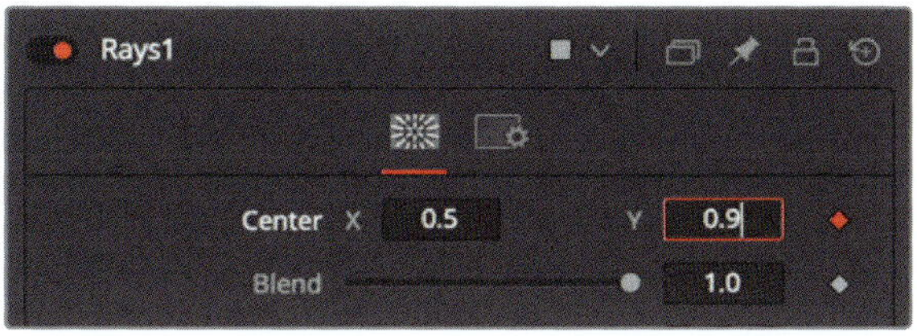

   Enabling the keyframe button of any parameter adds a keyframe at the current playhead location, and sets up auto keyframing: any time you adjust that parameter, a keyframe is added. Let's make the rays move up at the end of the render range.

3 Click in the render range to move to the end of the composite.

4 In the Inspector, drag the Center Y parameter to the left until it reaches around 0.0

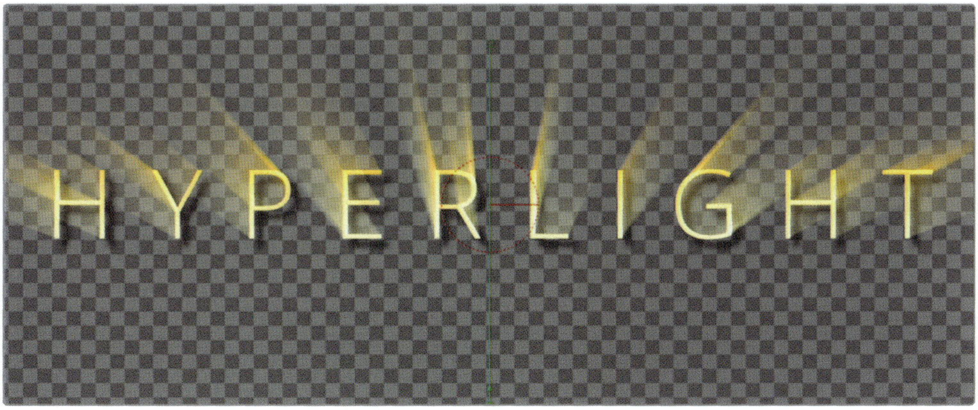

   Now, you'll set a few more keyframes so the rays are not visible at the start or end of the animation.

5 In the time ruler, drag the playhead to the start of the render range.

6 In the inspector, click the keyframe button to the right of the weight parameter, then drag the parameter to 0.

7 Position the playhead roughly halfway through the render range and drag the weight parameter to 3.0

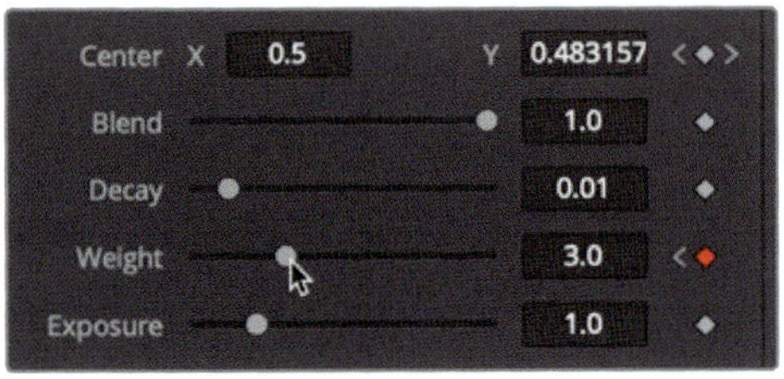

8 Move to the end of the render range and drag the weight slider back to 0 again.

To draw more attention to the title of the film, you'll animate the letters so they slowly spread out over the duration of the clip.

9 Select the template node, and In the Inspector, click the text tab.

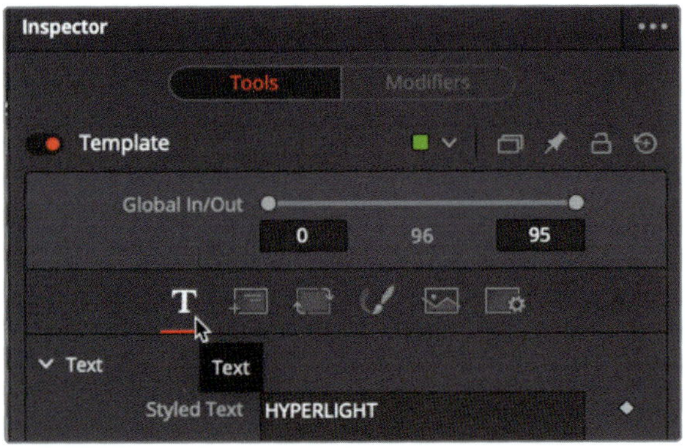

10 Press Cmd-left arrow (macOS) or Ctrl-left arrow (Windows) to move the playhead to the start of the render range.

11 Click the keyframe icon to the right of the tracking slider to add a keyframe on the tracking parameter.

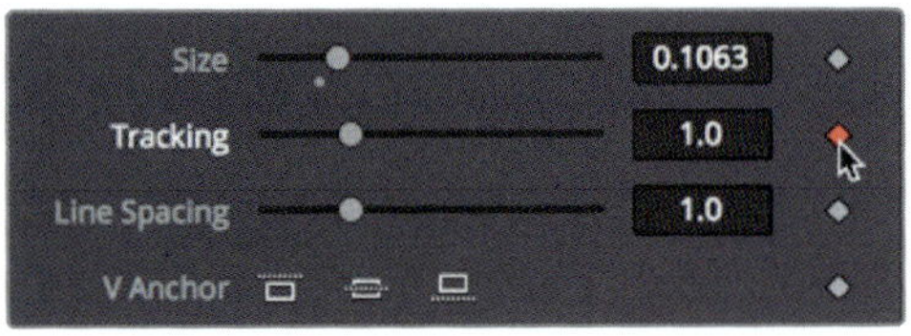

You'll start with the tracking at its default position and have it spread wide at the end of the clip.

12 In the time ruler, drag the playhead to the end of the render range, or press Cmd-Right Arrow (macOS) or Ctrl-right arrow (Windows).

13 In the Inspector, drag the tracking slider to the right to about 1.5

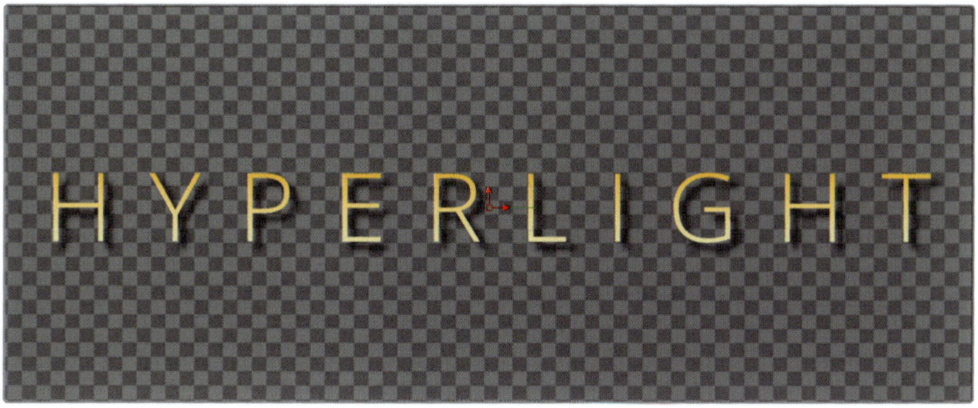

As soon as you drag the Tracking slider, a new keyframe is added at the current location of the playhead.

14 Press Cmd-left arrow (macOS) or Ctrl-left arrow (Windows) to move the playhead to the start of the render range.

15 Press spacebar to review the animation.

As you have seen, setting keyframes in the Fusion page Inspector is identical to doing so in the Edit page. So, it becomes incredibly easy to begin animating in the Fusion page. You'll encounter the main Fusion page differences compared to the Edit page when you want to view and modify keyframes. In doing so, you'll discover that the animating power of the Fusion page far surpasses the Edit page.

Viewing and Modifying Keyframes

The Node editor is used for organizing the image-processing operations in your composite, but it does not show keyframing information. However, the Fusion page includes a keyframes editor and a spline editor that are extremely powerful for viewing and modifying keyframes.

1 In the upper-right corner of the DaVinci Resolve window, click the spline and the keyframes buttons to show the two panels.

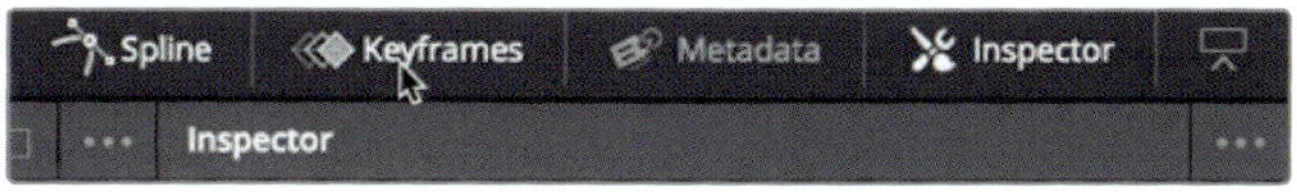

Both the spline editor and the keyframes editor give you tools to view and modify keyframes. Because you currently are interested only in modifying your keyframes, you do not need the Node editor. You can open more room for the keyframes editor by temporarily hiding the nodes.

2 In the upper-left corner of the Resolve window, click the nodes button to hide the node editor.

The keyframes editor shows each node stacked in a familiar timeline interface.

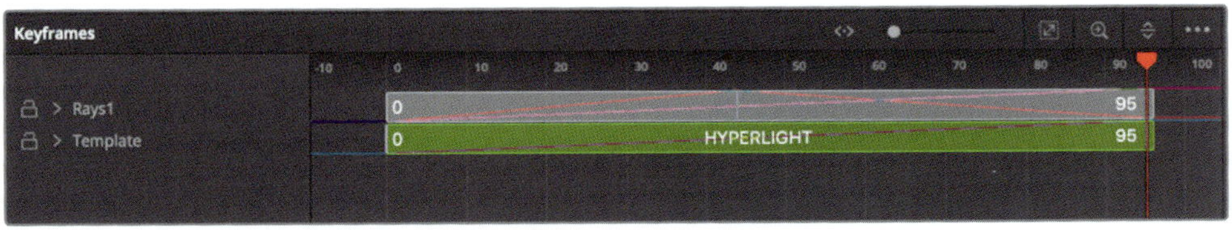

Even though the keyframe tracks are stacked like layers, the vertical order of these tracks has no impact on your composite. The tracks effect only when clips start, when they end, and the keyframes that they contain.

3 In the keyframes editor, click the disclosure arrow next to the Template and Rays1 nodes to show the start and end keyframes on both tracks.

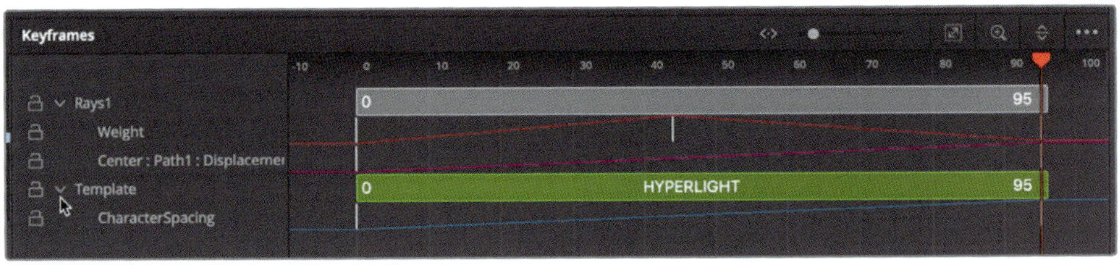

The white lines below the tracks indicate the keyframes for the Rays and tracking animations. Let's move the center keyframe on the weight track so it reaches the full force of the light rays earlier.

4 Click in an empty space in the keyframes editor, and press Cmd-F (macOS) or Ctrl-F (Windows) to fit the tracks in the window.

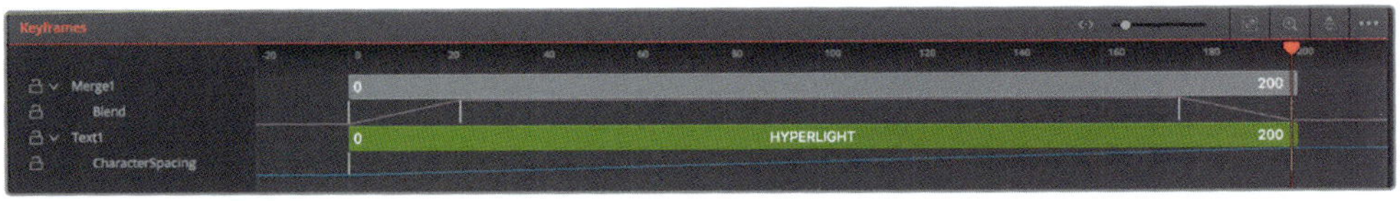

Expanding the tracks to fill the panels allows you to see the keyframes more clearly.

5 In the Rays Weight track, drag the middle keyframe to the left until the tooltip in the lower-left corner of the DaVinci Resolve window reads "Time: 20.0".

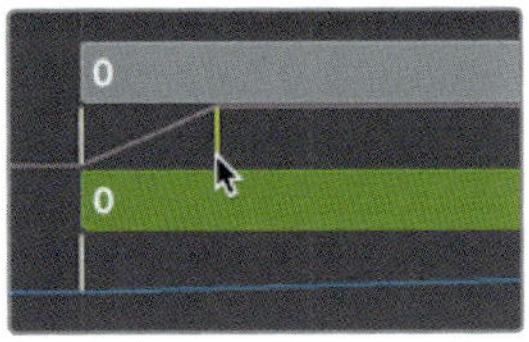

You have moved the keyframe to frame 20, making the light rays appear earlier.

6 Press Cmd-left arrow (macOS) or Ctrl-left arrow (Windows) to move the playhead back to the start of the render range, and press the spacebar to review the new adjustments.

The keyframes editor provides a straightforward way to adjust the timing of elements and keyframes. However, it doesn't provide any visual way to adjust the acceleration between keyframes. On a very basic level, that is what the spline editor does. Let's create a smoother animation for the character spacing by converting the keyframes from a linear acceleration to a smooth ease-in/ease-out acceleration.

7 In the spline editor, select the character spacing checkbox below Template.

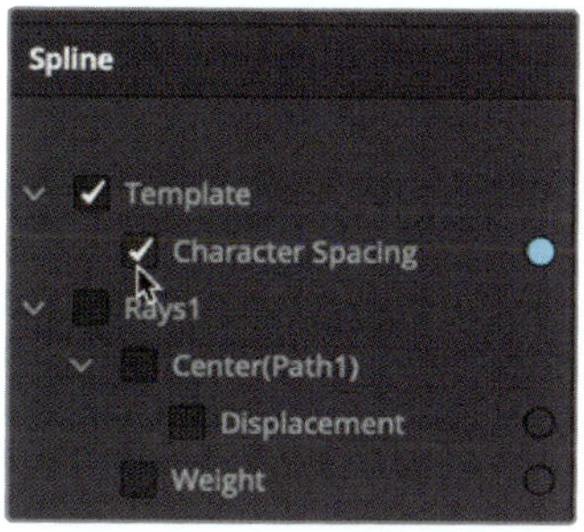

8 Move the mouse pointer over the spline editor, and press Cmd-F (macOS) or Ctrl-F (Windows) to maximize the spline in the graph area.

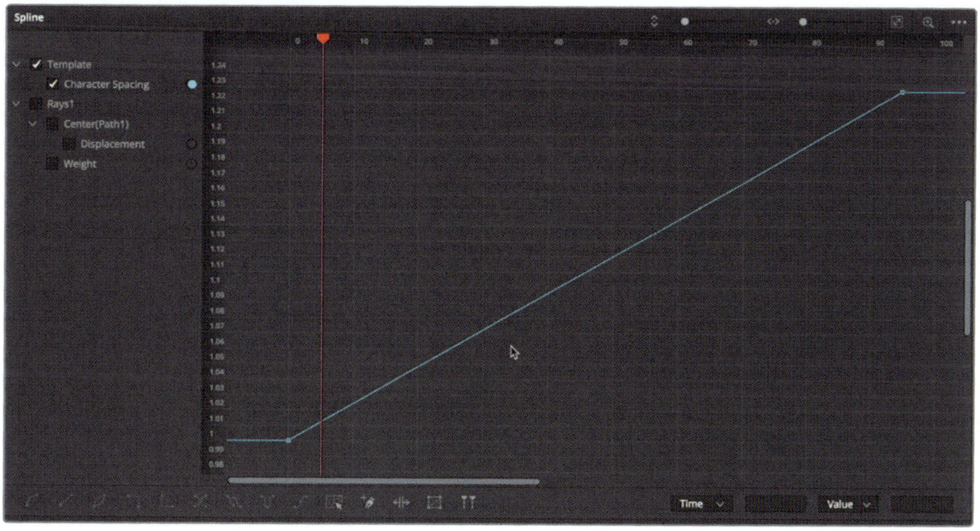

The animation spline for the character spacing is displayed in the spline editor. The starting keyframe is in the lower-left and the ending keyframe is in the upper-right. The straight line between the two keyframes indicates a linear animation, which means it has a constant, steady rate of motion. To create a more natural animation, you can smooth the motion between the two keyframes.

TIP You can pan and zoom in any panel of the Fusion page by holding down the middle mouse button and dragging to pan, and holding down Cmd (macOS) or Ctrl (Windows) and scrolling with the middle mouse button to zoom in and out.

9 In the spline editor, drag a selection rectangle around both keyframes.

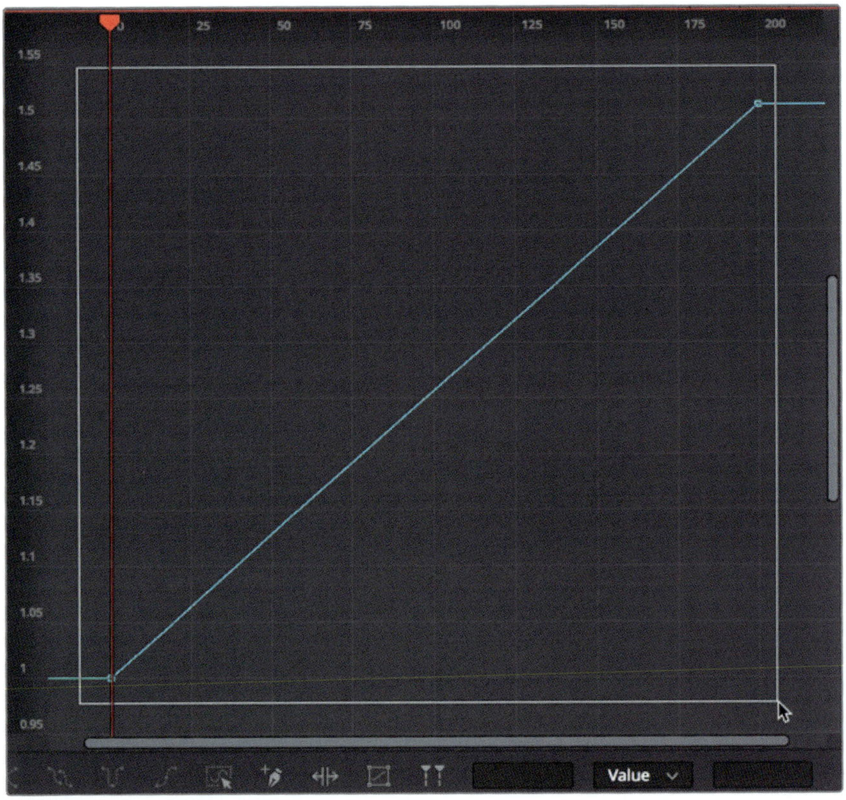

10 In the lower-left corner of the spline editor, click the Smooth button, or press Shift-S.

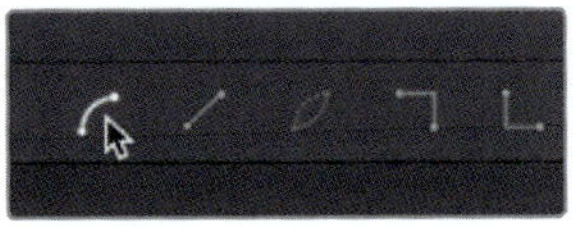

Smoothing the keyframes creates an S-curve and adds spline handles to each keyframe.

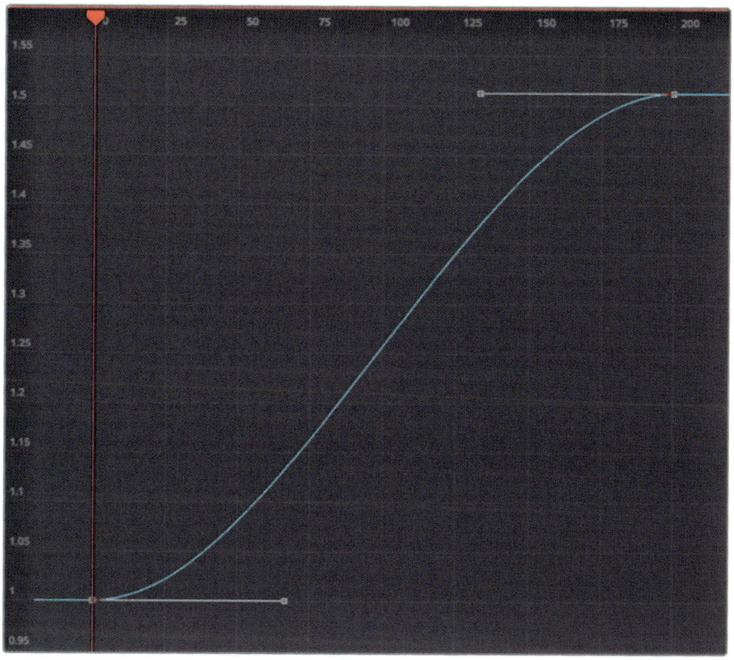

The result of smoothing both keyframes will be a more natural ease to the start of the animation and a nice ease at the end.

11 Press Cmd-left arrow (macOS) or Ctrl-left arrow (Windows) to move the playhead to the start of the render range. Press spacebar to review your new adjustments.

The Fusion page is a feature-rich, powerful compositing application that has been in development for several years. Don't expect to master it with a single lesson. If you are coming from a different visual effects or motion graphics application, you'll have a head start; but even if you are only familiar with compositing in an editing timeline, start off by applying simple effects to your own content and slowly experimenting from there. You'll be amazed how quickly your bag of Fusion compositing tricks will grow.

Lesson Review

1. In the Fusion page, how can you display the output of a node in viewer 1?
2. How can you move to the next shot in a timeline while remaining on the Fusion page?
3. What node would you use to blend two images?
4. What is the yellow input on a merge node?
5. True or false? When you are on the Fusion page, you can disconnect the media out node because you have no use for it.

Answers

1. In the Fusion page, to display the output of a node on viewer 1, select the node and press the 1 key.
2. To switch shots in the Fusion page, on the upper toolbar, click the clips button, and then click the thumbnail of the shot you want to work on.
3. A merge node is used to composite two images.
4. The yellow input on the merge node is for the background input.
5. False. The media out node is always the last node connected and it renders the node editor results back to the Edit page timeline.

An Introduction to Color Correction

Before you get into the technical side of color correction and learn how DaVinci Resolve 15's powerful color correction tools work, it's important to take a moment to understand color correction and the creative medium it is.

Color correction is not something you can do by learning the controls of the color corrector, and it's not something you can do well just using the scopes. It's a highly creative skill in itself. Just as a good editor can tell a story and bring a dramatic flow to a program, the colorist evokes an emotion in a viewer via visual manipulation of the image. While it can take time to learn how to be a top-level colorist, like all creative skills, it never gets boring because you'll always have something new to learn and a new creative style to explore!

When using DaVinci Resolve, you have the advantage of over thirty years of color correction experience. DaVinci pioneered the development of color correction hardware and software specifically designed to artistically enhance visual images acquired from film, video, and digital sources. As a result, DaVinci Resolve possesses an incredibly deep, sophisticated, and efficient toolset for adjusting the look of the clips in your program, and managing these adjustments over an entire timeline.

Furthermore, DaVinci Resolve has continuously evolved thanks to feedback from countless professional colorists worldwide working at all levels of the film and broadcast industry. So, the DaVinci Resolve Color page has been developed to work the way colorists think. Still, for all its technological sophistication, it's important to remember that DaVinci Resolve is merely a tool that requires an artist to realize its full potential. But of course, that's the fun part!

The following lessons cover the basics you'll need to learn to begin harnessing the power of the Color page in your own projects – be they feature films, episodic television, web series, short subjects, spots, promos, or corporate videos. No matter what you work on, these formats employ the same fundamental grading techniques and the same basic tools; so, if you're new to the world of professional color grading, don't worry. All rock star colorists once had to learn these first steps for themselves, and you'll use the fundamentals you learn here for the rest of your career.

Gone are the days when high-quality color grading was unaffordable. Blackmagic Design has put the powerful color tools of DaVinci Resolve within reach of any editor that has a reasonably capable workstation or laptop. The polish you'll need to achieve world-class results is only a click away on the Color page.

However, before you start getting into the specifics of color, it's important to step back and consider, what are these tools really used for?

Why Color Correct your Work?

It's a tempting question, and one that countless producers and directors have asked. "The program looks fine the way it was shot, why spend the time to grade it?" It's a good question in an industry where time is money; if the program you've cut in the Edit page looks fine, why bother grading it?

The answer is because your program won't look as good as it will after being graded.

The process of adjusting the contrast and color of every clip in a program is variously called color correction, color grading, or just grading. The difference in terminology is largely superficial, but most experienced colorists prefer "grading" because "correction" implies you only adjust things that are wrong, whereas "grading" implies that you're holding each clip in your program up to a higher artistic standard. A colorist doesn't ask, "Does this clip look good?" A colorist asks, "Could this clip look better?"

Setting the Tone of the Visuals

Much has been said about the emotional power of color to shape audience mood, and nobody would argue that a scene lit by cool blue lighting is going to have a very different vibe than one that's lit by warm orange lighting. The greenish tinge of fluorescent fixtures, and the salmon-hued wash of mercury vapor streetlights each paint the scenes of a show with different atmospheric feelings that, when done right, add to the narrative and how your audience perceives it.

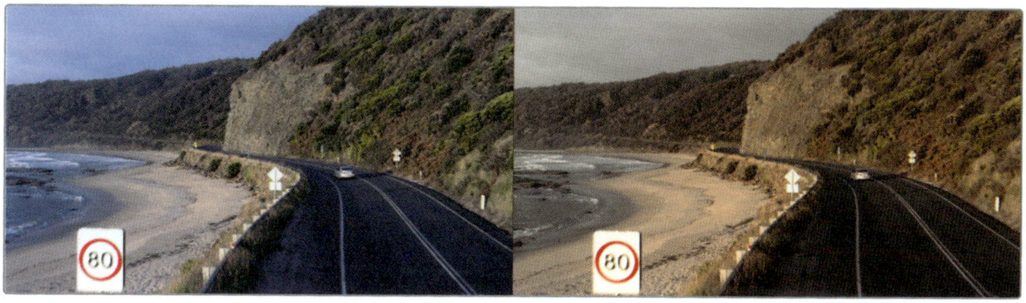

Cooler Warmer

Of course, what these varied illuminants mean depends on the visual palette you develop. Warm lighting that denotes romance in one film may instead portray roiling, desert-bound discomfort in another. Their impact, depends on the associations that your grading makes between the visuals and the story. Should this scene seem later in the day? Should the colors be more subdued? Should the sky be an inescapable presence? You control these audience perceptions when you exercise subtle control over the picture via color grading.

The important takeaway is that the Color page gives you the tools to mold these associations to suit your needs – intensifying, attenuating, or completely counteracting their effect, as necessary, to strike the right tone for each and every scene.

Portraying the World Subjectively

Narrative cinematography is rarely concerned with capturing objectively lit renditions of locations with perfectly accurate, neutral color and tonality. Instead, truckloads of lighting instruments and careful art direction manipulate the light and color of the location to make it look somber, magical, frightening, or sultry. These efforts extend to the grading suite, where your job is not to portray the world as it is, but the world that the cinematographer and director want the audience to see.

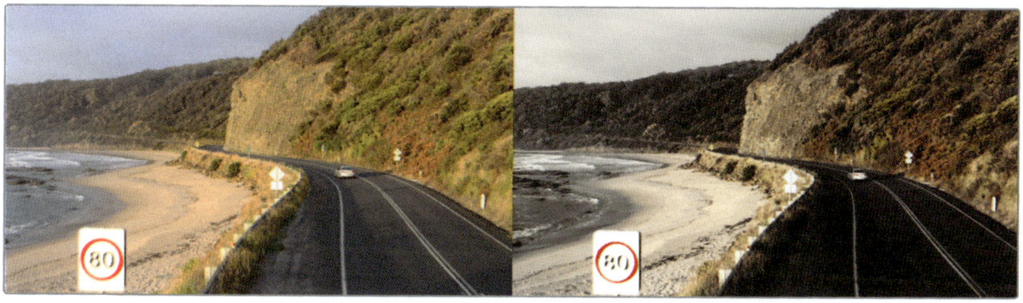

What the camera saw (left) What you want audiences to see (right)

Documentary photography may very often be concerned with presenting a supposedly unvarnished (yet gloriously rendered) look at the world. And yet, even this "realistic" look at the world is a fabrication, as every adjustment you make to improve the visibility of a subject, enhance the glory of nature, clean up some archival footage, or push the surroundings of the frame to recede artfully into the background, can be as carefully thought out and manipulated as any music video grade.

The point is, whether you're making a horror movie, an architectural documentary, a sales video, or an automotive spot, you're using the tools and techniques of color correction to create a subjective representation of the imagery. The more control you can exercise over this representation, the larger palette of emotional response you'll have to draw from.

Evolving to do High-end Work

If you want to learn and stay competitive, and especially if you intend to work on client projects rather than your own, it's good to make yourself aware of current styles and trends. You've no doubt heard that if you want to write, you should read as much as you can, and the same holds true for color grading. Watch movies, television, music videos, and web shorts. And if you're watching television, make yourself watch the ads. Once you've had a chance to learn the grading controls that DaVinci Resolve offers, you'll start to see how different looks correspond to adjustments you can make in your own projects.

And finally, get out into the world and look at other visuals. Flip through fashion magazines, go to art galleries, take a hike in the woods, and observe. Fill your mind with diverse images, and analyze them to see what inspires you. The more aware you are of other visual disciplines, the more ideas you'll bring to your own work.

A last issue to consider is the effect affordable color grading has had on the television industry. In most current episodic television production, the visual style is now as good as in a feature film. This dramatic change in quality has made television programming better than ever.

An unintended benefit of this change is that top-level feature film actors now move into television work and back to film with amazing freedom because television no longer looks like an inferior medium. Also, high-level film crews and facilities are able to do a wider range of both television shows and feature films, while still retaining their premium status. It's an exciting time when you consider the additional increase in the number of distribution platforms for high-quality work, such as streaming services. The industry is growing more quickly than ever, which means talented editors and colorists are more in demand than ever!

The Goals of Color Grading

Color correction can be considered the process of choosing which parts of the raw image data to display to create a pleasing image for the viewer.

Developing the Image

The latest generation of digital cinema cameras are almost all capable of either shooting raw color space image data, or at the very least, recording RGB image data with a log-encoded exposure. Doing so preserves the maximum amount of image data for manipulation during the color correction process. While this is great for flexibility in workflow and for making high-quality adjustments, acquiring media in this way forces you to take the extra step of transforming it into a viewable image for editing and finishing (in much the same way that film negative required development and printing to yield a viewable image.

DaVinci Resolve simplifies this task with built-in camera raw controls, DaVinci Resolve color management, and LUT support so you can quickly get your media to a sound starting point upon which to build the rest of your grade.

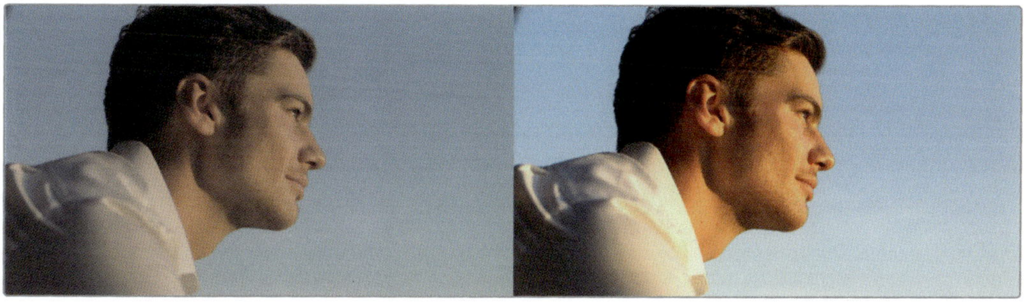

Log encoded source (left) The same source normalized and corrected (right)

Making Every Clip Look its Best

While the job of the cinematographer is to light and expose the image with an artistic intent, your job as an editor and colorist is to realize this intent by adjusting the color and contrast of the image of each clip so the final result is as close to the director's and cinematographer's intentions as possible. In the process, you can overcome inconsistencies with exposure and color balance that were otherwise unavoidable. Furthermore, you can subtly adjust warmth and contrast to realize looks that were not achievable during the shoot, but that the director and cinematographer would have liked.

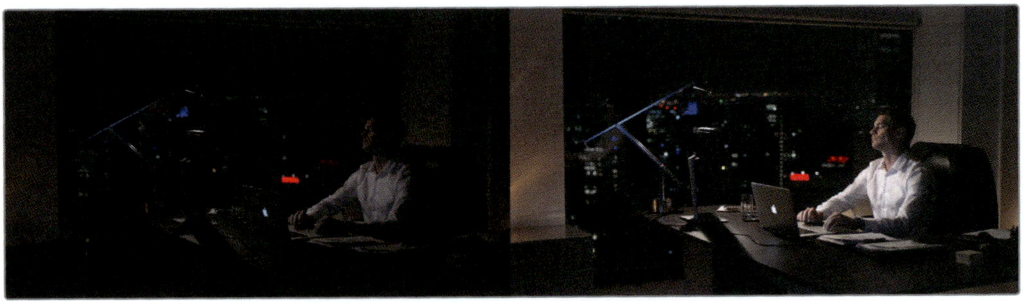

An underexposed image (left) The corrected image for the audience (right)

Of course, in some situations, you may find it necessary to fix media that has more substantial problems in color and exposure. In these cases, the tools exist to make far more involved changes to the image; however, the quality of your results will depend heavily on the quality and "latitude" of your source media. For example, Blackmagic URSA Mini cameras record quite a bit of image data within raw or minimally compressed media formats, allowing you to make extreme corrections that would be impossible on consumer cameras. Happily, in either case, the Color page provides the tools to process images in many different ways to adjust the image to achieve a better look.

Quality Control

While you're doing all this, it's important to keep in mind that for all the creative possibilities that DaVinci Resolve affords, it's still important that the deliverables you give to your client have appropriate signal levels relative to their distribution requirements. In particular, programs destined for cinema, broadcast, or streaming usually have very specific outer boundaries of luma, chroma, and gamut that you must not exceed, or you'll risk having a show kicked back to you for quality control violations.

DaVinci Resolve provides tools specifically designed to help you keep an eye on how the image data is affected, and to fine tune the image. In particular, the scopes display the standard Waveform, Parade, Vectorscope, and Histogram graphs that you can use to objectively analyze image data. These scopes let you see the boundaries of what's possible, and make it easy to spot subtle problems, and compare the characteristics of one image to another.

Balancing Scenes

It's rare for uncorrected shots to match one another seamlessly. Even the most carefully exposed angles of coverage can have small variances to be evened out. For example, run-and-gun programs using available light often result in edited scenes with huge changes in lighting and color as one shot cuts into the next.

Small or large, variations between shots can call undue attention to the editing, and jar the audience in ways that throw them out of the program. Balancing these differences is another fundamental task of the colorist. You know you're finished when every shot in a scene looks like the same time and the same place, and the color and contrast adjustments you've made flow unnoticeably from one clip to the next.

Adding Style or Custom "Looks"

Of course, it's not all about subtlety and correction. It's often appropriate, when grading music videos and commercials, for instance, to bring some radical visual style to a piece. Here, too, DaVinci Resolve provides an abundance of features for manipulating unexpected aspects of the image. For example, you can use custom curves to create an illusion of chemical cross-processing.

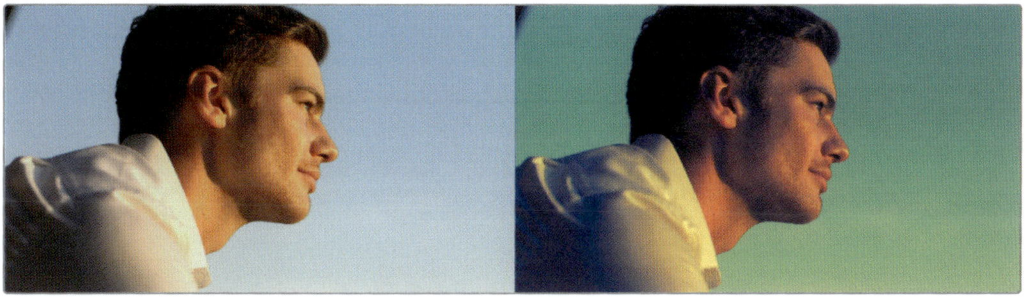

Grading an image (left) with curves to create a cross-processing effect (right)

The Tool Hollywood Uses

If all that isn't enough incentive to plunge forward into the next few lessons and exercises, keep in mind that DaVinci Resolve has become the tool of choice for some of the largest post-production facilities in the industry, worldwide. And yet, thanks to its accessibility, within the last several years, DaVinci Resolve has also become the go-to tool for a wide variety of smaller boutique post companies and individual artists. Considering only projects completed recently, DaVinci Resolve was used to grade blockbusters like "Independence Day: Resurgence" and "X-Men: Apocalypse," along with indie productions such as "The Big Sick" and "A Ghost Story;" not to mention television shows including HBO's "Westworld," AMC's "The Walking Dead," and the CW's "Arrow."

Whether you're looking to build a foundation of skills to enter the post-production industry as a contributing artist, or you want to develop the ability to finish your personal creative work in your own way, the following exercises will usher you into a much larger world of image manipulation and artistic expression than has ever been available in the average non-linear editing application.

Lastly, color grading is just fun! The feeling of resting your hands on the trackballs and holding the emotion of your images in your hands is exhilarating. It's like no other feeling in the world; you can make adjustments in real time, instantly see the results, and feel the emotional impact in your heart. We believe that color correction is one of those tasks that is more creative than cerebral. It's also one of those jobs that surprises you every day and has an emotional connection that reminds us why we fell in love with the film and television industry in the first place!

Enjoy the journey!

Lesson 11

Quick start: color correction

Like editing, color correction is an art form that takes time to learn and master. Color is an incredibly powerful creative tool that can define the style and convey the mood of your film. If you give yourself the time to practice and learn, you'll be able to master this exciting skill and create images that look amazing!

This quick start lesson will provide a fast overview of the most important color-correction tools to get you comfortable with how they work. You'll learn about the primary corrector, secondary adjustments, nodes and even applying DaVinci Resolve FX for special effects. Experience is key, and with so many controls at your fingertips, this lesson will give you the start you need toward learning this creative skill.

Time

This lesson takes approximately 45 minutes to complete.

Goals

Remember, DaVinci Resolve was originally developed for high-end color correction and finishing on feature films. That means you're about to work with the same tools that Hollywood's top colorists use to correct and finish the biggest blockbuster films, episodic television shows, and commercials.

Learning the Color Page Layout

The technical and creative process of color correction takes place within the color page in DaVinci Resolve 16. Let's start by examining the color page layout.

1. Open DaVinci Resolve to the project manager window.

   To begin exploring the color page, let's switch projects. The project you will use was archived using DaVinci Resolve. An archive is a self-contained project that includes all of its media. All you have to do is restore the archive and the project will be available with all the media already linked. You'll learn more about archives later in the book.

2. Right-click an empty area of the project manager window, and choose restore project archive.
3. Navigate to R16 intro lessons > Lesson 11, select the Lesson 11 Quick to Cook.dra folder, and click Open.
4. In the project manager, open the restored Lesson 11 Quick to Cook project, and from the timelines bin, open Quick to Cook promo into the timeline.

   This is a slightly modified version of the cooking show you created in lesson 1 and 2. This shows off one of the best aspects of DaVinci Resolve. Editing and color grading are completely integrated into a single application, so you can easily move between the two with a single click.

5. At the bottom of the DaVinci Resolve window, click the color button to go to the color page.

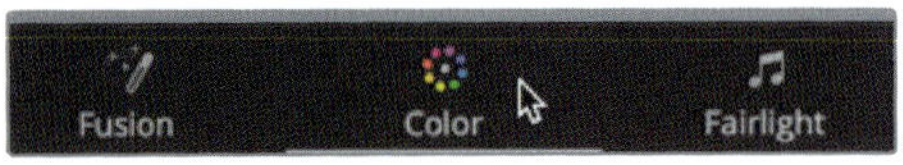

The color page is divided into seven main areas.

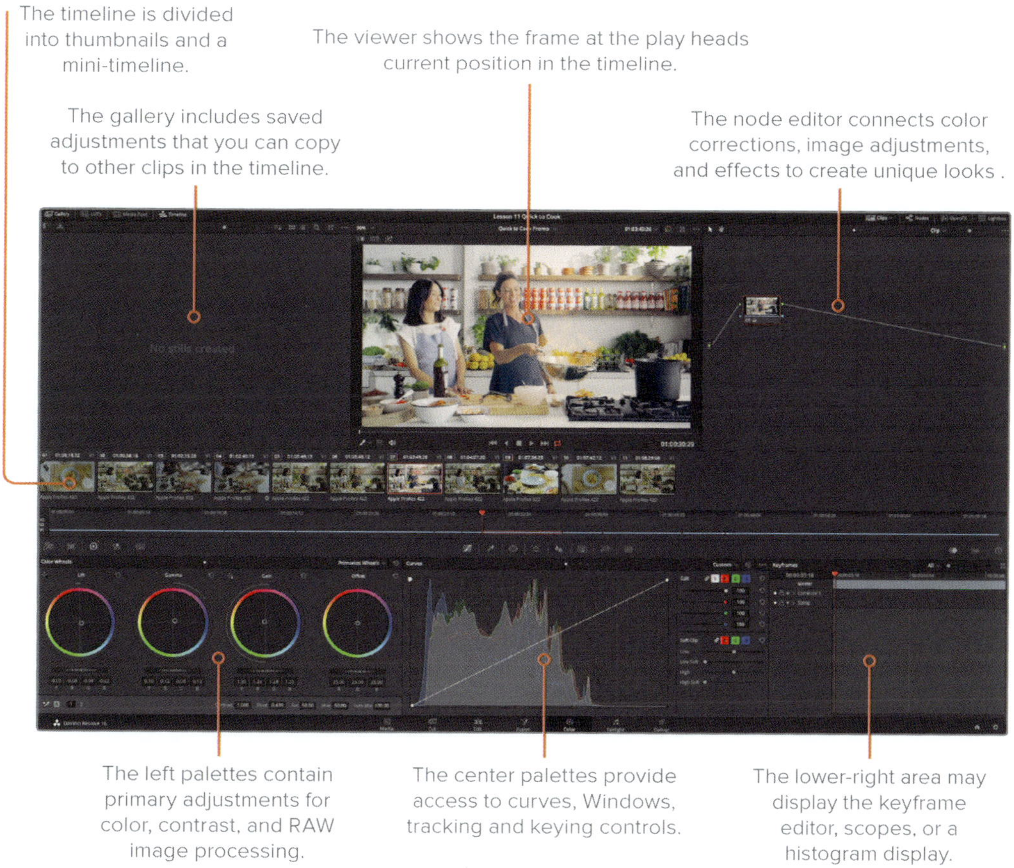

NOTE When you're using DaVinci Resolve on a computer display with a resolution lower than 1920 x 1080, some panels and buttons will be consolidated and not look exactly like the images in this lesson.

When you switch to the color page, whatever was loaded into the editing timeline is displayed in the color page timeline. The color page does not change or alter any cuts or transitions. It just provides a way of looking at your timeline that is more appropriate for color correction.

6 Select the last thumbnail in the timeline.

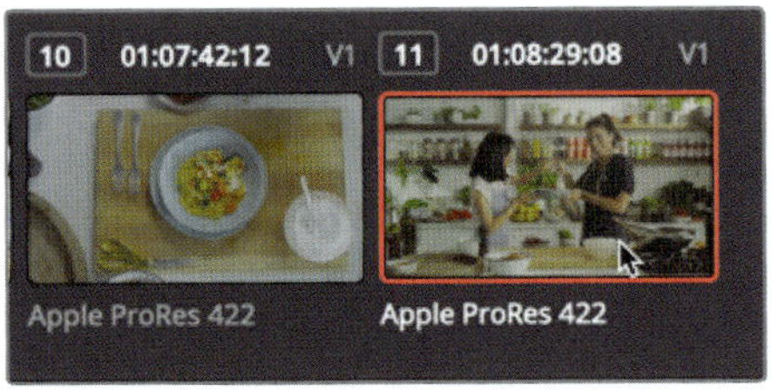

An orange outline appears around the selected thumbnail, and the play head jumps to the first frame of that clip.

7 Below the thumbnail, double-click the Apple ProRes 422 name to switch to viewing clip names.

The mini-timeline below the thumbnails displays thin bars to represent each clip. A bar's width is proportional to a clip's duration.

8 Drag the mini-timeline play head to the left to scrub through the timeline until you reach the first clip.

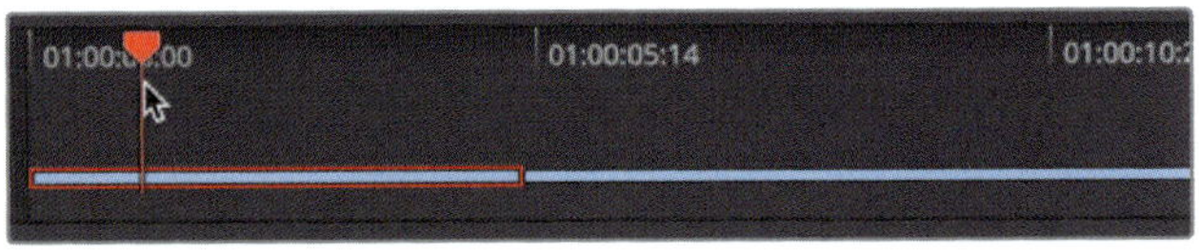

As you scrub through the timeline, the clip under the play head highlights in orange to show that it is selected, a behavior similar to the thumbnail display outline. The transport controls under the viewer, as well as all the playback keyboard shortcuts, are the same as you used on the edit page.

TIP If a track is disabled in the edit page, it will be dimmed in the mini-timeline.

Now that you have a basic understanding of the color page layout, you're ready to make some adjustments.

Modifying Lift, Gamma, and Gain

The most popular controls for creating styles and balancing your shots are found in the primaries corrector. Because DaVinci Resolve includes many controls in the primary corrector, you will find that you spend much of the time using the primary corrector while you are on the color page.

Using the primary corrector, you can achieve a refined result because you can divide the image into tonal regions.

The lift, gamma, and gain controls broadly correspond to the dark, midrange, and bright regions in the image. Within each region, you can adjust hue and luma values to create a wide variety of styles. For instance, if you wanted to adjust color or brightness in the dark areas, you would move the lift region.

Let's make a few adjustments to get the feel of some of the primary corrector's controls. In this exercise we'll use the color wheels controls.

1 In the timeline, click thumbnail 01 to relocate the play head to that clip.

The color wheels controls are divided into color wheels and master wheels. When starting to color correct an image you start with the master wheels to set the dynamic range between your black point and white point.

> **TIP** Adjustments made in the color balance controls are subtle. In most cases, the edge of the control will remain very close to or still touch the crosshair.

The master wheel controls, below the color balance controls, adjust brightness in the lift, gamma, and gain regions. Adjusting the lift wheel will increase or decrease brightness in the darker areas.

2 Drag the lift wheel to the left until the Y luminance value reads around -0.05.

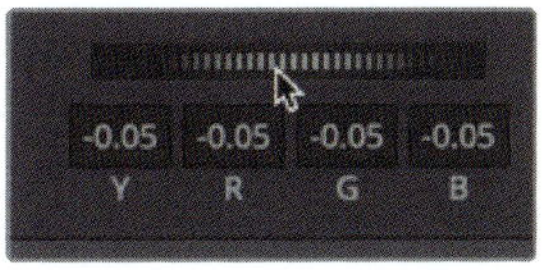

The master wheel under the lift color balance control adjusts the black point for the image. When dragging it to the left, the darker areas in the image become darker.

Let's look at the other end of the spectrum by adjusting the gain control.

The master wheel under the gain color balance control adjusts the white point for the image. When dragging it to the right, the brightest areas in the image become brighter.

3 Drag the gain master wheel to the right until the Y luminance value displays around 1.5.

By adjusting the lift master wheel and the gain master wheel, you have effectively adjusted contrast in the clip. Instead of using a simple contrast control, you have exercised greater control over the black point and white point using the lift and gain master wheels.

Now let's look at gamma.

4 Drag the Gamma master wheel to the right until the Y luminance value displays around 0.05.

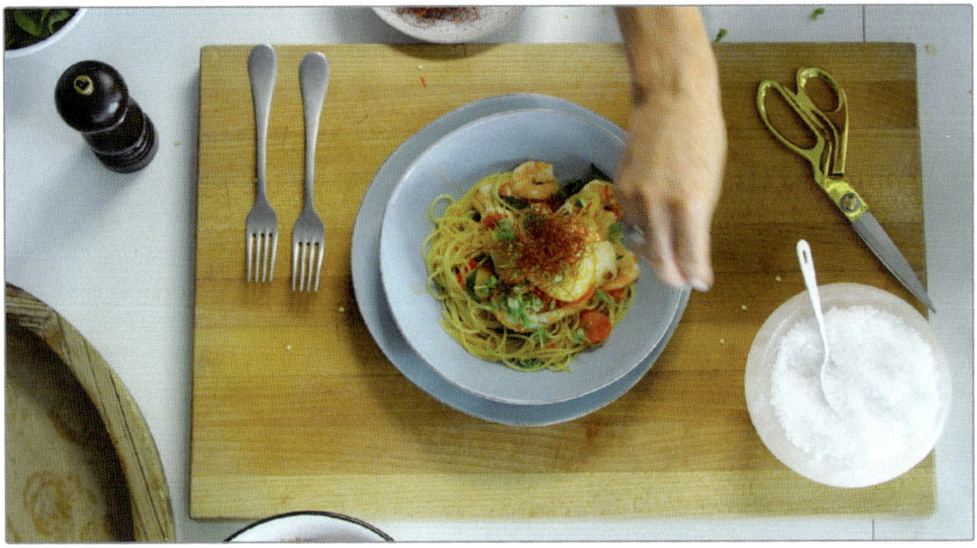

The master wheel under the gamma color balance control adjusts the overall brightness while maintaining the black and white points that you set previously. When dragging this control to the right, the overall image becomes brighter. When the tonal adjustments are made, you can then adjust color using the color wheels.

5 In the lift color balance control, drag the color balance indicator slightly toward blue to add blue to the darker areas.

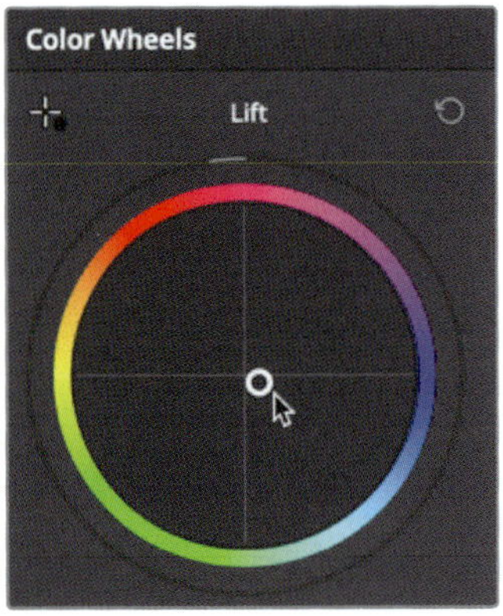

6 In the gain color balance control, drag the color balance indicator slightly toward orange to add orange to the brighter areas.

The gain color balance control tints the brighter areas of your image.

7 In the gamma color balance control, drag the control slightly toward magenta.

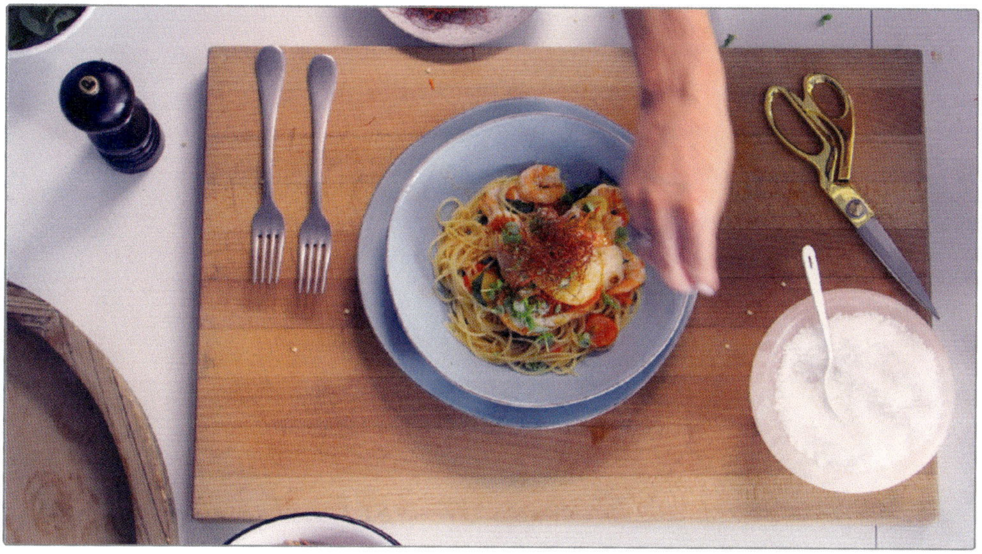

The gamma color balance control tints the midrange of your image.

Let's compare the corrected image you've made to the original image.

8 Click the Bypass button in the upper right of the viewer or press Shift-D, to see the original image. Then Click the Bypass button again, or press Shift-D, to view the corrected image.

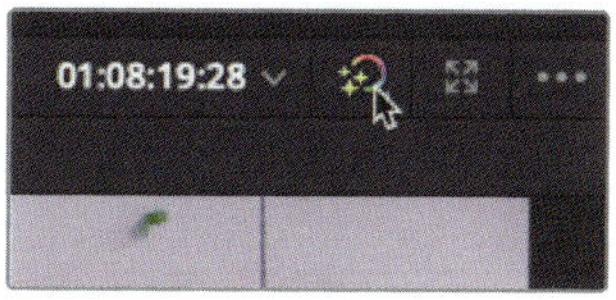

These adjustments were made only to give you a feel for the controls and what they do. They clearly didn't produce anything worth keeping. You can reset each control or the entire primary corrector using the reset buttons.

> **NOTE** In the color page, each clip has its own undo/redo history. That is, choosing Edit > Undo will undo previous changes depending on which clip is the current clip. The edit page also has its own undo history, which is separate from the color page. The edit and Fairlight page Undo/Redo commands operate on the entire timeline, not on each clip.

9 In the upper-right corner of the gamma color balance control, click the reset button.

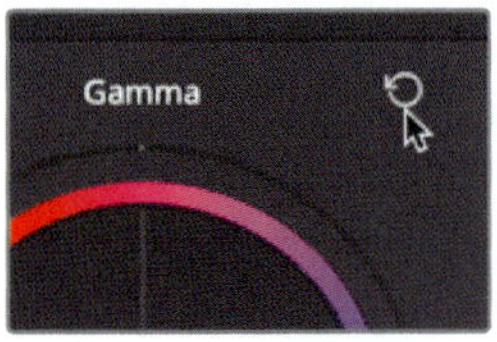

You can also reset the entire primary corrector using the panel reset button.

10 In the upper-right corner of the primary corrector panel, click the reset button.

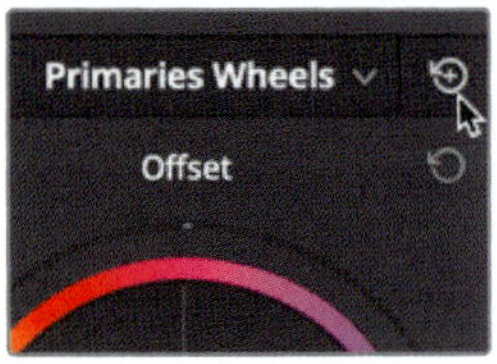

The lift, gamma, and gain controls are not isolated adjustments that change only the dark, midrange, and bright areas. In fact, their ranges overlap by a considerable amount. When you adjust the lift, for example, most of the adjustment affects the darker areas, but the midrange and even some bright areas also may be affected.

Similarly, when you adjust gain, most of the adjustment operates within the brightest areas of the image, but you'll also see a fall-off impact within the midrange and a small amount of dark areas. This overlap helps you make more natural, smoother-looking adjustments, but it also means that you'll need to move among the three color balance controls to achieve best results because making an adjustment to one control visibly impacts the others.

Using other Primary Corrector Controls

The primary corrector controls that you have used are adjusted mainly to achieve an overall look by controlling lift, gamma, and gain within the image. You can also make a few primary corrector adjustments that you may be more familiar with from other video or photo applications. The shared adjustment controls are located across the bottom of the primary corrector panel. These global adjustments affect the entire image, not just the lift, gamma, or gain.

1 Select thumbnail 02.

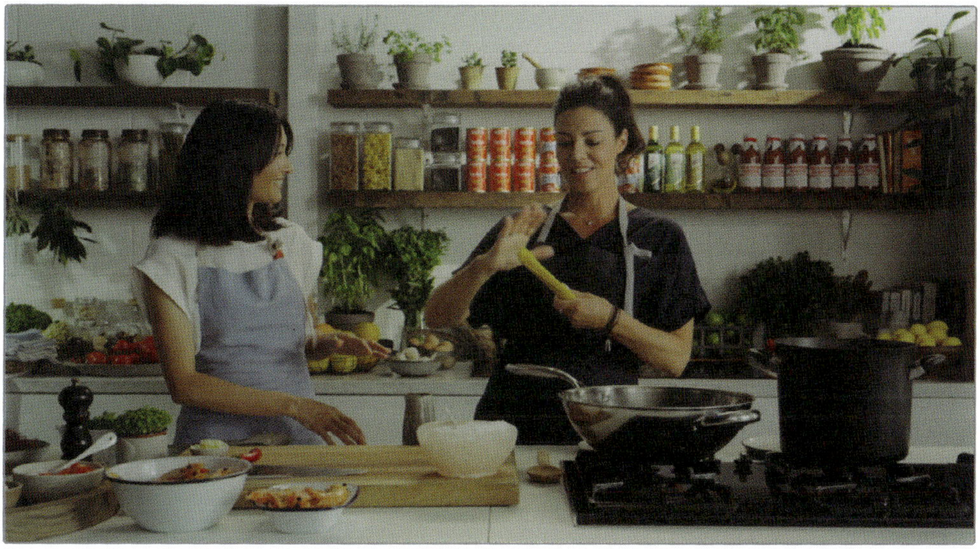

The color in this shot appears a bit dark and low in contrast. Although you can modify contrast using the primary corrector as you did earlier, the color page also includes some very quick and easy options.

2 In the adjustment controls below the color wheels, position the pointer over the contrast value field.

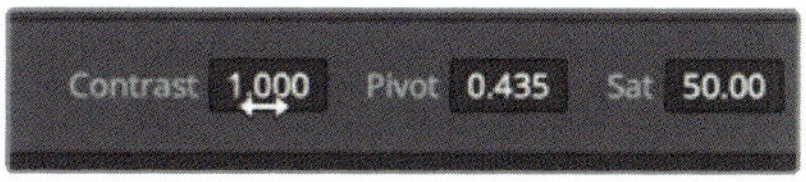

TIP Depending on your screen resolution, the names of each adjustment control may not be visible. Use the icons to identify each parameter, or hover your mouse pointer over an icon to view a tool tip of its name.

Dragging the contrast value to the right increases the spread of the shadows and highlights.

TIP As with all value fields in DaVinci Resolve, when the pointer is over the value field or the parameter's name, you can drag to modify the value.

3 With your pointer in the contrast value field, drag to the right until the value reaches 1.3.

The adjustment controls have a second page of parameters for globally improving your shot.

4 Click the 2 button to display the second page of the adjustment controls.

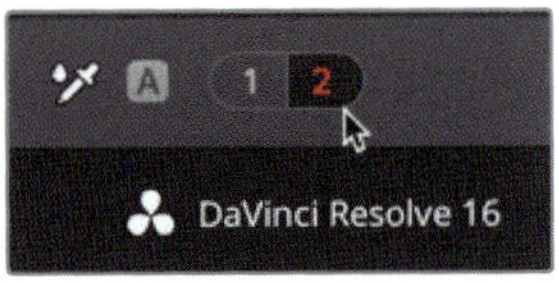

You can further refine the contrast using the shadow and highlight controls. These are similar to adjusting the low end of gamma and gain master wheels.

5 Drag the shadow control to the right to brighten the low end of the mid tones.

6 Drag the highlight control to the right to increase the brightness of the highlights.

Again, since you have set your tonal balance you can now work on color adjustments using the same adjustment strip.

You can perform straightforward white balance correction using the temperature and tint controls. Our current shot clearly has too much warm yellow tint to it. The white walls, which should be purely white, are the most obvious sign. Using the temperature control, you can shift the color in an image either warmer toward yellow, or cooler toward blue.

TIP For off-axis color casts that come from irregular light sources, you can use the tint control to shift an image away from magenta or green.

7 Drag the temperature value field to the left, until it is between -200 and -300, to push the image towards the cooler tones.

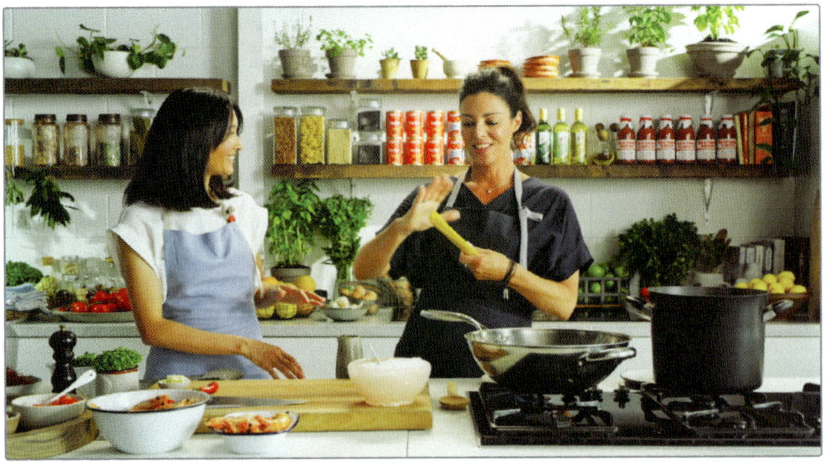

Making an image pop

On page 2 of the adjustments, color boost and midtone detail are two good adjustments that can add a nice visual punch to your shots. Color boost allows you to increase/decrease the saturation of lower saturated colors without changing high saturated colors as much.

This clip already has very saturated colors. We'd like to keep the vibrant colors of the of the yellow lemons, red peppers and red cans behind our host and chef but bring down the saturation in their skin tones to be more natural.

1 With your pointer in the Color Boost value field, drag to the left until the value reaches -20.

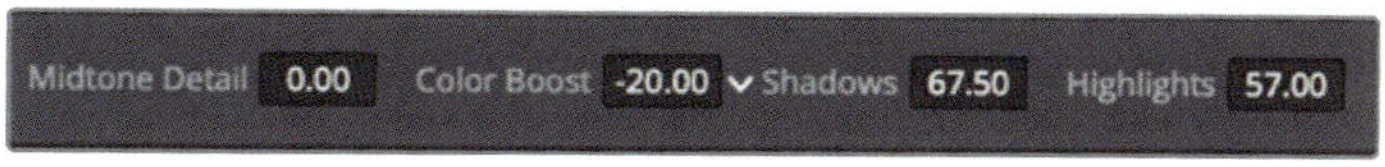

> **TIP** Double-clicking on any name in the adjustment controls will reset the value.

Now the pop of color from the food and cans behind them still add a colorful pop to the shot but their skin tones are much closer to normal.

The other adjustment that can add a good pop to your images is the midtone detail control.

The midtone detail control really is the best of all sharpen filters because it does a brilliant job of sharpening edges without increasing noise.

2 With your pointer in the midtone detail value field, drag to the right to increase the local contrast around edges in the image.(keep the value under 30)

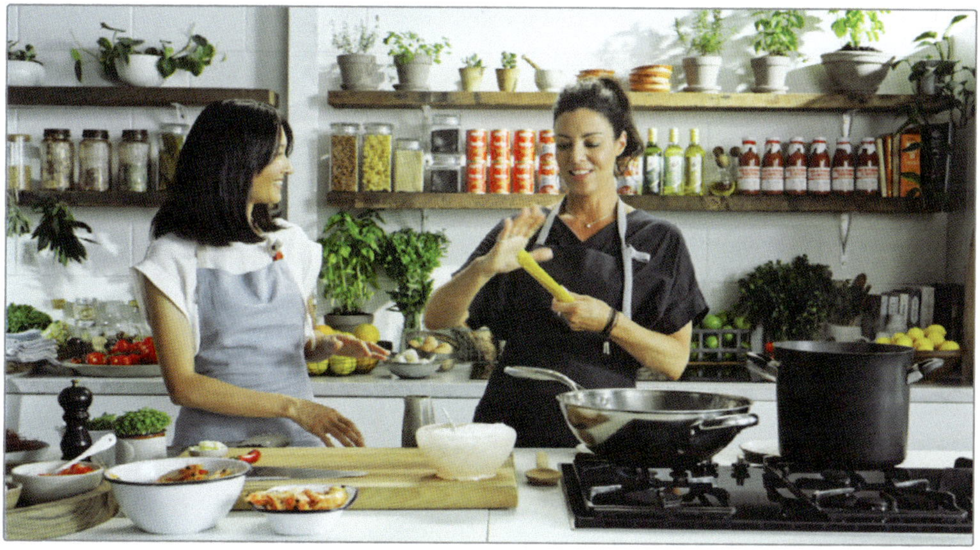

In both the color boost and midtone detail controls, a little goes a long way. A typical way to adjust these is to first add more correction than you want and then slowly back off until you find an acceptable result.

As always, when you make a significant adjustment, you should compare it to the original image.

3 Click the bypass button, or press Shift-D, to see the original image. Click the bypass button again or press Shift-D, to return to the corrected image.

> **TIP** You can use either the DaVinci Resolve Micro or Mini Panel with dedicated primary corrector hardware controls for quicker access to all of the most common tools.

With the adjustment you have made, this image now has a much better white balance.

In most color correction situations, you would likely bounce between the two images a few times while refining your adjustments. Rarely do you set a control once, compare it to the original, and move on. Color correction is an iterative learning process. It takes time; but the more you explore your options, the more you find the adjustments that work best for you.

Understanding Nodes

Like the Fusion page, the Color page uses nodes for multiple color corrections. Instead of stacking color corrections and effects as layers, you can add as many color correctors and filter effects as you like using nodes. You can view the nodes as a color correction flow chart for each individual clip. The clip, or the input, starts at the left, flows through each node, and ends on the right side of the screen with the corrected image output. Unlike Fusion page nodes, however, each node in the Color page is a full DaVinci Resolve color corrector and not an individual effect that performs only one type of image processing.

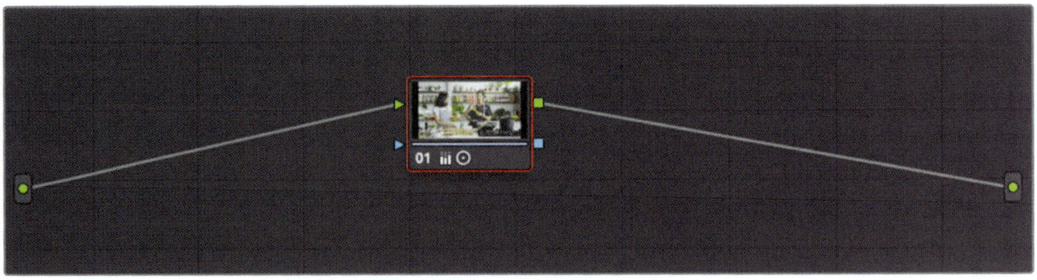

The adjustments you made in the preceding exercises were performed using the first node, which automatically is provided for you in the Node editor. As you create more sophisticated corrections, you can add more nodes that target different parts of the image or add effects.

Making Secondary Color Corrections

So far, you've made adjustments to an entire image, so-called primary color corrections. Secondary color corrections isolate only parts of an image to make very specific changes to a particular image area. A classic but extreme example is turning an entire image to black and white except for one object. Let's apply secondary color correction to a much more common task that you'll be able to use on many of your productions.

1 Click thumbnail 09.

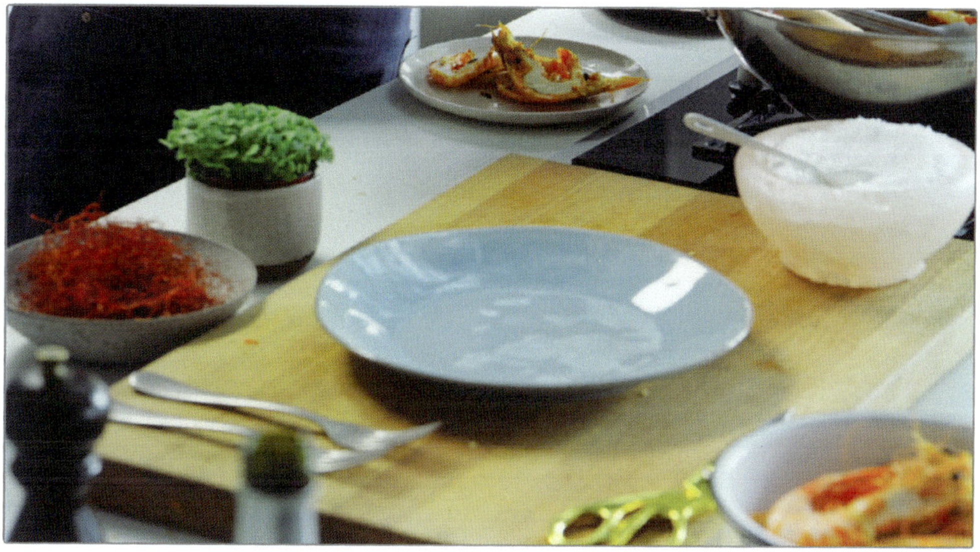

2 Press the spacebar to play the clip.

3 After you have viewed the clip a couple times, press the spacebar to stop playback.

This clip looks perfectly fine and it already as a node with some corrections on it. But let's say the color scheme is wrong and we want to introduce some magenta into the scene. Using DaVinci Resolve's color page controls, you can isolate colors very easily and shift them to other hues. Working on a specific area of an image or on a specific color is called secondary color correction.

Using Nodes and Curves

The first part of making a secondary color correction on one object is to isolate the adjustment to its own node.

Using the node editor (located in the upper-right quadrant of the DaVinci Resolve window), you can combine one or more individual nodes to create more intricate corrections.

By default, every clip has one node in the node editor that contains the initial adjustments you made. The node shown in the current project contains all the adjustments you previously applied to create the neutral correction.

However, you also have the option of creating additional nodes in which each node contains one or more corrections that affect the image. Using multiple nodes, each containing separate adjustments, you can exercise more precise control over the order of those adjustments and more easily track and modify them.

Let's add a second node to the node editor to separate the adjustment that you will apply to the teal dish.

1 Right click over the node in the node editor and choose Add Node > Add Serial, or press Option-S (macOS) or Alt-S (Windows).

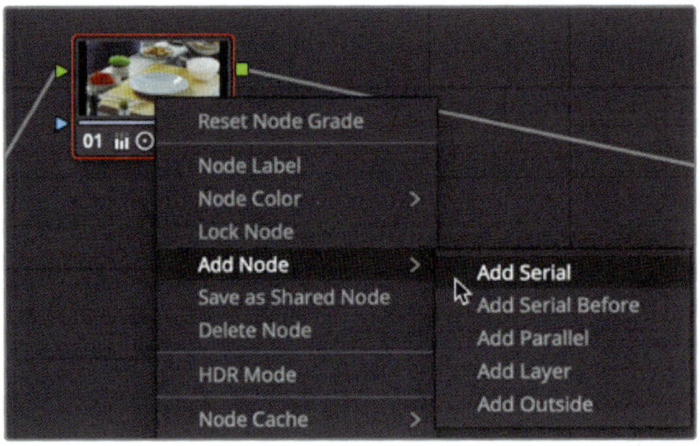

The node is added after the initial node in the node editor. The new node is given the number 02 and has a red outline to indicate that it is the currently selected node. You can rename the node to be more descriptive.

2 Right-click the node, and from the contextual menu, choose Node Label.

3 Type DISH, and press enter to rename the node.

With a new node in place, you can now use the curve controls to modify the color of the blue pole. The default curve controls are custom curves that you may be familiar using in Photoshop or other image-editing applications. However, DaVinci Resolve includes several curve controls for isolating various hues, as well as luminance and saturation levels. To adjust the hue of the dish and shift it to a different hue, you'll use a hue vs. hue curve.

4 In the curves pop-up menu, choose Hue Vs Hue to display the hue vs. hue curve.

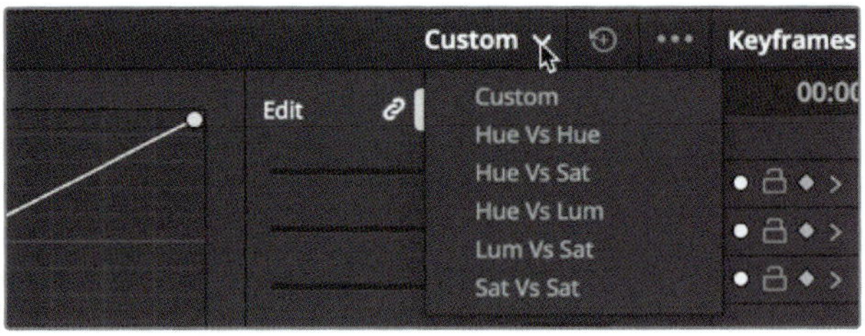

The hue vs. hue color spectrum is displayed under the timeline. These controls let you isolate a specific hue in the image just by clicking the image.

5 In the viewer, hover the mouse pointer over the teal dish.

The pointer changes to an eyedropper to indicate that you can sample an area of the image you want to isolate.

6 Click anywhere on the teal dish to sample its hue value.

Once you click the viewer, three points are added to the line in the hue vs. hue palette. The center point is the actual hue you selected. The other two points constrain the range of hues you will be adjusting as you drag the center point.

7 In the hue vs. hue palette, drag the center point down to shift the teal hue of the dish toward magenta.

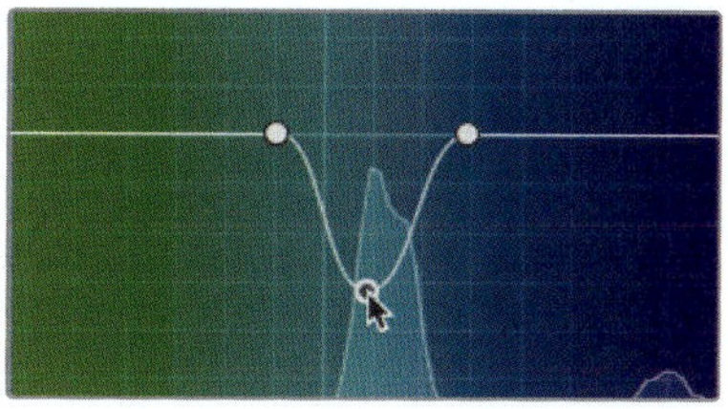

Only items with that specific hue you clicked on are affected by the shifted hue. In our case the teal color selected is too narrow to encompass all the various shades of teal in the dish. You can expand the hue to include a wider range by adjusting the outer two control points.

8 In the hue vs. hue palette, drag the outer two controls points away from the center point to encompass more green and purple until the dish is completed changed.

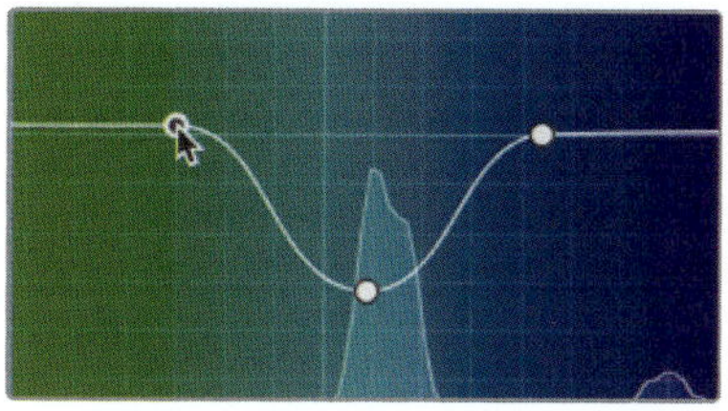

These hue, luminance, and saturation curves simplify a very complex process, so you do not have to worry about getting a perfect key or manually rotoscoping.

As always, after you make a significant change to an image, it is a good idea to compare your change with the original image. In this case, you want to compare only the changes to the dish. Previously, you were comparing changes to the original image. In this case, because you made the adjustment on a new node, you can temporarily disable the node to compare the change.

9 Click the number 2 on the node, or press Cmd-D (macOS) or Ctrl-D (Windows).

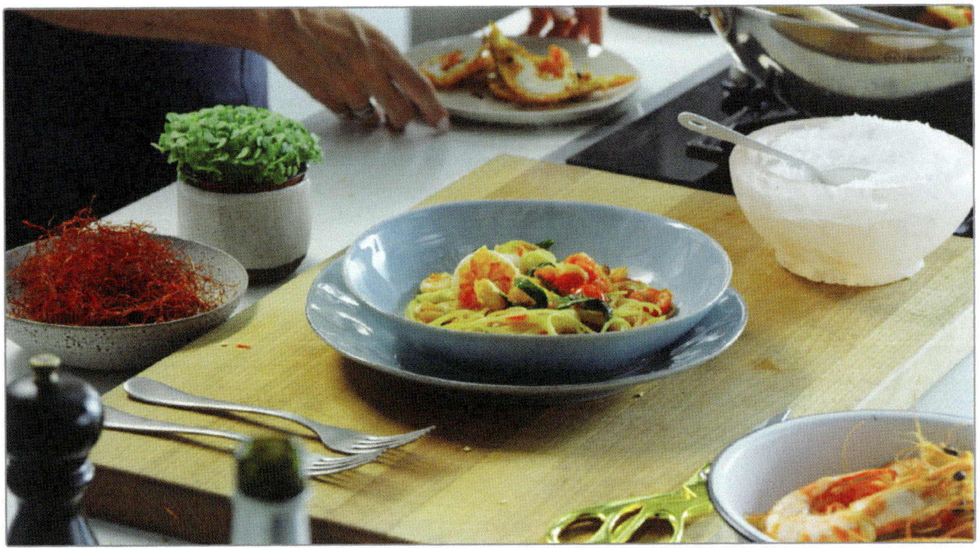

Now you are viewing the neutral correction without the shifted hue on the dish.

10 Click the number 2 on the node, or press Cmd-D (macOS) or Ctrl-D (Windows).

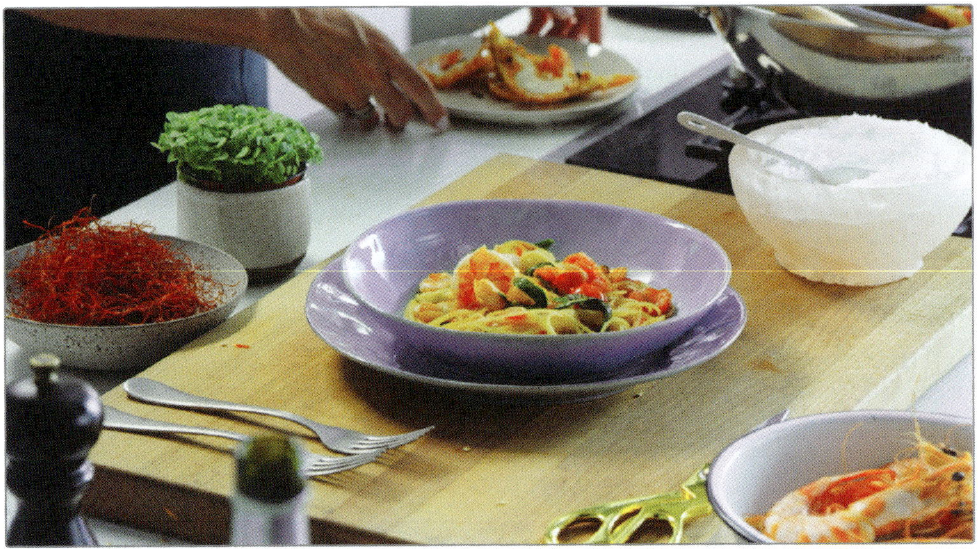

Although you selected the teal from the dish, teal (or shades of light blue) appear in other areas of the image and they are also affected by the hue adjustment. Narrowing the range can help this but in some cases more advanced techniques are required. You'll learn from of those techniques in later chapters of this book.

Applying Resolve FX

DaVinci Resolve includes many high-quality filter effects called Resolve FX that include blurs, glows, film grain, and lens flares. You can apply these effects to an entire clip or you can combine them with spline shapes called windows to isolate an effect to one area of the frame.

1 Click thumbnail 07.

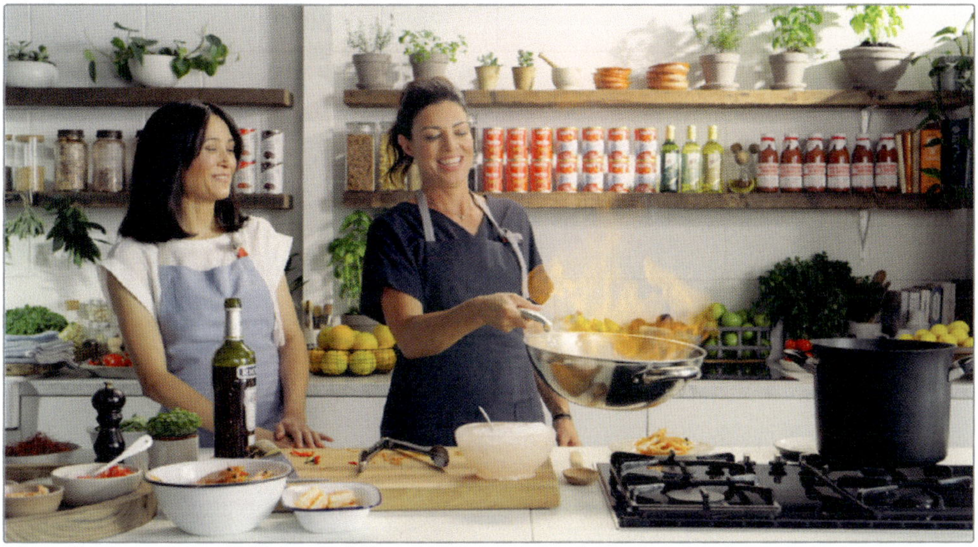

2 Press the spacebar to play the clip.

  This clip already has basic color correction on its first node, so you'll place a second node to add an effect.

3 Right-click the node, and from the contextual menu, choose Add Node > Add Serial.

4 Right-click the new node 2, and from the contextual menu, choose Node Label.

5 Type FACE, and press Enter to rename the node.

  The effect you'll add is a common one, although maybe not one you would think you need for this cooking show. Let's place our host in the witness protection program and obscure her face with a pixelated effect. This is something you frequently must do to hide people's identity or on logos to avoid violating copyright laws. The first step is to isolate the area you want to obscure.

6 Under the viewer, drag the play head to the start of the clip.

7 In the middle of the toolbar, click the power window button.

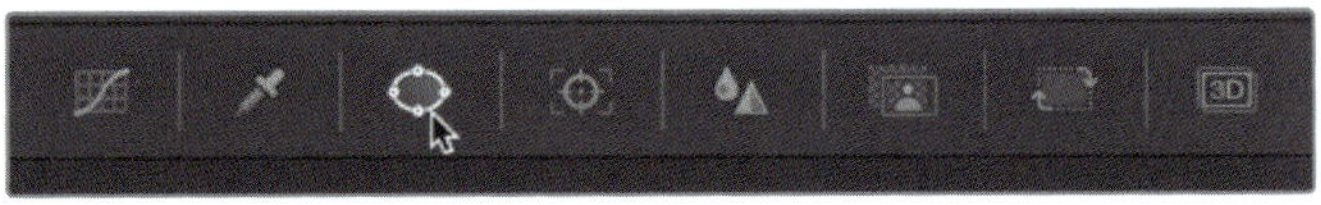

You can use power windows to isolate a part of the frame. Unlike the hue vs. hue curve, you use spline-based shapes instead of a hue selection.

8 Click the circular power window shape to add it to the clip.

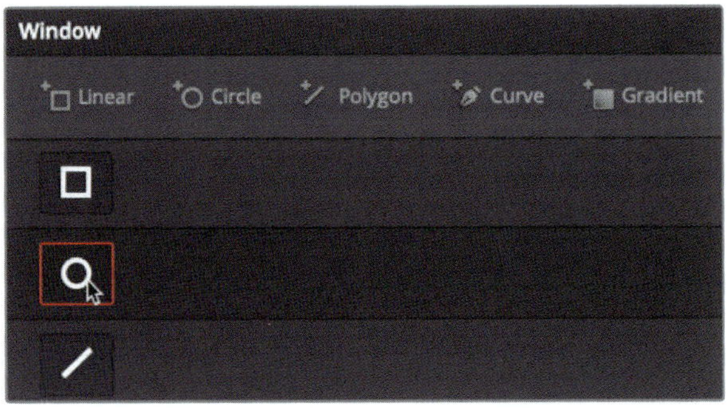

9 Drag one of the corners of the circular power window so that the inner circle is roughly the size of the host's head on the left.

10 Drag the center of the circular Power Window shape to cover her head in the frame.

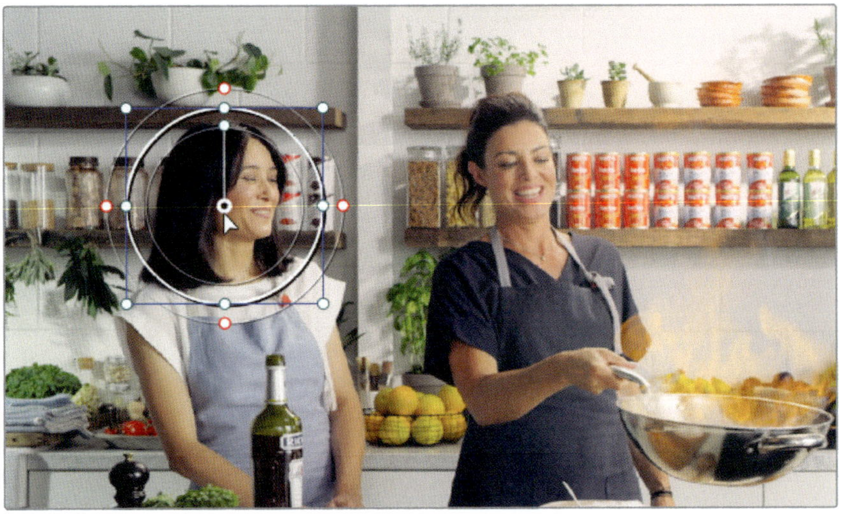

You can use a Resolve FX to "fill" the power window and obscure the woman's face.

11 Above the node editor, click the OpenFX button.

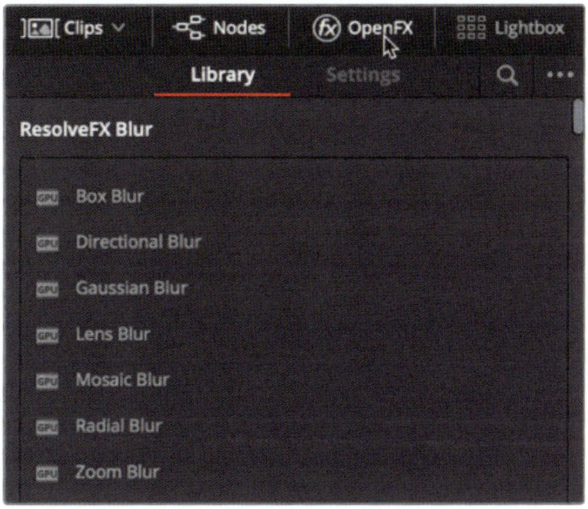

In the OpenFX panel, you'll typically find a list of the third party filter effect plugins that you added to DaVinci Resolve. However, it also contains a list of Resolve FX that are included with the application.

12 Scroll down the OpenFX library to find the Mosaic Blur effect. Drag the effect onto the FACE node that contains the power window.

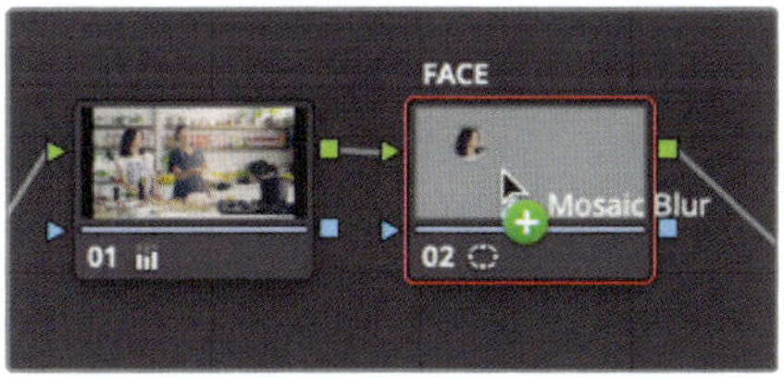

When the mosaic blur is added, it fills in the power window to obscure the face. You can modify the mosaic in the settings panel that automatically appears.

13 In the OpenFX settings panel, raise the pixel frequency to around 100 to increase the number of mosaic squares used in the power window.

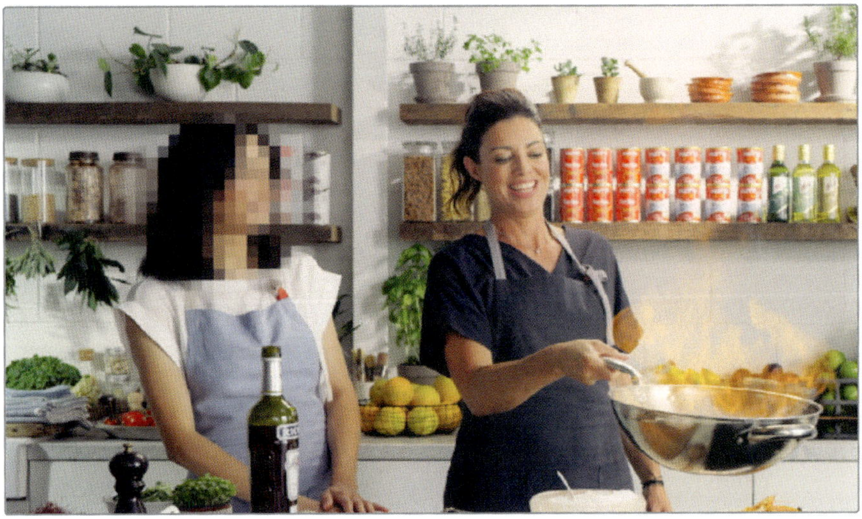

The mosaic is placed for this one frame only. Because the woman moves throughout the shot, you will need to track the power window to ensure that it follows her around as she moves.

Tracking Power Windows

The color page features an incredible 3D perspective tracker that not only follows objects, but can also determine if that object changes rotation or perspective. As a result, you can track the most challenging objects to apply Resolve FX or color correction.

1 In the toolbar, click the tracker button.

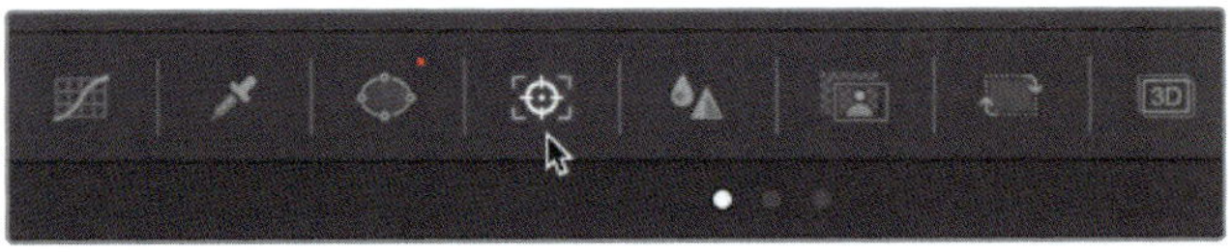

2 Make sure the playhead is at the start of the clip.

The tracker can track various aspects of objects within a clip. You can enable and disable the transform types using the checkboxes at the top of the panel. Disabling parameters can sometimes help improve tracking, so long as you needn't track those disabled aspects of the object. For instance, in this clip, camera does not zoom or rotate on her face; however, you do care about tilting and perspective changes.

3 Click the zoom and rotate checkboxes to deselect those transforms.

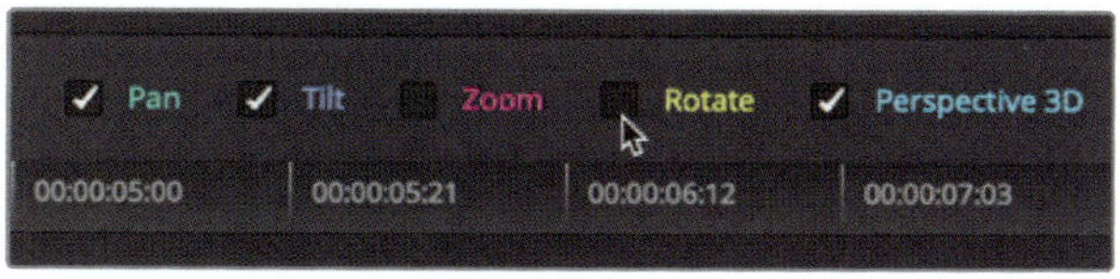

4 Begin tracking by clicking the track forward button.

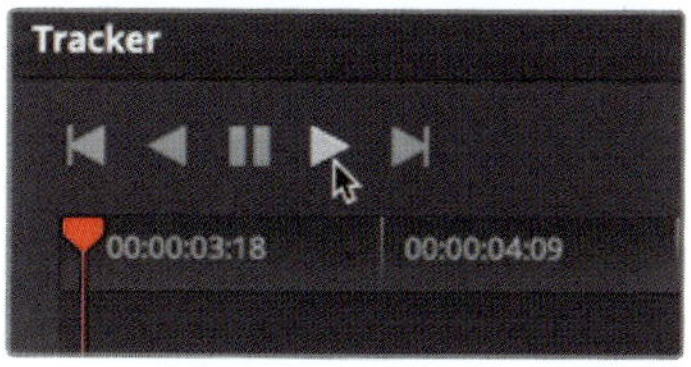

5 Once the track is completed, scrub or play through the clip to see the results.

The tracker causes the power window to perfectly follow the woman's face.

This quick start lesson was only a brief overview of how to use the controls in the color page. You'll explore the color page in greater detail in the next three lessons and learn more about controls in the primary corrector, additional secondary tools, and how to copy and save the creative looks you make.

Lesson Review

1 Below the lift color wheel, what does the master wheel adjust?
2 What control would you use to warm up or cool down a shot?
3 True or false? You cannot use the primaries wheels to change the color of a specific item in a clip.
4 What tool would you use to instruct a power window to follow a moving object?
5 On the color page, where is the mosaic blur effect located?

Answers

1 The Master wheel below the Lift color wheel adjusts the black point.
2 The Temperature control is used to warm up or cool down a shot.
3 False. You can use the Primaries wheels used to change the color of a specific item in a clip if a Power Window is used to isolate the item.
4 To get a Power Window to follow a moving object you would use the Tracker palette.
5 On the Color page, all ResolveFXs and third-party effects are located in the OpenFX panel.

Lesson 12

Performing Primary Color Corrections

With so many tools at your fingertips, the creative possibilities in DaVinci Resolve 16 are endless! In addition to the creative judgment you'll develop as a colorist, you'll also need to master some fundamental techniques. Along with stylizing the look and being creative, you're also responsible for ensuring a consistency, or color continuity for the entire project.

As a colorist, you'll need to fix image exposure and correct inaccurate color tints in shots. The ability to balance exposure and tint in shots is important because in a single scene the shots from one camera must match other cameras' shots.

This lesson teaches you how to create a base neutral grade and to balance shots. You'll use the primary corrector for most of this lesson and rely on built-in scopes to check your work. You'll save and copy grades, so you can quickly apply them to multiple shots.

Time

This lesson takes approximately 45 minutes to complete.

Goals

Using DaVinci Resolve Color Management

Filmmaking is technical, and can at times be complicated. Few aspects of the process illustrate this as well as cameras and their various file formats. Each camera manufacturer tries to give you the best-looking image possible, even if it means that image doesn't necessarily look great on your HD monitor right out of the camera.

Most professional digital cinema cameras produce images that are brighter and richer in their color palettes than an HD television can display. The result is that images directly from a digital cinema camera are often washed-out, and undersaturated.

However, these camera-original files are not intended for display on an HDTV. So, one of the first things you must do when color grading, or even editing, is to modify the contrast and color palette of those camera-original clips to display correctly on an HDTV (or whatever display tech you're targeting). You can do this manually using the color correction tools if you have the time or take a short cut using a LUT (look up table). However, there is a better alternative that will get you there quicker than the manual process and more accurately than a LUT. The best thing of all is that it will give you more flexibility in the end as well. It is called DaVinci Resolve color management. RCM, for short, excels by providing a project-wide solution for processing content from different cameras in different color spaces. Setting up a project from the start with DaVinci Resolve color management is the quickest and most accurate way to achieve better starting points for color correction and more normalized pictures for editing.

1 Open DaVinci Resolve 16 to the project manager window.

  In the next three lessons, you'll learn a color-grading workflow using a a documentary about cattle ranchers in the U.S. state of Wyoming. Once you restore the archived project, you will begin working with it just as if you had edited the project in DaVinci Resolve and were ready to color grade it.

2 Right-click in the project manager window, and choose Restore Project Archive.

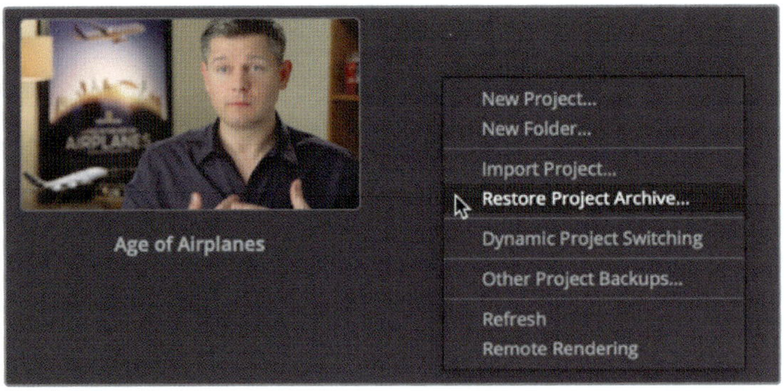

3 Navigate to R16 Intro lessons > Lesson 12. Select the Wyoming Ranch.dra folder, and click Open.

4 In the project manager, open the Wyoming Ranch project then in the timelines bin, double click the Wyoming Ranch thumbnail to load the timeline.

You are now ready to enable a color-managed workflow.

5 In the timeline, move the play head over the second clip.

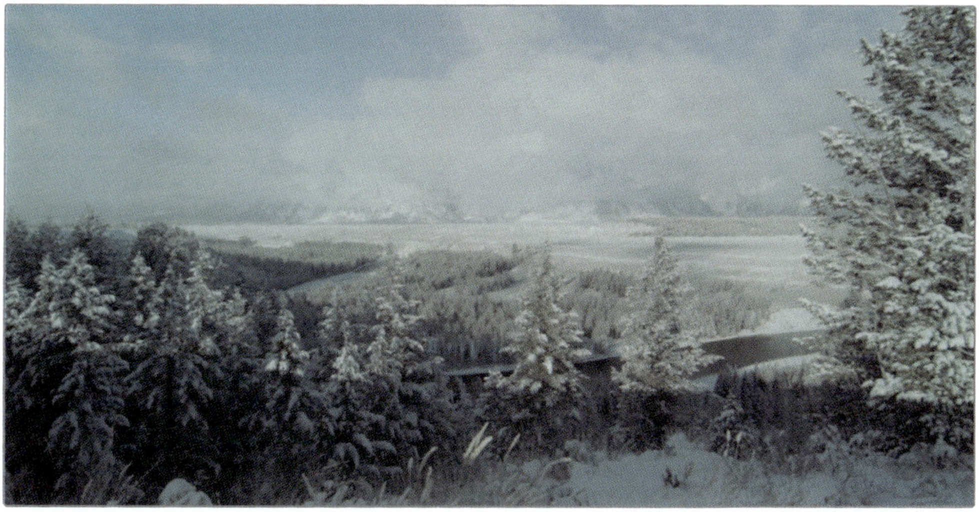

This shot is a good image in which to see the results of color management. This is a camera original file from a BlackMagic Pocket Cinema Camera 4K. Although it has a wide dynamic range and a large color palette (gamut) it looks flat and under saturated. The image was recorded perfectly but your monitor has no idea how it should look. That's where color management helps. The first step is just to enable color management.

6 Choose File > Project settings, and select the Color Management category.

7 In the Color science pop-up menu, choose DaVinci YRGB Color Managed.

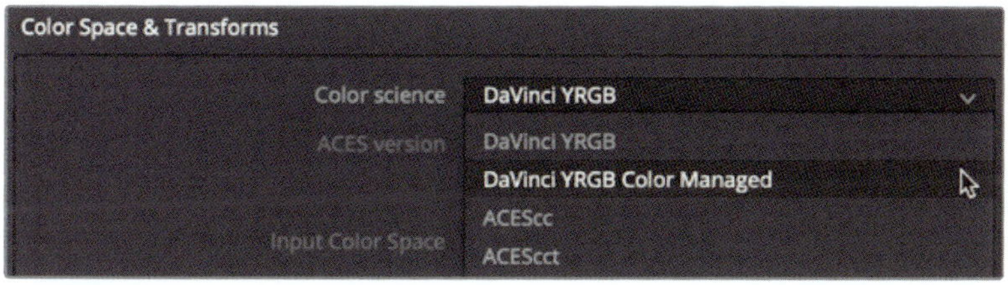

You won't see any changes to the image, but a few new pop-up menus are activated just below the Color science menu.

The three color management menus to be aware of are Input color space, Timeline color space, and Output color space. You will leave the Timeline color space and Output color space menus at their default values: Rec.709 Gamma 2.4. This is the standard HD color space and we will assume that your project is to be delivered in HD for television.

However, you want to change the Input color space value to match the device that recorded the imported clips.

8 Because these clips were shot with a Blackmagic Pocket 4K camera, set the Input color space to Blackmagic Design Pocket 4K Film Gen. v4.

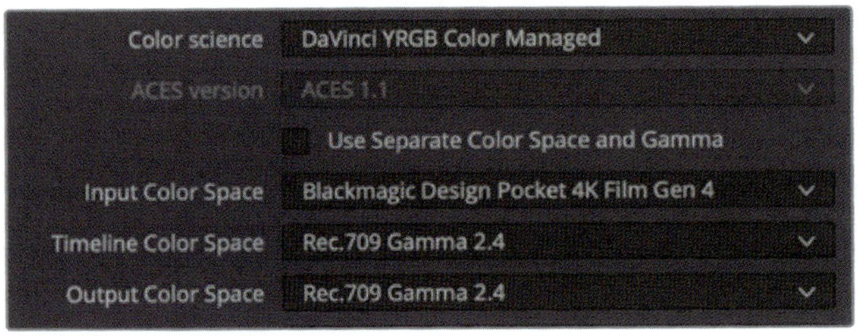

TIP Although you can change the Output color space at any time when you are delivering to different display devices, never change the Input or Timeline color space once you have started color grading your clips.

9 Click Save to close the settings, but keep an eye on the timeline viewer.

TIP When you have clips from multiple cameras, set the Input color space to the most frequently used camera. Then in each bin, right click the clips from each camera, and choose the appropriate Input color space.

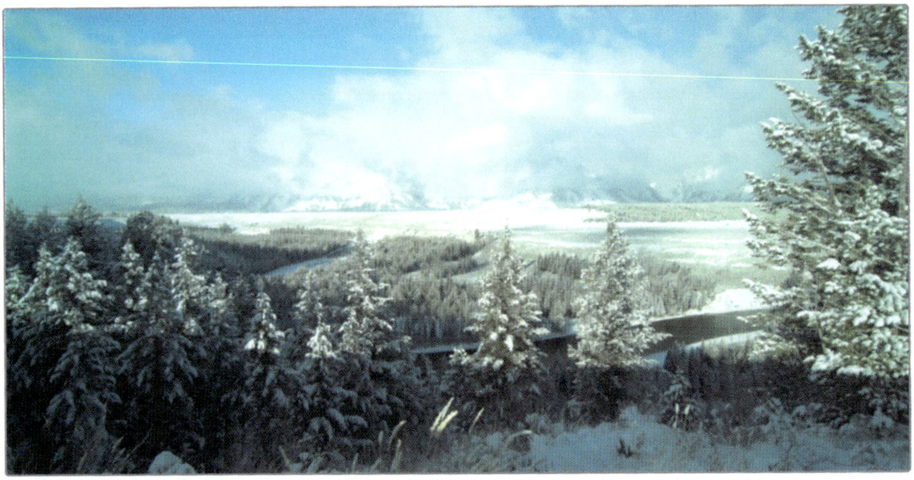

You may have to wait a second or move the play head, but you should notice that the shot now includes more contrast and color saturation.

10 Move the play head over the last shot in the timeline.

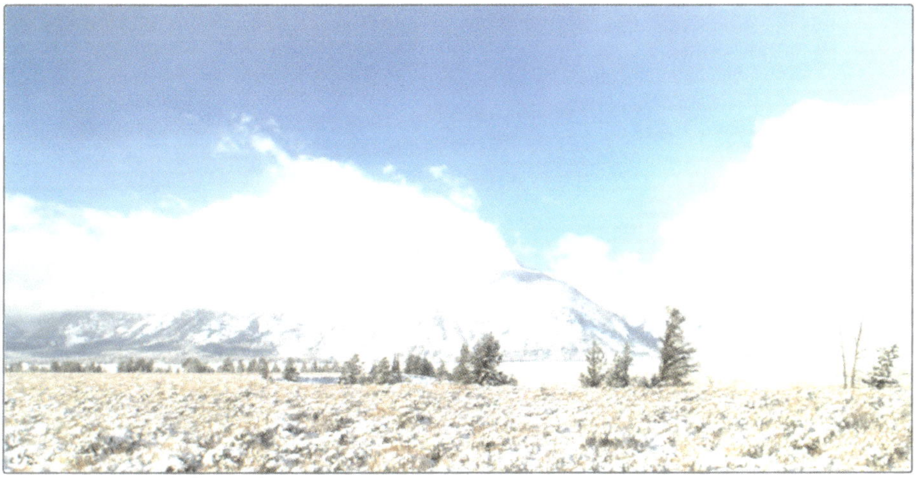

This shot has blown out highlights. At first it may appear that the blown out highlights are a color management mistake. However, Color Management only tries to match up equivalent tonal ranges in an image. Anything that falls outside the Output range will appear blown out.

When moving from a digital cinema camera that records a wide dynamic range to a smaller tonal range like Rec 709, you need to modify or remap the range to fit. Luckily, you can do that fairly quickly using the color correction controls in the color page.

11 Click the Color button to switch to the Color page.

In the previous lesson you learned about the lift, gamma and gain controls in the color wheels. For this overexposed shot you will use the color wheels again, but this time you will use the offset controls. The offset color wheel and master wheel modify the entire image. The master wheel will adjust the black point, white point and gamma allowing us to bring this entire image back into an acceptable tonal range.

12 Under the offset color wheel, drag the master wheel left until you can see detail in the clouds, somewhere between -30 and -40.

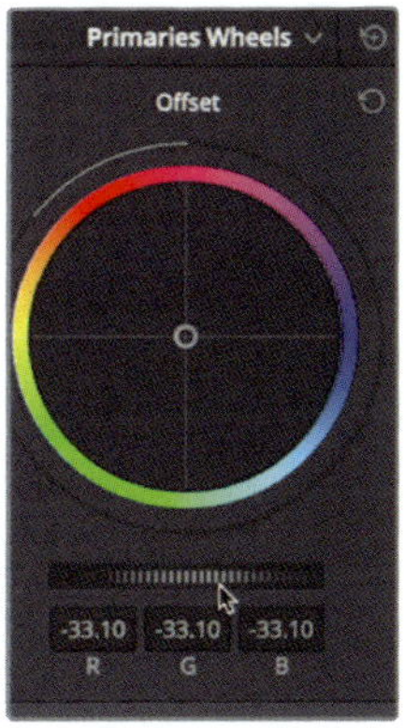

Sometimes the effects of DaVinci Resolve color management are subtle, sometimes they are very obvious like what we have just experienced.

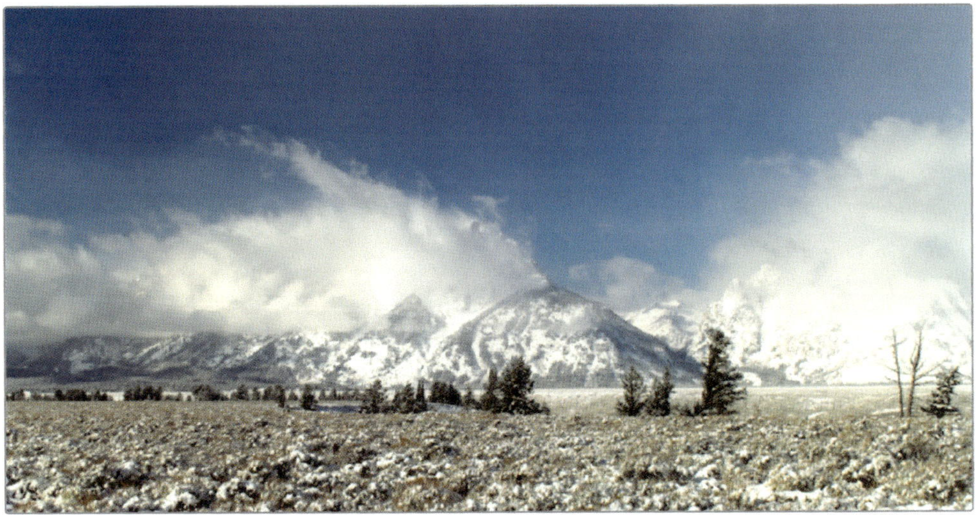

The results depend on the camera and how the image was originally exposed.

Since one setting cannot work for all cameras, when you have clips from different camera's you can override the project setting and set clips individually.

13 Click on the first clip in the timeline.

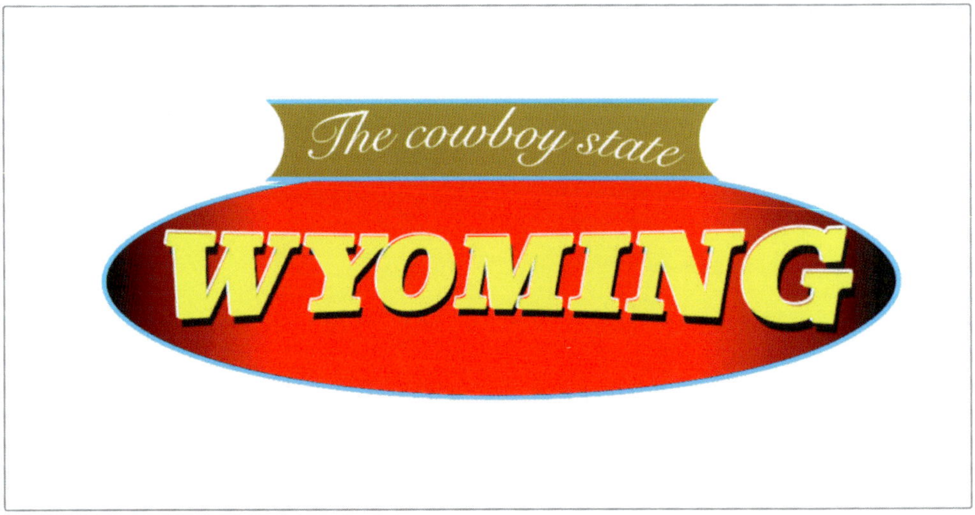

This graphic was obviously not created with the Blackmagic Pocket 4K camera. It was created using the sRGB color space. You can override the Input color space for any clip directly from the color page timeline.

14 Right click the thumbnail in the timeline and choose Input color space > sRGB.

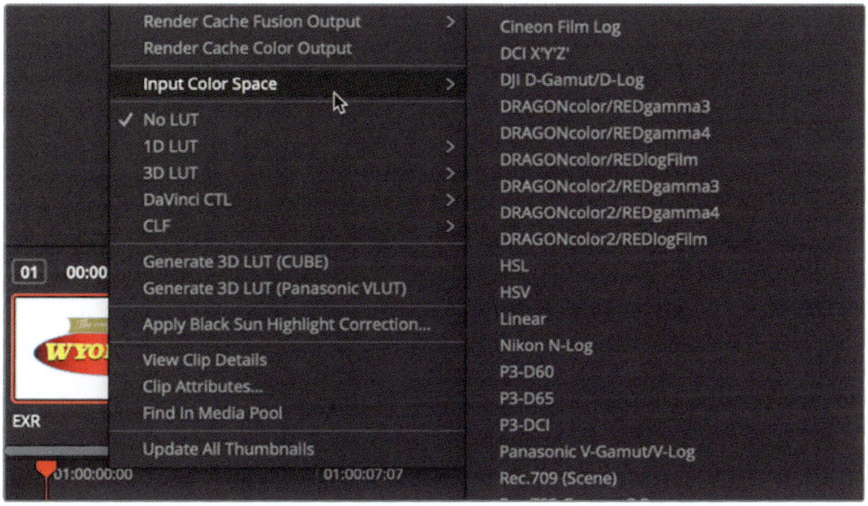

The graphic is now displayed with the correct colors but a slightly lower luminance values due to the simple remapping we did earlier. You can correct this at the end of the lesson when you have more knowledge about color correction and monitoring.

It is important to note that you have not color corrected these clips, although they may appear to look better. If the clips were shot overexposed, they will appear overexposed. If they were shot with the incorrect white balance, they will display incorrect white balance. All you have done is correct their gamma levels and color palette so they suit your HD display device. With that done, you can now begin the color correction process.

Using Tonal Mapping with RCM

Since digital cinema cameras can capture such a wide dynamic range, most cinematographers will set the camera to overexpose the images. This allows them to capture much more detail in the shadows without introducing noise. However, with RCM, what you capture is what you get so images tend to appear over exposed when you first enable the setting. If adjusting the offset on overexposed clips is too egregious for you, there are more advanced tonal mapping controls in the RCM settings that can wrangle those big highlights into a more acceptable range so you do not have to do a thing before balancing your clips. This topic is explored more deeply in the Color Correction in DaVinci Resolve 16 training guide.

Making Automatic Corrections

Because unforeseen or unavoidable situations occur during production, clips can be recorded with an incorrect color tint, have highlights that are dull, or shadows that are muddy. Therefore, you always start the color correction process by balancing every shot in your program.

Doing so unifies your shots for the creative look you may later apply to them. You can color balance shots using many techniques, but let's start with the easiest method: a method that makes the artificial intelligence engine in DaVinci Resolve 16 do the heavy lifting.

1 In the color page timeline, click clip 07 and move the playhead until you see the horses in the frame.

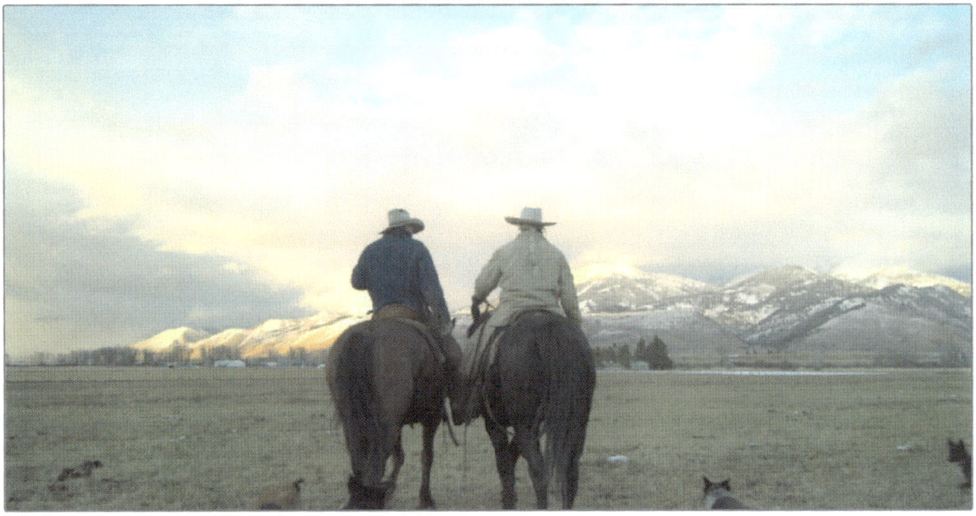

You typically start color correction by adjusting the contrast in a shot, setting the darkest and brightest points. You can do so using the black point picker and white point picker in the Color wheels palette.

2 In the upper-left corner above the Lift color wheel, click the black point picker.

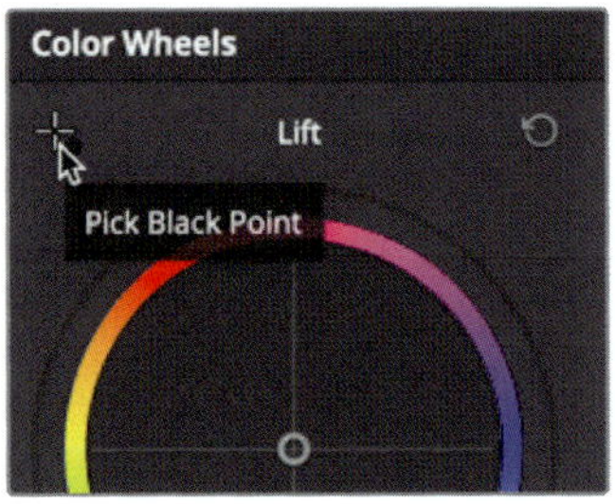

Using this control, you will locate and select the darkest point in the image. It should be in an area that you think represents absolute black in the shot.

3 Move the mouse pointer over the viewer, and click the darkest area of the horse on the right.

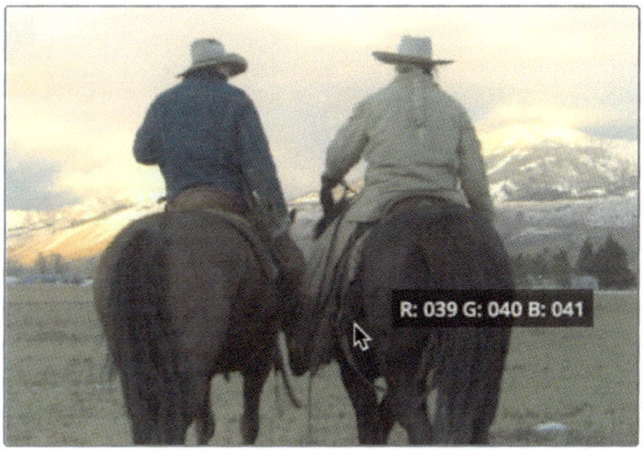

TIP If you need to zoom in to the viewer, position the mouse pointer over the viewer, and scroll the middle mouse wheel.

The image should become a bit darker. Clicking the shadow area identifies it as absolute black and corrects any tint in the black so that no single color channel dominates in the shadow regions. Now, you will do the same for the white point.

4 To the upper-left above the Gain color wheel, click the white point picker.

In the viewer, you will locate a bright point in the image and select it. The point should be an area that you think should be pure white in the shot.

5 Move the mouse pointer over the viewer, then click somewhere in the white cloud bank at the top of the frame.

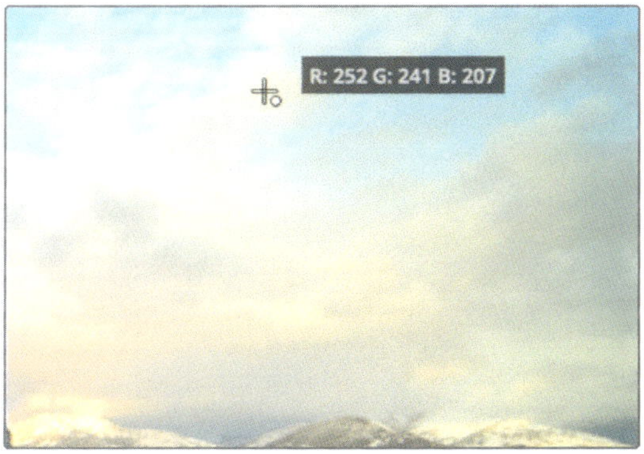

The image should grow a bit brighter but also becomes a bit warmer again. This shot now has great contrast and is also color balanced. You can compare it with the original image by disabling the changes you have made.

6 From the upper right corner of the viewer, click the Bypass Color and Fusion button to disable the grade.

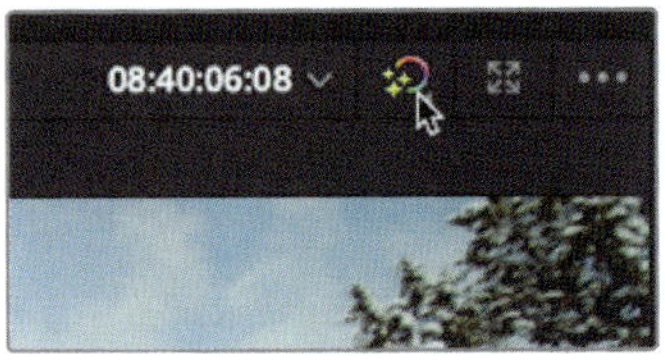

7 Click the Bypass button again to enable your grade.

When using the black and white point pickers it is important to click areas you know should be the purely black and purely white in the image or you risk making the image worse. You also do not want to select areas that are already clipped in the highlights since you'll find there is no image data there. All the information is already lost. That tends to be the problem with automatic tools. They work perfectly on optimal images but can be less effective when a shot lacks pure white or pure black. Then, you have to rely on your eyes and skills as a colorist to make the best choice.

Balancing Color and Brightness using the Color Wheels

On some shots, automatic corrections are either not effective, or you may just want more control over balancing your shots. In either case, the primary color controls in DaVinci Resolve give you ample ways to realize balanced contrast and color with minimal effort.

The standard approach is to tackle luminance correction first, and hue and saturation second.

1 Select clip 03 to display it in the viewer.

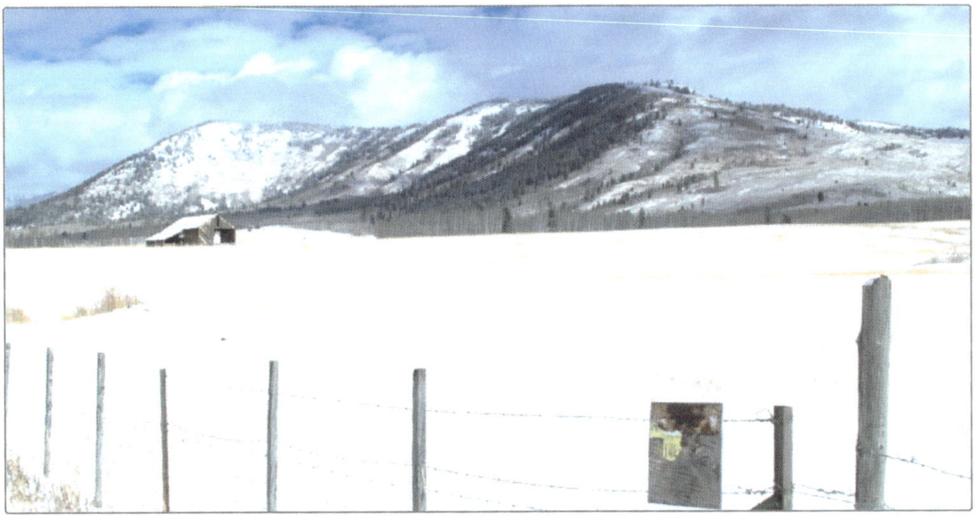

You can start evaluating this clip just by watching it in the viewer.

It is an over exposed shot in which the dark trees on the mountains appear muddy and the snow is super bright.

To improve tonal range, you can use the primary correction tools you used in the previous lesson.

2 Drag the Lift master wheel to the left until the Y luminance value is near -0.20.

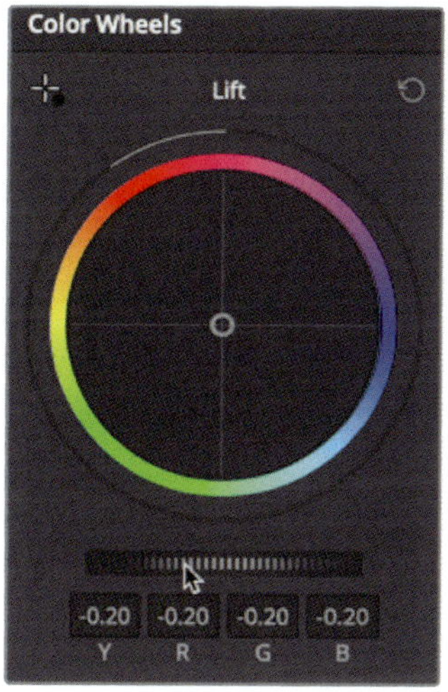

As you drag the Lift master wheel to the left, the darkest areas in the image become darker.

3 To decrease the highlights, drag the Gain master wheel until the Y luminance value displays 0.60.

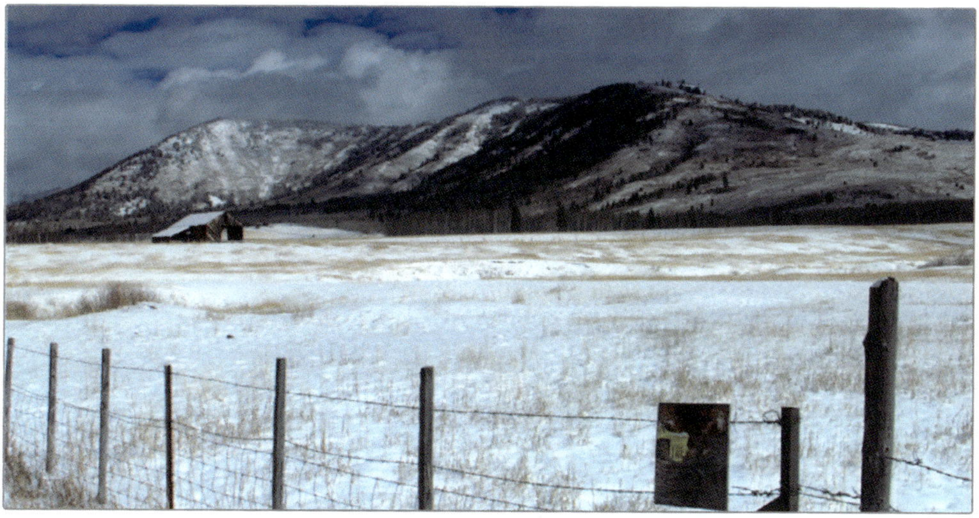

4 To brighten up the image, drag the gamma master wheel to the right, until it is around 0.15.

Now that you have maximized the contrast, you can compare those changes with the original image, this time using the menu option.

5 Choose View > Bypass Color and Fusion > Bypass All Grades, or press Shift-D, to see the original image; then press Shift-D again to view the corrected image.

With just a few simple adjustments you have created a better-looking shot in which the image shadows appear rich and dark while the highlights have detail.

Checking Adjustments on Scopes

As an objective way to evaluate adjustments made while color correcting, DaVinci Resolve includes five video signal scopes. You can use the Waveform, Parade, Vectorscope, Histogram and CIE scope to check the luminance, exposure, hue, saturation and color space of a clip.

1 Click the video scope button to the far right of the toolbar.

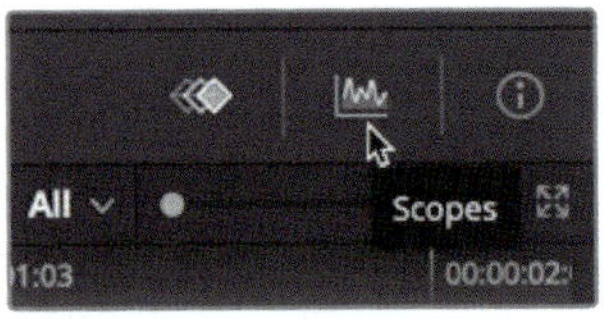

2 Click the disclosure arrow to open the video scope pop-up menu.

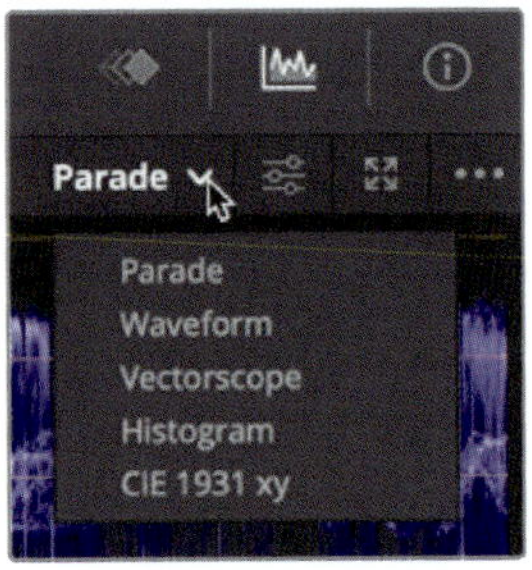

Using the menu, you can switch between the five different scopes depending on what you want to monitor.

shots, the image in the parade, called the trace, should not go below 0 or above 1023, otherwise the image will clip—cut off parts of the image data—and lose detail.

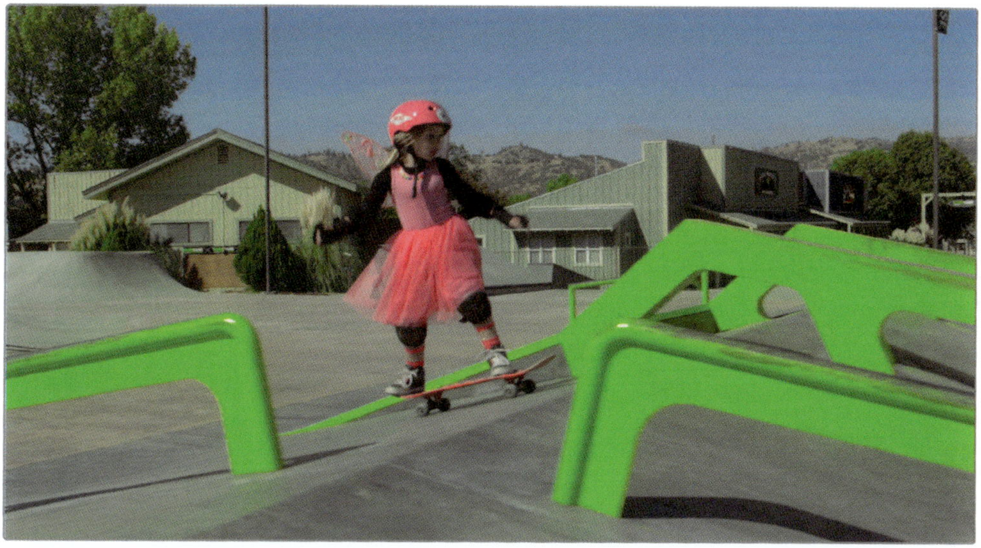

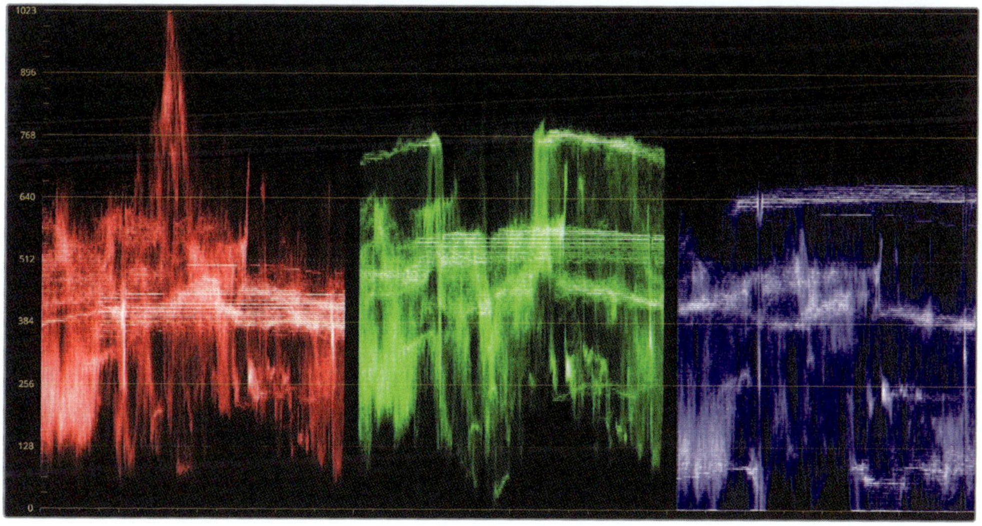

Reading the Parade from left to right, each channel corresponds to the image displayed in the viewer. For instance, the left part of the red, green, and blue trace corresponds to the left part of the image. This layout makes it easy to look at the scope and know exactly which area you are evaluating.

TIP You can switch back to the keyframe editor and hide the video scopes to free up your graphics card's processor and improve play back performance.

In general, the bottom of the trace should fall somewhere between 0 and 128 on the graph. If some elements of the shot are absolutely black, then the trace should fall closer to 0. If the darkest part of your image is more of a dark gray like the trees on our hillside, then it might fall closer to line 128 on the graph. For this shot, you can fine tune the Lift and Gain master wheels so your trace stretches between 0 and 1023.

4 Drag the Lift master wheel until the bottom of the green trace falls just below the 128 line.

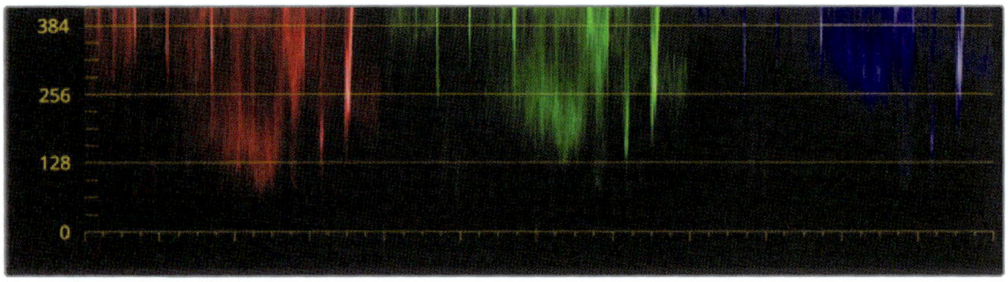

5 Drag the Gain master wheel so the top of the green channel just skims along the 896 line.

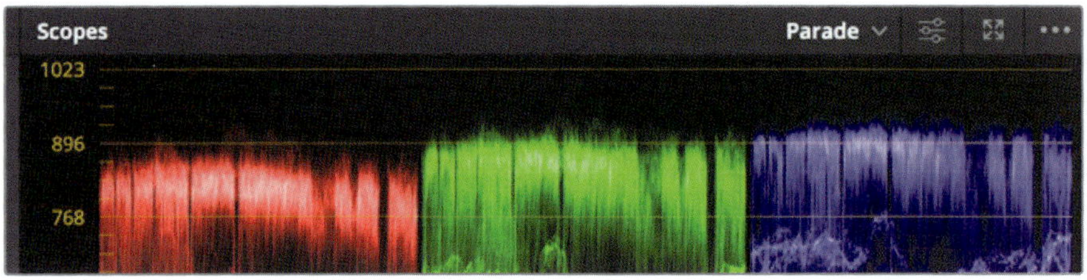

Next, you'll fine tune the color imbalance or cast in this shot. However, let's discuss a little additive color theory before you evaluate the color. To create pure white using additive colors, you mix an equal amount of red, green, and blue. On a Parade scope, a white image would have the red, green, and blue traces completely level along the top of the graph. Conversely, pure black would have the three color channels completely aligned at the bottom of the graph. That being the case, you'll use the white snow and the dark trees in your shot to make color balancing easier.

It is clear this image appears to have a blue tint. While the tint can be seen with your eyes, you can confirm it in the Parade.

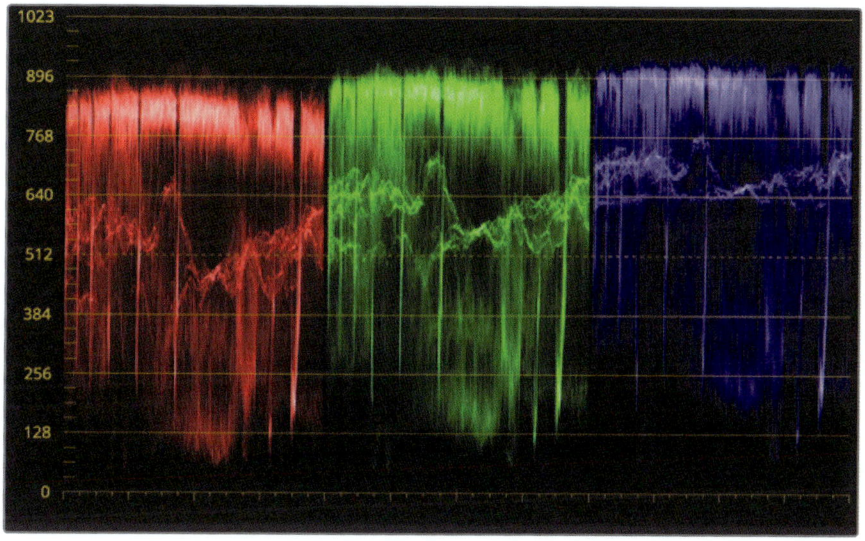

The blue trace is shifted higher than red or green which is an indication that a blue tint exists in the shadows and the highlights. Having a distinct blue or orange tint, or cast, in an image is a common white-balance issue. In the previous lesson, you used the temperature control to correct white balance, but you can just as easily use the primary corrector's Color wheels to deal with this common issue.

6 In the Lift color wheel, drag the color indicator toward yellow/orange until the dark trees on the mountains lose their blue tint; and the bottoms of the red, green, and blue trace in the Parade are fairly level with each other.

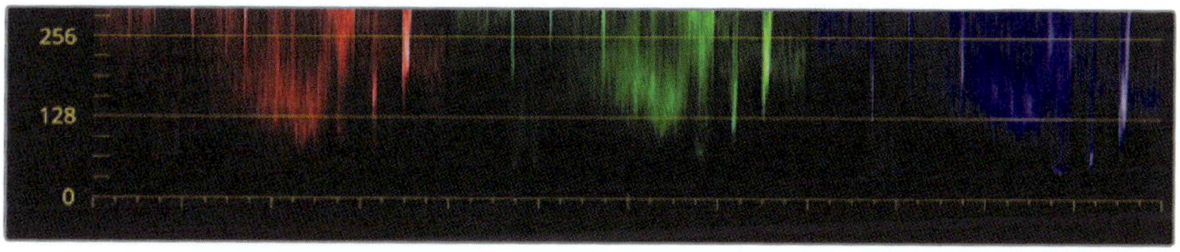

TIP Unless you have a completely black or white frame, a scope will always display some uneven areas. Use the trace as a guide but use your eyes to make the final decision when performing manual white balance adjustments.

7 Now remove the color cast from the highlights by dragging the Gain color indicator toward yellow/orange until the tops of the red, green, and blue trace in the Parade are fairly level with each other.

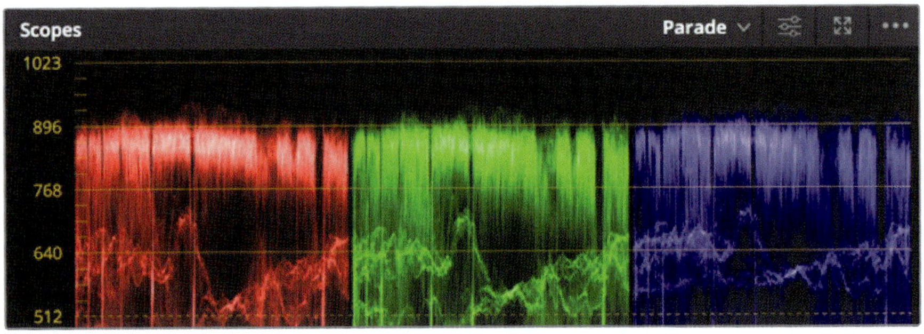

8 Press Shift-D to see the original image, then press Shift-D again to see your correction.

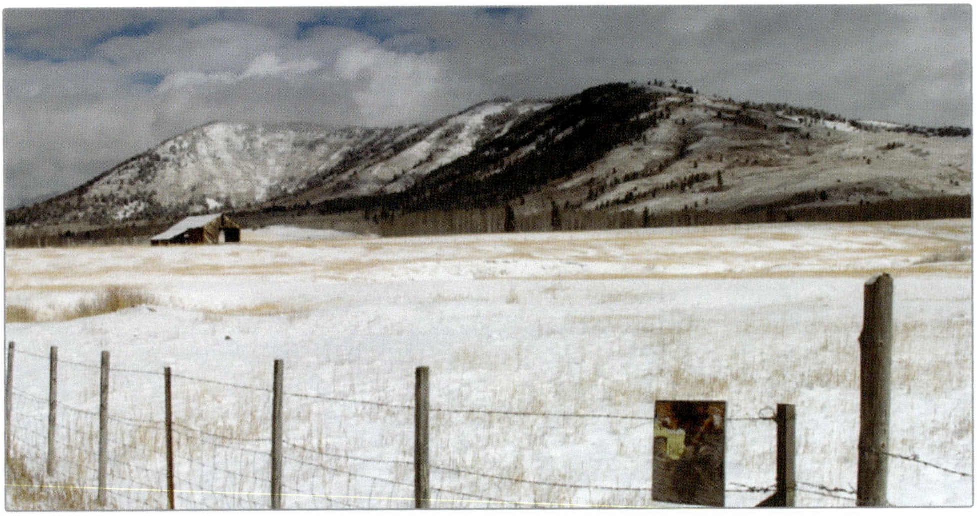

You've created a balanced, neutral color correction using the primary corrector on one shot. You repeat this for every shot in your timeline when you begin the color grading process. Doing so builds a consistent neutral starting point for your shots.

Using the Viewers for Color Grading

DaVinci Resolve's viewers are previews that are not intended to be color-critical displays, especially for projects intended for television broadcast or digital cinema. For those purposes, you can use a Blackmagic Design UltraStudio or DeckLink card to connect to a broadcast or digital cinema calibrated display.

Making a Neutral Color Grade with the Primaries Bars

A lot of the power in DaVinci Resolve comes from the flexibility of its toolset which provides many ways to do the same thing. To learn more about the primary corrector toolset, you'll explore another method for creating a balanced correction on a new shot.

1 In the timeline, select clip 06.

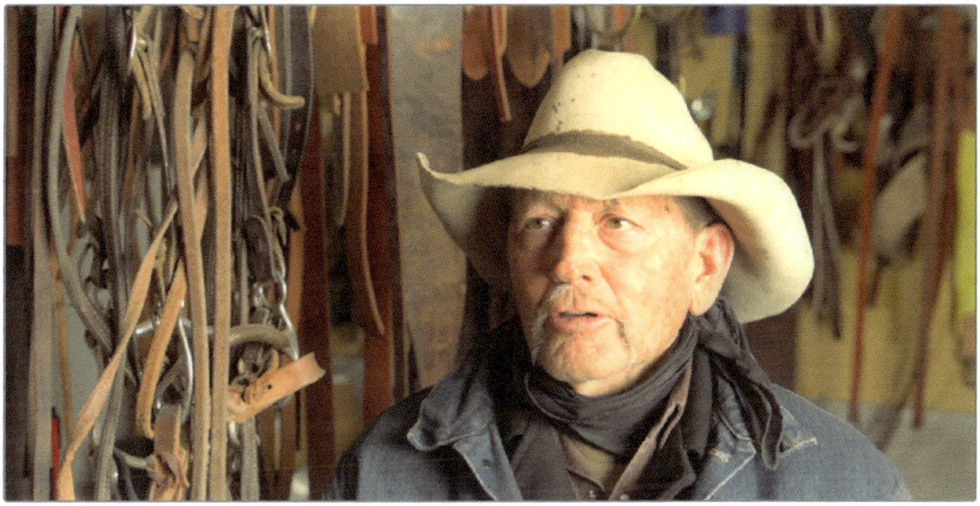

This is the first in a number of interview shots. As in the previous image, this also requires a tonal and color balance; but instead of using the Color wheels, you'll use another set of tools in the primary corrector called the Primaries bars.

2 In the upper-right corner of the primary corrector palette, in the pop-up menu, choose Primaries bars.

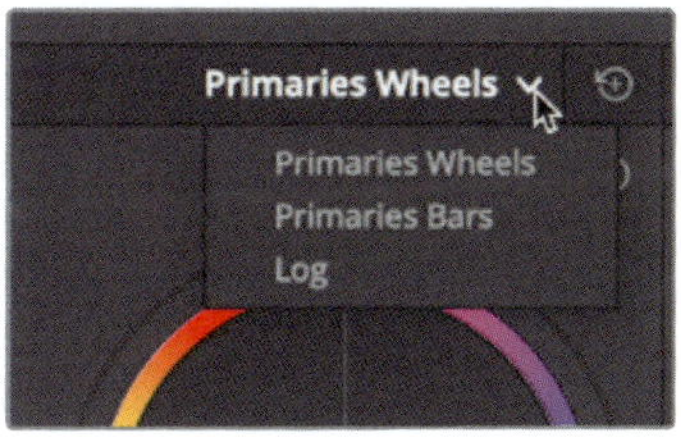

The Primaries bars allow you to make color and luminance adjustments similar to the Color wheels, but the bars provide explicit red, green, blue controls and separate luminance adjustments in the lift, gamma, and gain regions. That being the case, some may find them more effective tools for balancing specific color channels in different regions of a shot. For tonal adjustments, the Y or luminance bar allows you to adjust luminance without changing saturation.

3 Drag the Lift Y bar down until the Y luminance value is near -0.03.

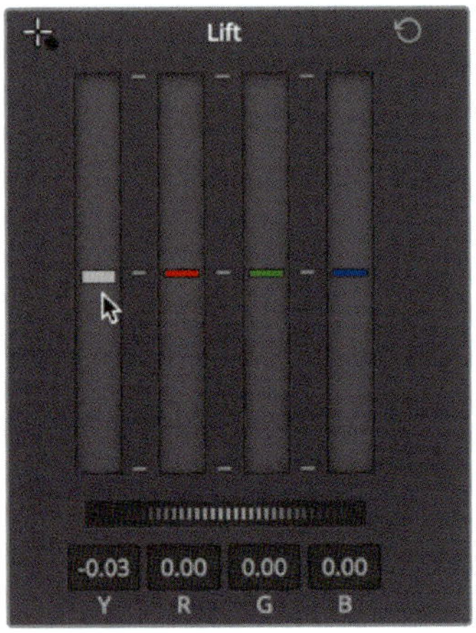

Once again, the darkest areas in the image become a bit darker. Unfortunately, the highlights in this image are trickier to adjust because, unlike the previous shot, this image has no white anywhere in the frame. However, using your eyes, you can see that you need to bring down the highlights.

4 To decrease the highlights, drag the Gain Y bar down until the top of the green trace falls just around the 896 line in the parade scope.

Not having white in any part of the image makes it more challenging to accurately correct for any white-balance issues. However, you do have areas of his scarf that provides a neutral dark gray tone. Just like white, a neutral gray consists of equal parts red, green, and blue. Because it is very difficult to see neutral gray on a scope, you'll need another method for measuring the red, green, and blue values. In this case, you can use an eyedropper to display RGB values for a region of pixels in the frame.

5 Hover the mouse pointer over the viewer until it becomes an eyedropper.

6 Right-click in the viewer, and choose "Show picker RGB value".

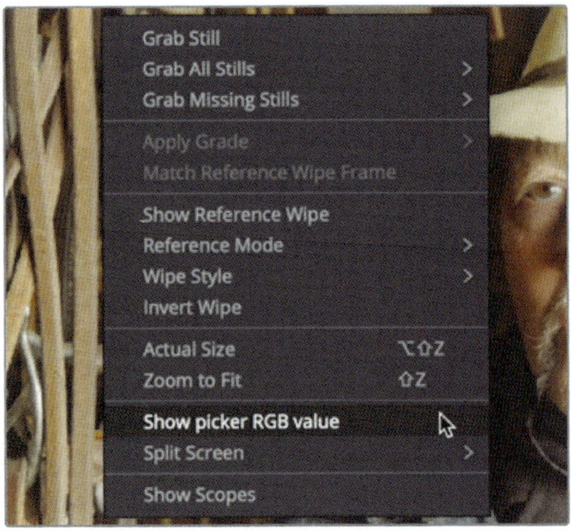

The 8-bit RGB values (0-255) are displayed as a tooltip next to the eyedropper. These values show you if a pixel has more red, green, or blue in it.

7 Hover the eyedropper over the brightest part of the gray scarf directly to the right of the man's face.

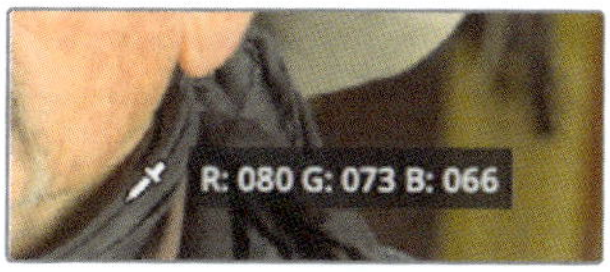

The RGB values show a higher level of red in the dark gray area of the scarf. If the scarf should be a neutral dark gray color (which you are assuming it should be), then you need to balance these RGB values.

TIP You can display 10-bit numeric values (0-1023) with the RGB picker by choosing View > Show RGB Picker Values In > 10 bit.

8 To increase the amount of blue in the mid tones—where the tone of the scarf lives – drag the blue Gamma bar slightly up and the red Gamma slightly down.

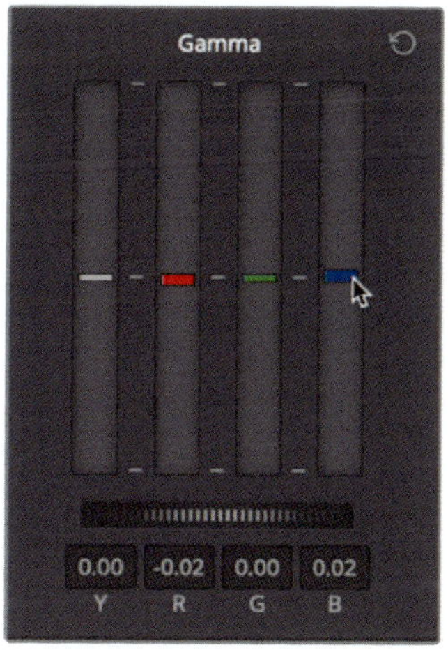

Once you have evened out the midtones, you can check that the values on the scarf again.

9 Hover the eyedropper over different areas of the scarf to see if it maintains relatively even RGB values.

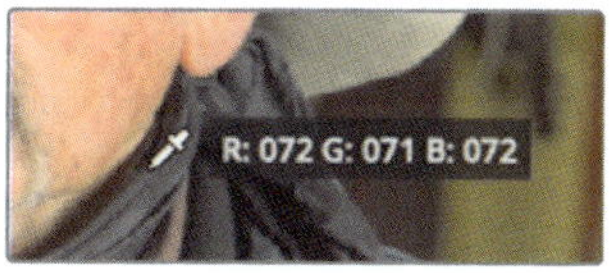

10 Keep making small adjustments to the red, green, and blue Gamma bars until the RGB values are nearly even.

After making critical adjustments, it's good to compare your changes to the original shot.

11 Choose View > Bypass All Grades, or press Shift-D, to see the original image; and then press Shift-D again to view your corrected clip.

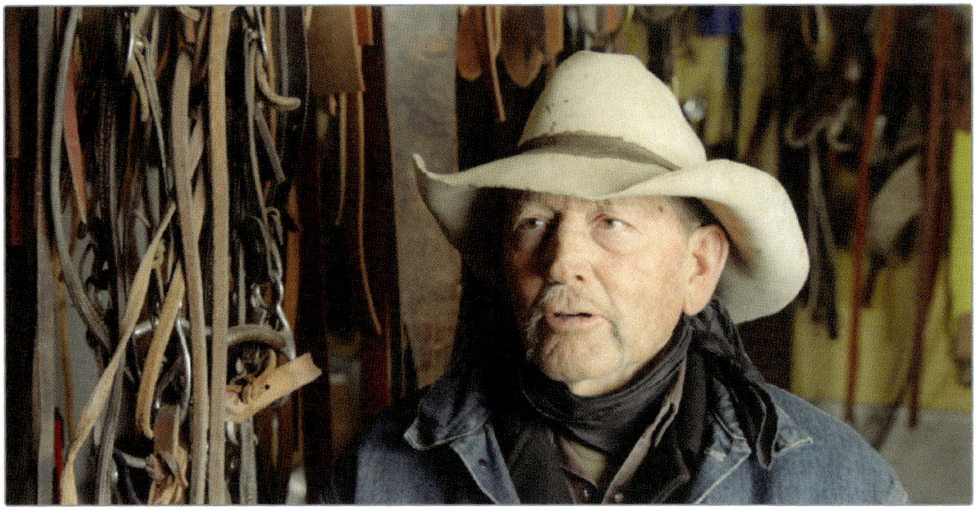

With these adjustments, the image now has a much better neutral balance and contrast. You did that quickly. Rarely do you set a control once, compare it to the original, and move on. Color correction is an iterative process—adjust, compare, adjust, compare. It takes time; but just like cooking or gardening, the more you explore, the more you find what works best.

Balancing with the Additional Primary Controls

The additional primary adjustments located under the master wheels can also be used to balance a shot. Although they do not have the precision or flexibility of the primaries controls, they do have a more familiar and direct approach.

1 Click clip 09 to move to that shot.

2 In the adjustments strip, click 2 to show the second page of adjustments.

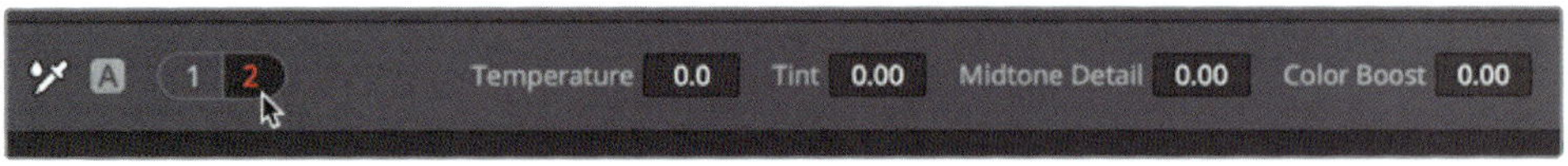

3 Drag the Shadows value to the left to slightly darken the shadows, and placing the bottom of the green trace just below the 128 line.

4 Drag the Highlights value to the right until the green trace reaches the 896 line.

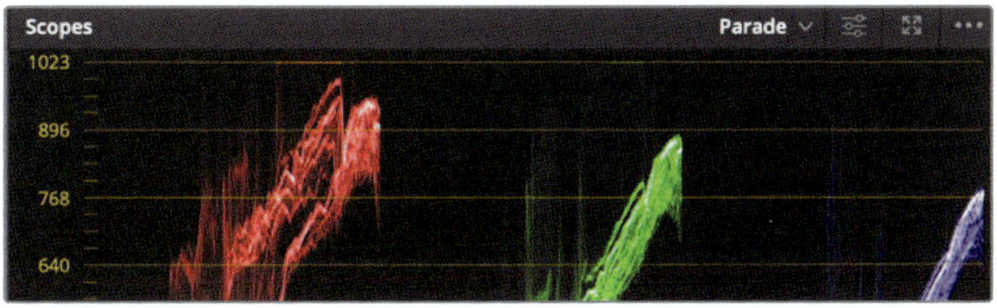

These two adjustments are similar to adjusting the master wheels under the lift and gain regions. To balance the color you can use the temperature control.

5 Drag the temperature value to the left to until the tops of each channel in the trace are more or less even along the 896 line.

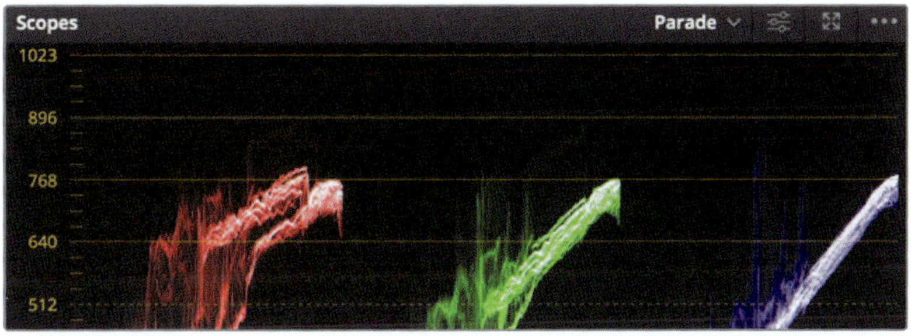

Mid tone detail used sparingly can add a nice pop to soft images like the one we have here. It adds local contrast to areas of sharp tonal differences which means regions with well defined lines and creases tend to become more pronounced.

6 Drag the Mid tone detail value to the right until it reaches around 20 or 30.

7 To compare the original with the balanced image press Shift-D.

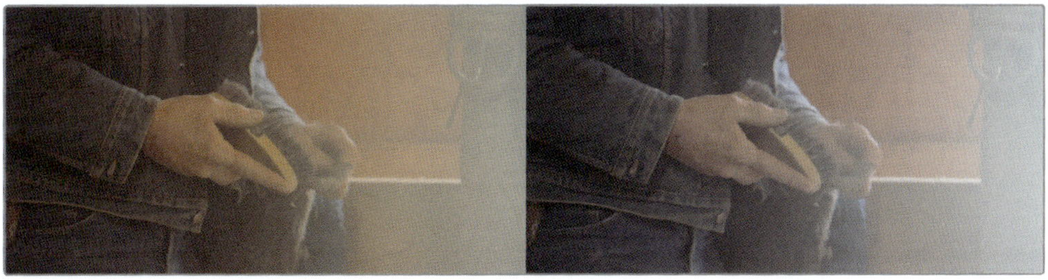

Before After

8 To return to the graded look, press Shift-D.

More often than not you will mix these adjustments with either the color wheels or primaries bars. It is common to use the flexibility in the primary controls to get the basic tonal and color balance but add to the grade using adjustments like mid tone detail and color boost.

Using Curves for Primary Color Corrections

In this exercise, you'll look at the last method of creating a balance shot. Using the Custom curves you'll have the greatest degree of flexibility for making tonal and color adjustments but it also requires a bit more finessing.

1 Select clip 15.

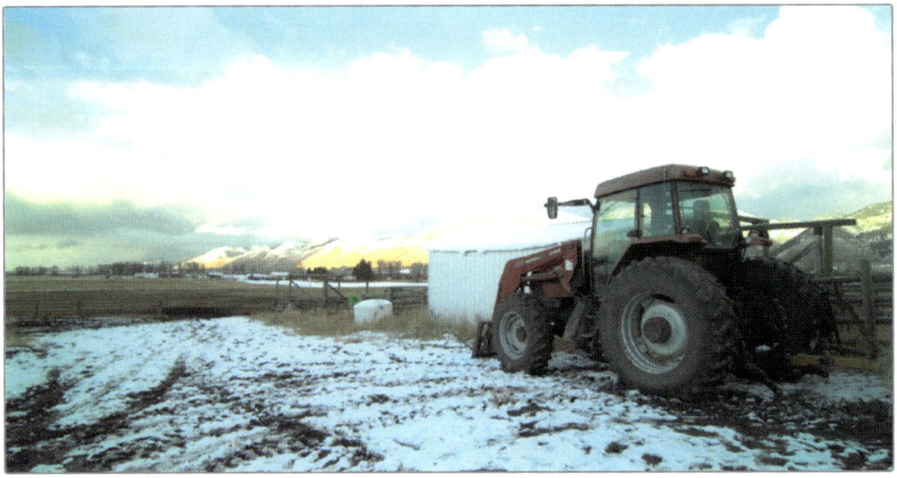

Looking at the image you can tell this shot is over exposed so we'll correct that first.

2 Drag the offset master wheel to the left until it is around 5.00 to fit more of the trace within the scope.

This shot has a wide dynamic range so the offset can only attempt to fit the majority of it within the HD scope. We'll have to do more work on the highlights and shadows to bring it all in range.

You will approach this shot in the same way you did the previous shots: first, you will correct luminance.

NOTE On computers with lower screen resolution, you may have to click the curves button to display the Curves palette.

The custom curve graph is a plot graph in which you can perform incredibly flexible adjustments on specific tonal ranges of images. The X axis represents the image's tonal values going from the darkest shadows on the left to the brightest highlights on the right. Along the Y axis are the output, or offset, values with darker adjustments placed lower in the graph and brighter adjustments placed higher.

TIP When you hear the terms tonal values or the tonal range, we are talking about brightness values.

TIP In the Color page, each clip has its own undo/redo history. That is choosing Edit > Undo will undo different steps depending on which clip is currently selected.

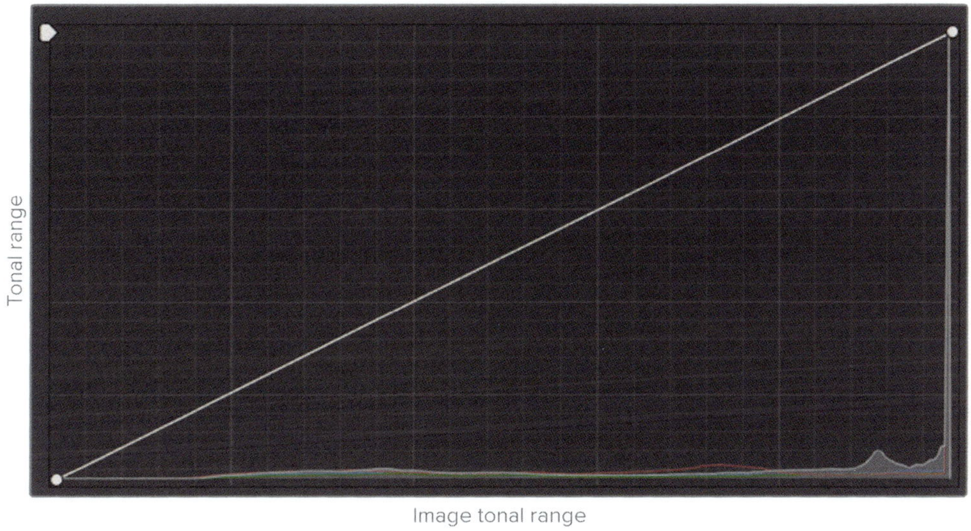

Like the Primaries bars you can adjust luminance separately from RGB channels. The end points in the custom curve graph are used to adjust the black and white points.

3 On the right side of the custom curves click the Y button to isolate the luminance channel.

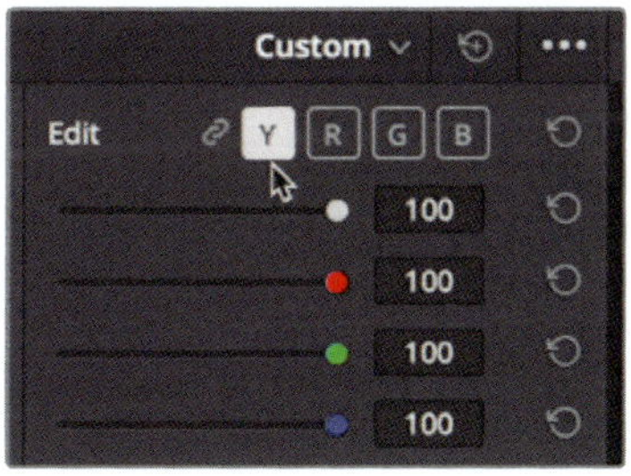

The shadows around the tractor truck should be fairly dark but arguably not completely black so we will set the black point in the custom curve accordingly.

4 Position the mouse pointer over the control point located in the lower-left corner of the custom curve graph.

This point is the black point control. Similar to the Y bar in the Lift primaries bars, adjusting this point raises or lowers the black point in a clip without modifying the saturation in the shadows.

5 Drag the point up until the red trace in the Parade skims along the 0 line.

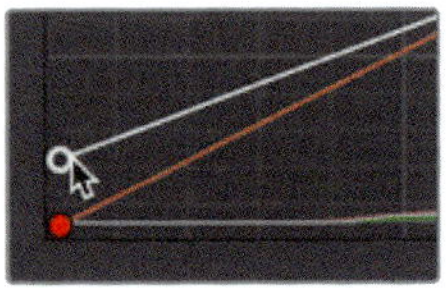

Moving the black point up lifts the black point, the darkest part of the image.

6 Position the mouse pointer over the control point located in the upper-right corner of the custom curve graph.

This point is the white point control. Similar to the Y bar in the Gain primaries bars, adjusting this point raises or lowers the white point in a clip without modifying the saturation in the highlights The highlights in this shot are already fairly clipping over the top so we will bring those down a bit.

7 Drag the point to the down until you have more detail in the bright clouds and the blue trace is no longer clipping at the top of the graph.

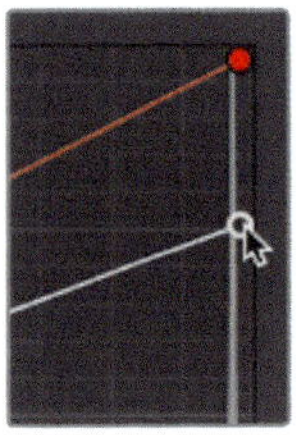

Dragging the control point to the left brightens the white point, the brightest part of the image.

Moving those two points as you did is a way of increasing contrast. But you still have a bit of clipping in the highlights. Instead of bringing the entire highlight region down, you can use the soft clip slider to softly bring that clipping back into range.

8 To the right of the custom curve, drag the high soft slider up until the clipped trace for the red and green channels are no longer clipping.

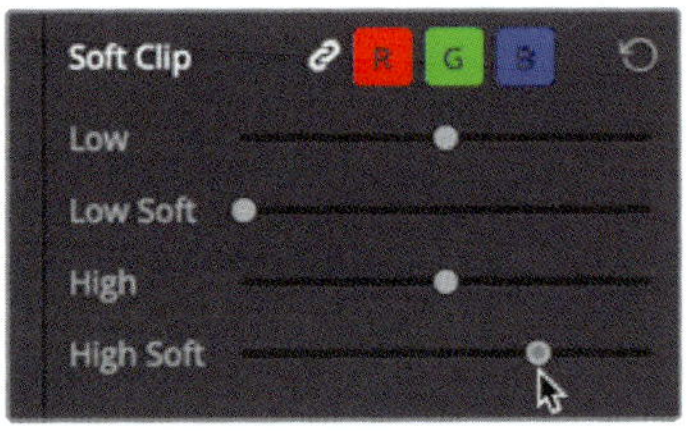

Soft clipping is ideal for a slight smooth roll off of otherwise harshly clipped channels.

9 Choose View > Bypass All Grades, or press Shift-D, to see the original image, and then press Shift-D again to compare your corrected clip to the original.

Now you can work on color balance by adjusting the curve for the individual channels.

Using nodes to separate tonal and color balancing

Looking at the parade scope, you can see the shadows in the blue channel trace appear slightly higher than the red and green channels. While the highlights in the blue channel trace appear lower. This indicates there is a blue tint in the shadow and a red tint in the highlights. So these are the first regions we will adjust. Sometimes, as you balance shots you may decide adjustments are best performed by isolating tonal problems from more complex color cast problems. You can separate the two parts of the balancing process using nodes.

1 In the Node graph, right-click node 01, and in the menu, choose Add Node > Add Serial.

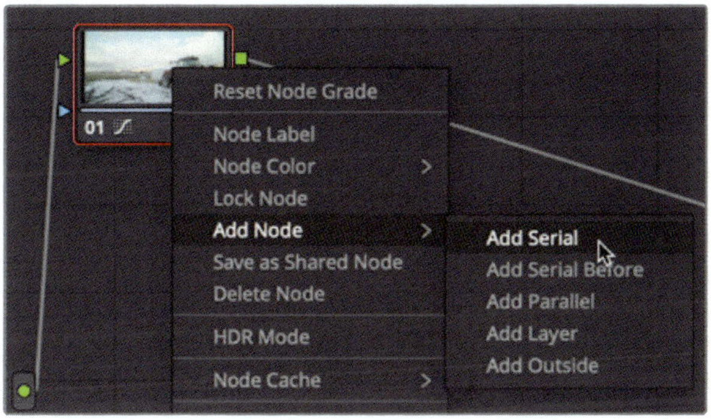

You can think of a node as a transparent layer stacked on top of your clip. When you make any color adjustment, those adjustments are applied to the node, and not to the clip. As a result, every adjustment in DaVinci Resolve is non-destructive because you can enable and disable a node at any time. We'll use the first node for our tonal adjustments and the new second node for color cast issues. Let's start by naming the nodes appropriately.

2 Right click over node 01 and choose Node label, then type TONAL BALANCE.

3 Right click over node 02 and choose Node label, then type COLOR BALANCE.

Since node 02 is the highlighted node, any adjustments you make will be contained in that node.

4 In the curve controls area, click the B button to activate the blue curve.

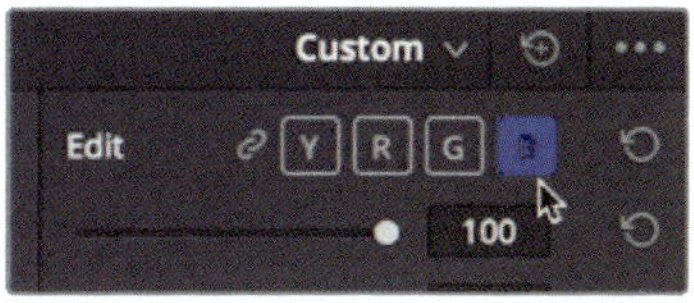

5 Drag the blue channel's black control point just a hair the right until the wheel on the tractor has less of a blue tint. The blue trace in the Parade scope will align at the bottom of the graph with the red and green traces.

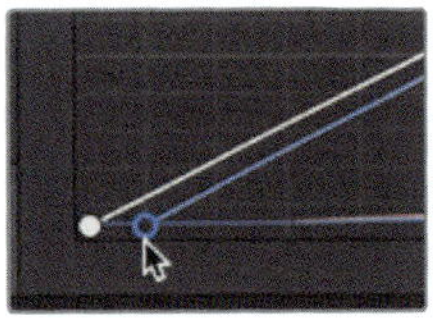

6 Drag the blue channel's white control point to the left until the blue trace in the Parade scope aligns at the top of the graph with the red and green traces. This will remove any green tint in the clouds.

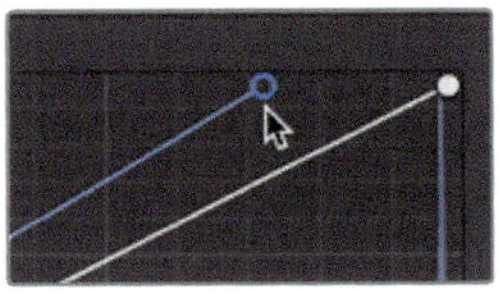

Since you have two nodes you can disable the color balance node without disabling the tonal balance. This will give you a better idea of how each node is changing the image.

7 Click 02 in the lower-left corner of the node, or press Cmd-D (macOS) or Ctrl-D (Windows), to see the image without the blue curve adjustment. Press Cmd-D (macOS) or Ctrl-D (Windows) again to view the corrected clip.

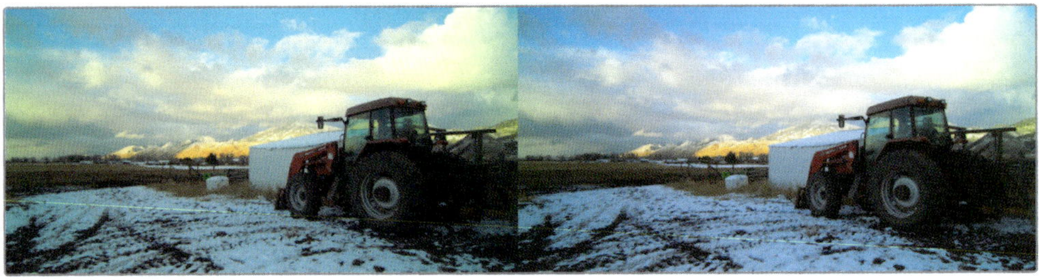

Before After

Sometimes balancing the white point, black point and color casts for shadows and highlights is not enough. Often you will come across color casts in midtones as well. The curves are distinctly capable at correcting color casts in mid tones because you can add control points anywhere along the line to pin point specific tonal regions that need correcting.

8 Click the G button in the custom curves to enable just the green curve.

Adding a control point anywhere along the line will allow you to modify regions other than just the white point and black point. Our image has a green tint in the darker midtones.

9 Click the green curve line about a third of the way up from the black point control.

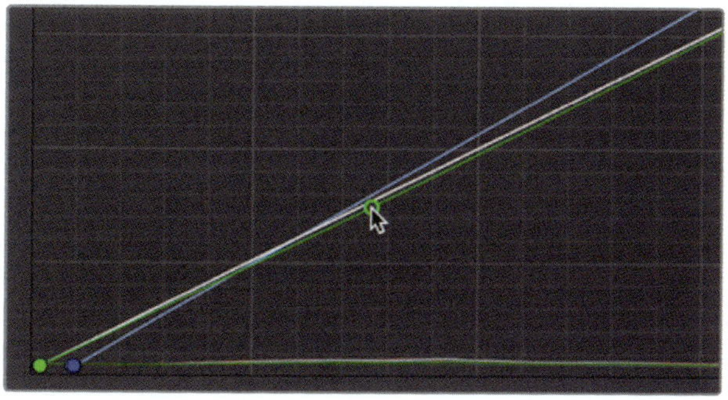

Adding a point here means we will be adjusting primarily in the darker mid-tones but not exclusively.

10 Drag the control point down slightly until the image no longer has a significant

Dragging the point lower in the graph decreases the green in the midtones by adding more red/magenta.

To compare the changes you just made, you can disable node 02, the node in which the changes were made.

11 Click 02 in the lower-left corner of the node, or press Cmd-D (macOS) or Ctrl-D (Windows), to see the image without the hue curves adjustment. Press Cmd-D (macOS) or Ctrl-D (Windows) again to view the corrected clip.

Nodes allow you to organize your color adjustments in flexible ways. On some simple grades, you may use only one node. For complete grades, you may add a dozen nodes. Using nodes, you can quickly navigate to the exact adjustment you are looking for and monitor

Copying Corrections between Similar Shots

Color correcting moving images gets very challenging the moment you edit multiple angles together into a single timeline. Not only does each shot need to look correct on its own,

it needs to look correct when compared to the shots immediately before and after it. This process of blending the look and feel of two or more shots is called shot matching.

The point of shot matching, or scene balancing, is simple: in real life, as you glance around, perhaps while having a conversation, you'll notice a consistency to what you see. Color saturation, skin tone hues, and brightness levels don't dramatically alter from glance-to-glance unless some external event forces the lighting to change. (For example, a light is turned on or clouds cover the sun.) If you want to maintain the illusion that your stories are real, then you need to mimic this consistency by matching shots and balancing your scenes.

In this exercise, you'll explore a few of the simplest tools that DaVinci Resolve provides for moving a correction from one clip to another. You'll use these tools to create a seamless flow of sequential shots.

1 In the thumbnail timeline, select clip 04.

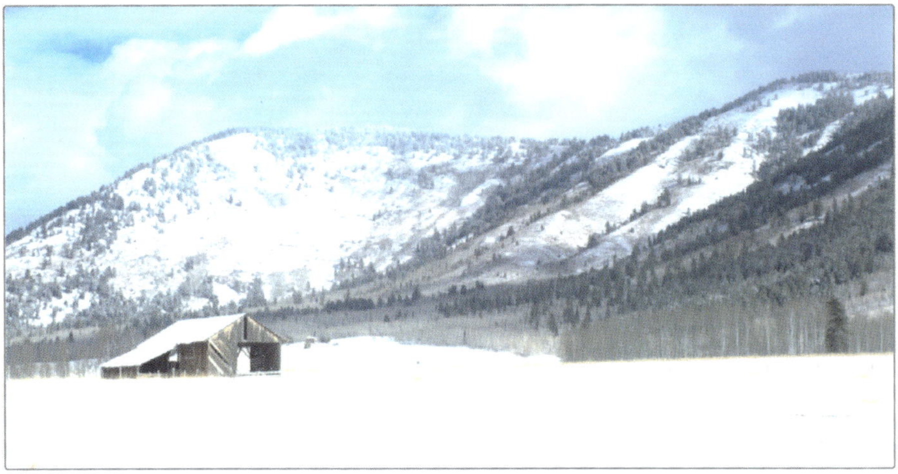

This is the second shot of the snowy field with the barn. One of the simplest shot matching situations is when you have clips that were recorded at the same time using the same camera. That's the situation you have with clips 03 and 04. Because you already balanced clip 03, you can apply the same correction to the close up shot on clip 04.

2 Select clip 03 and choose Edit > Copy or press Cmd-C (macOS) or Ctrl-C (Windows) to copy the node's settings.

3 Select clip 04 and press Cmd-V (macOS) or Ctrl-V (Windows) to paste the node's settings.

Copying and pasting works with one node, so the selected node's adjustments from the clip 03 is copied and ready to be pasted on to the selected node in clip 04.

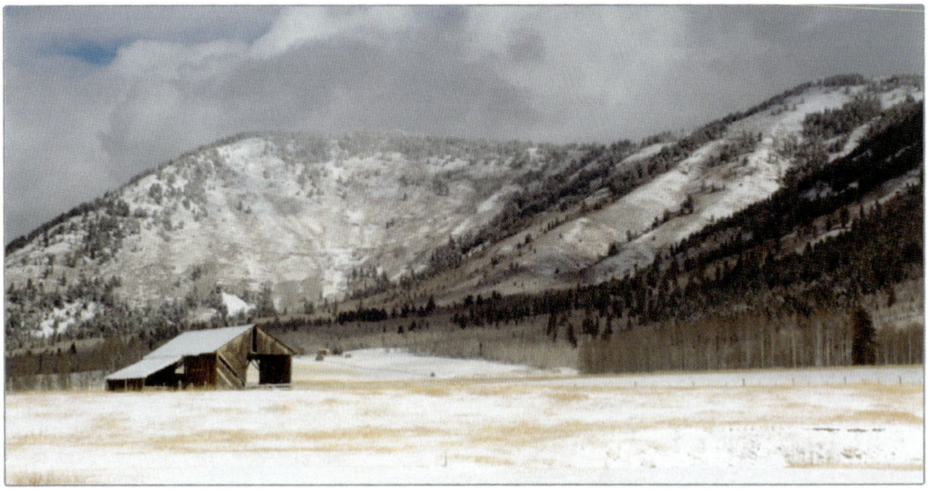

As long as you are only dealing with a single node then copy and paste is quick and easy. Now let's look at a method that can handle more than a single node.

4 Select clip 15.

This is the shot of the tractor that you balanced using two nodes. If you want to copy and paste an entire grade, there is an equally simple method.

5 Select clip 16.

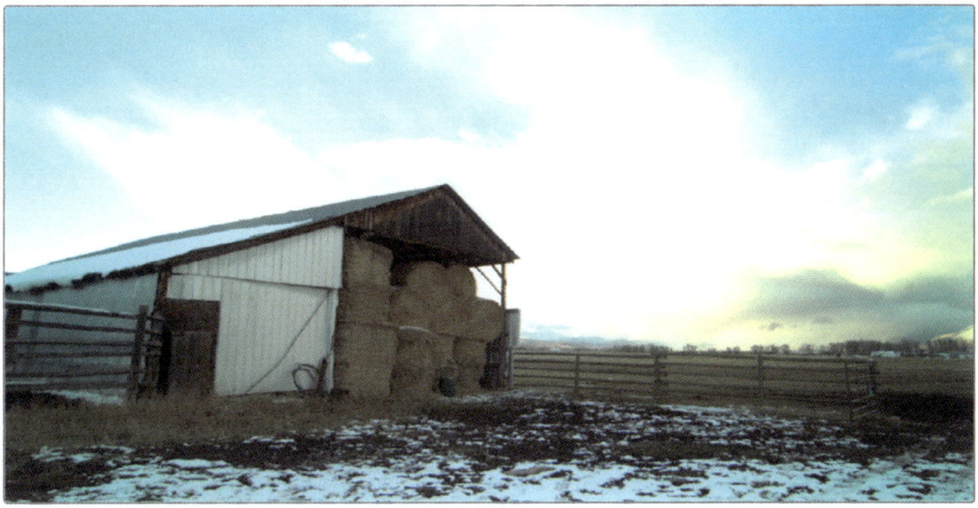

This is a similar shot to the tractor. It appears to be from the same area and the same time of day.

6 Move your mouse pointer over clip 15's thumbnail and click with the middle mouse button.

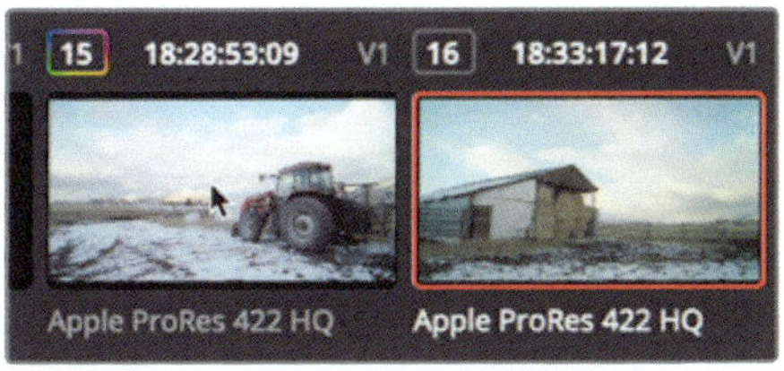

When a clip is selected, clicking over another thumbnail using the middle mouse copies the entire grade from the clicked thumbnail onto the selected thumbnail. The two nodes used to grade clip 15 are node copied onto clip 16.

7 Select clip 09.

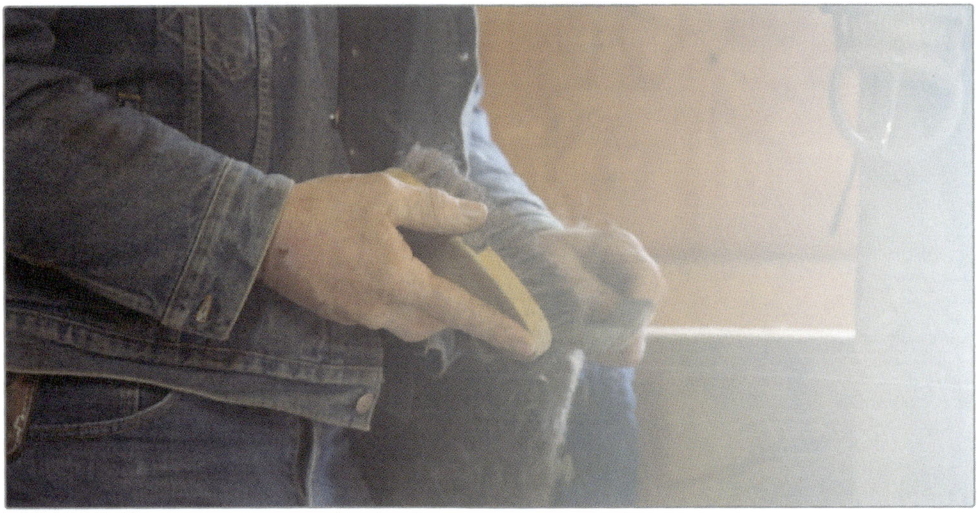

This clip is another shot you balance earlier and following it are two additional shots which appear to be from the same scene.

We'll use yet another method of easily copying entire grades from one clip to another.

8 Click on clip 10 and then clip 11 to see the two ungraded clips.

9 Click back on clip 10. This is the first ungraded clip we will work on.

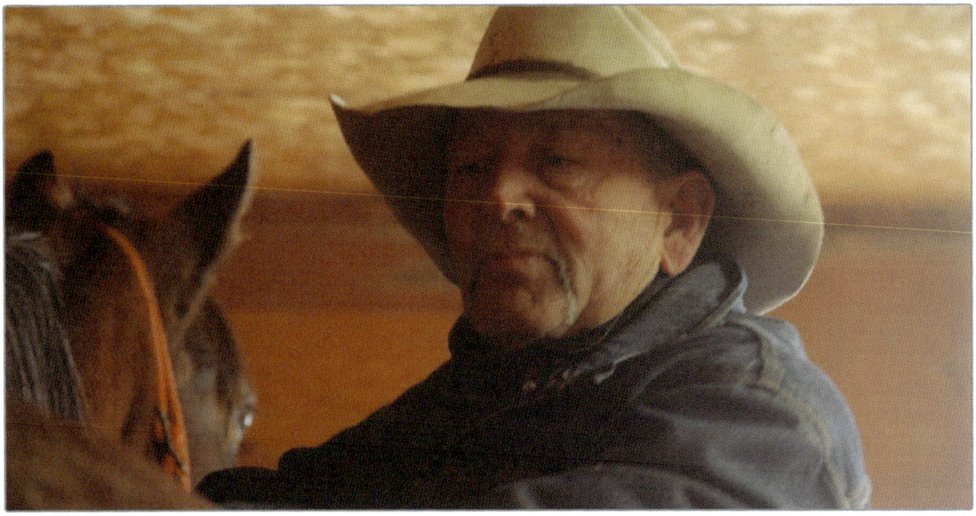

10 Choose Color > Apply Grade form one clip prior or press the = (equal) key.

The grade from clip 09 is copied onto clip 10.

11 Click on clip 11 and choose Color > Apply Grade from two clips prior or press the - (hyphen) key.

12 Play through the three balanced clips to ensure a consistent color continuity.

The shots all feel like one continuous sequence. Brightness, hue, and saturation look consistent. It may seem odd that there are two functions to copy a grade from one and two clips prior to the selected clip but if you think about a dramatic scene where you often cut back and forth between a shot and then a reverse angle of the shot, these two menu functions can come in very handy.

Saving and Applying Stills

Instead of copying and pasting nodes from one clip to another right on the spot, you can save your grades into the Gallery and recall them whenever you need them. Saving stills into the gallery has a few benefits over simple copy and paste. Most importantly, it allows you to compare the saved graded still with any clip in your timeline.

1 Select clip 06, which shows the interview of the rancher we balanced earlier.

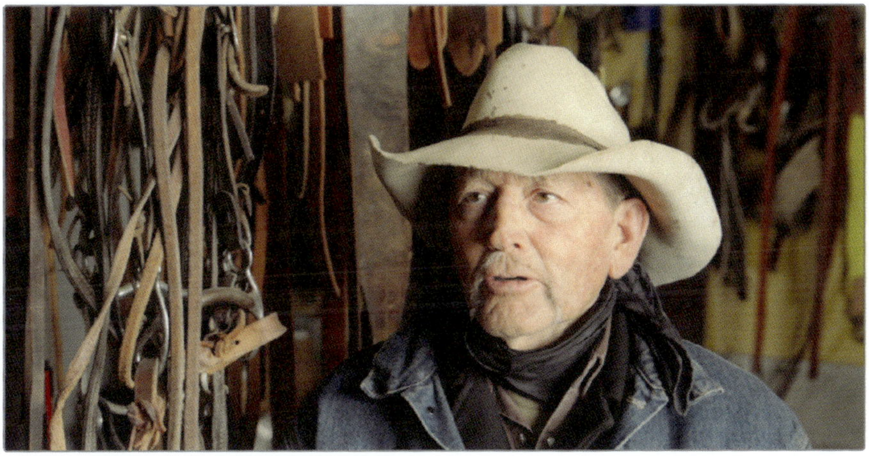

You can save the grade you created on this shot by saving a still into the gallery.

2 Right-click in the viewer, and choose Grab Still.

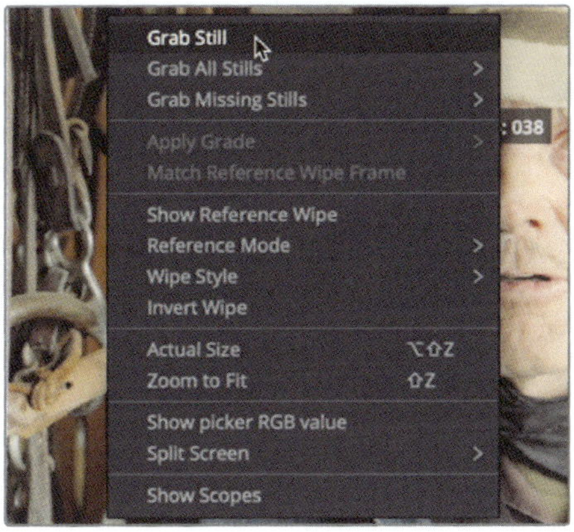

A reference still image is saved into the Gallery. The still image also contains all the instructions to rebuild the correction for that shot. It's helpful to name these stills so you will later know exactly what they do.

3 Right-click the still, and choose Change Label.

4 Name the still RANCHER BALANCED.

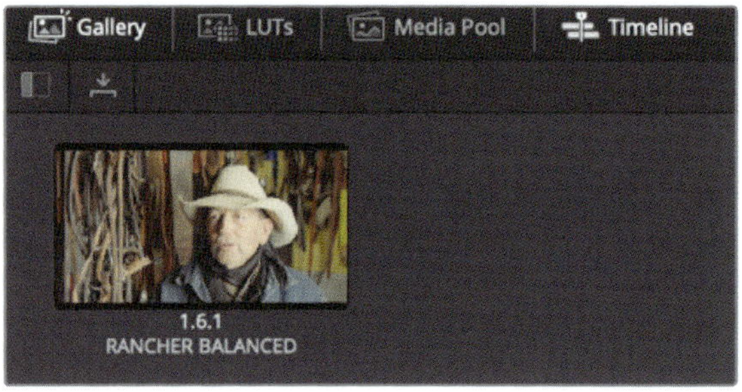

Gallery stills make it easy to apply an entire correction to one or more clips.

5 Click clip 17 near the end of the timeline.

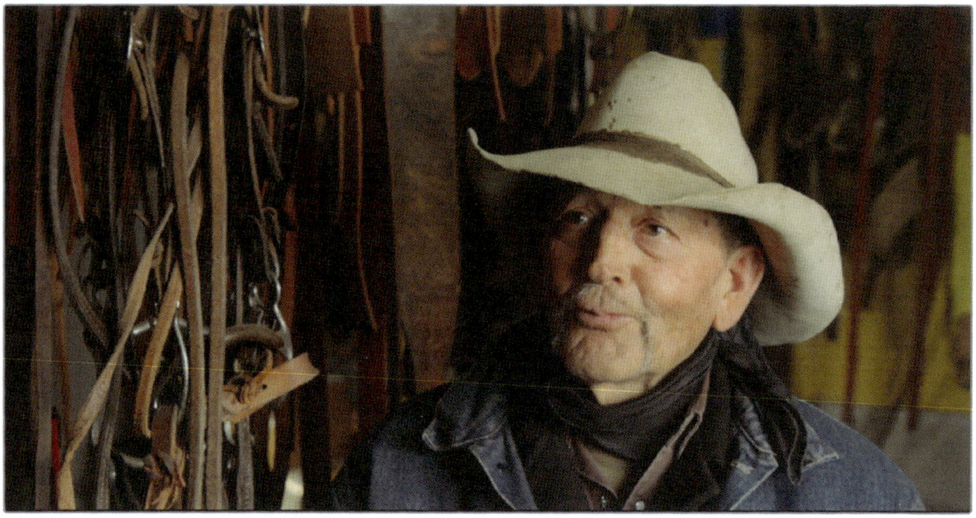

This is another shot of the rancher's interview so it should receive the same balance treatment as the first.

Before applying the grade, you can compare the still in your Gallery to this interview clip. This can help preview the differences and even help us improve the color continuity between the two interview shots. So, let's start just by comparing the two shots.

6 To compare clip 17 to the reference still of clip 06, double-click the RANCHER BALANCE still in the Gallery to open it into the viewer.

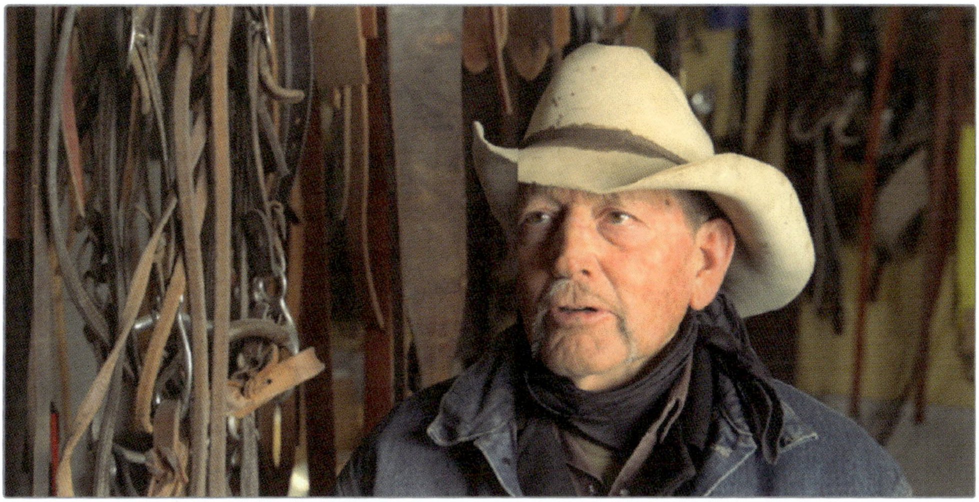

By default, a vertical split appears in the viewer. The shot from the timeline (thumbnail 17) is on the left. The selected still in the Gallery is on the right.

7 Choose Workspace > Viewer Mode > Enhanced Viewer, or press Option-F (macOS) or Alt-F (Windows), to expand the viewer.

8 In the viewer, drag to the left to position the split over the rancher's face.

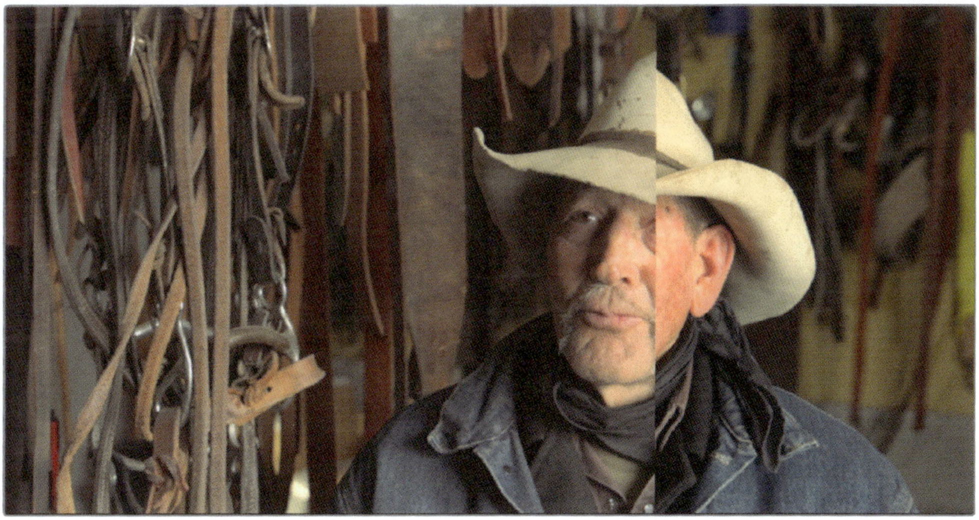

When comparing the two shots, the timeline clip appears darker and a bit cooler. So, let's apply your RANCHER BALANCE grade you saved in the Gallery.

9 Choose Workspace > Viewer Mode > Enhanced Viewer, or press Option-F (macOS) or Alt-F (Windows), to display the Gallery.

10 In the Gallery, right-click the RANCHER BALANCE still, and choose Apply Grade.

The timeline clip now has the color correction applied from the still. However, as is often the case, because the lighting is different between the original clips, the Apply the sill hasn't solved our issue completely. The color seems right but it is still too dark in comparison.

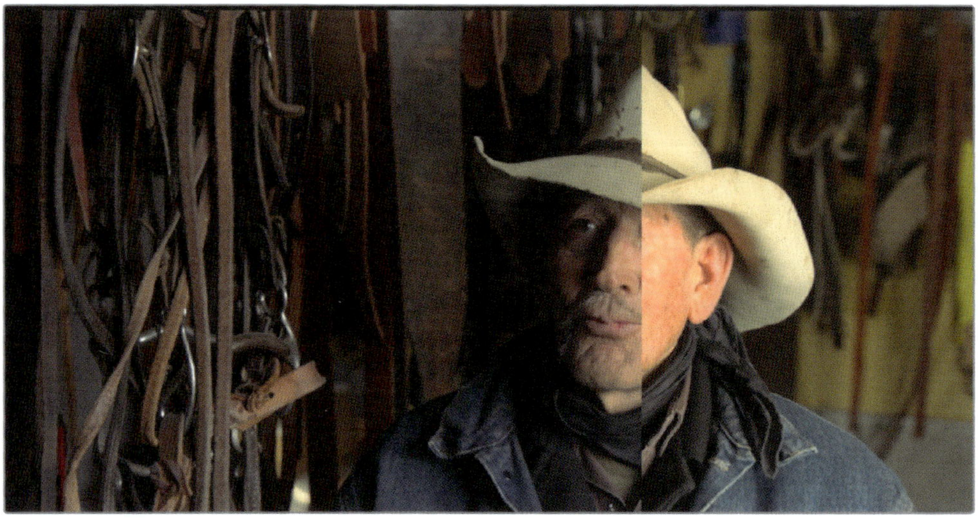

11 In the viewer, drag to the left, and then drag right to compare the tonal quality of the two shots in different areas.

As you drag, notice the parade scope shows the black levels fairly even but the highlights being much lower in clip 17. Because the timeline clip has lower highlights than the reference still, you can use the gain master wheel in the color wheels to brighten them up.

12 Using the Gain master wheel, drag to the right until the hat in the clip matches the brightness of the hat in the reference still. Use the parade scope to double check your adjustment.

Now that the overall tonality of the clip matches the reference, it is noticeable that the clip has less color saturation.

13 Under the master wheel, drag the saturation adjustment to around 55 or 60 until the two images in the viewer match perfectly.

14 To disable the image wipe in the viewer, click the image wipe button in the upper-left corner of the viewer.

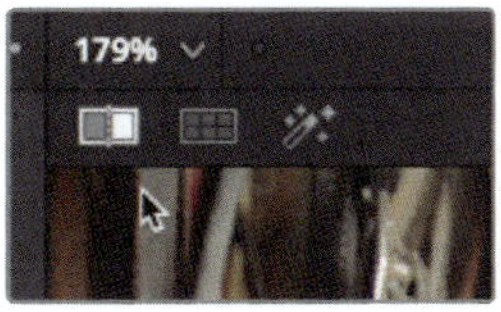

Shot matching is made easier when you start using the Gallery and reference stills to help your analysis and inform your color-correction moves. You should also use the scopes to minimize any visual quirks because your visual perception naturally tends to force the shots to match. The combination of reference stills and scopes will make the shot matching process more accurate, giving your entire project perfect color continuity.

Lesson Review

1 In the Color page, what does the 1023 line on the Parade scope represent?
2 True or false? Custom curves can adjust only the red, green, and blue channels.
3 How do you save a still to the Gallery?
4 If the RGB picker is over a neutral pixel, what should the red, green and blue values be?
5 What does double clicking a Gallery still do?

Answers

1 The 1023 line on the Parade scope represents pure white. Anything above the 1023 line is clipped and loses detail.

2 False. You can adjust luminance as well as the red, green, and blue channels using the custom curves in the Color page.

3 You can save a still to the Gallery by right-clicking the viewer, and choosing Grab Still.

4 Hovering the RGB picker over a neutral pixel, the RGB values should display the same or nearly the same values for red, green, and blue.

5 Creates a split screen in the viewer, with the timeline clip on the left and the still image on the right.

Lesson 13

Making Secondary Adjustments

Primary adjustments let you work on the entire image, whereas secondary adjustments let you isolate and work on specific parts of an image.

For example, you might want to change the color of a car from blue to red without affecting the rest of the shot, or add warmth and saturation to an actor's skin, or create a vignette to help focus the viewer's attention in a specific area of the scene. DaVinci Resolve features many powerful tools to do this.

In this lesson, you will use HSL Curves and qualifiers to isolate elements based on their color, as well as apply basic spline shapes to isolate areas of your frame. Then, you will use the tracker to follow a moving element and grade it as it moves throughout the scene.

Time

This lesson takes approximately 30 minutes to complete.

Goals

Making secondary adjustments with HSL Curves

The first part of making a secondary color correction is to isolate the adjustment to its own node. This allows you to make very specific adjustments without modifying the primary grade you have already completed.

Using multiple nodes, each containing separate adjustments, you can exercise more precise control over the order of those adjustments and more easily track and modify them.

1. Open DaVinci Resolve 16, if necessary, and then open the Wyoming Rancher project you have been working on.
2. Open the Wyoming Ranch timeline to load it into the viewer.
3. Click the color page and select clip 15.

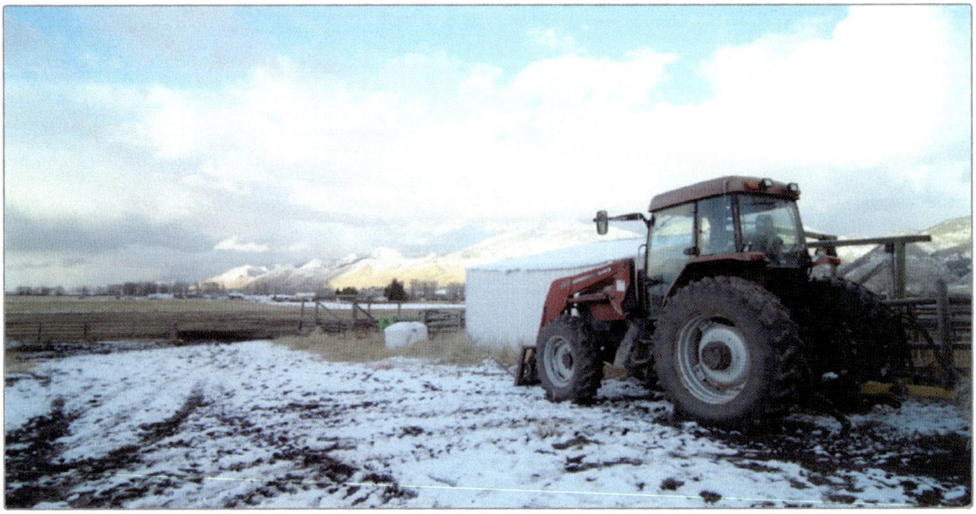

This clip has a nice old red tractor and it could be enhanced if we made the tractor's red color stand out a bit more. Isolating the red color of the tractor should be relatively straight forward since there is no other bright red color in the shot.

4. Select the Color balance node (node 02) in the node editor, right click over it and choose Add Node > Add Serial or press Option-S (macOS) or Alt-S (Windows).

   This third node in the node editor will be used for making the red tractor a bit more vibrant.

5. Right click over node 03 and label it RED TRACTOR.

   The easiest technique to use when you have a simple secondary color adjustment is to use the HSL curves. HSL Curves are located in the Custom curves palette.

6 In the toolbar, click the Curves palette.

7 In the upper right corner of the Curves palette click the drop down arrow next to the word Custom.

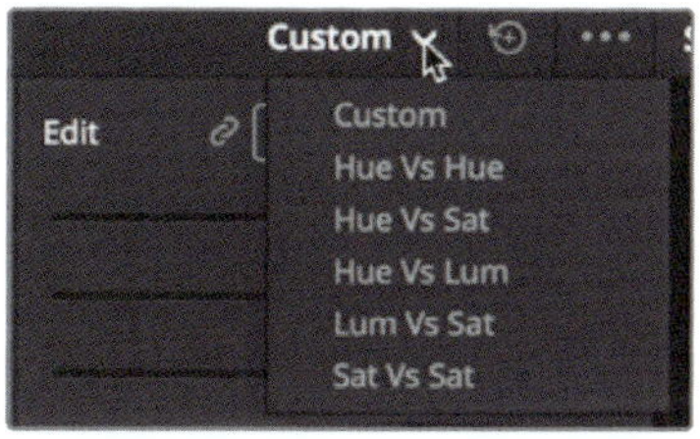

This menu shows the five different HSL curves that can be used to make simple secondary adjustments. The name of each HSL curve displays the property that will be selected and then how that property will be adjusted. For instance, Hue vs Sat will select a hue from the image and adjust the saturation of that particular hue. Let's try it out on our red tractor. Since we want to make the red tractor more vibrant, we will first select the Hue vs Sat curve.

8 Select Hue vs Sat from the Curves palette drop down menu.

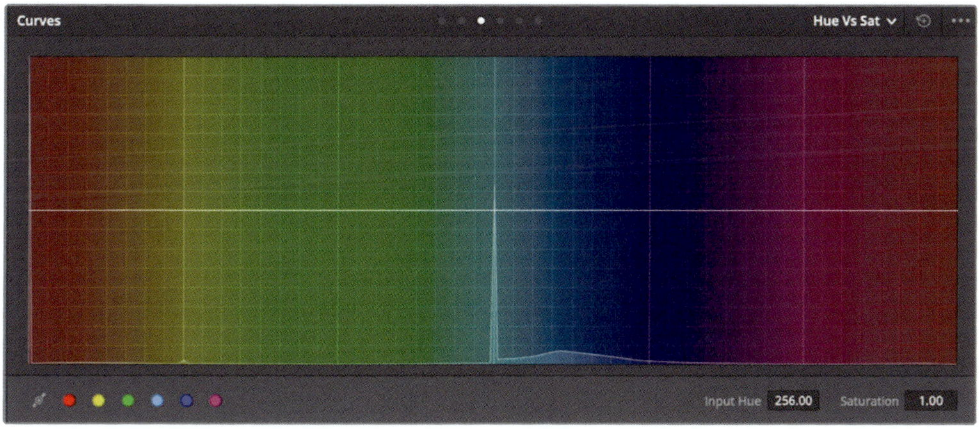

The graph displays a hue color spectrum with a line running through the middle. The next step is to select the hue you want to adjust.

9 In the viewer, click over a bright red area of the tractor.

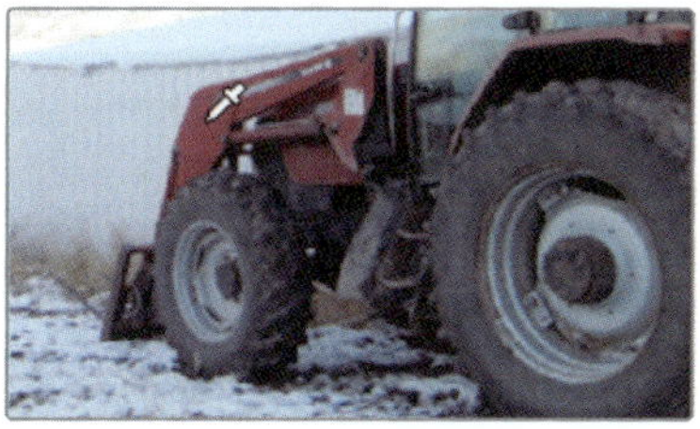

Clicking in the viewer adds three points to the line in the graph. In this instance, since red is at the end of the color spectrum, the last point loops around to the left side. The middle point is the precise hue shade you selected in the viewer. The outer two points limit the range of red hue that will be adjusted.

10 Drag the middle point in the graph up to increase the red saturation.

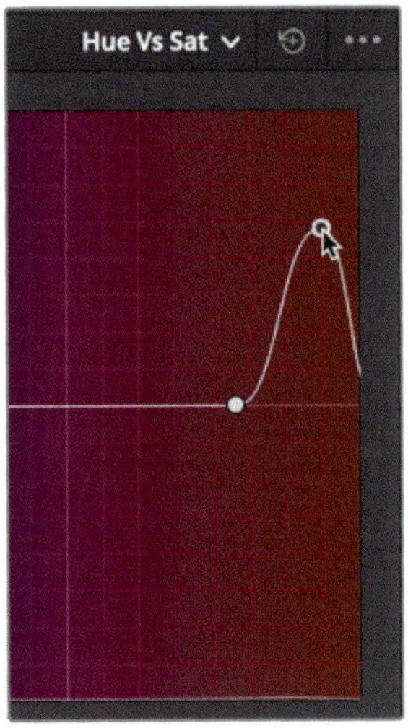

11 To see the change in saturation, press Cmd-D (macOS) or Ctrl-D (Windows) to disable the HLS curve adjustment, then press the keyboard shortcut again to enable it.

To increase the red a bit more, we'll adjust the luminance of the red hue.

12 From the Curves palette drop down menu choose Hue vs Lum.

The graph displays a similar hue color spectrum.

13 In the viewer, click over the bright red area of the tractor again.

The three points are added to the Hue vs Lum graph.

14 Drag the middle point in the graph up to increase the luminance of the red saturated tractor.

15 Again, press Cmd-D (macOS) or Ctrl-D (Windows) to disable the two HLS curve adjustments, then press the keyboard shortcut again to enable them.

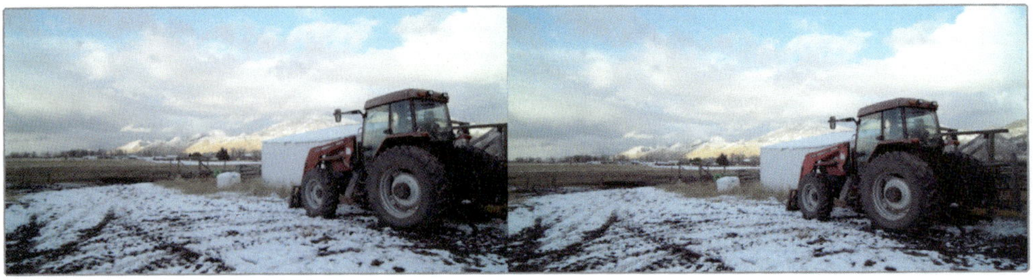

Before After

The computer mathematics behind the HSL curves create very smooth and natural results that are much trickier to get using other methods. However, the hue selection process is also limited in its control.

Selecting areas with Qualifiers

The qualifier palette is another method of isolating a color for secondary color corrections. Compared to the HSL curves, it is a more sophisticated palette that includes several ways to select that color using hue, luminance, and saturation. This detailed level of control enables you to get a clean isolation, or matte, of objects even when other elements in the shot are of a similar color.

> **TIP** Qualifiers are used only as a method of creating a matte. They are not color-grading tools in themselves, and you only start to see their effects when you begin adjustments in the color-grading palettes.

1 Select clip 08.

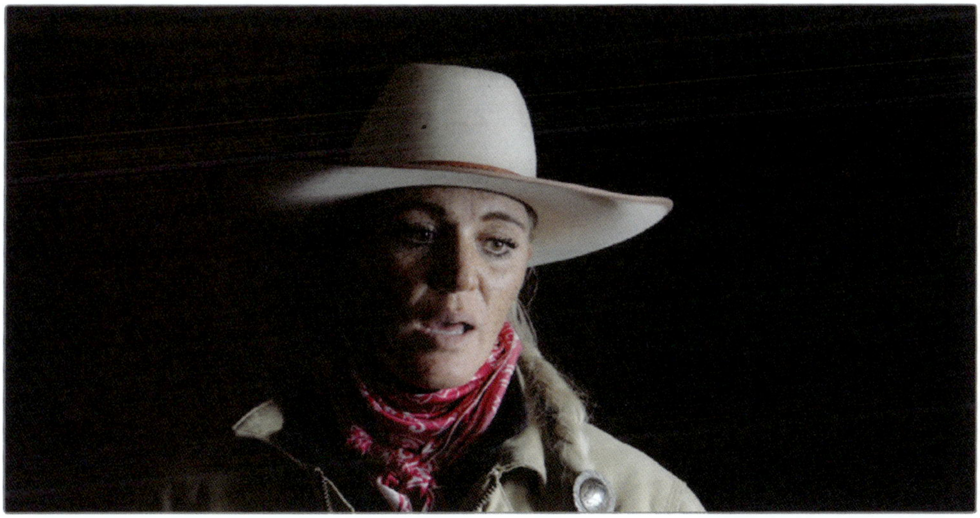

For this shot, you'll create a much-requested stylized image in which one color will be preserved, while the rest of the image is black-and-white. You've seen many movies with this effect and maybe even tried creating it in other applications. The critical task is being able to cleanly isolate the color you want to keep. You should keep this operation separate from the balance adjustments already created on the first node.

2 In the node editor, right click over node 01 and choose Add node > Add Serial.

3 Right click over node 02 and label the node PINK SCARF.

4 In the central palettes, click the qualifier icon.

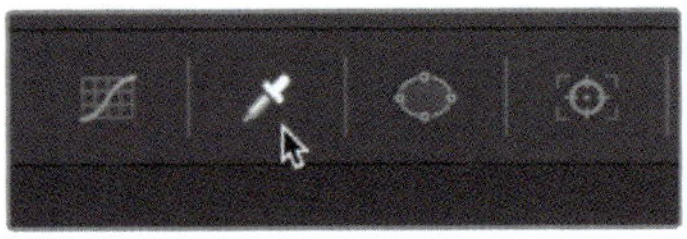

In this clip, you will want to preserve the pink scarf.

When the qualifier palette is selected, hovering your mouse pointer over the viewer will display an eyedropper that is used to select the color you want to preserve.

5 Drag over an area from under her chin to the bottom of the scarf.

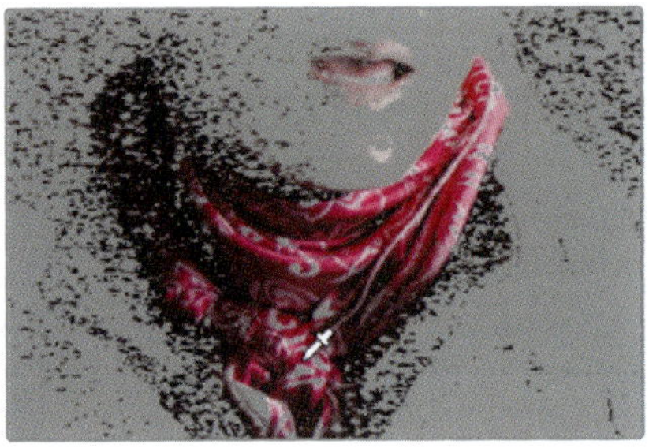

TIP The eyedropper is not only used with the qualifier palette. It will affect whichever palette you have open at the bottom of the Color page. If custom curves are open when you clicked your image, control points are added to the curve.

The clip in the viewer will not change, but you should see some activity in the qualifiers palette. The settings now reflect the information you have fed them by clicking the image. Your next step will be to refine and clean up your selection. To do so, you first must change the viewer's output to show your selection.

6 In the upper-left corner of the viewer, click the highlight wand icon.

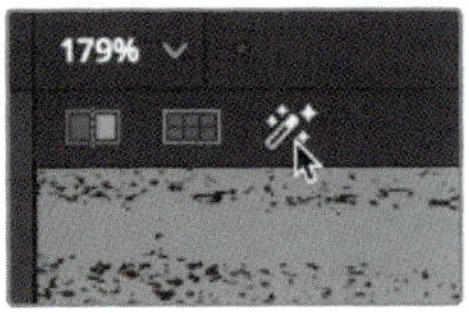

You are now seeing a representation of your selection against a gray background.

As you can see, the selection is not very clean. There's a variety of ways to improve it. The first will be to add additional samples of the color into the qualifier palette.

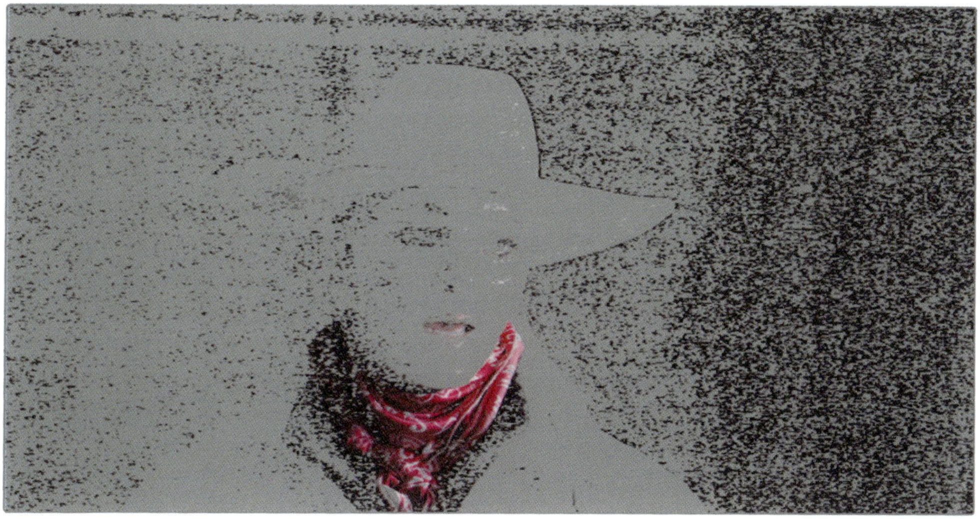

TIP You can change how your selection is presented using the three icons in the upper-right corner of the viewer. Next to the standard grayscale highlight icon, you also have the highlight B/W icon that outputs your image as a black-and-white matte. This might be familiar to users who have previously used compositing programs and have experience with keying.

7 Click the add color range button located in the Selection Range of the palette.

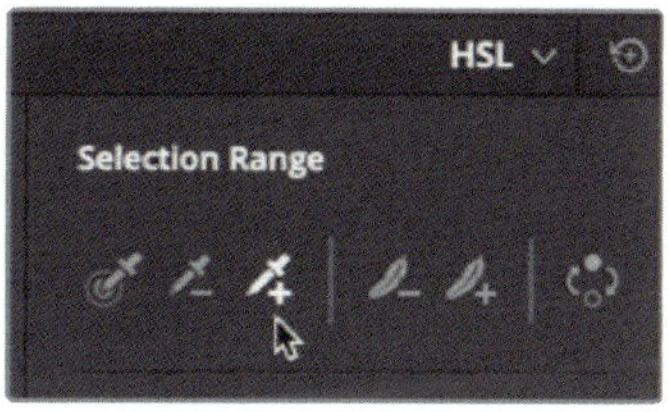

The add color range button allows you to append additional colors to the currently selected range.

8 In the viewer, drag over the upper right brighter side of the pink scarf down to the bottom.

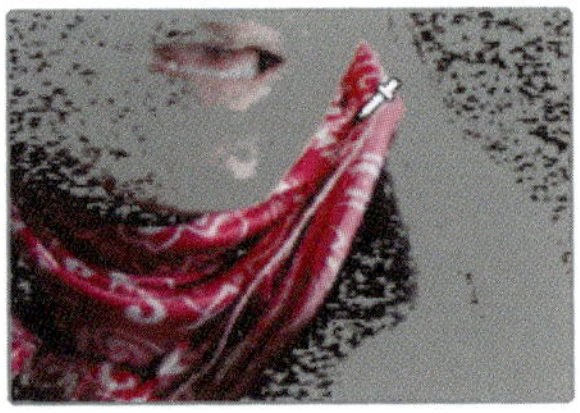

> **TIP** You can press Cmd-Z (macOS) or Ctrl-Z (Windows) to undo an incorrect selection.

9 In the Selection range palette, return to the default eye dropper picker on the left.

You should now see a fuller selection that still has imperfections.

You can now fine tune your selection by adjusting the Hue, Saturation, and Luminance values in the qualifier palette. The qualifier's controls are very sophisticated and powerful. It can take some time to master as you figure out how different shots react to different parameters. The best way to learn is to just start making changes.

10 Adjust the Hue Width and Hue Center. Then adjust the Low and High values under each Saturation and Luminance control bar to refine the range of the selection.

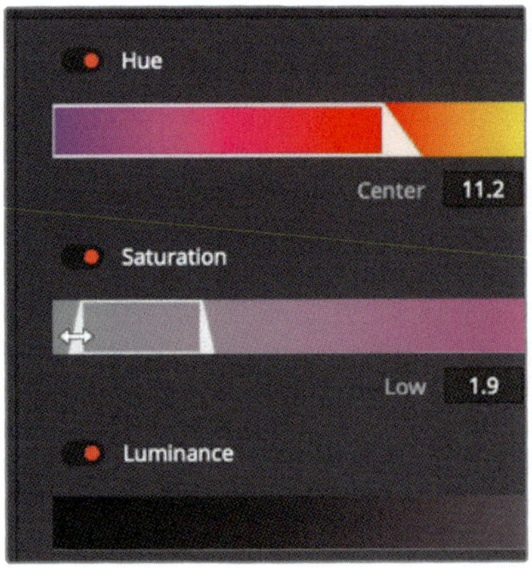

> **TIP** It can be helpful as you experiment to turn some of the sliders on and off by clicking the red dot to the left of the name. Doing so allows you to check if that change would improve the selection.

The last form of clean up would be to adjust the image matte. This technique does not rely on color selection as much as it manipulates the selection you have already made.

11 In the upper-right corner of the viewer, click the highlight B/W icon.

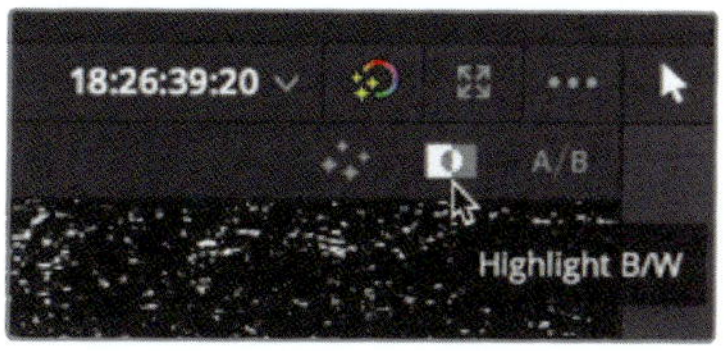

12 To the right of the Qualifier, adjust the Matte finesse controls Clean Black and Clean White to remove smaller, unwanted white and black specks that appear in the matte.

The goal when adjusting the Matte finesse controls is to produce a clean black-and-white image. Gray areas are seen primarily in transparent areas of which there are none in this shot.

13 Click Page 2 in the Matte finesse controls, and set Mode to Grow.

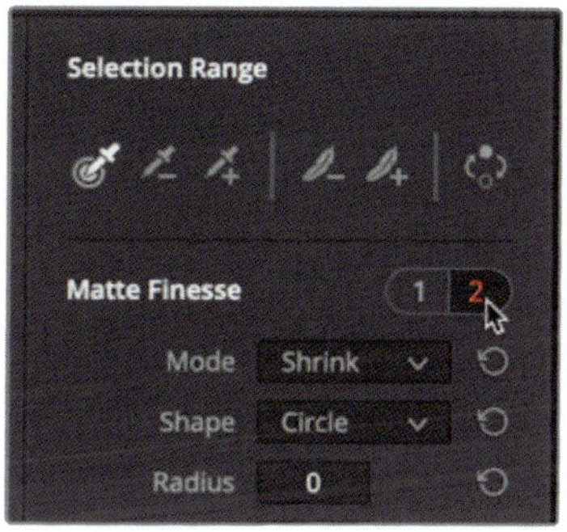

The Clean Black and Clean White parameters may have shrunk the matte around the scarf a bit too much. The grow parameter will allow you to increase the size of the matte.

14 Increase the Radius parameter to 4 to increase the matte size.

15 Turn off the Highlight view by clicking the Highlight Wand icon.

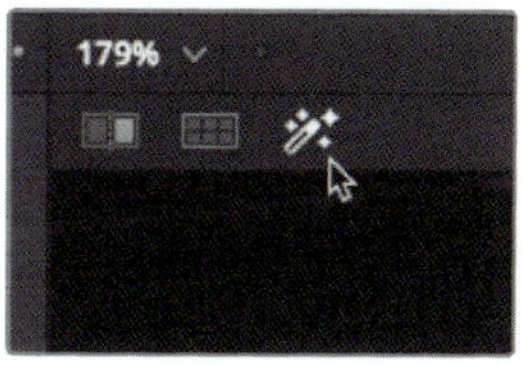

You can test to see if your selection includes all the colors you want by shifting the color of the selected area. A good method is to drag the Hue values at the bottom of the Color wheels palette.

16 In the adjustments strip below the Color wheels, drag the Hue value in either direction to shift the pink color in the viewer to another color.

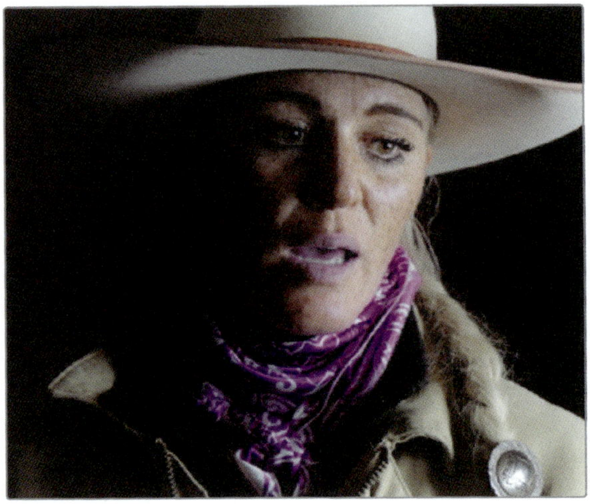

17 In the adjustment strip, double-click the Hue label to reset the value.

Notice how the lips are too close in color to the scarf to get good separation. We'll deal with that in a different way but If you notice other areas with the selection, return to the qualifier tool, and use one of the three methods described previously to clean up your selection.

Reversing selections with Outside Nodes

Occasionally, you will want to focus your attention on the area that are opposite of your selection. For example, in this shot, you might be happy to leave the scarf pink, and manipulate everything that isn't pink. With the pink selection already made, doing so will be easy. You will add an outside node, which will use your qualifier key to create an inverted version of the selection.

1 With node 02 selected in the Node editor, right-click it, and choose Add Node > Add Outside, or press Option-O (macOS) or Alt-O (Windows).

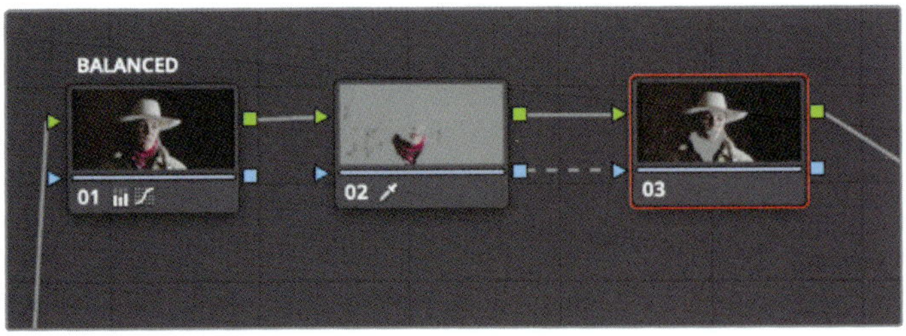

A third node is now present in the Node graph. As with previous nodes you've created, it will share a connection with the preceding node via the green RGB input/output circles. However, this time you'll see a new connection: the key input/output blue triangles. The key is the portion of the image that you isolated using the qualifier tool. When you create an outside node, it receives the key from the previous node and automatically inverts it.

2 With node 03 selected, in the adjustment controls strip, drag the Sat field to a value of 0.

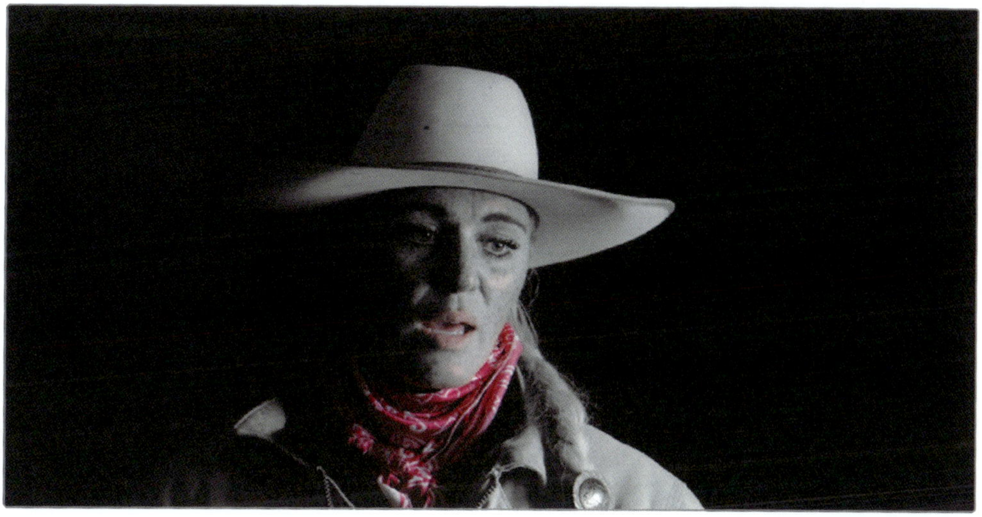

You can increase the drama in this shot by increasing the contrast in the black-and-white portion of the image.

3 With node 03 selected, in the adjustment controls strip, drag the Contrast slider to 1.1.

The ability to reuse key data is a beneficial component of node-based workflows. It speeds up the grading process by requiring you to perform only a single key, and reuse it multiple times.

Combining Qualifiers and Power Windows

Like qualifiers, Power Windows allow you to specify which area of the image you want to alter. Unlike using a qualifier, Power Windows do not rely on a selection of hues, but rather a spline shape within the frame that identifies the area you want to mask out.

You can refine an area of the frame you want to modify even more precisely by using qualifier and power windows together. Often, an image will have several instances of a hue that you are trying to manipulate. Instead of focusing your efforts on cleaning up the selection in the qualifier palette (and likely compromising the quality of the key), sometimes the best option is to use a Power Window to limit which part of the frame the qualifier operates on. For instance, in our shot you may notice her lips still showing a bit of color. Instead of fiddling with the Qualifier which would affect the scarf selection, you'll use a window to mask out everything except the scarf.

1 Select node 02 in the node editor.

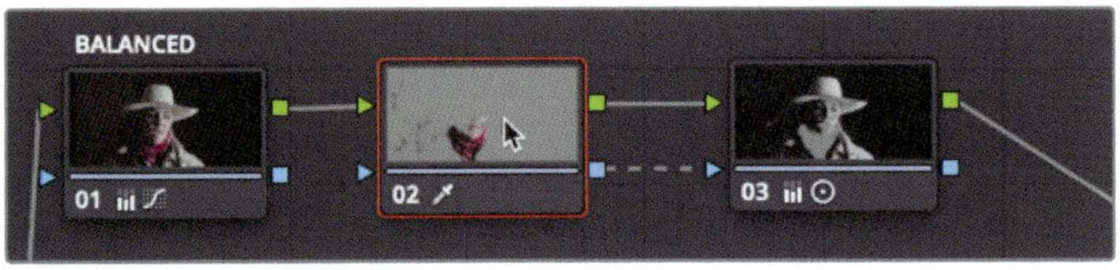

2 In the toolbar, in the central palettes, click the window palette icon

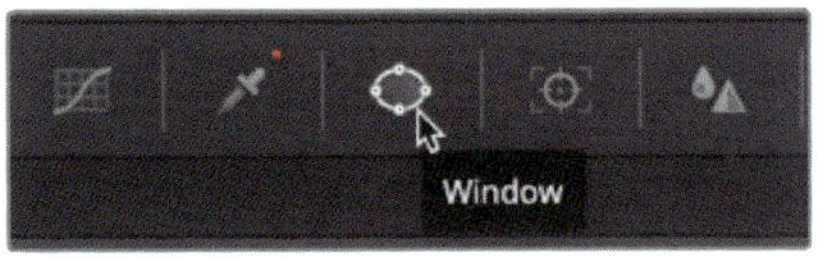

3 In the list of Power Windows, click the curve button to activate it.

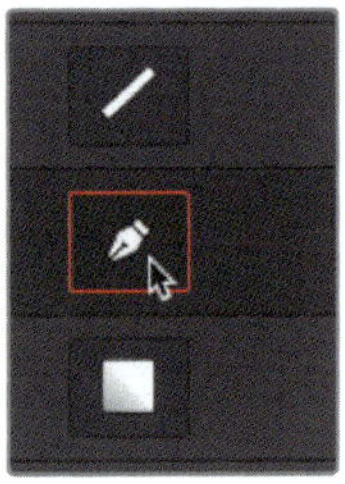

4 Double-click next to the curve button, and label the window as SCARF.

5 Move your mouse pointer into the viewer and make sure you can see the entire frame.

Now you are ready to draw a custom window shape.

6 Draw a shape by loosely clicking around the scarf, starting at the bottom of her chin, up to the dark left side of the face, down to include the dark part of the scarf, off the screen at the bottom of the scarf and finally up around the right side of the scarf.

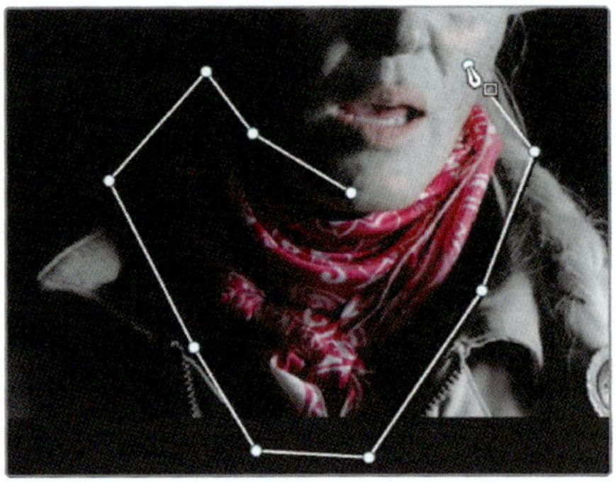

7 To complete the custom shape, click the first point in the shape to close it.

When the shape has been created, the Power Window will exclude the rest of the image, keeping only the selection inside the box.

Combining the qualifier with a Power Window has allowed you to quickly make a clean selection based on the hue of the element, while just as quickly excluding interfering elements from your selection. Using both tools meant that you didn't have to draw an overly precise Power Window around the box. Combining the two tools has saved time and resulted in the cleanest key.

Using the tracker

Now that you have one frame with a clean colorful scarf, you need to ensure it remains that way throughout the shot. One way to ensure the window follows the scarf as it moves is to track the scarf using Resolve's Tracker. The Color page features an incredible 3D perspective tracker that not only follows objects, but can also determine if that object changes rotation or perspective. As a result, you can track the most challenging objects so a window will follow it precisely.

1 In the toolbar, click the tracker button.

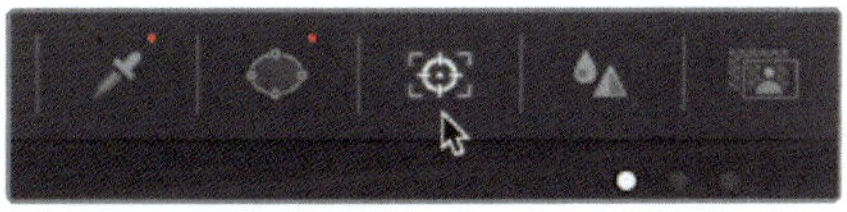

2 Make sure the play head in the tracker panel is at the start of the clip.

The tracker can track various aspects of objects within a clip. You can enable and disable the transform types using the checkboxes at the top of the panel. Disabling parameters can sometimes help improve tracking, so long as you needn't track those disabled aspects of the object. For instance, in this clip, the scarf does not increase in size so we can disable that property to potentially remove errors.

3 Click the Zoom checkbox to disable that transform.

4 Begin tracking by clicking the track forward button.

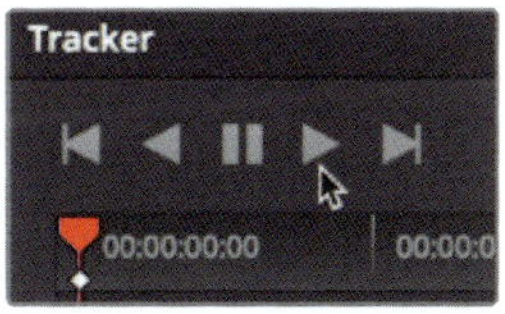

5 Once the track is completed, click on node 03 to hide the window outline in the viewer, then scrub or play through the clip to see the results.

The tracker causes the Power Window to perfectly follow the scarf as the woman shifts during the interview. You have one more interview shot of the woman that needs a similar treatment. You'll use a special copy and paste technique that will be able to reuse most of the work you have already done.

6 Select clip 14, the close up interview clip of the woman.

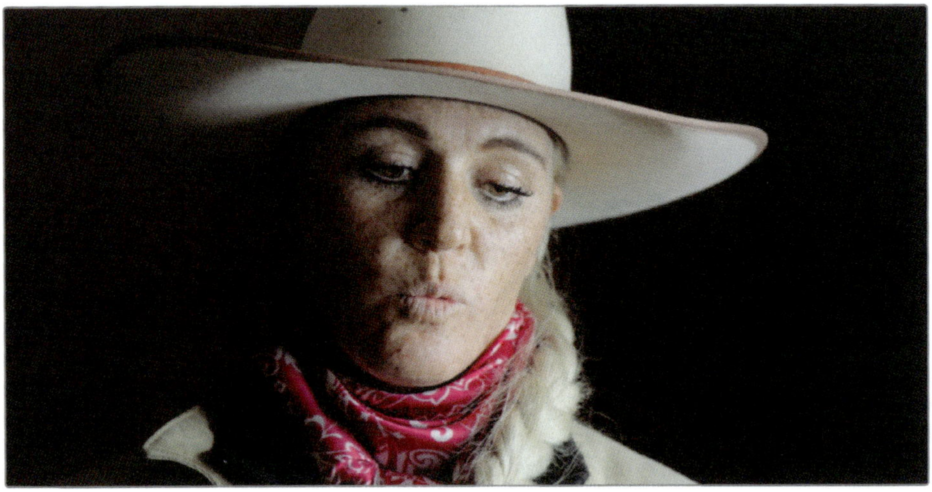

We'll first set up the nodes we will need for matching the previous interview shot.

7 Press Option-S (macOS) or Alt-S (Windows) to add a second node and label the node SCARF.

8 Right click over the second node and choose Add Node > Add Outside.

9 Label the outside node OUTSIDE.

Now we will copy over nodes form the previous interview.

10 Select clip 08 , select node 02 then press Cmd-C (macOS) or Ctrl-C (Windows).

11 Select clip 14 and select the SCARF node.

Instead of pasting the node directly, you can copy and paste only the properties you need.

12 Choose Edit > Paste Attributes.

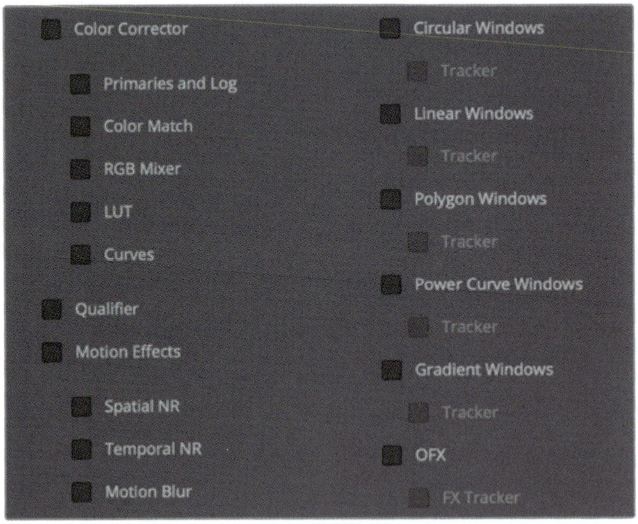

13 In the Attributes window select Qualifier and Power Curve Windows.

Selecting only these two items will ensure we do not copy over the tracking data, since she moves differently in this new interview shot than in the previous one.

14 Click Apply at the bottom of the window to paste the selected attributes.

The outside node is simpler since we want the entire node's changes.

15 Select clip 08 , select node 03 then press Cmd-C (macOS) or Ctrl-C (Windows).

16 Select clip 14 , select the OUTSIDE node, then press Cmd-V (macOS) or Ctrl-V (Windows).

The last piece is to just adjust and track the window on the new shot.

17 Select the SCARF node and adjust any of the control points so they fit more precisely around the scarf.

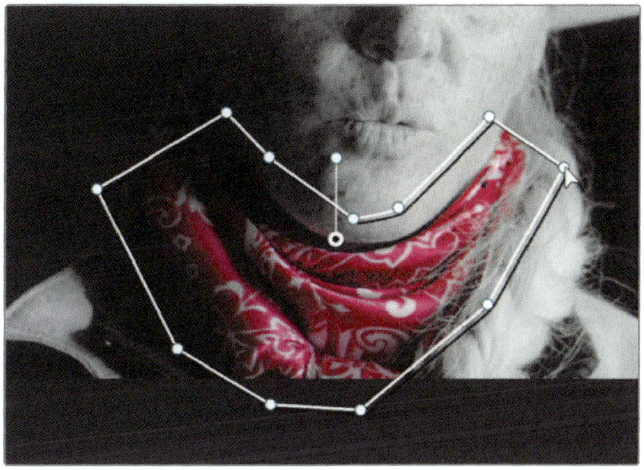

18 Select the tracker palette, make sure you are on the first frame of the clip and click the track forward button.

The tracker is a commonly used tool, most often when tracking windows for secondary color corrections. As simple as it is to use, it is a very advanced palette that can handle many tasks.

Stabilizing a Clip

Tracking is the process of analyzing motion in a clip and using that motion analysis to follow an element in the frame. That process can also calculate the camera motion in a clip. The color page's tracker can perform double duty: not only can it track movement, it can also stabilize clips.

1 Select thumbnail number 13, and play the clip.

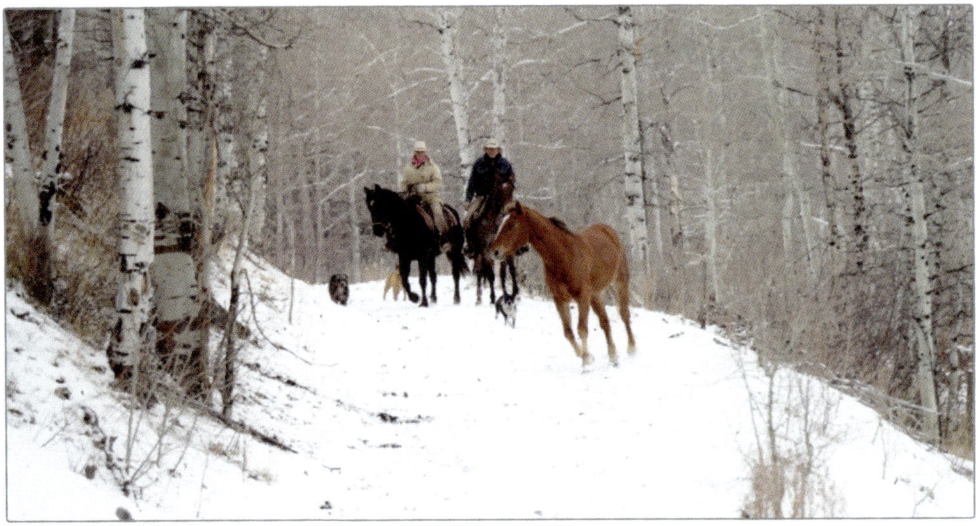

This is a nice shot but unfortunately the camera is a bit too shaky. You can use the stabilizer to either lock down the shot and remove all camera motion, or leave the general camera move but smooth out the motion. For this shot we would like to keep that hand held feel but smooth out the movement.

2 In the pop- up menu in the upper-right corner of the Tracker palette, choose Stabilizer.

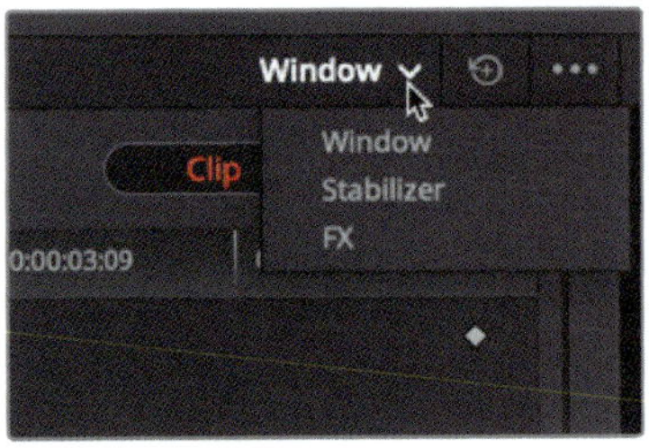

The Tracker palette now switches from tracking to stabilizer mode.

Like Cut and Edit page functionality, the Color page Stabilizer works without setting any points, which can be beneficial when you just need to perform a quick stabilize operation.

3 In the upper-right corner of the Tracker palette, click the Stabilize button to begin the motion analysis.

4 Once the analysis is complete, press the spacebar to view the smoother motion.

Although that worked well, it isn't as smooth as we would like it. You can make adjustments to the stabilizer using the Smooth setting at the bottom of the tracker panel.

5 Change the smooth setting to 0.75 to increase the amount of smoothing

6 Click the stabilize button again, then play the clip.

The stabilized clip is scaled a bit to fill the frame. Any time you stabilize a shot, the clip must move up and down, as well as side to side, to offset the camera movement in the shot. Moving the clip in this way obviously makes the edges of the clip visible as they move in and out of the viewer. To avoid this effect, the clip is automatically scaled until the edges are no longer seen. How much scaling is applied depends on how much camera movement is removed from the shot.

> **TIP** To see the amount of motion applied to the clip, you can deselect the Zoom checkbox at the bottom of the Tracker palette, and play the clip.

Understanding how to use tools such as the qualifiers, Power Windows, and the tracker palette enables you to perform secondary color grading with substantial control over the final look of your image. However, it is only when you combine these tools that their true potential is unlocked.

Lesson Review

1 What happens when you click the highlight button in the upper-left corner of the Color page viewer?

2 True or false? When isolating a color, the Color page qualifier is based on the Hue component.

3 In the Color page, what does an outside node do?

4 True or false? In the Color page, you can use a Power Window to select an area based on a spline shape or a luminance value.

5 When Stabilizing a clip you first draw a power window around the area you want to stabilize?

Answers

1. Clicking the Highlight button above the Color page viewer displays pixels that are selected by a qualifier or Power Window. These selected areas are displayed with their normal colors and will be affected by any color adjustment. Non-selected areas are displayed as gray pixels and will not be affected by color adjustments.
2. False. The default qualifier is based on Hue, Saturation, and Luminance.
3. The outside node inherits the alpha channel from the node before it and reverses the selection.
4. False. Power Windows select areas based only on spline shapes.
5. No, a window is not required when stabilizing a clip.

Lesson 14

Designing Creative Looks

Now that you're familiar with the primary and secondary tools, you should begin exploring the creative implications of grading. The colors within a scene can influence how your audience should feel. Cold tones denote a brooding character and warm colors tend to signify that everything is going well.

You can also use color to quickly communicate place and time by creating distinct looks for each location and/or time period. Finally, your grading can stylize your project and give it a unique, memorable look.

In this lesson, you will gain an understanding of how to employ these practices as you create, save, and compare three distinct looks.

Time

This lesson takes approximately 30 minutes to complete.

GoalsGoals

Mixing a Black-and-white Shot

When going through the previous lesson you saw that one of the adjustment controls was Sat, or Saturation. This simple setting sets the strength of your colors, allowing you to push them beyond their originally recorded values or to decrease them completely, thereby turning the image to black and white.

In the Color page, you have several methods for turning a color image to black and white. Setting your Sat adjustment control to 0 is the obvious way, but it happens to be the least flexible way.

In the RGB Mixer, you have the option to fine tune the strength of the individual red, green, and blue channels even for a black-and-white image, which can produce stark and interesting results. You'll experiment with this look by creating a new version for it.

1. Open DaVinci Resolve 16, if necessary, and open the Wyoming Ranch project you have been working on.
2. Open the Wyoming Ranch timeline to load it into the viewer.
3. In the timeline, select the last clip, thumbnail 18.

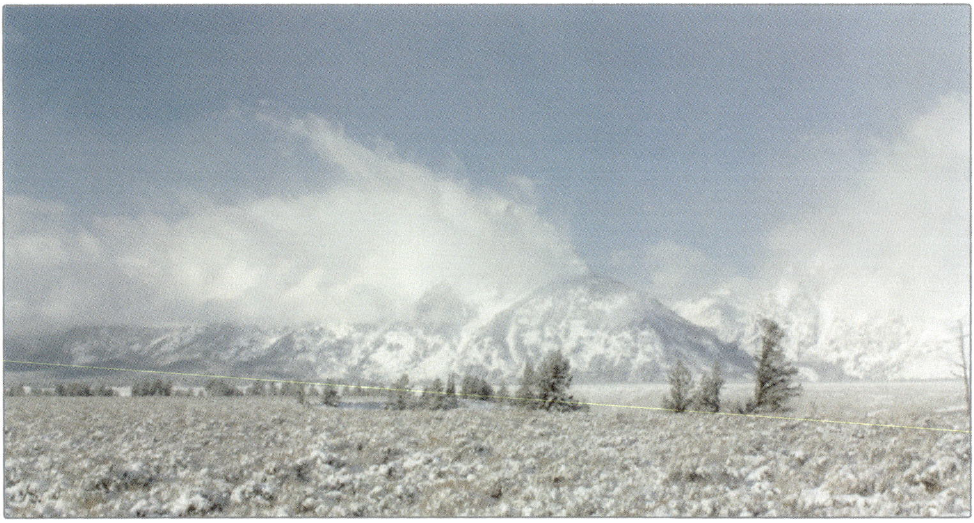

4. Since this clip has not been balanced yet, perform a quick color balance using any of the tools we have used in previous lessons.
5. Label node 01 BALANCED
6. Right click over Node 01 and choose Add Node > Add Serial node or press Option-S (macOS) or Alt-S (Windows)

7 In the toolbar, click the RGB Mixer button to open the RGB Mixer palette.

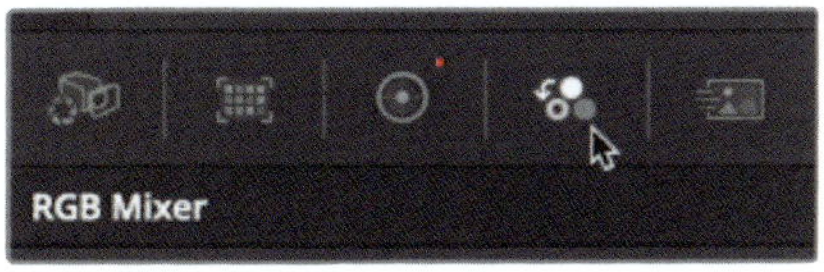

8 At the bottom of the palette, select the Monochrome checkbox.

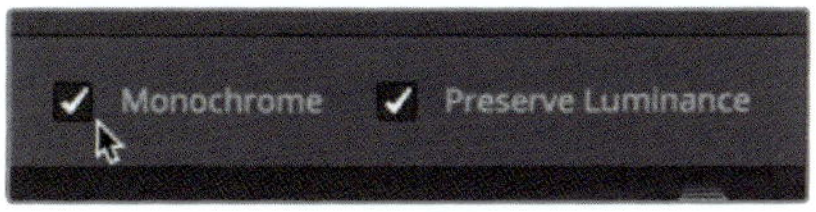

Doing so will turn your image black and white. Many of the controls under the individual red, green, and blue output bars will be dimmed and unavailable. When an image is set to monochrome, you can control only the degree to which red, green, and blue channels contribute to the black and white mix.

9 In the RGB Mixer, on the blue output bar, drag the blue bar up to the top, and then drag it down to the bottom.

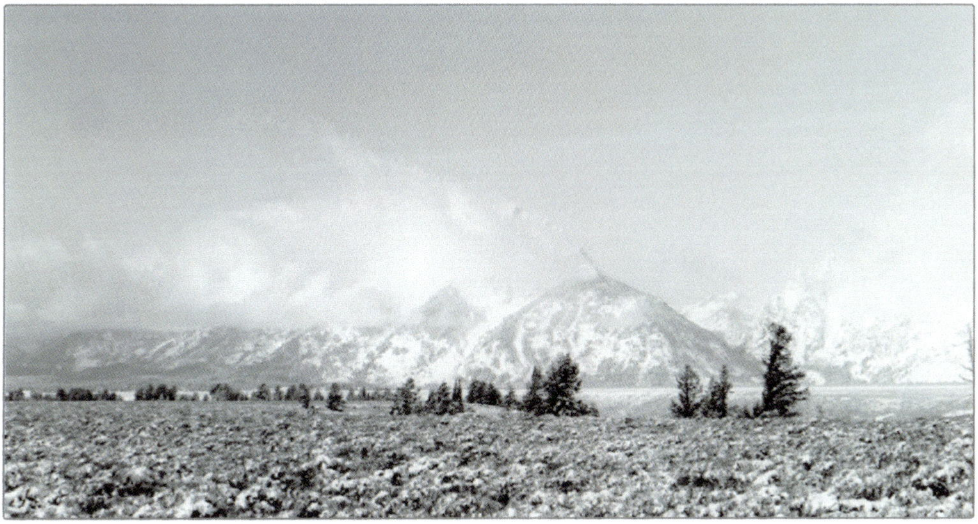

Notice that as you drag, the areas with the higher amount of blue, like the sky are the most affected.

You can repeat this step a few times while keeping your eye on the viewer to see the change.

10 Experiment by dragging the green and red output bars to see how they affect the image.

Notice how strongly some elements are affected when they directly correspond to the channel color. By adjusting the red output, you can make the sky darker since it has no red in it.

11 Set the red output around 0.90, the green output to 0, and the blue output to 0.10 to create a nice high contrast look.

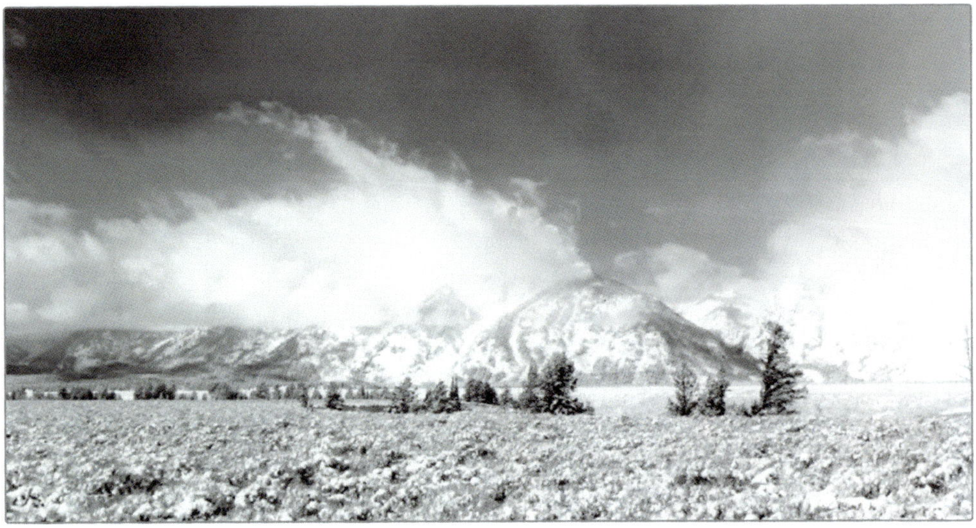

12 Right-click in the viewer, and choose Grab Still to save it to the Gallery.

As you can see, there is no such thing as a single, definitive black-and-white version of your image. Even when the colors are completely desaturated, you can still control the prominence of individual RGB channels. This technique can result in some carefully-crafted, highly dynamic monochrome images.

Using a Look up Table for Quick Looks

With a new look created and saved to the gallery, you can create another look using a look up table. At first glance, look up tables, or LUTs, appear very similar to color correction presets in that they affect the color and luminance of your image with a click of a button. However, look up tables have many uses: they are most often used on-set to give the production crew an idea of what each shot will look like once graded. LUTs can also assist with color space conversions and monitor calibration. They can also sometimes be used like filter effects for creating commonly used looks.

Loading LUTs

DaVinci Resolve comes with a variety of LUTs that you can start using right away. However, one of the strengths of DaVinci Resolve and its LUT workflows is the ability to create custom LUTs and share them with other colorists, as well as adding LUTs created by third-party developers.

You will begin by installing a third-party LUT. For this exercise, let's assume you downloaded a LUT from one of the popular LUT-creation websites.

1 Choose File > Project settings, and in the project settings, click the Color Management category.

2 Click the Open LUT folder button.

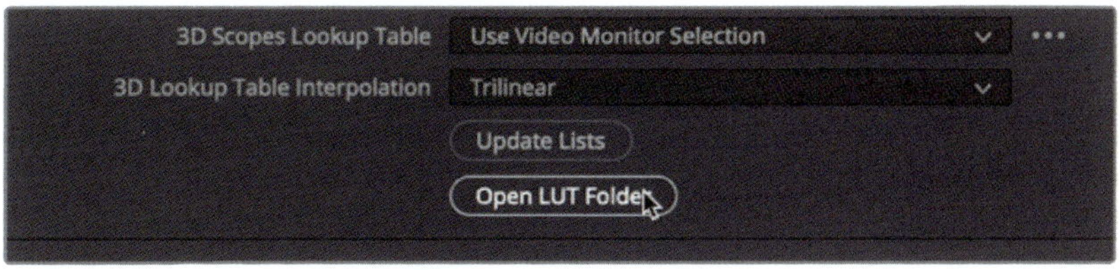

A window opens that contains a list of LUTs and folders of LUT categories.

3 In the window, create a new folder called Training.

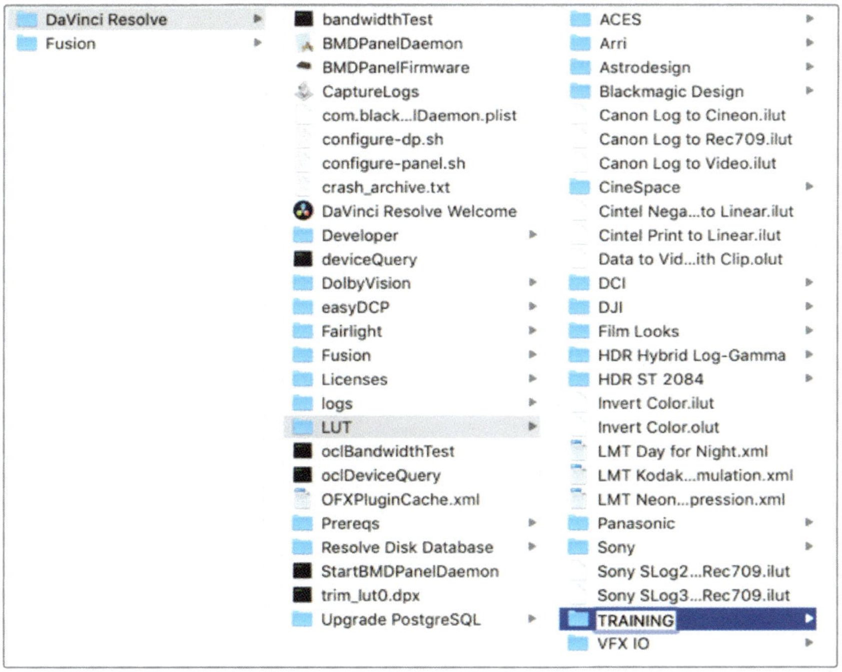

4 Open a second Finder (macOS) or Explorer (Windows) window, and navigate to R16 Intro lessons > Lesson 14.

5 From the Lesson 14 folder, drag the Lesson_14_LUT.cube file into the Training folder.

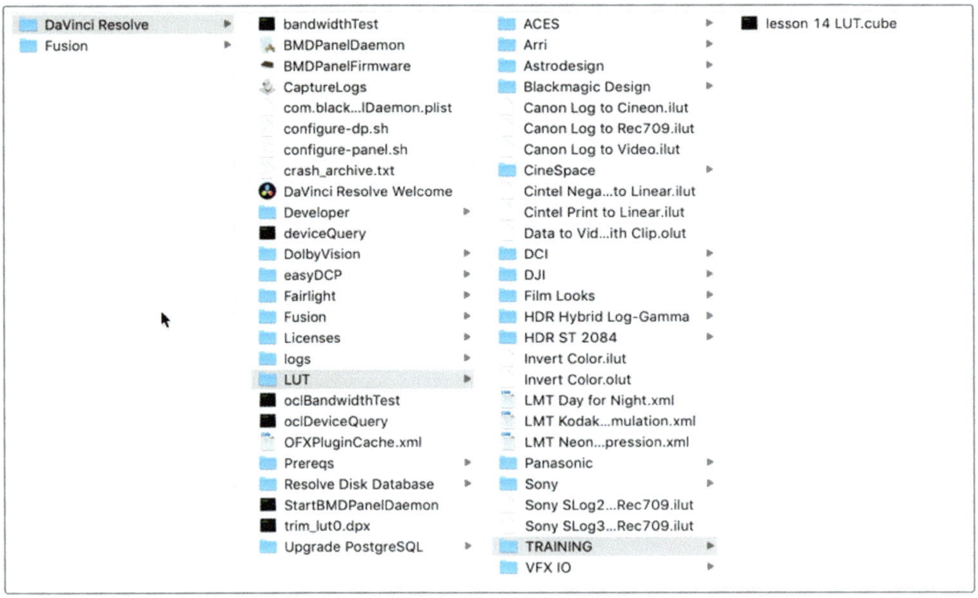

TIP DaVinci Resolve creates and uses LUTs in the DaVinci Resolve .cube format. This is an open LUT format and can be reviewed technically in a simple text editor.

6 Click in DaVinci Resolve, and in the color management project setting window, click Update Lists.

7 In the project settings window, click Save.

You now have a LUT loaded into DaVinci Resolve and you will be able to access it in the LUT browser.

Be cautious when downloading LUTs from third-party sources. Their implementation could result in your content looking very different from the originally intended adjustments. Since Post-production companies are able to generate LUTs that are precisely calibrated to their environments, they are popular for in-house use. However, taken out of those controlled environments and can cause results to vary widely.

LUTs for monitoring

LUTs are commonly used for monitoring on set. They allow you to change how a video signal displays when content is captured on camera. When the signal is captured using a filmic non-linear gamma curve, an HD monitor will display a very flat image with low contrast and saturation. If you apply a LUT to the display or camera view finder it can convert the signal to appear as HD (Rec 709)—the contrast will become much more pronounced, and the colors more saturated. If your project has a specific look, you can even create a custom LUT, save it, and upload it onto a Blackmagic Design camera, where you can shoot the scene while seeing an approximation of how the final footage will look.

The applied in-camera, monitoring LUTs will not alter the footage being captured. It will affect only how the image appears on the camera viewer. When the footage is transferred to DaVinci Resolve, it will still have full grading capacity.

Applying a LUT

Look up tables allow you to quickly recalibrate the way your color pixel data is displayed, essentially providing another form of grading. Conveniently, you can easily apply LUTs once they are installed in DaVinci Resolve.

1. Right click over node 02 and choose Reset Node Grade to remove the black and white look but keep the first balanced node.
2. In the upper left of the User Interface toolbar, click the LUTs button to show the LUT browser.

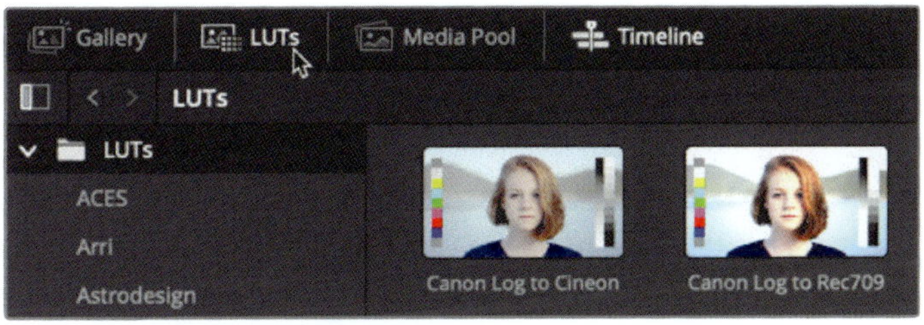

3. In the LUT browser, select the Training LUT category.

   You can preview any LUT by moving your mouse pointer back and forth over any LUT thumbnail in the browser.

4. In the browser, move your mouse pointer back and forth over the lesson 14 LUT thumbnail to preview the LUT in the viewer.

5 Right-click the LUT thumbnail, and choose Apply LUT to Current Node.

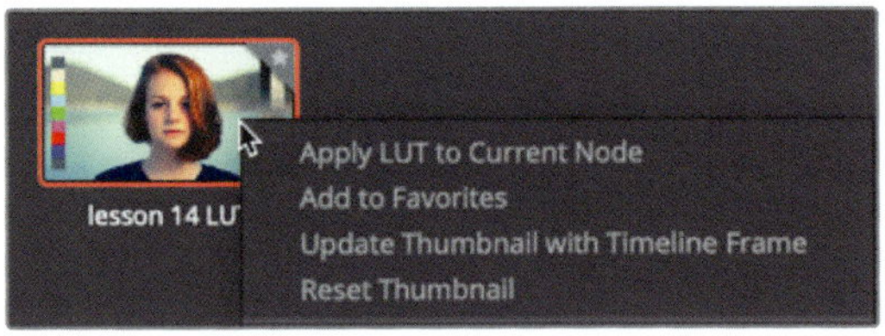

You have now applied the look up table you installed previously. The LUT has changed the look of the clip but as is common with LUTs, it has also clipped the highlights. It is up to you to bring the highlights back and then expand the dynamic range.

> **TIP** LUTs will change the appearance of your clip within a single node. They do not have node structures and do not employ secondary grading practices like qualifiers or windows.

6 Switch from the RGB mixer to the Color wheels palette and drag the Gain master wheel to the left until the top of trace in the parade scope is no longer clipped.

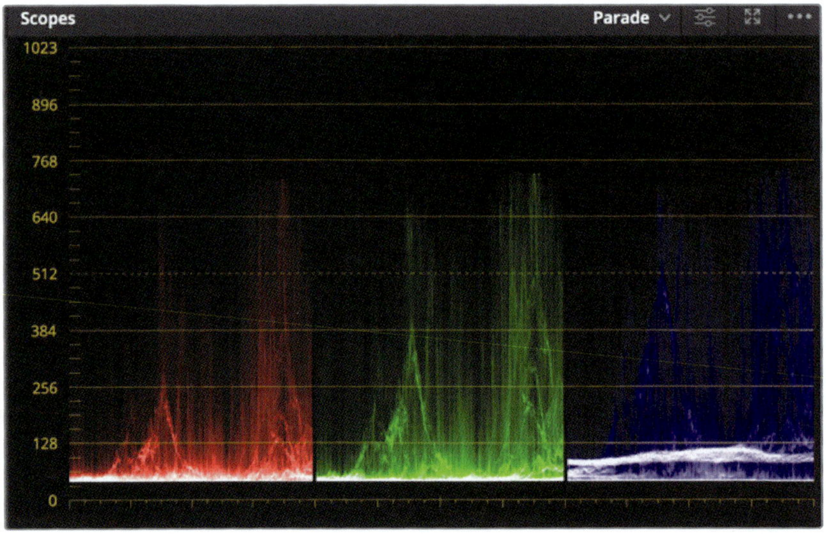

7 Drag the Lift master wheel to the right until the bottom of trace in the parade scope is no longer crushed along the 0 line.

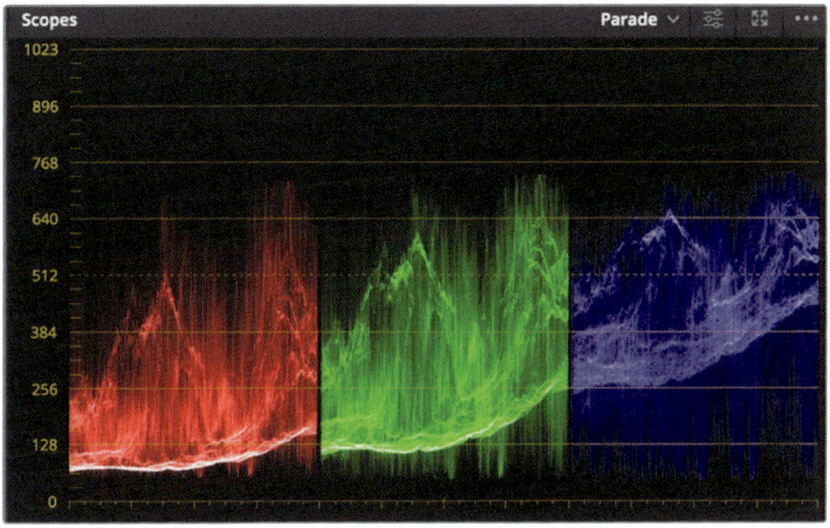

Now that you have the entire image data without any clipping, you can use another node to increase the contrast.

8 Right-click node 02, and in the menu, choose Add Node > Add Serial, or press Option-S (macOS) or Alt-S (Windows).

9 Again using the Gain and Lift master wheels, make adjustments so the highlights top out near the 1023 line and the shadows fall under the 128 line.

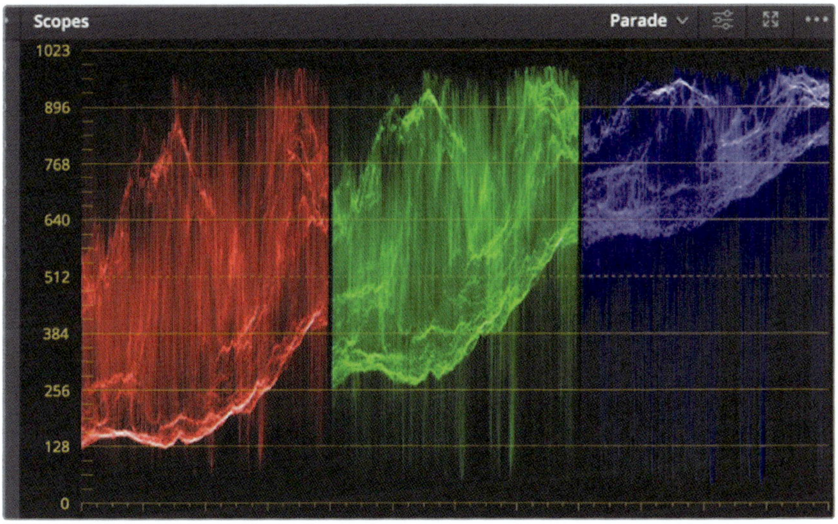

A node with a LUT on it is just like any other node. You can make changes to that node or add nodes after it to make changes.

Saving LUTs

Once you've customized some LUTs, you may want to save them for future use. Instead of saving this look to the Gallery, we'll save it back into the LUT browser.

1 Right-click thumbnail 18, and choose Generate 3D LUT (CUBE).

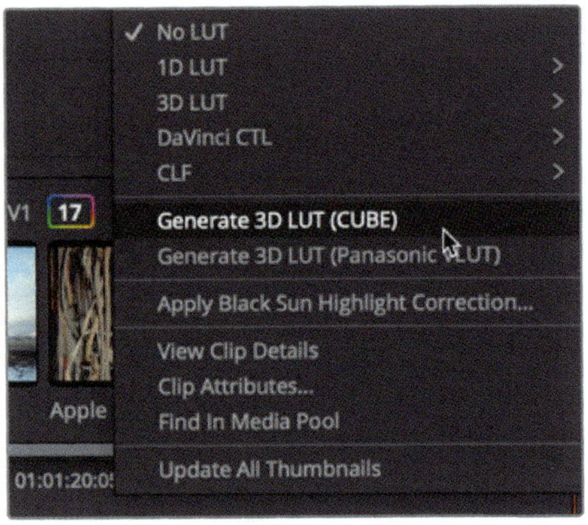

2 In the "Save LUT as" dialog, type the name Cold Air LUT, and save it into the Training LUT folder.

3 Click Save.

> **TIP** If you have difficulty locating where LUTS are saved, use the navigation paths below.
> macOS: Library/Application Support/Blackmagic Design/DaVinci Resolve/LUT
> Windows: C:\Program Data\Blackmagic Design\DaVinci Resolve\Support\LUT

You have now generated a LUT based on the configuration of your pixel color data

The LUT you created appears in the LUT browser.

In this exercise, you used look up tables to create a look for a clip. However, in DaVinci Resolve you can use LUTs in many parts of your image-processing workflow. You can add them to every clip and to the output of every timeline instead of using Resolve Color management, or just to your viewer or video monitor.

Creating a Bleach Bypass

In this exercise, you'll create a bleach bypass look for the same shot.

The bleach bypass process, sometimes called a silver retention or ENR process, is a low-saturation, high-contrast look. It stems from a film development process in which the bleaching stage was, well, bypassed. It can be seen in many television shows and films including Reds, Saving Private Ryan, and Seven.

1 Right click over node 02 and choose Color > Reset Node Grade to remove the LUT look and delete node 03 from the node editor.

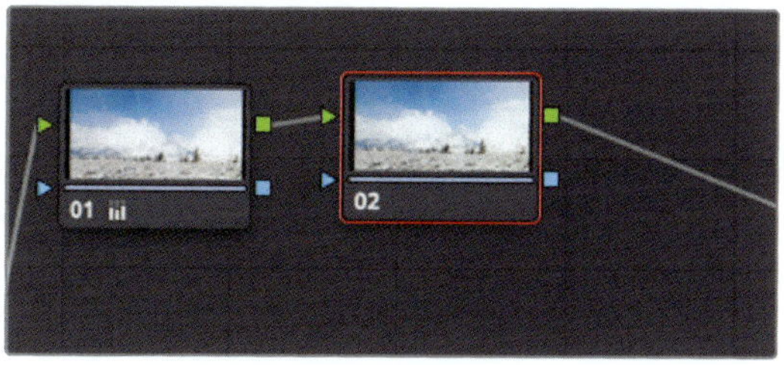

The bleach bypass look uses a low color saturation. So, you will start by decreasing the saturation using the shared controls under the master wheels.

2 In the shared adjustments controls of the Color wheels palette, lower the Sat value to 20.

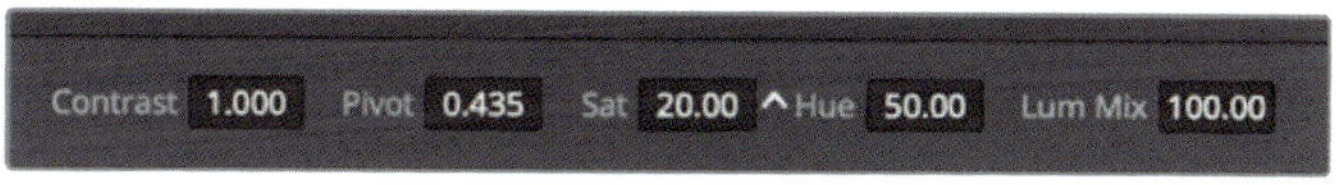

Up to this point, you have used the custom curves only to modify the black and white points and balance color. For this bleach bypass look, you'll use it to increase contrast.

3 In the toolbar, click the custom curves button and choose Custom from the pop up menu if the custom curve palette is still set to an HSL curve.

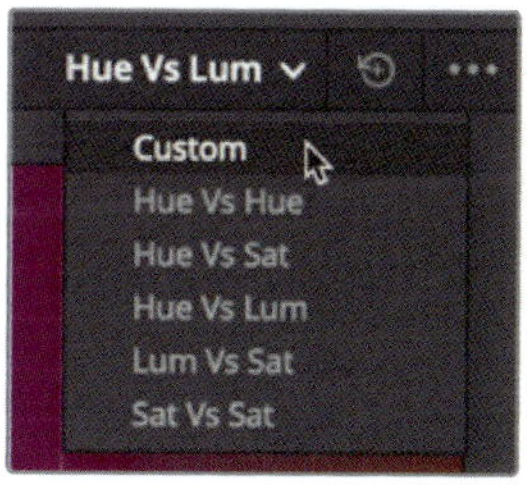

You can increase contrast using the custom curve palette by adding two control points to the curve: one point in the lower shadows area and one in the upper highlights.

4 Click the Y button to control only the luminance in this clip.

5 Click on the curve line about one-third of the way up from the bottom of the line to add a point to manipulate the shadows.

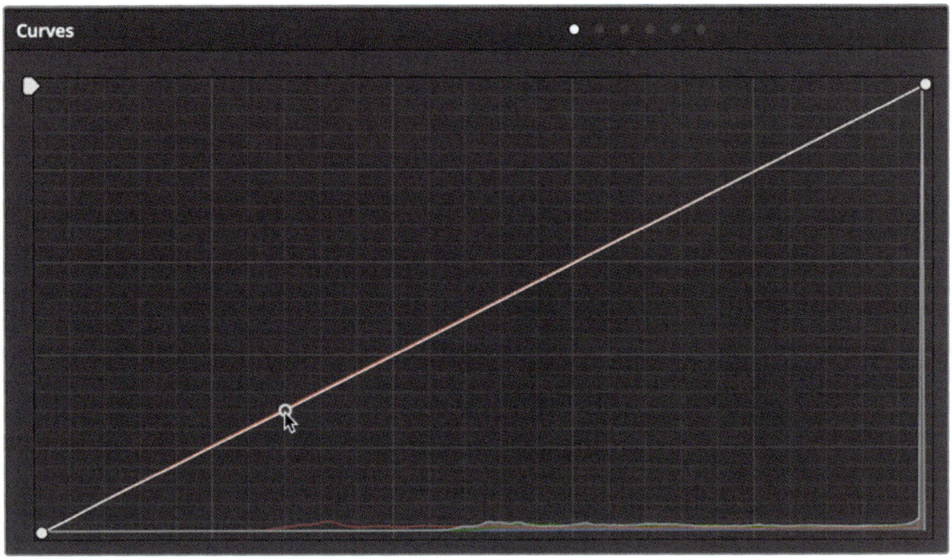

6 Click the curve line about one-third of the way down from the top of the line to add a point to manipulate the highlights

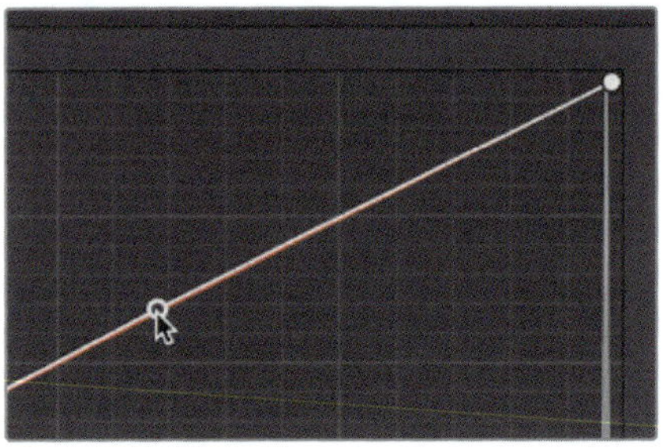

7 Drag down the lower control point until it reaches the first grid line to condense the shadows.

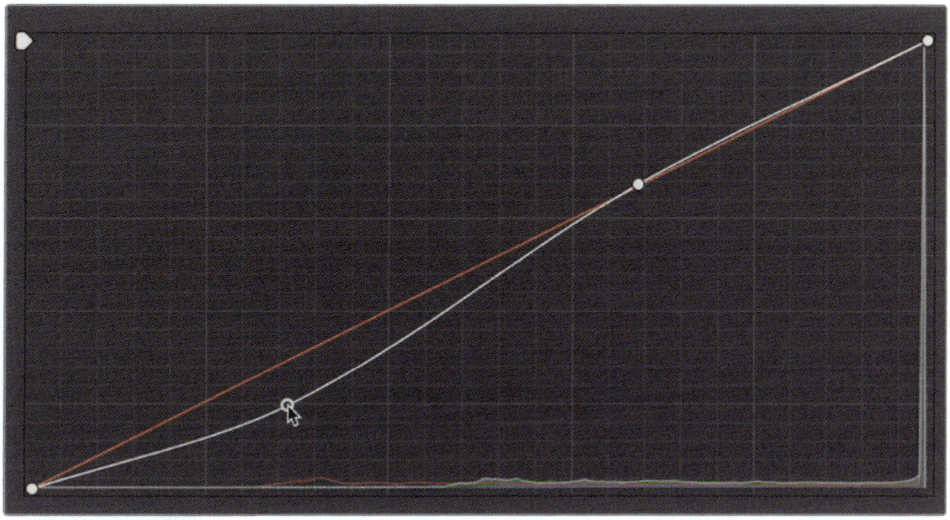

8 Drag up the upper control point until it reaches the grid line above it to condense the highlights.

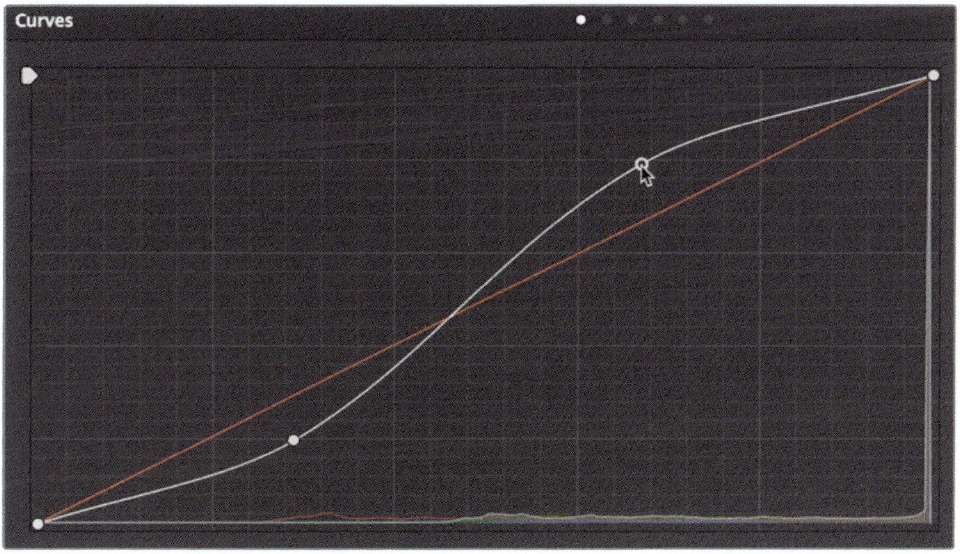

9 Right-click in the viewer, and choose Grab Still.

Moving both points into this S-shaped curve adds more contrast to your shot and produces a very simple bleached bypass look when combined with the low saturation.

Understanding additive color

What color do you get when you mix all the colors of the rainbow?

Some people will think of how light refracts from a prism and say that every color combined produces white. Others pause and think about what happens when you mix all the colors in your paint palette, resulting in a colorless gray sludge.

However, the true answer depends on whether you are treating colors in an additive or subtractive sense. Subtractive colors are used in painting and print mediums. Additive color is used in light-based mediums such as sunlight, stage lights, or computer screens.

Because grading is performed using a computer screen, it uses an additive color system; however, when grading, you think about color design in a subtractive system.

For instance, in a subtractive color space, complementary colors produce aesthetically pleasing combinations, so you tend to create looks using these complementary colors. But when it comes to grading, complementary colors combined on an additive color wheel will neutralize one another. Adding blue to yellow will produce white (or some variety of gray). This is a vital principle to understand for color correction workflows.

Saving Grades Across Projects

You will often want to access your previous grades when working on new projects.

A common reason could be that your work is episodic and requires a similar stylistic look from one episode to the next. Or, you might just like a specific grade you've created and want to use it again and again.

Previously, you used the stills gallery to save grades. You will now return to the Gallery to understand how you can share grades across projects.

1. In the upper-left corner of the interface, click the Gallery button to return to the Gallery.
2. In the upper-left corner of the Gallery, click the still albums icon.

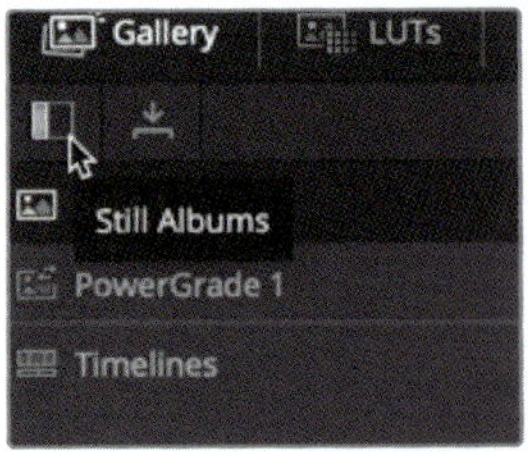

TIP If the resulting stills sidebar list is too narrow to read, drag the divider to expand the sidebar to the right.

In the list panel, you'll find a folder called PowerGrade 1. This folder can store Stills like a regular Gallery album, but the PowerGrade 1 folder is shared across all projects in your system.

3 Drag a still from your stills album into the PowerGrade 1 album.

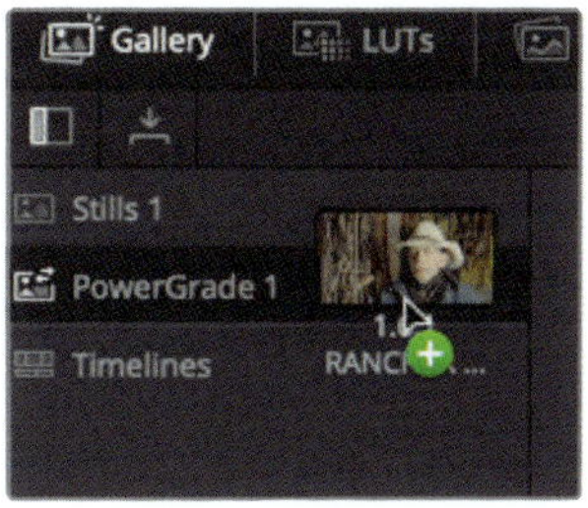

When you open your next project, the Color page will already have this grade present in the PowerGrade1 album.

With an understanding of the color page, you can now quickly assemble a variety of looks using your color-grading skills. You could also employ the use of LUTs, or export your own to share with fellow collaborators. By saving stills of your grades as you progress, you will be able to quickly balance similar shots and create looks that you can reuse in different projects.

Lesson Review

1. How does applying the monochrome adjustment on the RGB mixer differ from desaturating an image?
2. True or false? The merge node combines color corrections in the Color page.
3. Within DaVinci Resolve 16, how do you locate the directory where LUTs are stored on your hard drive?
4. In the Color page, how do you add a node to the Node editor?
5. True or false? In the Color page, you can use the custom curves only to adjust contrast. You cannot adjust the white point or black point using these curves.

Answers

1. Desaturating an image equally lowers the saturation levels of red, green, and blue. When the RGB mixer is set to monochrome, the resulting black-and-white image is created by independently adjusting the luminance of the Red, Green, or Blue channel, thereby yielding a more controllable black-and-white result.
2. False. The merge node is available only in the Fusion page and it is used to combine images.
3. To locate the directory where LUTs are stored, use the Open LUT folder in the Color Management section of the Project settings.
4. To add a node in the Color page, you can choose Color > Nodes > Add Serial node; right-click an existing node in the Node editor, and choose Add Node > Add Serial node; or press the Option-S (macOS) or Alt-S (Windows).
5. False. You can adjust contrast as well as the white point and black point using the custom curves in the Color page.

Lesson 15

Delivering a Final Program

Everybody's workflow is different, and the Deliver page is designed to give you flexible options for creating output from low-resolution editing proxies to the highest quality master files. You can batch render multiple files to multiple resolutions, compression formats, and destinations, all from the same project. With so many different options available on the Deliver page, you might think it would be difficult to learn. But it isn't.

In this lesson, you'll use the Deliver page to create two separate outputs: one for high quality web streaming, and another custom output to create files for visual effects work.

Time

This lesson takes approximately 20 minutes to complete.

Goals

Creating a Web Streaming File

Almost every project ends up on a web-streaming service in some form, even if it's just as promotional material. To output the most common file-based output formats, DaVinci Resolve includes easy setups, presets that automatically configure all the parameters for an output type that you select.

1 In DaVinci Resolve, open the Age of Airplanes project that you worked on in previous lessons.

2 In the Rough Cuts bin, double-click any of the timelines to open one into the timeline window.

   The currently displayed timeline is the one that you will prepare for export on the Deliver page.

3 At the bottom of the DaVinci Resolve window, click the deliver button to open the Deliver page.

   The Deliver page is divided into five areas.

The toolbar buttons switch between file rendering and tape output.

The viewer shows images from the selected timeline.

The Render Queue contains all of the jobs waiting to render.

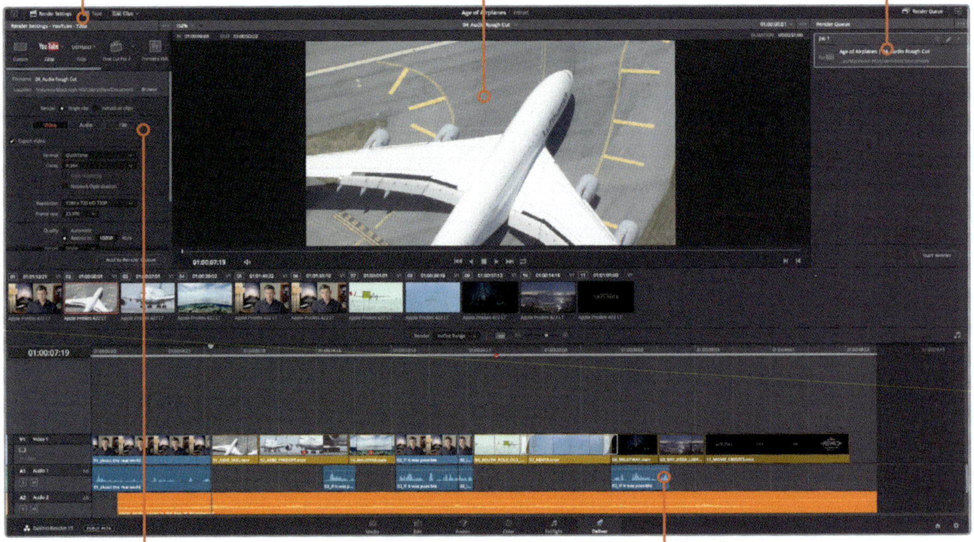

The render settings configure the output format.

The timeline displays a graphical representation of the timeline you are outputting.

You'll use the toolbar to select Render Settings for file-based output. When Render Settings are selected, as they are by default, you can choose a render preset to configure for your output.

4 At the top of the Render Settings, click the Vimeo preset.

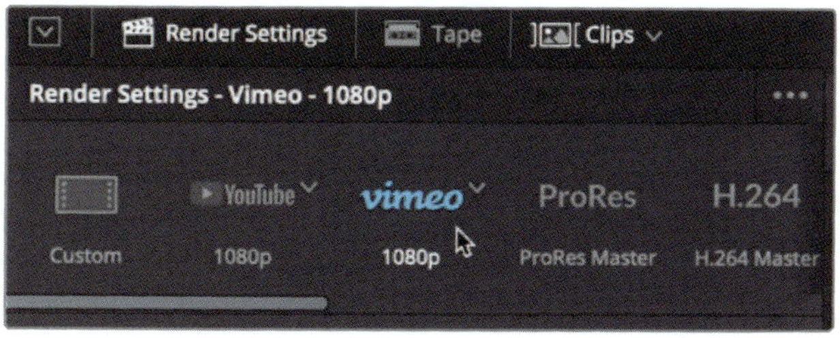

When you choose one of the presets, DaVinci Resolve configures the Render Settings to output a file that conforms to the destination's requirements. If you wanted to stop at this point and output the file, you could do so. The only parameter you would need to set would be the destination of the output file.

5 Just below the row of presets, enter the name of the file you want to create, then click the Browse button, and choose a location for the output file. Click the OK button on the dialog.

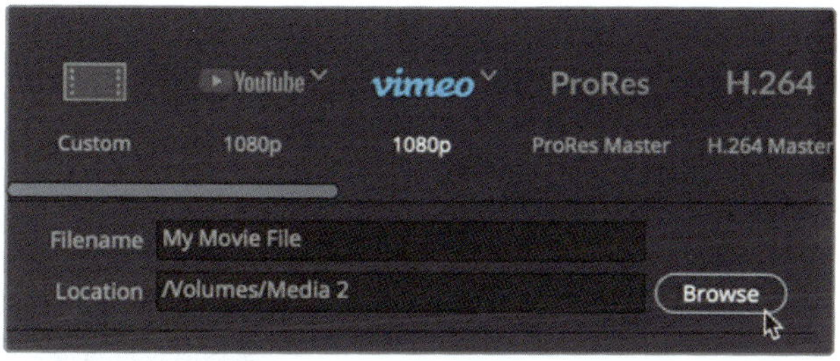

Since you selected a preset, that is all you must do to output a file, but you also have a few options that you can apply to presets.

6 Below the Browse button, set the Resolution to 1280x720 HD 720P since this is the resolution of the current timeline.

Although you can customize the video compression and format parameters in the Video tab, when you choose one of the easy presets many of the basic settings are optimized for you.

When the Vimeo preset was selected, QuickTime H.264 was chosen as the format and AAC Audio codec because those parameters are commonly used for web-streaming videos. The preset also configures the resolution to the current timeline settings.

Both YouTube and Vimeo allow for automatic uploads to the site.

7 Click the Upload directly to Vimeo checkbox.

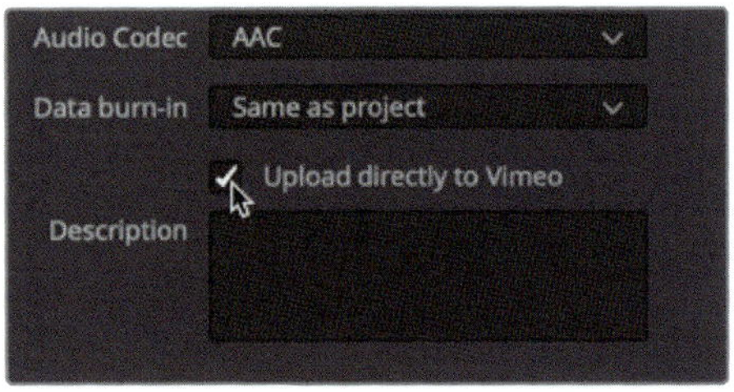

TIP In order for the automatic upload to work, you must enter your YouTube or Vimeo account information in the DaVinci Resolve > Preferences window.

8 At the bottom of the Render Settings panel, click the Add to Render Queue button.

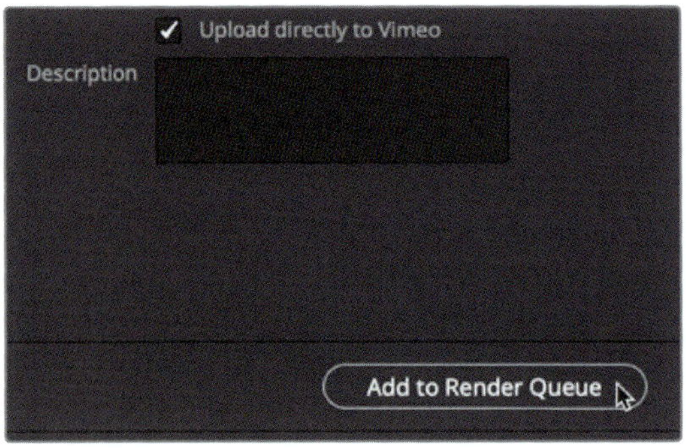

The job is added to the Render Queue on the right side of the window.

The Render Queue acts as a temporary holding area for jobs that you want to output from DaVinci Resolve. You can add as many jobs to the Render Queue as you need to output. Although you could render this file immediately, let's wait and prepare another job for the queue.

Creating a Custom Preset

In some situations, you will need to render out only a portion of your timeline for previews or for others to work on. When you have a few clips that need to be output or used for help in designing 3D visual effects, you will need to render just a section of the timeline and, usually, in a very specific format.

Let's render out a section of the timeline in a format that often is required by 3D animators. They need high-quality renders; but because DaVinci Resolve does not have a 3D animation preset, you'll want to create one of your own, and save it as a preset for later use.

1 At the top of the Render Settings, click Custom.

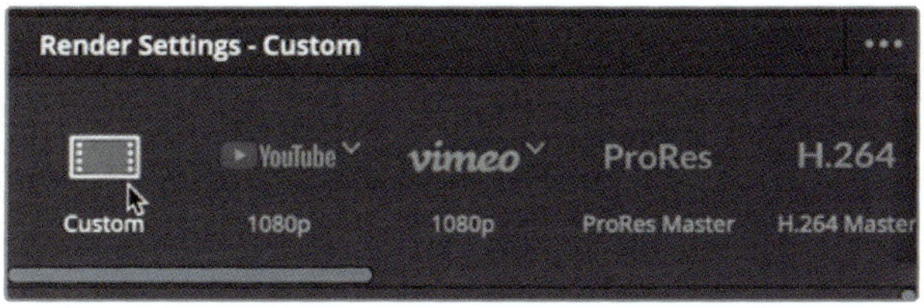

Clicking Custom makes all of the options in the Render Settings available for selection, and begins the process of creating a new preset. First, you can decide if you want every clip in the timeline to render out as its own individual file or as a single file.

2 At the top of the settings, click the “Single clip” button to output a single movie file.

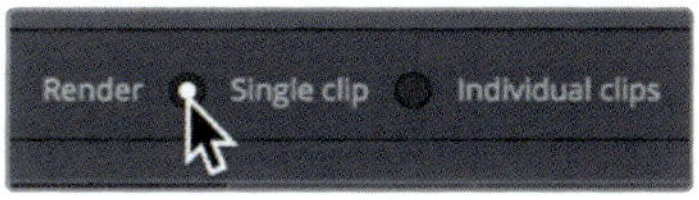

3 Click the Video tab, and in the Video Format menu, choose EXR.

EXR is a single-frame format like TIFF that is often requested by visual effects studios.

Because EXR files do not have audio tracks, you can skip the Audio tab and go to the File tab

4 Click the File tab to name the files.

5 Enter the Custom name, **Airplane VFX**.

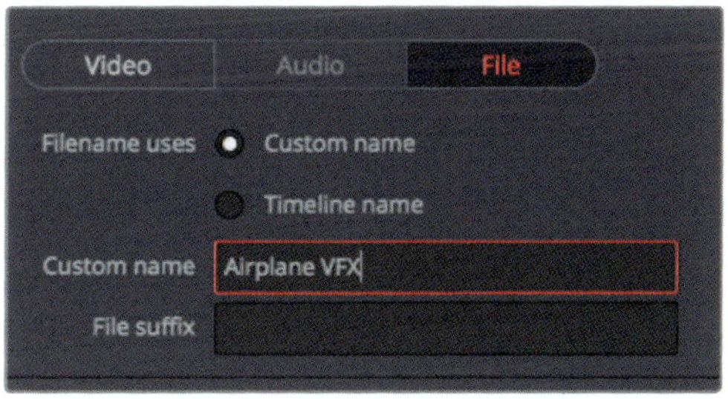

Because each frame will become an EXR file, you need to number the frames so that the visual effect artist will know the order in which the frames should appear.

6 Set “Use # digits in the filename” to 4.

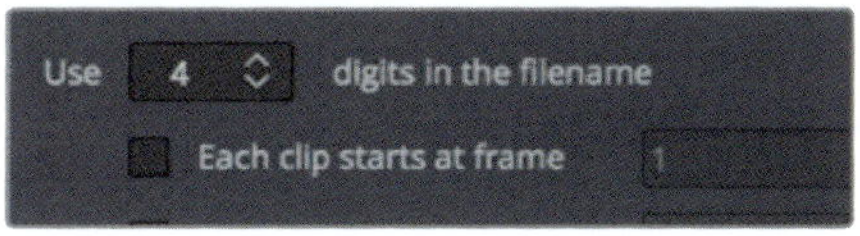

This value will add four numeric digits to the end of each file. None of our shots are over 1000 frames long so four digits should be plenty.

7 Select the “Each clip starts at frame” checkbox, and in the numeric field, enter **001**.

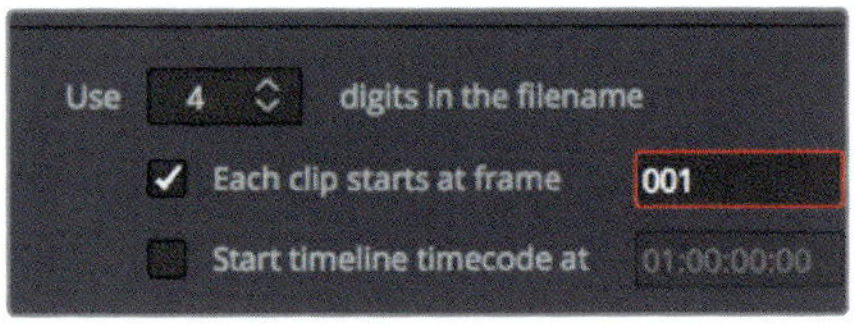

Next, because you want to send only one shot from your timeline to the VFX staff, you need to mark the range you want to render.

8 In the Deliver page timeline, move the playhead over the 08_SOUTH_POLE_DC3 clip.

9 Choose Mark > Mark Clip, or press X, to add in and out points around the South Pole clip.

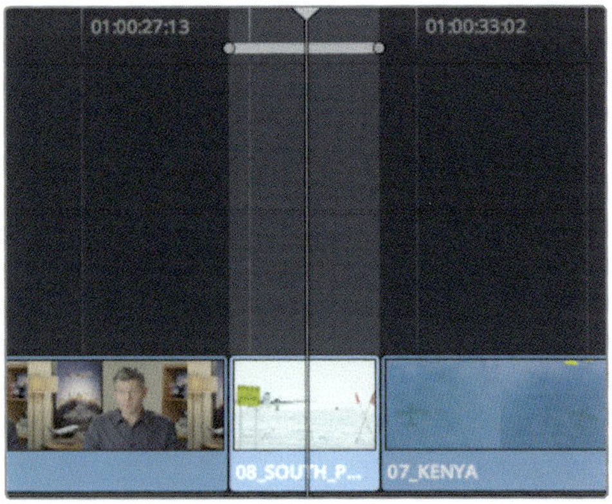

The marks in the timeline identify the region that you will render out. You can now save these settings as your own customized VFX preset.

Adding a Watermark

You can add a text-based watermark, similar to a title, that overlays the video. Most often this watermark is used to superimpose a “Do Not Distribute” text or to display a running timecode. The watermark is created and formatted using the Data burn-In controls.

1 At the top of the Render Settings, return to the Video tab.

2 Scroll down and click the “Advanced settings” disclosure arrow.

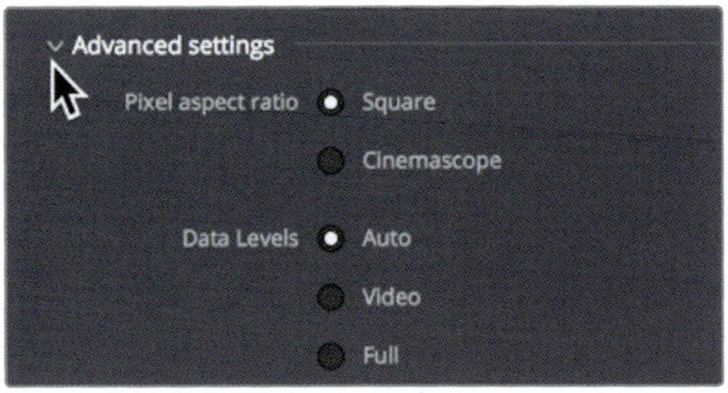

3 Set the "Data burn-in" pop-up menu to "Same as project".

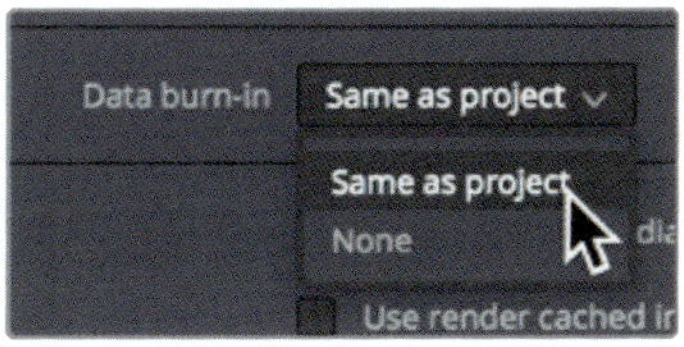

The Burn-in controls can be accessed from any page.

4 Choose Workspace > Data Burn-In to open the Data Burn window.

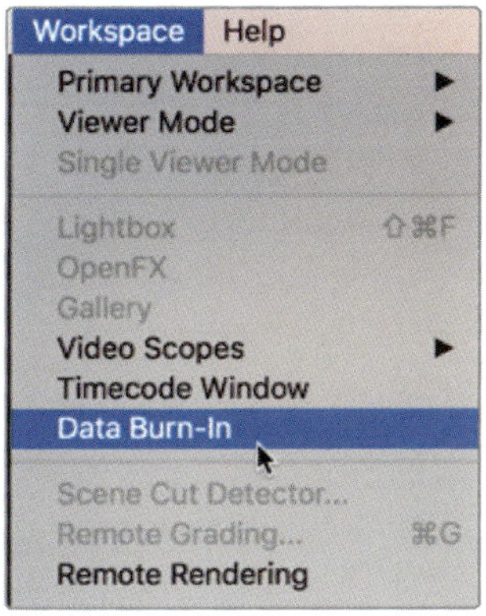

The left side of the Data Burn window includes a list of possible data types to overlay on the video. Selecting the checkbox next to any option enables it.

5 In the list of burn-in data, select the Record Timecode checkbox to overlay the record timecode on the output movie file.

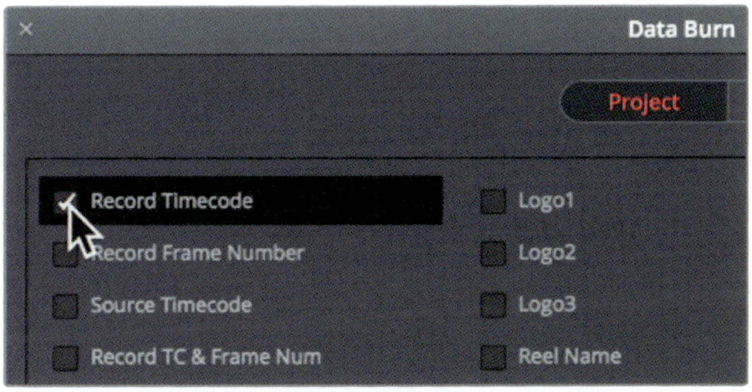

6 Select the Custom Text1 checkbox to add a text watermark.

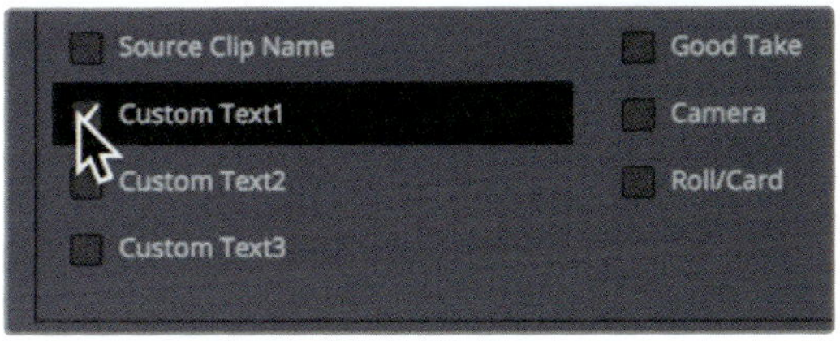

7 In the Custom Output Text field, enter **DO NOT DISTRIBUTE**.

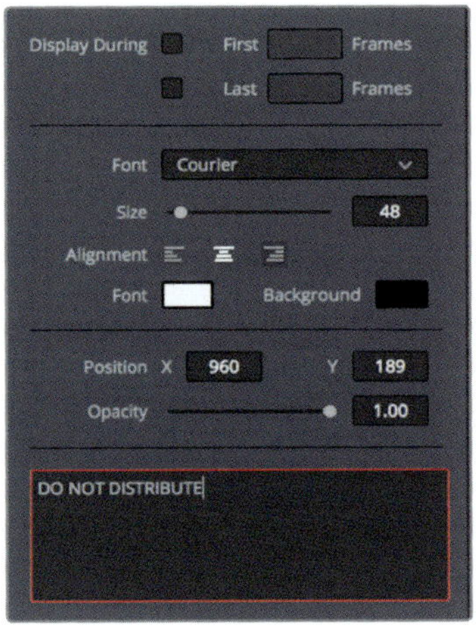

8 Drag the Size slider to the right to increase the text size to 55.

The viewer displays all the changes to the Data burn-In settings as you make them. You are now ready to output this vimeo file.

9 Close the Burn window to return to the Deliver page.

Now you can save the Render Settings preset in case you want to reuse it at some point.

10 At the top of the Render Settings, choose Options > Save as New Preset.

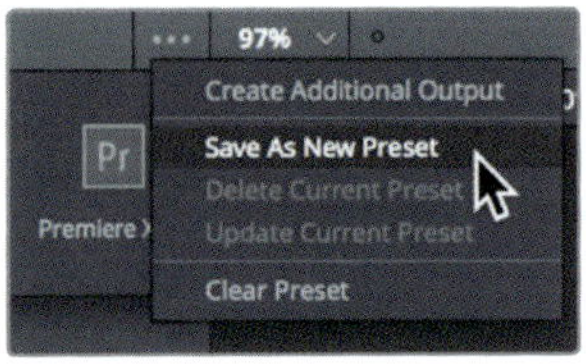

11 In the "Enter preset name" field in the dialog, type **VFX Output**, and click OK.

The new preset's name appears at the top of the Render Settings, indicating that it is the currently active setting. It also is listed in the row of presets.

With all of the settings configured, you can add this job to the Render Queue.

12 At the bottom of the Render Settings, click the Add to Render Queue button to add your second job.

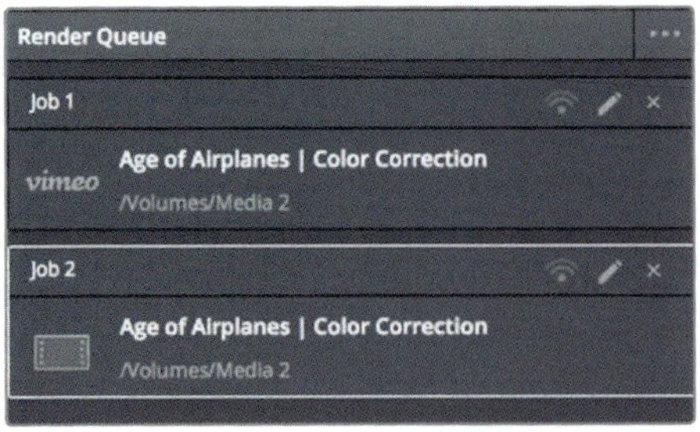

You now have two jobs in your Render Queue. If you save and quit DaVinci Resolve now and return later, those jobs will still be in the Render Queue. Because you may not want to devote disk space to these lesson results, you won't be expected to render them for this exercise.

13 When you do want to render one of your own projects, in the Render Queue, select the items that you want to render. Then click the Start Render button at the bottom of the Render Queue to begin the process. One by one, the jobs will render out and be marked as completed.

14 What you will find useful right now is knowing how to clear the Render Queue. In the upper-right corner of the Render Queue, click the Options pop-up menu.

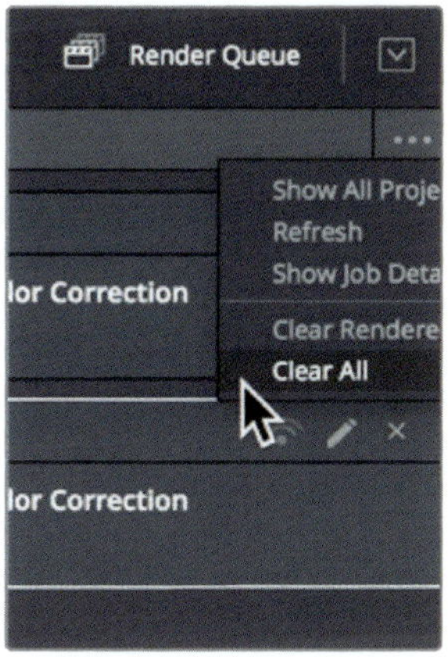

15 In the menu, choose Clear All to remove all the current jobs from the queue.

The Deliver page has many more options for outputting various file formats, and for supporting a variety of workflows; but you now understand the most commonly used workflows and how to set up your own custom presets

Lesson Review

1 In DaVinci Resolve, how do you add a watermark to a video?

2 What two online services have presets available in Resolve's Deliver page?

3 True or False, choosing the YouTube or Vimeo presets displays the most common options for creating movie files for those two online sharing sites?

4 Where would you save a customized preset for future use on the Deliver page?

5 After adjusting the Render Settings, how do you instruct Resolve to output a movie file?

Answers

1. Choose Workspace > Data Burn In.
2. YouTube and Vimeo are the two online services which have presets in the Deliver page Render Settings
3. True. Presets provide the most common options. To view all the options available, click the Custom render setting.
4. To save a custom preset on the Deliver page, in the Render Settings option menu (the three dots in the upper-right corner), choose Save as New Preset.
5. To begin rendering, click the Add to Render Queue button; and then in the Render Queue panel, click Start Render.

Lesson 16

Managing Media and Databases

Unlike almost all other editing, audio mixing, or color grading software, DaVinci Resolve uses an industry-standard database to store all of your projects, bins, clips and timelines-basically any item that is not an audio or video media file is kept in the database. As a result, DaVinci Resolve works a little differently from other apps when you want to move projects from one system to another or create backups of your projects. It is not any harder to do those things, and in some cases it can be a lot easier. But it is different.

In this lesson, you will explore ways to back up and move projects and media, as well as learn how to manage the DaVinci Resolve database.

Time

This lesson takes approximately 20 minutes to complete.

Goals

Consolidating Media

NOTE The following exercise uses a second hard drive for consolidating media. It is not recommended that you perform these steps on this project. However, you are urged to read through the lesson to gain an understanding of the process.

Before we explore database management, let's start with a topic that is a bit more down to earth: media management.

Almost every project will need some kind of media management. It might be just to copy media from one drive to another, or to convert files from one format to another. The media manager is the tool that performs these types of tasks in DaVinci Resolve. You can use it to copy, move, and even consolidate media.

When your hard drive cannot accommodate a complete copy of the original media, consolidating can help remove media that is no longer needed in your project. Using the media manager, consolidating gives you the option to copy only those pieces of media that are actually in use. For long-form projects with lots of media, consolidating is a great way to free up disk space and make backing up a project a quicker task.

Because the media manager can be used only when you are within a project, we will use the Age of Airplanes project.

1 With Age of Airplanes still open, click the Media page button; and in the Media pool, click the Rough Cuts bin. Select all the timelines.

2 Choose File > Media Management.

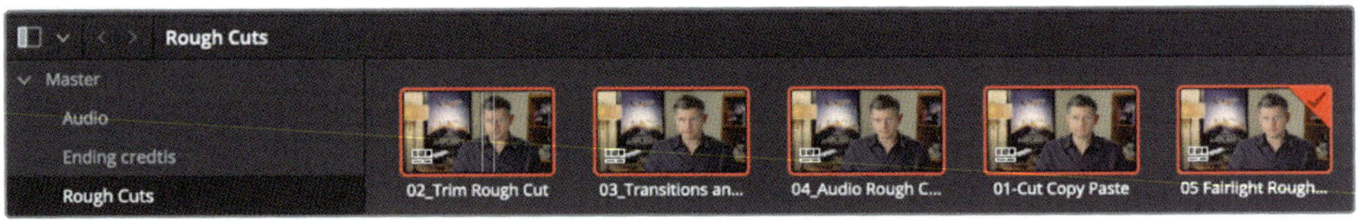

When timelines are selected, the Media Management window opens with the Timelines button selected.

3 Click the Copy button.

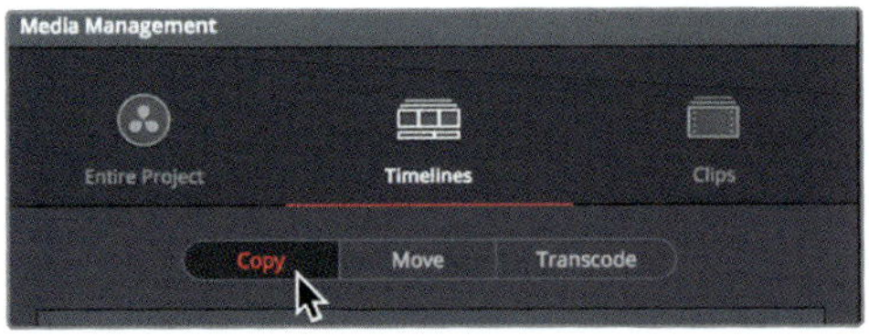

Choosing Copy first creates a duplicate set of media files on the portable hard drive, but leaves the originals in place.

4 Click the Browse button, and in the File Destination dialog, navigate to a location where you want to copy the media. Click OK.

> **TIP** You can click the New folder button to create a folder for the consolidated files that you create. If you don't do so, you might end up with too many files on the top level of a hard drive and no way to know which files to keep and which to delete.

The option to consolidate media requires that you select one or more timelines to determine which files to keep. You have two choices for consolidating your media: you can choose to copy the clips that you have used in the selected timelines in their entirety, or to copy just the portions of those clips that you have used in the selected timelines (including handles).

5 Choose "Copy and trim used media keeping".

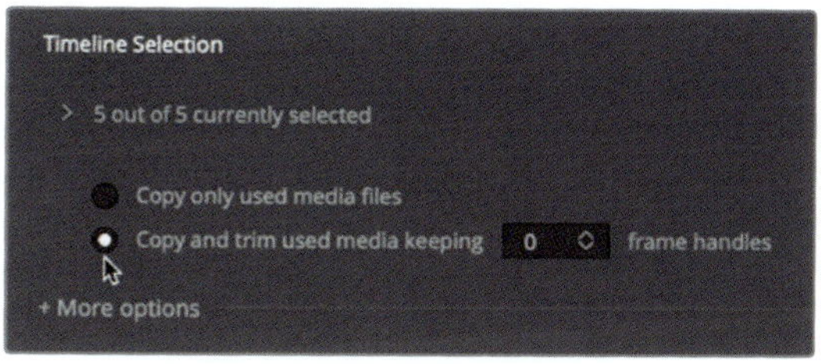

Choosing this option will trim the master clip files down to only those clip portions used in the selected timeline(s). A field is available in which you can enter the number of frame handles you would like added to each side of a clip in case you will later need to trim or create transitions.

> **TIP** Compression formats that use interframe, temporal compression, such as H.264, can now be used with the "trim unused media" option in the Media Management window.

6 Enter **12** as the number of frame handles to add. Because your project runs at 23.979 frames per second, entering this value this will enable a half-second of extra media on both ends of the clip for trimming and transitions.

7 Click "More options" to view additional settings.

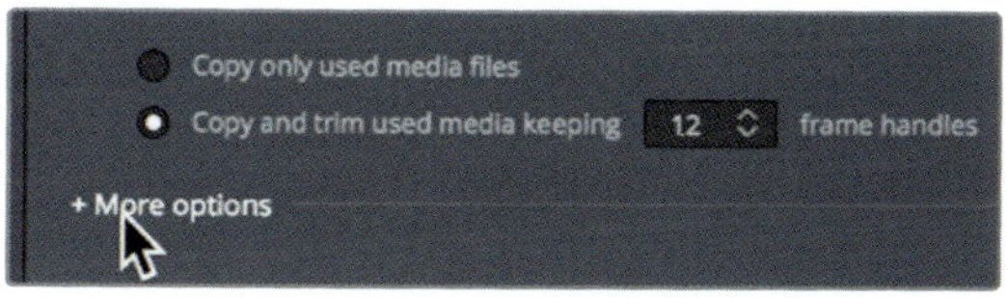

8 Select "Relink to new files" to use the new, copied media in the timeline instead of the existing media.

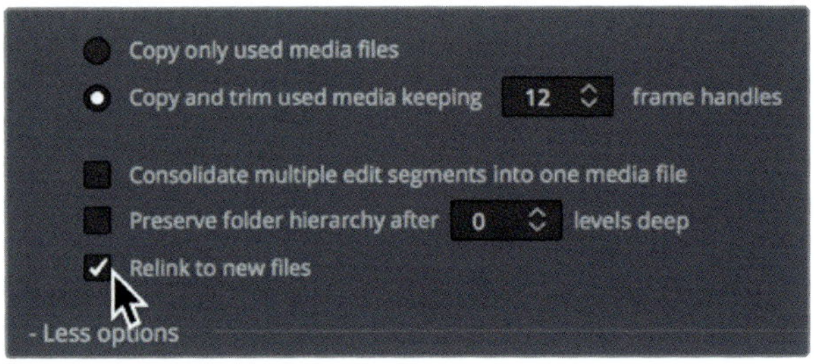

If you were finalizing these steps, you would now click Start to begin consolidating the media, but in this case do not do so.

After you started the consolidation process, the files used in the timeline would be copied to the destination drive, and then trimmed so that only the clip portions in use were saved to disk —along with a half-second handle on each side of a clip.

The clips in your bin would now link to these new, shorter media files, but all of the original clips would still remain in their original locations. It would remain for you to delete them when you were confident that you would no longer need them.

Copying Projects and Media to a New Hard Drive

Although consolidating media can save you the most storage space, it addresses only the media. Your timelines, clips, and metadata are not included. The easiest way to copy, back up, or move a single project and all of its content from one computer to another is to use DaVinci Resolve's archive and restore features. Archiving a project collects all your files (even if they are on different drives) and places them in the destination folder of your choice along with the project file. To archive a project, you must do so using the Project Manager window.

NOTE The following exercises use a second hard drive for copying and transcoding media. If you do not have a second hard drive or do not want to take up valuable disk space by copying and/or moving the training media from this book, you can still read through the lesson to gain an understanding of the process.

1 Open the Project manager, right-click the Age of Airplanes project thumbnail, and choose Export Project Archive.

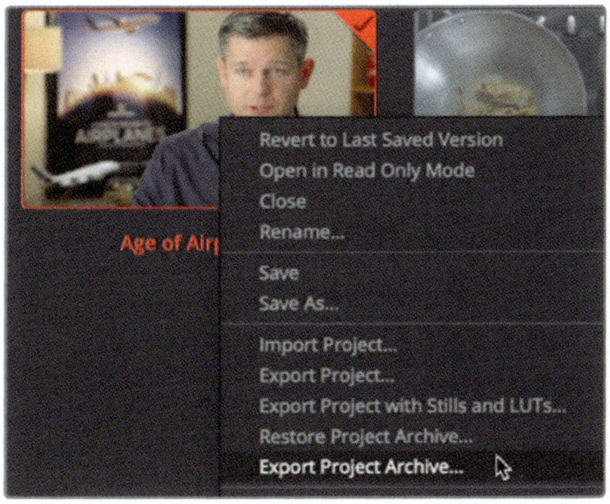

2 In the Archive dialog, navigate to a drive where you want to save the project, and click Save.

All of the media and the project file containing your bins and timelines are copied into a folder with the extension .dra. This folder contains everything you need to open your project on another computer.

Be assured that the original media remains in their original locations, and that the two sets of media are completely identical. It is up to you to decide if you want to delete the original media from those original locations or leave them to work on later.

When you copy the archived folder to another computer, you must restore it in DaVinci Resolve to begin working with it.

NOTE Because you already have the project from the archive on your computer, the following steps are included for educational purposes and are not meant to be followed.

3 To restore an archived project, you open the Project manager.

4 Then, you right-click anywhere in the Project manager, and choose Restore Project Archive.

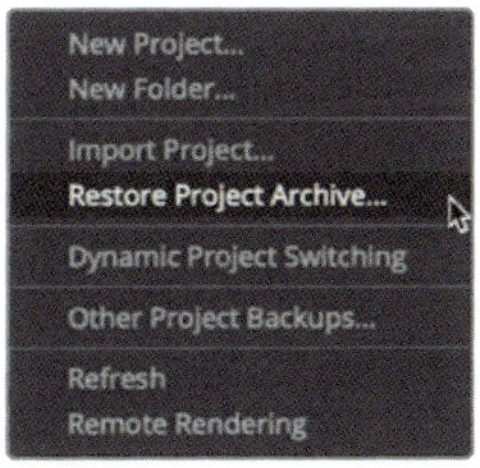

5 In the dialog, you navigate to the ".dra" folder of the archive you want to restore, and click Open.

The archived project opens into the Project manager and you can begin working on it.

Working with the DaVinci Resolve Database

If you want to move or backup all of your projects and timelines, then you must do so within the database. DaVinci Resolve must be open because projects and all their associated bins, clips, and timelines are not independent files that you can find (and freely manipulate) on your hard drive. And while that may suggest a process that is more complicated than you may be accustomed to, it brings a lot of benefits. A database adds a level of organization to your projects without you doing a thing. You don't spend time keeping track of projects and bins because they already exist in the database.

Also, because projects are kept in a database, they can be stored on a server that can connect to multiple DaVinci Resolve workstations with the flexibility to access any project on any computer or work collaboratively on any project.

Creating and Switching Databases

When you first open DaVinci Resolve, it automatically creates a disk database, so it is largely transparent to you that a database is in use. In macOS, the database is stored in the Library folder; whereas in Windows, it is in the Program Data folder. Even though you know where the database is stored, the first rule of databases is to not rename or modify any of the folders or files in a database and certainly not to delete them!

In this exercise, you'll learn the right way to switch between databases, create your own database, and back up a database without ever altering it at the operating system level. You'll start by creating a new database.

1 In the upper-left corner of the Project manager, click the databases button to open the list of available databases.

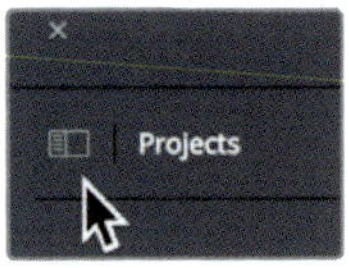

Notice the Local database listed in the sidebar. It is the current default database that DaVinci Resolve created when you first started.

2 Click the New Database button to create a new database.

The New Database dialog gives you two options that are displayed as tabs at the top of the window. You can either Connect to an existing database that you have not previously connected to, or Create a new database. Creating a new database can be useful for organization; for instance, you might create a new database at the start of every year or at the start of each school semester. We'll create a new database as if we are starting a new year.

3 At the top of the New Database dialog, click the Create tab to start creating a new database.

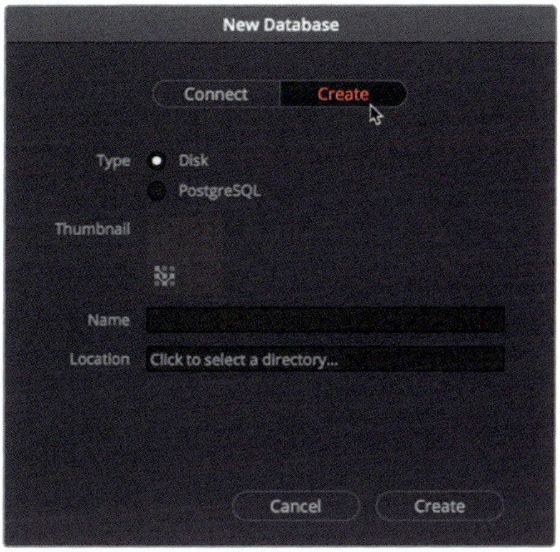

4 In the Name field, enter **resolve101**, and click in the Location field to locate where you want to save the database.

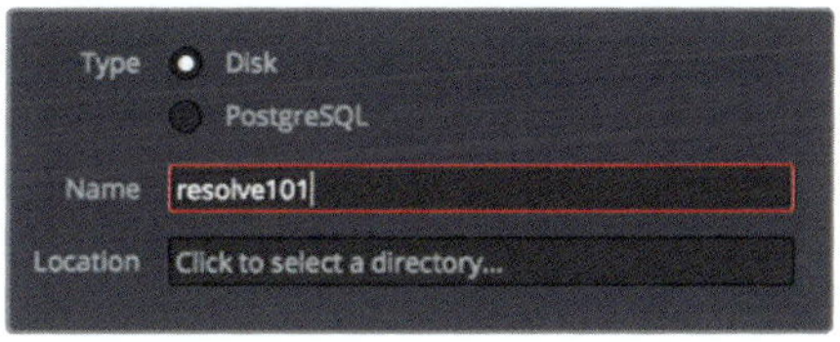

5 Navigate to Documents > 16 Intro lessons > Lesson 16.

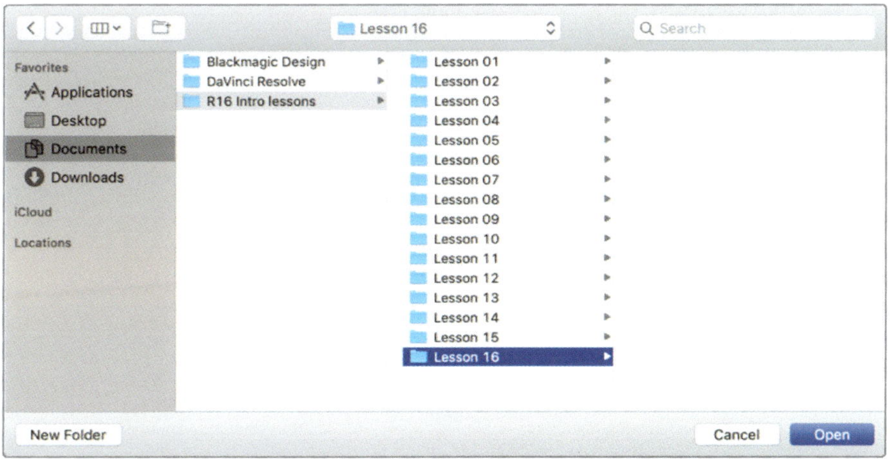

The location is added into the database dialog where you can now add it to DaVinci Resolve.

6 Click Create in the database dialog.

The resolve101 database now appears in your list of disk databases. Clicking any of the databases listed will switch to that database. The newly added resolve101 database is already selected and ready for your new projects.

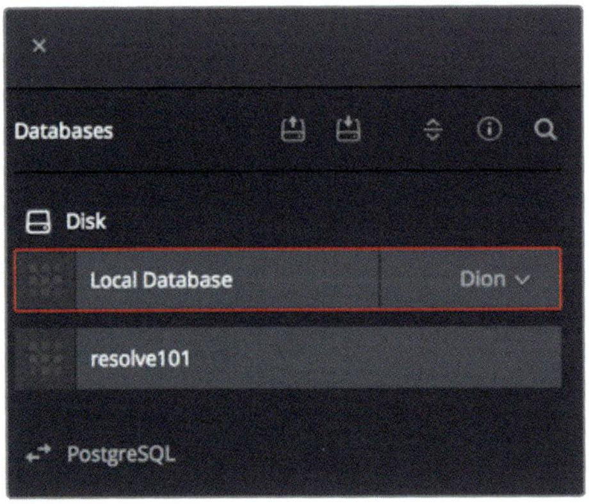

TIP Databases with fewer and smaller projects will save and operate faster than databases with a greater number of large projects.

Backing up Databases

Although databases do not contain media, they do contain all of the metadata for every project. What's more, they also contain all of the timelines for every project you have worked on. So, you'll want to regularly create a backup of that database to prevent your work from being accidently erased or deleted due to a hard drive failure or other mishap. Conveniently, you can back up your database within the databases sidebar.

NOTE The following exercise uses a second hard drive or cloud-based storage to store your database backup. If you do not have access to a second hard drive or cloud storage, you can still read through the exercise to gain an understanding of the process.

1 In the list of databases, make sure the **resolve101** database is selected.

2 At the top of the window, click the backup button.

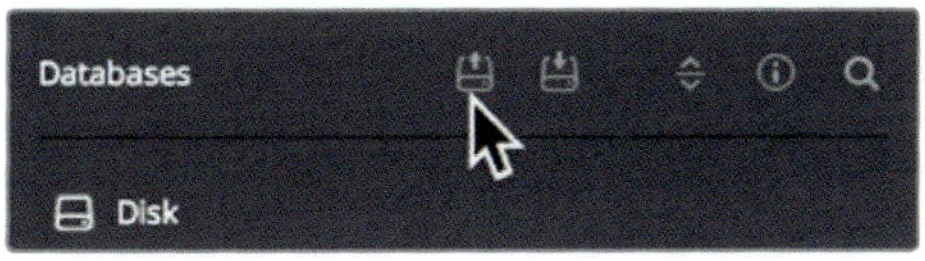

Generally, databases range in size from a couple of hundred megabytes to a couple of gigabytes; but unlike media, they can easily be saved to a cloud backup storage system or a small local hard drive.

3 Navigate to the hard drive or cloud-based storage where you want to back up your database, and click Save.

4 Once the save is completed, click the confirmation dialog, and click the databases button to close the database window.

After saving a backup, a .diskdb file is created. This file contains your entire database which you can simply copy to another drive if, for instance, you purchase a new computer and want to move your existing projects to the new hard drive. On the new computer, you can click the Restore button in DaVinci Resolve to open and use the database.

Lesson Review

1 True or false? The Media Manager manages clips, timelines, and bins.

2 What three operations can be performed on selected media in the Media Manager?

3 When using the Project manager, what's the difference between exporting a project and archiving a project?

4 How do you view the databases in the Project manager?

5 What's the advantage of having multiple databases?

Answers

1. False. The Media Manager manages only media; it does not manage bins.
2. In the Media Manager, selected media can be copied, moved, or transcoded.
3. Exporting creates only a DRP (DaVinci Resolve Project) format file which contains only the project metadata. Archiving creates a folder with the DRA extension that includes a DRP file for the project, along with all the media files contained in that project.
4. To view the databases connected to DaVinci Resolve, in the upper-left of the Project Manager, click the sidebar button.
5. You can create different databases to separate projects by year, by client, or by student/semester in an educational setting. Whatever criteria you use to create a new database, it is a best practice to back up databases daily.

Congratulations!

You have completed **The Beginner's Guide to DaVinci Resolve 16** and are ready to explore more editing, visual effects, color grading, and audio mixing functionality using the additional certified books in this series. Completing all the lessons in this book have prepared you to become a certified DaVinci Resolve user. You can take the online exam by following the link below to earn your certificate.

We also invite you to become part of the DaVinci Resolve community by joining the web forum on the Blackmagic Design web site. There, you can ask further questions about the creative aspects of editing, color correction and audio mixing.

We hope that you have you have found DaVinci Resolve 16's professional non-linear editing and world-class color correction tools to be intuitive to learn and a perfect fit to become the hub of your entire creative workflow.

Test your skills by taking the online assessment located on the Blackmagic Design DaVinci Resolve Training page — The Beginner's Guide to DaVinci Resolve 16 Online Exam:
https://www.blackmagicdesign.com/products/davinciresolve/training

Index

Numbers

Symbols

A

B

N

O

P

Q

R

S

T

About the Authors

Paul Saccone has been working in the post production industry for over 20 years and is an editorial workflow expert. He's based in San Francisco, California where he lives with his husband, Ryan, and their dogs, Chloe and Gracie. This is his second book, which means that someone must have read his first one. From 1998 to 2013 Paul worked at Apple and was the Product Manager for Final Cut Pro versions 2 through 7, including Final Cut Studio. He is well known around the world as a speaker, demo artist, and educator for his dynamic and witty presentations. Paul currently works for Blackmagic Design and spends his free time editing with DaVinci Resolve 16.

Dion Scoppettuolo is a Certified Blackmagic Design Master Trainer who has taught classes on DaVinci Resolve in Hollywood and New York City, as well as across Europe and Asia.

Mr Scoppettuolo has extensive industry experience in editing having held the postion of Product Designer at Avid technologies and more recently as Product Manager of Shake and Motion at Apple Inc.

Printed in Great Britain
by Amazon

33307465R00241